C + H
6 95

The Negro Vanguard

The

Negro Vanguard

BY RICHARD BARDOLPH

RINEHART & COMPANY, INC.

NEW YORK TORONTO

Published simultaneously in Canada
by Clarke, Irwin & Co., Ltd., Toronto

Library of Congress Catalog Card Number: 59-6571

For Dorothy, Ginny, Mark,

Ricky and Laura

Acknowledgments

Face-to-face interviews with 131 of the most famous Negro Americans made my search for data a fascinating experience. I made the major preparations for this book as a Fellow of the John Simon Guggenheim Memorial Foundation; and the Research Council of the Woman's College of the University of North Carolina, and President William C. Friday of the University of North Carolina placed at my disposal generous financial resources to enable me to complete the study. I am under heavy obligation, too, to the staffs of the New York Public Library, the Schomburg Collection, the Library of the Woman's College of the University of North Carolina, the Library of the University of North Carolina at Chapel Hill and the Widener Library of Harvard University.

I despair of calling the roll of all the persons who read portions of the manuscript in its several stages, but I am confident that I shall be forgiven if I name only those whom I pressed hardest to convict me of error. The whole manuscript, with the exception of the bibliographical essay, was read critically by James C. Evans, John Hope Franklin, Frenise A. Logan, William R. Ming, Doris E. Saunders and Robert C. Weaver. The first two thirds was subjected to the close scrutiny of George Breathett, William M. Brewer and Rayford Logan; and the prologue's argument was assayed by Roy Wilkins and Benjamin E. Mays. If I had followed more assiduously the advice of all of these counsellors—all of them in one respect or another better qualified to write this book than I—this would not have been *my* book but a composite, a report of a committee of eleven, each one of them differing at some points with me and with all the others. They may not recognize their contribution in the final form I imposed upon it, but I tell them with sincere thanks that they saved me from many errors. I beg them to indulge the vanity that prompts me to persist in what must seem to them my transgressions. At least my obstinacy absolves them from responsibility for the work's defects.

I owe more than I can say to William M. Brewer, editor of the *Journal of Negro History,* and to Boyd C. Shafer, editor of the *American Historical Review,* who published in their distinguished periodicals my articles which proved to be the ancestors of this book. Finally, I acknowledge once again my debt to my old teacher and friend, Fred A. Shannon, a master of the historian's craft. He is still at my elbow every time I face a classroom or put pen to paper.

8 August, 1959

RICHARD BARDOLPH

The Woman's College of the
University of North Carolina
Greensboro, North Carolina

Contents

The Negro Vanguard

Prologue

The time has come to lodge the Negro movers and shakers of American social history more firmly in the record, and to assemble, while they may still be discovered, the scattered and elusive facts about their social origins. Negroes, except *en masse* and as a "problem," are conspicuously absent from historical literature, both professional and popular, save that published by Negroes themselves. Whites can usually identify Ralph Bunche and some contemporary figures from the sport and entertainment worlds; they may, if pressed, identify Booker T. Washington or George W. Carver. A college man may recognize Paul Laurence Dunbar, Langston Hughes, Richard Wright, William E. B. Du Bois; perhaps even Frederick Douglass, Nat Turner, and Dred Scott. But there it ends. Most Negroes themselves, indeed, are surprisingly uninformed despite the efforts of their own publicists to press "famous" Negroes upon their consciousness. It does not follow, however, that the Negro's obscurity in the historical record is explained by a conspiracy of silence. His contribution has not, in all candor, been conspicuous in the whole American context; but this may only attest the inferior role to which the race was assigned from its earliest days here.

This study is offered not as a compilation of success stories but as an attempt to identify the most celebrated Negro Americans in the country's past. Available biographical data have been searched for generalizations in the hope that some light may be shed on the social origins of the group as a whole—their family backgrounds, their early economic and community environment, educational influences; the role of accident, sources of motivation, the importance of contacts with sympathetic whites and prominent Negroes upon their development; local and regional advantages and, so far as the data permit, some tentative conclusions about the development of the selective mechanisms and the social climate that favored their rise.

Even so, such evidence as may be found not only enables us to spell out some of the facts about the rise of the Negro vanguard; it is sufficient also to show that the record is sharply at variance with the stereotypes and facile generalizations from which the image of the tenth American has been compounded by the other nine.

The Negro's heroes are important not only for their objective contributions to American life; they also afford a convenient medium for studying the history of the whole Negro American group, both in its own internal evolution and in its changing situation in the developing American social frame. Especially important is the distinguished Negro's place in current discussions of the race's capacity for first-class citizenship, at a time when the resolution of the American Dilemma is our major domestic preoccupation, and when all of our people need, as never before, the knowledge and insights that inform sound judgment and prudent decision.

Perhaps the distinguished Negro is most significant as a symbol. When Gwendolyn Brooks took the 1948 Pulitzer Prize in poetry, she immediately became, like Roland Hayes and Marian Anderson, a moving appeal to whites to abandon their stereotypes. America loves the language of the success story and Negroes know how to profit by this propensity. The apparatus for bringing the story of the accomplished Negro to the attention of America is prodigious and, though it has not yielded the desired results, the harvest has been appreciable. This symbolic role of the colored genius as sponsor of the race's credentials has fired many a young Negro to fight his way to a plane where he could fling his trophies at the feet of the skeptic and the scoffer. Such enthusiasms are shared at every level. Cultivated Negroes who had no interest whatever in sports watched the fortunes of Joe Louis with as real a fascination as that which gripped the shoeshine boy, and the latter in turn is capable of a surprising enthusiasm for Dr. Bunche. Even Alain Locke, a high priest of Negro intellectuals, insisted that distinguished achievements in the arts is "the most persuasive and incontrovertible type of group propaganda, our best cultural line of defense."

But the leader-as-symbol is even more important in the Negro community itself. The old folk-belief that "white is right" is slowly losing its hold, but there still broods over Negro America a sense of inferiority, of resignation to a subordinate lot, tempered, it may be, by an astonishing capacity for exuberance even in that contracted sphere. Inherent inferiority of dark peoples has so long been forced upon the Negro's attention that he has been conditioned to doubt his own capacities. He sees his kind living in squalid rural and urban slums. A few athletes, entertainers and politicians aside, almost the only Negroes in the daily papers are buffoons, criminals and trouble-makers. From early childhood he learns that white folks own the country. The heroes in the comic books, in newspapers and radio, in the movies and television are whites, aided only now and then by a grinning colored domestic. The people in the schoolbooks and on the billboards are white. All his life he hears of Negro college graduates who became Pullman porters, and of white rail splitters, unlettered tailors and haberdashers who became President of the United States. He early learns that white is the hallmark of good, black the badge of evil. Adam and Eve were white, and so were the patriarchs and Moses, David and the prophets, Christ and the apostles. Heaven is a place of glittering white towers, while the smoky caverns of hell are governed by the black prince of darkness. God Himself is white, seated on a great white throne, and penitent sinners sing, "Wash me and I shall be whiter than snow."

From earliest youth, the Negro child is confronted by what seem overwhelming proofs of mortal attainder. "We were," said Pauli Murray, recalling a childhood in our own time, "bottled up and labeled and set aside. . . . We came to understand that no matter how neat and clean, how law-abiding, submissive and polite, how studious in school, how churchgoing and moral, how scrupulous in paying our bills and taxes we were, it made no essential difference in our place." And still, Negro Americans, from the poorest and most ignorant to the most highly placed, frequently affirm, despite all their distresses, that the condition and prospect of the Negro is better in America than anywhere else in the world. It is a mistake to suppose that the great mass of America's Negroes are morbidly preoccupied with their handicap. They have learned to live with it as most men everywhere learn to live with the constraints of a world they never made. All human beings, white and Negro alike, share outrage and injustice at the hands of capricious fortune. After all, as one brilliant, famous and prosperous New York Negro, now in his middle years, said to me:

> There are practically no unexplained deviations—the sort that biologists call "sports." Every successful Negro can be accounted for by family, by the people he gets to know, and any of hundreds of other variables. It's all a matter of people having a chance. There is no equality of opportunity for anybody, white or Negro, anywhere. Lots of people with immense potentials never get anywhere simply because they don't have the chance—the right parents, the right geographical and educational opportunities, accidental deliverance from the temptations that can ruin a man's chances in ten minutes. The people who don't have these breaks didn't have any choice in the matter, and neither did those who do.

Quite apart from the fetters that confine the generality of men, the additional shackles that bind the Negro contract his opportunities still further. The masses may resign themselves and live zestfully, even rapturously, however short the tether. They may even find it a relief to be able to excuse themselves from the white man's desperate strivings on the plea that the struggle will avail them nothing anyhow. Some see here one of the most tragic barriers to the rise of gifted Negroes. Doors are now opening unexpectedly only to disclose that there are few qualified Negroes to enter them; but until now, while these opportunities were exceptions, few could take the long risk of years of labor and sacrifice preparing to enter doors that very likely would never open. It was as if a man should train himself to be struck by lightning.

The hard truth remains that the low ceiling of aspiration in the ghetto must, in moments of introspection, raise doubts and anxieties for all; and for the talented, sensitive, ambitious, intelligent, educated and aspiring, from whom the vanguard must be recruited, it is a dreadful burden. In the encircling gloom that such thoughts inspire, the distinguished Negro sheds light and warmth. From Crispus Attucks to Martin Luther King, the heroes are held up before an afflicted people like the brazen serpent on the plain before Edom. In classroom, church and Sunday school, in the History Week kit for the Negro history club, on the wall calendar from the Negro insurance company, in the Chicago *Defender* and the *Pittsburgh Courier,* in popular magazine and scholarly journal, in the bookstacks and special displays at the branch library, the race's fairest ornaments are kept before its eyes.

With each new biography—frankly written to pluck up the hearts of a struggling people—the Negro press hails yet another boon for every Negro; in Gunnar Myrdal's phrase "a gloating consolation in his lowly status and a ray of hope." To those past hope, the Big Negro supplies vicarious fulfillment. For those who still face the battle, the annals of the great Negro doers, said one of them, put "at the disposal of the youth of the land stories of struggles and sacrifices which [are] . . . tremendous sources of inspiration and hope . . . [and] give them much-needed encouragement in facing the demand of American life."

"We know we are not weak, ignorant, frustrated, or cowed," exulted Langston Hughes, himself the best warrant for his words. "We know the race has its heroes. . . . Some day there will be many books and plays and songs that say that . . . Negro literature needs [its] heroes. Then it will come alive, speak, sing, and flame with meaning for the Negro people."

This preoccupation with heroes is a strongly American trait. The American, forever the romantic, forever the individualist, has small patience with the study of social change moving on broad fronts with glacial dignity. His history is a highly personalized drama of gallant men: Washington suffering with his troops at Valley Forge; Ethan Allen pounding the gates of Ticonderoga; Andrew Jackson defying Calhoun; Grant and Lee locked in combat in the Wilderness; Theodore Roosevelt bludgeoning the trusts; Wilson demanding strict accountability of Wilhelm II. But the Negro's heroes have the further function of proving to a skeptical world that the Negro, too, is a whole man, a whole American. No DiMaggio, no Hemingway, no Dulles, no Omar Bradley is needed to "bring credit" to his race and to attest its fitness to walk in dignity and to bear rule. But such is Jackie Robinson's burden, and Ralph Ellison's and Ralph Bunche's and Benjamin O. Davis's. The status of the Negro hero is often a lonely one. Estranged from his own kind by his very eminence, he is nonetheless rejected by the white community, for there he is still a Negro, still lumped with the coarsest elements in the enclave. Often he is the *result* of the "racial situation," and has to that extent a vested interest in its perpetuation. The white community expects him to be a "good Negro," but his kinsmen expect him to be a "race man," and he makes his way, pulled by competing allegiances, in constant peril of offending both.

The enthusiasm of the race for its heroes is, in fact, often qualified by complicated considerations. In recent years, sophisticated Negroes have been embarrassed over what seems to them a kind of racial chauvinism. They point out that many "celebrities" are all too often being judged by a patronizing standard ("first rate!—for a Negro"), and measured against their handicap; or they are cried up only by the brethren of the ghetto and a few latter-day Abolitionists. Others, who publicly push the claims of the Big Negro for the white man's applause, privately disparage his attainments. Just as whites explain their neighbor's wealth or eminence in terms of advantages which fortune denied to themselves, so the common—and even the well-educated—Negro is tempted to account for the uncommon Negro's success in similar terms, adding, moreover, another ingredient: a broad hint that such distinction is a product of fawning upon the white man. If my neighbor is a Somebody and I am a Nobody (so runs the argument), it is because he was willing to surrender his self-respect while I prefer, at whatever cost, to preserve mine. One prominent Negro author, Saunders Redding, goes so far as to aver that "the average Negro believes that the average Negro earning a salary of $2500 (. . . in no matter what capacity) can be bought out by whites for a few dollars more, or can be made to pull Mr. White American's chestnuts out of the fire."

Genuinely great achievement, wholly independent of white patronage, may still be drastically discounted by other Negroes because of its author's failure to adopt the "correct" racial position, a circumstance immensely complicated by the disquieting fact that there is no agreement as to what the "correct" position is. The same musician, journalist, educator, writer, bishop, brigadier general, scientist, physician, or athlete may be a militant race hero to one Negro—even to a highly intelligent, independent-minded Negro—while to another, equally sophisticated, the same "hero" may be an "Uncle Tom," "traitor to the race," "unspeakable handkerchief head," "vicious saboteur," "cheap race hustler," "shameless procurer." Such execrations rarely appear in print, but they spring readily to the lips of the best-informed folk in the Negro community.

Enthusiasms for this or that particular race interest or project are so infinitely variable that any position whatever exposes one to excommunication by some significant segment of Negro opinion. No prominent Negro is safe from this hazard. However irreproachable his record in every other regard, he may be ruthlessly read out of the communion of the saints by *some* Negroes, high and low, for one heresy or another. I have heard the most eminent Negroes defamed by others equally prominent for the most inconsequential deviations. A man may be the most famous Negro in a field dominated by whites (and *all* fields are dominated by whites, and a Negro's position in them is, with rare exceptions, determined by the white man's evaluation of him), but let him withdraw too far, physically or socially, from the ghetto, and he becomes a traitor to his race. When a private group in New York, with foundation backing, projected a first-class hospital for Harlem, there were enlightened folk on both sides who questioned whether acquiescence in such a plan was surrender to expediency, and distinguished New York Negroes on both sides of the dispute were belabored for impeding the progress of the race. A major official in the NAACP, after a lifetime of service to the race, is in some quarters, because of his prominence in certain interracial-co-operation and philanthropic agencies, "the wiliest race hustler of them all." One of the most famous of colored sociologists, when he deflates the pretensions of the "black bourgeoisie" or denies the persistence of the African heritage as a major force in Negro American culture, is taxed not with error but with the basest apostasy. It becomes a shameless bid for the white man's applause, by "the prince of academic Uncle Toms." One's very militancy may call down the execrations of the brethren, for "extremism" that "sets the Negro back twenty years" or "queers the race with its best friends."

The inability of its most eminent sons to agree has long been a standing jest in the intimacy of the family. Booker T. Washington was quite capable of undercutting rivals to his pre-eminence fifty years ago, and more than a century ago even the Negro Abolitionists, agreed as they were upon their goal, were divided by differences over strategy and tactics, reflecting both diverse philosophies and friction between racial leaders surprisingly jealous of each other. They disagreed (as well they might, for who could say what the precise formula was?) about the wisdom of working through political parties, about establishing an independent Negro Abolitionist press, and even about the pace of the campaign. Perhaps the fact that the segregated Negro community has afforded so few places of real eminence has been at the root of these contentions. Indeed the propensity for divisions in its leadership, combined with apparently irreconcilable wranglings over ideologies, had already exhibited itself in Negro America before the Civil War. Douglass, always sensitive to rival claimants to his title as the country's most famous Negro, taunted one of his eminent contemporaries, the freeborn, Amherst-educated Robert Purvis, for his "blood-soaked riches," wrung, he strongly hinted, from Negro slaves. Purvis's white father had in fact left his son a comfortable competence, but he was never connected with the slave interest; he was, indeed, an opponent of the institution. Purvis defended himself against Douglass's insinuations, branding his renowned detractor, in print, as "this meanly ambitious and foul-mouthed slanderer."

This book takes as its theme several hundred Negro Americans, from the days of the American Revolution to the present, who may fairly be counted among the movers and shakers of American social history. In compiling the roster, I have been at great pains to minimize my subjective judgments, for I have tried to assemble a list of those persons who appear most prominently in the written historical record. After sifting the available printed testimony and the oral evidence supplied me by numerous eminent living Negro Americans, I drew up a list of persons whose names seemed to stand out most conspicuously in the annals. This procedure largely exempts me, it is hoped, from defending my choices, but those who seek reassurance on the point are referred to the brief essay on authorities at the back of the book.

There is, at the outset, the thorny question of standards for identifying distinguished achievement. Many Negroes urge that their artists, writers, scientists and public servants be measured by the same standards applied to non-Negroes, but this is difficult to do when one is considering those who stood in the vanguard of the race as it climbed from slavery. Achievements less than memorable in the context of the whole population can be outstanding in another frame. A man equipped by nature to be a general or an industrial tycoon, but forced by man-made exclusions to be satisfied with the role of a bishop, can hardly be held to the same standards as a more voluntary divine. A poet's stature is properly judged by a single standard of performance, but a particular poet, say Paul Laurence Dunbar, can be a more significant mover of American social history than a white man of equal poetic stature, if he wins, for the first time, a respectful hearing for the Negro poetic voice.

There are, moreover, achievements that do not excite wide notice. A colored scholar who wins election to the presidency of one of the country's leading learned societies, or a Negro scientist who becomes director of a public health laboratory in Boston, member of the Harvard faculty, and author of a celebrated work on syphilology, is not likely to be mentioned in *American Heritage*. But men like these will be noticed here as more important shapers of American life than are white scholars of comparable attainments, precisely because they were moving and shaking the old order, changing its relationships, and shifting its center of gravity.

But even this qualification does not guarantee that the achievers singled out here are in every case more noteworthy than others who (because they do not figure prominently in the printed record) have been passed by. It is conceivable that some of the most significant heroes are the "firsts," unnoticed in this book and celebrated only in obscure corners of the Negro press—pioneers who, by their perseverance and a lucky instinct for putting themselves in the right place at the right time, entered doors hitherto closed to Negroes, and then so richly vindicated the faith of those who opened to their knock that the doors were never again closed to others of the race: the first buyer for Macy's, the first professors at white universities, the first policemen in Atlanta, the first Guggenheim Fellows, the first city councilman in Greensboro, N.C., the first stewardess for the airlines, the first manager of an A&P store.

Whites, too, have their own standards for defining a "good Negro" and have the additional advantage of owning the industries that shape reputations: press, radio, television and motion pictures. Even a list of distinguished Negroes compiled wholly by Negroes will strongly reflect the whites' preferences, either directly by including folk who have won notice in the white community, or indirectly by listing those who, by proving that a Negro can do just what a gifted white man does, have given the race another claim to fuller participation in the whole scheme of American life, a civilization compounded of values, ideas and institutions shaped largely by whites.

It has been steadily assumed in this study that "greatness" and "distinction" are only distantly related, that achievement is a function of opportunity, and fame is largely a matter of blundering into the right place at the right time, in the right company. Sometimes it is only a matter of a journalist snatching a man from obscurity, initiating a legend for others to magnify and distort; or it may be simply a matter of a favorable press granted to one Negro and withheld from another for reasons wholly unrelated to the merits of the case. One thinks of the differential treatment accorded to George Washington Carver and Daniel Hale Williams. Carver—whose public image is that of the quiet, self-effacing, deferential Negro who rose from slavery to world renown but preferred to live still in self-imposed segregation at Tuskegee and even dressed the part of the humble, conciliatory black—conformed to an image dear to vast numbers of whites. Williams, by contrast, deviated from the stereotype in nearly every detail. From the scientist's point of view a more important scientific innovator than the widely beloved Carver, he was almost wholly unnoticed by the country until, in 1956, long after his death, the Treasury of the United States used his picture and something of his story in advertisements for Savings Bond sales. Williams was a thoroughgoing professional, fastidious in dress, urbane in manner, fair-skinned and red-haired and, even more disturbing, a militant crusader for "Negro rights in medicine."

Discussion of Negro heroes is hag-ridden by attitudes that participants bring to the argument. Friendly whites, moved by sentimentality or enthusiasm for righting ancient wrongs, often overestimate Negro achievement, while Negroes egregiously overstate the case as a compensatory reaction, or because their very isolation has diminished their capacity to judge. Such overstatement may also be a form of the Negro protest. Others, Negro and white, surprised to find a Negro deviating from the stereotype, rush to acclaim him a prodigy. In my selections I have given primary consideration to the importance accorded to persons in the historical record, as measured by the amount of space allotted them and the regularity of mention in a wide variety of sources, balancing the sheer volume of such notice against the quality of sources from which expert judgments may be expected.

No trait has been more characteristic of our leading Negroes than their compliance with American culture patterns. Scholars of both races argue cogently the question of the continuity of African influences in America. Those claiming that African patterns persist, even go to the length of explaining Negro preference for the Baptist faith in terms of ancient African river cults. Some colored adherents of the doctrine vociferously scold the most eminent Negro American social scientists who reject it. The data assembled in this study invited the working assumption that the Negro people, uprooted and forcibly integrated into a slave economy, were in all essentials established here as a folk cut clean from their cultural base. In the transplanting, ancient ties were snapped; and after the initial shock gave place to adaptation to new realities, the evolution of a wholly new order went forward during two centuries of bondage, granting even that some ancient memories and immemorial usages might linger for some generations.

A central tendency in the evolution of American society has been the development of an order in which status was determined by achievement, not ascribed by birth or caste. That the Negro, segregated as the Great Exception, would prove in time to be no exception at all was decreed by the relentless logic of the unfolding American order—the steady self-assertion of an achievement society. A Civil War between white men wiped out the major institutional form of the separate culture. Then followed the agonizing task, still unfinished, of picking out the surviving devious and snarled strands so long woven through the underside of the social fabric. Barred by the color line from the established American order, the Negro began building a makeshift, black replica of white American culture on his own side of the line, an enclave stamped with the features of its model and carrying over familiar designs of social stratification, based eventually upon inheritance, wealth, vocation, education, and even upon color and family antecedents.

From the moment the facsimile emerged, Negro leaders turned their thoughts to the day when the line would dissolve and the copy merge with its original. The line is still there; Negroes throughout our history have in the main achieved their distinctions in the ghetto. Those who have been invited across the line to participate in the larger American community as artists or athletes, as writers, musicians, or public servants, are still to most Americans representatives of a separate people. The few may call them great American tenors or scientists or athletes; but many more—including Negroes themselves, and especially the Negro press—call them great *Negro* tenors or scientists, and "a credit to their race."

The effort to characterize several hundreds of eminent and widely diverse Negroes, drawn from a period extending across three centuries in a variety of fields of achievement—and all this in a social frame constantly, rapidly and profoundly changing under the urge of historical, legal, economic and moral compulsions—confronts one with baffling problems. We resort to the familiar artifice of dividing the narrative into historical periods, fully conscious that the device entails hazards, for personal histories do not arrange themselves in convenient time divisions, all running together in a pack and stopping short at the end of what historians are pleased to call "eras." There is also the disquieting disposition of some of the runners to conduct themselves as if they were still in an era already past, or, for that matter, in one that still lies before.

The impressions that accumulated as this study went forward suggested a crude frame of thirty- to thirty-five-year blocks, both because each of the segments thus spans a turnover of the Negro population as generations are usually reckoned, and also because each of them represents a kind of era in Negro American national development. For the three generations from 1770 to 1865 the task of selection, though difficult enough, was notably simpler than that for succeeding generations. Particularly after the First World War, the problem becomes progressively more complex, and for the contemporary chapter, 1936 to the present, the number and diversity of the company of prominent Negroes has become so overwhelming that a catalog of representative leaders—not a list that is in any sense plenary—must serve. The names for the middle twentieth century must still be sifted by time and history, and we are compelled to rely on suggestions from current sources, fully aware that they are suggestions only.

One problem that no student of Negro distinction can solve must be identified here. As Americans define the term "Negro," there is an undetermined and undeterminable number of distinguished Americans who are in fact Negroes, but who are not known to be so. State laws and constitutional provisions undertaking to define Negroes typically count a man a Negro even if only one of the eight ancestors (and that one himself may be of mixed blood) in three generations is a person of Negro descent; or, as some statutes more candidly word the formula, a man is a Negro if "he has in his veins any Negro blood whatever" (Arkansas), or if he is the descendant of any person "having any ascertainable trace of . . . Negro blood" (Georgia).

Even if there were no laws on the subject at all, no proportion of white ancestry, short of one hundred per cent, would in American parlance make one a white man. Now it is common knowledge that every year many persons of African descent successfully "pass" into white society and are assimilated. Such persons or their descendants have sometimes become prominent figures; indeed relatives of distinguished Negroes listed in this book are known to have disappeared into the white group. And since persons cross the line to raise the level of their aspirations, it may be assumed that some of the migrants have advanced fully as far as did their kinsmen who elected to remain in the Negro group.

Langston Hughes, in discussing the point with the author, expressed himself with characteristic humor. "Colored folks passing for white . . . I reckon you don't want to include—and there's no point in giving them away anyhow. That's just another technique of getting ahead." Walter White, himself unrecognizable as a man of color, declared that nearly every one of America's fifteen million discernible Negroes knows at least one who is passing. Some of them are prominent figures, he wrote, including "a few members of Congress, certain writers, and several organizers of movements to 'keep Negroes . . . in their places.'"

But if such demographic confusions make it difficult to assign a person to his race, they are equally confounding in the study of family backgrounds. A master fact in the Negro social heritage has been the precarious structure of the family among slave folk, shrouding the facts about the antecedents of individual Negroes. Even if it could have been expected that slaves should adopt at once the white man's centuries-old marriage pattern, slavery would hardly allow it, for usages must be flexible enough to permit slaveowners to manage their chattels to their own advantage. Moreover, slaves and their descendants who became free Negroes, North or South, carried with them the practices bred into them in the slave community. Negro marriages lacked the formality and deliberation that gave stability to the marriages of whites; they lacked the social and religious sanctions, the exact legal definitions which, if applied to the slave, would have crossed the white man's will.

William Wells Brown, the pioneer Negro historian and novelist, wrote that his mother had seven children, no two of whom were fathered by the same man. He added that most slaves did not know who their fathers were. "There is no such thing as slaves being lawfully married," he continued; "there never yet was a case where a slave has been tried for bigamy." Another wrote that "it is impossible for slaves to give a correct account of their male parentage. . . . There is no legal marriage among the slaves of the South; I never heard of such a thing in my life." Frederick Douglass declared that "slaves know as little of their ages as horses do of theirs." Douglass met his mother only a few times in his life after being separated from her in infancy, and she "left me without the slightest intimation of who my father was." That the same looseness of the marital tie naturally accompanied the slave into freedom and then persisted in significant measure to the twentieth century is acknowledged by scholars of both races.

No less disruptive of stable patterns of marriage and descent were the unendurable temptations to indulgence, so freely available to the white male, that made the chastity of his comely slave girl an early casualty and the plantation an uneasy hell for his wife and mother. The absence of legal protections for the colored female, the lack of social sanctions against seduction and concubinage, the encouragements to compliance that colored women could only with the utmost fortitude resist, and the economic value of mulatto children converged to the same result, rendering forever hopeless future progress in keeping the races "pure." As the decades advanced, the rate of illegitimate, mixed-blood births declined, but the white seducer still enjoyed his old immunities; indeed, the law encouraged the white man to repeat his offense, for it forbade him to marry the colored mother of his child. By 1850, mulattoes accounted for at least a ninth of the Negro people and a century later perhaps three fourths were of mixed blood. After Emancipation the increase came less from the direct infusion of Caucasian blood and more from the marriage of "pure" Negroes with those of mixed ancestry.

Most distinguished Negroes have been persons of mixed blood, a phenomenon now ascribed by scholars not to inherent white superiority but to the huge differential in the cultural heritage of the two races; the fact that the mothers of mixed Negroes have been the choicest colored specimens that the white man could commandeer; the reinforcement of this biological selection by a tendency for mulattoes to draw away from blacks by marrying their own kind, and for the most successful blacks to marry into the lighter-skinned group, so that Negro talent became increasingly concentrated there. More important still, the Negro of lighter skin, in slavery and freedom, was afforded far greater indulgence by the white man; and the Negro himself, urged by social environment, tended to defer to his half-white cousin.

Slave folk had always before them the evidence that laws and religious prescriptions as they applied to marriage and the family were not for them. Systematic slave-breeding that smacked more of the stock-raisers' manual than of the Catechism—at least in some quarters—put the slaveowner's economic interest before inconvenient considerations of conventional morality. For Negroes, no infidelity to the family relationship was known to law; and the white man's double standard for sexual excursions across the color line further affirmed that the family as a closed and stable circle was not for Negroes, that chastity was not to be taken seriously for the Negro male—except, of course, where white women were concerned. A truant glance at a white woman, though she were the meanest slattern, could bring down upon the Negro male the most awful judgment; but he must not show his anger when the white lecher prowled about the Negro quarter. Here again was proof that the closed, stable family was not part of the whites' design for Negroes.

Not only were slave marriages arrangeable and dissolvable at the master's pleasure, and without status in law; they also lacked what Professor Stampp calls the "centripetal forces that gave the white family cohesiveness." The wife was primarily a chattel and laborer, and only incidentally a wife, mother and homemaker. In the daylight hours her children were left in the keeping of another. She did not even, as a rule, cook the family's meals, make its clothing, or attend them in sickness. Real parental authority was impossible, for control of slave folk's conduct was vested in other hands. The family had no meaning as an economic unit; their exertions were not for each other. The father was not a farmer-enterpriser, not the *de facto* head of a family, not a provider, protector, or property owner. With the family so feebly developed, the wonder is that there were any stable families at all. They must be accounted for by conscientious masters, scrupulous in keeping families safe from dispersion and so far faithful to their own religious and moral professions that they communicated them to their wards by precept and example. After the Emancipation, progress was immediately accelerated as the Negro's scruples and religious sensibilities were permitted freer play and as the whites' laws and attitudes were gradually modified by the new circumstances. Still, some of the old factors continued to touch the lives of individual Negroes straight down to the mid-twentieth century.

That family disorganization would continue long after the Emancipation was further guaranteed by the Negroes' relegation to the lowest economic and social stratum, precisely the locus of greatest family instability regardless of race. Further reinforcement for old ways came also from the persistence among whites of the freely expressed belief that Negroes are congenitally amoral, if not immoral, and hence not to be expected to share the white man's ideals of chastity and marital fidelity. Most Negro notables of the period as late as 1900–1936 were born in the decades immediately preceding and following 1865, many in slavery or as children of ex-slave parents. Autobiographies by famous Negroes—when they do not simply pass over discussions of their forebears, or trace their descent from white slaveowners—candidly confirm William Pickens's assertion that most Negroes who are as much as thirty years old (it was published in 1923, hence for thirty years now read sixty-five) know nothing reliable of their ancestors more than one generation back. His own case was an example.

The evolution of a personality, to say nothing of several hundreds of them, cannot be really accounted for. The historian can discern only the grosser outlines. The influences that play upon the rise of any Negro who achieves a degree of distinction cannot conceivably be described in all their complexity in a work of this scope. One can only point out to his readers the rapidly accumulating fund of testimony on matters affecting the race as a whole that are afforded by the sociological, anthropological, psychological and historical studies of a lengthening list of scholars.

The progenitors of the Negro vanguard were for the most part illiterate folk. They left little by way of a written record, and the absence of stable family patterns by which an oral historical and genealogical tradition might have been transmitted from father to son further deepens the obscurity. Knowledge of the leading figures of the remoter past comes to us, not primarily from their own testimony, but through remoter witnesses, the story undergoing successive changes with each retelling to fit the ends that the narrator subserved. For the most recent past, when the data are more abundant, the shadows still persist. Many recent or contemporary notables who wrote autobiographies or who were interviewed for this study, whose parents or grandparents were born in the slave era, were unable to declare whether their immediate forebears—particularly the male ancestors—had been slaves, whether they had been literate, and what their social circumstances were. Sometimes the ambiguity was a consequence of the loose character of the family relationship, but in other cases the matters had never, in the memory of these persons, been discussed in the family circle, and no dependable tradition on the subjects survived.

Part One

1770–1900: Out of the House of Bondage

The first two generations in our story, the folk in the years 1770 to 1831, saw momentous changes in the status of the Negro in America. At the opening of that period, slavery was in legal existence in all the colonies and everywhere on the defensive. Informed estimates for 1776 indicate that in that year, in a total population of two and a half million, more than a fifth—about 570,000—were Negroes, and of these perhaps not more than 40,000 were free persons, the South accounting for approximately nine tenths of the slaves and roughly half of the free Negroes. By 1830, slavery had been abolished in the Northern states, and the country's Negroes numbered two and a third million, still comprising nearly a fifth (18 per cent) of the nation's total population of just under thirteen million. By now six of every seven Negroes in the country were slaves in the South, and of the free persons of color, numbering nearly 320,000, some 57 per cent were in the Southern states and the District of Columbia, and the rest in the free states. Just as important as these growing disparities and shifting proportions was the transformation of the nation's attitudes during these decades, a mutation that marked a turning point in Negro social history as the 1830's opened.

Conditions of slave life varied enormously from time to time, state to state, and plantation to plantation, a circumstance which in itself compounded the insecurities of the bondmen. Slave codes differed markedly both on paper and in practice, and masters varied from brutal tyrants to kindly heads of closely knit households. The work routine ranged from a lifetime of brutalizing toil in the fields to responsible managerial functions in the Big House (and, in extreme cases, as plantation overseers), and even dignified arrangements whereby a slave was permitted to hire out his services on his own time, in some instances with a fair prospect of buying his liberty and that of his family. But the slave condition, even at best, was manifestly not a context in which a man could distinguish himself. For the vast majority it was a monotonous round of toil, relieved, it may be, by elemental pleasures of a sort and by bland day-to-day sabotage that must have had its fascinations. It was a life without books, without intellectual and aesthetic opportunities, without worldly aspirations; a life lived within a severely contracted geographical compass, a shadowed hinterland separate from dominant whites who could scarcely bring themselves to believe that the Negro was in all respects a whole human being. There was, to be sure, a status system of a kind in the slave population. The house Negro, the artisan and the coachman lorded it over the field hand. The master's favorites (perhaps his kinsmen) and the "bright mulatto"; the storied matriarch and the preacher; the man who could read, and even the bondman with a high price tag—these commanded the deference of the humbler denizens of the quarter, but of no one else.

If the record offers no instances of genuinely distinguished achievement that won for its authors during their bondage anything more than local celebrity, it is noteworthy that a large proportion of our Negro notables for the period before 1865 were those who had managed to rise out of the slave group, by flight, manumission, or emancipation, and who had, while still slaves, enjoyed opportunities not available to the great mass of their fellows. There were, after all, disparities in the condition of slaves—advantages available to only a minority of the whole slave population, but a minority large enough to comprise a kind of elite from which unusual individuals could be recruited.

Some slaves had indulgent masters, solicitous for their mental, moral and spiritual development. Where a servant was the natural child of the master himself or of his kinsman, understandable indulgence was shown either from natural affection or in obedience to the claims of white superiority. Now and then it worked quite the other way. If only to appease an outraged wife, it might be necessary to avoid every appearance of partiality or even to sell such offspring to a distant purchaser and thus remove an inconvenient reminder of old infidelities. Sometimes indulgence sprang from genuine scruple, sometimes from economic considerations. A conscientious master with more slaves than he could at a given time keep profitably employed, might authorize the vocational training of his wards. A favored few slaves, typically on large plantations in the cotton states where specialization was economically justified, became skilled craftsmen or personal servants who were hired out by their owners to urban employers or were permitted to seek employment, keeping for themselves whatever they might earn above their stipulated obligation to the owner and using the savings for their own eventual redemption.

Slaves in the household group—particularly those who grew up in it—had advantages far beyond those of the field hand. Opportunities for acquiring literacy and other refinements and for encountering ideas and cultivated whites, though still limited even for the most fortunate house servants and craftsmen, were infinitely better than those within reach of the more typical slave. Frederick Douglass described them as "a sort of black aristocracy. . . . In dress, as well as in form and feature, in manner and speech, in tastes and habits, the distance between these favored few and the sorrow and hunger-smitten multitudes of the quarter was immense." Lighter skin likewise conferred impressive social advantages upon Negroes, quite apart from the leverage it gave them in the slave quarter. Negroes of mixed blood were preferred over blacks as house servants, and it was from the mulattoes that masters selected young Negroes for training in trades with a view to hiring them out to city employers, who preferred light-skinned servants in their homes and shops.

Residence in the upper South and the border regions was another fortuitous advantage, for it greatly increased the chances for successful escape. Even there, of course, the prospects were very dismal indeed, but even so, the race heroes encountered in this study who had successfully fled their bonds were almost invariably from the border South. And again, Negroes who grew up in stable families, thanks to their owners' disinclination—whether from scruple or other considerations—to separate families by sale or other means of dispersion, had the boon of a superior social heritage compared with that of less happy bondmen.

The status of slaves changed, moreover, as the generations succeeded each other. In the early decades of the eighteenth century, when the first of the notables identified in this study were born, slavery had already passed through a significant century-long evolution, marked by progressively clarified differentiation of the white from the black servant class, followed by ever sharper definition of slavery as distinct from less permanent forms of servitude. Slave codes had been elaborated before the Revolution; by 1770 the slave's status was clearly delineated both in statute and in the public mind. Libertarian and equalitarian influences excited by the Revolution, together with certain economic and social developments, weakened the institution, and by the close of the century it had been virtually extirpated from the Northern states. In the South, however, with the appearance of the cotton gin in the final decade of the eighteenth century and the astonishing rise of the cotton kingdom in the early decades of the nineteenth, the drooping establishment was re-energized and became a uniquely Southern phenomenon, open to Northern censure. New and accelerating events and tendencies precipitated a minor revolution in the attitudes of the slaveholding South and in the rules under which slave society lived, and the institution became the focus of political controversy, leading quickly to the explosion of war and the outlawing of slavery from the American order.

The bondman's time, in the best of circumstances, was almost never quite freely his own, but if it were, and even if he were inclined to bestir himself in his own and his family's behalf after spending his strength for his owner, his preoccupation would be with survival values, improving the physical plane of living or, more rarely, looking to possible self-purchase arrangements. He could scarcely busy himself with creative activity that could win him in time the sort of prominence that biographical dictionaries celebrate. He lived constantly on the ragged edge of subsistence; with the rarest exceptions education was categorically denied him; and he had, manifestly, no bargaining power, no social leverage by which he could pry himself upward a notch or two.

There were further barriers perhaps even more decisive. It cannot be too firmly stressed that the slave was a captive in a white society and that the great mass of whites, slaveowner and non-slaveowner alike, believed no less with their hearts than with their wills that the Negro's role in America was inescapably that of the common laborer. This, many quite honestly believed (the qualification is important), was divine fiat and unvarying natural law. A people deeply persuaded that a minority in their midst literally cannot rise because of congenital deficiencies will scarcely encourage the hapless underling to attempt the impossible; indeed, if he does perform the impossible, the achievement will either not be recognized for what it is or it will be explained away in terms that leave the initial assumption unscathed.

That a slave could not in such a climate rise to extraordinary heights is a point that need not be labored. What is less generally remembered is the continuing momentum of these influences in the two or three generations following the Emancipation—until the time when the distinguished Negroes of our own generation were born and reared. Despairing attitudes and expectations, so long the lot of slave folk; habits of deference, assumptions of inferiority, and long experience with a world where additional exertions brought no reward—these hardly afforded a school for resolute and enterprising strivers. Such legacies survived in a man's reflexes and were communicated to his sons and thence to *their* sons, particularly when important segments of the dominant group had an interest in keeping the man of color permanently under enormous necessities to court the white man's favor and subjecting him to grievous penalties for crossing his will.

That the slave's condition was a barren one for a gifted man will scarcely be disputed. It is not so widely understood that the free Negro was, until the end of the slave system, in little better case than his fettered kinsmen. As his numbers increased from perhaps less than forty thousand at the time of the Revolution to nearly half a million before the end of slavery, his condition deteriorated in proportion.

Sources of the free Negro population varied. A few were descendants of free persons of color, already making up a tiny fraction of the American population as early as the first half of the seventeenth century. More commonly, they were the offspring of Negroes more recently freed, or themselves first-generation freedmen. A few were immigrants from the West Indies or their descendants, and a very small fraction were runaways. Occasionally they were persons who had been manumitted by legislative act as a reward for some public service, as, for example, exposure of a slave conspiracy. Slaveholding regions lived in constant dread of slave risings and it was, obviously, good policy to convert every slave into a potential informer. Other freedmen in the Northern states were the beneficiaries of legislative emancipation after the

Revolution, when all the commonwealths north of the Potomac except Maryland and Delaware abolished slavery either at a stroke or by gradual liquidation.

The most typical source, however, was the voluntary act of the slaveowner. Thousands were freed by last will and testament for such widely varying reasons as conscience, the declining productivity of slave labor in particular areas, the desire to reward faithful servants, or even the wish to liberate one's offspring. Others freely manumitted individual slaves or whole groups of them, usually after securing express authorization from the state legislature, for much the same reasons that disposed others to free their chattels by last will. Perhaps the most dramatic avenue of liberation was that of self-purchase. This resort was closely dependent upon the good will of the master, and often the real initiative lay with the master rather than with the slave. In some cases the purchase price agreed upon was a mere token fee; in others, slaves were even permitted to assume free status at once and pay for it later in easy installments.

Purchase arrangements were often placed on an unsentimental, hard-bargain basis. Sometimes when the bondman was ready to consummate his self-purchase the owner withdrew the offer, even confiscating his chattel's savings; sometimes he cruelly raised the price after the original sum had been saved; sometimes he died before the bargain was executed and his heirs refused to be bound by it. Always the slave's power to make enforceable contracts was so limited as to make these transactions a precarious business at best, and they were, in fact, rare.

Usually a newly freed man's first concern was the liberation of his family, an enterprise which left little time for anything else. Here again survival values laid the first claim upon him. Some of the redeemed slaves had been bought out of bondage by third parties, perhaps by Quakers or other Abolitionists, and then promptly liberated. Not all slaves purchased from their masters by such humanitarians or by their own kinsmen were subsequently freed. Sometimes they were retained as nominal slaves of their own husbands, or fathers, to defeat the common legal requirement that newly manumitted Negroes must emigrate at once from the state, or to protect them against the very real hazard of forcible re-enslavement either by kidnapping or on some legal pretext. (The price that a kidnapped free Negro could fetch was a more tempting prize for slave hunters than was the reward for the capture of a runaway slave.) Negro slaveowners listed in the federal census are in considerable degree explained by this species of spurious slaveholding.

The free Negro population was steadily augmented by aged and infirm ex-slaves who were an economic burden to their owners, a group from which distinguished Negroes could obviously not be recruited. Even those in the prime of life were scarcely in an enviable position, for they were, after all, an incongruous element in a society that contemplated only free whites and Negro slaves. Particularly as their numbers increased, the disabilities laid upon them by law and usage steadily contracted their liberty.

In the South, fears multiplied that free Negroes threatened the slave system and white supremacy itself, that they spurred slaves to rebellion or escape, both actively and by the envy they excited. The free Negro's preference for urban life made him, moreover, a competitor of white labor, and his enforced willingness to accept lower standards of living than those to which white workers were accustomed exposed him to mounting resentments.

As the generations passed, restrictions upon the free Negro multiplied, in both North and South. Property rights were cancelled, the franchise was denied him, his mobility was greatly circumscribed and freedom of vocational choice stifled. If he escaped the slave hunter, he was still in peril of being snatched back to slavery by courts ready to be persuaded of technical defects in their "free papers." Public provision for schooling was in Northern states all but wholly neglected; in the South, the teaching of any Negroes was made a felony subject to surprisingly severe punishments. And by 1860, it should be recalled, fully half of the nation's free persons of color were in the slave states, and two thirds of these were concentrated in Virginia, Delaware and Maryland.

As hostility to the class grew, means were sought to rid the country of them, chiefly by resettlement in Africa, especially through the agency of the American Colonization Society. Another resort was the effort, by multiplying restraints upon the manumission process, to curtail their further increase. Very few colonists were in fact sent to Africa; and though the number of manumissions dwindled after 1830 as the result of hostile legislation and the changed attitude of slaveowners, natural increase of free Negroes guaranteed constant growth. The last ante-bellum generation even saw the enactment of measures looking to the re-enslavement of free Negroes, including laws to facilitate their voluntary re-entry into slavery. The fact that some free men really acted upon their suggestion affords at least some evidence that the lot of the free Negro could be even more unendurable than that of the slave. He was not wanted anywhere; on that, North and South were agreed.

"If there is one fact established by steadily accumulating evidence," said the Southern *De Bow's Review* in the 1850's, quoting with evident approval from a Northern organ, the Philadelphia *North American,* "it is that the free Negro cannot find a congenial home in the United States. He is an exotic among us." And though nearly all of the "famous" Negroes of the period before 1865 were drawn from this class, it is not to be supposed that it was an environment that fostered talent and achievement. Pitifully few of them made themselves memorable. If it can be assumed that slaves who won their liberty were in some measure a selected company, it may also be concluded that the overwhelming majority of free Negroes inherited from their slave antecedents the slave's attitudes, assumptions and expectations, the slave's habits and reflexes. Even the maverick who did break away from the herd did not, it may be supposed, wholly escape that heritage.

Slaves at middle age in 1770–1800 had, of course, been born near the middle of the eighteenth century. The slave system had by that time undergone a long seasoning. Codes more severe in their bare statement than in their enforcement had been adopted. The individual colonies had now emerged from their experimental stage; settlements were stable and permanent, economic and social patterns were hardening. The last decades of the century were dominated by libertarian doctrines and, once political separation from the empire was achieved, by the quest for cultural independence.

After the Revolution one Northern state after another moved to abolish the remnants of the fast-disintegrating slave-labor system, and by 1800 slavery was virtually a Southern institution exclusively. Even in the South, where it had by no means escaped local criticism, moral and philosophical considerations were so powerfully reinforced by economic change that the early demise of the peculiar institution seemed likely until, in the last decade of the century, its term was extended as a number of developments in the technology of the textile industry, of which the patenting of the cotton gin in 1794 was the most spectacular, quickly modified Southern attitudes.

Slave discipline in the late eighteenth century was moderate. Instruction of slaves was tolerantly permitted, though not encouraged, for it was assumed that the black man's incapacity to profit by it rendered such provision futile if not mischievous. Preachers were allowed considerable latitude, and an excess of hands in the upper South multiplied instances of the hiring of slaves to urban employers (in defiance of legal discouragements), and of training them to skills. Except in the North, the condition of the bondmen saw little change during the generation, and such change as there was in the South was perhaps in the direction of amelioration. Then the century closed on a discordant note with the Gabriel Prosser insurrection in Virginia, in 1800, that moved Southerners to reconsider the whole structure of slave controls.

The free Negro population meanwhile grew very rapidly. In the 1790's alone it increased 82 per cent, while the expansion of the slave population was only 28 per cent. Some of this is explained by the emancipation in the North, but more of it is ascribable to the liberalization of manumission by deed, will and paid-redemption arrangements, supplemented by a vigorous natural increase. This growth promptly evoked legal and social constraints as misgivings about the free Negro in a white man's country deepened. After 1800 even liberal Pennsylvania, as it saw with alarm the accelerated growth, tightened restrictions. It stripped its large free Negro population of the right of trial by jury and energized existing vagrancy laws. Maryland, with the largest free Negro population in the several states, in 1783 revoked the franchise granted them by the constitution of 1776, forbade persons of color manumitted after that year to give evidence against white persons, and in effect denied them all other rights of "freemen" (a category then deemed not to include free Negroes), except those of property holding and the right of redress at law and equity for injuries to person and property. Educational provision for Negroes was supplied in Maryland before 1800 by Quakers and Methodists without restriction, and a statute of 1793 required that apprentices be taught to read and write. In the next generation, however, the latter practice fell into disuse as feeling against Negro apprentices mounted.

If a central tendency in American social history in the six decades following 1770 was the effort to found a native American order, the same effort engaged the Negro leader. Denied full participation in that process in the white man's institutions, he proceeded to build his own, beginning with the fraternal order, the church and the school. Other members of the race found self-expression in letters and learning, and still others began the assault upon slavery and caste. The years 1770–1831 saw the emergence of the first Negroes destined to win some sort of renown in America, some twenty-six names that have survived the sifting of time and upon which historians can roughly agree. The next generation, extending to the end of the slave system, brought forward about forty more, yielding a total of less than seventy names for the whole century spanning the eve of the Revolution and the close of the Civil War.

The roll call begins with a flourish. At its head stand the names of Crispus Attucks, first to fall in the celebrated "Boston Massacre" of 1770, and Peter Salem and Salem Poore, who distinguished themselves at Bunker Hill. Cynics play down Attucks's conduct on that stirring day as simply the accident of stumbling out of a barroom and into a British bullet, but his place among Negro heroes is assured, thanks to his dramatic identification with the cause of American liberty. He was, in a sense, the first American to perish in its defense, even while he was himself not wholly his own man. Statues are erected in his honor and schools named for him, but Peter Salem and Salem Poore are remembered only by close readers of Negro history, honored, one suspects, above many a white soldier of similar performance precisely because they were Negroes. All three had evidently begun life as slaves. Attucks, usually described as a mulatto, was a fugitive, and there is evidence that Salem and Poore had been manumitted to permit their service with the Continental forces. All were from the vicinity of Boston, where the social climate for Negroes was perhaps the best to be found in America, and Attucks, who is believed to have fled his bonds when he was past the age of twenty-five and then worked for twenty years as a merchant seaman, may well have been familiar with the burdens that British imperial policy saddled upon American shipping.

Two other heroes of the period prefigured the experience of others who would follow. James Derham, the first Negro physician in America, and Benjamin Banneker, a gifted amateur mathematician and astronomer, were both the product of native gifts nourished by sympathetic whites, and both moved intellectuals to see in their achievement evidence of a Negro potential heretofore unsuspected. Derham, though a slave, had the advantage of a childhood in Philadelphia, including a basic education. As an assistant to a succession of physician-owners, he acquired a medical knowledge that moved the last of his owners, a New Orleans doctor, to offer him his freedom on liberal terms and to help him set up a practice of his own. Banneker, still often designated as the most distinguished Negro of his day because of his unusual intellectual powers, won wide notice as an almanac-maker, designer of what may well have been the first clock to be manufactured wholly in this country, pamphleteer for the peace movement, and member, selected at the instance of Thomas Jefferson, of the commission appointed by President Washington to survey and lay out the projected federal capital.

Both were men of atypical ancestry and far removed in social origins from the lowly plantation hand. Derham was the child of mulatto parents, and Banneker, following the condition of his maternal ancestors, was freeborn. His grandmother was a free white woman said to be one Molly Welsh, an English indentured serving girl who had been deported for a trifling misdeed. Arrived in America, she served out her indenture and then bought a small farm and two slaves, whom she purchased from a slave ship. One of these, named Benneky, believed to be of royal lineage, she promptly married and freed. Their daughter, Mary Banneker (as the name had been Anglicized), subsequently married a native African, who had been purchased from a slave ship by a neighboring planter, baptized into the Christian religion and eventually freed by his master. It was this pair who became the parents of the famous Benjamin. The boy gained a scanty education from an obscure country school for free Negroes and was for many years assisted in scientific studies by George Ellicott, a Quaker and Maryland planter of broad learning and humanitarian interests.

Banneker's deportment while functioning with the Washington survey commission is of some interest. His biographers report that while he was treated with respect by his fellow commissioners, the situation posed an early form of the question of "social equality." His relationship to the commission of course removed from dispute his sitting in with his associates at their conferences and labors, but when, during the stay of the body at their official quarters, he was invited to dine with his fellows at the same table, he demurred and at his own request was served his meals separately. Perhaps more significant is the influence of Derham and Banneker upon public assumptions concerning the race's capacities. Both excited the interest of Benjamin Rush, America's foremost professional man of science at the time, and in the case of Banneker occasion was provided, thanks to Jefferson, for discussion among intellectuals on both sides of the Atlantic.

Prompted by a consciousness of the effect that his history could have upon public estimates of the intellectual endowments of Negroes, Banneker wrote

Jefferson on August 19, 1791, appealing for a more liberal attitude toward the race, invoking his own work as evidence that the "train of absurd and false ideas and opinions which so generally prevails with respect to the Negro should now be eradicated." Earlier writings of Jefferson testify to uncertainty in his mind, but in 1791 he wrote Banneker that no one was more eager than he to see proofs "that nature has given to our black brethren talents equal to those of other colors of men." He was, he said, sending a copy of Banneker's almanac to Condorcet, then secretary of the Academy of Sciences in Paris, as evidence on the point. A generation later, when Banneker had long since died, the old sage of Monticello—to the subsequent confusion of students of the Jeffersonian mind—wrote Joel Barlow of reservations he entertained concerning Banneker's intellectual gifts.

Whatever his final resolution of the matter, Jefferson's vacillations are revealing, for they suggest how tenacious was the assumption of the inherent inferiority of darker peoples, even in the mind of one of the most emancipated spirits of the age. They suggest, moreover, the bearing that the performance of outstanding Negroes might come to have in forcing reconsideration of old tenets. If Jefferson doubted that the case for the equality of all races of men was unproved, he had not closed his mind to the possibility; he only doubted that Banneker proved it. And Banneker, meanwhile, had served the historic function of turning the attention of thoughtful men to reflection upon a question of the highest importance to the young republic.

The chief literary figures of these years were Phillis Wheatley, Jupiter Hammon and Gustavus Vassa. Phillis Wheatley, the most gifted of the three, is much the most famous. Her talent and accomplishment are reiterated in every history of Negro America; she is a favorite theme in inspirational literature and Negro History Week celebrations, and countless women's organizations are named for her. Hammon's reputation was relatively local in his own day and he dropped into obscurity soon after his death, to be rehabilitated as a man of mark because scholars now usually name him as the first published Negro writer in America. Vassa is still more obscure, known only to historians and other specialists.

All three began life as slaves, all achieved their note in the North, and all were evidently unmixed blacks, as Negroes, constantly nettled by white explanations of Negro genius in terms of infusions of Caucasian blood, are fond of pointing out. All three benefited by sympathetic aid and sponsorship of white owners and guardians, and all were devout folk, given to writing in the Christian idiom. Their social origins marked them off from the nation's colored masses, and advantages not available to others were clearly operative in the selective mechanisms that thrust them forward.

Hammon was a beloved slave of the Lloyd household on Long Island. They provided him with a rudimentary education, kept him close to the church, and helped him place his verse before the public, arranging for its publication at Hartford at a time when that city could be considered the literary capital of the fledgling republic. His verse was preoccupied with the salvation-epic, and though Negro scholars have never claimed for him the rank of a poet of serious consequence, he is honored for his priority in the chronology of Negro literature. A remarkable circumstance in his story was his evident satisfaction with his lot as a slave. His long obscurity is often explained by the race's disappointment over his meek acceptance of his bondage. Here then, if this analysis is correct, is an early manifestation of the race's disposition to judge a potential hero in terms of his status as a "race man," apart from the merit of his achievements, and to require that a great Negro use his talents for the amelioration of his people's plight. That Hammon was so quickly forgotten by his people, otherwise so assiduous in keeping alive the memory of those who achieve any sort of distinction, cannot otherwise be explained.

In his surprising *Address to the Negroes of the State of New York,* Hammon exhorted Negroes to be faithful and obedient to their masters. He conceded that liberty ought to be the lot of all men, but admonished slaves to endure their bondage in patience and humility until such time as the race earned its freedom by honesty and good conduct. "For my own part," he said, "I do not wish to be free; for many of us who are grown up slaves, and have always had masters to take care of us, should hardly know how to take care of themselves; and it may be for our own comfort to remain as we are."

Gustavus Vassa's reputation rests upon an autobiography, marked, like Hammon's verse, by a fresh artlessness, and this memoir provides us with the fullest account we have of an eighteenth-century Negro as well as a major contribution to the antislavery cause, an appeal to the nation's conscience. It was originally published in England, where he had removed in order to engage in antislavery work.

Vassa's social origins were far from average. Born in Nigeria, he was kidnapped by slavers in very early youth, taken to America, and placed in service on a Virginia plantation. Subsequently he had the good fortune to become the property of a British officer, and then of a Philadelphia merchant, who took him along as a helper on voyages to the West Indies and aided him generously in his efforts to purchase his freedom. Phillis Wheatley's antecedents were somewhat similar. Like Vassa, she was snatched from Africa in very early childhood and brought in a slave ship to Boston, where she was lucky enough to be purchased by one John Wheatley, a prosperous tailor, to be trained as a personal servant for his wife. Under the family's tutelage, Phillis quickly learned the English language and began acquiring the fundamentals of a classical education. While still a child, she was producing remarkable verse, and when she was twenty, a first volume of her poems was published, not in Boston, but in England, where she had been taken by her master's son because of her failing health.

During her stay in London she was immensely popular, but on her return to Boston her fortunes began to decline, evidence, doubtless, of the dependence of her career on the patronage of her white folk. Her patroness died, she herself contracted an unfortunate marriage, and became estranged from the Wheatley family. In her last years she was earning her keep as a drudge in a cheap boardinghouse. She was considered a prodigy in her time, a sophisticated and competent imitator, and her reputation was kept alive by antislavery writers and publicists of succeeding decades, who knew the symbolic value of an unmixed Negro slave girl lately from Africa to whom General Washington himself had taken the trouble to write a gracious note and whom that august commander later received at his headquarters in Cambridge.

The history of American slave conspiracies parallels the entire history of American slavery itself, but all accounts agree in giving first importance to the risings of Gabriel Prosser (1800), Denmark Vesey (1822) and Nat Turner (1831), all elaborately conceived plots, swiftly put down. All three rebels were hanged. Prosser, who belongs to this period and died with it, is shrouded in obscurity. We know only that he was a Virginia slave, evidently not yet twenty-four years old; that he won adherents by impressing them with testimony from the Bible that God would deliver them as he had delivered the Israelites; and that, judging from the elaborate organization and ingenuity with which the revolt was planned, he was a man of more than ordinary gifts. His plot was foiled by slave informers and a cloudburst. Once captured, he went to his death steadfastly refusing to implicate any of his accomplices.

The one religious leader among this generation's most noted Negroes is Prince Hall, who, though a clergyman, was not a pioneer in the establishment of the independent Negro church, as were religious leaders of the next generation. Remembered as the founder of Negro freemasonry, his reputation is further bolstered by his role as an early, if temperate, champion of Negro rights. Efforts to represent him as a militant "race man" are confounded by surviving writings in which he urged the race to bear its lot with patience, submitting to God's will; but he is known to have been active in a campaign to rouse opinion against the kidnapping of free Negroes for sale into slavery, and in 1787 he petitioned the legislature of Massachusetts to provide for the education of colored children.

Hall came to Boston as a youth, a near-white West Indian emigrant from Barbados, the son of an Englishman and a free woman of French and Negro admixture. He had been apprenticed in the islands as a leather worker. With such advantages over the average American black, he easily became a property owner and voter, a soldier in the patriot cause during the Revolution, and a Methodist minister with a congregation in Cambridge. Early in the war he and a dozen other free men of color were taken into a Masonic lodge attached to a British regiment then stationed in Boston, and when the city was abandoned by the British in the next year, Hall undertook to organize the first lodge of Negroes in America. After repeated rebuffs in this country, he succeeded in obtaining a charter from England in 1787, and African Lodge No. 459 was formally organized with Hall as master. From that time forward, the lodge was to be a major social institution in Negro America.

All of these figures in the Negro vanguard except Banneker and Gabriel Prosser flourished in the North, and all save Prosser and Hall were persons who won their distinction not by what might later have been called "race effort," but by demonstrating that such qualities as courage, intelligence and artistry could be Negro attributes. Not yet fully launched upon the experiment of constructing the Negro replica of American society on his own side of the color line, the Negro of that generation could perhaps make his greatest contribution to the amelioration of the race by proving to the white man that the Negro was a whole man, capable of high achievement. It is doubtful, however, that gifted Negroes were aware of such considerations or motivated by them. In any case, the next generation's leader was to show a significantly different preoccupation.

The years 1801–1831 define an epoch in Negro American history. The young republic was laying the material base for a remarkable civilization in a political climate where the philosophical-libertarian principles of the Jeffersonians were shading off into the coonskin-democracy and equalitarianism of the Jacksonians. In the South, where the cotton kingdom took its phenomenal rise in these three decades, misgivings about the incongruity of slavery in republican society troubled the public mind, urging slaveowners and lawmakers to soften its rigors. Few presumed to justify it without qualification.

The outlawing in 1808 of new importations of Negroes from Africa, however, and the growing demand for hands on the new cotton lands raised the price of slaves, and the massive shift to cotton planting beginning about 1800 led to larger slaveholdings and greater specialization of function. The rising value of individual slaves, together with the fright occasioned by the Vesey Plot of 1822, directed by a free Negro of Charleston, led in the last of these years to some tightening of precautions against slave risings and a notable diminution of manumissions. By 1860, the ranks of free Negroes were being recruited largely by natural increase and by escaped and rescued slaves.

Even so, free Negroes tripled in number in this period. They were found in town and country (the great majority of them still in the latter), and in a wide range of employments, chiefly as common laborers, farm hands, servants and washerwomen. Growing disinclination of whites to countenance assimilation of these folk into their society, rising anxieties concerning race mixture —the mulattoes were always far more numerous among free Negroes than among slaves—plus the threat they seemed to afford to the stability of the slavery system, now evoked new laws and other devices for the more effecutal control of the group. In the North, provision for education of free Negroes made its first effective gains at the opening of the century, but it was in separate schools; and it was mounting prejudice against free Negro worshippers in Methodist churches of Philadelphia, hitherto noted for their hospitality to Negroes and antislavery views, that led them to establish the first separate denominations of their own. Word of brutalities and insults to free persons of color in Philadelphia began to appear in the press during these years, and segregation in public places was becoming common.

Virginia, sobered by the Gabriel (Prosser) Insurrection, began to stiffen its Black Codes. By 1806 it required newly manumitted Negroes to leave the state within twelve days. When states as far afield as Illinois and Indiana retaliated with laws forbidding the entrance of these outcasts, the freedmen could have had few remaining illusions about the hospitality of white society toward their kind. By this time masters otherwise disposed to free their slaves sometimes abandoned the intention when they contemplated the unhappy lot of ex-slaves in a white man's world. New legislation and enforcement of older laws fallen into disuse now insisted more firmly on proof of a free Negro's right to his liberty. He was required to register, to carry "free papers" at all times, and to confront everywhere the presumption, now found in law and the public mind, that all Negroes were slaves who could not, upon demand, furnish incontrovertible proof to the contrary. The period saw, too, the rise of the American Colonization Society and its individual counterparts, and energetic efforts, mainly in the states where free Negroes were most numerous, to rid the country of these folk by inducing them to go as colonists to Liberia.

The Black Codes, constricting Negro education, religious observance, and the whole range of Negro life, slave and free, during these years, were, though increasingly ominous in their tendency, still mild compared with those yet to come. It was in fact the intensification of Southern attitudes and repressive measures that introduced the new era about 1831.

Our sixteen notables for these years, born naturally in the previous era or earlier still, are wholly contained in two categories. No less than ten are associated with the founding and development of the Negro church, and all the rest are remembered principally as militant champions of Negro rights: four as articulate spokesmen for race advance and the other two as leaders of desperate insurrections. While the first contingent in the Negro vanguard had been persons whose attainments might win from the dominant group a respect for the race's fitness to share in a common humanity, the second company, confronted by growing evidence that such a change in the attitudes of whites was not forthcoming, were characteristically folk whose works were directed toward organized protest and correcting the wrongs under which the race groaned, and to doing so by Negro initiative. Whether they were like the embattled Denmark Vesey, Nat Turner, or David Walker striking boldly for the end of chattel slavery, or like Richard Allen or Absalom Jones building a religious structure to enable free Negroes on their own side of the color line to escape the affronts they now suffered as unwelcome communicants in the white man's churches, each was in his way an agent for raising the colored man's condition and pushing forward his quest for dignity.

The four early champions of the race's social redemption exhibit extraordinary differences in their histories, their attitudes toward the problem and the strategy and tactics best calculated to achieve their objects, the nature of their roles and their relation to white humanitarians interested in Negro advance. So great, indeed, are these diversities that here, as in so many instances to be chronicled in succeeding chapters, is evidence of the fatuity of casting Negro leaders into some common mold, contriving some credible stereotypes, and seeking to discover some official Negro position on any question whatever.

The four, Paul Cuffe, James Forten, Elijah Johnson and David Walker, had one trait in common: they were all freeborn men, living in the North, all of them born there except Walker, who was born in Wilmington, North Carolina, the posthumous son of a slave father and a free mother. Cuffe, born near New Bedford, Massachusetts, was the son of a prosperous self-bought ex-slave who had married an Indian woman. Nothing is known of Johnson's parentage, but he is presumed to have been born in New Jersey, while Forten was a native of Philadelphia, the son of free parents whose ancestors had lived in Pennsylvania for generations.

All were literate men. Cuffe learned reading and writing by his own efforts in late adolescence; Walker attained literacy only as a mature man after making his way to Boston. Johnson had a brief common-school education, and Forten, after a few years at the school for colored children conducted by the Quaker Abolitionist, Anthony Benezet, left to go to work at the age of ten, and at fourteen entered the navy in the service of the patriot cause.

Their labors for Negro betterment were equally diverse. Cuffe became a shipowner and, as a prosperous and respected citizen, exerted a steady pressure not upon slavery itself but upon discrimination as it bore upon free men of color. He is best remembered for challenging in the courts (unsuccessfully, as it proved) the exclusion of tax-paying Negroes from the franchise. Like his father, he married an Indian woman and was so far identified with whites that he was received into the Westport Society of Friends. Disillusionment over the outlook for free Negroes drew him for a time—he was to repent of it before he died—into the immigration movement, and in 1811 he sailed to Africa with a small group of Negroes to plant a "friendly society" at Freetown. He intended to return periodically for additional colonists. Ill health supervened, but in 1815 he sent nearly forty more migrants and invested some of his considerable fortune in the enterprise.

Johnson's race efforts were identified wholly with colonization. After serving in the War of 1812 and preparing for the Baptist ministry, he went to Africa as a missionary and colonist in a company of a hundred Negroes, and three whites representing the United States Government and the American

Colonization Society. He labored for the colony in the face of grave reverses and desertions and lived to see it become the Liberian Republic with a Negro as its first elected president.

James Forten, the most celebrated of the four, was, unlike Johnson, a passionate foe of colonization. He was in his day the wealthiest Negro in Philadelphia, the owner of a sail loft employing both Negro and white workers. Like many of the white reformers and philanthropists of that remarkable epoch of reform enthusiasms, he gave his time and wealth to a wide range of humanitarian causes, and though not himself directly touched by the slave system, he came to be regarded as the most important Negro abolitionist of this generation. When not crusading for temperance, peace and women's rights, he threw himself, as an organizer and pamphleteer, into various efforts for Negro progress. In 1817 he presided over a meeting in the African Methodist Episcopal (AME) "mother church" in Philadelphia, called to denounce the designs of the American Colonization Society; and in 1830 he was responsible for assembling a national convention of free Negroes, the first in a notable series, to consider the plight of the free Negro, to plan his social redemption, and, incidentally, to strike again at the colonization idea.

His influence was a major factor in consolidating Northern Negro opinion against emigration and preparing it for the abolitionist doctrines of the antislavery societies just then perfecting their organization, and in the conversion of William Lloyd Garrison and Theodore Dwight Weld to belief in racial equality—a revolutionary mutation in the development of abolitionist ideology which Professor Ray A. Billington has called "the most important single event in the antislavery crusade."

While the American Colonization Society staked its case upon the doctrine of ineradicable racial inequalities, the Garrison-Weld movement was ultimately grounded on equalitarian assumptions, much as Forten and his free colored associates based their demand for first-class citizenship on the premise that Negroes were old American stock, who resented the emigrationist insinuation that they were a threat to the country. Far from abandoning their brethren in slavery, the Forten group called for their emancipation, persuaded that the welfare of all Negroes waited upon the extinction of the peculiar institution. A militant champion of Negro rights like Forten, a man of large means and the scion of several generations of free men, is a less appealing historical figure to the white community than, say, the gentler Phillis Wheatley, for he deviates too drastically from stereotype. But the greater importance of Forten as a shaper of the American tradition can scarcely be questioned.

David Walker had as a free man travelled extensively in the South during his youth, and then gone to Boston as the proprietor of a secondhand clothing store. He read widely in the literature of human slavery, steeping himself also in the history of resistance to oppression, and in 1829 he published his incendiary pamphlet, *Walker's Appeal in Four Articles. . . .* It exploded with shattering force. In the South extreme measures were taken to prevent its circulation, not only by scrutinizing the mails and searching ships putting in at Southern ports, but even, as in the state of Georgia, by setting a price on Walker's head and making the circulation of his work a capital offense.

The *Appeal* was a closely argued, if strident, philippic against slavery, a trumpet call to bondmen to rise in force against their oppressors. It became at once the most widely discussed book yet written by a Negro and the most widely circulated, until others surpassed it ten years later. Two increasingly radical editions followed. Few slaves could have been moved by it, for the overwhelming majority were illiterate, and extraordinary pains were taken to keep the pamphlet from falling into the hands of those who could read. So general was the rejection, by antislavery leaders of both races, of Walker's counsels of violence that he circulated the work at his own expense.

His name was conspicuous enough in his time, but few paid him honor until after his mysterious death in 1830, three months after the appearance of the third version of the booklet. Unproved rumors that he had been poisoned were persistent enough to make a martyr of him. After the Emancipation his stature as a hero increased, however, in militant Negro circles, while white opinion, except that of radicals and some New England reform enthusiasts, was slow to accord him approbation. Thirty-six years after Walker's death his son was elected to the Massachusetts legislature, and sober historians of both races now attach great importance to his contribution, especially because of its timing, for it came at a moment in American history when organized abolitionism was girding for battle and when, on the other hand, majority American opinion was persuaded that the Negro was incapable of self-expression.

If Gabriel Prosser's was the first of the three most famous insurrections, Denmark Vesey's (1822) and Nat Turner's (1831) quite surpassed it in the terror they conjured up. Vesey, a handsome and intelligent young mulatto subject to epilepsy, had been born and reared in the West Indies. He became at the age of fourteen the favored servant of a Charleston slaver, trading between St. Thomas and Saint-Domingue, and sailed with his master's slave ship for twenty years. When he had the incredible luck to win $1,500 in a lottery, he purchased his freedom, became a carpenter, and, goaded by his children's inheritance of their mother's slave status (and his imagination fired by slave risings which had taken place in Saint-Domingue), he matured his famous plot, which so terrorized South Carolina. He gained a considerable influence as an AME Church lay teacher, greatly given to dwelling on the analogy between Negro slaves and another oppressed people led at last out of the house of bondage. A literate man who quoted scripture with telling effect, he was able as a free Negro to carry his message to plantations scattered over a belt a hundred miles wide.

As a plantation Negro, Nat Turner had far fewer advantages. His mother was an African native, and his father deserted his family, fleeing from his bonds back to Africa. Nat was a precocious child, taught to read by his owner's son. He was a deeply religious zealot with a propensity for exhorting his fellows and believed himself called of God to liberate slaves. The divine appointment was revealed to him, he said, by signs upon leaves and in the heavens and by voices that he heard in the air.

The place of such rebels in the annals of Negro notables is a dubious one. Historians and popular writers accord them attention in print, but Negro scholars point out that most Negroes seeking acceptance in American society are under pressure to mute their admiration for some of their historical heroes and martyrs. Vesey is a vivid case in point. Such men do violence to the myth of the Negro's inherent docility and the slave's contentment with his lot; and because he symbolizes a spirit offensive to whites, says Charles S. Johnson, no colored schools are named for him "and it would be [considered] extremely poor taste and bad judgment for the Negroes to take any pride in his courage and philosophy."

That nearly half of the Negroes whom we found most prominently mentioned in the record for 1801–1831 should be religious leaders reflects the fact that the church was the first, and for many years the only, major social organization in America that the race could call its very own. The church's early development was, of course, more extensive among Northern free Negroes, but from the middle of the eighteenth century forward there were colored preachers in the South, many of them slaves, exhorting their own folk and even mixed audiences, as local plantation evangelists or itinerant revivalists. Fears of the growing influence of such preachers over their flocks gave rise to uneasy feelings among whites. In the North a disposition to segregate free Negroes in the Methodist and Baptist churches led to the movement for independent Negro denominations. In 1816, Richard Allen and a number of associates made a dramatic withdrawal from the Methodist Church—in liberal, humane Philadephia—after they had been pulled from their knees during prayer and ordered to the gallery. In time they established what came to be a national African Methodist Episcopal Church, and soon thereafter other denominations, like the African Methodist Episcopal Zion (AMEZ) and the African Baptist were initiated.

In the South, Negroes long continued—in some areas until the Civil War—to worship in segregated sections (or at a separate hour) in white churches, but the Vesey plot and the Turner Insurrection precipitated repressive laws to check the teaching of Negroes to read and write and, incidentally, to cut off the source of literate Negro preachers. Other restrictions, both legal and social, placed existing colored religious leaders under close surveillance, if it did not silence them altogether.

The Negro church was the parent of other social institutions, notably schools and fraternal orders, and it is perhaps not too much to say that these three agencies, the church, the school and the lodge, were the principal organizations comprising the Negro's social structure until the twentieth century. In the ante-bellum period, as now, the church was far more than a religious organization. It was the center of the social life of free Negro communities, providing as well an important vehicle by which these folk might attain status and exercise leadership.

After 1830, the few remaining preachers in the South and a growing number in the North had to find ways to supplement the small provision that their poor parishioners were able to accord them, and in the North the preacher had, besides, to give time to teaching the fundamentals of literacy to children and adults alike. Institutions of higher learning for Negro ministers were not yet available, but despite their lack of professional training, the preachers were the class best equipped to furnish leadership to the race, and it was they who were expected to be the spokesmen for their people to the whites. Many of them stood fearlessly for the emancipation and elevation of the race. Preachers served the abolitionist cause in various ways and were conspicuously identified with the Free Negro Convention Movement. Relatively few associated themselves with the colonization program. Many were active Underground Railroad agents and a goodly number were fugitives themselves.

From an early date, the Negro's aspiration to status and authority found its best chance of realization in the church. The colored minister, in the North from the beginning and in the South after the Civil War, enjoyed wider freedom of expression and influence than any other Negro in his community, for he derived his authority from his own people. Until well into the twentieth century, the ministry was more attractive to the ablest men of the race than was the case among whites because of the Negro clergyman's primacy in his community, not only as its spiritual leader but also as its most learned member—"counselor of the unwise, the friend of the unfortunate, the social welfare organizer, and the interpreter of the signs of the times," as Carter Woodson has said. Some were, in all candor, not religious men at all, but other avenues of preferment were closed to them. Though in the twentieth century the clergyman lost some of his old pre-eminence to other professional men, he was often able to retain his foremost position because the urban Negro churches were becoming vast social agencies with secular functions that invested their pastors with new importance.

For the period 1801–1831, ten pioneer religious leaders stand out. Richard Allen was the founder and first bishop of the African Methodist Episcopal Church and James Varick of the African Methodist Episcopal Zion connection; Morris Brown and Daniel Coker were associated with Allen in the establishment of the AME Church, and George Liele and Andrew Bryan were early Negro Baptist organizers. Absalom Jones is identified with the origins of the Negro Protestant Episcopal churches (not a separate denomination) and Lemuel Haynes, a Congregationalist, was the first regular Negro pastor to white congregations. John Chavis was a Presbyterian clergyman and schoolmaster in North Carolina, and Lott Cary was an early Baptist missionary to Africa. Schools also sprang up in the shadow of the church, but they were of such modest character that as yet not a single name in our list for this period is that of an educator except John Chavis, the master, not of a Negro school, but of a school for whites.

Pre-eminent among these religious leaders was the patriarchal Richard Allen, who, by his leadership in the establishment of a separate denomination for Negroes, attained at once the stature of a race leader hitherto not achieved by any other Negro and thereafter unequaled until the rise of Frederick Douglass. In laying the foundation for a national denomination, Allen was founding the first permanent interstate association of Negro Americans. Thirty years earlier he and Absalom Jones had taken a first step leading to the independent Negro church when they initiated the Free African Society in Philadelphia. This, though a local body, was in fact the first mutual-aid society for Negroes in the land, a quasi-religious reform organization that included in its program for the "free African's" social redemption the systematic building of a fund for mutual aid, burial assistance and the relief of widows and orphans; co-operation with the abolition societies of the city; resolutions and regulations looking to the strengthening of marriage customs and the raising of standards of personal conduct; and correspondence with free Negroes of other cities with a view to extending this movement far beyond the borders of Philadelphia.

Devout Methodist though he was, Allen was thinking in secular terms as well as religious. Both through the Free African Society and as an independent pamphleteer, he was an early and courageous antislavery spokesman, and he gave his denomination a decided abolitionist orientation from the outset. "I entreat you," he said, in a characteristic *Address to the People of Color* (1831?), "to consider the obligation we are under to help forward the cause of Freedom." He threw himself into the cause of developing Negro education and was an outspoken opponent of the American Colonization Society. He was a principal organizer, with Forten, of the Free Negro Convention Movement; indeed, its first convention was held at his Bethel Church, with Allen himself as its elected president. He was particularly insistent that Negroes must become group-conscious; that the initiative for the crusade for final freedom must come from within the Negro group itself, working in association with sympathetic whites; that group solidarity would be an indispensable element in resisting further affronts.

Absalom Jones was long a coworker with Allen in the Free African Society and in the effort to organize independent Negro church establishments, but the two eventually parted amicably to enable Jones, who felt drawn to the Anglican tradition, to become rector of the first separate Protestant Episcopal congregation for Negroes, the first of many Negro parishes eventually organized. Like Allen, he was identified with a variety of secular activities. When Philadelphia was swept by a fearful yellow-fever epidemic in 1793, Allen and Jones organized relief measures for the Negro population, and two decades later the pair raised a company of militia for service in the War of 1812. Jones became also the first Negro Grand Master of Masonry in the United States as well as founder and director of an insurance company and of a society for the suppression of vice, and cofounder of a school for colored children in Philadelphia.

Liele, Bryan, Varick, Coker, Cary and Brown stand out less prominently in the historical record than do Allen and Jones, but the whole company have a number of attributes in common. All were evidently born in slavery except Morris Brown, who had the very considerable advantage of birth among the "free people of color" in Charleston. In the extraordinary social structure of Charleston, this group had such close relations with the aristocratic whites, with whom they were connected by ties of blood, that they were for all practical purposes exempt from the usual incapacities imposed on their kind. Before the Vesey scare they had their own schools, and Brown had a fair education for that day.

The other seven, though born in slavery, also had advantages that eased their ascent. Allen, for example, the son of mulatto parents, was born in Philadelphia and sold as a boy to a farmer of Dover, Delaware. In his youth he underwent a conversion and almost at once became a religious worker with permission to hold services in his owner's home. As a self-taught pastor, he preached to whites and Negroes and was allowed by his owner, meanwhile, to "work out" to buy his liberty. He and his brother contrived to purchase their freedom with savings earned by hauling salt, cutting cordwood and working in a brickyard.

Jones enjoyed similar advantages, and scarcely felt his bonds. He was an unmixed black, born in Delaware, but as a child was encouraged to learn to read and to purchase a speller and a Testament with the pennies that a favored young slave could save. At sixteen he was taken to Philadelphia as a handyman in his owner's store, and there a clerk promptly taught him to write. A few years later a period of instruction at an evening school completed his formal education. He married one of his master's slaves and purchased her freedom with money he and she earned by working for wages in the evening. The pair's industry enabled them to buy a home and then Jones's own freedom. (Because the slave or free status of children was by law determined by the status of the mother, the redemption of a wife was sometimes placed ahead of that of the husband.) The couple continued in the employ of their former owner, and in time built two more houses and rented them.

Daniel Coker's rise also illustrates the importance of fortuitious advantages. He was born in Maryland, the son of a white, English indentured serving-girl and a slave of the same master. His owner's little son (or, by some accounts, Daniel's white half brother by a previous marriage of his mother) was his inseparable companion, and refused to go to school unless Daniel accompanied him. It was thus that Coker acquired his basic education. For reasons now not clear, Daniel himself was counted a slave, but at an early age he fled to New York. Here he joined the Methodist Episcopal Church and, like so many colored pastors of his day, was quickly ordained a deacon —in his case by no less a dignitary than Bishop Asbury himself. When he returned to Baltimore to take up religious work, he concealed his identity until he had been freed by friends who collected funds to buy him, a precaution later to become fairly common among fugitives who became conspicuous targets for slave hunters. He became, with Allen and Jones, a co-founder of the AME Church and subsequently managed a school operated by the Bethel Church in Baltimore. In 1814, Coker was sent as a missionary to West Africa with ninety Negro emigrants who sailed under American Colonization Society auspices, and there he won his reputation both as the AME Church's great missionary and, to the disappointment of his early abolitionist friends, as an organizer of settlements for free Negro expatriates.

Another of the missionary pioneers was the Baptist leader, Lott Cary. Born in Virginia, he was hired out to a Richmond tobacco warehouse where he fell under corrupt influences until he was stopped short by an overwhelming conversion experience, one of whose fruits was a desire to learn to read that he might study the Bible. He learned largely by his own efforts, supplemented by occasional hints which he wheedled out of his fellow workers. He saved his earnings, adding to them by selling the tobacco scraps which he was permitted to salvage. Soon he bought freedom for himself and his family and was promptly licensed to preach by the First Baptist Church of Richmond. In 1815 he helped organize the Richmond African Baptist Missionary Society and was sent by the Baptist Board of Foreign Missions as a missionary to Africa. Though not himself sympathetic to emigration schemes, he sailed with a shipload of colonists and co-operated with the American Colonization Society in the founding stage of the Liberian Republic.

Virtually nothing is known of the social antecedents of James Varick beyond the fact that he was born near Newburgh, New York, probably about 1750, and presumably as a slave. George Liele and Andrew Bryan were both Southern slaves, apparently of mixed blood, and it appears that their education did not carry them beyond modest literacy. Soon after his youthful conversion, Liele began exhorting his own people, and after a trial sermon before a quarterly meeting of white Baptist ministers, he was licensed as a local preacher. When these men first emerged as preachers, there were as yet no Negro denominations, and Methodist and Baptist exhorters were characteristically untrained men, ignorant of theology. The leadership in both denominations in the eighteenth century was, moreover, inclined to antislavery, equalitarian and humanitarian views, so that the ordination of Negro ministers was as casual as the recruitment of white laborers in the vineyard.

Whites were, for conscience's sake, disinclined to place obstacles in the way of the growth of a Negro clergy, at least until the Vesey plot and the mounting alarms of the early 'thirties, and there was, furthermore, the conscience-soothing argument that slavery was the means of snatching the savage from heathendom to the fold of grace. Even hardened slavocrats were loath to sacrifice a consideration so congenial to American sensibilities. All of the ten we are here considering were in some way significantly helped on the road to religious leadership: they were converted under the preaching of white men, admitted to worship in the white churches, assisted to literacy and manumission, and even, as in the case of Bryan, defended by their owners against hostile whites alarmed over the rise of Negro churches. The slave condition may in the case of men like Liele and Bryan even have been an advantage. Like many a Negro pastor, Liele was long unsalaried and supported himself by hiring out his labor, but he continued as a slave until his pious master freed him. Bryan bought his wife's freedom long after their marriage, but for many years was content to remain the property of an indulgent master who aided him in the organization of churches, and only upon his master's death did he purchase manumission from his late owner's estate.

However indulgent the attitude of some toward Negro preachers and the developing Negro church, there were from the beginning folk who viewed them with misgivings. In the North these doubts, as we have seen, took only the form of increasing hostility to the admission of Negroes into white congregations, an affront which led Negroes to create their own denominations. In the South, however, notably in South Carolina, resistance steadily hardened. At Savannah, Andrew Bryan and his followers met overt opposition, but he continued his efforts despite being twice imprisoned by whites determined to silence him. At least once he and his slave followers were whipped, but their master interceded for them and the presiding magistrate ruled that they were entitled to freedom of worship during the daylight hours. The owner then offered the worshippers one of his barns as a sanctuary. Liele escaped similar resistance by moving to Jamaica and establishing Negro Baptist churches there.

Even Morris Brown was compelled to flee his favorable Charleston environment and transfer his labors to the North. He had served as a travelling minister, acquiring considerable influence around Charleston, and became so interested, after the manner of AME leaders, in the improvement of the Negro's lot that he was once imprisoned for displaying too much sympathy for slaves. Then, in 1822, the Vesey plot brought all Negroes of influence under suspicion and it was pointed out that the independent status of the

AME Church made it suspect, to say the least. As the pressure on articulate Negroes increased, Brown fled to Philadelphia in 1823 and quickly took rank there as a leader in every concern of the race. Five years later he was made a bishop and upon Allen's death in 1831 was left as the sole bishop of the connection.

In our group of ten religious leaders, Lemuel Haynes and John Chavis are sufficiently unlike the others to warrant special attention. Chavis's career sprang from a fortunate coincidence of talent and opportunity. Evidently a "pure" Negro and born free in North Carolina, he was sent by a white North Carolina gentleman, it is said, to Princeton University to study privately under President Witherspoon to demonstrate whether a Negro could assimilate higher learning. He later passed through a regular course at Washington Academy and became a Presbyterian clergyman in Virginia. About 1805 he returned to North Carolina, where he joined the Orange Presbytery, ministering to whites and slaves in various churches. The dignity of his manner, the purity of his speech and his classical education won him a reputation that enabled him to establish a preparatory school for sons of prominent whites, some of whom he boarded in his own house. His young charges included the future United States Senator Willie P. Mangum, Governor Charles Manley, the Reverend William Harris, two sons of Chief Justice Henderson of the North Carolina Supreme Court, and others who became lawyers, doctors, teachers, preachers and politicians. Even he was forced to yield to the legislation evoked by the Nat Turner rising, by which Negro teachers and preachers were silenced.

Here was an unusual Negro hero, celebrated not for a direct contribution to the elevation of the race, but for demonstrating the Negro's capacity to play a white man's role in the white man's society, and in fact more frequently instanced as a "Negro leader" than are several other notables of this era.

Much the same may be said for Lemuel Haynes, a hero to Negroes because he succeeded in identifying himself fully with the white community. His father was an unmixed Negro slave and his mother a white woman of respected New England family, the hired girl of a Connecticut farmer. The shamed and hapless girl abandoned the baby, and the Haynes household, to spare her family, gave it their own name and that of Lemuel, "consecrated unto the Lord." The child was bound out to a pious deacon of Granville, Massachusetts, in whose home he lived for more than thirty years. The indenture stipulated that he was to have the usual district-school education; and after absorbing what the poor backwoods school had to offer, Lemuel continued his education by private study, encouraged by his employer. After serving in the Revolution, he returned to the Haynes home, apparently was enrolled for a time as an irregular student at Dartmouth, and then studied theology under a white preacher in Canaan, Connecticut, laboring in the fields for his keep. In 1780 he was licensed to preach. He married a white schoolteacher—after prayerful consideration—and throughout his life served a succession of white pastorates in Connecticut and Vermont. He lived his life among the whites and as a white man, though never attempting to conceal his race. Widely beloved and respected in Congregationalist circles, he was befriended by Presidents Dwight of Yale and Humphrey of Amherst, and a few years after his death a leading Congregationalist divine published a full-length biography of Haynes. None of his published writings allude to his Negro connection. Some Negroes criticized him, then as later, for his preoccupation, in the tradition of Jonathan Edwards and George Whitefield, with sin in the abstract to the exclusion of any concern for particular evils like slavery and discrimination, and there were those who felt that his talents could have made him an earlier Frederick Douglass. A more typical judgment was that of the *Colored American,* which declared on March 11, 1837, a few years after his death, "He is the only man of *known* African descent who has ever succeeded in overpowering the system of American caste."

These then were the nation's first Negro heroes. Diverse though they were, the group of twenty-six, drawn from the two generations spanning 1770–1831, present at least three notable uniformities. First, all were in some sort Negro pioneers: the first to die for America, to win glory in her wars, to become published writers, to initiate an independent Negro church, or to establish congregations for Negroes in the white man's denominations, and the like. Second, such distinctions as they achieved were not won in direct competition with whites. Though they fall into two general groups from this point of view—those who demonstrated the Negro's capacity to make some contribution to society and so furnished their race with new claims upon their white countrymen, and those who made some overt attack upon the white man's arrogations—they had in common the fact that each is remembered for furnishing leadership somehow in the struggle to raise the Negro's condition. Third, these folk typically made their mark on their own initiative, often encouraged by sympathetic whites, to be sure, but not as sponsored agents of white organizations or their programs.

Twenty of the twenty-six were born in slavery and grew up under the handicap of family instability and want of responsible direction, and the rest, though free men, were with an exception or two not far removed from bondage or beyond its influence. Such eminence as was achieved, however, was typically won in freedom, not in chains; the three insurrectionaries who purchased a place in history on the gallows and the dubious case of Jupiter Hammon were the melancholy exceptions. It was, chiefly, the rare Negro who was born free or who made a successful flight to freedom, or who was manumitted, purchased, or snatched into liberty or at last emancipated by law, who recruited the tiny company who made their names memorable, while their less-favored kinfolk, often literally without family name, would live and die in deeply shadowed obscurity. They were, with few exceptions, folk who had contrived somehow to appropriate some of the white man's education and a great deal of his religion, to learn a faltering use of his social instruments and to work with him sometimes for common goals.

In every case the "racial situation" was the critical element—indeed the occasion—for such celebrity as they attained, whether it was Richard Allen and Absalom Jones creating an independent Negro church in protest against white affronts, or Lemuel Haynes or John Chavis winning applause for breaking through the barrier of caste; whether it was Nat Turner striking in awful desperation at the peculiar institution, or Benjamin Banneker, Phillis Wheatley, or James Derham furnishing proofs of the consonance of high intellectual achievement with Negro blood; whether it was James Forten, capitalist-equalitarian-abolitionist, or Lott Cary transporting the gospel and colonists to Africa. All of them, finally, exhibit variations that must have been involved in the origin of the species. Formidable though their handicaps were, it must appear that the great mass of Negro folk were vastly more hard-favored than these—so much so that by contrast the typical prominent Negro was the fortunate possessor of advantages which, pitiful though they were, enabled him to raise himself above his fellows.

The prominent Negroes who had emerged in the sixty years before 1831 were primarily men who had absorbed as much of the culture of the whites as their limited opportunities allowed. In the next generation, a somewhat larger company were characteristically people who found economic and social disabilities increasingly intolerable precisely because they had assimilated so much of America's civilization and had come to share its values and expectations. Such men, even if they were free, moved naturally into the antislavery crusade because, through racial discrimination, they were identified with the enslaved Negro.

The years 1831–1865, now to be surveyed, were in American social history pre-eminently the time of the rise of the common man, heralded by fresh winds of religious and philosophical doctrine, quickened humanitarian impulses, and a new hospitality to levelling tendencies. Liberalization of the franchise, organization of the emergent industrial working class, multiplication of free schools, enlargement of women's rights, more humane social provision for society's wards, and a host of other conscientious concerns were in varying degrees effected by wide-ranging reform efforts. Small wonder that the slave should have excited this American generation's liveliest attention, particularly in the Northeast and the new states north of the Ohio, where not only was the far-flung reform movement more vigorous anyhow, but where there were, besides, fewer considerations of economics, class structure and social control to muffle the call of conscience.

The reform enthusiasms of these years were increasingly channelled into the antislavery movement and the Negro leadership adjusted itself easily to this formula. Convinced of the futility of slave revolts, they worked now in close association with a growing army of Northern abolitionists. Just as the religious leader, typified by Richard Allen, had dominated the previous period, so the next saw the Negro-rights crusader, epitomized by Frederick Douglass, move to the fore—the rocklike Douglass whose pre-eminence as race leader was to persist until his death in 1895, the very year when Booker T. Washington was thrust into the role of the nation's most famous Negro by his celebrated "Atlanta Compromise" address, signalizing a strategic retreat which a changed national attitude then compelled.

By 1831 slaves were, to the satisfaction of Southern opinion, a permanent element in the life of the region, while the free Negro was everywhere an unwelcome exotic. Although the preceding generation had subjected both classes to increasing surveillance, the opening of the 'thirties saw a series of events that so greatly accelerated this process that it is customary to consider the year 1831 a turning point in Negro history. The fact that these reactionary developments went forward in an age of new and generous cultural, intellectual and humanitarian strivings only threw into sharper relief the issues that the illiberal aberrations raised.

Southerners took fresh alarm at the mounting resistance of slaves to their bondage; and the institution had, moreover, fallen under increasing free-Negro attack, ranging from Walker's *Appeal,* which struck as much terror into Southern hearts as did armed insurgents, to the annual sessions of free Negroes to consider the plight of the race (the Convention Movement), from 1830 forward. The year 1831 saw not only the blood-chilling Turner Insurrection but the establishment by William Lloyd Garrison of the inflammatory *Liberator* and the organization of the New England Antislavery Society as well, followed two years later by the founding of the American Antislavery Society.

Multiplying threats to the security of the slave system drove Southerners to its aggressive defense. It was now no longer to be tinctured with apology and reservations as a permissible institution in the South's peculiar circumstances. From now on the defense was to rest on the bold affirmation that the institution was a positive good for both white and Negro, a fateful development signalized by the appearance in 1832 of Thomas R. Dew's *Review of the Debates in the Virginia Legislature of 1831 and 1832,* later (1852) reissued as *The Pro-Slavery Argument.*

As the argument waxed ever more shrill, the whole machinery for holding the race under control was further elaborated to keep Negroes ignorant, dependent and cowed, and their society primitively atomized.

The years 1830–1832 brought a rash of such legislation. Instruction of slaves was forbidden, colored preachers were muzzled, and the assembling of three or more Negroes, slave or free, except under supervision of whites, was categorically prohibited. Slave-hiring was now rigorously circumscribed, and the possession of drums, whistles or musical instruments interdicted lest they serve as signals for revolt. Slaves found as little as eight miles from home were presumed to be runaways and subject to awful discipline.

The free-Negro class in the South saw a corresponding degradation, and new obstacles were put in the way of manumission. The chances for the freeing of a slave living in Virginia, for example, in the generation preceding 1800 were about one in ten; in 1800 to 1832 about one in twenty; in 1832 to 1860 about one in fifty. Prompt deportation of newly freed slaves was required in many states in the early 1830's and sharp checks were placed on the mobility of persons long free, extending even to prohibiting their crossing county lines. They were forbidden to marry slaves, to teach or to preach, or to receive instruction from any person of whatever race, and vocational choice was progressively constricted. They were kidnapped back to slavery or re-enslaved by legal subterfuges, a stratagem which their steady loss of rights in court did little to obstruct, for they might now not give evidence against whites. On the other hand, a slave could testify against a free Negro—so far had the latter's status deteriorated.

In Northern states the decay was less vividly marked, but even here social encroachments, actual or feared, fed a tendency to repressive laws and race prejudice. The most liberal states, though quick to improve every opportunity to assist fugitive slaves to freedom, perversely closed more and more doors of opportunity to the class whose numbers they were helping to swell. In the 1830's, yearly meetings of Philadelphia Quakers deplored the general disposition to regard Negroes as "an inferior and degraded race . . . [who] had made no progress, could make none, and . . . should not be allowed to make any," and it was becoming clear that many a zealous opponent of slavery—or of slaveowners, perhaps—was remarkably susceptible to color prejudice. "It was true in Pennsylvania as elsewhere," wrote one careful student, "that for no one did a darker future seem in store, for no one did there seem less hope, than for the Negro." Such was the environment in 1831–1865 out of which that generation's leading Negro-Americans had to rise. It was also the social context in which those who came to prominence in the years until 1900 and even beyond were born and grew up.

Of the thirty-nine individuals in the roster for this period, some thirty are remembered chiefly for contributions to the Negro protest and race-advance effort. The other nine include four writers, an actor, a concert singer, an inventor and a "hunter, squaw man, and raconteur." The absence of religious leaders contrasts sharply with the roster for the generations immediately preceding and following this one. At least ten of the thirty-one Negro-rights contenders were or had been clergymen, but only one of them was a church leader whose fame lay outside the race-advance movement. This is not to say that the influence of the Negro church waned, for it remained more than ever a dominant force in Negro America. But with the pioneer work accomplished, independent denominations or congregations founded, and a network of other religious agencies in being, even the most important divines were less likely to stand out than their predecessors had been. Meanwhile in the South, the work was virtually halted by the legal and social pressures evoked by the Vesey and Turner risings.

The thirty celebrities* of this period, whose chief claim to the historian's notice lay in their contribution to race-advance effort, are an extremely various company as well from the point of view of the nature and importance of their reform achievements as that of their social origins. Some were historical accidents. Dred Scott, for example, was at best an illiterate, good-natured, shiftless slave, whose successive removals about the country by his owners furnished the pretext for the fateful court battles that he himself scarcely understood. After the case in which he was the central figure had dragged its way through years of litigation, until finally disposed of by the Supreme Court in 1857, he remained a slave, a lazy and amiable porter at a St. Louis hotel, where he was pointed out to staring guests as a historical curiosity.

Anthony Burns was another leaf swept up by a whirlwind and pinned for a moment upon an eminence that must have startled him. A Virginia slave who had picked up his alphabet from white playmates, he became after an ecstatic religious experience, a slave-preacher. His big chance came when his trusting owner hired him out to an employer in Richmond from whence, in 1859, he fled on a vessel aboard which he happened to have a friend. Not many months later he was arrested in Boston. The city, already inflamed by the Fugitive Slave Law of 1850, was further excited by the presence of suffragettes and abolitionists just then holding anniversary conventions there. Crowds, urged on by such venerated crusaders as Wendell Phillips, Theodore Parker, Thomas Wentworth Higginson and Richard Henry Dana, endeavored to block Burns's return to his master, but the combined resources of federal and local governments, including military escorts and a revenue cutter to transport the captive back to Virginia, finally effected his return to slavery at a cost to the taxpayers variously estimated as being from forty to a hundred thousand dollars.

The fame of Josiah Henson rests similarly on slender personal achievements. He escaped from bondage into Canada where he became a preacher,

* James Madison Bell
Henry "Box" Brown
William Wells Brown
Anthony Burns
Samuel E. Cornish
William and Ellen Craft
Alexander Crummell
Martin R. Delany
Frederick Douglass
Henry Highland Garnet
Josiah Henson
Lunsford Lane
Jermain Loguen
William Cooper Nell
James W. C. Pennington
Robert Purvis
Charles Bennett Ray
Charles L. Remond
Joseph Jenkins Roberts
Edward James Roye
David Ruggles
John B. Russwurm
Prince Saunders
Dred Scott
James McCune Smith
William Still
Sojourner Truth
Harriet Tubman
Samuel Ringgold Ward
James M. Whitfield

participated in slave rescue work, helped establish an industrial school for people of color, did some speechmaking in behalf of antislavery societies in New England and even in Britain and, with a great deal of assistance, wrote one of the autobiographical "slave narratives" that abolitionists were so willing to sponsor. His real renown springs from a chance meeting with Harriet Beecher Stowe to whom he related his story, for he became the prototype of her famous Uncle Tom. Though his title to the dubious honor has been disputed, his peculiar place in history rests on the success with which he exploited his identification with Mrs. Stowe's hero.

Others in this generation were memorable only because their dramatic escapes from slavery were capitalized for propaganda purposes. Henry "Box" Brown, by his own account a well-favored slave, was finally aroused by separation from his wife and children to escape. He had a sympathetic white merchant nail him up in a crate and ship him over the Adams Express Company's lines to an Underground Railroad agent in Philadelphia. After a rough twenty-six-hour journey by rail, steamboat and wagon, he was claimed at the Philadelphia baggage room by the consignee. Antislavery agitators promptly adopted him as a lecturer on the iniquities of the slave system, and Negro history had another hero.

In the following year, William and Ellen Craft, a Georgia slave couple, made an equally audacious bid for freedom. Ellen was to disguise herself as a white gentleman. (She was the daughter of her owner by his light-skinned slave, and herself so nearly white that she was constantly mistaken for her mistress's own daughter, a circumstance so annoying to that lady that she finally presented the child to her daughter as a wedding present in order to rid the community of her.) Her husband was to be passed off as her slave. After carefully accumulating articles for the disguise and wheedling a "Christmas pass" from their mistress, they made their perilous way from the interior of Georgia, gravely handicapped by their illiteracy. Travelling through slave states and emerging at last in the North, they were quickly taken in hand by antislavery groups and sent on tours to appear at meetings not only in the United States, but also in Canada and England where reformers kept up a steady agitation to mobilize antislavery opinion in the whole Anglo-American community. The inevitable slave narrative appeared under the title *Running a Thousand Miles to Freedom* (London, 1860).

Such autobiographies were an important staple in the antislavery crusade. They varied greatly in quality and originality. Several were written by lesser figures than those in our roster, but the heroes we have identified were also responsible for a few of them. Some, like those of Frederick Douglass, William Wells Brown, James W. C. Pennington, Samuel Ringgold Ward and Jermain Loguen were competently written by the heroes themselves, while others were manifestly ghosted and still others, like the narratives of Lunsford Lane, Sojourner Truth and Harriet Tubman, were set down in the third person by whites. Publication and circulation of the books were vigorously pushed by organized abolitionists.

Still more extensive exploitation of these folk was made by antislavery societies in sponsoring them as speakers, organizers and officers of local, state and national groups. Frederick Douglass became a polished orator, but others pressed into service as speakers could offer little more than halting versions of their stories. Some who served as lecturers and organizers were not ex-slaves at all but highly articulate free Negroes, striking effective blows against slavery and for the advancement of free Negroes. Abolitionist leaders were moved to enlist these Negro spokesmen in active abolitionism because in some cases their moving stories, and in others their intelligence and commanding personalities, afforded compelling propaganda for the Negro rights cause. "Can anyone longer say," cried Wendell Phillips, as he rose to adjourn a meeting that had just heard from Frederick Douglass one of the majestic oratorical efforts in which that generation delighted, "Can anyone longer say that this is a *thing!* Can anyone now deny that this is a MAN!"

At least sixteen of the thirty-two race champions were conspicuous on the antislavery lecture platform, and Douglass, Garnet, Nell, Purvis, Remond, Still and Ward were among those who served as organizers, agents and officers for the major abolitionist groups as well. Douglass was in the high command of the American Antislavery Society, Purvis was one of its founders; and others, like David Ruggles and Charles Bennett Ray, in addition to labors for the larger cause, were important officials in state vigilance committees to protect free Negroes from kidnapping and, in defiance of the Federal Fugitive Slave Law, to shield fugitives from recapture.

The principal service of some lay in their literary contribution to the struggle while they were at the same time involved in other forms of protest. On a more sophisticated level than the slave narratives was a budding race-conscious literature in the periodical press, in pamphlets and in books that multiplied as the period wore on, much of it by men with ideas of their own, quite independent of white abolitionist confederates. Indeed, the poverty in "pure literature" in this generation is largely explained by the crusading preoccupations of potential literary talent that might well have flourished in more tranquil times. James Madison Bell, the radical antislavery lecturer who found it prudent to reside in Canada during the six years preceding the Civil War (and even at that distance helped John Brown assemble men for the 1859 raid), is often listed among the early Negro poets, but his single-minded allegiance to antislavery propaganda thwarted the development of any real technical excellence. James Whitfield, another example of these untrained poets, was similarly preoccupied, and died en route to Central America on a mission in behalf of an emigrationist project over which Martin R. Delany, physician and antislavery writer, presided. Meanwhile, the successive editions of Douglass's autobiography were supplemented by his spirited addresses in pamphlet form, to say nothing of his famous weekly *North Star*.

William Wells Brown was a literary pioneer militantly identified with the race as its first considerable novelist and playwright and one of its first historians. All of his works dwelt on Negro themes: history, biography, sketches of slave life, miscegenation—a steady stream of articles for the antislavery press and, after the Civil War, a history of the Negro's part in that conflict. Brown was, in fact, a professional reformer, a Negro associate of the remarkable company of crusaders who gave the pre-Civil War generation one of its most vivid qualities. He was active in the rescue work of the underground, an associate of Garrison and Phillips, and for several years a lecturer for the New York and Massachusetts antislavery societies. He was deeply involved in the temperance, woman-suffrage, prison-reform and peace movements. In 1849 he represented the American Peace Society at a world peace congress in Paris, and before returning to America spent five years in England, where he delivered nearly a thousand abolitionist lectures.

Others were impressed by the propagandist value of historical records. William Cooper Nell, another organizer and speaker for abolitionist groups, for many years connected with Garrison's *Liberator,* began collecting Negro historical data and produced in 1852 the brief *Services of Colored Americans in the Wars of 1776 and 1812,* followed four years later by the more impressive *Colored Patriots of the American Revolution*. . . . Meanwhile, William Still, a principal conductor of the Underground Railroad in Pennsylvania, was assembling records of the fugitives who were slipping over into Canada, a treasury of documents later to be turned into his *Underground Railroad*.

Negro journalism took its rise in this period also and gave its major stress to protest. Samuel E. Cornish and John B. Russwurm founded the country's pioneer Negro newspaper, *Freedom's Journal,* in 1827, and though Russwurm soon emigrated to Africa, Cornish continued to edit it and its successors with vigor for the next twenty years. One of the major figures in abolitionist journalism, his organs campaigned stoutly for full citizenship and equality for the Negro. He, too, was a participant in various reform programs: a trustee of the schools for free Negroes in New York City, a member of the executive committee of the American Antislavery Society and an energetic promoter of higher education for persons of color. Although abolitionism and the case against colonization claimed his columns' main attention, they spoke for all the humanitarian causes of the time. Charles Bennett Ray, another of these many-sided freedom fighters, conducted the *Colored American;* and Ruggles, the radical free-Negro-rights pamphleteer, was a travelling agent for the *Emancipator,* an Abolitionist paper, and conducted a bookstore heavily stocked with antislavery literature, in addition to being so assiduously active in slave rescue work that he is said to have assisted a thousand fugitives to freedom. It was Douglass, however, who became the most famous of the Negro abolitionist editors, after founding the *North Star*.

The figure of Douglass now overshadows his contemporaries, but students of Negro heroes see in men like James McCune Smith, Alexander Crummell, Martin R. Delany, Henry H. Garnet and David Ruggles, crucial innovators in the early shaping of a social philosophy for the race and in the evolution of a strategy for raising its condition. Their writings afforded an early debate on the fundamentals, a tentative formulation of assumptions and conclusions later to be refined by experience. Smith, a dignified and highly trained physician, identified with numerous forms of race endeavor, was important for his pioneering in the scientific study of race. With Crummell, one of the two most highly educated Negroes of his day, he brought a scholar's temper, a knowledge of history, and a familiarity with the sciences, languages and literature to the writing of essays and articles on a remarkable range of Negro themes. His work significantly directed sober thought to the controversy over the Negro's physical and moral equality with the rest of the human race.

The more radical Garnet, whose following diminished after his address to the annual meeting of the Convention Movement in 1843, where he called upon slaves to mount a general strike and to slay if need be, was another whose contributions to antislavery literature helped to clarify issues and define alternatives. One authority sees in Garnet the originator of "the idea which Frederick Douglass tempered and presented to the world in more . . . acceptable form." Ruggles was another whose radicalism, especially respecting free Negroes, frightened readers away; but he, too, helped to clear the air. Martin Delany, a Harvard-trained physician who rose to the rank of major in the United States Army immediately following the Civil War, was another significant voice in the ante-bellum battle-of-the-books over the plight of the Negro, but his volume, published in 1852, was not well received in his day because it preached emigration to Central America as a solution to the free Negro's dilemma.

Crummell's most productive years, 1853–1873, were spent in Africa as a clergyman, political leader and agent of the American Colonization Society, but he was a major figure in Negro America in the decades both preceding and following his African sojourn. Modern interest in him centers on his reputation as a literary stylist, but in his own day he was more noted for his contribution to the emergent ideologies of race adjustment. It was he above all others who, before the Emancipation, preached an optimistic view of the Negro's prospects, a buoyant self-confidence as a challenge to the sense of inferiority to which the Negro in America had so long been conditioned. His inspiriting exhortations to independence of mind and confident aspiration—impressively validated by his own example—struck a note that anticipated the counsels of militant Negro leadership a century later. He has been a hero to disciples of the doctrine of challenge ever since William E. B. Du Bois in his

Souls of Black Folk (1903) devoted a chapter to Crummell and another to Booker T. Washington, a comparison to the decided advantage of the former.

Among the miscellaneous efforts of these early champions of Negro progress was the development of schools for persons of color. Cornish was a trustee of the Free African Schools of New York and assisted the Tappan brothers in founding a secondary school at Cheyney, Pennsylvania; Henson established an industrial school in Canada; Russwurm became the first superintendent of schools in Liberia, and Nell led a campaign that ended separate schools for Negroes in New York in the middle 'fifties. Pennington and Still were early heroes in the fight against discrimination on public conveyances. The latter led what was to prove in 1867 a successful assault upon segregated streetcars in Philadelphia; and, in New York City, Pennington and his parishioners, insisting on their rights, precipitated a court battle that ended in a ruling in favor of equality for all races on the cars. In the same spirit Nell attacked discriminatory employment practices of the United States Government, and in 1861 had the satisfaction of being appointed by the postmaster of Boston as a clerk, the first Negro to hold a post in the federal bureaucracy.

Nearly all of the group were prominent in the Free Negro Convention Movement, the annual congresses where every affront to first-class citizenship was denounced and the outlines of an ideology and tactics for the Negro protest were hammered out. Some were, in fact, more strenuously occupied with the Free Negro Movement than they were with abolitionism, but in almost every case reformers active in behalf of either cause were active in the other as well. This disposition to join the fortunes of all Negroes, bond and free, like mountain climbers roped together, was a dominant note in the race effort of this generation, much as race leaders a century later were to reiterate the thesis that every accomplished Negro was a living argument against Jim Crow.

A few of the number were involved in promoting colonization to Liberia (or, as in the case of Delany and Whitfield, to Central America or Nigeria), typically in collaboration with the American Colonization Society, but this was always a minority cause, not only among Negro leaders but among the masses of free Negroes as well. Individual Negro-rights champions, the abolitionist press, the Free Negro Conventions, and even the rank and file of white humanitarians not especially engrossed in Negro problems, opposed the scheme—sometimes with astonishing vehemence. When Russwurm, the race's first American college graduate, resigned as editor of the stoutly anti-emigrationist *Freedom's Journal* and went over to Africa to promote colonization, having concluded that it was a "mere waste of words to talk of ever enjoying citizenship in this country," he was roundly damned for his treason by his former abolitionist friends in both races. Other members of the group besides Russwurm, Delany and Whitfield, who braved such criticism and cast their lot at least for a time with emigrationist programs, were Roberts and Roye (both of whom became presidents of Liberia) and Prince Saunders, who made a name for himself in Haiti but came to be regarded by Negroes generally as something of a fraud and a self-seeker.

The most dramatic form of race redemption was the rescue operations, carried on usually—as in the case of William Wells Brown, Henson, Loguen, Purvis, Ruggles and Still—in conjunction with the famous Underground Railroad. Easily the most celebrated of them, however, was Harriet Tubman, the "Moses of her People," who preferred the role of a lone operative. After her own escape from Maryland, she embarked upon an incredible career of forays into the South to lead fugitives—the number eventually exceeded three hundred—to freedom. A gaunt, illiterate woman, persuaded that she was led by God, she threatened with death any of her "passengers" who wavered. She was sometimes drafted as a speaker at antislavery meetings and during the War served with Union troops in the South as a laundress, cook, nurse and guide for scouting parties and raids. She remains one of the most venerated of Negroes, one of the trio—with Frederick Douglass and Sojourner Truth—in this period who are always assigned topmost places in any compilation of Negro notables.

Douglass is perhaps familiar enough to the literate American, but Sojourner Truth—so widely did she deviate from the white community's image of the "good Negro"—is so little recognized among whites that she was not included in the *Dictionary of American Biography*. After her emancipation by law in New York (1827) she became a half-legendary "sojourner," preaching abolitionism, women's rights and other reforms at gatherings, secure in the knowledge that she was a chosen vessel of the Lord. Though illiterate, she had the reputation of an oracle.

Nearly all of the thirty-two are usually described as persons of mixed blood. Probable exceptions were Crummell, Delany, Ruggles, Scott, Tubman and Henson, though even these are, in some accounts, represented as having at least some Caucasian admixture. Ward, for example, is often called a "full-blooded" Negro. Wendell Phillips said of him that "when he shut his eyes you could not see him," and he was for that reason a favorite with abolitionists who were always on the alert for evidence to confute those who attributed to white ancestry any talent that a Negro might exhibit. Ward himself pointed out in his autobiography, however, that he was one-sixteenth white, the remote descendant of a Maryland slaveowner.

At the other extreme were persons fair enough to "pass": some of them the children of light-skinned parents whose white forebears were some generations removed; others, the immediate descendants of whites. William Wells Brown and Ellen Craft were the children of white masters by mulatto slaves, and Douglass was the son of an unknown white father and a slave whose mixed blood included an Indian strain. Loguen was the natural son of a planter whose slave, named Cherry, was for many years his mistress and bore him several children. Cherry, in turn, was a freeborn "pure" African, who had been kidnapped from her childhood home in Ohio and sold into slavery. Roberts was presumed to be at least seven-eighths white, and Purvis, a "voluntary Negro," was extremely fair. He was the freeborn son of an English merchant who had settled and prospered in Charleston, and his mother was the daughter of a German-Jewish merchant and a Moorish girl, a white woman by European standards, who had been kidnapped in Morocco at the age of twelve and sold into American slavery. Russwurm was born in Jamaica, of a white American and a native woman, and when the elder Russwurm moved to the United States, he sent the boy to Canada. To conceal their relationship he renamed him John Brown, but the white woman whom he later married insisted that the boy be taken into the family. Others in the group were also the sons of white fathers, and some were the fruit of casual slave marriages in which one or both of the partners were of mixed blood. Charles Bennett Ray was proud of his descent from Indians, English settlers and the first Negroes brought to New England.

Fifteen began life in slavery, but all of them, Dred Scott excepted, escaped its bonds. One was free under the New York law ending slavery in that state, only one was freed by purchase, and the others were runaways, all of them except the Crafts from the upper, border South. Some of the runaways had been moderately well off compared with slaves generally. Box Brown wrote that he had never been whipped, overworked, or mistreated by his unusually kind master, and the Crafts gave similar testimony, but all three were finally spurred to rebellion by the dispersion of kinfolk through sales. Others traced their revolt to cruelties to themselves or relatives, while still others never made the decision for themselves but (like Ward and Garnet) were carried to freedom by parents. Autobiographies of fugitives indicate that slaves who were relatively well off were just as restive as those whose lot was especially hard, that the will to freedom was strong in intelligent slaves, and that it was other factors, particularly fair prospects of success, that were determinative.

Some of the fugitives, like William Wells Brown, Douglass and Loguen, failed in their first attempts but persisted in spite of severe punishments. The perils were not over when they reached free territory; there was always the danger of recapture, particularly after 1850 when the law gave every advantage to the slave hunter. When they did not take the still greater precaution of settling in Canada, runaways commonly changed their names and dropped into obscurity. The decision to join the Negro-rights crusade rather than lie low in discreet anonymity was a heroic act in itself.

William Wells Brown happened to be in England on a lecture tour when the Fugitive Slave Act was enacted, but he found it expedient, even though he had made his escape as much as sixteen years earlier, to remain in Britain until 1854 before venturing home again. Ward, snatched to freedom in infancy by his runaway parents, did not learn until he was twenty-four that he had been born a slave, so fearful were his elders that an incautious word might lead to their recapture. Pennington kept even from his wife the secret that he was a runaway, and following the act of 1850, sought safety in England, while a friend negotiated for the purchase of a deed of manumission from the estate of his owner. Even the intrepid Douglass, more than a decade after his escape, took out this insurance against re-enslavement, a step regretted by some abolitionists because it seemed to concede the property right of slaveowning. Douglass, upon completing the first draft of his autobiography, was warned by Wendell Phillips to burn it lest it lead to his capture, but abolitionists generally urged him to bring out the book to reassure skeptics that so gifted and lionhearted a man was an ex-slave. Long after his escape, Loguen's mistress had the temerity to write, offering to accept one thousand dollars to cancel his obligation to her, but she received only a magnificently indignant letter in reply. Long ago, when still a slave, he had scorned self-redemption, vowing that he would never pay for what was his birthright, and he was severely critical of others who used that resort particularly after they had made good their escape.

In making the break, many of the escapees were helped by white humanitarians in the Underground Railroad and by personal assistance at both ends of the journey. Box Brown, we have noted, was unchained by a Southern white merchant. William Wells Brown, when he finally succeeded in getting over into Ohio, fell into the hands of a Quaker who took him in while he prepared for the next leg of his journey to Canada. Hitherto known only as William, he adopted the name of his benefactor, William Wells Brown. Many found shelter and some their introduction to literacy at the hands of Quakers. Pennington, after a harrowing flight, was taken in by a Quaker for six months and taught to read. Even Harriet Tubman, the most daring saboteur of them all, planned her escape with the aid of a Southern lady.

The life these escapees had lived in slavery rarely afforded opportunities for education or other personal development, but in several cases it did supply motivations for their later contributions to the cause of race advance. Box Brown wrote that he was kept in such profound ignorance that he and his fellows believed that their master was God and his son was Jesus Christ. Still he had his advantages, for his duties were in and around the house, not in the field, and he was also hired out to a factory in Richmond and after a time permitted to live there. William Wells Brown was hired to a succession of employers, including steamboat lines, and no less a humanitarian than Elijah P. Lovejoy, the abolitionist editor soon to be martyred. He was even leased for a year to a slave trader who "neither loved his Maker nor feared Satan," and it was then that he saw slavery at its worst.

He had also known it at its best as the pampered companion of a little white cousin whose mother had died and who was being brought up by William's owner. His determination to run away was nourished during his years of river-boat service, when, as he said, "continued intercourse with educated persons, and meeting on the steamer so many travelers from the free states, caused me to feel more keenly my degraded and unnatural situation." Eventually his owner, in need of cash, offered to sell him his freedom, but the proud young slave declined. Loath to sell his own kinsman to a trader, the planter ordered William to find a buyer himself, but the young man and his mother ran off instead, only to be recaptured. The owner now decided to sell William's mother but to retain him, and even tried to forestall another flight by purchasing a handsome slave girl of whom William was very fond and offering her to him as his wife, but the youth refused the bait for he was already determined upon another trial for freedom.

Douglass, separated in infancy from his mother, suffered under cruel masters as a child, but he had at least the advantage of being sent to Baltimore as a very young house servant. There he learned to read from white playfellows, with some help from his mistress over her husband's objections. His first escape attempt brought him a jail term, but his master soon sent him off again to Baltimore, this time to learn the ship calker's trade—a real boon to him later in freedom. He was still only barely literate when he escaped, but his training by antislavery groups as an abolitionist agitator turned him shortly into a lucid and forceful speaker, autobiographer, journalist and pamphleteer.

Sojourner Truth and Harriet Tubman were lifelong illiterates. The former, a near-black and one of twelve children, was owned by a succession of masters in New York State and early separated from her kinfolk. She had five children by a husband forced upon her by her owner, but the family was dispersed before slavery was ended by state law in 1827. Harriet Tubman likewise was one of eleven children widely scattered by sales. At her own insistence she was returned to field work after a period as a hired houseworker, and some years later was injured by a blow on the head from an iron weight hurled by an overseer at a slave whom Harriet was trying to shield from his rage. She suffered from "sleeping seizures" for many years thereafter, and because she was not considered a "breeder" she was not required to take a mate at the usual early age.

Josiah Henson's conditioning as an abolitionist was simple and direct. As a child, he saw his mother brutally assaulted and his father lashed, mutilated and sold south, for striking an overseer who was thrashing her. Soon she, too, was sold, leaving the lad without parental care. His hostility to slavery was apparently concealed, for as a young man he was given supervisory duties on the farm and even became the overseer. Once he came to his master's rescue in a tavern brawl and then was waylaid by the adversary, who beat him so severely that he was partially disabled for life. In a lawsuit brought against the assailant by Josiah's owner for damages to his property, Henson, as a slave, could not testify and the court accepted the ruffian's plea that he was only defending himself against a slave's insolence.

Sometime later his owner entrusted Henson with the responsibility of conducting twenty slaves to a kinsman in Kentucky. There he worked under favorable conditions for three years, when, badly cheated in a self-purchase bargain and learning that he was to be sold to New Orleans, he fled with his wife and two infants by the Underground Railroad to Cincinnati. Here he found his situation rendered precarious by the Fugitive Slave Law, so he continued until he was safely in Canada. He was already forty years old and now learned to read from a son who preceded him in school.

Such schooling as the others enjoyed came only after they had escaped to the North. Garnet and Ward, carried in childhood by their parents to New York, happily had access to the African Free School on Mulberry Street. Ward was able to pursue his studies further when Gerrit Smith, the philanthropist, helped him with funds for classical studies at Oneida Institute, but Garnet's efforts to secure further education encountered less hospitality. With two other Negro youths (one of whom was Alexander Crummell) he matriculated at an academy established by abolitionists in Canaan, New Hampshire. The trio incurred the hostility of townsfolk when they participated in the speechmaking at a Fourth of July celebration. The aroused patriots hitched forty-five yoke of oxen to the school building, dragged it to a swamp and fired a parting salute to the Negro boys as they rode off to New York atop a stage coach.

Loguen secured his only formal training at Oneida Institute. Pennington, already a grown man when he escaped, had his first instruction in literacy from the Quaker who took him in for several months after he crossed the Pennsylvania line, and when he found employment on Long Island he added some night-school work, supplemented later by private tutoring. Within five years after his escape from Maryland as an illiterate, he was teaching school and preparing for the ministry. He later recalled that in his earliest years his father was separated from the household by some two hundred miles, that he was afforded only the barest minimum of parental oversight, and that, while suffering for want of security and affection, his unhappiness was compounded by the tyranny of the slaveowners' children.

The roads to freedom taken by Lunsford Lane and Anthony Burns—the only persons in this group who were manumitted—deserve notice. Burns, after the bold attempt of the Boston mobs to rescue him, finally fell into the hands of a friendly master who sold him to individuals in Boston interested in freeing him with funds raised by public subscription. He enrolled in the preparatory department of Oberlin and stayed on, thanks to the generosity of a Boston woman, for several years at the college, before becoming a Baptist pastor in Canada, serving the abolitionist cause with occasional speeches.

Lane was born in Raleigh, North Carolina, one of the 250 slaves of Sherwood Haywood, and had the advantage of being brought up in the special quarters for house Negroes. His playmates were the children of both planters and slaves, and he was quite unaware of the difference until he reached school age and noticed that his white companions were now put to studies while he was assigned instead to a full round of chores. Even so, in the manner of bright young house Negroes, he picked up an education of sorts from his youthful white playfellows as well as from frequent contact with cultivated whites in and about the home.

As these gentling influences separated him ever further from the humbler field hands, he coveted his freedom. He began saving the tips that a bright young slave could pick up in a household that entertained a constant stream of guests and soon he was supplementing this income by selling peaches, cutting firewood and turning his hand to whatever employment offered, far into the night.

Meantime he married a young slave of a covetous master who skimped her on food and clothing, knowing that Lane's growing hoard of cash would supply the deficit. Despite this burden, Lane undertook to conduct a business of his own in the spare time that his kindly owner allotted him, for the young slave had learned from his father how to put up an excellent preparation of pipe tobacco. Unfortunately for the young tobacconist, his owner died and the less amiable widow now ruled his destiny. She did, however, allow him to hire his time for $120 a year, provided he supplied his own subsistence. He redoubled his efforts, distributing his little fifteen-cent packets of tobacco from his own shop in Raleigh and through agencies as far away as Fayetteville, Chapel Hill and Salisbury.

In eight years he amassed one thousand dollars besides paying a like amount for his time and providing his own and part of his family's keep. He now approached his mistress to discuss terms of self-purchase and she coolly demanded his entire capital. He had no choice but to accept, but a new obstacle supervened. The legislature was by now disinclined to authorize manumissions except for "meritorious service," so he transferred his money to his wife's owner, who "purchased" him and held him in nominal slavery until he could take Lane with him on a business trip to New York, where formal emancipation was made.

Returning to Raleigh, he enlarged his enterprises by acquiring a firewood business and serving as messenger for the governor at the capitol. He now engaged to buy his wife and six children. Their owner had acquired them for less than six hundred dollars and had had their labor for years and only part of the burden of their keep, but he now asked three thousand dollars for them, reducing the figure, upon the earnest pleas of the harassed Lane, to twenty-five hundred dollars, payable in annual installments of five hundred dollars. Lane was allowed to take his family under his own roof at once, but title to the woman and children was to pass to him when the debt was extinguished. Hardly had the happy family begun its life together when a new difficulty presented itself, for a number of white townsmen, alarmed by the ex-slave's rise, were determined to be rid of him and to offer an example to others who might emulate him. Lane was confronted by a court order peremptorily directing him to leave the state conformable to the state law of 1827 forbidding Negroes from other states (Lane was now a "free Negro of New York") to tarry in North Carolina for more than twenty days. He had made every effort to avoid giving offense, keenly aware that he had far too many irons in the fire to be risked against the hostility of the community, but it was the young bloods and poorer whites who induced a magistrate to invoke the statute. Influential citizens intervening in his behalf delayed execution of the order for four months, but he was at last compelled to leave.

Taking one child with him for the payments already made, the distracted freedman fled to New York and Boston where, by telling his story before abolitionist meetings, at churches and even from door to door, he raised the funds to meet his obligations. Assured by the governor that he could safely come to claim his family, he returned to Raleigh, only to be arrested for delivering abolitionist lectures in Massachusetts. A hastily contrived "court" failed to convict him, but he was warned by sympathizers that it would be unsafe to remain in the state. The Mayor of Raleigh agreed to conclude the final purchase of Lane's family and to look to their safe conduct to Philadelphia, but Lane himself barely escaped with his life after having been dragged by a mob in the direction of the public gallows and then, on soberer second thought, to a wood where he was stripped, tarred and feathered. He slipped away the next morning by train, minutes before the mob learned he was aboard. Once in the North, he served extensively as a lecturer in New England antislavery groups until the Civil War.

Sixteen of the thirty-one race champions were drawn from the free-Negro class; only three of them were born in the South and even these had fled the region early in life. As a child, Delany, a grandson of slaves, moved to Chambersburg, Pennsylvania, after his parents found color prejudice unendurable even in relatively liberal western Virginia. Purvis moved from Charleston, South Carolina, to Philadelphia when he was only nine; and Roberts, another near-white, migrated as a young man with his mother and younger brothers from Virginia to Liberia.

With the exception of Russwurm, a West Indian, the thirteen remaining were freeborn in the North. Some, like Remond, the son of a West Indian hairdresser who had been admitted to full citizenship in Salem, Massachusetts, boasted that not a drop of slave blood coursed through their veins, while others descended from parents newly freed. William Still, for example, was the son of a Maryland slave who had lately come North after redeeming himself, and whose wife and older children had escaped. Once established in New Jersey, the reunited family changed its name to elude slave hunters and settled in a thinly inhabited area where William was born, the youngest of eighteen children. James McCune Smith's father was freed by the New York statute of 1827 and his mother was self-emancipated. Crummell's maternal ancestors had been free for generations, but his father's people had been recently liberated.

The educational histories of the group showed wide disparities. Bell had only a token schooling and was apprenticed to a plasterer, while Russwurm's white foster mother (even though his father had died and she had remarried) sent him through Bowdoin College as the first Negro to take a degree at an American college. Purvis earlier attended Amherst, but did not finish his course, while Crummell and Smith attended the Free African Schools in New York City and built impressively upon this foundation. Crummell, after the disastrous Independence Day incident, enrolled at Oneida Institute, founded by the Quaker abolitionist, Beriah Green, for colored youth. After finishing there he was refused admission to an Episcopal seminary, but accepted at another in Boston. Then, in England, where he was soliciting funds for a church he hoped to build in New York, some distinguished liberals, recognizing his talents, helped him through Queen's College, Cambridge, where he took a bachelor's degree in 1853. Smith took an A.B. at the University of Glasgow in 1834, an A.M. in 1836 and a medical degree in 1837. Delany's earliest education in western Virginia was at the hands of book peddlers and other clandestine instructors, and he later studied under a clergyman employed by a society of free Negroes. When he had already made a reputation as an antislavery journalist, he entered Harvard Medical School, after being denied entrance at the University of Pennsylvania and at medical schools in New York State.

William Still apparently had no formal schooling, while Saunders, after two years at a charity school associated with Dartmouth College, taught colored children in Boston and there enjoyed education of a kind by association with such cultivated men as William Ellery Channing. Ray and Remond in Massachusetts and Roye in Ohio attended common schools while Ruggles in Connecticut attended a manumission society school. Ray, after learning the shoemaker's trade, prepared for the ministry at Wesleyan Seminary at Wilbraham, Massachusetts, and Wesleyan University at Middletown, Connecticut. Nell studied at a colored school in Boston, but finished at a mixed school where painful discriminations motivated his subsequent battles for equal educational rights for all children. He read law in an attorney's office, but at the urging of Wendell Phillips did not seek admission to the bar because it would require him to take an oath supporting the Federal Constitution and thus compromise himself with the slave power.

Of the thirty-nine notables of these years, only nine were outside the category of Negro-rights champions. Three (two writers and an inventor) derived from the Creole-Negro stock of Louisiana where the French culture tolerated the curious *plaçage* system. The years had seen the emergence of a caste of handsome "octoroon" women, some only one thirty-second or one sixty-fourth Negro. They were barred from marriage with whites by law and custom that refused to give religious and legal sanction to this uninhibited miscegenation, but they were at the same time too conscious of their Caucasian heritage to countenance mating with Negroes. Like their mothers before them, they became the mistresses of white men—almost invariably French—as the only course open to them. These alliances were often arranged at the "quadroon balls" in the old *salle D'Orleans* after candid discussion of credentials and terms between the girl's mother and the prospective "protector." Sometimes the affair was terminated when the protector married, but often enough he preferred not to encumber himself with a wife, or, not infrequently, he undertook to maintain two households at once, quite without loss of caste.

The education of the children of these exotic unions was virtually interdicted by custom on the ground that every educated Negro was a potential inciter of servile revolt. As a result, such sons of wealthy fathers were sometimes sent to French universities where they lived as Europeans and the peers of their schoolfellows. When they returned to ostracism and segregation in New Orleans, the adjustment proved most painful.

Victor Séjour and Camille Thierry, both included in the *Dictionary of American Biography,* but almost never noticed in histories or anthologies of Negro American letters, were representatives of this Negro-Creole strain. Séjour was the offspring of a liaison between a quadroon of New Orleans and a French Creole who had come to that city from Saint-Domingue and prospered in business. The elder Séjour diverged somewhat from the classical *plaçage* pattern, for he had apparently a tiny admixture of African blood himself and many years after the birth of his son actually married his handsome concubine. Victor was sent to a college in Paris and established a permanent home there, returning briefly only after his father's death to look after his property and to acquire an octoroon mistress to take back with him to France. He enjoyed enormous popularity in Paris as a playwright and was a friend of another celebrated author-dramatist of mixed French and Negro blood, Alexander Dumas.

Thierry, a poet, was another who found folk beyond New Orleans unsympathetic to writers of color and, indeed, unable to read their works, for they wrote only in French. Removal to France seemed their only recourse. Thierry, the son of a Frenchman from Bordeaux and an octoroon mistress, was prepared for a French university by private tutors in New Orleans, but the death of his father put an end to these plans. He inherited his father's lucrative business interests, but found the drudgery so unendurable that he let affairs get out of hand while he made repeated trips to Paris, wasting his patrimony in epic dissipations. Convinced that he could no long bear the social isolation to which his color condemned him in New Orleans, he left his affairs in the hands of agents and after several years of high life in Paris became a Bordeaux recluse, the best of the remarkable group of Louisiana writers of French verse in the ante-bellum period. Neither Séjour nor Thierry wrote in the tradition of social protest, but the theme of racial persecution now and then emerged in their work.

A third exotic was Norbert Rillieux, a machinist whose inventions transformed the sugar-making industry. He was the natural son of a white Frenchman by a New Orleans quadroon. His father, an engineer, sent him to school in Paris where he became an instructor in applied mechanics at l'Ecole Centrale. When French manufacturers rejected his vacuum pan for the evaporation of sugar, he returned to New Orleans and in the decade 1845–1855 had the satisfaction of seeing his machinery widely installed. By this time, racial tensions made life in New Orleans unthinkable and he returned permanently to France. In his later years his system was adopted by at least 150 factories in Europe.

Two others also achieved their reputations outside the normal American environment. Ira Aldridge, famous for his role in Shakespeare's *Othello,* was born and reared in the United States, but made his dramatic career and his permanent home abroad. He was a mulatto, the reputed grandson of a Senegalese prince. He attended the Free African School in New York, a theological institute in Schenectady and Glasgow University in Scotland. As attendant of the English actor, Edmund Kean, he perfected his talent and quickly became a popular success in England and Ireland. Failure to win an audience in Baltimore, where he had spent much of his youth, persuaded him that his own countrymen were not ready to recognize a colored dramatic artist, and he returned to England, resuming his success there and on the continent, honored as a leading interpreter of Shakespeare. He maintained a palatial home near London, married an English woman and, after her death, a Swedish lady of distinguished family.

James Beckwourth is another peripheral figure, quite withdrawn from his group. He was the son of a white man and a mulatto woman with some Indian admixture and himself more Indian in appearance than African. For six years he even abandoned his white associates to live with the Crow Indians and had a succession of Indian wives. He was only a picturesque frontier figure—fur trader, horse wrangler, squaw man and raconteur, whose memory survives, even in the *Dictionary of American Biography,* because of a colorful biography said to have been written at his dictation.

Four others remain to be noticed.

This generation saw the first Negro American musician to achieve more than local distinction: Elizabeth Taylor Greenfield, a concert singer. She was born in slavery in Natchez, but passed as an infant to the care of a Quaker woman of Philadelphia, who reared her and whose friends gave her elementary instruction in singing. She was later sponsored by an army officer's wife, but brief concert tours in the Northern cities and England brought her more praise from critics than support from the public.

The other three were poets. George B. Vashon was trained as a lawyer, a graduate of Oberlin who read law for a time under a future American Secretary of the Treasury, but the attention historians give him derives from his poetry and from his having been one of three Negroes on the faculty of a white college established by abolitionists in McGrawville, New York. His professional duties left him little leisure for writing, and when he did turn his hand to poetry, it was to plead his race's cause.

A second poet was George Moses Horton, a full-blooded black slave. More celebrated for the circumstances of his career than the merit of his verse, he was wholly self-taught—he learned to read by studying hymnbooks—and showed in his best work a talent that might have issued in greater verse had it not been thwarted by the shiftless and bibulous life that his situation did little to discourage. His owner had found him unproductive as a farm hand and permitted him to hire his time and to take employment as a janitor's assistant at the state university at Chapel Hill, where he added to his meager earnings by writing rhymed *billets-doux* to order for the college boys.

Much the most popular poet was Frances Ellen Watkins Harper. The verse and fiction that entitle her to consideration as a writer came after the War, but because her greatest fame derives from her antislavery work she is mentioned here. She was born in Baltimore of free parents, orphaned at an early age, cared for by an aunt, and attended her uncle's school for colored children. She began to work for a living at thirteen and a decade later was teaching domestic science at a seminary in Ohio. By 1853 she was in Pennsylvania, actively associated with the Underground Railroad and soon thereafter with the Maine Antislavery Society as a full-time lecturer. Her booklets of antislavery and religious verse sold by the thousands because of her fame as a reformer and because she circulated the books with the aid of whites at her abolitionist lectures.

The Civil War heralded a major turn in the American road. The country entered an era of fabulous economic expansion, bringing in its train a business civilization that transformed our social climate. New forces were in the ascendant as politics became venal, corrupt and subservient to the business community and as earlier reform enthusiasms faded into nostalgic memories.

For the jubilant Negro it was the Emancipation, of course, that marked the transformation, but the freedmen, lately the wards of a cradle-to-grave paternalism, soon learned that the felicities of freedom were offset by new anxieties. After a fitful season of trial and error, a new order was imposed upon them, differing remarkably little in its externals from prewar antecedents, even though the dislocations attending the confused readjustment were so catastrophic that for a year or two the bulk of the Negroes were reduced to utter want and tens of thousands quite literally perished.

But while the servile relationship was reincarnated in tenancy and sharecropping, Negro family structure, buttressed at last by social and legal sanctions, began to approach American norms. If at first many neglected the formality and some grasped the opportunity to dissolve alliances of which they had tired, thousands of households were regularized by formal "re-marriage." Progress was slow but, at least for the future, marital fidelity and the family as a biological, social and economic unit sustained by law, religion and custom were to mean the same thing on both sides of the color line. Such social mutations always proceed slowly. Liberation, moreover, found thousands of freedmen in the condition of displaced persons so far as family affiliation was concerned. Families had been so long and so widely dispersed that it was hopelessly impossible to dissolve subsequent connections, reunite scattered kinsmen, and define family ties with accuracy. The absence of stable family names among slaves also baffled attempts to trace family connections, and the confusion was compounded when the ex-slaves, at their pleasure, adopted their late owners' surnames (so that Carter's George became George Carter), or chose new names or modified old ones to suit themselves.

This generation saw America's Negroes double from approximately 4,500,000 to nearly 9,000,000, while their proportion to the total population remained roughly constant at about 13 per cent. These years saw also the beginnings of the shift of Negroes cityward and northward, though at the end of the period, nine tenths of the colored population were still in the South, five sixths of them rural folk.

Now began also the emergence of common schools for Negroes in the South, the expansion of modest facilities already in being in the North, the mushrooming of denominational colleges and the appearance of "industrial institutes" and, late in the era, Negro land-grant "colleges." The new day in Negro education dawned too late to be a factor in the rise of those whose careers came between 1865 and 1900, but a few were the beneficiaries of new opportunities provided by Northern missionary-teachers, and all of them shared in the development in the sense that their careers matured in a community changing from an unlettered folk to a moderately literate people. Only a tenth of the country's Negroes, most of them in the free-Negro class, could read in 1860, but in 1900 more than a half of the entire group were literate.

While new doors opened to the Negro, new barriers were thrown up and old ones reinforced to contest his advance. Once federal troops were withdrawn, Jim Crow patterns and a new etiquette of race relations were elaborated; and even more fateful than this evolution—too familiar to require description here—was the tightening hold upon the national mentality of certain attitudes and assumptions. The common Negro's doubts of his own capacities now operated to fix his level of aspiration. Formerly the question had been academic, for he was not his own man, but now old feelings of inadequacy persisted into the new era of freedom as whites with new reasons for perpetuating the sense of inferiority affirmed—indeed *legislated*—it, and as Negroes themselves faced the hard facts of a life in a hostile community for which they had been so pitifully ill-prepared.

Whatever Negroes might think of their capacities, it was white opinion on the point that counted more. This was as yet an era when whites honestly believed the Negro to be congenitally inferior. When the brilliant Joseph C. Price, educator and race leader, died at thirty-nine, his case was cited, even by admirers and by Northern white professors in Negro colleges, as proof that "no Negro can master a college course and devote himself to study without shortening his life. Price was a wonder, but he paid the cost by his early death." Outstanding Negroes of mixed blood were invariably explained by Caucasian ancestry. Booker Washington was accounted for on these grounds and he repeatedly pointed to the pure African Price as a refutation, just as others mentioned Phillis Wheatley or Paul Laurence Dunbar, until then the most gifted poets of the race, both presumed to be of pure African blood. "I am just as much opposed to Booker Washington as a voter with all his Anglo-Saxon re-enforcements," declared a United States Senator from Mississippi, "as I am to the cocoanut-headed, chocolate-colored, typical little coon, Andy Dotson, who blacks my shoes every morning. Neither is fit to perform the supreme function of citizenship."

This was the day of the Anglo-Saxon cult, of the White Man's Burden, of the Chinese Exclusion Act; this was the high-water mark of social Darwinism. It was the era when the image of the bestial, "burly Negro" was fixed in our catalog of stereotypes and when writers were creating the models that Sterling Brown has identified: the Contented Slave, the Wretched Freeman, the Comic Negro, the Tragic Mulatto, the Local Color Negro and the Exotic Primitive. A leading Negro historian, Rayford Logan, in his book significantly titled *The Negro in American Life and Thought: the Nadir, 1877–1901,* has described the era and its sterility, so far as Negro social gains were concerned, in richly documented detail. It is against such a backdrop that the principal figures in the Negro vanguard for the post-Civil War generation should be judged.

Nearly a hundred in this book's roster fall in this period. More than half owed their recognition to political "careers" in the South, a forced growth, burgeoning only briefly under the protection of federal troops during the chaotic Reconstruction. While it lasted, political disabilities laid upon whites, enfranchisement of Negroes, aggressive party organizing by white Republicans, and the overwhelming concentration of the Negro voters in Republican ranks gave the race its first political opportunity. Free at last from lawful slavery, the race was increasingly deserted by the Northern white allies who had heretofore provided leaders and shock troops in the campaign for their social redemption. Its adjustment to the new environment was cautious and prudent. A few might revel in new-found power, some might even match the white man's rascalities in politics, but this generation's notables were typically dedicated to their people's improvement so that they might rise to the responsibilities and opportunities which the law now gave them.

The majority of Negro officeholders in the Reconstruction served in state and local government, but the best remembered were the twenty-two who reached Congress.* Six others of the most prominently noticed held state offices, two were party officials, and a few were minor diplomatic appointees.

That Negroes were far from controlling Southern politics is attested by the small number sent to Washington. In the four years following the war, Congress contained no Negroes at all, and in the next eight years the average was six. During the twelve Reconstruction years, 1865–1877, only two Negro Senators were seated (one for a year), and fourteen Representatives, six from South Carolina, where the black population was heaviest and political activity most aggressive. Nine of the fifteen former slave states had no Negro Congressmen at all in the Reconstruction years. In the fourteen years, 1877–1891, after termination of the Radical program, Negroes averaged only two seats per Congress, and in the next decade there was never more than one to represent the nation's Negroes, by that time grown to more than eight million.

For solid achievements in making public policy, the careers of these national legislators were not important for the race or for the nation, but their names, ignored by white historians, are conspicuously inscribed in Negro annals, though even there they are celebrated more for managing to occupy these high posts with dignity under hostile pressures than for objective accomplishments. Most of them had been members of postwar state constitutional conventions and state legislatures before going to Congress. All were Republicans and came from "black belt" districts where Negro voters were strong enough to insist at district nominating conventions upon a share of offices.

Both of the Senators succeeded to the seat of Jefferson Davis of Mississippi, who had vacated it to become President of the Confederacy. Negroes made up more than 90 per cent of the Republican party in Mississippi, but in the legislature where Senators were chosen they had only a fifth of the seats. Three senatorships were at stake in 1870: one for a full term; one for an unexpired term of five years; and, to precede the full term, a mere year-long remnant rounding out Davis's unfinished service. The legislators, at the

* Blanche K. Bruce
Richard H. Cain
Henry P. Cheatham
Robert C. DeLarge
Robert B. Elliott
Jeremiah Haralson
John A. Hyman
John Mercer Langston
Jefferson Long
John R. Lynch
Thomas E. Miller
Charles E. Nash
James E. O'Hara
Joseph R. Rainey
Hiram Rhoades Revels
Alonzo J. Ransier
James T. Rapier
Robert Smalls
Benjamin S. Turner
Josiah T. Walls
George H. White
George W. Murray

time willing to give the Negroes only token recognition, bestowed the one-year term on a man of color, Hiram Rhoades Revels.

He was a preacher, recently and reluctantly drawn into politics. It is said that he became the choice of the Negro legislators because he had opened the session with a resounding prayer. A few weeks later he was in Washington, famous overnight, claiming his seat as the first Negro to sit in either house of Congress. Republican extremists, preferring some full-blooded Negro ex-slave to the mulatto, freeborn Revels as heir to Jefferson Davis's seat, were disappointed. Democrats vainly argued that he could not constitutionally be seated because a Senator must have been nine years an American citizen, whereas, by their tortured logic, Revels, being a Mississippi Negro, could not have been a citizen before the Civil War.

Blanche K. Bruce, the only Negro ever to serve a six-year term in the Senate, was selected in 1874 at the age of thirty-three after holding minor offices and acquiring a state-wide reputation as a Republican leader. He even won a few votes from white Democrats in the assembly. No one seriously doubted that the Senate would seat him, but there was an awkward moment when his white colleague from Mississippi declined to escort him to be sworn. The attendant embarrassment was quickly eased, however, for the lordly Senator Roscoe Conkling of New York strode briskly down the aisle to the lonely Senator-elect, grandly offered him his arm, and marched him to the rostrum.

Both Negro Senators had unusual backgrounds. Revels, never a slave, was born the son of free parents of mixed blood, in North Carolina. After some years as a barber, the youth went to the Middle West where he absorbed some formal education, it is said, at Knox College. After ordination as an AME minister in 1845 and a few years of pastoral work in the Midwest, Tennessee and Kentucky, and as pastor and principal of a Negro school in Baltimore, he moved to Mississippi. Bruce, born in slavery, never knew its rigors, for he was the light-skinned son of a wealthy Virginia planter by a slave woman. He shared a tutor with his owner's son (whose body servant he was), but when his young master took him—he was now twenty—as his valet to the Confederate Army, he ran off to Missouri, established a school for Negroes, and made his way to Oberlin College, where he spent two years in study. After the War he became a Mississippi planter, accumulated property, taught school occasionally and entered politics.

An unassimilated minority in the majority party, and denied key committee roles, the twenty-two Negro members of Congress, 1869–1901, were not able to influence legislation, but they were by no means inarticulate. Some were as undistinguished as hundreds of whites who have served in Congress, but others, like Bruce and Representatives Langston, Lynch, Rapier and Elliott, were able, cultivated men. Some felt keenly their responsibility as spokesmen for both a particular congressional district and a disadvantaged race of many millions, especially in 1891–1901 when there was but a single Negro in Congress. They concerned themselves particularly with civil rights and education for their group, but their exertions extended also to the more conventional legislative interests. At a time when the nation was learning of brazen corruption in Washington an ex-Congressman, ex-Confederate general remarked upon the Negro lawmakers' innocence of any scandal, and James G. Blaine declared that the colored Congressmen were "studious, earnest, ambitious men whose public conduct . . . would be honorable to any race."

Most of these men reached Congress by routes usually travelled by Congressmen-in-the-making, though they were for the first time, and only briefly as it proved, open to Negroes. Comparison of their biographies in the *Congressional Directory* with those of their white contemporaries shows no startling disparity in educational backgrounds. In both were university men and men of minimal training. Ten of the colored Congressmen had attended college; half of them were graduates—and this was more than could be said of several Presidents, cabinet members and Senators in these years.

The twenty-two included six lawyers, three clergymen, four farmers, two "public officials," a barber, a teacher, a tailor, a bricklayer, a river pilot, a liveryman and a shipping clerk. Nine were freeborn and only four were considered pure Africans, including Elliott and Cain, two of the ablest. Elliott was perhaps the most brilliant in the entire company. He was a very black man with pronounced Negro features and such purity of speech that he is often ranked above the mulatto Frederick Douglass as an orator. Nine of the slaveborn Congressmen apparently continued in bondage until the Emancipation and the other four achieved freedom only by running off during the War.

Some owed their election to earlier renown. The urbane John Mercer Langston, for example, who represented Virginia in 1889–1891, had already been professor of law, dean and acting vice-president of Howard University, and then for eight years minister-resident to Haiti and *chargé d'affaires* of the Dominican Republic. In 1883, he became the first president of the newly established Virginia Normal and Collegiate Institute, and by the time he sought election to the House, he had been widely known for a generation. When the votes were counted, after a vigorous campaign in which he made a frankly racial appeal, he was counted out by a narrow margin. He contested the returns, and inquiry revealed that many Negroes had been kept from voting, but the hearings were so thwarted by obstructive tactics that it was twenty months before he was permitted to take his seat.

Not only did white Democrats fight to keep Negroes out of power; white elements in the Republican party were scarcely less determined to keep it for themselves. Some were legitimately elected, but on one pretext or another kept from assuming their seats. Some, like Jefferson Long, of Georgia, the first Negro to be elected to the House, found their campaigns hobbled by intimidation. On election day in 1870, Negro voters were set upon by angry whites. Seven were killed and Long himself took refuge in the courthouse belfry until friends spirited him away to even greater safety in an uncompleted sewer section. He carried the district by only nine hundred votes. It is hardly surprising that his first speech in Congress should have been a plea for retaining the test oath as a means for protecting blacks, or that the typical colored Congressman served only one or two terms. Joseph Rainey and Robert Smalls served five, but of the other eighteen, ten served a single term, six two terms, and two had three.

As a member of the crew of a Confederate dispatch boat, Smalls one day steered the ship within federal lines and became a pilot for the United States Navy. His fame made his rise in South Carolina politics easy, despite his lack of education. His moderation, intelligence and self-possession made him acceptable to white Republicans, while his prestige with the Federals deeply impressed Negroes. Richard Cain was another whose road to high office was relatively easy. An AME clergyman in New York, he was sent by the denomination to South Carolina to assist in religious work among the freedmen. As founder and editor of the *Missionary Record,* a denominational organ that soon became the "most influential paper ever published in South Carolina," he naturally became a spokesman for his race, serving as a member of the Constitutional Convention, the state senate, and two terms in Congress, where he made an excellent record. An unmixed black with strong racial feelings that kindled active particiption in every reform movement which he felt would improve his race and protect them from carpetbaggers, he was often praised in the white press and even enemies regarded him as an inflexibly upright man. After his congressional career he became an AME bishop and college president.

Several of the Congressmen had the untraceable ancestry so common to ante-bellum Negro history. Some, like Senator Bruce, were the sons or grandsons of white men. DeLarge and Rainey were light mulattoes of uncertain lineage and Miller was related to good Charleston stock. The strongly Caucasian Cheatham regularly associated with the better white element and Ransier, a passionate advocate of equal rights, was nearly white. He had earlier served as lieutenant governor of South Carolina, and the skill with which he presided over the state senate was uniformly attributed to his white ancestry.

Langston of Virginia and Lynch are examples of mulattoes benefiting from white parentage. Langston was born on a large plantation in Virginia, the son of its owner, Ralph Quarles. His mother was Lucy Langston, of white, Negro and Indian ancestry. A slave, she became Quarles's mistress and bore him four children. He emancipated her after the birth of Maria, their first child, and three sons were born to the pair in the succeeding quarter century. John Mercer Langston, endowed with his mother's name, was the youngest. Quarles had strong abolitionist leanings, but when Maria married a man of her own choice, he bought her husband for her and several slaves besides. Both he and his colored mistress died when John was scarcely five years old, but Quarles had made liberal provision for his children and John was sent to a friend of his father in Cincinnati, who reared him as a son.

John R. Lynch was the son of a slave woman by a wealthy white man of Louisiana. The latter arranged to free the woman and their child but died before the formalities were completed, and instead the child and his mother, against their dead kinsman's will, were sold and taken to Natchez. By this time, John was sixteen and had already enjoyed a privileged childhood, including some tutoring. Like Langston, Lynch was a strikingly handsome man of aristocratic bearing and fluent speech, wholly free from the accents of the "quarters." He was a Negro celebrity for over half a century after his retirement from his third term in Congress, for he lived until the Second World War.

In some instances Congressmen who began life as slaves had acquired clandestine grounding in literacy because some member of the slave-owning class believed that the white man's burden included a duty to teach blacks to read the Bible. DeLarge, Haralson, Hyman and Long, however, were largely self-educated men, whose only formal education came in their adult years after the War, when schools, often conducted in the evenings, were hastily set up by Northern missionaries, Union troops or the Freedmen's Bureau. There were also those who had received secret instruction in childhood from the children of planters and yeomen who drew their playmates freely from slave children. Smalls had an indulgent master who so far defied the law as to permit him some formal instruction. Murray and Cheatham were born late enough to profit from the schools emerging after the War. Cheatham, born in 1857 near Henderson, North Carolina, where his mother was a privileged house slave, attended schools taught by ex-slaveowners before graduating from Shaw University. Murray, born in 1853, attended public schools in Charleston and then, on a scholarship won in a competitive examination, studied at the reconstructed University of South Carolina until an anti-Negro administration recovered control in 1876. Rainey had been redeemed before the War by his father, a barber, who bought his whole family's freedom. Rainey himself became a barber in Charleston and acquired the kind of private instruction available there to well-connected light Negroes.

Two of the eight freeborn Representatives were native Northerners, but can hardly be called black carpetbaggers. O'Hara, born in New York City, had come to North Carolina as a very young man and practiced law in New Bern until his death in 1905. Nor was Elliott, born in Boston, the opportunistic vulgarian that the term "carpetbagger" connotes. Educated at an academy in London, England, and at Eton, he studied law under a London barrister. He decided to establish himself in South Carolina where colored clients vastly exceeded those in New England. He was reputed to be a remarkable linguist and the owner of one of the finest law libraries in the state. Estimates of his political principles differ, but all accounts agree that he was a man of unusual intellectual gifts.

The freeborn native Southerners had, of course, substantial educational advantages over the slaveborn. Cain's family had moved to Ohio when he was only six, but even there he had, until after his marriage, only such education as he could absorb in a Sunday school, and only after becoming a pastor did he enter Wilberforce University, when he was thirty-five. Miller's family moved to Charleston, where "bright mulattoes" attended public schools even in the 1850's, and then he was sent to Lincoln University. Ransier and Walls had only the most limited schooling in their home states, but Rapier, whose father, like Langston's, was a comparatively wealthy man, was educated first by private tutors and then trained in Canada as a lawyer. Eight years there, where discrimination was minimal, made him one of the strongest spokesmen for civil rights in Congress.

After their congressional careers, several were given appointive posts by Republican national administrations. Senator Bruce was mentioned for the vice-presidency or a cabinet post and was made Register of the Treasury and Recorder of Deeds for the District of Columbia by Presidents Garfield, Harrison and McKinley. Like Frederick Douglass and Langston, Bruce had more lecture invitations at a hundred dollars per appearance than he could accept, for Negroes thrilled to see one of their number who had served a full Senate term.

Senator Revels later became president of Alcorn University, a Mississippi state school for Negroes, and Elliott, after his career in Congress, resumed his career in South Carolina state politics. Others were given minor federal posts while some became conspicuous figures in Republican national conventions and in the party's committee structure, thanks to the "rotten borough" framework of the party's Southern wing. Lynch was temporary chairman of the 1894 convention and a member of the national committee. The plums shrivelled rapidly after 1880, however. Ransier, for instance, had been a member of his state constitutional convention, presidential elector, lieutenant governor of South Carolina and a delegate to a national convention before he went to Congress. By the time he died in 1882 at the age of forty-eight, he had become a mere day laborer in the streets of Charleston.

As party regulars, they could be advocates of civil rights for Negroes, but Negro intellectuals were often disappointed by "their" Congressmen's illiberal propensities; Southern Reconstruction politics hardly propelled the most militant Negroes into office. Bruce's enthusiasm for migration to Liberia won him little applause from Negroes, and others were accused of being too friendly with whites and siding with reactionaries on the tariff, currency and civil service reform questions. Only Langston had held elective office in the

North. Upon his graduation from Oberlin in 1853, he was denied entrance to law schools in New York and Ohio, and had to be content to read law in an attorney's office. When he offered himself for the bar, the referees agonized over his eligibility, and finally ruled in his favor on the novel theory that he was more white than colored. He soon established himself as an attorney in an all-white community in Ohio and was elected (1855) township clerk, perhaps the first Negro to attain elective office in America.

There were some Negro officeholders at state and local levels who were in their time more famous than some of the Congressmen. Three were lieutenant governors of Louisiana. One was C. C. Antoine, a freeborn Creole Negro, whose father had fought under Andrew Jackson at New Orleans in 1814 and who himself raised a colored company for a Louisiana Union regiment and served as its captain. After the peace he became a Shreveport grocer and politician, serving in the state constitutional convention, the state senate, and finally as lieutenant governor. Oscar J. Dunn and P. B. S. Pinchback preceded him in that office. Dunn had run from slavery and purchased his liberty, having achieved a basic education before he was free. Pinchback, the best known of the three, was the son of Major William Pinchback, a Mississippi planter, and Eliza Stewart, a very light mulatto. The boy was the eighth of ten children that Eliza bore to the major, and by that time the planter had taken his "wife" and children north for manumission. The boy was tutored at home and then sent when he was ten to school in Cincinnati. Major Pinchback died the next year, however, and his executor hastily sent Eliza and five of her children to Cincinnati to forestall any attempt by white relatives to disinherit and re-enslave them. The precautions proved fruitless, so far as the inheritance was concerned, for the white kinfolk succeeded in appropriating it.

He was now destitute and left school to become a cabin boy on the river boats. During the War he reached Union-occupied New Orleans, where he raised a colored company of Union volunteers. He could pass easily as a white man, but outraged whites forced him to resign the captaincy of his company. After Appomattox, he probably held more public offices than any other Negro of his generation. For a month he was acting governor of Louisiana. He was a handsome, shrewd, aggressive man—a practical politician playing the politician's game, but preserving a reputation for integrity.

Francis Louis Cardozo is better remembered than several whom his state of South Carolina sent to Congress. Here is another freeborn mulatto with white family ties, who had the advantage of growing up in Charleston. The son of a Jewish economist by a woman of mixed blood, he was urbane, splendidly groomed and nearly white. After his elementary schooling, he became a journeyman carpenter. His carefully husbanded savings, eked out by summer employment and a one-thousand-dollar scholarship, enabled him to go to the University of Glasgow and then for two years to a theological school in London. At the outbreak of the War he was a Presbyterian minister in New Haven, but when the conflict ended he went as principal to Avery Institute in Charleston and entered politics, rising in time to be South Carolina's secretary of state (1868–1872) and then treasurer (1872–1876). Jonathan Jasper Wright, another celebrated officeholder, was born to free, probably unmixed, blacks in Pennsylvania. After some college training in Ithaca, New York, he studied law in a private office in Pennsylvania, and in 1866 became the first Negro to be admitted to the bar of that state. He went to South Carolina as an appointed legal adviser to the freedmen and in 1870 was elected to a full six-year term as associate justice of the state's supreme court, but was forced to resign shortly before the end of his term when the Republican regime was overthrown.

Jonathan C. Gibbs was another prominent Reconstruction officeholder, for several years Florida's secretary of state and superintendent of public instruction. He was born in Philadelphia, a light mulatto, and educated at Kimball Union Academy, Dartmouth College and Princeton Theological Seminary. He had been sent to direct religious work among Negroes, but his superior education led him naturally to political leadership. Norris Wright Cuney held the place of boss and patronage dispenser of the Republican party in Texas for nearly twenty years and national committeeman for ten, but was finally unseated by white factions. Like many other Southern Negro Republican party politicians, of his own and the succeeding generation, he was related to the white planting class. He was born on the Texas plantation of his father, Col. Phillip Cuney, the fourth of his eight children by a woman of mixed blood. Norris and his brothers went to school in Pittsburgh, but the War blocked plans to send the boys to Oberlin. After the War, Norris returned to Texas, married the quadroon daughter of a white planter, and began his political rise, drawing his livelihood meanwhile from a stevedoring business in Galveston.

Another political figure was James C. Napier, a mulatto with Scots-Irish antecedents. He attended Wilberforce and Oberlin until a minor clerkship took him to Washington, enabling him to complete a law course at Howard University. A competitive examination started him up the ladder through successive promotions until the returning Democrats retired him. He then went back to Nashville as a lawyer and was for twenty years a member of the state Republican committee and four times a delegate to national conventions. He married the daughter of John M. Langston and for some years was Register of the Treasury.

These years also produced Benjamin "Pap" Singleton, a leader in the migrations from the cotton states to Kansas, the so-called "Exodus of 1879." Singleton was a slave who, after earlier unsuccessful attempts, escaped to Canada. He was all his life a simple, unlettered Negro who, though a mulatto, preached separate racial communities, persuaded that the race could rise only through its own industry in an environment where they would not have to compete with whites. He was hostile to educated Negroes, doubtless because they opposed his movement.

Republican administrations were disposed to reward Negro politicians for their services to the party, both as a matter of desert and to purchase increased allegiance, to say nothing of flattering the Negro voter. We have mentioned the plums distributed to Negro ex-Congressmen; similar provision was made for state politicians and for personalities whom Republicans recognized as symbols. The venerated Douglass, for example, held posts under several Presidents including the Democratic Cleveland: as Police Commissioner, Recorder of Deeds, United States Marshal for the District of Columbia, and as minister to Haiti.

The diplomatic and consular service took more Negro appointees than did any other branch of the federal service. They were sent to Haiti and Liberia, which cynics called the "Negro beat," but patronage dispensers were quick to point out that the government properly sent Negro diplomats to posts where they would be welcome. In the quarter century before 1900 more than a dozen became ministers to Haiti and Liberia. Beginning with Ebenezer D. Bassett, appointed as Haitian minister by President Grant, the office was filled in turn by John Mercer Langston, J. E. W. Thompson, John S. Durham, Henry M. Smyth, William F. Powell and Henry W. Furniss, while the Liberian ministership was held by James Milton Turner, John H. Smyth, Henry Highland Garnet, C. H. J. Turner, E. E. Smith and William H. Heard. The best known in the groups were Basset, J. M. Turner, Langston, J. H. Smyth, Garnet and Heard.

Heard, later an AME bishop, affords a sharp contrast to the courtly Langston. The walls in the slave cabin in which he was born were so loosely timbered that his mother chinked and unchinked them in season. The chimney was a wattled makeshift, there was but a single door and window, and young William could count the chickens under the house through the cracks in the floor. His mother was a "breeder" whose function was to produce and nurse babies. William's father, the slave and son of a neighboring planter, was permitted only brief semi-weekly visits with his family. The boy's mother died when he was nine and he worked as a field slave from the age of ten until his emancipation at fifteen in 1865. His rural community threatened mutilation of the right hand of any slave who learned to read and write, so the future diplomat and bishop learned only Bible lore at Sunday school. The close of the War found the region wholly destitute of teachers for ex-slaves, but Heard's father opened a little wheelwright's shop and this enabled the boy to pay a white boy to pass on to him, at ten cents a lesson, what he was absorbing in the shabby little school for whites.

In 1866, he was hired by a farmer named William Henry Heard, and from him he took the name he was to carry through life, for he had been the property of successive masters and had not yet acquired a stable name. The farmer paid his hand five dollars a month plus a nightly lesson. The boy worked in the fields till dusk, studying during the lunch period while the other hands slept. Soon a school for freedmen was opened and he attended in the afternoons, working for his father in the mornings and evenings. In a matter of months he was teaching a school himself. He used part of his earnings for instruction from a white man, and then entered the University of South Carolina. The Reconstruction legislature had established a program which entitled a county to five scholarships for which all boys between sixteen and twenty-one might compete. He won one of these and received from the state, besides, an allotment of twenty dollars a month for the support of his family.

At twenty-one he was Republican county chairman, organizing the Negro vote and fighting frauds and election irregularities. In 1880 he was appointed railway postal clerk by the efforts of a Democratic Congressman for whom he had canvassed, and then, entering the ministry, he became politically inactive until 1895 when, with the aid of the vigorous Negro Bishop H. M. Turner, he was appointed by President Cleveland as minister to Liberia.

Ebenezer Bassett, born free in Connecticut, attended public schools and Yale University, and at the time of his appointment as minister to Haiti was headmaster of the Institute for Colored Youth, a Quaker school in Philadelphia. James Milton Turner was, like Heard, born in slavery, but his father, who had been taught veterinary medicine by his owner, accumulated sufficient savings to redeem himself and later his wife and child. The master had in fact decided to sell the slave woman for more than her husband could raise, but before a purchaser was found she fractured a bone in her wrist. When the attending physician, an abolitionist, strongly hinted that her hand could not long be saved, her owner put her up for whatever she would fetch, and her spouse seized the opportunity to buy his wife at a bargain price and his little son as well for an additional fifty dollars. The child's parents smuggled some instruction to him and then sent him to Oberlin's preparatory department for a year. He served as valet to a Union Army officer, was wounded at Shiloh, and devoted himself after the War to promoting Negro schools in Kansas City. His oratorical gifts soon made him the leader of Missouri's Negroes and a power in Republican politics. As minister to Liberia he was perhaps the first Negro in the diplomatic corps.

John Henry Smyth was born in Richmond, the son of a slave who had married a free woman so that his children would be freeborn. He was then purchased by his wife, and because Virginia law forbade her to manumit him, she willed him to their own son. John became perhaps the first colored newsboy in Philadelphia and soon thereafter, the first Negro student in the Pennsylvania Academy of Fine Arts. A few years later he graduated from the Institute for Colored Youth, where Ebenezer Bassett was teaching. After putting himself through Howard Law School by holding clerkships in federal bureaus in Washington, he was made cashier of the Wilmington branch of the Freedman's Bank, and when that institution failed, he opened a law practice and became prominent in the Republican party. His exertions in behalf of the Hayes ticket in 1876 brought him the ministership to Liberia.

Minor consular posts were also being filled by Negroes in South America, Europe, Africa and Asia, and the period saw, in addition, the placing of Negro partisans in domestic federal offices. James Monroe Trotter, for example, was made an important officer in the Boston post office and then Recorder of Deeds for the District of Columbia, a post reserved for Negroes until the Wilson administration. The Treasury Department similarly afforded plums for deserving Republicans, in clerkships and collectorships in the Internal Revenue service in Washington and the South. The most conspicuous of these appointments was that of Senator Bruce as Register of the Treasury. Three other Negroes followed Bruce in that high office before Wilson restored it to whites.

The political celebrities we have mentioned stirred the pride of Negro America during their brief tenure simply by the fact of their holding office; it is not to be supposed that their objective accomplishments excited much notice. In any really significant sense they touched the lives of the Negro people but little, and scarcely influenced the course of American social history except as symbols. And while the company of religious leaders of this period is somewhat smaller than the roll of public men (many of whom were also clergymen), the greater importance of the church leaders is clear. They were more widely known in their own day and their surviving reputation is also greater. Their total influence upon the life of their people, both inside the ghetto and in the slow obliteration of the lines that defined the Negroes' cultural isolation, was certainly more significant.

These years restored the religious leaders to something like their old pre-eminence. After the politicians, they supplied once more the largest contingent in the vanguard. A notable contrast with the earlier decades is the fact that the great majority of them won all or most of their renown for labors in the South, a region where before the War religious observance by black folk had largely passed, as a means of social control, under the surveillance of whites, but where after the War a new social frontier beckoned colored religious leaders to assume control of the one major social institution that the race could call its own. The extraordinary concentration of these clergymen in the South is explained also, of course, by the concentration of the nation's Negroes in that area where few other avenues for social advance were open. In the North, the major religious structure had been completed and members of the far smaller Negro population were now aspiring to other callings as well.

The Baptist polity made the multiplication of independent churches easy, and Negro Baptists soon comprised the largest single body of colored communicants in the country. Negro Baptists in the South quickly established state conventions and by the early 1880's the National Baptist Convention was created. Competition for place among churchmen precipitated schisms, withdrawals and reorganizations and in 1917 this huge religious structure split into the National Baptist Convention, Incorporated, and the National Baptist Convention, the former retaining two thirds of the membership, and the latter the balance. Meanwhile the decentralized structure of the Baptist group operated to reduce the number of its leaders who could achieve national prominence.

The Methodists have provided a far larger proportion of celebrities in the persons of their bishops. Before the War the bulk of the AME and AMEZ membership was found in Northern congregations which had withdrawn from the main Methodist body; however, after 1865, most Negro Methodists were in the AME or AMEZ Church. In 1866 the remaining 78,000 Negroes in the Southern Methodist church were eased out to form a denomination of their own—the Colored Methodist Episcopal Church, established in 1870. Meanwhile a remnant of Negro Methodists, both North and South, remained with the Northern Methodists, in what is essentially a separate wing, with bishops of its own. By 1936 separate Negro sects accounted for nine tenths of the country's Negro church members, and of the latter in turn, nine tenths were contained in five denominations alone: the two major Baptist conventions leading with nearly 3,800,000 members, and the AME, AMEZ and CME bodies following with about 500,000, 415,000 and 270,000 respectively.

While denominational lines were being clarified, there began the evolution of the means for educating the growing army of clerics. The religious leaders in this generation came upon the scene too late to be served by these facilities, but many participated in their creation. The Negro educational "system" that began to emerge in the South was at every level, from the earliest grades upward, bent toward training ministers to elevate the Negro masses. Northern philanthropists, the white denominations and public authority participated in the development. Not professional training but literacy and "Bible study" was the program, and the first waves of teachers who flowed into the schools were mainly Northerners, themselves trained in the theological tradition and inclined to turning their best students to the ministry. In the 1890's the Southern states acquired land-grant schools for Negroes through federal aid, and these at once began to overshadow the sectarian schools because their fiancial resources, small as they were, were ampler. Industrial schools like Hampton and Tuskegee also began to outstrip the church schools.

The American Missionary Association (Congregationalist) founded or helped to found twenty-one schools including Talladega and Tougaloo colleges, Hampton Institute, and Fisk, Howard, Atlanta and Straight universities. Their religious emphasis slowly faded and by 1923 only two of these still had theological departments; and in some cases, like Howard, Fisk, Hampton and Atlanta, the AMA surrendered control to independent trustees. Similar enterprise engaged the American Baptist Home Mission Society, the Methodist Episcopal Church's Freedmen's Aid Society, the United Presbyterians and the Board of Missions of the Presbyterian Church USA, but all of this effort was soon outstripped by the Negro denominations. Even in 1923, when many of the shakier institutions had been abandoned, there were still far too many Negro theological schools or schools with theological departments. There were no less than 52 "major" institutions, most of them established by the Negro denominations after 1880, doubtless as one manifestation of growing race-consciousness and a desire for independence from sporadic white philanthropy. Standards, even in the principal institutions, were pitifully low. A study of the 52 "majors," completed in 1924, revealed that of the 1011 theological students enrolled, only 34 were graduates of colleges and 214 of high schools. They were largely taught by whites and graduated in two or three years even though most had entered the theological course after a mere fifth- or sixth-grade education.

Private, church-supported Negro colleges and universities without theological divisions were also multiplying recklessly, invariably in the South, while provision for public secondary schools for Negroes lagged. On the eve of World War I, fourteen of the eighteen Southern states had an *aggregate* of thirty high schools. The colleges looked to this pre-collegiate training in high-school departments, and, indeed, elementary grades as well, so that statistics about attendance at what are called colleges and universities must be used with great caution.

Twenty-five of the men* most frequently encountered in the record of this generation were leaders—virtually unnoticed by whites—in the Negro denominations and segregated colored adjuncts of white churches: eight from the AME, eight in the Negro Baptist, three in the CME and two in the AMEZ connections; and one each in the white Methodist, Presbyterian and Episcopal folds. Another was Bishop James Augustine Healy, unique as the only colored American to be a Roman Catholic bishop and for labors wholly outside the ghetto.

Bishop Healy's father had come to Georgia as a poor Irish emigrant in

* Benjamin W. Arnett, Richard H. Boyd, Edward M. Brawley, John Miflin Brown, Levi J. Coppin, Elias Cottrell, Wesley J. Gaines, James Augustine Healy, James T. Holly, Lucius H. Holsey, James W. Hood, John Jasper, Isaac Lane, Emanuel K. Love, Christopher H. Payne, Daniel A. Payne, Rufus L. Perry, Joseph C. Price, Daniel J. Sanders, William J. Simmons, Benjamin Tucker Tanner, Marshall W. Taylor, Henry MacNeal Turner, Charles T. Walker, Alexander W. Wayman

the early days of the cotton boom. By 1831, he had amassed 1,600 acres and seventeen slaves and was still on the rise. In 1829 he had taken a sixteen-year-old mulatto slave girl, evidently the daughter of a Southern aristocrat, as his common-law wife and by her had ten children, of whom James, born in 1830, was the eldest. Anxious to shield them from insult, he sent his sons North for their education. After several academies rejected them, they entered a Quaker school in Long Island.

When the Healy boys felt their inferior status at the Quaker school, they transferred to the College of the Holy Cross at Worcester, Massachusetts, where the student body was so cosmopolitan that a swarthy skin excited no remark. Here James kept near the head of his class and had altogether a pleasant time of it except for the fear that one day some Georgia students might enroll and divulge the secret of his origins. The moment never came, but there were difficulties in assembling the necessary papers when he entered the Sulpician Seminary in Montreal; and when his father died, there were questions about inheritance rights. The mixed-blood offspring of Southern whites were commonly disqualified by legal action brought by white relatives. The Healy boys eventually surmounted this difficulty, but for a time it appeared that they would lose the inheritance and that James as the eldest would be compelled to leave the seminary to support the numerous family he now headed. In 1852 he went to the Sulpician Seminary in Paris and from there to Boston as a priest, an assignment he approached with no small apprehensions. Indeed, he was prepared, if the reaction proved too strong, to give up the priesthood and enter a religious order. Again the crisis was safely passed.

He was now a Negro priest in a white parish in abolitionist Boston, the coowner of fifty-seven slaves. In a sense, he and his brothers were their own and each other's chattels. The law prohibited manumission, so the Georgia slaves were sold and the proceeds distributed. The early years of Father James's priesthood coincided with the anti-Catholic outrages of the early 1850's, but he somehow escaped the persecutions. As secretary to the Bishop of Boston he lived in the bishop's residence, and when his superior died he became pastor of the new St. James Church. While serving as the bishop's secretary he had been one of the two principal candidates for the rectorship of the projected new Cathedral of Boston. His aged rival made slurring allusions in the pulpit to Father James's lineage. Though he missed the rectorship, his stature in Catholic circles in New England rose steadily and his pre-eminence as a beloved pastor was challenged only by his younger brother, Sherwood Healy. The latter became rector of the new cathedral in 1870, but four years later Father James attained the papal appointment as Bishop of Maine. Another brother, Patrick F. Healy, served as president of Georgetown University, in Washington, D.C., from 1872 to 1883.

Father James's biographer describes him as the model bishop: hard-working, devoted, beloved. The circumstance that he ministered wholly to whites occasionally evoked whispers about the diocese, such as, "the Bishop is a Nee-gar!" and sometimes in the confessional children confided "and I called the Bishop a nigger." When church business took him into the South, he risked insult as he registered at hotels under the critical eyes of clerks, but he usually escaped affront, thanks in part to his reluctance to appear in public among folk likely to take offense. He was not a second-class bishop in a second-class diocese; his own successor, William H. O'Connell, became archbishop of Boston and ultimately cardinal. Only the "historical unknowns" which must necessarily keep the great majority of bishops from reaching the cardinalate denied him that ultimate elevation. He must have come near it, for before his death he had been promoted to the rank of Assistant at the Papal Throne.

The other twenty-four Negro religious notables of this period follow a more familiar pattern, all of them laboring in the Negro vineyard, most of them in the South where the Negro millions were massed. All twenty-five were, of course, born during the slavery era, fourteen as slaves, eleven as free persons of color. Only three of the latter were born in the North: James W. Hood, Benjamin W. Arnett and Benjamin Tucker Tanner, all of them in comparatively liberal Pennsylvania, and all apparently sons of stable families who had already enjoyed some generations of freedom. One of them, Tanner, was the founder of a veritable clan who were to add luster to the name in succeeding decades. All but two of the twenty-five made their principal careers in the South, both of the exceptions (Arnett and Tanner) being drawn from the trio of Northern freeborn persons.

Of the eight Southern freeborn, all but one were natives of the upper South or the Charleston environment, perhaps none in families long free. Irregular ancestry and family instability were as common to the heritage of freeborn Negroes as to that of slaves. Christopher H. Payne, for example, was the grandson of a white planter who had freed his comely slave and the daughter she bore him. The child later became the mother of Christopher, born free under the rule that a child followed the condition of its mother. Marshall Taylor and Henry MacNeal Turner also descended from unconventional unions. Joseph C. Price's father, one Charles Dozier, had married a free woman to insure that his children would be free, but by the white man's rule that a slave's marriage had no sanctions in law that an owner was bound to respect, the union was dissolved when Dozier, an illiterate but skilled ship's carpenter, was sold off to a distant city. Joseph's mother then married one David Price, whose surname the boy assumed. Ten of the fourteen who are known to have been born slaves remained in bonds until the Emancipation; none was redeemed by purchase, none—with the arguable exception of Healy—was manumitted, and only one managed to escape by flight.

Some who spent their childhood in slavery had advantages of a sort. Rufus L. Perry's father was a slave-preacher and a skilled artisan, permitted to hire his time and move with his family to Nashville. Here Rufus attended a school for free Negroes until his father ran off to freedom in Canada. The boy was restored to his owner who, believing the young slave had been rendered dangerous by education, sold him to a slave trader when he reached the age of eighteen. He was scheduled for resale in Mississippi, but broke away and fled to Canada. Richard Henry Boyd, whose lineage combined old Southern white stock with a slave inheritance, was a privileged hand on a Texas plantation. He was with his master and his three sons—all of whom perished—in the Confederate force around Richmond. He was at his master's side when he fell and brought the body back to Texas, assuming, though scarcely twenty, the management of the farm for his late master's widow, and perfecting, one supposes, the skills that later marked his career as director of the National Baptist Publishing House.

This generation of religious leaders were in the main roughhewn, plainspoken men, far less preoccupied with theological refinements than with the practical spiritual and social improvement of their uncultivated folk, now free at last to elevate themselves. Several were very much involved in politics and most of them lent their energies to some effort or other to improve the Negro's condition in the here and now. Most were active in the promotion of higher education for Negroes, often as founders or presidents of the new institutions, and others contributed to the maturing of the religious press or the proliferation of vast mission, church-extension and Sunday-school programs.

Not all were denominational leaders. Rev. John Jasper, slave-preacher until the Emancipation, won a surprising reputation in the 1870's and 1880's as a free-lance exhorter and "philosopher"; and Charles T. Walker, an unmixed black ex-slave, was widely regarded as the ablest Negro preacher in the country. This fiery evangelist was for many years a pastor in Georgia. He drew enormous crowds everywhere, even in Europe, where, incidentally, curious folk, fascinated by a full-blooded American Negro, crowded forward to touch his skin to see if the color rubbed off. He was an editor of religious periodicals, founder of a colored YMCA, director of banking, insurance and real-estate companies, a perennial member of the Republican state committee of Georgia and a delegate to several Republican national conventions.

Other clergymen, even more than Walker, were influential race leaders. The pure African, Price, founder of the AMEZ's Livingstone College in Salisbury, North Carolina, was a man of extraordinary force and eloquence, bridging the period between the decline of Douglass's influence and the preeminence of Booker Washington. Josephus Daniels, who knew him well, called him "unquestionably [one of] the two most remarkable Negroes of their day." James Weldon Johnson and W. E. B. Du Bois shared the view that the history of Negro America would have been different if Price had lived longer, for he would have exerted a significant counterpoise to the dominant Tuskegeean.

Some notice should be take here of the range and disparity of the race-advance efforts and viewpoints that these clergymen represented, as proof again of the fatuity of lumping Negroes together in generalization. There simply was no official Negro position on any issue. Because the church was the race's major social institution, responsible for a vast complex of secular functions which in non-Negro society could be left to other agencies, and because the Negro clergymen had the ear of more Negroes and had it more steadily and with greater authority than any others, they could scarcely escape the role of chief mentors and uplifters of the race. On the basic needs all were agreed, and each in his own way was in the vanguard of an untiring crusade for the race's progress through thrift, cleanliness, sobriety, literacy, purity of conduct and refinement of tastes. But on the ultimate means and ends of Negro social policy opinions were extremely various.

Price advocated education for broad culture instead of the industrial education of Booker Washington, but he died before the issue was joined. Some counselled patience until time softened the hearts of the whites, but others like Daniel A. Payne, an emaciated little man weighing less than a hundred pounds, stoutly defied Jim Crow regulations. He insisted on having trains stopped so that he might be put off rather than submit to indignity.

Payne's unique position as elder statesman of the church deserves notice. By the time he became the senior AME bishop he was regarded as a sort of archbishop with extraordinary power. A wraithlike tubercular for forty years, he was a moral giant, the embodiment of the spiritual purity and ideals which he labored to foster, a perfect counterpoise to an equally important kind of leadership afforded by men like the blunt Henry MacNeal Turner, his younger contemporary, and the last of what Du Bois has called the "mighty men, physically and mentally, men who started at the bottom and hammered their way to the top by sheer brute strength . . . the spiritual progeny of ancient African chieftains and the fruit of the African church in America." In his earlier days as a politician and Georgia legislator, Turner was often obliged to take to the woods to escape violence from enraged whites. The gentle Payne, by contrast, college-trained, sometime president of Wilberforce and chief advocate of an educated ministry when such advocacy still invoked fierce denunciations, brought his denomination steadily around to his view. He gave, in fact, more of his effort to educational advance than he did to purely ecclesiastical affairs.

Turner belabored both white oppressors and colored laggards, but saw so little hope for improvement that he favored the Negroes' return to Africa. Bishop Holly, who finally settled in Haiti, was a Negro nationalist boldly challenging Anglo-Saxon pretensions and exhorting Negroes to live their own lives in a country where there were no whites to cow them. The great majority, however, were persuaded that the Negroes' best hopes lay in America, though they differed among themselves. Marshall Taylor, for example, a leader of the Negro wing of the Methodist Church and editor of its *Southwestern Christian Advocate,* supported segregation in his denomination's churches and schools and urged Negroes to work out their own destiny apart from whites and to abandon aspirations for social parity, while a different tack was taken by Bishops Gaines and Tanner, who wrote books to make the race conscious of its potentialities and accomplishments.

Bishop Healy aside, not one of the clerics had first-class theological training. Several were, like Price, supported in school by white humanitarians. For several decades following the War, wealthy Northern whites commonly included Negro students in their charities, preferably ministerial students recommended by Negro college heads. In 1874, C. T. Walker enrolled at Augusta Institute (later to become Atlanta Baptist College), then headed by a former slave-owning clergyman. He lived with a private family for two dollars a month, doing his own cooking and washing, but even so his tiny capital soon ran out and he prepared to leave the school when some fellow students laid his plight before the president, who in turn found three wealthy Ohio humanitarians willing to subsidize him. One of them explained that he had been left for dead on a Civil War battlefield but had dragged himself to a Southern home for succor. The white householder refused him but suggested that he try the slave folk in the quarters. The bondmen nursed him back to health, and now ten years later he repaid the kindness.

Even those who had some "higher" education acquired it usually after they had become pastors, while others, including some of the most eminent, had none at all. The normal pattern was a conversion experience in youth, a "call" to preach, and a trial sermon before a local conference or board, and then a license to exhort. These men grew up when mere literacy itself was an achievement. The struggle to acquire the rudiments was often the most absorbing chapter in their histories. A few examples may illustrate the diverse factors playing upon the development. For those who had spent their youth in slavery, training had been categorically interdicted, but in the South similar prohibitions lay upon free Negroes as well. Even in the North scarcity of educational provision for Negroes, combined with rising hostility of whites, and the colored folks' own poverty and doubts of their abilities, held back the development.

Even Richard Boyd, a slave entrusted with the highest responsibilities, was permitted no instruction until 1865, when, a man of twenty-two, he induced some whites to teach him to read. E. M. Brawley, born free in Charleston, was in early childhood given sound instruction at private schools until the fright kindled by John Brown closed them. His parents were so well situated, however, that they were able to send him, before the outbreak of the

War, to the Institute for Colored Youth, at Philadelphia. John Miflin Brown was a homeless mulatto child taken at last into the home of Quakers, who sent him to a white private school, and he later joined the household of two whites, a physician and a lawyer. He learned the barber's trade in Philadelphia and this enabled him to support himself later at school.

Elias Cottrell got his early training from a parent. When he was only four, his parents and their seven children were placed on the block in Holly, Mississippi, and dispersed among five owners. Happily, little Elias was sold with his literate father, who taught the one child left to him. After the War he added to this foundation two years of evening instruction from a German, and then, in the early 'seventies, some training under Northern missionaries before entering college. Another kind of good fortune attended Wesley Gaines. Born a slave of the Toombs family of Georgia, he was the youngest of fourteen children and so sickly that he was excused from labor and permitted to puzzle over copybooks and a Bible until he became a fluent reader. He lived to have a long career as a bishop and a builder of sectarian colleges.

Bishop Holsey, a slave until he was liberated by the Emancipation at the age of twenty-three, confessed: "I have no complaint against American slavery. It was a blessing in disguise to me . . . (and) made the Negro race what it could not have been in its native land."* His mother was a pure African and his father a highly educated Georgia planter who never married but availed himself freely of his slave women. When his father died, Lucius, then only six, was sold as houseboy first to one new master and then another. Separation from his family seemed to disturb him little, for he later wrote that he considered his masters unusually kind and that he served them with deep affection. His last owner was a Georgia State College professor. While Lucius served this family, he conceived an inclination for learning too strong to be denied. As a boy he had learned reading from white playmates and an old colored man. Now in spare hours he hunted up rags to sell and thus acquired books like the Bible, Webster's *Blueback Speller* and Milton's *Paradise Lost,* over which he pored at night by firelight. Converted by Henry MacNeal Turner in 1858, and a decade later a tenant farmer licensed to preach, he added to his stock of books and studied by himself, a dictionary constantly at his side.

Isaac Lane, patriarch of the CME Church and founder of Lane College, still incredibly listed in *Who's Who in America* in 1938 at the age of a hundred and four, spent an obscure slave childhood without parental care on a large isolated plantation. The use of book and pencil were forbidden, but

* William M. Brewer, who knew Holsey, cautions me that this sentence from the Bishop's autobiography (page 10) is sharply at variance with his subsequent attitudes as a resolute foe of discrimination. I have, in fact, found a widespread disposition among Negroes, both famous and obscure, from that and the succeeding generation, and even in our own time, to suggest that slavery had in the end proved a fortunate accident as the means of the race's advance. That view is now rejected by many liberals and intellectuals, both Negro and white.

he somehow picked up the rudiments, and after the War, when he was thirty, he was plodding through the Bible and such theological works as he could lay his hands on. He had married at nineteen and was licensed to exhort at twenty-two. While still a slave he conducted prayer meetings on the plantation and sometimes suffered violence from whites hostile to Negro preachers. The Southern Methodist Church first granted him permission to preach only as a lay exhorter, but during the War he applied again to a quarterly conference and found that it had relaxed its earlier rule against licensing Negro ministers.

Lane left a full account of his rise and it strongly parallels the story of others who came out of slavery. He continued to work on the land after the War, confining his pastoral labors to Sundays and odd hours. He preached to both white and colored folk and was so bitterly resented by whites who preferred to silence all Negro preachers that they burned down the rude sanctuaries in which he held services. His people, he confessed, were extremely crude and harbored the most grotesque notions concerning religion and the ministry. The freedmen's excitements were so few that they would travel great distances (and, fortunately for the impecunious denominations, would even pay an admission charge) to see a bishop or a new preacher. The dignitaries themselves were hardly prepared for their new roles. They affected the frock coat, plug hat, long hair, and pompous manners that were to amuse whites who had the benefit of a longer genteel tradition. "I was too big a fool to know that I was a fool," confessed Bishop Holsey, commenting on this propensity in after years. The same pomposities and overstrained social pretensions, the same slavish aping of what they conceived to be the white dignitary's courtly standards, the same punctilious insistence upon their "entitlements" enmeshed the political leaders, so unused were they to the standards of the new realms into which changed circumstances had thrust them.

Even bishops were never quite emancipated from poverty. In the first year after his consecration as a bishop in 1873, Lane's paid-in salary was under two hundred dollars and many years later it was still less than four hundred dollars. To make ends meet, his enormous family—he had eleven children—joined him in raising cotton and cutting firewood for the local market. When he was not scrounging for subsistence, he worked equally zealously for his young denomination, soliciting funds and selling books, tracts and religious pictures. His colleague, Bishop Cottrell, long the chief fund-raiser for the CME colleges, was also obliged to support his family as a farmer and businessman, and Bishop Holsey, Secretary of the CME College of Bishops, wrote in 1920 that he had been in debt ever since he had become a bishop at the age of thirty-one, half a century before.

Henry MacNeal Turner's free childhood in Abbeville, South Carolina—he was descended from white and royal African ancestry—was hardly distinguishable from that of a slave except that from the time he was twelve he fiercely resisted any efforts of overseers to whip him, proudly conscious that he was a free man exempt from the rawhide. Upon his father's death the boy had been bound out to a planter to work side by side with slaves, but he ran away at the age of fifteen and by that time had been taught his letters by a white woman and a white playmate. Angry whites cut short this instruction, but, the foundation laid, he taught himself by means of a speller, a Bible and a hymnbook—and, by his own account, by an angel who came to him in visions to help him with the difficulties of pronunciation and grammar which he never fully mastered. The deficiency was to expose him and his kind for many decades to the ridicule of whites who made no allowance for the circumstance that a self-taught Negro was constantly accumulating new expressions which he encountered only in print and never in the speech of his associates.

After his escape he became a messenger in an attorney's courthouse office, and made the most of his constant exposure there to books, periodicals and literate men. Not long thereafter he was a handyman at a Baltimore medical school where a stock of books on medicine, law and theology engaged him in private study until an Episcopal bishop guided him through more formal classical and theological studies. Such was the education of the first Negro to be an army chaplain (of a Negro Civil War regiment), the holder of public offices during the Reconstruction, the manager of the AME Book Concern, a bishop, chancellor of Morris Brown College, founder of several denominational periodicals, compiler of a catechism and a hymnbook, recipient of an honorary degree from the University of Pennsylvania, and one of the most forceful personalities in Negro America in his time.

Our roster for these years lists very few educators. Negroes were not yet on the staffs of white and "mixed" institutions, and in their own schools and colleges it was still a day of modest beginnings. There was no reservoir of Negro teachers and scholars with suitable professional training and, moreover, the foremost Negro colleges, as well as many of the weaker ones, were still dominated by white clergymen, philanthropists, trustees, presidents, deans and professors. A few colored educators by sheer length of service were becoming familiar to literate Negroes. William H. Crogman, for instance, was for forty years a beloved figure at Clark "University" at Atlanta. He was not recruited from a typical background. He was born a freeman with a strong Caucasian inheritance in the Danish West Indies in 1841, ran off to sea at the age of fourteen, and for eleven years served a Massachusetts seafaring family named Boomer, who took a strong interest in the colored orphan's progress. One of his benefactors induced him to make the United States his home, and in the winter months, between voyages, took him into his home in Middleboro, Massachusetts, where he sent him to the common schools. William saved his earnings for an academic education and in 1868 entered

Pierce Academy for a two-year course. In 1876 he completed the classical course with the first graduating class of Atlanta University and, now thirty-five years old, joined the faculty of Clark. When a city ordinance finally segregated the races in the streetcars, Crogman, though seventy years old and living four miles from the city, never again set foot in an Atlanta car.

George William Cook, another whose career extended into the twentieth century, was born a Virginia slave of mixed ancestry in 1855, but escaped during Sheridan's Raid and made his way to New York, returning in the middle 1870's to Howard University where he was graduated in 1881. He remained to serve for the next half century as teacher and administrator. Like Crogman, he was a militant "race man," identified with NAACP as an officer during the last two decades of his life.

No Negro leader had a stranger background than did William Jefferson White, the foremost cultural leader among Georgia Negroes in his time. He was the originator of the public-school system in Augusta and of the influential Negro periodical, the *Georgia Baptist,* and the founder of Augusta Institute, later to become Morehouse College. Du Bois said of him: "he held a hundred thousand (Negroes) in the hollow of his hand," yet it is by no means certain that he was in fact a Negro. He was the son of a white planter and an Indian girl with a possible Negro strain. After becoming a prosperous cabinetmaker, he fell in love with a slave girl. Unable to persuade her owner to sell, he married her, moved into her master's home, and became identified with the race, though remaining free and going about his own affairs. Before the War he had boldly taught colored folk reading and ciphering, and in the Reconstruction years his zeal for helping the Negro people increased still further despite attempts to lynch him.

Another educator won far greater laurels. In 1895, the year that Douglass, the old Abolitionist hero, died, Booker T. Washington's "Atlanta Speech" at the Cotton States Exposition opened a new era of leadership. "In all things social we can be as separate as the fingers, yet one as the hand in all things essential to mutual progress," he declared. The compromise evoked an enormously favorable response from the country. It was a comfortable doctrine, the more widely accepted for its calculated ambiguities; diverse groups found in it what they sought. "I think," he said, "that the whole future of my race hinges on the question as to whether or not it can make itself of such indispensable value that the people . . . will feel that our presence is necessary to the happiness and well-being of the community. No man who continues to add something to the material, intellectual, and moral well-being of the place in which he lives is long without proper reward. This is a great human law which cannot be permanently nullified."

With Tuskegee as his working example, Washington preached industrial education for the Negro. His thesis that the race should now begin to *earn* eventual first-class citizenship rather than press for further immediate concessions made him not so much a leader of Negroes as an intermediary, interpreting the races to each other, and the most powerful national politician in the South in his day, with an immense influence in the patronage system and in all questions affecting the Negro. He was a useful emissary for practical politicians who knew how to reward him with power and patronage, and for Northern philanthropists who found him equally serviceable in distributing largesse and conserving racial attitudes and practices of which they approved.

As the years went by—and particularly after his death in 1915—he was increasingly criticized for his "accommodation-with-a-price" on the ground that the price he exacted was simply not high enough. A recent authority grants that Washington minimized the extent of discrimination, counselled his people against pushing for first-class civil and political rights, lectured them on their shortcomings and exhorted them to thrift, industry and the self-reliant capitalistic virtues of the Protestant ethic. But, says this scholar, conservatives mistook his short-range for his long-range goals; he was in fact sabotaging the American race system, and the picture that emerges from Washington's own correspondence is distinctly at variance with the ingratiating mask he presented to the world.

Washington's role was, inescapably, tailored to the times. He believed as firmly as Douglass that the American Democratic Credo ordained that it can never be necessary for a man to "earn" or prove his fitness to receive what is his birthright. He believed it, but did not preach it, precisely because the white man preached it, but did not believe it. Douglass, moreover, had been a fugitive when his race was still in slavery, but Washington had been freed by the white man's laws and came to maturity at the time when the definition of the relationships between the races was the central issue—an issue all but irrelevant heretofore. Douglass as abolitionist was indeed sponsored by whites when he stressed the Negro's rights and the white man's sins, while Washington's generation preferred an emphasis on the Negro's duties and shortcomings; and it is Washington, not Douglass, who is still the only Negro in the Hall of Fame.

His advice to Negroes to make the most of what they have, where they are (and this meant the rural South), and his dictum that "the opportunity to earn a dollar in a factory is just now worth infinitely more than the opportunity to spend a dollar in an opera house," anticipated what latter-day liberals still maintain: that the Negro's social redemption waits upon his economic emancipation. The controversy between Du Bois and Washington over the relative merits of industrial training and the higher education of a "talented tenth" obscures the fact that intellectuals like Du Bois and John Hope were not opposed to industrial education but insisted only that it was not enough, and that denial of training for political, social and cultural leadership for the race's most gifted sons would condemn the whole Negro community to permanent vassalage. Perhaps the Du Bois attack upon the Boss of the Tuskegee Machine with his incredible power over the country's racial matters (ranging from educational and editorial policy-making and the allocation of philanthropy's dollars to political appointments, major and minor) was less an attack upon Washington's ideas than a demand that other Negroes have a right to ideas, too. Even so, Washington's outburst against color prejudice in his Spanish American War celebration address, his dinner in the White House, and his anti-segregation article, published just after his death, in the *New Republic,* must have disenchanted many Southern admirers.

His *Up From Slavery,* a minor classic of the American tradition, has made his story too familiar to bear repeating, but some facts may be summarized with profit. He was born a slave in Virginia, probably three-fourths white, the son of an unknown white father and a woman of whose parents he also professed ignorance. He was not even sure of the year of his birth. His mother's cabin was the plantation kitchen and he did not sleep in a bed or eat at a table until after the Emancipation. The James Burroughs family with its thirteen children lived in a log house hard by the two cabins which housed the small farm's bondmen—three adults and four children, the latter still too young for the field. Booker's mother, Jane, cooked for the entire ménage and her children romped freely with the younger white Burroughs brood while the kindly master with his older sons worked side by side with their tiny complement of adult Negroes. Their happy situation fixed in Jane and little Booker an optimistic estimate of the white man's intentions toward the race, and long after he became famous, Washington still declared that the Negroes profited as much from slavery as did their owners. The contrast with Douglass's harder lot as a slave boy is instructive.

Booker was to have further reason to be kindly disposed to whites as he struggled for an education. After the War he and his foster father found employment in the West Virginia salt mines, where Booker soon met an Ohio Negro who could read, a marvel that prompted the boy to begin his self-education with Webster's *Speller* which his mother had somehow obtained. Soon the first colored school in the neighborhood opened, taught by a Northern Negro. These were not as yet free schools, and the desperately poor Negro families had to pitch in for their support. Colored folk from five to seventy-five years flocked to daytime and evening classes, some because they yearned to read the Bible and all of them, doubtless, eager to see what was in the books that had formerly been so sedulously kept from them.

Booker's wages were so sorely needed that his father kept him in the mines, but the lad was so persistent that his father finally allowed him to go to school if he worked five hours before nine o'clock in the morning and two more in the afternoon after school, an appalling schedule that the nine-year-old boy entered upon and followed for five years. In the mines he overheard talk of Hampton Institute where Negroes learned trades, and at once he had a new goal. At fifteen, after a stint as houseboy for a Yankee woman who encouraged his educational ambitions after instilling in him exacting standards of workmanship, he set out for Hampton with his own little savings, augmented by nickels and dimes of adult well-wishers in the community.

He worked his way through the school as a janitor and a painter, profiting immensely from his association with the dedicated white instructors and particularly the founder, Gen. Samuel C. Armstrong. The young master of Hampton and the rustic slave boy from the salt mines developed a strong friendship that deepened with the years. After Booker's graduation, Armstrong placed him on his faculty, and when he was asked to send a teacher to a new industrial school at Tuskegee, Alabama, the general dispatched Washington, and a notable career began.

A few personalities belonging to this era may be cited as outstanding members of learned professions in addition to those already accounted for. Richard T. Greener, the race's first Harvard graduate ('70), made a substantial career as an educator, lawyer and consular officer. Born in Philadelphia and reared in Boston, he attended the common schools at Cambridge and preparatory school at Oberlin and Phillips Andover before entering Harvard, where he won the Boylston Prize in oratory in his sophomore year and again as a senior, as well as the Bowdoin Prize for a dissertation. He served during the Reconstruction as a professor of philosophy at the University of South Carolina until 1877, completing a law course there at the same time and securing admission to the bar of that state and of Washington, D.C. Upon his return to Washington, he became dean of the Howard University Law School but resigned to become a law clerk in the office of the first Comptroller of the United States Treasury. He practised law privately in Washington from 1882, until he entered the foreign service in 1898, having become in the meantime a prominent Republican political figure. Himself an extremely fair man, he married a near-white woman and both could readily pass as white. His children are said to have gone over to the white race and are no longer traceable among Negroes.

Another prominent lawyer of pronounced Caucasian appearance was Archibald H. Grimké. His brother, Francis, was a famous Negro clergyman of the early twentieth century, and his daughter, Angelina Weld Grimké, was recognized as a poet and playwright. Archibald and his brothers were born near Charleston, the sons of Henry Grimké, a South Carolina planter of excellent family, and Nancy Weston, a beautiful slave whom he apparently emancipated. Nancy sent her boys to a school conducted by white Southern gentlemen of Charleston for children of free colored folk, and after the War the boys attended a school for colored children opened by Gilbert Pillsbury, Charleston's Reconstruction mayor, a Northern abolitionist. The Pillsburys resolved that the boys should go north for higher education and enabled them to enter Lincoln University, in those days still conducted by whites. It was the old story of consecrated white teachers stimulating the intellectual growth of gifted young Negroes.

Arch's father was the brother of the famous Grimké sisters, Sarah and Angelina (Mrs. Theodore Dwight Weld), who were living in Washington, long since out of touch with their Negro kin. When Mrs. Weld, startled by a newspaper account of Arch's triumphs at Lincoln, confirmed her guess that he was her nephew, she shocked Washingtonians by acknowledging the kinship and welcomed him as a house guest. In 1872 she helped him enter Harvard Law School. She subsidized the first year of his two-year course and a scholarship carried him through the second. His aunts insisted that his opportunity lay in the South, but he declined to return there and through the assistance of his Cambridge landlady was taken into an attorney's office. He was soon in a partnership, associating meanwhile with renowned Boston liberals.

He now launched a career that was to extend to 1930 as lawyer, editor and crusader against racial discrimination. He wrote creditable biographies of Garrison and Sumner, contributed to the Boston newspapers, campaigned for full Negro suffrage, served under Cleveland as consul to Santo Domingo, lectured and wrote for race-welfare causes, and became prominent in the American Negro Academy and the NAACP.

George Washington Williams was the foremost Negro historian of the period. He was born in Pennsylvania of mulatto parents and moved to Massachusetts where he left school at fourteen to enter the Union Army. After being discharged for wounds, he re-enlisted. He became in 1874 the first Negro graduate of Newton Theological Seminary. It is said that gunshot wounds received in the lung during the War rendered the New England climate unsuitable to him, compelling him to resign a pastorate in Boston, but he assumed another in Cincinnati where he also attended law school and read law for two years in the office of Alphonso Taft. He gained admission to the Ohio bar, a term in the Ohio legislature and a succession of federal offices, including a brief appointment from President Arthur as minister to Haiti.

Williams's reputation rests upon his two-volume *History of the Negro Race in America* and his *History of the Negro Troops in the War of the Rebellion*. They suffered somewhat for lack of formal training and occasional uncritical treatment, but they are based on extensive library research. If they do not measure up to modern standards of historical scholarship, they show a marked advance over the earlier Negro historians, Nell, Brown and Still, and judged by historiographical standards of his time Williams was "as ardent a devotee to the cause of truth as any of his contemporaries," according to John Hope Franklin.

Negroes noticed beyond the ghetto for achievement in the arts showed some increase in these years. Edwin M. Bannister was destined to be remembered as the race's first distinguished artist, though he was preceded by a few engravers and portraitists who may have had a greater claim to the honor. Joshua Johnston, whose work still hangs in Baltimore museums, painted portraits for leading citizens of that city, and Patrick Reason was a gifted portraitist and engraver at mid-century, patronized by New England abolitionists. A number of Louisiana *gens de couleur* also showed remarkable talent in painting and sculpture, but perhaps the ablest pre-Civil War painter was Robert Duncanson, the natural son of a Scotsman by a Negro woman. He was trained abroad and won his fame as a landscape artist in Europe. Bannister's was a solid but unspectacular talent, and it was his identification with a white artists' group in Providence, rather than his gifts, that gave him his priority. He was a native of the province of New Brunswick, born of preponderately white ancestry, orphaned at an early age and reared by a lawyer. He began sketching as a child and went as a young man for training in the 1850's to Boston, where he was ostracized by white artists but worked at his art in the rear of the barbershop where he earned his living. He was trained at Lowell Institute and in 1867 was challenged to an artist's career by a newspaper's observation that "the Negro seems to have an appreciation of art, while being manifestly unable to produce it." Three years later he moved to Providence and there made his career, though not his living, as a painter. He was a founder of the Providence Art Club, and advanced his reputation by winning a competition at the Philadelphia Centennial Exposition of 1876. When he stepped forward to claim the award, a hurried and awkward colloquy by the judges to "reconsider" the choice was thwarted by other contestants who stood resolutely by their colored rival.

In sculpture, Edmonia Lewis was the foremost figure. Her father was a Negro and her mother a Chippewa Indian. She was orphaned at an early age and brought up first by Indian kinsmen and then at an orphanage until sent by a group of abolitionists to Oberlin College. Thereafter, William Lloyd Garrison brought her to the attention of the Boston sculptor, Edmund Brackett, who trained her until she was sent to Rome for further instruction by white patrons, the Story family. Her best work was "Forever Free" for the Hariett Hunt Mausoleum at Mount Auburn Cemetery, Cambridge, and busts of Wendell Phillips, Sumner and Longfellow.

In music, the most celebrated Negro was "Blind Tom" Bethune. Born blind, the twentieth child of a slave woman in Georgia, he was considered worthless and thrown into the bargain when his mother was sold to a Colonel Bethune. As an infant Tom was enthralled by the piano playing of Bethune's daughters, and early demonstrated a fantastic talent for complete recall and for reproducing on the piano whatever music he heard, besides contriving extraordinary improvisations. As the boy matured, his owner conceived the idea of presenting him on concert tours and is said to have accumulated a fortune.

Bethune steadily increased his prodigy's repertoire by hiring professional musicians to play for him, and his handbills boasted that the boy knew more than five thousand numbers. Bethune shrewdly required the young slave to act the part of a feeble-minded boy upon whom occult forces played. Years of heartless exploitation on one-night stands finally stifled his genius. In 1860 he played, it is said, for President Buchanan. After the War, Bethune persuaded Tom's mother to designate him as guardian of the "idiotic Tom." He was now driven harder than ever and even taken on a highly profitable European tour. When Colonel Bethune died, the guardianship was transmitted to his son. Many years later Tom was found in obscurity in Hoboken, New Jersey, and once more came under the control of his guardians, who arranged one more tour in the year before he died in 1905 at the age of fifty-nine.

His contemporary, James A. Bland, one of the greatest minstrels of his day, had a vastly different background. He was born on Long Island of a long line of free Negroes deriving from Charleston. His father had attended Oberlin and Wilberforce and after the War moved his family to Washington where he was the first Negro examiner in the Patent Office. James began his musical history with a banjo which he made himself and was soon playing and singing for pennies near the White House. His father, an early example of the rising Negro bourgeoisie, opposed his strumming, preferring to make a scholar of the boy. When he was fourteen, however, a hotelkeeper employed him as a musician, to the great detriment of his record in the common schools and at Howard. He was virtually self-trained except for informal instruction from an old Negro.

Bland continued the musical tradition of Stephen Foster, who had only recently died. His melodies were in fact often ascribed to Foster, and Bland's publishers were often ignorant of his race. At first he performed at Negro dinners and weddings, barred, like other Negroes, from theaters, until colored entertainers took over the minstrel business, even blackening their faces and perfecting the "Negro talk" that was heard only on the stage. He outlived the minstrel vogue and died penniless. At his prime he went abroad, and for a twenty-year period spent most of his time there. Some of the best known of his hundreds of songs—immensely popular in their day, and still well known—were "Carry Me Back to Old Virginny," "In the Evening by the Moonlight" and "Oh, Dem Golden Slippers."

At least three concert singers achieved some prominence. Sisieretta Jones was born in Virginia but taken as a child to Providence. She studied at the New England Conservatory and her early concerts led to two tours in the West Indies. Once back, the "Black Patti" found that in spite of her sound training (reputedly financed by a Vanderbilt), critical acclaim and a concert at the White House, the public was not ready to support a Negro concert singer, and she stepped down to a role in her own musical-comedy company. Flora Batson was a gifted soprano who had to be content with church singing and Redpath circuit performances until she married a white manager who arranged modest tours for her in the South and abroad. Marie Selika had some professional training in Boston and made American and European tours, but did not reach the audiences she deserved.

More readily accepted were vocal groups recruited from the Negro colleges for fund-raising tours. Confining themselves to "spirituals" and "Negro music," they conformed pleasantly to the folklore about the Negro's propensity for simple piety and song, and college administrators knew how to profit by this predilection, even though the stereotype exasperated the more cultivated Negroes and sometimes provoked students to open rebellion. Much the most successful of these groups were the Fisk University Jubilee Singers, trained and directed by George D. White, the school's treasurer. After a modest success in America they appeared in England under missionary auspices, billed as the "ex-slave students of Fisk University, Tennessee." As usual, European acclaim increased their vogue at home, but they still encountered serious resistance at hotels and dining rooms in the South and to no small degree in the North. In Washington the barriers were so firm that President Arthur invited them to sing at the White House in an effort to thaw out the hotels. In Europe they were relatively free from such discrimination, but there they were exhausted with the strain of too many concerts, too many demands for benefit performances and the constant ordeal of playing the role of exotics whom curious Europeans crowded forward to gape at, even touching the ebony skin and woolly hair that they found so fascinating.

The day when Negroes should hold conspicuous rank in business and industry, the country's major preoccupation, was still far in the future. Here and there a Negro, like the near-white, slaveborn Scott Bond of Arkansas, who rose to become a wealthy planter and merchant, attracted local notice; but it was not real distinction, for thousands of whites of equal achievement excited no remark. Still, there are four in this generation's commercial sphere who were prominent enough to be listed in the *Dictionary of American Biography* (James Wormley, Thomy Lafon, Elijah McCoy and Jan Ernst Matzeliger), and another, John Jones, merits notice.

Jones was one of America's wealthiest Negroes and a prominent citizen of early Chicago. He had been born free in North Carolina, taught himself to read and write, served a tailor's apprenticeship, and arrived in Chicago in 1845 with an octoroon wife and $3.50. He was a militant reformer, a friend of John Brown and Frederick Douglass, and made his home an Underground Railroad station. After the War his wealth, gained in his tailoring business, enabled him to head the fight to repeal the Illinois "Black Laws" and he was twice elected Cook County Commissioner.

James Wormley was a flourishing hotelkeeper in Washington whose light-skinned, free parents had been domestic servants for a wealthy Virginia family before 1800. His hostelry was the scene of the so-called "Wormley Hotel Conference" associated with the disputed electoral count of 1876 and for two decades the Washington home of American and European dignitaries. In 1868 Wormley had accompanied Reverdy Johnson to London as steward for the American legation. He was never servile in manner but associated easily with the patrician Sumner and other reformers of the time.

Thomy Lafon was a New Orleans capitalist, born in that city of French-Haitian and American Negro blood. After an education that qualified him as a schoolteacher he became a merchant, moneylender and investor in real estate. He was a semi-recluse, constantly mistaken for a European, for his skin was white, his manner polished and he spoke French and Spanish fluently. He was devoted to the arts, a devout Roman Catholic. The city itself borrowed money from him on occasion. His chief interest was philanthropy and he gave his whole fortune to charities and religious and educational institutions, wholly without reference to race.

Two inventors are in this era's roll: Jan Ernst Matzeliger, born in Dutch Guiana, the natural son of a Dutch engineer and a native black woman; and Elijah McCoy, born in Canada to Kentucky slaves said to have been unmixed Africans who fled by way of the Underground Railroad. Matzeliger's father had his son apprenticed to a government machine shop where he developed his skill in mechanics. He came to the United States in his youth and found employment in a shoe factory in Lynn, Massachusetts. Here he studied the possibilities for increasing mechanization and eventually transformed the industry, for it was the Matzeliger laster that completed the series of machines now used in the manufacture of shoes. McCoy was a self-educated tinker with a flair for invention which he applied to the problem of automatic lubrication. He developed his ideas in a small shop in Michigan but, lacking both capital and an inclination for business, he assigned his patent rights to others to raise funds to enable him to continue his work. He secured his first patent in 1872 and in 1881–1925 took out forty-four more, principally for devices for supplying oil to machinery and engines without stopping them.

The most gifted literary artist between Phillis Wheatley and Paul Laurence Dunbar was Albery Allson Whitman. After a dreary slave-orphan boyhood in Kentucky, he became an itinerant laborer in shops and railroad yards. After less than a year at school, he became a teacher himself and then went to Wilberforce University, where he remained for six months under the tutelage of the great Daniel A. Payne. He did not graduate but served the university as financial agent before becoming an AME pastor. His poetic models were Byron, Tennyson, Bryant and Whittier; and his favorite themes were mixed blood and the vanishing Indians. The work is intellectually unimpressive and painfully conventional, but often fluent, its sympathies and emotions unforced, giving evidence of wide reading and great aspiration for one of his limited educational opportunities. He was a man of non-Negro appearance and his own mentor, Payne, confessed that Whitman's frail health and a predilection for alcohol thwarted his rise in the church.

The emergence of Paul Laurence Dunbar near the end of the century is often called the most important event in the history of Negro American letters. No Negro writer has been so universally approved by Americans, and for Negroes he was, because of his presumed unmixed African descent, a proud retort to the usual explanation of Negro genius. He made his finest contribution in dialect poems, but he tried with disappointing results to rest his reputation on classical English verse with non-racial themes. One poem asserts that he "sang of life" and his song now and then had "a deeper note," but the world only praised a "jingle in broken tongue." His stories enjoyed a moderate success, but less notice was taken of his novels dealing with whites. Like Booker Washington, he falls in that generation's "accommodationist" pattern, trimming his labors to white expectations. He suffered keenly from the conflict of emotion that entrapped the sensitive Negro between two cultures, and died at thirty-four, his end hastened by tuberculosis and whiskey.

That Dunbar was able to live by writing was owing in part to help from influential whites and the temper of the times. He was born in Dayton, Ohio, in 1872, the first in our roster to be born after the War. His father was a plasterer who fled from slavery to Canada, learned to read and served in a Massachusetts regiment during the War. Paul lost his father at the age of twelve. He went through the public schools, and in high school, where he was the only Negro, he was senior class poet and editor of the student publication. The best job he could find was that of elevator operator in a Dayton office building at four dollars a week. Disappointment over his inability to secure a college education led to profound, almost suicidal, depression, and as the years passed he turned to liquor as a solace for his frustrations and his lung troubles, and to steel himself for public appearances. Overuse sometimes brought him to grief as at a program of readings at Northwestern University where he appeared very late, stupefied with drink.

As elevator boy he found both time and encouragements, and began placing verse in the newspapers. His former high-school teacher retained her interest in him and when the Western Association of Writers convened in Dayton in 1892 she saw to it that he was invited to write a verse of welcome. At twenty he had ready his first book of verse, *Oak and Ivy,* which he published at his own expense and distributed as best he could. He sold the book to elevator passengers and to admiring Dayton High School students for a dollar. Another hundred copies were sold by Reverdy Ransom, then still a young AME pastor, but soon to become a bishop and race leader. Ransom pressed the book upon his parishioners with the admonition that Negroes have a duty to support their artists. Dunbar was employed in the Haitian Exhibit at the Columbian

Exposition in Chicago by Frederick Douglass. More help came when Dr. and Mrs. H. A. Tobey of Toledo made him their protégé and in 1897 he was given a trip to Europe by the daughter of a lecture bureau head who helped to bring him to the notice of publishers. Upon his return, Robert G. Ingersoll and others secured a position for him in the Library of Congress.

When his second volume, *Majors and Minors,* was published with help from the Tobeys, William Dean Howells, the literary arbiter of the era, gave it an enthusiastic *Harper's Weekly* review that touched off a veritable Dunbar vogue, and when in the following year Howells wrote the introduction for a third volume, *Lyrics of Lowly Life,* his reputation was made. Ill health, overwork, financial improvidence and racial affronts, however, quickly sapped his strength, and as he struggled against deadlines and ground out his poems, stories, novels and newspapers articles, the quality of his work declined. He went to Denver on his doctor's advice, but found it necessary to leave because of the vexing delays in moving copy and proof between Denver and the New York publishers. Later his home was graced by a souvenir portiere made of corks from whiskey bottles he had drained in Denver.

He was never a Negro-rights spokesman, but colored Americans forgave him, proud of his achievement as the first Negro to succeed as a professional writer. "In Dunbar's time," wrote Benjamin G. Brawley, "black was not fashionable. The burden still rested upon the Negro to prove that he could do what any other man could do, and in America that meant to use the white man's technique and meet the white man's standard of excellence. . . . This was the test . . . he had to satisfy, and not many will doubt that he met it admirably."

Charles W. Chesnutt is usually called the most competent Negro writer of fiction before the 1920's. He first came to notice when he published a story in the *Atlantic Monthly* in 1887, and the next two decades saw the publication of a biography of Frederick Douglass, a collection of short stories and three novels. Though he lived until 1932, he published his last major work in 1905, and left off serious writing for want of an audience for racial themes. Though it was on the color line that he found his materials, he did not, in the manner of the later realists, use the novel for propaganda but for dramatizing human conflicts, aspirations and anxieties. His work won high praise from Howells and critics generally, and even Southern papers, unaware of his race, published favorable reviews. Publishers were careful to make no allusion to his race, but the public clearly drew the color line at his subject matter.

He was nearly white, descended from free folk of Fayetteville, North Carolina, who found the condition of free Negroes in the middle 1850's so unendurable that they moved to Cleveland, Ohio. Here Chesnutt's future mother met and married Andrew Jackson Chesnutt, a light-skinned, thoroughly literate man. Because they coveted a good education for their son, born in 1858, they removed to Oberlin, but at the end of the War returned to Fayetteville to be near the elder Chestnutt's ailing father. Charles attended a freedmen's school and witnessed a lynching when he was nine. A new world opened to him when a prominent Fayetteville citizen took an interest in him and offered him the run of his library. When reduced family circumstances put the boy to work at fourteen as a bookkeeper in a saloon, his white teacher, a Robert Harris, contrived to have him appointed as a pupil-teacher at the school he attended. That year he published his first story in a small Negro weekly. Soón Harris found Charles a better post as assistant to his brother, Cicero Harris, who kept a school in Charlotte. Here Charles remained for three years, living in the Harris home, surrounded by books and cultivated folk. A mere youth, he was appointed to the staff of the state normal school at Fayetteville; by the time he was twenty-two he was principal, but by that time he found intolerable the restrictions of life in the South. Before making the break he became, by self-training, an expert stenographer and then resigned his position and set out hopefully for Cleveland. It was then that he entered a prize contest sponsored by McClure's magazine syndicate. He did not win the competition, but the sponsors bought his story and invited him to send more. After studying law and passing the Ohio bar examination, he thought for a while of emigrating to Europe but lacked the means, for he now had a wife and three children.

While building a practice as legal stenographer he plunged back into writing, encouraged by the prompt acceptance of a story by the *Atlantic*. His court-reporting business prospered. He was befriended by George W. Cable and Walter Hines Page, and when his volume of conjure stories was brought out in 1899, critics hailed him as a major American short-story writer. He gave up his business as attorney, court reporter and stenographer and set up offices as a professional writer. His novels were well reviewed, but they were not commercially successful, and he had to support his family by lectures and readings. After 1900 he became increasingly depressed by the worsening of the Negro's plight. He was loosely attached to the Tuskegee faction but deplored Washington's readiness to sacrifice the ballot, and his sharp attack upon a major publisher for bringing out an anti-Negro book induced the company to withdraw it. He sent his two daughters to Smith College and declined to allow one of them to go South as a teacher.

Disillusionment ended his career as a professional litterateur but with men like Kelly Miller, T. Thomas Fortune, Charles W. Anderson and J. W. E. Bowen he gave his time to fighting prejudice. His high reputation in Cleveland (he was a member of the chamber of commerce and of fine clubs) and, away from home, his Caucasian appearance insulated him from affront, but the family when dining in restaurants far from Cleveland sometimes conversed in French to insure being served. He was an informal consultant on

Negro affairs to publishers and a race champion, scolding writers who traduced Negroes.

In T. Thomas Fortune the era had its leading journalist, pre-eminent until World War I. He made his important career with the *New York Age* and its predecessors, from about 1880 until 1907, when it was bought by Fred R. Moore. He was identified with Booker Washington, but in his last years was an editor of the publications of the Garvey Back-to-Africa movement. At his peak he was an intimate of the race's most celebrated men. Nominally Republican, but often an independent crusader, he was a pragmatist, opposing proposals for segregated schools in New York, but at the same time a leader in the establishment of New York's colored regiment, later known as the 369th. He was a founder of the United Colored Democracy, a voters' group, and in 1890 an organizer of the National Afro-American League, which quickly expired but faintly foreshadowed the NAACP.

Here again was a man of uncommon background, strongly Caucasian in appearance. He was born in Florida of Indian, Irish, Jewish, Negro and Anglo-Saxon stock, allied both to slave and prominent white families. After the Civil War, he attended a Freedmen's Bureau school in an AME church until hostile whites drove the family away. He was a Sunday-school superintendent at the age of twelve, the only colored boy in his neighborhood who could write. His father, a tanner and independent shoe merchant who never knew slavery, served several terms in the Florida Reconstruction legislature and his influence secured for his son an appointment as page boy in the state senate. The family's political activities and its close friendships with many whites evoked so much animosity on the part of other whites that the household moved to Jacksonville where the elder Fortune was soon elected city marshal.

The boy went to Washington to attend Howard University, but found his financial resources inadequate until his Congressman found him a place as a special customs agent in Delaware for a year. Then, after two and a half years at Howard and a brief period of newspaper work and schoolteaching, he went to New York in 1879 to take up his career. In the late 1880's he was an editorial writer for the New York *Sun*.

Such then were the names that stand forth in the record of the first generation out of slavery: a little company of political officeholders, some elected in the prostrate South under the protection of Yankee guns, and some appointed as the pawns of partisan warfare; a cluster of religious leaders, shepherds of a separate Negro flock; a tiny company of educational pioneers embarked upon a still-uncharted course; the first lonely figures in the learned professions and the arts, still largely contained in the ghetto, still outside the American mainstream, still curiosities in the larger American community.

Part Two

1900–1936: Cloud by Day and Fire by Night

The Negro generation of 1900–1936 began with the Tuskegee Idea in the ascendancy: purchasing peace for their time by deferring social and political aspirations. It ended with the achievement of much of what the truce had thought to barter away. Hardly had the Atlanta Compromise become the "settled" policy of the country when tightening segregation and an appalling resurgence of violence—the first decade of the new century saw nearly a thousand lynchings, to say nothing of such riots, in roughly the same period, as those at Wilmington (1898), Atlanta (1906) and Springfield (1908)—signalized the white community's bad faith and the breakdown of the bargain. Such a catastrophic turn for the worse, a full generation after Emancipation, evoked a revolt of Northern Negro intellectuals, who now renounced the Washington program of reliance upon Southern whites' benevolence and heralded a militant drive for full civil, political, economic and educational opportunity, a program bold enough to frighten timid Negroes as well as white conservatives. It resulted in 1910 in the establishment (with white liberal co-operation) of the National Association for the Advancement of Colored People.

Not only was there a fateful shift of Negroes from tenant farms to cities in the South during these years; there was, after 1910, an even more massive migration from the South to the North, magnetized by widening employment opportunities and the promise of comparative freedom from discrimination and Jim Crow. They flooded Northern urban centers by the thousands, faster than the region could assimilate them, and there followed a mounting white resistance to their absorption, and the concentration of these teeming thousands in the Harlems and Bronzevilles, where the Negro was to find more than he had known in the past but considerably less than he hoped for. The cityward drift heightened Negro self-respect and race-consciousness, a development also accelerated by the maturing of a Negro press, broadening of educational opportunity, decline in illiteracy (from roughly 50 per cent in 1900 to less than 20 per cent, most of it by 1936 confined to Southern rural Negroes, and urban folk over forty years old), and by the emergence of a Negro middle class.

With waxing urbanization, education and economic differentiation, came the familiar American counterpart of growing specialization and expertness. Gone now was the era when a man, because of rocklike character or a few years at Oberlin could step forth as a "spokesman for the race." And with the new aggressive Americanism of whites, intolerant of difference and suspicious of alien influence, there developed that chauvinistic hundred-percentism which, because it had no place for the Negro, evoked from him the response so familiar in the history of colonialism. The colonial had grown too much like the national to be held to second-class citizenship. There emerged the aggressive Negro Americanism that saw first the Tuskegee Idea challenged by the emergent NAACP, and then a mounting determination, energized by the race's participation in the War to Make the World Safe for Democracy, to become Negro Americans as well as American Negroes. And, though not themselves in office, they were now voters—especially after World War I—aware that candidates were under new necessities to court colored votes with promises of the amelioration of all Negroes, even those in the deep South.

The maturing of Negro American civilization, moreover, fostered by well-defined Negro communities in Northern cities and by advances in education and occupational differentiation, rendered it an ever more faithful facsimile of white society with all its stratifications. Facile generalizations about "the Negro" no longer hit the mark, if indeed they ever had. Such a social order produced "functional leaders" (the phrase is Professor Frazier's) instead of another Booker Washington. A man would now be a leading Negro writer, or artist, or scientist, rather than a "Negro leader," and his position in the race would be determined more by the ideology of his group than by his own tendency to conciliation or challenge.

The standards for eminence were now much higher. It was no longer possible in the twentieth century, by being the first to enter a field, to astonish the world with proof that here, too, the Negro could perform like a man. In the new era the Negro artist, scientist, or scholar was to be less and less an untaught prodigy pushed forward by latter-day abolitionists beseeching the nation to measure him against his handicap. In growing measure he was the trained specialist, competing now in the whites' exhibitions, scholarly journals and professional associations. The distinguished Negro, to be sure, still felt constrained to confine himself to Negro themes, working usually in the ghetto and under Negro auspices, but the standards of excellence began to match those of the whites. The price of eminence in the white man's world rose steadily, but it *was* now, at least in some small degree, eminence in the white man's world. The change is more qualitative than quantitative. Perhaps the number of Negroes who by 1936 were "famous" was not much larger, proportionately, than the number a century earlier; but the point is that the celebrity in the past (unless he stood astride the color line as a negotiator for both sides) was a hero only to the Negro and a small fringe of reformers and radicals, and for works that promised to raise the condition of the race. But at the end of the era here under review, a few who did break through the barriers of caste emerged on a different plane, regarded by white colleagues in their fields of achievement—though not yet by any sizable segment of the American public at large—as American artists, scholars, writers and religious leaders rather than *only* as "outstanding Negroes."

Although World War I brought new discriminations in war industries and the armed services, older disabilities were moderated in response partly to the Negroes' loyal support of a war that promised them few rewards (even Du Bois urged colored America to close ranks in the nation's hour of peril), and in part to articulate Negro protest. The war, indeed, greatly strengthened the Negroes' own Americanism and their determination to achieve fuller participation in American life.

Postwar reaction brought new disillusionments. Nearly 350,000 Negro troops had served, and whites were fearful of the effects of this adventure upon the mood of colored veterans. Some 400,000 migrants, moreover, had swarmed up out of the South into Northern cities in 1914–1917, and the strains engendered by the population explosion were vastly increased in the years following the war, when the flood grew ever more torrential. In 1900, nine tenths of the country's Negroes lived in the South, five sixths of them rural folk; but by 1936 21 per cent were in the North, nine tenths of whom were concentrated in great urban centers. Even in the South a third of the colored population was now in urban communities.

The nation was, moreover, gripped by a psychosis marked by hostilities against all strangers, all exotic influences. The hysteria expressed itself not only in a new rash of lynchings, the Scottsboro case, race riots and new refinements in Jim Crowism; it boiled up also in the Lusk Laws, the Soviet Ark, the Red Scare and a resurgent Ku-Kluckery, this time as strong in the North as in the South and directed against a whole catalog of "undesirables" of whom the Negro was only one.

Paralleling these reactionary growths was the extraordinary interest in the Negro on the part of Northern intellectuals, especially in New York, now that they were for the first time coming to know him at close range and in considerable numbers. The remarkable, if somewhat misnamed, "Harlem Renaissance" or "New Negro" movement, is at least in part explained by this vogue, for it provided a market for the Negro literary and artistic genius's wares, to say nothing of the applause and sponsorship it accorded Negro writers and artists who scarcely deserved it.

These forces, however, had largely spent themselves by 1930 when the Great Depression engulfed black and white alike in common ruin. The Negro was, as always, hit first and hardest, but it was essentially a levelling catastrophe; the gap between the races was narrowed, and then the New Deal operated to prevent the inequalities from reasserting themselves in quite their old degree, and, incidentally, to shift the Negroes' historic party allegiance. They had, in fact, long since been disenchanted with the Republicans. Theodore Roosevelt, after spurring Negro hopes by dining with Booker Washington, found it prudent to appease powerful white interests he had thus offended. He exhibited his repentance by his peremptory discharge of three companies of colored troops for allegedly "shooting up the town" at Brownsville, Texas, and by speaking tours in the South in which he urged Negroes to stay out of the professions, and to put their confidence in their Southern white friends. President Taft was even more aloof, and in the 1920's the Coolidge and Hoover administrations supported Southern Republican "Lily-whites" in forcing Negro party officials out, in the effort to rid Republicans of the handicap of being the Negro's party in the South.

The notables of this era, some three hundred of whom we identify, were recruited from this changing society. Many began life as slaves; others were a short generation removed from bondage, the great majority the children of ex-slaves. All of them were born and grew up before the great Northward migrations, and most were themselves born and reared in the South. Except for those who made their careers in the Negro church and school, they were typically persons who came up out of the South and made their reputations in the North. Perhaps, like all migrants, they were less firmly in the grip of their social heritage than were their fellows who elected to remain behind, but it is clear that their minds and emotions still responded powerfully to stimuli in patterns to which their lately abandoned social environment had conditioned them.

The momentum of the past continued to define the conduct of whites toward the freedmen. Habits and attitudes crystallized in preceding generations lingered in assumptions of inherent Negro inferiority, in the old social distances between the races, in antagonism of white against colored workers, in condescending white paternalism, and in the Northern missionary and philanthropic spirit. For Negroes who moved North, the process of urbanization was complicated by the hostility of the older Negro urban folk, the Old Families who, when Negroes were still rare in great Northern cities, had made a comfortable *modus vivendi* but now saw their tranquillity threatened by the "low-class" Southern Negroes swarming into their peaceful neighborhoods, certain to bring squalor and strife and to alter the social attitudes of whites.

The list of notables in the half century after 1900 continues to include sons of white fathers, but by this time white ancestry was more frequently a generation or two removed. The disproportion of light-skinned Negroes among the elite had also diminished: intermixture in the race as a whole had become so great as to reduce the seeming preponderance of light complexions among distinguished Negroes, and complexion was becoming notably less relevant in a growing number of fields of achievement.

The white fathers rarely acknowledged their natural sons, though some, to be sure, did so. In 1950 *Ebony* Magazine identified a surprising number of eminent Negroes in this category: Fred Moore of the New York *Age,* for instance, was the son of a white man by a household slave in a very prominent family, and Daniel Hale Williams is said to have been the sixth child born by his mother to a white man. Among those in recent decades who tried to conceal such descent were a leading legislator, a prominent Eastern race leader and well-known college presidents, including one "known to be the son of a foremost white leader in the field of race relations." The pair bore a startling resemblance. The father, says *Ebony,* was a Methodist minister from Atlanta, who founded a leading racial organization after the boy's birth, and later helped push him into the college presidency. John Hope and his father, on the other hand, never concealed their kinship. The article names a president of Virginia State College, and a president of Selma University, reportedly the son of a Southern governor by a slave woman whose time he hired. It also repeats the familiar report that William J. Hale, for over thirty years president of a state college in Tennessee, was the son of a governor of that state, and adds that Henry A. Hunt, a very prominent Negro educator and public figure, for thirty-four years president of Fort Valley Industrial School in Georgia, was one of seven children of a Georgia judge (his name is given) by a Negro woman.

Distinguished Negroes were now recruited from all levels of colored society, but showed increasing tendency to derive from the emergent middle class rather than from the humbler strata, for Negro society was undergoing steady stratification. Even in slavery, special deference was paid to light-skinned house slaves, particularly to those known to be blood relations of good white families, and free Negroes had another claim to status. After Emancipation, stratification became still more marked. Among the indices of social priority, family descent stood first, but in the North it was perhaps no more decisive than length of residence in a particular community. The time elapsed since the family's emancipation was another factor, and color was a consideration of very great weight. Next came occupation, education, general behavior and wealth. As the decades passed, the increasingly complex Negro status system, though faithfully duplicating that of whites, was steadfastly ignored by the latter, for they were disinclined to see differences between one Negro and another. In the ghetto, however, it was determinative for the emergence of persons of distinction, though the rigidities that assigned rank often yielded to the characteristically American social mobility that so frequently permits Tom, Dick and Harry to become Thomas, Richard and Henry.

The presumption of whites that Negroes are inherently inferior still blocked the race's progress, but important breaches were being made in this wall by the findings of social scientists, and as the proportion of college-trained whites exposed to the new scientific data on race became larger. But if white Americans abandoned old beliefs slowly, the Negro proved little more educable in this regard. Perhaps nothing so effectually choked off the young Negro's ambitions as the constant reminder of disability and "inherent" incapacities by which both whites and Negroes (and even his own parents) exhorted him to abandon his illusions.

It was against this mentality, as much as against overt discriminations, that the attack was directed by Negro prophets of the race's redemption: the religious and educational leaders, the race-advance agencies, professional associations, the writers and artists—all of them perpetually hammering away at the Negro's despairing disbelief in his own abilities. It was the Negro press particularly that became the chief scold of the race, berating it for its shortcomings, exhorting it to greater exertions and self-confidence, and deploring what Carter Woodson, the race's foremost historian, called "the Negro's conspicuous belief in his own inferiority . . . the . . . barrier between him and the progress he might now be making." The lack of "race pride" and of group solidarity which derived from the same inferiority feelings kept them from rallying to agencies like the NAACP and the Urban League, from patronizing their own lawyers and doctors, from supporting their own businessmen and authors and artists, from voting for their own candidates for public office. The shadow of the plantation still lay athwart Harlem and Bronzeville in the early twentieth century.

Because the passing of the first full generation since slavery times coincided with the completion of the Jim Crow structure—its building began two decades after Emancipation and was completed only about 1910—it was difficult to avoid the conclusion that economic and social exclusion for the race was to be the fixed policy of the country. It would be an uncommon Negro, with uncommon advantages, who would presume to defy such odds. The gloomy view of the race's prospects seemed confirmed by the plane of life in urban and rural slums. On every hand were the familiar evidences, regardless of race, of life at the bottom socio-economic layer, where the Negroes were concentrated: brutalizing poverty; filthy and incredibly overcrowded housing; shiftlessness and improvidence; heedless abandonment to elemental pleasures, coarse conduct and hooliganism; family disorganization and instability; intemperance, gambling, sexual promiscuity and illegitimacy; cutting and shooting scrapes; low educational attainments; crude tastes and gaucheries in clothing, personal adornment and religious observance.

The tragic circle tended to confuse cause and effect. The recent slavery past had accustomed them to life at the mudsill and to a low ceiling of aspiration. Then, after freedom, the rigidities of caste and the denial of opportunity perpetuated and intensified the familiar incidents of slum life, confirming both whites and Negroes in their declining expectations of the Negro's prospects and capabilities. The degraded condition of the Negro quarter had the effect, moreover, of cutting off avenues of future amelioration because it strengthened the resolution of whites that segregation must be preserved, that the blight must be contained, that the Negro must be interned, lest all be contaminated together.

It is in this generation that students remark the growing tensions inside the Negro group, generated by the pressures from without. The Negro male, powerless to protect his women from the white man's double standard, was rebuffed at every turn in his quest for dignity and economic independence, "climbing a mountain of yessirs" and eating the bread earned by his wife in domestic service. Prevented from being a hero in his family's eyes, he found desperate catharsis in animal excesses to prove his manhood to himself and his fellows, and in violence against friend and kin (which the law somehow winked at) to discharge emotions excited by strangers, ending finally with a hatred of his own Negroness, or, if he was more fortunate, with escape into the delusions described in Franklin Frazier's *Black Bourgeoisie*. If by some wonderful conjunction of perseverance and good fortune he rose to some eminence, insistent tugs pulled him away from his own group who, in their low estate, hung like a millstone around his neck. Withdrawn from his own folk and branded a snob, but rejected by the white community, he was often a lonely figure. Yet, however such gloomy reflections might paralyze the hopes and efforts of great numbers, there always remained a hopeful and energetic company, thoroughly imbued with conventional American values and expectations, who achieved personal successes that triumphantly vindicated their faith and in some degree raised the condition of all Negro Americans by dramatizing to the Negro his capacities and opportunities and, at the same time, persuading a growing company of whites of the Negro's title to their respect and steadily augmented participation in American life.

In this generation, religious leaders once again comprised the largest single group we have sifted from the historical record. It was perhaps inevitable that the church should continue to attract able young men. It was the one institution where their ambitions to rule, to express themselves freely, to exercise—independent of white pressures—a major influence in Negro America could most readily be realized. Both saints and sinners flocked to the church, the substitute for the clubhouse, theater and amusement park; the meeting place for friends, the clearinghouse where one picked up the gossip, courted one's sweetheart, kept abreast of economic opportunities. It mobilized the slender resources of the faithful to send promising young members to college, supported their artists, writers, musicians and lecturers, by paying for their training and providing them with audiences. The larger metropolitan congregations undertook vast institutional programs that supplied their gigantic parishes with welfare and social-service agencies from kindergartens, summer camps, playgrounds, visiting nurses, gymnasiums, temperance societies and family-counselling agencies to homes for working girls, music schools, children's handicraft clubs, evening industrial schools, employment agencies and credit unions, to say nothing of political and social-action groups.

The more than fifty* whom we found most conspicuously mentioned labored exclusively among Negroes. They were most likely Methodist bishops, or, in the case of the Episcopal Church, "suffragan" (assistant) bishops. Baptist leaders, except for the heads of the National Convention, Baptist publishing agencies, the foreign-mission board and the Baptist Young People's Union, were far less numerous because the decentralized Baptist policy, mentioned earlier, kept leading Baptist divines from becoming national figures.

The roads to leadership were various. Vigorous personalities and men of distinguished intellectual, oratorical, administrative and political gifts forged ahead. Often it was as editors of denominational organs or as college presidents that the clergymen achieved the sort of national prominence that made them eligible for high ecclesiastical office, and sometimes pastorates in the huge congregations of New York or Chicago proved the steppingstone. Competition for high office in the Negro Baptist groups and in the major Methodist connections (the "Central Jurisdiction," the Negro wing of the Methodist Episcopal Church North, was an exception) was often incredibly lively. All the characteristics of political contests were there, including well-oiled machines, preconvention electioneering, campaign funds and efforts to capture or stampede delegates by all the devices known to party warfare.

The long tenure of National Baptist Convention presidents attests the firm hold that leaders achieved. Rev. L. K. Williams, pastor of the huge Olivet Church in Chicago, was re-elected annually from 1922 until his death in 1940; one of his predecessors had held the presidency for nearly thirty years. The place of this office in Negro America is suggested by the fact that the largest Negro newspaper conducted a poll to discover the "people's choice" to succeed Williams.

The annual contests over the Baptist state and national presidencies were often tumultuous, but the AME and AMEZ national conferences suffered

* W. E. Beckett
William Y. Bell
Shelton Hale Bishop
George L. Blackwell
J. W. E. Bowen, Sr.
Henry A. Boyd
George F. Bragg
James B. Caldwell
Archibald Carey, Sr.
Randall A. Carter
Matthew W. Clair, Sr.
Nelson Cleaves
George C. Clement
George W. Clinton
James N. Conner
William N. De Berry
Henry B. Delany
Edward T. Demby
Elijah Fisher
Robert F. Fisher
Joseph S. Flipper
William A. Fountain
Theodore M. Gardiner
John A. Gregg
Francis J. Grimké
William H. Heard
Richard B. Hudson
William H. Jernagin
J. Albert Johnson
Joshua H. Jones
Robert Elijah Jones
Lorenzo King
Willis J. King
Lynwood W. Kyles
Benjamin F. Lee
William L. Lee
Charles H. Phillips
Adam Clayton Powell, Sr.
Henry H. Proctor
Reverdy C. Ransom
James S. Russell
Alexander P. Shaw
B. G. Shaw
David H. Sims
Evans Tyree
William T. Vernon
William J. Walls
Alexander Walters
L. K. Williams
George F. Woodson
Richard Robert Wright, Jr.

even more from these dissensions in electing bishops to fill vacancies. Unfortunate choices were sometimes made; successful candidates fought too hard for preferment and took revenge on opponents. Sometimes the new bishop was exiled to a hardship post as a reprisal from fellow prelates. Earlier bishops had often been plain, blunt men, painfully conscious of humble origins and want of preparation, but skillful in their use of power and politics in the episcopal office, for ends that were ultimately unselfish. As a new leadership, more refined by education and gentler antecedents, replaced the old slaveborn warriors, competition for office grew even more strenuous.

The hundredth AME general conference, assembled at the historic Bethel Church in Philadelphia, in 1916, was the most boisterous the denomination had yet seen. Selection of two new bishops proceeded calmly enough, but the storm broke over the indictment of one of the body's most prominent bishops on counts of "maladministration, stealing, lying, and conduct unbecoming a Christian gentleman." He was spared the disgrace of suspension, but in 1932 was again the center of a frenzied floor fight where, with another leading bishop, a former Register of the Treasury of the United States, he was ousted on charges of misappropriation of funds. Another bishop escaped by politics and tears, while two others were saved only by a disposition of the delegates to conceal the church's disgrace. One was involved in a widely publicized bastardy case and the other, eighty-four years old, a former United States Minister to Liberia, was charged with embezzling Wilberforce University funds. The latter's reprieve was only temporary, for he was in the following year declared guilty.

At the 1936 AMEZ quadrennial conference, the pastor of a huge parish, an extremely able man who had succumbed to amorous and bibulous propensities, was made a bishop primarily, it was said, to save his congregation by removing him. A bishop was found guilty of maladministration and misappropriation, but given a year to make good the losses. When the verdict was reported the delegates stampeded until police restored peace between the contending factions. Earlier in the proceedings the unhappy bishop's brother had tearfully offered to write a check for the amount if the affair were dropped.

Candidates for high church office commonly announced well in advance and even made ringing speeches on the convention floor, appealing for votes on the score of their services to the denomination and its institutions, and their success as fund-raisers, membership builders, public servants and race champions. They were usually men of mixed blood, but this could be a handicap. Once a candidate of very fair complexion was openly disparaged for that shortcoming but he surmounted the obstacle by presenting his wife, a very dark woman to the delegates' view and then pointing out that his rival had preferred a light-skinned wife. The delegates were predominantly dark Negroes, but he was elected.

None of this generation's best-known religious statesmen was a noted theologian; their chief efforts were devoted to the building of Negro Christianity, however sorely parishioners may have been tempted to doubt this when newspapers reported the misdeeds of some of them. But besides the ecclesiastical responsibilities, secular functions increasingly engaged them.

Holders of high denominational office were drawn to non-ecclesiastical work by the strong disposition of both whites and Negroes to seek Negro leaders among the clergy and educators. L. K. Williams, for example, was the head of an insurance company and a prominent Republican party figure besides. Bishops Kyles and Tyree were connected with business institutions; R. R. Wright, Jr., a leading AME bishop and editor, was a cofounder and later president of a bank in Philadelphia; and in 1916 one Negro life insurance company had five bishops on its board of directors.

Once arrived at positions of leadership or as heads of great urban institutional churches, they became leaders in a bewildering variety of enterprises. Bishops Bell and Walls were life members of the NAACP, and the elder Bowen, another NAACP and Urban League leader, headed the drive to bring the first Negro high school to Atlanta. Bishop Clement was chairman of the interracial commission of the Federal Council. DeBerry's civic labors while pastor of America's largest Congregational church, in Springfield, Massachusetts, brought him an award from the city itself. The venerable William H. Jernagin, vigorously active until his death in 1958 at eighty-nine, had a record as a race leader that spanned nearly seventy years. At twenty-one he was organizing Negro farmers in the Alliance Movement, crusading for temperance laws and challenging the new Jim Crow legislation. A founder of the Fraternal Council of Negro Churches, he was prominent in the race relations work in the Federal Council, which in 1919 dispatched him to the Paris Peace Conference where, with Du Bois, he helped organize the Pan-African Congress. From the vantage point of his Washington office he set up a "Washington Bureau," as a watchdog for the Negro's legislative interests.

Robert E. Jones was another leader with immense prestige, greatly respected by both Negroes and whites, and appointed in 1920 as one of the two first Negro bishops in the Methodist Episcopal denomination. He came to national prominence as the editor of the *Southwestern Christian Advocate*, as a trustee of denominational colleges, a founder and director of several Methodist institutions for Negroes, a major officer in Negro YMCA and Boy Scout work, a 33rd-degree Mason, a leader in the Federal Council and in the Inter-racial Commission, and a prime mover in the National (Negro) Business League. In 1929 he was awarded the Harmon Medal for developing Gulfside, a sort of Negro Chautauqua-resort at Waveland, Mississippi, where he still resides in 1959 at the age of eighty-seven, still a man of weight in his denomination's affairs.

The elder Adam Clayton Powell, who came to the Abyssinian Baptist Church in 1908, became a formidable enemy of organized prostitution in

Harlem, a director of the NAACP, a Republican leader who switched to Roosevelt in 1936, taking thousands of New York Negroes with him. Reverdy Ransom was yet another of the giants in the Negro vanguard. Assigned to a parish in Chicago in 1896, he plunged into politics and reform, associating himself with Clarence Darrow and Jane Addams. After an unsuccessful race for Congress in New York in 1916, he aspired to a bishop's post. He was elected in the 1924 conference and came to be one of the most famous AME leaders. During his war against Chicago policy gamblers, his church was dynamited and he preached with a loaded revolver within reach. He was a forthright opponent of the Tuskegee Idea, and the Tuskegee press attacked him openly, even hinting that an appalling humiliation he suffered on a Pullman car in the deep South was attributable to his own misconduct. Ransom had the last word on the matter, however, for he denied the imputation in his autobiography in 1950 and even added a story about Booker Washington's own misconduct. The sage of Tuskegee, he said, was beaten in a New York hallway after calling on a white woman, and fled for refuge to Ransom's home.

Multi-phase civic and social service marked the careers of all of these churchmen, as a glance at their biographies in *Who's Who in America* amply shows. They threw themselves into campaigns to stop radio programs like *Amos 'n' Andy* and movies like *Birth of a Nation*. Many were political party officials and public officeholders. Jernagin conferred with Presidents at the White House from Wilson to Eisenhower as a spokesman for Negro opinion, and others consulted by Presidents included Walls, Ransom, Wright, Gregg, F. J. Grimké, R. E. Jones, the elder Powell. Many held offices in national religious bodies, like the Federal Council, and occasionally one would head a predominantly white group, as when H. H. Proctor became moderator of the New York Congregational Church Association. Some participated in ecumenical congresses abroad and in the World Council of Churches, where they pressed hard for resolutions against racial discrimination.

Two thirds of the fifty-odd made their careers in the South, and the balance in the Northeastern states, in Africa, or in both North and South. Four fifths were born in the South, one in Canada, one in Africa, and the rest were Northerners, usually children of parents recently come from the South. About half were born in slavery times, at least sixteen of them in bondage. Another sixteen are known to have been (and it may be presumed that most of the remainder were also) children of ex-slaves. A few were sons of white planters by slave women, several were the known grandsons of white slaveowners, and most of the rest had unstable family backgrounds in which white and Negro blood were freely intermixed but where the lines of descent are uncertain. Several, because they were descended from the loose slave unions so common to the plantation economy, knew nothing of their paternal ancestry, but at the other extreme a very few came of regular ancestry that could be traced through generations of stable families. At least one had legal, mixed marriages—in the South—in his pre-Civil War ancestry.

The life histories of these men present so few generalizations that any effort to squeeze them into a stereotype is absurd, but for our purposes the variations and uniformities may perhaps be outlined by selecting ten of the most famous for closer scrutiny, five of whom, still active in early 1958, were interviewed by the writer: William Yancey Bell (1887–), William H. Jernagin (1869–1958), Robert Elijah Jones (1872–); Willis Jefferson King (1886–) and William J. Walls (1885–); and five who left autobiographies: Charles H. Phillips (1858–1951), William H. Heard (1850–1937), Reverdy C. Ransom (1862–1959), Henry Hugh Proctor (1868–1933) and Adam Clayton Powell (1865–1953).

Heard's antecedents were discussed in the preceding chapter because of his nineteenth-century political career, though his AME leadership extended to 1938. Ransom was born during the Civil War in his maternal grandmother's hewn-log home in Flushing, Ohio. He had fair skin and fiery red hair. He never knew who his father was, but supposed him to be white. His mother, a bright girl who had learned to read, was liberated long before the War but illegally held in bondage for several more years, until she was given a small sum of money and sent to Ohio. Young Reverdy went to school in an AME church, while his mother worked as a domestic. For a while they slept in their employers' attic, and it was when the latter sent their sons off to college that Harriet Ransom resolved that her son, too, should make something of himself. The boy wondered why all Negroes were poor, why he could not go to school with his white playmates, why the teacher wept when he was assigned to her class in the white Presbyterian Sunday School. The cause, his mother explained, lay in the ignorance of the Negro people, and his hope of improvement lay in education.

Reverdy delivered his mother's laundry bundles, worked as a brickyard helper, a porter in a barbershop and a houseboy, and then, his savings supplemented by funds his mother raised by mortgaging the home, he went to Wilberforce University.

Phillips was one of twelve children in a secure, pious, hardworking, closely knit Georgia slave family, whose humane owner permitted the elder Phillips to hire his time and ply his trade as an independent blacksmith and to be a rural preacher. Only after the War, when he was past fifty, did he learn to read, however, at an evening school taught by Northern women. The boy's mother, a woman of sturdy character, knew nothing of her ancestry, but his white paternal grandfather was a Col. Zachariah Phillips, a gentleman of some repute. Freed at the age of three, Charles worked on his father's farm until he was sixteen and had his first formal education from Northern women at a missionary school in the local Negro Baptist church and then under the pioneer Negro educator Lucy Laney, at Haines Industrial

Institute in Augusta. At the close of 1874, the holidays over and the crops garnered and sold, he went, prompted by a religious ecstasy, to Atlanta University to prepare for the ministry.

Adam Powell, Sr., was born in direst poverty in a one-room slave cabin in Virginia, less than a month after Lee's surrender. His autobiography mentions no natural father: "On my paternal side I know less than little about my ancestors," he wrote, but on the maternal side his grandmother was predominantly Indian and his grandfather was a German. Adam's mother was a huge, independent tyrant who hated poor whites, and her spouse was a branded slave with a huge letter *P* burned into his back. Adam was one of seventeen children in a family of sharecroppers who subsisted sometimes for weeks on dried apples and black-eyed peas until new crops restored their credit with the country merchant. At seven he entered a little log school, five miles from home, taught by a white man who at once became his dearest friend. His foster father accelerated the boy's progress by taking a weekly Washington newspaper, but two or three school texts and a Gospel of St. John were the only books in the house. He never saw a timepiece or a train until he was ten. Before he was twelve the family moved to West Virginia, where they found a better share contract, but no schools. After a few years in the coal mines and a religious conversion, he entered an academy, earning his tuition as a janitor, and resolved to go to Congress.

Scarcely less humble were Proctor's beginnings. He first saw the light of day in rural Tennessee, the son of newly emancipated parents of mixed blood. The community's school was a cabin. "One could throw a cat between the logs and never touch a hair," he wrote. The backless benches were made of rails, and desks were unknown. The school had a session of three months and the instruction was as poor as the supplies were meager. When two brothers passing through the community demonstrated their ability to read, young Proctor was at once aflame with ambition to emulate them and soon afterwards his parents decided to move the family to the city where a good nine-month school, with a competent teacher, was available. Upon finishing school, he became a teacher until he felt a call to preach. When some Negro teachers from Nashville came to hold a teacher's institute in the county, he thought one of them the most cultivated and high-minded man he had ever met. Education, he reasoned, had made this man, so he worked, saved his money and spent seven years at Fisk.

Jernagin's parents were Mississippi slaves. His father, the son of his master by a slave woman, had seventeen children by two marriages, and though he was a privileged house servant and acknowledged kinsman of his owners, he was never taught to read. William's mother, also illiterate, was of Indian-Negro blood. Once free, the Jernagins acquired a small farm and were well regarded by neighbors of both races. It was the trust that whites reposed in him that moved William at fifteen to vow to God a blameless life. His noble father was the dominant influence in his development, and while there were no books in the crowded little house, the elder Jernagin constantly boarded teachers and visiting ministers to inspire his children. William absorbed such common-school training as the community afforded. As a youth, leading forty-five hands chopping cotton, he felt called to preach, and after teaching school and preaching for five years attended an academy, took some instruction from a New York correspondence school and theological training at Jackson.

Robert E. Jones exhibits some notable variations, for his people were urban Greensboro, North Carolina, folk for generations, remote from the slave environment. His free grandfather had married a white woman (and after her death a second), and his free great-grandfather is believed to have fought in the Revolutionary army at Guilford Courthouse. All of his Negro ancestors for several generations were free persons, many of them with strong white strains. The bishop himself was at least seven-eighths white. Not only was his paternal grandmother not a Negro; his maternal grandfather was also a white man who had four children by a handsome, light-skinned Negro named Isabella Dunn, whom he maintained but never married. The bishop's mother, a daughter of Isabella, believed herself a granddaughter of John Jacob Astor.

Jones's mother was perhaps the first colored schoolteacher in Guilford county, but it was his semiliterate father who was the principal inspiration for his sons and who forbade his daughters to demean themselves with domestic service. Dallas Jones was a proud, restless, forceful man, by turns a grocer, shoemaker, city lamplighter, convivial saloonkeeper behind the old Federal Building in Greensboro and a Republican politician who could divert enough votes from an organization candidate to his own man to elect a Democrat when his party leaders slighted him. He bought an encyclopedia and an eight-volume Shakespeare for his boys, and took into the household a Negro college graduate to provide them with intellectual stimulation.

Sharply different were the antecedents of Willis J. King, who traces an ancestry unmixed with whites back to 1785. His parents were reared in what was essentially the slave pattern. On his mother's death when he was only three, his father disappeared, and little Willis and his sister went to an ex-slave grandmother. His forebears were Virginia slaves, resettled in Texas when their owners followed Sam Houston into the new cotton lands of the Southwest. His grandmother toiled over the washtubs of white folk, a gaunt, black, unlettered woman scarred by the lash, the reminder of long years in slavery at its worst. She was the major influence in the bishop's life—a woman of heroic character and deep religious faith. When he was a lad of five, he was awakened in the night and strangely moved by her deep-voiced prayer for guidance in the rearing of her little brood in an evil world. She presided over the family with dignity, and when her strength ebbed, young

Willis, now thirteen, left his one-room rural school and took the responsibility for the household's support, laboring thirteen hours a day for less than a dollar. The four years of schooling he had had were exceptionally good, thanks to his Negro teacher, a man of amazing gifts, still living in 1957. When he was seventeen, his long-absent father returned to support his family, and Willis, now able to give his attention to his further education, went off to Wiley College in nearby Marshall, Texas.

Walls, now the senior AMEZ bishop and all his life a staunch foe of racial bias, but still persuaded that America is the Negroes' best home, is a dark Negro, born of rural North Carolina folk. His father, presumably born in bondage (the bishop is not sure) died when William was eight; his mother, who lived with him until her death in 1956, was born a slave. Upon his father's death, William was sent to his grandparents in Asheville, where his mother worked in a laundry to support her children and parents. He attended a small colored school and, in a day when the Sunday school was an equally potent educational force, he was simultaneously enrolled in four of them of varying denominations, meeting at different hours.

Like the other churchmen, he spent his boyhood at the usual chores that robbed the Negro poor boy of his play—especially the never-ending fetching of laundry bundles. Some of his instructors were Northern missionary women, but his early evangelical bent was most influenced by his mother's religious ecstasies and by the funeral of a little playmate. Before he was ten he was assembling his playfellows in a pine wood for imaginary church services, and he soon fell into the habit of retiring to his wooded retreat to rehearse his boyish sermons. Once he was overheard by a reporter whose interview with him was published in the Asheville papers and given wider circulation by the wire services. His sudden notoriety as a boy-preacher moved his church and Sunday school to gather funds for his first year at Livingstone College.

In his earliest years he was unconscious of racial strains in segregated Asheville until, when working as a houseboy for a prosperous white widow, he was startled one day to see an angry mob hustling a Negro to the edge of the city. He saw no more, but the next day learned that the wretch had been hanged. It was his first—and only—brush with a lynching, but the shock produced a marked fear of whites that required several years to dispel.

The Colored Methodist Episcopal (CME) leader, William Y. Bell, typifies some additional factors. His grandfather was a pure African, a North Carolina slave-blacksmith, hired out to neighboring planters. He was so defiantly independent that his owners found him a troublesome property and, with some relief, allowed him to "buy out." Soon thereafter he drew up in a carriage before his former mistress's home and calmly asked for terms for his wife. The outraged lady refused, but in the confusions of the Civil War he slipped off with his family to Union-occupied Memphis.

On the maternal side, Bell's people were the light-skinned offspring of white South Carolina folk, and related to a number of good Charleston families. His mother was light enough to cross over to the white group; her brothers actually did. After the flight to Memphis, Bell's father, eighteen at the time, worked as a helper for his father and then became, without formal training, a CME pastor, with an extraordinary knowledge of theology and homiletics. He remained a minister the rest of his life, and it was in a succession of neat, if severely modest, parsonages that William grew up in a Negro middle-class family respected for the minister's prestige and his reputation as a "race man."

Bishop Bell traces his early racial attitudes to several influences. His high-spirited grandfather exhorted the household to isolate themselves from whites and in no case to work for them, and his parents harbored equally strong hostilities. Life in small Jim Crow towns, with grossly inferior colored schools, generated further misgivings. When he was still a small boy, the entire family saw a naked, freshly lynched Negro hanging from a tree. By the time he went to college his hostilities were steadily disciplined by his religious feelings and a resolute quest for balance between self-restraint and self-respect, but fresh shocks disturbed the equipoise the youth fought to achieve. One day, on his return from college, when he made his way to the rear of a Memphis Jim Crow car, he courteously reminded a white man, sitting in the colored section, of the new laws. The passenger cheerfully moved to comply but the conductor rushed to the spot, ordered him to keep his seat, and roared at Bell for insulting a white man. The young college graduate, suddenly overwhelmed with rage, firmly ordered him to the front. Passengers begged Bell to relent, but he was now beside himself with anger, and only the intervention of a policeman (who reprimanded the conductor) prevented real violence. Calm was restored in a matter of minutes, but the incident persuaded Bell to leave the South, and the recollection of it is as vivid in his mind fifty years after the event as it was on the day it occurred.

His ambition, he says, was often stimulated by racial affronts, and all the while his desire to dedicate his life to Christian service and to "do something about the racial situation" sustained him as he advanced to leadership.

In the larger company of fifty-odd, each was a child of poverty; all in their several ways felt the sting of the slavery past and the newer racial discrimination, and the childhood of none was exempt from labor. The pattern of family disorganization was never far in the background, and their education was perhaps the major selective factor in their rise above the generality of their fellows. Separation from white playmates, in inferior schools, prompted fleeting misgivings, but less surprise than did the fact that they were in school at all. These men hardly dreamed in their school days before the close of the nineteenth century that the races could or should be educated together. Some were wholly untutored until maturity; others had only rudimentary instruction in public or white missionary schools.

The number who called themselves "self-educated" had now, in contrast to the previous generation, dwindled to three or four, but the proportion without college degrees was still high, and few had formal theological training. As in the past, there was usually an early conversion, a "call to preach," accompanied sometimes by dramatic signs or visions, and then a regular pastorate before the young preacher had reached his majority. Eighteen or even sixteen was not an uncommon age for licensing, but Bishop Wall's first application at twelve was, happily, refused. Several returned to school many years after entering the ministry by taking leave or by holding pastorates where there were nearby colleges or seminaries of whatever denomination, and then their superior educational pedigree proved the major factor in their preferment.

Biographical dictionaries show that more than half of the group attended colleges, universities, or theological schools, but many of the schools listed were dubious institutions with extremely low standards. A "college" was frequently still an elementary and "normal" school with a "collegiate department," and several years at a college often meant attendance in the lower grades plus a few feeble theology courses. College courses were still directed by largely self-taught Negro "professors" and white missionary teachers who (with notable exceptions) had more zeal than competence. The few Negroes who were actually earning theological degrees showed a preference for the stronger seminaries, where instruction was comparable to that at scores of white sectarian schools of the day, but it was an era when the Negro masses were still so suspicious of highly educated preachers that a ministerial candidate often took pains to make clear that he was innocent of such contamination.

Of our fifty-odd church leaders, only two listed A.B. degrees from white institutions (the universities of Kansas and Toronto), but several were sharply distinguished from the vast army of Negro preachers by divinity degrees from Northwestern, Boston, Chicago, Yale, Harvard, Union, Princeton, Garrett and Drew. Several of these, born slaves or children of penniless ex-slaves in the rural South, found their humble educational backgrounds no obstacle to success in the Northern schools, but some doubted that professors held them to normal standards. The group also included some of the earliest Negro Ph.D.'s. The doctorate was earned by J. W. E. Bowen, Sr., at Boston University in 1882; and Wright, after an A.B. at Georgia's state Negro college, won B.D. and A.M. degrees at Chicago and the Ph.D. in sociology at Pennsylvania. These higher academic and professional degrees were, however, still unusual, for education of most of the group fell short of junior-college levels and theological training was even more modest. Those who took degrees at Northern schools felt less strain on the score of race than did others a few decades later. Bowen at Boston excited friendly admiration for defying the myth that his race was congenitally unequal to higher training; and Proctor, one of twelve Negroes at Yale in the 1890's, wrote that they were accepted as first-class campus citizens by all except a few Southerners.

Experience in Northern institutions was uneven. Bell, in 1914, found Northwestern more hospitable than did his son a quarter of a century later when Negroes were more numerous there; and King, looking back upon his years (1910–1918) at Boston University remembers an "excellent social situation." Others, studying theology at the University of Chicago, found the atmosphere far more comfortable than that in the rural South whence most of them came. Ransom, after a stimulating year at Wilberforce under such notable Negroes as B. F. Lee, Daniel A. Payne, William S. Scarborough and Bishop Arnett, and visiting lecturers like Douglass, Bruce and Langston, accepted a tuition scholarship at liberal Oberlin. He made his expenses by campus jobs and as a porter in a barbershop for twelve hours on Saturdays until his scholarship was withdrawn as a rebuke for addressing a student meeting to protest the assigning of colored women to separate dining tables. After this demonstration that life at Oberlin was not so pleasant for Negroes as it had once been (and was to be again), Ransom was happy to return to Wilberforce.

These were still days when whites were convinced that education "spoiled" a Negro (if, indeed, he was capable of college training), and that it was a kindness to dissuade him, for there were no suitable vocations for college-bred Negroes anyhow. Still, despite poverty and these discouragements, they broke through. Sometimes it was because ex-slave parents—perhaps a mother with a cabin full of fatherless children—labored to exhaustion to help their children get on. Sometimes it was because they had middle-class parents—perhaps teachers or preachers. Or again, the telling factor might be a white benefactor or the accident of living near a college. In every case where the record supplies details, the college-educated clergymen in our group worked at some employment, usually menial, to meet costs. One of them wrote boldly—and successfully—to a New York philanthropist, inviting him to test his devotion to good works by helping a colored boy prepare for the ministry. Two won scholarships to the University of South Carolina when the Reconstruction legislature established these awards, and remained there until 1877 when "home rule" once more closed the university to Negroes.

Wright studied at leading American and European universities by supporting himself as a dishwasher, janitor, farm hand, factory employee, book salesman and laundry agent. When Fisher and his wife determined upon the ministry, the young bride worked as a washerwoman while her ex-slave husband applied himself to study and taught a rural school. During their first pastorate at Atlanta, Fisher took a few courses at Baptist Seminary and began his rise as a Baptist leader.

When Joshua H. Jones completed the academy and college courses at Claflin Institute in South Carolina, whites, angered by his commencement oration in which he denounced racial discrimination, warned him to leave town before sundown. He fled to Howard University and, while serving as a local pastor, was invited by an AME bishop who heard him to come to Wilberforce as pastor of the college church. After graduating there, his location at Lynn, Massachusetts, enabled him to study at Boston University.

Phillips cut cordwood and carried water for dormitories, and in summer taught in the rural schools. The college and common-school calendars in these years were arranged to enable needy college students to conduct county schools in search of teachers. Proctor dug ditches, set type and preached to pay for his excellent education at Fisk, and his years at New Haven were financed by weekend song-recital tours of the small band of Negro Yale students of which he was a member. Walls, after initial assistance from his church and Sunday school, was Livingstone College's lamplighter, and during his years as a theological student there paid his way as college pastor, an office in which he succeeded the future Bishop Clement.

As a boy, Robert E. Jones drummed up trade for his father's saloon by working mathematical problems on the floor. He dug ditches, laid sewer pipe and delivered produce from the city market. During his nine years at Bennett as a preparatory student and collegian, he taught in the town's first common school for Negroes, painted houses, operated the college dining hall and served as pastor of churches in two neighboring towns. His belief in his "call" was strengthened when one day he prayed desperately for funds he needed if he was to remain in school, and then learned when he reached the campus that the college had, only hours earlier, heard from an Iowan eager to support a Negro ministerial student and that he, Robert, had been selected as the beneficiary.

King made his way at Wiley College (Texas), as student supply pastor, travelling on weekends to his congregation a hundred and eighty miles away. His decision to enter Boston University for advanced training was largely accidental. He had been impressed by an advertisement and, when a Negro seminary professor rebuked him for preferring a white Northern university, King promptly accepted the challenge. Returning to Texas after finishing the Ph.D. residence requirements at Boston, he was handicapped in writing his dissertation by want of a library for Negroes. A local Jewish rabbi, however, opened his library to him, and with the help also of books mailed from Northern seminaries he completed the thesis. Later a Rosenwald Fellowship took him to Oxford and the Holy Land.

Bell, after working his way through Lane College (Tennessee) as a porter for white families, joined a brother in Chicago, at that time the goal of many a Negro who had been aroused by Abbott's *Chicago Defender* to flee the South. He took a job at the post office with a view to going through Rush Medical College, but when he found that Negroes could not advance in the postal service, despite civil service laws, he reluctantly withdrew to Northwestern University for theological study. The outbreak of World War I prevented him from utilizing a scholarship he won there for study abroad, and he went instead to Yale for a Ph.D. in Semitic languages.

Powell, who also won an advanced degree at Yale, in his undergraduate days worked his way through Wayland (now Virginia Union) Seminary, in Richmond. There a Massachusetts visitor was so impressed by him that he authorized the president to offer him a $1,500 scholarship if he would give up self-help employment, devote his full time to studies and agree to make his career in the South. Powell declined and begged for the one job for which there were no applicants, cleaning the college's privies. The astounded president, a white man, dismissed him abruptly, but recalled him minutes later to give him the best student job on the campus—that of dining-hall headwaiter.

The fifty-odd were notably free from bitterness. Most of them were in the tradition of Booker Washington or slightly to the left of it, but somewhat more candid than he in declaring for the ultimate goal of equality. Several argued that Washington's shrewd conciliatory strategy had won more than had the exertions of more impassioned men. Some, however, like Ransom, Walters, Walls, Clinton, Bowen, Heard and Jernagin, repudiated the cautious counsels of Tuskegee in favor of stronger pressure upon the color line.

Bishop Bell's adjustment to racial injustice was typical of the group as a whole. Though a respected champion of Negro rights (he is a life member of the NAACP and cochairman of its Life Membership Committee), he is innocent of rancor, an evolution he ascribes to his religion, to deepening appreciation of the tragic forces that produced the "racial situation," to the greater kindness shown by whites to Negro clergymen than to other leaders, to prudent avoidance of inflammatory situations, and to his own need for keeping his temper, lest, by flailing angrily at a self-possessed and resourceful adversary, he waste his strength and destroy his usefulness. Some of the group even declared that if the positions of the two races were transposed, the Negroes would be the discriminators.

They were, of course, never wholly safe from insult, nor were they always patient in adversity. Once a group of Negro church leaders en route to a religious conference were compelled by white tormentors on a Southern Railway platform, at the point of a pistol, to sing and dance. Jernagin, under the governance of "vows" to God which regulated his conduct, remained serene under affronts in public facilities (his denominational travels included twenty-two Atlantic crossings, several transpacific trips, and frequent journeys into the South), but he could, when opportunity offered, defy discrimination. When he was denied unsegregated accommodation on a trip out of Washington in 1943, after the courts had forbidden such treatment, he insisted upon being put off the train, and retained the foremost Negro law firm in Washington to bring suit.

Bishop Wright was stranded in Liberia in 1940 when the only steamship line operating in wartime declined to book a Negro, but a telephone call to President Roosevelt brought instant results. King was assigned to Liberia by the Methodist Episcopal (M.E.) Church, and obliged to accept Jim-Crow accommodations on American and British vessels after the war. He accepted philosophically the church's separate Negro wing, but believed that time would erase the line, as did Robert E. Jones, who could remember M.E. general conferences in which Negro delegates drank from paper cups while whites used glasses.

Some emphatically declared that the Negro's opportunity to rise in America was better than the white man's in Europe, and testified, upon returning from visits abroad, that the deference shown them in Europe did not increase their impatience with their countrymen. Besides, the color bar was there too. When Bishop Heard, attending a religious conference, was refused hotel accommodations in 1937 in Edinburgh, he was not the first to be so injured. Such treatment, accorded a Negro who had been nearly thirty years a bishop, and four years American Minister to Liberia, and who was nearly ninety, persuaded many that color prejudice is not a peculiarly American failing.

Here at home the national capital was the scene of numerous incidents. Bishop Walls, when refused unsegregated service in the Union Station's restaurant in 1925, joined his friends in a vigorous protest and they won their point after three hours of remonstrance. For many years thereafter, the station was the only place in the city where Negroes could obtain unsegregated meal service. Twelve years later, as far North as Portland, Maine, where he had gone to address the Interracial Fellowship of America, Walls found hotels closed to him until a white judge intervened privately in his behalf.

Some Negro bishops resident in the South concluded that individual Southerners were more enlightened than they dared profess to each other, and that "the solution" will come when the South comes to know itself and ceases to fear a myth that it does not quite know how to put aside. Bishop Bell illustrated his point from his experience. When a wave of police brutality against Negroes struck a Southern town where he lived briefly, he sought out over thirty of the town's most prominent citizens for support. Each made fundamentally the same response: promised his support, provided that Bell keep the citizen's name out of the affair. A number of police officers were promptly dismissed, the cruelties ceased, and the bishop learned from city authorities that numerous leading private citizens, "acting independently and without each other's knowledge," had brought insistent pressures upon city officials for immediate reform. On another occasion in the same town, a prosperous citizen called on him to leave a substantial donation for the scholarship fund of the Negro academy that the CME denomination maintained there. His only stipulation was that Bell keep the matter quiet because, he said, "the people here, and especially my wife, have such strong Southern views that they would explode if they heard of this." Very soon thereafter his wife appeared with a similar offer of funds but begged him to conceal the matter from her husband, "because of his old-fashioned Southern feelings."

About fifty persons* in this period's roster were in the category of educators identified with Negro higher education. By 1900, institutions calling themselves colleges or universities numbered about ninety-nine, and in 1936 the number was about the same. Founded in the post-Civil War decades by Northern philanthropy, missionary enterprise, the Freedmen's Bureau and state authority as well as by denominations, one group was under public control, another under white sectarian boards, and one cluster in the hands of Negro denominations. As late as 1922, 85 per cent of the enrollment in the so-called "colleges" was in the elementary and secondary department, for all but three or four of the colleges were in the South, where common-school provision for Negro children was still minimal and public high schools wholly absent. By the end of the period, more than three fourths of the enrollment was in the collegiate departments, which, incidentally, often afforded only a two-year course.

The school's objectives were confused by the assumptions that their task, because of the Negroes' supposed mental and moral deficiencies, and because of very real social and economic discriminations against them, was to afford

* James A. K. Aggrey
Mary McLeod Bethune
James M. Bond
Ferdinand Bluford
Maudelle Bousfield
Benjamin G. Brawley
Charlotte Hawkins Brown
Nannie H. Burroughs
Eugene A. Clark
Joseph S. Clark
John W. Davis
Matthew W. Dogan
William E. B. Du Bois
James B. Dudley
George W. Ellis
John M. Gandy
William G. Goler
William J. Hale
Gordon B. Hancock
Leslie P. Hill
Joseph W. Holley
Dwight O. W. Holmes
John Hope
Benjamin F. Hubert
Zachary T. Hubert
Henry A. Hunt
Mordecai W. Johnson
David D. Jones
Gilbert Haven Jones
Laurence Clifton Jones
James F. Lane
Lucy Laney
J. R. E. Lee
Alain Locke
Henry L. McCrorey
Kelly Miller
Lewis B. Moore
Robert R. Moton
Joel A. Rogers
William S. Scarborough
Arthur Schomburg
Emmett J. Scott
James E. Shepard
William J. Trent
Robert S. Wilkinson
William T. B. Williams
Carter G. Woodson
Monroe N. Work
R. R. Wright, Jr.
R. R. Wright, Sr.
George Young

Some of the foregoing were writers of scholarly or quasi-scholarly works, rather than being "educators" in the usual sense. Perhaps this is the place to note Hubert Henry Harrison, a figure not easy to catalog. He was a Virgin-Islands-born, self-educated author, lecturer, journalist and critic, and a staff lecturer for the New York City Board of Education.

"moral" and religious instruction. Further conflict arose from the competing claims of a race-conscious sort of curriculum, and one that minimized the fact of race and proposed with limited facilities and staffs to ape the offerings of conventional American colleges without regard to the kind of world that awaited the young Negro after graduation.

Colored educational leaders were caught in the cross fire of these divided counsels, and sorely pressed by those who gave them their office and provided their college's funds. They often became autocrats, not only to enforce the fiats of their superiors, but also to ease frustrations imposed upon them from above, by lording it over those beneath—wielding their petty dictatorships over faculties powerless to resist, for the only alternative to submission to the tyrant who determined tenure, rank and salary was to leave the profession.

Opportunities for Negroes to rise to prominence as educators were extremely small. There were only 23,000 students, most of them woefully ill-prepared, in the Negro colleges in 1932, and the supply of adequately trained professors and administrators was microscopic. Whites, moreover, were reluctant to see these colleges operate outside the orbit of white control. Until the close of this era, most of the best Negro colleges were in the hands of white trustees, faculties and administrators and even those which had Negro professors and presidents were controlled by white boards. The most notable exceptions were the schools founded by Negro denominations. Howard, already sixty years old, acquired its first Negro president in 1926; Hampton was still run by whites in the early 1940's; Fisk, then eighty years old, inaugurated its first Negro president in 1947. Several did not see the transfer until the 1950's. After the 1920's Negro students were increasingly insistent upon the change, and in some cases as at Fisk, Howard and Hampton, feeling on the point led to spirited demonstrations.

Of the fifty-two educators on our roster for the era, all but a tiny minority were college presidents (or, in a few cases, deans), and, of course, resident in the South. All but two were born in the South, the only exceptions being Du Bois and Locke. Negroes distinguished in fields other than religion and education, by contrast, were nearly all residents of the North.

At the end of the era, the institutions were still seriously deficient as to library facilities, equipment, preparation of instructors, administrative skill and all the other indices of academic status. Their symbol was the begging bowl; they were from the beginning dependent upon alms, first from religious and relatively unorganized benefactors, and then from foundations and philanthropic agencies.

In 1916, the United States Office of Education considered only three of the schools worthy of the name "college" from the point of view of equipment, student body, income, and teaching staff, and found thirty-one "leading" institutions offering college-level work to only 2,132 students. In 1932, the Southern Association of Colleges and Secondary Schools placed only six Negro colleges in its class "A" group—all of them founded by whites, and all but one by missionary enterprise. Twenty-two were placed in class "B"—eleven founded by white sectarian boards, nine by public authority and one by the Roman Catholic Church. The only one established by Negroes was Tuskegee. Except for extremely modest master's programs offered at four of the schools, there were no graduate departments and hence little opportunity for scholarly distinction for Negro professors, the overburdened instructors of underprivileged undergraduates, with crushing teaching loads, inadequate libraries and departments without research budgets.

The state Negro colleges were starved as to funds and controlled by white politicians who conferred the presidencies upon deserving Negro politicians or men who knew how to play the white politicians' game. Administrators of the all-Negro denominational colleges enjoyed far greater independence than did heads of state schools and of colored colleges maintained by white denominations, but even they felt the firm hand of higher-ups and the gentler pressure of the foundations. The leaders of denominational colleges were nearly always ordained clergymen, often bishops. Even those in quasi-sectarian and public institutions were trained in the theological tradition, and men like the celebrated Charles S. Johnson, for example, whose professional roles were purely secular, were very prominent churchmen.

The school and church leaders provided the largest reservoir of race leaders. They attracted the bulk of the most highly educated Negroes, for there were as yet few alternatives, and these were, besides, the areas in which gifted Negroes could best minister to their people's most pressing needs and in which white men were not their rivals—while in the arts, the sciences and business, in politics, the army, the law and medicine, they faced the crushing handicap of the white man's competition in a white man's world.

Although precariously stationed between the Negro's need and the white man's displeasures, the educators served numerous race-advance agencies, preferably milder, semi-religious uplift groups, and several were forthright spokesmen and officers in the NAACP even though they did not find it prudent to advertise the connection. They were still outside the national professional associations, and their infrequent scholarly publications were invariably preoccupied—at the behest of their thesis-directors in graduate-school days and of editors and publishers thereafter—with Negro themes.

A glance at their biographies in *Who's Who in America* suggests the immense range of public, semi-public and community enterprises into which the educators, like the clerics, were drawn. They were college and hospital trustees; chairmen of the Negro divisions of state cancer societies; leaders in the "colored work" of the YMCA and the Boy Scouts; members of city, county and state public health and welfare boards and commissions; supervisors for Negro affairs in New Deal welfare agencies; directors of state tuberculosis and Red Cross groups; and occasionally members of county school boards and councils of social agencies. Such public offices and advisorships were almost invariably appointive, and the Negro usually sat in as the only person of his race, selected one supposes, as a spokesman from the Negro enclave rather than simply as the tenth American.

The immense variety of data concerning the social origins of the group compels us to be content with a few examples. Dean Hancock was typical of many in ascribing a good start to family connections. His father was a minister, his mother one of the first Negro schoolteachers in South Carolina, and a great-uncle, with whom he lived after his father's death, was an enthusiast for education. Mary McLeod Bethune's parents were illiterate slaves. She was one of seventeen children, all but the three youngest of whom were born in slavery, but she pointed to advantages that set her apart from the great mass of Negro children. Her parents had been house servants, "upper-caste" slaves who continued to serve their ex-owners after the Emancipation as contented tenant farmers and even acquired a little farm where Mary was born in 1875. Maudelle Bousfield, the first Negro high-school principal in Chicago, was a member of the eminent Tanner clan, and her father was for over fifty years a teacher in the St. Louis schools.

Benjamin Brawley's freeborn, light-skinned father, a college president himself, furnished young Ben with decided advantages, while Charlotte Hawkins Brown enjoyed no less tangible odds. Her father deserted the household when "Lottie" was born, but the white Hawkinses of Henderson, North Carolina, had conscientiously helped their beloved former servants make a good beginning in freedom. Lottie's mother was a woman of wonderful energy who, to improve the prospects of the whole clan of twenty, of whom she was the majestic matriarch, led them up into Massachusetts about 1890, and there operated a hand laundry to support them.

The eminent John W. Davis, president of West Virginia State College, was born of Georgia parents, light Negroes, and his maternal grandfather was a white man, whose mulatto daughter was raised under the refining influences of a white pastor's manse, where Davis himself was also reared after his fifth year, when his parents moved with their other children to Savannah. Matthew Dogan, head of Wiley College for more than forty years, was the son of bright, energetic Mississippi slaves who had earned enough money to redeem themselves in the middle 1850's. Matthew grew up in a family of "Negro aristocrats," owners of a barbershop whose all-white patrons took a kindly interest in the lad who swept out the shop, blacked their boots and devoured such books as they put in his hands.

The background of David Jones, younger brother of Robert E. Jones, and molder of Bennett College in his own home town, of Greensboro, North Carolina, has already been noted. He had, of course, the additional advantage of having his older brother as a mentor. When the boys' father died, Robert assumed responsibility for David's development and eventually sent him to New England for a superior education. Like advantages came to R. R. Wright, Jr., president of Wilberforce, who was the son of a college president. Robert Shaw Wilkinson derived from Charleston free folk who, before the Civil War, had profited from blood ties with one of South Carolina's proudest families. His father was the proprietor of a butcher shop and later custodian of a church whose white rector joined Robert's father in urging the boy to secure the best education available.

Both William T. B. Williams and Emmett J. Scott enjoyed in their youth an easy familiarity with their white kinfolk. William S. Scarborough, president of Wilberforce and the race's first notable classical scholar, was a slave like his mother, but his free father spurned a tender of nearly three thousand dollars (offered to establish him in the North) in order to remain with his fettered family.

Some of these men—like President McCrorey, who was one of an enormous brood of children born to illiterate slaves—were sons of the most obscure and impoverished field Negroes; but this was unusual. Slave parentage was common enough, but there was usually some uncommon factor in the background of those who rose to prominence. Dwight O. W. Holmes, for instance, came of ex-slave parents, but his father had become a pastor and his mother in her youth had been a Sunday-school pupil of that pentecostal West Pointer, Thomas J. ("Stonewall") Jackson.

Joseph W. Holley, founder of the state industrial college in Georgia and an extremist in his acquiescence in segregation as a means of purchasing concessions, was also a son of a slave. His mother was denied training in literacy but was otherwise extensively educated by her mistress, and his father was the son of his owner, a Scots immigrant. The young mulatto was trained as a leather craftsman in his slavery days, and then became a sharecropper after the War, an arrangement under which James fared so well as a boy that he later insisted that croppers who failed to prosper had usually only their indolence to blame.

Laurence Clifton Jones, head of another industrial school in Mississippi, and an extreme accommodationist, was born in Missouri, where his father was a hotel porter and his mother a domestic. The latter had been raised in Wisconsin, attending good, unsegregated schools, but the industrious elder Jones had grown up in rural Alabama without schooling.

Another accommodationist was Robert R. Moton, Washington's successor at Tuskegee. He was born less than two years after the Civil War, and reared on the Vaughan plantation in Prince Edward County, Virginia, where Robert's father led the plantation hands, and his mother served as cook. Young Robert, from his earliest days, benefited from his position as a family favorite, and as soon as he was old enough was made general houseboy—a distinction rarely conferred upon Negro boys as dark-skinned as he.

His otherwise generous employers were opposed to Negro literacy, so he was secretly taught by his mother who concealed from her mistress the fact that she could read. Her solicitude proved unnecessary, for when the secret was discovered the astonished mistress praised her Negro wards for their industry and permitted her daughter to provide the boy with an hour of instruction daily and to supply him with books. Thus Moton, like Washington, was early encouraged to believe that the Southern whites were fundamentally well disposed toward Negroes.

The Hubert clan, which produced college presidents Benjamin Franklin Hubert and Zachary Taylor Hubert, and several cousins and brothers scarcely less notable, sprang directly from bondage. Paul, the founder of the line, had been a leader among the slaves of Warren county, Georgia, and his sons, Zachary and Moses, immediately after the Emancipation purchased land in Hancock County. Hardly had they built their log cabin when they created a brush-arbor church and a log school. All twelve of Zack Hubert's children made their way to college and notable careers.

Far different was the origin of John Hope, certainly one of the two or three most distinguished Negro university presidents in America. A strikingly handsome man—blue-eyed and delicately featured—whom one took instantly for an eminent professor or clergyman, his heroic efforts for Negro advance were a constant surprise and even an embarrassment to whites who found it difficult to believe that he was a Negro. He was the product of generations of light-skinned Negro women prevented by the rules of caste from marrying the fathers of their children.

His father, James Hope, came from Scotland to America and prospered in mercantile enterprises before establishing a cotton mill with several others in Augusta, Georgia, in 1845. He subsequently sold out for a hundred thousand dollars and became a wine importer in New York. On a Christmas visit to Augusta in 1860, the secession and War interned him there, and it was then that he entered an informal union with a beautiful young quadroon named Fannie, of excellent white ancestry and formerly the common-law spouse of his deceased friend and business associate, a Dr. Newton. After the War, Hope established his family in Manhattan, but because Fannie pined for her home and kinfolk, they returned, against the earnest advice of Frederick Douglass, to Augusta, where John Hope was born in 1868, the third of the couple's children.

Fannie's mother, Alethea, had been the slave of Judge Taylor of Sparta, Georgia, the owner of several plantations. The child Alethea, the constant companion of little Mary Elizabeth Taylor, sprang from one of the casual adulteries so common to the Cotton Kingdom. When Alethea's mother was a girl, a planter guest remarked upon her beauty and was rewarded when she was sent to him as he retired for the night. Alethea was eventually inherited by Mary Elizabeth when she became the mistress of the principal plantation. Like her mother, she was made available to a friend of the family, a Virginia planter, but this time the casual sexual excursion ripened into an acknowledge liaison which endured until the planter died. Alethea was freed and provided with a house in Augusta, where she passed on to her seven children the cultivation that long intimacy with white aristocrats had afforded.

Mordecai W. Johnson remains, after more than thirty years as president of Howard University, one of the most famous Negroes in America, renowned also as a Baptist leader, a platform spellbinder, and a familiar figure in agencies devoted to the advancement of the race. He attributes his career to his parents, with acknowledgement also for his teachers, John Hope, Benjamin Brawley and Samuel Archer. He was the only child of Wyatt Johnson, a dark man, reared in slavery in Tennessee, who emerged with a knowledge of farming that no common field hand could have achieved, but left the farm when slavery was abolished to assist a white man in a planing mill. Mordecai's mother was the child of a white planter and his bondwoman. Mrs. Johnson never spoke of her father; she was scarcely out of infancy at the Emancipation, and he never made the slightest provision for her. When Wyatt Johnson, many years her senior, took her to wife in the late 1880's, he had, besides his skilled work in the mill, become a self-trained Baptist minister for a tiny congregation he had organized. The pair afforded an excellent example of the so-called "Black Puritans." Wyatt Johnson was an austere man, strongly grounded upon religious foundations. By industry and frugality, the Johnsons soon owned their home and a five-acre plot, complete with orchard and livestock, within the town limits. They kept themselves and their little son meticulously groomed and laundered, and their home place tidy and in good repair. The old man was fanatically devoted to discipline and order, both moral and physical, while his wife, more effusive, though no more sincere in her affection, overwhelmed the boy with love and anxious solicitude. It was she who encouraged him toward lofty aspirations and in time took the responsibility for his training by working as a seamstress until failing eyesight compelled her to turn to laundering. It was she who praised and soothed him, prayed over and admonished him to a life of prayer, and took his part when he was expelled from college for playing cards.

The stern rectitude of one and the gentler religious sensibilities of the other, and the fidelity of both to spiritual values was a rare heritage. They never discussed The Problem in the boy's hearing. They never borrowed, but faithfully paid every bill out of the weekly wage, both as an obligation in honor and as a stratagem for keeping whites at a distance. They chose their friends meticulously. Only once did a white man enter their home with disrespect, a physician and former governor of Tennessee. He pushed his way into the house, kept his hat on, and carried himself with a hauteur that his Negro patients could not mistake. He was never called in again.

Johnson's childhood was uncomplicated by racial strains. There were occasional boyish taunts, and play groups were invariably segregated, but it did not occur to the youngster that the separation was a mark of inferiority. The gentle mother, solicitous over the racial affronts that the boy would ultimately face, took pains to teach him to avoid thinking of white folk *en bloc* or permitting occasional injuries to overshadow kindnesses he received at their hands. When the day came for Mordecai, as it must for every Negro child, to have the epithet "nigger! nigger!" cast into his teeth, she explained without hinting at the word's contemptuous overtones, that it was a rather poor sort of joke, and that the standard retort was "Caucasian! Caucasian!"

The renowned William E. B. Du Bois, still at ninety-one in 1959 the dean of Negro intellectuals, traces his generations through "Negro blood, French, a bit of Dutch and thank God! no Anglo-Saxon!" His French Huguenot great-great-grandfather came to America in 1674 by way of Leiden, and the latter's son, a slave-owning planter in the Bahamas, had a son by a brown-skinned woman of the Islands, and it was he, Alexander, nearly white, who became Du Bois's grandfather. Alexander was sent with his brothers to an Episcopal school in Connecticut, but when their father died intestate, his property passed to a white cousin. The boys were bound out as apprentices and "dropped" from the white Du Bois family. Alexander subsequently married into the colored group and made his way to Haiti, where William's father was born in 1825. The family soon returned to America.

William's fair-skinned father, who served in the Civil War, was a footloose barber, merchant and preacher. In 1867 he wandered into the Berkshire Valley and married a brown woman sprung from the Dutch colonial Burghardts, and a year later William was born. The Burghardts had long ago come into possession of a native African named Tom, born about 1730. Tom had earned his freedom by serving in the Revolution, and a son served in the War of 1812. His son Jacob married a woman freed under Massachusetts law in 1780 and their child, Othello Burghardt, Du Bois's maternal grandfather, married the mulatto daughter of an unknown Dutchman. Before marrying, William's mother had been a domestic.

William's childhood in Great Barrington was a happy one, no thanks to his father who drifted off and "faded out of the family." William attended a common school where he was "one of the boys," but increasingly conscious of alienation. In the little schoolhouse in the New England hills, the sense of rejection first smote him when he was sharply snubbed in a childish game.

Several in our roster of educators ascribed to poverty and discrimination a formative influence in early life. Almost all were compelled to work at a tender age to help bear the family support, and some left us accounts of early initiation into color trauma. Contrasting treatment of Negroes by Northern missionaries and Southerners awakened qualms in Mary McLeod Bethune's childhood. Others first met The Problem when white playmates went off to separate schools, renouncing forever their former colored chums. Dean Hancock's association with white boys persisted longer. They trudged down the same dusty road together to their separate schools to be joyfully reunited in the late afternoon. There came a day when, after he had revelled under a tree in his white playmates' barnyard with the after-school bread and butter so dear to schoolboys, his alarmed parents angrily forbade the uncomprehending lad to repeat so rash an act. Soon came another shock when some rustics in a country store, callously indifferent to the little Negro boy who stood by, guffawed over their low opinion of "niggers." The incidents never faded from his mind.

Moton's autobiography passes over childhood indignities except to note such painful estrangements. Once an especially dear friend left for college and upon his return for the Christmas holidays ruthlessly ignored his old playfellow. The heart-wound had at least the merit of whetting Robert's hunger for education, for it was the Negro's ignorance, he reasoned, that underlay his rejection.

Charlotte Hawkins Brown traces her awakening race-consciousness to the chance remark of a well-meaning white woman, addressed to Charlotte's mother. "Caroline, if there be anything like a colored *lady,* I want you to be one." Later when she returned to North Carolina, after college in Massachusetts, she learned that white and colored folk alike now distrusted her as a "Northern nigger."

Introduction to color prejudice came to Dwight Holmes through the familiar cry of "nigger!" from youthful tormentors when he was a lad of six, accustomed to the sheltered life of a Methodist manse. A half century later he could remember the street in Annapolis where it happened. When he was nine, his father was transferred to Staunton, Virginia. Because there was no Negro high school there, he was sent to the Howard University preparatory school, where homesicknesses daily reminded him of the penalties for being colored. In the previous summer, his parents had put him on a train for a visit to Chicago. When it stopped at Clifton Forge, Dwight joined the other passengers in alighting for refreshments at the long counter in the shabby railway lunchroom. As the waiter moved down the row, he stared hard at the light-skinned boy, lest he be mistaken, and bellowed, "We don't serve niggers . . . get out of here!" The boy was crushed not so much by this cruelty as by the total indifference of his traveling companions to his discomfiture.

Until his father's death, John Hope had a secure childhood, but when he was a mere eight years old, he witnessed the 1876 "Hamburg Massacre" in Atlanta, a sharp race incident involving an attack upon Negro militia who had stood up to white ruffians. The clash precipitated an armed assault upon

Negro houses and a terrorization of the region, in which some Negroes were killed before peace was restored. Sixty years later, Hope had not fully shaken off the shock he had sustained.

The struggle for education was, as usual, the crucial chapter in the early history of these folk. Richard Robert Wright, Sr., for example, was ten when freedom dawned. A year later he and his mother walked the nearly two hundred miles from Cuthbert to Atlanta, Georgia, to enter a primitive academy that ultimately grew into Atlanta University. (There were no public schools anywhere in Georgia.) It had been established in a battered Confederate commissary car by the American Missionary Association with a gift of eight hundred dollars from a Cincinnati congregation. Four hundred ex-slaves from six to sixty years of age were enrolled and instructed in shifts. Whittier's poem, "Black Boy of Atlanta," evidently grew out of a visit of Gen. O. O. Howard to the school. He asked the eager learners what message he might carry back to the children of the North, and Wright sprang to his feet to exclaim, "Massa, tell 'em we'se risin'!" When the boy and his mother were too poor to continue, he went to work as a houseboy for an Atlanta hotel man, but before long a benevolent white sent him to Atlanta University, where he was graduated as valedictorian with its first college class.

Said Dean Hancock, "the struggle to get an education was the best part of my education. . . . I had the good fortune to earn every dollar of it." McCrorey, also self-made, undertook at sixteen to train himself. While giving his days to hard field labor to support the enormous household crowded into their shabby, poorly lit cabin, he spent the first fifty cents he owned for an arithmetic and studied it at night. Other books came to his hand and after six years of study by firelight he set out for Biddle University, North Carolina. He completed the collegiate and theological courses, joined the faculty, and eventually became president in 1907. He became in time the first Negro on the Presbyterian Board of Christian Education.

Not until she was eleven did the rural South Carolina community where Mary McLeod lived have its first colored school, provided by the Presbyterian Board of Missions. The fact that it was five miles away did not deter Mary from trudging the distance in whatever weather. She later recalled that her zeal for learning flamed when a little white child snatched a book from her hands with the taunt that no Negro could possibly learn to read. When she had exhausted the resources of the school, a scholarship donated to the Board of Missions by a schoolteacher, who had accumulated the money by dressmaking, sent her to Scotia Seminary in Concord, North Carolina, and after eight years there she was again the beneficiary of white benevolence at the Moody Bible Institute in Chicago on a two-year scholarship.

Charlotte Hawkins Brown was another object of white charity. After the family's removal to Cambridge, Lottie, with her teacher's help, found a place as a nursemaid. While wheeling a baby carriage one day and reading snatches from a volume of Vergil, she met Mrs. George Herbert Palmer, wife of the Harvard philosopher. Her interest in the child led her to assume the responsibility for the girl's education at the state teachers' college at Salem. A few years later when Charlotte, influenced by an address of Booker Washington, returned to make her career among her own folk in North Carolina, it was the memory of her benefactress that inspired her to establish Palmer Memorial Institute at Sedalia.

During his student days at Atlanta Baptist, John W. Davis was fortunate to come to the notice of John Hope, the "maker of college presidents," when Davis was polishing the floor of the president's house, for Hope elevated the bright and energetic youth to reponsible duties in the college's business office. Davis's choice of the University of Chicago for graduate work, like that of several others of his generation, is explained by the presence in the Union Stockyards of a Negro of some influence with a remarkable record for securing summer and after-hours employment for colored boys who came to Chicago for university training. It was Davis's association with Hope that later led to his long presidency at West Virginia State.

A perceptive teacher and an ambitious mother had steered Du Bois into the college preparatory course in high school at a time when few whites in Great Barrington aspired to college, and when he graduated as the only Negro, he was awarded a scholarship to Fisk by four Connecticut churches. After his stimulating, happy years there, he entered Harvard on a scholarship and again additional scholarships and prizes kept coming to him. He was granted a fellowship for study in Europe and had an exhilarating year abroad. After earning his doctorate at Harvard, he had the satisfaction of seeing his dissertation published as the first volume of a notable series, the *Harvard Historical Studies.*

The ultra-conciliatory Holley had his early schooling from white Northern missionaries in rural South Carolina, where his family were sharecroppers. Then after several years at Northern academies, again under sectarian boards of missions for freedmen, he came upon a catalog of Phillips Andover Academy, while working at a Rhode Island summer resort. Noting that an Andover trustee, Rowland Hazard, lived nearby, the young Negro called upon him and laid before him his desire to prepare himself for service to the Negro people. Hazard and his family, which included Caroline Hazard, president of Wellesley College, like many heirs of the abolitionist tradition, found an outlet for philanthropy in helping Negro students. They arranged his matriculation at Andover, paid his initial fees, and provided him with loan funds and a job as custodian of teachers' cottages.

After two fruitful years at Andover, Holley was urged by New England friends to go on to Harvard and then to Andover Theological Seminary, but the seven-year program seemed interminable to the young man, now in his middle twenties and eager to return to South Carolina. (He was persuaded that "at heart the Southern people were the best friends the Negroes had.") The Andover authorities were appalled by his decision, but he was not to be dissuaded. Before returning to the South, however, he entered Lincoln University for a degree in theology. Again it was the Hazards who lent him the necessary funds, and years later they came to his aid once more with funds for the industrial college he was establishing.

Lawrence Clifton Jones was another whose Northern education failed to make of him a militant race man. His father encouraged him to seek a college education, but was hardly prepared for his departure for the North at fourteen. He enrolled as the only Negro at the public high school in Marshalltown, Iowa, supporting himself by working in a restaurant and hotel, his years there sweetened by a teacher sufficiently interested in the boy to befriend him and to place him in Iowa State College. There, in the venerable American tradition, he worked his way by waiting on tables at a fraternity house. After graduation he was sorely tempted by an appointment from Tuskegee, but his original intention to establish an industrial school in the most backward region he could find prevailed.

For Dwight Holmes, the quest for education was a constant battle with poverty. He interrupted his course at Howard by withdrawing for a year to earn some funds. He was unhappy over the necessity to choose teaching as his career; he much preferred engineering, but the field seemed to offer as yet no opportunities for Negroes. W. T. B. Williams first finished at Hampton and then took four years at Phillips Andover and an A.B. at Harvard. Wilkinson, like Holley and Jones, though educated at centers steeped in the abolitionist heritage, returned to the South to be counted among right-wing "moderates."

The preponderance of moderates among the forty-eight educators is hardly surprising. Whether a school was dominated by public authority, Northern philanthropy, Northern missionary or denominational influence or even the Negro sects, circumstances favored the conciliatory and the diplomat rather than the rebel. Still, strong presidents did come up from both Southern and Northern backgrounds. John Hope, never a trimmer (he was a prime mover of the NAACP and brought his redoubtable friend Du Bois to his faculty), was a product of Northern schools. Mordecai Johnson, on the other hand, another forceful man who (though disparaged for his evangelical fervors) has long been conspicuous in an astonishing array of militant and liberal agencies, got his basic college training in a Southern school.

After the death of his father, John Hope gave up all expectation of further schooling until, after five years of work in a restaurant, he went off to Worcester Academy, in Massachusetts, under the prodding of a minister and with a loan from his brother. He earned expenses by serving meals and building fires, and in the summers as a waiter at hotels and resorts. The headmaster at Worcester, a trustee of Brown University, saw to it that Hope was given a scholarship to Brown. There he again worked at meal jobs, as he did during the summer of 1893, at the Columbian Exposition, where his meeting with the girl he was to marry determined his choice of the University of Chicago for graduate work. Financial hardships haunted him at Brown and a vast amount of effort went into the struggle to stay in school. It was precisely then that a wealthy white uncle died, leaving a million dollars, not a penny of which went to his colored nephew. John was dangerously underfed, but his cheerful demeanor and splendid academic record concealed his private distresses.

Mordecai Johnson had an easier time, but was not wholly exempt from working for his subsistence. Help from his oversolicitous mother smoothed his way at college, but he supplemented this modest resource by working in a print shop.

Leaving his ex-slave parents and their enormous brood of children, Kelly Miller came to Howard at seventeen with a few dollars in his pocket, the gift of a missionary society interested in training boys for the ministry. A reading of Darwin and Huxley changed his goal, however, and he directed his efforts toward a teaching career. He worked at miscellaneous jobs and as a waiter at summer resorts, but found a more satisfactory arrangement when, in the summer months after taking a Civil Service examination, he received a wire offering him a six-hundred-dollar job in the Pension Office. When a companion read the telegram to him, Miller dropped the tray he was holding and hurried back to Washington. The new-found security enabled him to complete his degree requirements at Howard, take graduate work in mathematics by extension from the Johns Hopkins University, and to get some instruction at the United States Naval Observatory.

As usual, the personal histories and racial philosophies of the forty-eight noted educators and scholars forbid stereotypes. The group included intrepid fighters like the near-white Hope, who dared to differ with benefactors upon whom his Atlanta University depended; he was the only prominent Negro educator at the conference of 1906 that foreshadowed the NAACP. On the other end of the scale stood accommodationists like Holley and Clifton Jones and the ebony, humbly born Moton. In between stood men of every degree of conciliation and challenge. Even those elude definition who presented a smiling face to the world while cruelly squeezed between their own and their constituents' conceptions of the Negro's need, and between the imperious expectations of whites and Negroes, churchmen and philanthropists, politicians and social theorists, all fingering the purse strings, and all with ideas of their own as to the Negro's "place" and the true end of his education.

How is one to judge (to take a notable example) James E. Shepard of North Carolina College, as complacent before white backers in the North, politicians in Raleigh and pompous Negro fraternal leaders, as he was dictatorial on his own campus? Between his dubious college training at a tiny school in North Carolina and his long college presidency, he was a Republican payroller in Washington and Raleigh, and a field agent among Negroes in the International Sunday School Association. The dismay of impatient reformers, and denounced by white and colored liberals as a time-serving Uncle Tom, he elicited, nevertheless, far different estimates from outspoken race champions like Du Bois and Benjamin Mays. Like many of his kind, they point out, he was, while seeming to capitulate, a supreme strategist, sabotaging the arrogations of whites and forcing them to pay a stiff price for segregation. He habitually opened his biennial plea for funds before the state legislature with: "Gentlemen, segregation comes high." A Shepard could, by his enormous industry and intricate beguilements, always in the open and with a philosopher's disregard for the jeers of sidewalk superintendents, build a first-class college where a zealot would fail.

John W. Davis of West Virginia State, with less ingratiation and more educational statesmanship, played the game so ably that whites crowded into his college during his last years there in such numbers that it lost its identity as a Negro school. To him it had never been a "Negro college," just as he had never been a Negro, but always an American. He became president of the state's association of colleges and universities, and upon his retirement, administrator of the Point Four Program in Liberia.

Several, in founding schools, looked to white generosity. Palmer Institute began with little gifts that Charlotte Hawkins Brown assembled, and continued to derive support from tours she organized for her musical groups. Mrs. Bethune won aid from capitalists like James N. Proctor and Marshall Field, III, and Holley had the blessing of Negro-baiter "Pitchford Ben" Tillman, and latter-day ultra-conservatives like the Talmadges and Senator Russell. Jones's Piney Woods school was supported by whites who approved its mild program, but his biggest boost came when his appearance on the popular *This Is Your Life* television program moved sentimentalists to pour a fortune into the school—folk who would not have responded to appeals from first-class universities like Fisk, Howard or Atlanta.

The eminent educators were mainly college presidents. A few were deans and three or four agents of white foundations subsidizing Negro education. Less than a dozen achieved their distinction in scholarship. The latter included William Scarborough, celebrated as the race's first classical scholar of considerable reputation. A graduate of Oberlin, he wrote a textbook and monographs that were long used to refute the myth that the Negro is incapable of the intricacies of Greek conjugations and mathematical exercises.

The self-trained Joel A. Rogers's vigorously polemical books and newspaper column on Negro history made startling claims unfortunately ignored outside the ghetto, but Carter G. Woodson, a Harvard Ph.D. and a son of ex-slaves, was venerated by scholars of both races as founder of the Association for the Study of Negro Life and History and father of modern Negro historiography. The dour bachelor edited the association's publications, originated Negro History Week, and produced a flood of books and papers to present the Negro in a better light and to stir his race pride. Du Bois was another scholar, his reputation as historian and sociologist already established in early manhood by his one-man survey of Philadelphia Negroes and his earlier study of the African slave trade.

Alain Locke, another of the race's chief intellectuals until his death in 1953—aesthete, critic and art historian—was, like Du Bois, a Harvard graduate. The tiny exotic bachelor had the further distinction of being the first (and still the only) Negro American Rhodes Scholar. Benjamin Brawley, another Harvard graduate, was best known for his social history of the Negro in America and for works of appreciation of colored writers and artists. Others, like the West Indian Arthur Schomburg and George Young, were noted as amateur bibliophiles and collectors of Negro historical materials; and George W. Ellis was a lawyer, student of race and sociologist in the federal service. Monroe N. Work at Tuskegee collected historical records, compiled a Negro yearbook, and a monumental bibliography of the Negro with a view to promoting appreciation of the race's attainments; and Kelly Miller, the Howard dean and articulate sociologist-mathematician, was long one of the best-known Negroes (among Negroes), though unsuccessful in his efforts at race leadership and disappointed over his failure to achieve the presidency of Howard.

Opportunities for distinguishing themselves as scholars were, as we have noted, severely limited for the Negro academician. Most had themselves attended colleges where the emphasis, when not upon industrial preparation, was upon training for "character" and "the Christian life." Trustees, donors and visitors expected to hear Negro spirituals, not conjugations. In after years these men, appraising the education afforded by their Negro colleges, were by no means agreed. Woodson, who never attended one, wrote them off as tragically misdirected, dispensing "education for self-contempt"; but James Weldon Johnson (Atlanta '99), recalled that it was "education as a means of living, not of making a living." They were being taught in those days, he remembered, for lives of service and dedication to noble values, not as vulgar strivers and "go-getters."

Graduate scholarships and fellowships were as yet rare, and the prospect of teaching graduate students hopelessly remote. When they entered college teaching, exhausted from the struggle to win an adequate training, they found microscopic salaries, crushing teaching loads, undergraduates with little interest in scholarship and no scholarly tradition. Libraries were pitifully inadequate, research funds wanting and the atmosphere uncongenial to sustained creativity. Even the rare Ph.D. surrendered to an intellectual untidiness which there was no incentive to check. And still there were those accepting the life of genteel poverty, who fought the uphill fight; and out of the struggle came a company of strong men with a lofty vision—some of them sprung from the meanest social backgrounds—creators of a Negro scholarly tradition: Du Bois at Atlanta; Hope, Archer and Brawley at Morehouse; Dogan at Wiley; Scarborough at Wilberforce; McCrorey at Biddle; Miller at Howard; Crogman at Clark; Bowen at Gammon.

Some forged to the top by sheer politics; some were theologians to whom their denominations entrusted the keeping of their seminaries; and some caught the inspiration from dedicated teachers now long forgotten. Two thirds of them secured their baccalaureate training in the small Negro colleges of the South. A few attended white institutions: Chicago, Williams, Harvard, Colgate, Brown, Iowa State and Oberlin. Less than half took master's degrees, and only a half dozen earned Ph.D.'s, three of them at Harvard, and the others at Columbia, Pennsylvania and Jena. Let it be remembered that by 1920 (when all of the educators we have listed for this period had already begun their careers), only twenty Negro Americans, not all of whom became educators, had earned the Ph.D. degree.

In the age of accommodation, 1865–1900, any kind of distinction—be it only the attainment of a college degree—thrust a Negro into the role of "race leader," but the maturing Negro community in 1900–1936 concentrated responsibility for "race work" in the professionals of the NAACP, the Urban League, the institutional church, the press, the inter-racial commissions. The race's achievers had not abdicated such responsibility, but they exerted their pressures now through the organized agencies that a more specialized age demanded. The "talented tenth" were in fact the principal reliance of these organizations, for the masses showed a surprising inertia. In 1936 the membership of the NAACP (much of it white) stood at less than 75,000, and its income (at least a fourth of it from whites), fell short of fifty thousand dollars—an average of a mere penny per year from each Negro family in the land, for the principal instrument in the struggle for their social redemption.

In this new category, nine names which this investigation found most prominently noticed were Du Bois, Walter White, A. Philip Randolph, Channing Tobias, Mary Church Terrell, Mrs. Bethune, William Pickens, Eugene Kincklé Jones and George E. Haynes; and seven other outstanding leaders were Elmer A. Carter, Frank R. Crosswaith, Elizabeth Ross Haynes, Daisy Lampkin, Mary Talbert, Ida Wells and Max Yergan.

Du Bois, the dominant figure in the NAACP and editor of its publications, was the race's chief warrior, but while the NAACP fought lynching and pleaded the race's cause in the courts, the Urban League stressed interracial co-operation and greater economic opportunity, while other groups exhorted colored folk to self-discipline or appealed to the conscience of whites.

Walter White, already prominent as a writer and relentless investigator of lynchings, succeeded Du Bois as the dominant figure in the NAACP, and Pickens and Mrs. Lampkin served the association as organizers, fund-raisers and speakers. Randolph was (and remains in 1959) the race's foremost labor leader, and was prominent, with Chandler Owen and Crosswaith, in the Negro intellectual-socialist left. Crosswaith, greatly respected by whites—he was appointed to two five-year terms as a member of the New York Housing Authority—was also a pioneer organizer of Negro labor.

George E. Haynes founded the Urban League, Jones captured it from him and developed it to maturity, and Carter edited its magazine (which had been founded by Charles S. Johnson). Haynes was, in addition, a race-relations expert for the United States Department of Labor, the Federal Council of Churches and the Congregational Church, while his wife, Elizabeth Ross Haynes, was a New York social worker. Yergan and Tobias were YMCA officials, the former noted for work among South African students, and the latter as a churchman and inter-racial leader, appointed in 1946 to President Truman's Commission on Civil Rights.

Of the women in the group, Mrs. Bethune, Miss Talbert and Mrs. Terrell had enormous followings as leaders of colored clubwomen. Mrs. Terrell was still actively fighting Jim Crow in Washington at the age of eighty-nine. Ida Wells, another intrepid campaigner, as a newspaper editor and lecturer, was driven out of Memphis for her anti-lynching zeal. She relocated in Chicago and there joined Jane Addams and other humanitarians in a number of liberal causes.

The careers of most of the sixteen extended beyond 1950, and several are still active. All but Mrs. Terrell lived in the North, though nearly all were born in the South, the children or grandchildren of slaves. The exceptions, besides Du Bois, were Crosswaith, reared in the Virgin Islands, and Carter, a Long Islander whose great-grandfather had been bought into freedom from a slave ship at a Northern port by Quakers. Carter's mother was herself a protégé of a Quakeress who helped several Negroes through college.

Carter, for many years editor of *Opportunity,* was from early childhood conditioned to optimistic racial views, for his father, no less than his mother, enjoyed associations that endeared the white race to him. The elder Carter had been born to Georgia slaves—he probably never knew his natural parents—and was picked up by one of General Sherman's cavalrymen and eventually carried to Elmira, New York, where he became the houseboy of an industrious German-American family. As an AMEZ preacher, he and his Northern-born wife frequently took their son to lyceum and Chautauqua meetings, in addition to introducing him to the classics which white friends supplied for the pastor's library. The churches that the senior Carter served derived much of their financial support from kindly whites, and the friendly white school Elmer attended further supported his sanguine expectations. Only occasionally was there a hurt—as when his hard playing with his high-school football team elicited from a cheering teacher the shout, "Look at that coon play!"

One of the strongest advocates of inter-racial co-operation and good will bore during his childhood the name of his white father, an affluent merchant and landowner, who offered to provide his higher education. The lad declined, even though at least seven of his classmates at a foremost Negro university were subsidized by their white sires. After college, his father offered to employ him in his business or to send him to Europe, but the young man preferred to make his own way. His mother, emancipated in infancy, was sixteen when he was born, and broke off her relationship with her child's father when she embraced religion.

Jones's father was a slave and his mother freeborn, but both became college teachers in Richmond, where the elder Jones prefigured his son's career by agitating for wider employment of Negro teachers. Eugene, grieved by the failure of Negroes to back their champions, concluded in his youth that it was the Negro's economic instability that cowed him before every social pressure, and that his salvation lay in merit employment.

Mrs. Haynes's father ran off to the Union Army and later used his bounty to buy part of the Alabama plantation where he had been a slave. His widow, at eighty, still operated the plantation, by then grown to 1,500 acres. The pair could provide little intellectual stimulation for their child, but their high aspirations moved them to send her to Fisk University.

Pickens, the near-black field secretary of the NAACP, had no knowledge of his ancestry beyond his parents, except that his maternal grandmother was grotesquely deformed from the beatings of her slavery days. His ex-slave parents had, by the time William was eighteen, moved twenty times and during these years in near-peonage as sharecroppers the children worked the land instead of going to school, until a fortunate move to a place near Little Rock made a good elementary and high school available. Here William received, over the surly protests of the family's supply merchant, the preparation for his subsequent career at Yale, rising at four for a half-day's work before school began, and going back to work when classes were over for the day.

Another extreme was represented by Mary Church Terrell, born in Memphis at the end of the Civil War. Her mother had been extensively educated in slavery and her father, Robert R. Church, Sr., was the extremely fair-skinned natural son of a pro-Union slaveowner. Beginning as a cabin boy in his father's river boat, Church made a fortune from saloon and real-estate interests in the Memphis tenderloin district. His wife was a vigorous woman of business in her own right. Church left, at his death in 1912, a fortune of nearly a million, and his wealth and prestige had purchased a superior status for his children. Mary was sent North for schooling at six, finishing at Oberlin, where, she later wrote, her situation left nothing to be desired, and where she was powerfully impressed with the importance of welcoming the friendship of whites of good will. So steeped was the elder Church in the Southern white man's attitudes that he forbade Mary to become a schoolteacher, an occupation he considered beneath her station.

Tobias, chief of the inter-racial co-operation faction, during his long career as a YMCA official, Phelps-Stokes Fund Director and now chairman of the NAACP's board—to say nothing of his membership on countless committees, boards and agencies, and his role as perennial intermediary between Negroes and the White House—has all his life been surrounded by favorable white influences. A man of impressive appearance, with blue-gray eyes, fair skin, polished manner and impeccable diction, his forebears, beyond his parents, were principally white folk. When he was orphaned in childhood, he was befriended and helped through college by the white President Walker of Paine College, Georgia, who shaped his racial attitudes and trained him for the ministry. He entered YMCA work, resolved upon a career that would combine Christian with race-relations endeavor.

Walter White was so nearly pure white that his Negro critics often cast this shortcoming in his teeth, but his influence as head of the NAACP was so great that James E. Byrnes once publicly taunted him as the most powerful lobbyist in Washington. An urbane, sparkling man, he was sharply marked off from the millions whom he championed. His mother was one-sixteenth and his father one-fourth Negro. The latter, a mail carrier in Atlanta, provided the family with a home of their own, the tidiest house and grounds in the neighborhood, on the rim of the white community, where they were the objects of sullen envy from both races. It was a grimly Puritan home, dedicated to religion, sobriety and cleanliness, the shelves well stocked with Bibles, classics and lugubrious tomes from the church library.

Atlanta was, in Walter's childhood, a racial powder keg, menaced by inflammatory editors and politicians. When he was thirteen, he and his father were suddenly trapped in a race riot that killed a dozen Negroes. The pair escaped because they were taken for whites. (Years later his protective coloration made possible White's famous on-the-spot lynching investigations, in at least one of which he was deputized by a Negro-baiting sheriff!) On the following day, however, mobs descended upon the Negro quarter, and when they moved to burn the Whites' house as a hated symbol of the "uppity nigger," Walter and his father posted themselves at the windows with borrowed pistols until shots from a neighboring house dispersed the rioters.

Years later he ascribed his escape from racial hatred to the "unselfish and dedicated men and women who had forsaken their homes in New England to . . . teach in . . . Atlanta University," where he drank in the crusader's spirit. His career was sustained until the end, for all its militancy, by a remarkable optimism, amply manifested in his final book, *How Far the Promised Land?*

All of these persons confirm Gunnar Myrdal's observation that Negro race leaders must be emissaries, standing not at the head of the Negro people but between the races, acceptable to important segments of both. Militants like Weldon Johnson, Du Bois and White were closely associated with whites in the NAACP. Inter-racial good-will champions like Jones, Carter, Haynes and Tobias, and valiant warriors like Randolph, Crosswaithe and Ida Wells, no less than a matriarchal symbol like Mrs. Bethune, were important to the degree that whites in the power structure took them seriously. And it must not be supposed that any of them was well known to the Negro millions in this period; not one of them could draw an audience like a leading jazzman, prize fighter, or fraternal potentate.

Du Bois's brilliance as a scholar and writer, his Harvard Ph.D. and his flaming passion placed him far ahead of any conceivable rival for leadership in the Niagara Movement (1905) and the NAACP which grew out of it, as an undertaking of white and colored intellectuals, far removed from the black *Lumpen*. Mass popularity had no part in his rise. When James Weldon Johnson became the association's secretary, he had a solid reputation with the intelligentsia of both races who knew him as a writer and diplomat, with all the graces and urbanities that whites prized in their own leaders, and peculiarly available as a negotiator on the color line.

Once in key positions, such leaders shared with whites the recruitment of other leaders. It was Johnson who sold White to the NAACP after the poet, as a dinner guest at the White home in Atlanta, met young Walter. When Pickens succeeded Johnson as field secretary he was well known to white reformers for his brilliant Yale record and years as an educator and lecturer. Noteworthy too as avenues to race leadership for many in this group were the church (particularly interdenominational bodies like the Federal Council), the YMCA and YWCA, and federated Negro women's clubs, commonly supplemented by ties with political parties, quick to recognize the value of persons in touch with so large a block of voters. Mrs. Bethune, Mrs. Lampkin, Mrs. Terrell and Mrs. Haynes, for example, were accorded conspicuous place in the two major parties.

The case of Mrs. Bethune raises interesting questions. A big, dark, ungainly matron, conspicuous in her later years for magnificent indignations and for her walking stick and magniloquent affectations, she came to prominence as the heroic founder of a school and then as a leader of Negro clubwomen and a member of the "black Cabinet" in the Roosevelt-Truman era. She was a faithful, articulate participant in every liberal cause, frequently linked with Mrs. Roosevelt. And yet, some colored intellectuals regarded her as an opportunist with a sure instinct for the telling phrase, the defiant gesture, with precisely the degree of impudence that whites would admire, while she gave to the Negro masses the appearance of splendid courage and resolute militancy.

If Mrs. Bethune resists analysis, the others are no less baffling, for scholars have yet to explain the mechanisms by which Negro leaders are chosen and enabled to exercise influence. One thing seems clear: without racial discrimination there would be no "Negro leaders." (Colored wags jest that the NAACP fears that someone may stumble upon The Solution, and that peace may break out.) Interesting, too, is the acknowledgment of several of the leaders that they had come up through kindlier environments than were the lot of their contemporaries, or even of those who followed them and faced in their youths a stiffening of Jim Crow patterns precisely because the color line showed signs of yielding.

Because the stories of the leaders' struggles for education do not differ markedly from those in other categories, a few observations will serve. Some confessed that they chose Northern white colleges because Negro schools were inferior, but Du Bois, who took degrees at both Fisk and Harvard, declared that at Fisk only was the race problem squarely faced and the essential equality of races affirmed. There, he wrote, a young Negro could enjoy normal social contacts, uncomplicated by tensions and irrational barriers, and build his defenses against future outrage. Many years later Elmer Carter was often unhappy at Harvard, where he worked hard to support himself and constantly encountered racism among students and professors. As a child he heard much of heroes like Douglass and Harriet Tubman, both of whom lived near his boyhood home, but when he reached Harvard, he was shocked by discussions—as in the classes of F. W. Taussig and Albert Bushnell Hart—in which the immutable inferiority of the Negro was presumed. James Weldon Johnson and White, as we have noted, looked back with satisfaction upon their Atlanta University course with its stress upon the intellectual virtues and high-minded conduct as preparation for the good life in the days before Negro colleges capitulated to the American stress upon material success.

Most of the group were in some way pushed forward with white help; several—Du Bois, Haynes, Pickens, Johnson, Bethune and Tobias come to mind—by scholarships and handsome private benefactions from folk always on the lookout for promising colored youth. Pickens at Yale was far happier than Carter at Harvard. After he finished at Talladega, where the white faculty had provided him with campus jobs, the white President Andrews arranged for his admission to Yale, again with good self-help jobs in New Haven. In addition, the coal-black sharecropper received occasional fifty-dollar checks from a New York benefactor whom he never met—once more through the mediation of his faithful sponsor, President Andrews. The importance of these New England heirs of the old Puritan-Abolitionist tradition in the molding of Negro leadership over several decades can scarcely be exaggerated.

Pickens earned scholarships during all four years at Yale, and when he won the Ten Eyck oratorical competition, the glee club gave him fifty dollars to express its pleasure. A flood of congratulatory letters followed, one from Grover Cleveland, and one, with a check, from the sister of Theodore Roosevelt. "An Unknown Well-wisher" sent three fifty-dollar gold certificates. When he was graduated with Phi Beta Kappa honors, a lecture bureau offered him an American and European tour, but on the advice of Paul Laurence Dunbar, whose experience as a travelling exhibit had been unhappy, he declined and became a college teacher and an active associate of the newly formed NAACP.

We have made repeated reference to Du Bois, the most commanding figure in the race's struggles during the first third of the twentieth century, and still the Grand Old Man of Negro leaders, despite his unpopular Marxist views. We have said less of A. Philip Randolph, since World War I and to this day one of the most influential Negroes in America.

Randolph has had a multiple importance as a democratic radical, pacifist, head of the Pullman Porters' Union, central figure in the 1941 "March on Washington" movement, enemy of segregation in the armed forces and officer in an enormous number of humanitarian agencies, including the NAACP and the American Civil Liberties Union. Impervious alike to vanity and intimidation, he has long been feared and hated, respected and loved, as few Negroes have been. When, in June, 1958, President Eisenhower summoned four Negro leaders for a "summit conference," on racial affairs, his choice of Randolph was inevitable.

His Virginia slave forebears settled in Florida after the Civil War. His father, a minister, and his mother eked out their tiny pastoral salary by running a small shop for cleaning and mending clothes. Here again were Black Puritans who took endless pains to instil in their two boys the ancient virtues of piety, industry, respect for learning, purity of conduct and impeccable respectability. Randolph's childhood was free from racial friction, and while his mother dominated the home, his father, a homespun philosopher, impressed upon him the achievements of Negroes and the doctrine of racial equality.

After attending Cookman Institute, Florida, where a consecrated bi-racial faculty confirmed him in these values, he sought work in New York City, where he had already spent summers as a hallboy in apartment houses. Subsisting on odd jobs, he attended City College at night, browsing in economics, literature, political science and philosophy, greatly stimulated by warmly interested professors, including the young Morris R. Cohen. His excursions into social theory, his experience in the rough-and-tumble of workaday Harlem, and his intense moralism led the ascetic youth into native American socialism, while exposure to racial bias and a reading of Du Bois's *Souls of Black Folk* deepened his zeal for racial justice.

Soon he was having difficulty keeping his jobs because of his efforts to organize his fellow workers. With Chandler Owen, a law student, he joined the Socialist party, organized street meetings and a political discussion group for colored students, and established the monthly socialist *Messenger,* which, under his direction, became one of the most brilliantly edited magazines in the history of Negro journalism. He also studied public speaking and earned part of his living as an "elocutionist" in Negro churches, developing meanwhile his orotund platform style.

Now his reputation as a crusader brought him an invitation to organize the Pullman porters. His final victory is one of the most dramatic chapters in the history of American labor. The railways—and, curiously, Negroes worried about preserving one of their few monopolies—used every tactic to thwart him, from attacks upon his integrity to the proffer of a fat sum for an extended "vacation" abroad. (It came when he was hard pressed to pay his rent, but the check was instantly returned.) During his first twelve years with the porters, his income was so precarious that his wife worked as a hairdresser to meet household bills. He later ceased to be actively associated with socialism, and Mayor La Guardia invited him into his administration, but he preferred to keep his role in the liberal-labor, anti-Communist left.

Newspapers had made a modest beginning toward becoming a major influence in Negro America before 1900, and then multiplied rapidly. By 1920 there were some two hundred, and thereafter growth was principally in the expanding circulation of existing papers. Like other professions, Negro journalism owed its sudden burgeoning to the maturing of free, separate colored communities in the new century, and particularly in the wake of the great northward Diaspora after 1914. After World War I circulation per capita was at least four times as high in the North as in the South, and perhaps a third of the country's colored families subscribed. The papers passed from hand to hand before they were discarded, for their cost was comparatively high, and their influence was increased because those Negroes who took the papers were the most ambitious and literate third of the race.

In the 1930's the combined circulation had reached well over a million and a quarter, much of it accounted for by a dozen leading journals in Pittsburgh, Chicago, New York, Baltimore, Norfolk and Philadelphia, all of them weeklies designed for national circulation. Individual papers strongly reflected the personalities of their editors and publishers, though the day of personal journalism was beginning to give place to standardizing influences such as columnists and other "chain" features, and the emergence of the Associated Negro Press, and, more recently, the Negro Newspaper Publishers' Association.

It was above all a fighting press, offering only "race news": Negro achievements, Negro crime, Negro business, Negro hardships and an astonishing quantity of "society news" of the black bourgeoisie that white America declined to recognize—materials, in short, which the white press either did not present at all or offered in tiny quantities and with distortion. Editorials, cartoons and other features were equally preoccupied with the race's improvement and with the struggle for first-class citizenship.

It exhorted the race to industry, sobriety and thrift; to neatness, cleanliness and refinement; to a more dignified religion, a more disciplined morality, greater family regularity. It denounced gambling, improvidence and a foolish predilection for skin and hair conditioners. It warned its readers against neglecting their opportunities in a country rich in promise. "Be Ready!" was a constant refrain, for the press never doubted that the triumph of full justice—soon—was inevitable in the logic of American history. In a word, the church in these years was losing to the press and the "race agencies" its old responsibility for voicing the aspirations and indignations of the race, for keeping it informed of its opportunities and responsibilities, organizing and co-ordinating its efforts for betterment.

It was a bootstrap operation, for the men who built and ran the press faced the usual lack of opportunity for training and experience and for acquiring capital. National advertisers passed them by, for buyers of Negro papers bought white papers, too; and the big department stores were reluctant to invite Negroes to come in and shop. In the early days, Negro papers took subsidies from politicians and other interest groups. The principal advertising income came from vendors of dubious products: hair straighteners, skin lighteners, lip reducers, luck charms, patent medicines, hair pieces and sartorial oddities. Two thirds of the money had to come from subscribers, however, and that meant a selling price five times above that of the white daily. This freed the Negro press from advertiser domination, but also compelled the publisher to pander to low-class interests to boost circulation. Especially after 1910, when Robert Abbott, founder of the Chicago *Defender,* demonstrated its appeal, the trend was toward mixing the paper's sober crusading content with lurid headlines, and heaping portions of scandal, sex, crime and vulgarities, for readers with a feeble literary tradition. Still it remained, far longer than the white press, a highly personal journalism, not yet dominated by the business mentality that would in the next generation make the Negro newspaper an increasingly faithful facsimile of the white tabloid.

Besides Du Bois of the *Crisis,* Charles S. Johnson of *Opportunity* and Randolph and Owen of the *Messenger,* all of whom we are noting elsewhere, thirteen leaders* of the Negro press stood out in our study of the years 1900–1936. Only two were Northern-born. Schuyler's parents were middle-class Negroes in Providence, and then Syracuse, by turns operators of a hand

* Robert S. Abbott, Claude A. Barnett, John "Grit" Bruce, Wendell P. Dabney, Roscoe Dunjee, Fred R. Moore, Carl Murphy, Percival L. Prattis, George S. Schuyler, William Monroe Trotter, Robert L. Vann, Lester A. Walton, Plummer B. Young

laundry and hotel cooks, descended through stable family lines from free folk antedating the Revolution. Trotter's father, the Mississippi-born son of a white slaveowner, was a Federal officeholder under President Cleveland, in Boston, and his mother, a fair-skinned woman of color, claimed descent from Thomas Jefferson. It was an upper-class Negro household, and young Monroe was constantly admonished to excel whites as a means of breaking down color barriers.

The other eleven were Southern-born. At one extreme, Robert Vann, builder of the impressive *Pittsburgh Courier,* was the child of ex-slave tenant farmers in North Carolina, so submerged in the back country that he was ten before he saw his first train. Fred Moore, on the other extreme, the son of a white scion of the Virginia Randolphs, passed his first years in a plantation mansion in Loudon County, and then grew up in Washington. Abbott, founder of the vigorous Chicago *Defender,* was the son of a slave-butler who, when he married a field Negro, was rebuked by his kin for "marrying down." Her father, however, though snatched from Africa into slavery, had been resourceful enough to buy his liberty. Robert's father had been taught to read by his master, and his mother also attained literacy in slavery. After the Emancipation the pair operated a little grocery store for freedmen, and when Robert's father died, his mother married a man of mixed German and Negro blood, one John H. Sengstacke, a sometime schoolteacher and clergyman and editor of a little newssheet in whose publication the boy assisted—an introduction, as it proved, to his life work.

Wendell Dabney's parents were grandchildren of their owners. His father, a jockey and waiter, had bought his own and his wife's freedom, and as hotel employees in Richmond they provided their child with superior environment. Lester Walton, of untraced mixed ancestry, was similarly fortunate; his mother was a schoolteacher and his barely literate father a hotel bellman, notable among St. Louis Negroes in church and school affairs.

John "Grit" Bruce and Moore never progressed beyond the grades; Schuyler and Walton had a brief high-school course; and all the others had some college education. Abbott was instructed by whites under American Missionary Association auspices, first at an academy, where his light-skinned fellows spurned him, and then at Hampton, where his dark complexion was an asset for the travelling glee club on its fund-raising tours, and where he came under the influence of the same General Armstrong who had molded Booker Washington. When he moved to Chicago, he completed a law course at an evening school, but his dark skin and rustic background proved an insurmountable barrier to establishing a practice.

Claude Barnett absorbed Booker Washington's philosophy during a year at Tuskegee, while Roscoe Dunjee and P. B. Young attended Negro liberal arts colleges. Dabney had all of his higher education at Oberlin and others studied at white schools after attending Negro colleges. Carl Murphy, of the

Afro-American chain, followed his Howard A.B. with a Harvard A.M., and summer study in Germany; and Vann went from Virginia Union to the University of Pittsburgh for A.B. and law degrees, supporting himself by summer bell-hopping at Bar Harbor. Trotter was valedictorian and president of his class in a white Massachusetts high school and took A.B. and A.M. degrees, with junior-year election to Phi Beta Kappa, at Harvard, where he was on the debating team and president of a temperance society whose secretary was William Lloyd Garrison, Jr.

Abbot recruited his staff from porters, barbers, waiters and assorted bright young men, and, for all his lack of technical training, had a remarkable knack for recognizing talent. He made youthful Willard Motley his young-peoples' editor and printed scores of the early poems of Gwendolyn Brooks, then a gangling high-school girl living a few blocks from the *Defender's* office. His technique for building circulation among lower-class folk with uncultivated tastes, while keeping close to the role of the race's "defender," revolutionized Negro journalism. In his Chicago office sat the South's chief scold, campaigning ceaselessly to induce Negroes to flee the region as for very life, and in parts of the South his paper was an under-the-counter commodity. And yet, his aversion to blackness drove him to an irrational loathing of black clothes, to the avoidance of dark companions, and to excluding from his pages for years on end not only advertisements for Negro cosmetics but the very words "Negro" and "black." When his efforts to buy a Rolls-Royce were repulsed because so black an owner would destroy the car's snob appeal in Chicago, he acquired one through a ruse and employed a liveried chauffeur lest he himself be taken for a white millionaire's flunky.

Before building his news-gathering service, Barnett sold photoprints of famous Negroes, and Dabney was a musician and amateur poet until he found his mission with the Cincinnati *Union* and as an appointed city official. Dunjee served several Oklahoma City papers before beginning his lively career with the *Black Dispatch*. He was conspicuous in the NAACP, but happiest when he held the leading strings himself. Political hacks more than once tried in vain to buy him off with a share of the swag from the police-protected colored underworld.

Forbes, associated with Trotter on the Boston *Guardian,* was better known as an official of the West End Branch of the Boston Public Library. Moore, a spokesman of Tuskegee-Republicanism, had been a deputy collector of United States Internal Revenue and Minister to Liberia before becoming editor and publisher of the New York *Age,* and during his editorship was elected Alderman. Trotter, just out of Harvard, began in the real-estate and mortgage business before dedicating himself to race effort through journalism. The fiery editor of the Boston *Guardian* became an implacable critic of Booker Washington and was once jailed for heckling him during a speech in Boston. After World War I, he joined a group of Negroes at Versailles to place the American Negroes' plight before the Conference. To obtain passage it had been necessary for him to sign on as ship's cook.

He was one of the projectors of the NAACP and from his Boston office he railed against every conceivable form of racial prejudice, including some usages—such as the training camp for Negro officers at Des Moines during World War I—against which other liberals had no objections. As an influential voice of the Negro left, he was frequently called into consultation with other Negro leaders, and with high public officials. On one occasion his sharp face-to-face criticism of Woodrow Wilson for his bias in the Civil Service so enraged the Virginia-born President that he lashed out at Trotter with a savage rebuke and forbade him to return to the White House. Wilson's successors did, however, call him in again.

The milder Walton worked as a reporter and staff writer for white dailies in St. Louis and New York before joining the staff of his father-in-law's *Age,* and then after long service to the Democratic party, notably as director of Negro publicity in presidential campaigns, he was appointed by President Roosevelt as Minister to Liberia, a post he held with dignity and quiet efficiency for nearly a dozen years. Vann built his giant *Pittsburgh Courier* upon a little two-page sheet initiated by a Negro worker in a pickle factory, who wrote poetry in his spare time and saw in the University-trained Vann an opportunity to convert his personal journal into a major newspaper. When he took his paper out of the Republican and into the New-Deal camp, Vann was made an assistant to the Attorney General, but long before the Roosevelt era had ended he was back in the Republican fold.

These years saw fewer Negroes in public office than did the preceding era, when federal bayonets had enforced the race's political rights in the South. But such share in government as the newer generation did show was more promising. Republican administrations continued to give Negroes posts that were coming to be regarded as traditional Negro plums, and strategic party offices were still held by colored politicians. In the North, things had progressed to the point that when, by 1936, a dozen states were sending colored members to the legislatures, such office-holding excited little notice, even in the Negro press.

The highest place held by a Negro in this period was a seat in the United States House of Representatives. When George H. White of North Carolina, the last of the post-Civil War Congressmen, finished his term in 1901, he predicted, in a moving valedictory, that the Negro would return. His prophecy was fulfilled when Oscar De Priest of Chicago was elected in 1928 to the first of three terms. A Caucasian-featured Southern Negro, De Priest was born in Alabama shortly after the War, to ex-slave parents who moved to Kansas when Oscar was a boy. Elementary schooling and a brief business course at a normal school were all his formal education. He became a house painter, but when he moved to Chicago, he switched to real estate and politics for a living and soon became Chicago's first Negro alderman. His importance to the Thompson machine of Chicago enabled him to dole out fistfuls of appointments to Negro payrollers and he became a delegate to Republican national conventions.

His parents had been poor but proud folk who exhorted him to stand up to Jim Crow insults, and when goon squads from the Jim Crow painter's union tried to drive him from his jobs in Kansas, he stood his ground with a pistol in his hand. When he arrived in Chicago, he was so destitute that he lived for weeks on the free lunches that saloons of that day served free with five-cent schooners of beer.

The district that sent him to Washington was at least four-fifths Negro but thoroughly satisfied with its white Congressman, Martin B. Madden. It was Madden's death, after his renomination in 1928, that brought De Priest the nomination, not at the hands of voters, but from a committee of five ward politicians—including De Priest himself.

When he assumed office, some Negroes of the better class repudiated him as a hack of the most vulgar sort, harking back to the old Reconstruction politicians, but others argued that he was a courageous, if clumsy, fighter against racial bias, despite his deficiencies in training and native endowments. Even the austere Du Bois rallied the *Crisis* to his defense, insisting that—for all his coarse speech, tossing of his white mane and flailing of his arms—he stood "solidly and unwaveringly" for enforcement of every legal guarantee of Negro rights. He spoke out bluntly, not only in Congress, but to Negro audiences in the Deep South and at such peril that he carried pistols on the lecture platform while he denounced race-baiting whites and timid Uncle Toms alike.

De Priest lost his seat to Arthur Mitchell in 1934, thanks to Negro defections to the New Deal and to the foot-dragging of Republican leaders alarmed by his militancy. Mitchell was an Alabama farm boy, the son of ex-slaves. At fourteen he walked sixty-five miles to Tuskegee where, as Washington's office boy, he absorbed the leader's views. He later took a degree at Talladega, taught a rural school in Alabama, and read law in a Washington attorney's office. Upon moving to Chicago, he joined the First Ward Republican machine until the shifting party preference of Negroes moved him into the Democratic party. Like De Priest's, Mitchell's nomination was a last-minute substitution by party bosses after the primary's nominee had died.

Once in Congress, he disavowed any intention to be the race's spokesman, deplored his predecessor's "extremism," and became the target of the Negro press, the NAACP and Negro intellectuals for his compromising position. Except for an occasional speech for Negro rights, his eight years in Congress were not remarkably different from those of many undistinguished

Representatives. Perhaps his most important service was his suit against the Pullman Company and a railway after the Congressman had been hustled into a Jim Crow car despite the precaution of buying two Pullman tickets to secure a compartment to himself. He bore the protracted and expensive litigation unaided and argued the case himself. The Supreme Court unanimously reversed the pro-Jim Crow ruling of the Interstate Commerce Commission. Though Mitchell's victory only confirmed that a Negro who purchased first-class accommodations could not be denied them, and did not touch the Jim Crow car *per se,* it was a milestone in the history of minority rights. When he retired after a fourth term, the Chicagoan established his home in Virginia, where he became a gentleman farmer.

While Mitchell sat as the first colored Democrat in Congress, the Roosevelt administration was bringing into the New Deal agencies several able Negroes who had little connection with politics, but this had only just begun at the close of the era. Negroes continued to serve as ministers to Liberia, as in the post-Civil War generation, but the Haitian post was restored to whites by the Wilson administration. The Wilson years in fact witnessed a sharp decline in traditional Negro appointments, but most of the ground lost was recovered in the 1920's. Throughout the thirty-five years, the Negroes appointed to the Liberian and Haitian posts were respectable, if unspectacular, men from the professions: Ernest Lyon, a clergyman; J. L. Johnson, chairman of the board of trustees of Wilberforce; George W. Buckner, an Indianapolis physician; W. T. Francis, a Minneapolis lawyer; Solomon Porter Hood, an AME educator and clergyman, and Charles E. Mitchell, a banker and former business manager of a leading Negro state college.

Two men were consular officials: William H. Hunt was a consul at Madagascar and St. Etienne, France; and William J. Yerby became an official for twenty years at consulates in Africa, with briefer service at French and Portuguese cities. More widely noticed were domestic appointments given William H. Lewis and Robert H. Terrell. Lewis, a Virginia-born lawyer, came to Boston as a boy and was educated at Amherst (where he was a schoolmate of Calvin Coolidge, captain of the football team and class orator) and at Harvard. He opened a law practice and became a Cambridge City Councilman, a state representative, and Assistant United States Attorney before his appointment by Presidents T. Roosevelt and Taft as Assistant Attorney General of the United States. Terrell, another Harvard graduate, was made Municipal Judge of the District of Columbia by Roosevelt, Taft and Wilson. He had been a law partner of former Congressman John R. Lynch and an official in the Treasury. Both appointments encountered strong opposition in the Senate, but the Southern irreconcilables succeeded only in calling attention to the solid qualifications of both men.

Several state and municipal officeholders were notable. Ferdinand Q. Morton, a party leader rewarded with office, was a pioneer New York Negro

Democrat and a founder of the United Colored Democracy, a voters' group. As a member of the New York Civil Service Commission (originally appointed by the grace of Tammany Hall and later made president of the commission by Mayor La Guardia), he worked effectively to eliminate discrimination in public employment and in the welfare services of the city. Though born in rural Mississippi, he was, as a graduate of Exeter, Harvard College and Boston University Law School, one of the most highly educated working politicians in America.

A half dozen Republican party officials, all but one of them products of the South's pocket boroughs, had a major voice in party councils. At least one made little effort to conceal that he was a white man's son, and all were markedly Caucasoid in features. Two—Perry Howard, of Mississippi, and Henry Lincoln Johnson, of Georgia, Republican National Committeemen and patronage dispensers—lived in Washington, with only occasional visits back home to fight the Lily-whites bent on unseating them, while Benjamin J. Davis of Atlanta, Robert R. Church, Jr., of Memphis, William H. McDonald of Texas and Roscoe Conkling Simmons of Chicago, kept close to home. The hands of all six were firmly on party controls in the state and national structure. Church and Johnson were perhaps the most influential, and after Johnson's death in 1924, Church remained until 1932 the most powerful Negro politician in the land, not only as party boss in Tennessee, but also as chief dispenser of Negro patronage in the country at large. He derived his living meanwhile from the real estate he had inherited from his wealthy father.

The group's influence had important limits, however: Johnson, for example, hoped for appointment as Assistant Attorney General but never attained higher office than that of Recorder of Deeds for the District. The others, perhaps by choice, were manipulators without public office. Each was criticized for wire-pulling and patronage-peddling, but this was squarely in the American political tradition. More important was their genuine participation in party mechanics; and, for all the vilification that they suffered from liberals of both races, they were, with their leverage, purchasing significant recognition for the race's aspirations and claims.

Their styles varied. Church and Johnson were cultivated men, working quietly in the background, sometimes with the President himself. Howard, also well educated, played the game from his Washington law office, while Davis, as a lawyer, fraternal potentate and editor of both the *Atlanta Independent* and the *National Baptist Review,* was in touch with a vast constituency. McDonald was the salaried associate of the son of the eccentric millionairess, Hetty Green, in a curious bi-racial political partnership that dominated the Texas Republican machine from 1896 to 1912. In Chicago, Simmons, a tiny, frail redhead, whose spellbinding oratory was the Negroes' answer to the fire-eating Vardamans, Bilbos and Heflins, was as much at home in the smoke-filled room as in the packed convention Hall.

Besides kinship with whites, these men had other advantages to improve their chances. McDonald, born of slave parents, had formed his partnership with E. H. R. Green in his youth. He had sufficient education to become a school principal, and his tutelage under Green enabled him to dabble with great success in banking and real estate. Simmons was the nephew of Mrs. Booker Washington. He left his Mississippi home for Washington as a boy and became a protégé of the Mark Hanna and Medill McCormick families. In his maturer years he was a guest of Republican presidents from Roosevelt to Hoover, and with Johnson, Howard and Church, he directed Republican national campaign strategy among Negro voters. Johnson, a more urbane man (he married the poet Georgia Douglas), was born in Augusta, Georgia, and educated at Atlanta University and the law school of the University of Michigan. He chose the law, he said, because it seemed the best arena for fighting for the race's improvement, but he left his Atlanta practice to accept President Taft's appointment as Recorder of Deeds in order to devote himself to politics in Washington.

Church, like his famous sister, Mary Church Terrell, was reared in wealth and educated at Oberlin. Davis, born in rural Georgia, attended the high-school department at Atlanta University, and then learned the bricklayer's trade, but became a schoolteacher before launching his career as a lodge official and editor. Perry Howard, a tall, blue-eyed, light-skinned Mississippian, was born a decade after the Civil War to a slave father who had been "sold South" for his intransigence and compelled to abandon his first wife in the transfer.

When Perry was born, the Howards were well regarded in the town of Ebenezer, where they were the only colored family, and when freedom came, the elder Howard took the lead in bringing a teacher from the North for Negroes of the area, and became a member of the legislature. Perry was one of seven sons, all of whom went to college and into professions. Working his way in Pullman, hotel and restaurant service, he studied at Rust College and Fisk University, then still strongly under the influence of Northern missionaries, and spent a year studying mathematics at the University of Chicago before entering legal practice. He was untroubled by a sense of racial exclusion and discrimination in his youth and in maturity was firmly in the Tuskegee camp. So thoroughly acceptable was he to white Southerners, that in his first political contest in Mississippi he defeated a white rival with the support of the Ku Klux Klan, who burned a cross to warn voters against voting for Howard's opponent. He was hotly attacked in the middle 'twenties when he was retained by the Pullman Company to frustrate unionization of the porters, but he is also respected for the vigorous role his law firm has played in Negro civil-rights cases in the federal courts.

In this era, twenty-two widely various writers claim our attention.* They chose principally "racial themes," ranging from the passionately protestant to the purely lyrical, but a few avoided race altogether. Some were university-educated, some self-taught. Some were born to advantages; others, of uncertain lineage, came up through bleak years of struggle. The essays and fiction of Du Bois and Schuyler were frankly polemic, but the group as a whole seriously aspired to literary reputation and only incidentally to advancing the race, and in some cases to literary eminence alone.

Before the 1920's, the Negro poet or novelist was still so much a curiosity that he was thought of not as an American writer, but as a "Negro genius." The 'twenties witnessed a notable retreat from this mentality, but it remained for the years following 1935—with its more liberal social climate and the help of the Federal Writers' Project—to accord an occasional colored writer the real status of author. Publishers, editors and white and Negro readers deplored the poets' efforts to break away from the Negro idiom in favor of standard English, and even the best of those who made the break—like James Weldon Johnson, Georgia Douglas Johnson, McKay, Cullen, Hughes, Braithwaite and Toomer were often taxed with being merely (however competently) imitative. It was only (so ran the argument) when it preserved the "tang" of Negro speech, as in the best of Sterling Brown and Langston Hughes, that their poetry was said to be "successful."

Fiction writers were also under pressure to confine themselves to Negro themes, on the plausible ground that their enforced isolation disqualified them as commentators on other facets of American life. The white man's preferences, moreover, had to be accommodated, for the poor and socially disadvantaged Negro folk were not buyers of books. Du Bois aside, all the pre-World War I authors of this generation were primarily writers of verse: Braithwaite, Corrothers, Cotter, Grimké and James Weldon Johnson. Braithwaite, editor of an annual anthology of magazine verse, literary historian and critic, produced only non-racial verse, while Johnson, though choosing racial themes, was a pioneer in defying the old predilection for dialect. The poetry of the so-called "Harlem Renaissance" or "New Negro Movement" repudiated the old dialect tradition, and ranged from racial themes—with and without social protest— to the polished lyrics of Countee Cullen. The most warmly applauded was the verse of the then very young Langston Hughes, already in the early 1930's, as he remains today, the unofficial laureate of the

* Arna Bontemps
William S. Braithwaite
Sterling Brown
James D. Corrothers
Joseph S. Cotter
Countee Cullen
W. E. B. Du Bois
Jessie Fauset
Rudolph Fisher
Angelina Grimké
Langston Hughes
Zora Neal Hurston
Georgia Douglas Johnson
James Weldon Johnson
Nella Larson
Claude McKay
Alice Dunbar Nelson
George S. Schuyler
Wallace Thurman
Jean Toomer
Eric Walrond
Walter White

race, perennially young, ebullient and amused. His work—a compound of humor and pathos, realism and protest (some of his readers worried about his leftist and his heterodox religious views), almost always unmistakably Negro—included, besides his verse, novels, plays, biography, lyrics for stage productions and a delightful newspaper column, unhappily confined to the Negro press, built around a Negro Mr. Dooley, Jesse Semple.

Though the fiction produced by the group rarely strayed from the Negro milieu, it found a variety of themes: slave insurrections, folk tales, "passing," Northern upper-class urban life, the West Indian environment, racial violence and discrimination, Harlem life and the plight of the very dark woman in the color-conscious Negro community. Preoccupation with such Negro characters exposed authors to constant rebuke from their own race, for colored folk insisted that writers stress the race's better side rather than confirm the misgivings of both whites and Negroes by dwelling on their shortcomings and vulgarities.

Almost every one of the twenty-two had an urban childhood. Not one was an unmixed African, but three or four were very dark. Some (like White, who chose not to) and Toomer (who eventually did) were fair enough to "pass." McKay and Walrond were immigrants from Jamaica and British Guiana, far removed from the conventional slave heritage. Seven were born in the North, and of the eleven native Southerners, several came from the atypical border South, and some moved to the North or far West in early childhood. All but two matured in the North.

Several sprang from unstable family circles. Cullen was turned over soon after his birth in New York City to a Methodist minister who gave him his name. Another poet was born in Atlanta, the child of a woman of mixed blood and a white man whom the poet never met. Others could point to similar ancestral irregularities in recent generations.

Braithwaite's father, university-trained in Barbados and London, was the son of a distinguished colonial family of British Guiana, of Negro, English and French noble ancestry. He migrated in early manhood to Boston, where he married the daughter of an ex-slave by a white man, whose identity the poet's mother never knew. She had fled North after Appomattox and became the housekeeper of a Boston family "on terms of absolute Christian equality." The senior Braithwaite established himself as a physician's assistant, and confined his friendships to Boston gentlefolk, excluding all Negroes from his house, and forbidding his children to play with any others, white or colored, or to attend public schools, so conscious was he of rank. He educated the little Braithwaites at home, and Willie was obliged to wear the curls and Fauntleroys that befitted a little son of the Empire.

Willie was eight when his father died, leaving the family destitute. His mother became a domestic, and the lad, after four years of public school, went to work, never again to enter a classroom until he went to Atlanta as a visiting professor, forty-five years later. He worked with his mother in fashionable seashore resorts, managing a bookstore which put books at his disposal and multiplied his associations with cultivated whites. From the beginning his writing carried no hint of his Negro ancestry, and long after he had acquired a reputation as a critic with a flair for discovering young talent, many, including Negro poets familiar with his work, were startled to learn that he was a Negro, if they learned it at all.

As a free-lance critic for the Boston *Transcript,* a lyric poet, and a prime mover in the effort to revive American poetry around the time of World War I, he urged Negroes to disengage themselves from "Negro writing," lest they be judged by a double standard, but the advice only offended Negro intellectuals, exasperated by his "repudiation" of his "heritage."

In sharp contrast was the race-consciousness of the foreign-born McKay and Walrond, and the proud Negroism of Hughes, whose own father had rebelled so passionately against his status as a Negro that he forsook his family for life in Mexico with a German *hausfrau* as his second wife. Young Langston was reared by his mother and grandmother in Midwestern and Northern communities, where he often had no Negro schoolmates, and found enough defenders among his generally hostile white companions to learn not to dislike whites *en masse*. Pride in his own race was fostered by his majestic grandmother, the last surviving widow of the Harpers Ferry raid, and fiercely disdainful of the conventional Aunt Jemimah jobs for Negro women; she eked out her living by renting rooms to Kansas University students. Both of Hughes's paternal grandfathers were white Kentuckians, one a slave trader and one a distiller, and on his mother's side his great-grandfather was the planter Ralph Quarles, who had fathered, by Lucy Langston, several light-skinned children, including the poet's grandfather and his great-uncle, the arrogant and color-struck educator and Congressman, John Mercer Langston.

Others in the group were equally atypical. Bontemps derived from cultivated free French-Negroes who had migrated from New Orleans to California; Angelina Grimké was the Boston-born, classically educated daughter of Archibald Grimké. Corrothers, orphaned in early infancy, was the only Negro boy in his neighborhood in Michigan, and brought up by his grandfather, a devout white man with Indian admixture, who had married a Negro woman. James Weldon Johnson, a light-skinned, gray-eyed Negro, was born in Florida six years after the War. His father, a freeman of Richmond, had removed before the War to New York, and his mother, of French and Negro stock, passed her childhood in the Bahamas before migrating to New York with her mother. She was the first female colored schoolteacher in Florida. Never reconciled to Southern race ways, so foreign to her own tradition, she instilled a strong pride of race in her sons.

Toomer was born in Washington of upper-class Louisiana Creole-Negro parents. He became, with the publication of *Cane,* a volume of poems and short stories, one of the most celebrated "New Negro" writers, but little more was heard from him thereafter, for he withdrew from Negro society. He married first a white novelist, and, after her death, another white woman, the daughter of a New York broker, renouncing his Negro ancestry, declining to permit his poems to be printed in anthologies of Negro verse, and even averring that his illustrious grandfather, P. S. B. Pinchback, called himself a Negro only for political reasons.

Sterling Brown's maternal grandfather was white, evidently a judge, and both of his parents were, like their son, extremely fair. His mother was valedictorian of her class at Fisk, and his father, a Fisk and Oberlin graduate, was a Howard professor. The boy thus grew up in an atmosphere of extraordinary cultural advantages, and was sent, as a matter of course, to one of the finest colleges in the country. Others had more modest beginnings. Zora Hurston's father was an Alabama mulatto and her mother was a dark Negro whose family owned land and deplored her marriage with "an over-the-creek nigger, and a bastard at that." Zora's was a sheltered childhood in the Negro town of Eatonville, Florida, her poverty brightened by reading and eager inquiry, but buffeted between her mother's encouragements and her father's dire predictions. "The white folks were not going to stand for it," she wrote; "I was going to be hung before I got grown. Somebody was going to blow me down for my sassy tongue."

Several in the group attended white elementary schools, and all but two were college-trained, most of them in Northern, white colleges. Hughes attended Lincoln, in those days still in the hands of whites, and Du Bois, who took an A.B. at Fisk, took another at Harvard before earning his A.M. and Ph.D. there. Zora Hurston finished her college training at Barnard, after beginning at Howard, and White and J. Weldon Johnson, both Atlanta graduates, took advanced work at New York City College and Columbia. Walrond was educated in Panama, and McKay, on a Jamaican Government trade scholarship, entered Tuskegee, but finding it uncongenial to his rebellious spirit, transferred to the University of Kansas.

A majority had their whole college training in leading white institutions. Sterling Brown followed a pattern traced by several colored notables. He had a superior preparation at Washington's Dunbar High, to which highly trained Negro teachers, reluctant to associate themselves with feeble colored colleges, were drawn. Promising Dunbar graduates annually received scholarships to Williams and Amherst. Brown was one of the Williams scholars and, after graduating with Phi Beta Kappa honors, he won the college's graduate scholarship to Harvard. Cullen, a New York University Phi Beta Kappa, had graduate training at Harvard also, and Jessie Fauset at Cornell. Angelina Grimké studied at superior Northern academies and Boston Normal

College, while Fisher won a battery of prizes and scholarships, a Phi Beta Kappa key, and A.B. and A.M. degrees at Brown.

Like most white authors, these folk relied for their livelihood on other vocations. Nearly half were teachers in high schools and colleges. Corrothers was a clergyman, Fisher a physician, Walrond and Schuyler, journalists. Georgia Douglas, a housewife, was for a time an official in the Department of Labor, a post given her by Republican administrations upon the death of her husband, the renowned politician, Henry Lincoln Johnson. Du Bois, J. Weldon Johnson and White were salaried NAACP officials, and Johnson also held a consular post in Latin America. Thurman, a brilliant bohemian, was a reader for a major New York publisher.

Four found in writing (with occasional lecturing) a major source of income. Braithwaite's literary efforts came close to supporting him, and Miss Hurston was eventually able to devote the bulk of her time to writing. McKay made a precarious living as a writer and editor when he was in America, and Hughes, in his mature years a genuine professional, earns an adequate living by his versatile pen. He began writing as a boy, worked at menial occupations, and after several years as a happy vagabond abroad returned to finish college at twenty-nine. The writers gratefully acknowledged that editors and publishers were an enlightened lot, and that much the same was true of the sort of people who bought poetry, novels and the "highbrow" magazines that carried their work: journals like the *Atlantic, Poetry* and *Story*. Sometimes they felt that the publishing industry was too reluctant to resist popular prejudices, but these misgivings were tempered by the sobering example of Chesnutt's commercial failure, despite vigorous promotional efforts of Walter Hines Page and the house of Houghton Mifflin.

Several benefited by encouragements of whites. A widely reported "plug" by Vachel Lindsay boosted the youthful Hughes, who was carrying trays at the Willard Hotel when the Springfield poet stopped in Washington. Others acknowledged help from literary folk that included Martha Foley, William Dean Howells, Frank Harris, I. A. Richards and Max Eastman. Many of the most successful in the group had reason to be grateful to the NAACP and the National Urban League, both for providing them with vehicles for publication and for sponsoring through the *Crisis* and *Opportunity* annual prize contests in the arts. They freely acknowledged a great debt to Du Bois and Charles S. Johnson, for their untiring efforts to discover and encourage young Negro writers.

Most of them were beneficiaries of the New Negro vogue and in some cases (Hughes and Hurston were examples) there were white "angels" in the background, helping them through college and subsidizing them directly for a while as promising young authors. Organized philanthropy also came forward, notably the Rosenwald Foundation and the John Simon Guggenheim Memorial Foundation. Guggenheim Fellows in the group included

Bontemps, Brown, Cullen, Hughes, Hurston, Larson, Walrond and White. Indeed, so favorable were opportunities, that several came to feel that the only serious surviving obstacle by the later 'twenties was the double standard of criticism.

Braithwaite's struggles at the opening of the century afford an instructive contrast to these later hospitalities. There were no fellowships available in those days and he had a wife and child to support when he burnt his bridges and embarked upon a literary career. When publishers offered to bring out his first book of verse only at his expense, he tramped the streets of Boston for months drumming up subscribers among the aging survivors of the New England reform tradition: people like Thomas Wentworth Higginson, Julia Ward Howe, Thomas Bailey Aldrich, Bliss Perry, Mark A. De Wolfe Howe and Edward Everett Hale. When the book was published in 1904, he delivered the volumes himself in a handbag.

Serious reception of Negro concert musicians began with this period and at the end of the era was still largely restricted to three vocal artists: Roland Hayes, Paul Robeson and Marian Anderson—soon to be followed by a fourth, Dorothy Maynor. A crude measure of their acceptance is afforded by the fact that by 1941 Robeson, Anderson and Maynor were among the ten most highly paid concert artists in America, while Hayes, then past fifty, was still near the top ten. All four are pronouncedly Negro in appearance and the fact that there was one for each of the four conventional vocal ranges elicited the observation that the country would accept only one in each category.

There were others who may be mentioned as first-rank concert-artist material, like Abbie Mitchell and Etta Moten (both of them notable also in the theater), Lillian Evanti, Jules Bledsoe and Harry Burleigh. Bledsoe appeared as a soloist with the Boston Symphony Orchestra, but—except for European tours and an occasional Town Hall or radio guest performance—he was submerged as a "Negro singer" in such vehicles as *Show Boat* and *Porgy and Bess*. He was by no means the untutored "born" singer of the stereotype, but a liberal arts college graduate with a professional degree from a leading conservatory and private study in Paris and Rome.

Harry Burleigh is honored as a trail blazer who, without attaining the concert stage himself, helped place Negro artists before white and mixed audiences—a genuine professional, earning a comfortable income from music. He was for over fifty years soloist at Saint George's Episcopal Church in New York City after winning the appointment in competition with a large, otherwise all-white, field of candidates—to the dismay of some of the parishioners and with the sturdy support of others, the elder J. P. Morgan among them. He served as an editor in a music publishing house and earned steady royalties from arrangements and compositions, nearly three hundred spirituals, anthems and secular songs in the light-classical idiom.

His grandfather was a runaway slave, and his mother had been born in a wagon as the family trekked northward to free territory. Reared in Pennsylvania, she became an educated woman, reduced upon the death of her husband to supporting her five children by working as a charwoman and laundress. Harry's talent was awakened by music he heard in homes of his mother's employers, one of whom arranged for his admission to the National Conservatory of Music and to fruitful association with Victor Herbert and Anton Dvorak, both of them on the conservatory's staff.

Lillian Evanti, again a product of social advantages and thorough training, was the fair-skinned daughter of Washington schoolteachers. She came up through childhood music lessons, church singing, a musical degree at Howard and professional operatic training in Europe to emerge—thirty years too soon—as a candidate for grand opera. She found roles abroad, but in America gave concerts mainly for Negro colleges, churches and fraternities, and was proud, despite disappointments, to serve the State Department as a cultural ambassador abroad in 1940.

Roland Hayes was the real pioneer. He was born in 1887, in Georgia, in a cabin which his father—an amiable, illiterate carpenter and craftsman of sorts—had built on an indifferently cultivated ten-acre patch. It was at an encampment of liberated slaves streaming out of Atlanta at the close of the War that he met and married Fannie Mann, who with her mother was en route to Chattanooga to celebrate their freedom by learning to read. The elder Hayes passed on to his son a fondness for song, but died when Roland was eleven. Another influence was the itinerant conductor of local singing groups, who lived with the Hayeses when he was in the neighborhood. Roland's maternal grandfather was a rebellious bondman who once hid out in the woods for eighteen months, subsisting on food smuggled to him by his friends, and Fannie, all her life a hard worker, was a pantry-maid in slavery. Even when she lived with her famous son in Boston she took in ironing.

Father Hayes' death impelled his widow to take her three boys to Chattanooga, where she took in washing and Roland found work in a sash-weight foundry. He had had only a few three-month sessions at school—where he disliked everything except the stories of Negro heroes—and after some years at the foundry, he returned, a strapping sixteen-year-old, to the fifth grade. He sang, inevitably, in his church choir and had some instruction from a local Negro, Oberlin-trained "Professor" Calhoun, who introduced him to a white Cincinnati music lover. The latter stoked his ambition with praise and by letting him hear his recordings of Caruso, Melba and other virtuosi of the period.

He entered Fisk's preparatory department on probation, supporting himself as a houseboy for the family of a white Fisk professor, where, again, phonograph records enriched his training. He did not learn until his fourth year at Fisk that a white woman teacher was paying his fees, and when she withdrew her support, evidently because he neglected his work in favor of the Jubilee singers, he was dropped. Soon thereafter, he boldly set out for Boston to try for a career. He combed the city for menial jobs and secured introductions to five voice teachers, all of whom warned him that no Negro could succeed as a concert artist, and only two of whom were willing to teach him. Eight years later, when he was his own manager, and had sung in Negro churches and schools across the country, he asked a Boston manager to take over his bookings. "Hayes," he said, "you know that I'm your friend. . . . You have got about as far as you can go."

Years of excellent training, an indomitable spirit and one of the finest voices in the world still required white benevolence like that supplied by Annie Cleaveland Bridgman, secretary in the Boston office of the American Missionary Association, who helped him secure engagements. Ready for his first full professional season, he sought in vain for a manager to launch him, so he sponsored a Boston debut himself. It proved a financial disaster and attracted almost no critical attention.

More determined than ever, he accumulated funds by self-managed tours of Negro churches in Southern cities and, rejecting the remonstrances of his teachers and friends, announced a concert at Boston Symphony Hall. This time there were excellent reviews and a cash balance, but he had not emerged from obscurity. More years of self-managed tours on the Negro circuit, punctuated by an occasional white-church recital, persuaded him that he needed another credential—a European tour. He sailed for London.

His search for hotel rooms found the color bar as rigid there as in New England, but his musical reception was hospitable and when, after triumphal tours and a performance at Buckingham Palace, he returned home in 1923, his greatly augmented reputation preceded him. He placed himself under professional management and entered upon a crowded annual schedule that included an extremely full American itinerary and some months abroad. Except in the South (where overtures from his manager once elicited a telegraphed reply, "Atlanta is not interested in niggers"), he sang for full, unsegregated houses, balancing his programs with Negro spirituals, classics and lieder. By the middle 'twenties he was all but universally recognized as one of the nation's foremost singers.

As he prospered financially, he included low-cost programs on his itinerary to enable the poor of both races to hear him—often at segregated concerts where local circumstances required, for he was not yet (as he and other Negro artists were to be later) under pressure from liberals to defy Jim Crow. He was keenly aware of his role as a Negro symbol, however; he repeatedly emphasized that he was a "pure black," and often found white audiences curious, skeptical and even hostile. Managers protected him from humiliations by making his reservations far in advance, but even so, unpleasantnesses arose, some of which led to criticism from Negroes who felt that he understated his grievances. When he reached an age when others retired, he felt he "must go on, for now more than ever the case for the Negro must be brought to the public; by the Congressman and the lawyer and the writer in their way, by me in mine." At seventy he was still making extended concert tours and recordings.

That international fame did not purchase exemption from outrage was made clear in 1942 when Hayes was struck by a policeman, hurled into a patrol wagon and taken to the city jail at Rome, Georgia. He was visiting at his six-hundred-acre estate (he had long ago bought the farm where his mother had been a slave), and on a hot afternoon went with his wife to shop in town. When she sat near the fan in a local shoestore instead of taking a "Negro place" at the rear, the clerk ordered her out, and Hayes, who had stepped across the street to the bank, hurried over to speak for her. The charge against him was later dropped, but he sold his Georgia property and never returned. Repeated injuries did not shake him, however, and long before the end of his career he saw many Negro concert artists advance to fame with little sense of strain through doors that his artistry, his perseverance and his confidence in the essential good will of his countrymen had opened for them.

Marian Anderson was the first. She had a happy childhood in reduced but respectable circumstances in Philadelphia, where she lived with her parents, a sister and her grandmother. Her mother, an ex-schoolteacher and her father, an unskilled worker, were pious, hard-working people, devoted to the Puritan-bourgeois values. Father Anderson died when Marian was very young, and his widow struggled to keep her household in dignity.

The church was the center of their lives, and it was there that Marian had her first experience as a child soloist and choir member. She was deeply stirred when she chanced to hear a Negro woman play a piano expertly. Her mother sent her to high school—still unusual in those days—and she began to be invited to sing in churches other than her own. When Roland Hayes first heard her in Philadelphia, he urged her grandmother to see that the girl was trained, and began recommending her for singing engagements. Before the fees came, her church took up a collection for a suitable dress, but soon she began picking up five-dollar fees for recitals before colored congregations and "socials." When she was still in high school, she was already making with her mother little tours of Southern colleges. On the first of these trips, when the pair were compelled to move to the Jim Crow car as the train reached Washington, Marian was overwhelmed with a sense of shame, her first experience with the tensions that threatened a young Negro artist's equilibrium and integrity.

She was singing "naturally," but soon recognized the need for training. A family acquaintance introduced her to a good Negro voice teacher—who refused to accept a fee—and, as her talent matured, she aspired to a music-school course. Screwing up her courage, she applied at a Philadelphia conservatory, only to be told bluntly: "We don't take colored."

She continued to sing at churches, appearing as early as 1916 in cantatas and oratorios with Roland Hayes. When an excellent teacher agreed to accept her for lessons, but at a fee she could not pay, her church again came to the rescue with a benefit concert (that included Hayes) which raised six hundred dollars. When the sum was exhausted, the teacher carried her for another year. Marian enlarged her circle of church and college concerts in the South, with occasional appearances at neighborhood theaters and now and then a house with a sprinkling of whites. Then, emboldened by her rising prospects, she tried a Town Hall appearance in 1925. Her performance before the tiny audience was a failure, and the reviewers candidly said so. She decided to give up, but her spirit revived when she was invited to sing at the NAACP's Spingarn Award dinner honoring Roland Hayes, and her victory at a major competition in New York City brought her both an appearance with the New York Philharmonic Orchestra and an upturn in her fortunes. She was soon singing for three-figure fees and came under the management of Arthur Judson. The agency found it difficult to book her, however, and she was urged to acquire a European reputation.

Earlier trips to Europe, with the help of Rosenwald funds for study and experience, were followed by a two-year stay in 1933–1935 with full bookings. Not much money remained in the end, but two immensely fortunate accidents befell her: in Paris she met Sol Hurok—her manager ever since; and at Salzburg, Toscanini's extravagant praise of her voice brought her extraordinary notice. By 1936 she was one of the nation's foremost concert artists, like Hayes constructing her programs of spirituals, classical arias and lieder, and appearing in the principal concert halls of America and Europe. The color line kept her from the major circuits in the South, but when the Daughters of the American Revolution denied her the use of Constitution Hall in Washington, Secretary of the Interior Ickes and other officials (at the instance of Charles Houston, who sold the idea to under-secretary Oscar Chapman) arranged an Easter Sunday morning recital at the Lincoln Memorial that assembled a huge audience. The Constitution Hall snub stirred millions of white Americans, including leading concert performers who pointedly cancelled appearances at the Hall, and Mrs. Roosevelt, who withdrew her DAR membership. Miss Anderson subsequently made several concert appearances at the hall.

A dark, stately woman of quiet dignity, she had an excellent press and became one of the most beloved of all Negro Americans. Hurok's staff took great pains to insulate her from humiliation on tour, and she made a point of taking her meals in her rooms. She became the first Negro to sing at the Metropolitan Opera, and though this came too late to alter her career, it quickly brought similar roles to younger Negroes. In 1957 she toured the Orient as America's "good-will ambassador," and high lights of the tour were presented over a widely admired television documentary program by Edward R. Murrow.

Her earlier audiences were all-Negro, but later she was heard primarily by white or unsegregated groups, and eventually she declined to sing at all before houses where segregation was enforced. The decision cut out many potential engagements, but did not exclude her from the South, for she sang occasionally before mixed audiences in college, church and town auditoriums in scattered Southern cities. When her city gave her the ten-thousand-dollar Bok Award, annually given to the year's most distinguished Philadelphian, she established a scholarship that has enabled several young Negroes to secure musical training.

More honored even than Miss Anderson was Paul Robeson, until the middle 'forties, when his racial militancy and leftist affinities cost him the bulk of his following in both races. His father was a fugitive slave, who worked his way through Lincoln University and became pastor of a church in Princeton, New Jersey. He married the college-trained daughter of a proud Indian-Quaker-Negro family who had lived in Philadelphia for generations. One ancestor served in the Continental Army, another had been a cofounder of the Free African Society in 1787, and others of the clan were teachers, artisans and otherwise distinguished from the mass.

Paul was the youngest of several children in the Robeson parsonage, and though his mother perished in a fire when he was very young, her strong religious convictions, intellectual and humanitarian interests, and vigorous character vividly stamped her children, complementing the sturdy heritage passed on to them by their father. The children attended segregated schools, unmindful of the discrimination, but were occasionally stung by the slurs of Princeton students, and chafed at the absence of a high school for Negroes. The older boys left home for secondary schooling, but when the family moved to Somerville, New Jersey, a mixed high school was available to Paul. He made an excellent record there, working meanwhile with his father's Sunday school as superintendent and leading the singing with his robust, untutored voice.

He won a competitive state scholarship to Rutgers and became the third Negro to be admitted to the university. His singing was not impressive enough to gain him a place on the glee club, but his performance on the football team (though he was repeatedly "slugged" by opposing teams, who singled him out) won him "All-American" honors. This, plus four varsity athletic letters, in addition to junior-year election to Phi Beta Kappa and a dazzling record in oratorical competitions, brought him unstinted praise.

At Columbia University Law School his formidable reputation as athlete and scholar, his personal warmth and his gifts as a mixer insured friendly acceptance by the great majority of his classmates. A proud, sensitive young man, accustomed to adulation, and showing a strain of indolence, he took his law degree with honors but declined flattering opportunities to gain a foothold in the profession. Earlier successes in the theater stirred an ambition to make a career on the stage, but because opportunities were few, white liberals and bohemians—this was the day of the Harlem Renaissance—who had helped him make a beginning in the theater pressed him to try singing. The Provincetown Players, with whom he had worked in O'Neill plays, organized a concert for him at the Greenwich Village Theater in 1925, with energetic promotional assistance from Carl Van Vechten, Heywood Broun and the NAACP's Walter White; and when the reviews proved favorable, a second concert was staged.

Now came a critical step: he found a professional manager. Later artists found this easy, but predecessors and contemporaries of Hayes, Anderson and Robeson failed at this juncture. After an appearance in London with *Emperor Jones,* his reputation enhanced by the European experience, he embarked upon his first American tour with Hayes's former accompanist, Lawrence Brown. A conspicuous failure in Boston, where he went on stage with a heavy cold, almost killed his career, but still pressed by admirers, he intensified his efforts and in 1928 was again in London for the role of "Jim" in *Show Boat*. He was so warmly applauded that he decided to make his home in England.

Much of the next decade he spent abroad as an actor (notably in *Othello*) and a baritone, spaced by American tours that brought him immense popularity despite (and in some quarters *because*) of his militant race attitudes. He was aware that his serious acceptance in America had waited upon a European imprimatur and he chafed also under the strong expectation of audiences—in Europe as well as America—that he concentrate upon "Negro music": spirituals and such hardy perennials as "Old Man River" and "Water Boy." It was thirteen years after he first played Othello in London that his first opportunity came to play the role in New York, but by the middle 'thirties, disillusioned by what seemed the no less real, if more sophisticated, color prejudice in England and on the Continent, he returned to the United States. However, he sent his son to school in Switzerland and the Soviet Union.

The precipitous collapse of his fame belongs to a later chapter, but it may be noted here that even so gifted, proud and indignant a man as Robeson felt constrained to accept parts in American motion pictures that brought strident criticism from some Negroes and white intellectuals offended by his willingness to be cast in "Uncle Tom" roles. These dissenters were few, however, and the nation acclaimed him as a fabulous sucess, his comparative lack of training more than counterpoised by his big, resonant voice, his moral intensity, his magnificent, dark and smiling physical presence, and his fine sense of theater.

Other gifted musicians were so deeply hidden in the enclave that they can hardly be called famous. Even Marian Anderson was not really a heroine to her own people until her reputation in white America was established, and she was not accepted by whites until she had been acclaimed in Europe. Only shortly before she became a national celebrity, a fraternal organization, thinking to promote cultural advance in Harlem, sponsored her at Carnegie Hall, but spirited publicity brought only a tiny sale of tickets, at a time when she needed all the help she could get.

Even so, at least seven more musicians may well be cited. John Work, a collector, arranger and choral director, noted for his success with the Jubilee Singers, was a major mover in establishing the reputation of Negro spirituals as an art form. Descended from upper-class free Negroes, he was a college graduate, and for a while professor of Latin and history at Fisk. Hall Johnson is also identified with the spirituals idiom. He came to prominence as musical director in *The Green Pastures* and *Run Little Chillun,* and for his choral group's association with the motion-picture industry. His father, an AME pastor and college president, was freeborn, but his mother and grandmother were slaves, and it was their remarkable knowledge of slave music that laid the foundation for his career. He began piano lessons as a child in Athens, Georgia, but his efforts to enter a music conservatory in Philadelphia were repulsed, so he studied at the University of Pennsylvania. Carl Diton had a limited success as a concert pianist but, like Nathanael Dett, another pianist, made his more important contribution in the composition and arrangement of both non-racial anthems and Negro spirituals. Both earned their livelihood as musical directors at Negro colleges, both were Northern-born, and both had liberal-arts degrees from leading Northern colleges and professional training at foremost conservatories.

William L. Dawson (a cousin of the Illinois Congressman of the same name) and William Grant Still, easily the best-known Negro composers of symphonic music, are important figures in the vanguard. Dawson, until 1955 the director of music at Tuskegee, won serious notice as an American composer when his *Negro Folk Symphony No. 1* was performed by the Philadelphia Symphony Orchestra under Stokowski at Carnegie Hall in 1934. On both sides of his family his forebears were Deep South slave folk, with the usual history of family dispersions and a strain of Caucasian ancestry. His father never learned to read, but his mother and an uncle were college-bred.

He was born in 1898 in Anniston, Alabama, a small city where industries and a larger Northern-born population than was common to Alabama towns offered a wider range of opportunities for Negroes than was ordinary. William's resolve for higher education brought strong opposition from his father, whose faith in a Negro boy's capacity to profit from such instruction was as weak as his need for the lad's wages was strong, for William was the oldest of seven children.

But one Sunday morning while his father was at church, the lad made the break and caught an early train for Tuskegee. He had less than two dollars when he reached the Institute, but Booker Washington, who rarely turned away a boy whom he saw was in earnest, enrolled him as a special agricultural student, to work on the school farms by day and attend classes by night until he had earned enough to become a day student. There came a day when he was made office boy for the school's bandmaster and given general oversight of the instruments. With virtually no instruction he learned to play them all, and the bent of his life was determined.

When he took a teaching job at Kansas City, the Horner Institute of Fine Arts permitted him to enroll for a limited program as an irregular student. Then, taking a leave of absence, he went to Chicago and entered both a municipal junior college and the American Conservatory of Music. While carrying this double program he made his living by playing at a dance hall, directing a Negro church choir, and playing the trombone as the only Negro member of the Chicago Civic Orchestra. Returning to Kansas City, he completed the course at Horner, graduating with honors but not permitted to sit on the platform with his white classmates when the governor of the state distributed the diplomas, or to acknowledge the spirited applause that followed the Kansas City Symphony's performance of the composition for which he had been awarded a prize in Chicago. Sitting beside him in the audience, speechless with amazement, was Roy Wilkins, then a young Kansas City journalist.

When his *Folk Symphony* had its Southern premiere in Birmingham, Alabama, with the Birmingham Orchestra, the composer, with the prior consent of the municipal authorities, was permitted to sit in the all-white audience. The orchestra had in fact asked the city fathers to permit Dawson to conduct the performance, and after an initial flat refusal they relented far enough to approve on condition that a separate platform be built immediately in front of the stage so that Dawson could conduct without physically sharing the stage with the white orchestra. The musicians declined, of course, to subject Dawson to the humiliation.

In the summer of 1956, he was sent to Spain by the United States Department of State to conduct Spanish choral groups in the singing of American Negro spirituals on the occasion of the four hundredth anniversary of the death of Ignatius Loyola. Dawson sometimes admitted that Negro artists expended so much energy and anxiety upon The Problem and its daily attritions that the creative urge—quite apart from the struggle to secure a hearing—was all too frequently stifled, but he was never embittered or disposed to abandon his fundamental optimism about the prospects of the Negro American.

While Dawson made his living as director of the Tuskegee Singers, William Grant Still was a professional composer for motion pictures and radio networks. Still was born in Mississippi in 1894 of Indian-Spanish-Irish-Scottish-Negro stock. His slave ancestors had been house servants and his parents were schoolteachers. His father had been an amateur musician, his stepfather had a library of classical phonograph records, and his mother engaged a violin teacher for the boy, so he was surrounded by good books, music and upperclass Negro folk from the beginning. Hoping to make a lawyer or doctor of their son, they sent him to Wilberforce, but his preoccupation with music kept him from graduating. He became a drifter until he came into a small inheritance on his twenty-first birthday, and then entered Oberlin Conservatory. His achievements there soon won him scholarships and admission to the New England Conservatory, and subsequent commissions as an arranger for Broadway productions, W. C. Handy's music publishing firm, Paul Whiteman and radio and motion-picture firms.

Two Guggenheim Fellowships freed him for more intensive creative effort and he began writing operas, symphonies and short works, some of them highly abstract and some (like his *Pages From Negro History, African American Symphony* and *Fanfare for the 99th Squadron*) pointedly racial. Sympathetic whites helped him with scholarships, fellowships and free tuition at crucial points in his career, and courageously put his music before the public; he became, indeed, more intimately associated, socially and professionally, with whites than with Negroes, and he married a white woman. He made his home in Los Angeles, and though he could not purchase a home in precisely the neighborhood of his choice, his social situation as an associate of the film industry was comfortable. It was on the road that he was poignantly reminded of The Problem. When he drove with his family to Ohio to receive an honorary doctorate at Oberlin, they were refused sleeping and restaurant accommodations en route and had to buy materials for sandwiches in grocery stores.

Though Still's operas, requiring all-Negro casts, were steadily rejected by producers, his symphonic compositions have been performed by America's foremost orchestras, and he became the first Negro to lead a major symphonic organization when he was guest conductor for the Los Angeles Symphony Orchestra in the Hollywood Bowl in 1936. Like Dawson, he expresses optimism over the Negro American's prospects and strong appreciation of the progress he has seen in his lifetime.

While a few composers won limited notice, instrumental artists were virtually ignored. The tardier success of instrumentalists is variously ascribed to the country's preference for singers of spirituals, to the cost of instruments and long tutelage, and to the lack of opportunity for gaining experience with orchestras (vocalists had their church choirs). The road to vocal virtuosity, arduous enough, was simply shorter and less costly than that for a violinist or pianist. Marian Anderson sang almost as well at twenty as she did at forty-five.

Clarence Cameron White's reputation as a violinist was solid enough to place him for several years in *Who's Who in America,* but he emerged a generation too early to attain the status he deserved in musical America at large. He derived from the same light-skinned, long-free folk at Fayetteville, North Carolina, from which his distant cousin, Charles W. Chesnutt, sprang. His parents, both Oberlin graduates, were professional folk—his mother a teacher and his father a physician—and when the latter died, his widow married another physician, a medical examiner for the Pension Office in Washington, where the family went to live when Clarence was ten. He went to a segregated school with no feeling of discrimination, and public conveyances, concert halls and theaters were then still unsegregated.

He entered Oberlin with a view to a violinist's career, and though he was the only Negro there until he was joined, in his senior year, by Nathanael Dett, no one presumed to discourage him. He was giving recitals at Negro churches before he finished Oberlin Conservatory. He next went to Boston for advanced private instruction, paying his way with the twenty-five-dollar fees from still more church and college concerts in the South and West.

A musical scholarship from a group of women's clubs sent him to London for a year of study, and funds for a second year were supplied by advance payments from his old church and college clients whom he promised concerts upon his return. Back in Boston, he lacked pupils until an aging white violinist turned over to him several of his white students, a bonanza that quickly stimulated colored enrollment as well. He kept up his concert tours —still mainly at Negro colleges, churches and clubs—during many years of teaching, including periods as director of music for Negro colleges and for the National Recreation Association's program at scattered Negro recreation centers. A Rosenwald grant took him abroad to write (with Professor John Matheus) a Haitian opera, and some of his livelihood came from royalties for his arrangements of spirituals.

It was in the thirty-five years reviewed in this chapter that jazz and its affiliates arose from small beginnings to a conspicuous place in American culture. Here was one field in which the Negro's pre-eminence was acknowledged and where, far from aping the white man, he was himself the model who was copied. But because evaluations by enthusiasts vary hopelessly, both as to what "real" jazz is and as to who have been its chief makers, selection of the leading names in jazz and popular music is so hazardous that one can only post his list and run for cover. Millions of Americans even deny that it is worthy of consideration as an area of significant achievement, and would insist that no jazzmen have a place on a roster of distinguished Negroes. Others make extravagant claims for the importance of jazz as a modern art form; and still others, who dislike it, grant that it is the one innovation that America has contributed to the world's musical heritage.

All that can be ventured here is a conscientious listing of names I found most prominently mentioned* in book-length histories, periodicals devoted to popular music, the general Negro press, and a recent, carefully edited *Encyclopedia of Jazz*. Beyond reporting that a panel of "experts" cited in the *Encyclopedia* designated Duke Ellington, Louis Armstrong, Lester Young, Count Basie (all of whom emerged before 1936) and Charles Parker as the greatest of them all, I shrink from arranging our group of fifty-four in any order except the alphabetical.

The Negro's uncontested rise in "light music" is sometimes—by uneasy whites, eager to believe that he is a happy childlike creature equally given to exuberance in this life and buoyant expectations for the next—explained by a presumed incapacity for intellectual and moral maturity which directs his "instincts" into emotion and sentimentality, primitive impulses and unabashed animalism, and hence into jigging ragtime, work ballads, blues, spirituals, booming gospel hymns and the abandoned spontaneities of jazz.

White America's Puritan proclivities, moreover, made it still easier for whites to give place to Negroes in the early days of a musical idiom that had about it the odor of the dance hall, the boozy, smoke-filled cabaret and the sporting house; and then the very exclusion of Negroes from many other segments of American life operated to attract a disproportionate number into this area where there was some expectation of success. Born and cradled in the bordellos of New Orleans and rendered nearly homeless through the purging of that port city by a cold-water Secretary of the Navy, the dispersion of the jazzmen northward and westward ushered in a new era in the history of the art at precisely the time of the "New Negro" Movement and of the roaring 'twenties: the Jazz Age, with its thrill-bent, frenzied search for the exotic, the bizarre, the pandemonious and the perverse.

Important was also the growing number of serious white devotees, a

* Louis Armstrong
William "Count" Basie
Sidney Bechet
Eubie Blake
Buddy Bolden
Thomas "Mutt" Carey
Johnny Dodds
Warren "Baby" Dodds
Edward K. "Duke" Ellington
James R. Europe
George "Pops" Foster
Adelaide Hall
W. C. Handy
Jimmy Harrison
Coleman Hawkins
Fletcher Henderson
Bertha "Chippie" Hill
Jack "Jay C" Higginbotham
Earl "Fatha" Hines
Tony Jackson
"Blind Lemon" Jefferson
James P. Johnson
Lonnie Johnson
William "Bunk" Johnson
Scott Joplin
Freddie Keppard
Andy Kirk
Huddie "Leadbelly" Ledbetter
Jimmie Lunceford
William Mckinney
James "Bubber" Miley
The Mills Brothers
Ferdinand "Jelly Roll" Morton
Jimmie Noone
Joseph "King" Oliver
Edward "Kid" Ory
Alphonse Picou
"Ma" Rainey
Andy Razaf
Don Redman
Noble Sissle
Bessie Smith
Clara Smith
Mamie Smith
Clarence "Pinetop" Smith
Johnny St. Cyr
Art Tatum
Thomas "Fats" Waller
Ethel Waters
William "Chick" Webb
Clarence Williams
Spencer Williams
Teddy Wilson
Jimmy Yancey

happy company recruited from every social level, from sober-sided intellectuals and esthetes to very ordinary folk surprised to find themselves sharing an enthusiasm with the long-hairs and the gentry. Here were people whose relish for the product rendered them indifferent to race—or perhaps they were an emancipated, bohemian sort to begin with.

Especially in the 'twenties did colored entertainers move into the big Northern cities, concentrating in the theaters and night spots of the black belts, which drew a clientele from both races, but appearing also in downtown theaters, where colored patrons were either excluded or segregated, or in ballrooms, cabarets, niteries, dinner clubs and bordellos catering to whites.

We cannot trace here the sinuosities of jazz history, or apportion individual laurels, measure the rival claims of ragtime and blues, swing and boogie-woogie, bebop and rock'n'roll, hot and cool jazz, or determine whether "sweet" music or the big commercial bands qualify for honors. We only record the names the written record thrusts forward and take note of the uniformities and disparities that mark the diverse company. Some have long been among the best-known Negroes in the world; others achieved fame only among zealots, often after their "discovery" by specialists who unearthed half-forgotten recordings when their makers had long since fallen back into obscurity or died. Some were rich and others never escaped poverty or even sought an income from jazz. Some were unknown to whites until the legends and recordings that lived after them elevated them to the sainthood. It was, as Max Lerner has said, a sacerdotal cult, with its saints and devils, Old Believers and Modernists, reprobate and regenerate, orthodox and schismatic. Its essential spontaneity and improvisation thwarts documentation of its past, minimizes the composer and arranger and, except as recordings illumine the obscurities, throws the student back upon the witness of old-timers. Inevitably, myths clustered about the patristics, fostered sometimes—one thinks of Jelly Roll Morton and Bunk Johnson—by the testimony of the participants themselves.

Negro performers were not, of course, exempt from Jim Crow. They were segregated in separate unions, but appeared before white and mixed audiences in the North and sometimes, if the races were clearly separated, in the South. They played white dances in both sections; but only rarely in the North and never in the South did mixed bands or Negro soloists with white bands perform for either race. Even in the 1940's Artie Shaw, for example, cancelled his Southern engagements because he could not take "Hot Lips" Page, his trumpet virtuoso with him. Colored musicians encountered the color bar in hotels and restaurants all over the country and, whether bandleaders, vocalists or instrumentalists, they found it prudent to leave bookings and business affairs to white agents and managers.

They were a remarkably cohesive group, frequently joining forces or learning from each other. The links between the old New Orleans pioneers were intricately forged, and the same kinship later characterized the rising generation in Chicago, Kansas City, St. Louis, Memphis and Harlem. When white jazz burgeoned on the other side of the color line, the Negro jazzmen bred an *esprit de corps* that accentuated differences, and only later would musicians associate so freely that the difference in style would evaporate.

The origins of New Orleans jazz are variously traced to Creole influence, march music, quadrilles and Negro funeral processions, but spirituals and work songs are also brought into the line of descent, and it is the brothels of the wide-open Storyville of the 1890's that are emphasized. By that time a New Orleans ordinance confined the roaring trade in Eve's flesh to that area, and there it remained until a nervous Navy Department ruled otherwise.

Brown's Dixieland Jass [*sic!*] Band had early established itself in Chicago (union officials were worried about its name, lifted, they understood, from the argot of pornography), and while jazz moved to Chicago, Jim Europe, who had led a regimental band in France, returned to New York and promoted the vogue of colored musicians playing syncopated dance music for whites. The 'twenties saw a remarkable growth of the market for "race records," and the early 'thirties brought both a rising number of "name bands" into the big ballrooms of Chicago and New York and the first successful European tours by Armstrong (1932) and Ellington (1933) followed by Cab Calloway and Coleman Hawkins. In 1932 came "swing music," and by 1936 name bands, small combos and individual performers had multiplied, and the subsidiary vogue of boogiewoogie had appeared. By then the cult had also begun to proliferate a literature, distinguished by the establishment of the magazine *Downbeat* in 1934, increased notice of jazz in the older *Metronome,* and the publication of the first sober, book-length historical and critical treatments.

At least twenty of the fifty-four were born in the Delta (sixteen in New Orleans alone), eleven in other corners of the Deep South, eight in the border South, and only twelve were native Northerners. Several in the Delta group were Negro-Creoles who felt superior to common blacks and mulattoes. Many were children or grandchildren of slaves who had pushed the slave heritage into the background. Sissle's parents, for example, were former slaves, who had established a respectable household in their Indianapolis parsonage; Waller's father was pastor of a huge Harlem church and Ellington was the son of a blueprint technician for the Navy shipyards, a member of the rising Negro middle class in Washington. Henderson came from Southern bourgeois folk who sent their sons to college; and Webb's childhood in a close-knit, proud Baltimore family, dominated by his forceful mother and grandmother, afforded insulation against other handicaps. They were extremely poor, and Webb was burdened all his life (he died at thirty-two of tuberculosis) with a deformed little body plagued with pain and fever, but he became a brilliant band leader and a drummer of incredible vitality. The frail cripple was peddling papers at nine, saving his money for a set of drums. In his early teens he was already earning twelve dollars on Saturday nights with his drums.

Most of the group were born to poverty, many in irregular family groups. Candid testimony on the ambiguous consanguinities of Morton's clan are in the tapes made for the Library of Congress by that loquacious piano-thumper. Louis Armstrong had at least six "stepfathers" in his cruelly squalid New Orleans boyhood, and Ethel Waters, born the illegitimate child of a black girl in Pennsylvania, grew up in a brutalizing milieu of prostitution, thieving, dope-addiction and violence. Others were literally raised in brothels and many more owed their first instruction to the stews and dives that offered them opportunity.

From the evidence in hand, there is simply no accounting for the flowering of the talents of most of these musicians. Some showed a precocity that can only be explained by inborn talent, and some were born into "musical families." Jim Europe grew up in a family of amateur instrumentalists; Bechet had a talented brother and Johnny St. Cyr's father was an expert flutist. James P. Johnson's mother was skilled in "hot piano" and Redman, a trumpeter at three, had a father who played in a brass band and a mother with a local reputation as a contralto. Ma Rainey was the daughter of touring minstrels. Both of Hines's parents were musicians and Count Basie had his first music lessons from his pianist mother.

While these could build early upon such advantages, others, less fortunate, had to look elsewhere for opportunity. The fabled Armstrong acknowledges a debt to his church and Sunday school, where he "did a whole lot of singing," but owed even more to a "Professor" Davis who, he says, taught him to "blow cornet" at the New Orleans Colored Waifs' Home for Boys, to which the young Satchmo had been dispatched after a New Year's Eve fracas when he was thirteen. Nearly all began at a very early age to master some instrument, frequently a banjo or guitar fashioned from a cheesebox, or a drum made from a tin can or a barrel. Several, while children, listened to the early inventors of the idiom in marching bands, funerals and bistros, and others were lucky enough to have access to several instruments at home. Handy, inspired by the accompanist for a church choir, yearned for a trumpet, but decided to content himself with a cheap guitar, purchased with the pennies left over from his earnings as janitor for a white church after the major portion was surrendered to his parents. His hopes were dashed, however, when his preacher-father ordered him to return so worldly an instrument, and then revived somewhat when he was given lessons in playing hymns on the reed organ.

A good proportion picked up informal instruction from maturer performers who recognized their gifts and ambition. A "natural" like Armstrong was well advanced upon his career before he read music easily, and Spencer Williams, one of the most prolific of blues composers, never had a lesson in his life. His aunt, the madame of a Storyville sporting house, looked after her orphaned nephew and let him practice on the establishment's piano. At the other extreme, Waller and Blake had extensive professional training and Henderson and Lunceford had college degrees as well as substantial musical educations. Lunceford, like Andy Kirk, studied under the father of Paul Whiteman, and Redman completed studies at the Boston and Detroit Conservatories.

Sissle enjoyed competent coaching in the choir of a Cleveland public high school where he was one of the few Negroes enrolled, and even more important was the experience in his father's choir. Like so many before and after him, he credited much of his musical start to the church choirs that afforded opportunity to sing with unashamed fervor. He also received free music lessons from a Negro singer who had a studio in Cleveland. Ellington began desultory piano lessons at seven, but it was when he was in high school that he resumed private instruction with a view to a pianist's career.

Entrance into the profession was by numerous bypaths. Armstrong, after driving a coal cart and playing small engagements in New Orleans, worked the river boats, while Basie was an organ accompanist for silent movies. Baby Dodds was another who played New Orleans night spots and the river boats. Ellington, out of high school in 1917, dropped in at "rent parties" (where guests, bidden and unbidden, paid for drinks to help the host pay his rent) to study the style of colored jazz pianists. Occasionally he played the piano himself, developing a reputation that emboldened him to get up a little band. A musical catering service, which he advertised in the telephone book, prospered, and two years later he was commanding substantial fees at white parties. At the suggestion of Waller he shifted to Harlem.

Henderson worked as a "song demonstrator" for Black Swan Records; Hawkins and Miley began by touring with the earthy Mamie Smith; Morton, Oliver and Jackson started at New Orleans brothels; and Bessie Smith was a trouper with Ma Rainey's Rabbit Foot Minstrels, carnivals and tent shows until a Columbia agent heard her in an obscure club and decided to make a recording artist of her. Tatum had a radio program in Toledo in his early days and Pinetop Smith was a young pianist, comedian and tap dancer for vaudeville and Negro night clubs in Pittsburgh. Bunk Johnson toured with minstrels and played with Bolden in and around New Orleans at fairs, picnics and gin mills. Ma Rainey herself got her start on a road show with a man she married at fifteen; then followed years in minstrels, levee camps and tent shows for the Theater Owners Booking Association, a Negro vaudeville circuit.

Some performers clowned and pandered to the uninitiate to win favor, but many showed an artistic integrity surprisingly indifferent to the lure of commercial rewards. Beginning about 1921, recordings became an increasingly important outlet. Perhaps the brisk business in "race records" for Negro buyers is to be set down to burgeoning radio and movie industries that made no concession to Negro tastes. Even though reproducing techniques were still woefully primitive—high fidelity was still in the future—enough of the music came through to satisfy buyers of the discs, and even now these early platters still find a steady market. Still, many of the foremost personalities in jazz derived a very scant income from their art. Though some Negro jazz musicians by the mid-'thirties were competing successfully with top-ranking whites, more of our group never broke out of "small-time" clubs, cabarets, niteries, rent parties, medicine shows and the well-worn Negro theater and vaudeville circuit.

Recordings brought Ma Rainey belated notice, and her protégée, Bessie Smith—like others in the Rainey blues tradition: Clara, Mamie, Trixie and Laura Smith, Ida Cox and Chippie Hill—had a limited face-to-face audience. Bessie's chronic financial distress stemmed in part from her dissolute habits, but another factor was her steadfast artistic fidelity. Despite her big, warm, honest voice, her earthy art was too direct for the "respectables" of both races, and her vast following was always concentrated in the Negro rural South and the urban ghettos. When Columbia launched her recordings, her popularity among these folk was instant, and in five years her sales climbed to ten million. Her deepening addiction to alcohol and a collapse in the record business during the Depression hastened a decline already under way, and by 1933 she was singing pornographic songs for drinks and tips in a wretched little Philadelphia gin mill.

Other jazz "greats" earned their living as waiters, day laborers, porters and dock hands. Bolden was a barber; St. Cyr repeatedly left music to resume his trade as a plasterer; the Dodds brothers drove taxicabs in lean years, and Ory dropped out of music to become a chicken farmer. Yancey left when he was twenty-four to become—with only an occasional musical appearance thereafter—a groundskeeper in a Chicago baseball park. Carey worked for over twenty years as a Pullman porter and mail carrier but came back to music in the 'forties. Chippie Hill sank into obscure poverty for fifteen years until, like Bunk Johnson (who had returned in the early 'thirties to labor in the Louisiana rice fields), she was "rediscovered" by devotees and briefly restored as a performing artist. Even the gasconading Morton was relegated to a third-rate night club in Washington. But to dwell overlong on these hardships is to obscure the commanding position that Negroes were winning in the popular arts. Many were achieving renown—destined to be augmented in the next generation—that was to make them some of the most famous Negroes in America and, indeed, some of the most famous Americans in the world.

The day when Negroes would be regular entertainers at first-rank hotels, restaurants, night clubs and in radio was still in the future. Networks occasionally aired Negro bands like Noble Sissle's from hotels where they played extended engagements, but it was not until 1937 that the first contract directly between a network and a Negro artist for a sustained run was concluded, when Armstrong was engaged for a thirteen-week series. Leading Negro bands were now appearing in big Northern ballrooms, but only at the end of the period did they begin playing white college proms in the South. As late as 1939, when Basie made a six-week run at Chicago's College Inn, the event was startling news in the Negro press.

At the end of this era the musicians also began making European tours, sometimes for extended stays. Sissle for several years spent more time abroad than in America and Adelaide Hall tarried in Europe for years on end, but only rarely did even the most warmly applauded Negro performers elect, like Bechet and Spencer Williams, to cast their lot permanently in Europe. Josephine Baker became a French citizen and an articulate, if waspish, critic of American racial practices, but her popularity among Negroes was diminished by the racial discrimination she herself manifested in selecting a succession of white husbands.

More often musicians declared that their European experiences convinced them that the deference paid them sprang from fascination with the strange and exotic—or from pharisaical anti-Americanism—rather than from sincere equalitarianism. Ellington's pioneering tour in 1933 met ugly barriers. The Duke's personal fame opened London's finest facilities to him, but his men were compelled to hunt up such rooming and dining facilities as they could find in the shabbiest quarters of the city. Worse difficulties were encountered on the Continent. Six years later, however, Ellington's second grand tour noticed marked improvement, particularly in France, Holland and Scandinavia.

The attitudes of a few of the period's popular musicians to the realities of racial bias are in the record, and they suggest that these men did not in early youth suffer keenly from the sense of racial proscription. It was in maturity, when their encounters with whites multiplied and when they achieved some celebrity, that the double standard began to plague them as they saw whites of lesser attainments win greater rewards, or when, after an all-night performance for wildly cheering whites, they packed up their instruments and made their way in a gray dawn back to the squalor of the ghetto.

Perhaps the comparative absence of angry racial militants in this as in so many other categories of "successful Negroes" is to be explained by the hypothesis that their achievement and their surface acquiescence were cause and effect in both directions. Some insisted that the loss of this composure would stifle their creativity and the opportunity to make their contribution to racial justice through their art. Only later could some of the most eminent join the struggle directly by declining segregated engagements, when they could trade upon the strong demand for their talents.

Handy, born in poverty in rural Alabama in 1873, was hardly aware of

The Problem until as a youth he heard a candidate for governor shouting abuse upon the race. In later years it was the economic exploitation that colored musicians suffered from white publishers that moved him to join Harry Pace in establishing a Negro music-publishing house and the Black Swan Recording Company. Handy lived until 1958, extravagantly honored by the American people, and always effusively loyal to America. He insisted that Jim Crowism had been far less an obstacle to his youthful musical aspirations than were his own folk, who looked upon show people as social outcasts. Morton was another whose chief obstacle was the resistance of his kinfolk, and he more than justified their apprehensions, for he became in early youth the pianist at a Storyville house of prostitution.

Jelly Roll Morton, as a Creole, constructed his life around his denial of his Negro status, according to Alan Lomax. He rarely played a colored engagement, and at his peak, when colored establishments could not meet his price, he imagined that his white patrons were conceding to him the social superiority over blacks which he claimed. In the end Morton became, like many of the other great innovators, the victim of a new commercial spirit that operated to squeeze out the inspired Negro jazzman in the 'thirties. The reorganization of jazz as a big business was already discernible in the 'twenties, but in the 'thirties the newer tendencies were accelerated, and there was less hospitality for the "inspired and careless talent" of the "pure" performers, and a growing commercial demand for "efficient music machines."

Ellington's childhood in segregated Washington was a comfortable one, spiced by the usual fights between white and colored boys not animated by serious racial rancors. It was when his band moved up to Harlem that the color line grew sharp, but then rather than dissipate their creative impulses in hatred and futile heroics, they moved to fatalistic acceptance of race differences, absorbing also the neo-Africanism and race pride that marked the "Harlem Renaissance" of those years.

Sissle was hardly aware of discrimination in his Indianapolis boyhood. When the family moved to Cleveland they settled in a melting-pot section with only a small scattering of Negroes. In high school he was one of a half dozen colored students. One of his teachers was a daughter of Charles Chesnutt, and the principal was a liberal reared in the Abolitionist tradition. In his maturer years, Sissle retained his optimistic view of race relations. His long career began before the First World War (when, in uniform, he was once beaten by toughs determined to put him in his place), but in 1952 he was still prominent enough to be invited to lead his band at the first Eisenhower Inaugural Ball.

Armstrong's candid autobiography, carrying Satchmo's story to his arrival in Chicago, shows him quite unscarred. He met outrage and absurdity now with good-natured resignation, now with pungent disparagement, now with waggish sally, but never with craven surrender.

There were many durable masters of the art, but a surprising number were early casualties of the frenetic pace, the hard night driving in private bus and automobile (in preference to Jim Crow trains), from one engagement to another, the late hours and the boozy revelries. This was, of course, not peculiar to the colored jazzmen. (The epic dissipations that killed Bix Biederbecke at twenty-eight are a case in point.) Some died violently, some suffered protracted disintegration, others quietly collapsed at the peak of their careers. Before he was forty, Jim Europe was stabbed to death by one of his drummers at the conclusion of a concert at Symphony Hall, Boston. Pinetop Smith, not yet twenty-five, was killed by a stray bullet at a dance in Chicago's Masonic Hall. Chippie Hill and Bessie Smith met death in automobile smash-ups. Bessie bled to death from a nearly severed arm, presumably because of the delay in medical aid. She had been rushed to the nearest hospital but refused entrance because of her color, and then died en route to the Jim Crow ward of another.

Some of the pioneers like King Oliver and Bunk Johnson lived to old age, but were virtually incapacitated when still young because of physical deterioration. Bolden left no recordings of his mighty trumpet blasts, because, before the day of jazz recordings, his career was over at twenty-eight when a brain infection sent him to a state mental hospital for the rest of his days. Henderson was incapacitated by a stroke at fifty-two, and Lunceford died of a heart attack, on tour, at forty-five. Waller died at thirty-nine of heart failure and drink, while James P. Johnson was silenced by a stroke before he was fifty. Shattered health brought death to Morton and to Ma Rainey in their fifties; to Johnny Dodds, Keppard, Jackson, Noone and Jefferson in their forties. Harrison died of ulcers at thirty-one, Webb of tuberculosis at thirty-two and Miley was dead at twenty-nine.

Negro stage shows were, in 1900, still confined to minstrels (patterned, ironically, upon earlier buffooneries by white comedians in burnt cork) and to a few Negro musical comedies where the staples were still the shuffling "darky" and the "coon song" full of razors, chickens and watermelons. The famous Williams and Walker team was billed significantly as "Two *Real* Coons," and when Walker died, Williams became the star for "Mr. Lode of Koal."

About 1900 Ernest Hogan, a singer-actor-composer-producer, was remaking the silly end man into a more credible harlequin, while the most notable of the musical-comedy composers were Bob Cole, J. Rosamund Johnson and Will Marion Cook, all of them men of great talent improved by extensive training. They often collaborated, sometimes with the further aid of Paul Laurence Dunbar or of Johnson's brother, James Weldon Johnson. Cole's *A Trip to Coonville* broke sharply with the old minstrel tradition, and with Rosamund Johnson he later found a brief commercial acceptance. Johnson had been born in an upper-class Negro family in Florida and studied at the New England Conservatory, supporting himself as a piano teacher and church choirmaster.

Cook came from a free-Negro background. His mother was an Oberlin graduate and his father secretary and acting dean of law at Howard as well as a practicing attorney in Washington. Will was born in the family home on the Howard campus, and when his father died, Mrs. Cook taught sewing in the university. She sent the boy to the Oberlin preparatory school and, after a year at the Conservatory there, Will received funds for professional training in Germany, from the members of an unsegregated Washington church who arranged a benefit program. Cook himself was later noted for encouraging young Negroes of promise.

After studying with the renowned German violinist, Joachim, he settled in New York. He quickly learned that America was not ready for a Negro concert violinist, so he turned to popular "Negro music," convinced that the Negro artist should preserve his racial identity. His first success, *Clorindy,* for which Dunbar wrote the lyrics, appeared in 1898, and twenty years later he took his band to Europe and helped to create the vogue for Negro music there.

Bert Williams and George Walker were the chief Negro vaudeville fixtures, widely known to whites. Indeed, colored entertainers were dependent upon white acceptance, for there were virtually no Negro theaters, no experienced managers, nor even an adequate Negro audience. They played for whites, in white theaters, under white management, except that in the South they played the Negro circuits of such agencies as the Theater Owners' Booking Association.

Walker, a very black, dapper man with a row of gleaming teeth, was a perfect foil for the great Williams. In his prime, Williams achieved large financial success during ten years with the Ziegfeld Follies, but when he died at forty-six, one of America's favorite stage personalities, he had not realized his ambition to "interpret the real Negro on the stage." The antithesis of the buffoons he was obliged to portray, he was born in the Bahamas, the grandson of the white Danish consul at Antigua and his quadroon wife. Their son and another quadroon were Bert's parents. He migrated to California and, too poor to enter Stanford University, drifted into theater. He was a tall, handsome, scholarly man of refined speech, and looked like a swarthy white. He always performed in blackface, and spoke on stage the so-called "darky dialect" that he mastered by close study. One can only guess his thoughts when the country applauded him for his "realistic" portrayals by "simply being himself."

The 'twenties brought a brisk vogue of all-Negro reviews like *Shuffle Along, Chocolate Dandies* and the annual *Blackbirds* shows, which provided roles for (among others) Florence Mills, Ethel Waters, Josephine Baker and Bill Robinson. All of these derived from humble origins. The elflike Mills, whose singing and dancing electrified New York, had been a child prodigy in

Washington. She toured the shabby Negro vaudeville circuit and advanced, by way of Harlem cabarets, to Broadway and extended engagements in London and Paris and a dazzling eminence in the entertainment world before her early and widely lamented death. Josephine Baker was the daughter of a St. Louis washerwoman. A childhood of bitter poverty followed by hard years as a waitress and a hoofer in the chorus line in dingy honky-tonks preceded her appearance in Harlem theaters and cabarets and her association with *Shuffle Along*. Thereafter, her magnificent carnality, piquant song and brazen strut carried her to still greater triumphs in the *Folies Bergères* in Paris.

Bill Robinson came out of poverty and squalor in Richmond, where his mother was a church-choir singer and where as a child he was the despair of the ex-slave grandmother who reared him. Incorrigible at school, he ran off when he was only eight to hang around a race track near Washington, and soon found himself employed as a juvenile dancer at five dollars a week in a road show. He was past thirty before a manager rescued him from the tank towns and cheap amusement halls, and turned him into a "single." In time he was booked in New York houses at three thousand dollars a week and made several motion pictures. He was a simple-minded man, easily imposed upon, and though he is said to have earned three million, died in debt.

Ethel Waters made her first disastrous marriage at thirteen. At seventeen, when she filled in for a singing bump-and-grind act at a party in a Philadelphia saloon, she was offered a ten-dollar-a-week spot with a Negro vaudeville troupe touring the South. Accommodations were so difficult to secure that the group put up in stables and brothels. Upon her return to Harlem she resumed her work as a chambermaid, interrupted by road tours, before her eventual success on the stage. Her first important role in *Mamba's Daughters* moved several leading theater people in New York to place a large advertisement in the *New York Times* over their signatures, praising her performance as a "magnificent example of great acting."

Abbie Mitchell was born a generation too soon to achieve the kind of recognition that a colored vocal and dramatic artist of her talents could realistically aspire to a generation later. Her people were Baltimore folk, freed well before the Emancipation. Orphaned at an early age, she was sent to live with an aunt in New York, and at twelve had already had stage experience with a Negro review. At thirteen she was a member of Will Marion Cook's road troupe, and a year later she was his wife.

She toured the white vaudeville circuit in the North and West, appearing usually in theaters with mixed audiences. She was able to secure good hotel accommodations, but took her meals in her room. In 1905–1907 she toured Europe by herself, appearing with European orchestras, singing operatic arias and classical songs. Europe gave her also the opportunity to study under competent teachers, and when she returned home she abandoned vaudeville and years later appeared in concerts and Negro shows such as *Porgy and Bess* and

In Abraham's Bosom, as well as other Broadway productions with stars like Tallulah Bankhead and Helen Hayes. On Broadway she cheerfully accepted parts as a maid, for she was, she declared, "not built for anything else." She felt that a colored actor should accept any part that he could do well, so long as it called for creative talent, and argued that doctrinaire opposition to unflattering stereotypes would only exclude the Negro from the theater altogether. Succeeding years brought her radio network engagements, but the widening opportunity for colored actors on the stage and later on television passed her by because she was too fair to be plausible as a Negro.

Meanwhile, several factors enlarged the opportunities for colored entertainers—among them the maturing of motion pictures, Harlem's Lafayette Players, a little-theater movement and the appearance of Negro plays by white writers, like Connelly's *The Green Pastures,* Heyward's *Porgy and Bess,* Green's *In Abraham's Bosom* and O'Neill's *All God's Chillun Got Wings* and *Emperor Jones.* At the end of the era another important impetus came from the Federal Theater Project.

Developments such as these opened a few doors for Negroes, but the movie roles were confined to bit parts as domestics, witless comics, Orientals, or other exotics. The stage roles were, if more plausible than those in earlier productions, still racially tailored. The public's understandable predilection for regarding a Negro in a "non-Negro" role as unrealistic and distracting, the lack of suitable Negro parts and the unavailability of professional training and experience stifled development of a very considerable number of Negro dramatic stars.

Stepin Fetchit (Lincoln Perry), whose bumbling gait, head-scratching, eye-rolling bewilderment and drooping dialect convulsed millions of whites, became the most popular colored motion-picture personality in the country, to the distress of proud Negroes who were outraged by his clowning, however vigorously some Negroes applauded his commercial success and his undeniable comic gifts. A race-track habitué as a boy, jailed for larceny as a young man, he became a vaudeville bit actor, billed as "Rastus the Buck Dancer." He was earning one hundred dollars a week on the road when Metro-Goldwyn-Mayer picked him for a comic Negro role in *In Old Kentucky,* and before his eclipse he had earned and squandered more than a million dollars.

Hattie McDaniel and Louise Beavers, neither of whom ever had a dramatic lesson, appeared in hundreds of films as maids or mammies. Miss McDaniel was drawn into dramatics by her brother—she joined him in his traveling tent show when she was thirteen—and by a prize she won in a declamation contest sponsored by the Woman's Christian Temperance Union. She appeared in more than three hundred films before she died in 1952. For her mammy role in *Gone with the Wind* (1939) she won an "Oscar" from the Academy of Motion Picture Arts and Sciences, and she later starred in the *Beulah* show as a handkerchief-headed character, on radio and television. Miss Beavers also had an endless succession of maid and mammy roles, and now and then the part of a prisoner or a vagrant, and drew strong commendation from critics for her part in *Imitation of Life*.

Ethel Waters eventually achieved real eminence in show business, but it had been a long, hard road, and not until the end of this period did she find truly satisfactory roles. Meanwhile, an Etta Moten, a handsome, light-skinned cultivated woman, never attained the position for which her gifts equipped her. A talented singer and actress, her very refinements were obstacles to her success, because she deviated too widely from the stereotype of the artless, simple black. Her career was largely restricted to concerts for Negro groups and the role of Bess in a *Porgy and Bess* revival, with only an occasional chance at a dignified part in the movies or in radio. She was a well-educated daughter of a clergyman, never exposed to the brutalizing struggle with poverty and squalor that was the portion of so many Negro entertainers.

Fredi Washington was another actress whose gifts increased her hardships. She had toured with *Shuffle Along* for three years and worked as a night-club entertainer in New York and Europe, but after many years of bit parts in Hollywood she accepted the fact that dignified roles were as yet not forthcoming, and left the film capital to become a drama editor. Rose McLendon was yet another of the actresses who found only a limited opportunity despite genuine talent and solid training by Franklin Sargent of the American Academy of Dramatic Art.

The best-known male actors were Charles Gilpin, Paul Robeson, Richard B. Harrison and Leigh Whipper. Gilpin, born in the South in 1878, was the son of a day laborer and a trained nurse. He worked in the printing trade while playing brief song-and-dance engagements in restaurants, variety theaters, county fairs, vaudeville and minstrels. In 1903 he began a slow rise that brought him, by 1916, the directorship of Harlem's Lafayette Theater company. His first Broadway part was that of a Negro clergyman in Drinkwater's *Abraham Lincoln* (1919), and his most important role was the lead in a four-year run of O'Neill's *Emperor Jones*.

In 1924 the Provincetown Players pushed Robeson into the leading role in O'Neill's *All God's Chillun Got Wings,* a story with an intermarriage theme. The play evoked a storm, and established Robeson's dramatic reputation. An essentially untrained actor, but equipped with intelligence, excellent university training, a magnificent physique, an emphatically Negro face and a superb voice, he was a "natural" for roles like Othello and Emperor Jones. Still, his major successes came in Europe. He declared early in the 1930's that he found it necessary to go to England to find out if he could act, because in America many of his countrymen who were not hostile to Negroes injured them by according first-class applause to a third-rate performance out of sentimentality or indignation, or even out of surprise at finding a Negro capable of anything above buck-and-wing dancing. After a few years abroad, however, he told American reporters in 1935 that he had grown weary in England of being "Mr. Robeson, every hour of every day," and tired of being successful *because* he was a Negro, tired of sham hospitality that did not even extend to his family. "My own father," he protested, "my own brother cannot go where I go. They cannot come in behind me." In American movies, Mr. Robeson had the usual cruel choice: to play along with the stereotype or make no movies at all. Like most Negroes before the middle 1930's, he sadly concluded that the former offered a more promising road to eventual acceptance than did the latter.

Richard B. Harrison, without Robeson's advantages, fought all his life for a place on the stage, but in the end all his perseverance counted for far less than did the accident of the publication of Marc Connelley's *The Green Pastures*. He was born in Canada of parents who had fled there from slavery. As a youth, persuaded that the Negro had a better future in the United States, he went to Detroit to work as a waiter and porter. He haunted the gallery seats at stage productions and, with the assistance of his railway employer and other interested whites, secured some professional dramatic instruction. He later declared that he was challenged to his career by the efforts of Negro friends to dissuade him. He worked up a repertory of Shakespearean scenes and miscellaneous readings, but no booking agency would take him. While working as a dining-car porter and railway mail clerk, he tried without success to arrange recital tours until a lyceum bureau booked him as a dramatic reader for Negro groups and Chautauqua.

There followed years on the road as he trained dramatic groups in Negro churches and schools and kept steadfastly to his classical readings. Harrison's Shakespearean scenes, in which he took all the parts, once moved an astonished Hammerstein to suggest that he spend a year in Mexico and return to the States as a Mexican so that Hammerstein might cast him in a Shakespearean role. Finally the summons to play the Lawd in *The Green Pastures* called him from his summer school of dramatics at North Carolina A. & T. College. His first appearance on the legitimate stage came when he was past sixty-five, and from that time until his death he was famous. But reminders of the handicap persisted. When the National Theater set aside a "Special Night" during the play's run in Washington, so that Negroes might see the all-Negro play, Harrison was rebuked for "capitulating." The Negro Elks, who sponsored the event, pointed out that refusal to countenance segregated houses only denied to the race the opportunity to see its most distinguished artists; and, they added, every Negro who delights a white audience undermines prejudice. The cast encountered during its immensely popular five-year run, on Broadway and on tour, the usual discrimination in hotels, restaurants and public carriers. In the last year of Harrison's life, his fame at its zenith, the company sometimes—as far north as Madison, Wisconsin—sat up through the night in railway stations.

Leigh Whipper was another who struggled against the mixed feelings of Negroes concerning roles that tended to reinforce disparaging clichés. He was a brilliant character actor in a long list of stage, movie and radio dramas, usually as a Negro or other non-white type. His background was one of advantages that few Negroes could match. Born of upper-class Negro folk in Charleston, South Carolina, he was the son of William J. Whipper, a lawyer who had gone to South Carolina after the Civil War and had become a legislator and judge. Leigh Whipper himself was graduated cum laude from Howard University.

Earlier pioneers in the fine arts had worked in liberal white environments, isolated from their race; they were artists primarily—though severely imitative—and Negroes incidentally. By the late 1890's, however, they were forced increasingly, by the fact of race, into "academic cosmopolitanism" or into equally conservative, sentimentalized portrayal of racial types. Then in the 1920's, this conservatism provided the race-proud generation a rallying point for rebellion.

In the ghetto, where the sense of beauty was blunted by squalid struggle for survival, there was no market for Negro art, and confusion as to what was expected of the Negro artist compounded his dilemma. Racial subjects, before 1920, were virtually tabooed by potential white patrons; and yet the Negro artist, thus diverted from themes he knew best, was censured for imitation and for stifling honest self-expression. Besides, feelings of inferiority rendered Negroes half ashamed to treat Negro subjects, or, if they treated them at all, they did so with apology or false sophistication.

For the years 1900–1936, sixteen artists stand out in the record: painters such as Henry O. Tanner, Aaron Douglas, William E. Scott, Archibald Motley, Edward A. Harleston, Palmer O. Hayden, Laura Wheeler Waring, James L. Wells, Malvin C. Johnson and Hale Woodruff; and sculptors like Richmond Barthé (also a painter), Meta Warrick (Fuller), May Howard Jackson, Sargent Johnson, Elizabeth Prophet and Augusta Savage.

Two thirds of these were Northern-born; the rest came North in early youth. All made their reputations in the North, usually in Harlem. Although they showed childhood precocity, not one was an untutored "primitive"; all were professionally trained—often in Europe—and all were aided, in one way or another, by benevolent persons eager to document the Negro's capacity for artistic achievement. They were people of brown or lighter complexion, somewhat further removed from the slavery past and higher in the socioeconomic scale than the average of their contemporaries. Tanner, for example, much the most famous of them, was the son of the eminent Bishop Benjamin Tucker Tanner. Douglas's father was a baker and Harleston's a funeral director. Meta Warrick was the child of Philadelphians in good circumstances. Some, to be sure, came from very poor homes. Augusta Savage was one of fourteen children in a needy family, but even she had the advantage of growing up in a parsonage. Malvin Johnson's boyhood in Greensboro, North Carolina, was singularly barren of advantages. Scott's irregular ancestry included whites, Indians and free Negroes who had come up from North Carolina to Indianapolis by oxcart before the War. Woodruff descended from Alabama slaves whose blood was mixed with white and Indian strains. His father, a semi-literate farmer and free-lance musician, died in Hale's childhood, and his mother was a lifelong domestic. Several of these born in the North grew up in communities where Negroes were still so rare that no considerable hostility against them had yet accumulated.

Tanner, with the help of his father and two other bishops, was trained under Thomas Eakins at the Pennsylvania Academy of Fine Arts, where Laura Wheeler later had her instruction and where Miss Jackson also spent four years on a generous scholarship. Scott was one of the first Negroes enrolled at the Chicago Art Institute. As the only Negro there he received more attention than his classmates, and, besides paying his way by sweeping floors, he earned three thousand dollars in prizes and commissions.

As a boy in New Orleans, Barthé had to leave school at fourteen, but was encouraged in his art by the white family he served as butler, and by the art editor of a New Orleans daily who tried in vain to persuade the paper to run a story about the Negro boy's talents. Finally, a Catholic priest, unable to secure the youth's admission to a local art school, solicited funds to send him to Chicago. There he studied at the Art Institute for several years, supporting himself as a waiter in a downtown restaurant. Like Scott, he found that being a Negro brought him more, rather than less, attention from artists and collectors.

Motley, while studying privately in Chicago, labored as a dining-car waiter, steamfitter and coal heaver, and Woodruff made his way through a private art school in Indianapolis by his own and his mother's hard labor, encouraged by the example of Scott. Douglas studied art at the University of Nebraska before working with Weinold Reiss, Harleston at the Boston Museum, Sargent Johnson at the California School of Fine Arts and Miss Prophet at the Rhode Island School of Design. Miss Savage broke out of the rural South when her exhibit at a county fair brought from interested spectators funds that enabled her to go to New York. There, with the help of scholarships, she completed the art course at Cooper Union.

More than half of the fifteen had higher training in Europe, assisted usually by scholarships and private gifts. Most of them found their professional progress advanced by prizes in the yearly contests for writers and artists conducted with help from white benefactors by the Urban League's *Opportunity* and the NAACP's *Crisis*. Some were helped by Harmon and Spingarn Awards (both directed by white philanthropists), and seven received either Rosenwald or Guggenheim Fellowships, or both, and in some cases more than one of each.

Some of those who went abroad elected to stay there. Tanner and the 1929 Harmon Award winner, William H. Johnson, settled permanently in Europe and married white women. Woodruff considered staying, but found the economic squeeze too uncomfortable; while Miss Jackson maintained a semi-permanent studio in Paris. Barthé established his residence in Jamaica. When Tanner went over in 1891, with funds earned in teaching and photography, the struggle for a livelihood in France was grim, and without help from some wealthy Americans he might not have been able to hold out. Years later, Scott, his pupil, found the move easier, thanks to the prize money from his Chicago days, eked out by working as Tanner's assistant, and as a commercial artist on visits back home. He had three stays abroad before he settled down in America. Meta Warrick's private resources were adequate, but she had great difficulty finding lodgings available to colored girls in Paris.

Augusta Savage won a scholarship to Fontainebleau, but the committee of American artists who allocated the scholarships for the French Government cancelled it when they discovered her race for fear that a Negro among scores of white American Fellows might cause friction. The action brought protests in the American press and offers of free instruction from white sculptors. W. E. B. Du Bois induced the Royal Academy in Rome to award her a scholarship, but, despite an offer of help from the Baptist Young People's Union, she lacked sufficient funds for the trip. Eventually the Urban League secured for her a Rosenwald grant for two years abroad.

Woodruff's four years in France were made possible in part by assistance from Otto Kahn, through the mediation of the NAACP's Walter White. When Woodruff returned to this country to teach at Morehouse, the move to Atlanta (he had never lived in the South) proved a massive shock. Laura Wheeler, also a Harmon Award winner, spent two years at a Paris academy on scholarships. Hayden was a houseboy for a Park Avenue woman. She was thunderstruck when she learned that he had won the Harmon Award for 1926, and soon sent him to Paris at a cost to her of more than five times the prize he had won. When Elizabeth Prophet, still another Harmon winner (1930), submitted some work for a Providence show, she was asked not to appear at the showing. Outraged, she went to Paris for study and to open a studio there.

Tanner, Scott and Barthé were full-time professionals, but others earned their living on college faculties, and still others kept up their art as an avocation. Their commissions included both racial and non-racial subjects, for both white and colored patrons. Barthé had sufficient notice from an exhibit sponsored (with encouragement from a Chicago lawyer) by the Chicago Women's Club to win commissions for several portrait busts. Douglas executed murals for Negro colleges, and now and then for white institutions, as did Scott.

Douglas also did illustrations for Negro and general magazines and books, and Meta Warrick's chief works were Negro busts for individuals and for colored YMCA's, colleges and hospitals. Her most ambitious work was a group of Negro figures for the Jamestown tri-centennial exhibit. When she returned from Paris, she had great difficulty finding patrons, not so much because she was a Negro but because she was not a European. Tanner was the most extensively exhibited, and Negroes never tire of pointing out that some of his works, usually Biblical scenes, were purchased by European governments, and hang in distinguished galleries on the Continent.

Some of these artists who are still living assured the writer that by 1936 genuinely talented Negroes could no longer plead that they were excluded from the creative arts. Like white artists they were usually obliged to work at something else for bread and butter, but they had come to feel that they were more fortunate than most other colored Americans because first-rate art was recognized for what it was, regardless of race, and because a Negro artist could find expression and full recognition in a field that was not essentially competitive and where the folk associated with it were singularly free of bias and ill will.

Fourteen of this generation's vanguard were from the realm of science and medicine, but only one, George Washington Carver, was widely known beyond the ghetto, and even his reputation in the scientific community fell far short of his stature as a Negro curiosity. It is conceivable, of course, that some might well, but for the color bar, have achieved more, and so become really celebrated Americans by non-racial standards.

The leading white American scientists of 1900–1936 were men associated with big university and industrial laboratories, and trained principally (about 1880–1920) in the country's best graduate departments and technological institutes in the Northeast. Studies have shown, moreover, that they were drawn from upper-class families with a tradition of scholarship nourished in the nation's finest colleges. These specifications were not, manifestly, met by Negroes in these years. The ablest Negro scientists were, furthermore, isolated from the scientific environment in impecunious undergraduate colored colleges, or even in high schools, where serious research was virtually unthinkable.

In the special case of medicine, the exclusions were no less inexorable. By 1900 there were only half a dozen Negro medical schools, all of them sub-standard and soon only Howard and Meharry remained. The financially insecure Negro students worked their way during the school year and in the summer as waiters, porters, redcaps and bellhops. When they finished a course administered with inadequate staff and equipment, they found internships and residencies in shabby little hospitals. Paths to specialties were blocked; even the rare student lucky enough to be admitted to a large hospital for postgraduate training found patients averse to the presence of Negroes, even as mere observers. The young practitioner found his clientele confined to the poorest and most superstitious patients in the land, if indeed he could win them away at all from white doctors, whose superior training and general air of competence commanded the Negro's preference. Exclusion from the local medical association and the fellowship of white colleagues completed the isolation and compelled the race's doctors to found their own National Medical Association, with meetings and a journal of its own.

Some physicians on our list owed their prominence to unusual circumstances. Numa P. G. Adams, for example, was noted chiefly as the first colored dean of the Howard Medical School; and Midian O. Bousfield as an outstanding Chicago civic leader, insurance executive, and officer in fraternal circles, the Urban League and the National Red Cross. U. G. Dailey was a genuinely distinguished surgeon, however, at Chicago's inter-racial Provident Hospital, and a Fellow of both the American and the International College of Surgeons. In New York, Peter Marshall Murray was—and remains—a recognized specialist in gynecology, and became the first Negro member of the House of Delegates of the American Medical Association, as well as president of the non-segregated but preponderately white New York County Medical Association. Louis T. Wright was best known as a crusader for Negro medical rights for doctors, nurses and patients, and a chairman of the board of the NAACP, but he was also for many years the dominant figure at Harlem Hospital, the author of important monographs and an authority on several surgical procedures.

Daniel Hale Williams was the most famous surgeon on our roster. A very important pioneer in radical heart surgery, he was also conspicuous in the establishment of Provident Hospital, the country's first inter-racial hospital for the better training and employment of colored doctors and nurses. He subsequently withdrew from Provident because of differences with associates, and became the only Negro on the staff at St. Luke's, Chicago. He was elected in 1913 as the first colored Fellow of the American College of Surgeons; years later, Louis Wright was the second.

Every one of the seven doctors was of Caucasoid appearance, and all came from better than average backgrounds. Adams was a graduate of Rush, an outstanding medical school, and Bousfield and Dailey were trained at Northwestern, where Bousfield worked his way as a barber after learning the trade in his father's shop. Murray alone secured his medical degree at a Negro school. He was born in New Orleans of ex-slave ancestry, and went to a school of the Methodist Freedmen's Aid Society. It was at his mother's urging that he went into medicine, and it was by her efforts that he was, he says, "washed through college" in New Orleans. At Howard Medical school he was helped by federal employment and by summer work as a dining-car waiter. He was prompted to establish a practice in New York because Harlem offered a better opportunity than did the South for his wife's pursuit of professional musical interests.

Williams, born in Pennsylvania, the sixth child of a free colored woman and a white man, was on his own at the age of twelve in Janesville, Wisconsin, where he was employed in a Negro's barbershop for whites. There the milk-white Negro boy caught the fancy of an ex-Surgeon General of Grant's staff, who took him into his office, tutored him and arranged for his admission to the Chicago Medical College, and an internship at Mercy Hospital. Such extraordinary advantages account for his rise; they may have accounted also for the difficulties that bedevilled him. His inability to work with others, Negro or white, may have been, as some suggest, the consequence of being trapped between two cultures and rejected in both. He never had the kind of practical training that other colored youths picked up in Negro schools, churches, lodges and social groups, the "folk schools in which [Negroes] learned to obey rules and manage men." He was in his later years a bitter man, criticized for his withdrawal from Provident Hospital and his marriage with a white woman, and accused of "resigning" from the race.

Wright's career was also the product of fortuitous circumstances. A man of "refined" features and light skin, he was born into an upper-class family in Atlanta where his mother was a schoolteacher and his stepfather a physician. After taking a bachelor's degree at a Negro college in Atlanta, he went to Harvard Medical School, finishing fourth in a class of a hundred—an achievement which did not suffice, even in Abolitionist Boston, to admit him to any of the city's hospitals as an intern, so he went to Freedman's Hospital in Washington.

The most applauded scientist was Carver. Negro schools, lodges, clubs, banks and insurance companies were named for him; a postage stamp was issued in his honor. Here, in fact, was a genuine national hero, a legend in his own lifetime. But no white scientist with precisely the same achievements would have been called a "wizard" or "the greatest industrial chemist in the world." Despite his productions from peanuts, sweet potatoes and pecans in fifty years at Tuskegee, he was chiefly a symbol, and particularly acceptable to whites. He never published a single paper in a standard professional journal in his life.

Far less adulation came to a "scientist's scientist" like Professor Ernest E. Just, once elected vice-president of the American Zoölogical Society. He made his whole career at Howard, where, despite extensive help from reduced teaching chores and foundation grants, he labored under disabilities with respect to equipment and "research atmosphere." He published two impressive books and over sixty scientific papers, and participated in scholarly meetings of regional, national and international professional associations, but never permitted himself to be drawn into impassioned "race-work," preferring to work off his frustrations in his laboratory and at the Woods Hole

Marine Biological Laboratories in the summers. Once, as he returned from research in Europe, a shipmate asked if he had a position in Washington. "No," he replied; "only a profession." Foreign scientists were adroitly fended off by his distraught wife, to avoid the humiliation of entertaining them in the ghetto. When famous visitors called at Howard, he had to be content—sometimes taking Kelly Miller or Alain Locke along—to go to the Union Station for a cup of coffee, for not even in a nearby ten-cent store could such groups stand at a counter to be served.

Charles H. Turner ground out an incredible stream of papers for biological journals. Never more than a high-school teacher, he published nineteen papers in the brief span from 1917 to 1921 and a total of fifty articles for professional journals in his career. Thomas W. Turner was another competent biologist held down by duties as a department head at Hampton; and Elmer Imes, an authority on spectroscopy, was similarly isolated at Fisk.

Two scientists made careers outside the colored milieu. Julian Lewis, after taking a Ph.D. and an M.D. at the University of Chicago, was placed on the faculty there, but eventually became a professional pathologist, serving hospitals in Chicago, and the author of *The Biology of the Negro*. William A. Hinton, a Harvard Medical School graduate, was for many years on the Harvard faculty, but he was best known for his work as a syphilologist and as director of the laboratory of the Boston Dispensary, and chief of the Wasserman Laboratory of the Massachusetts Department of Health. Patients who had occasion to call at his office, obviously annoyed at being received by a Negro, would sometimes insist upon being taken directly to Dr. Hinton.

All of our seven scientists profited from some early partiality. Carver was born a slave—as an infant he was traded for a horse—but a few years after the Emancipation he moved to Kansas with the Negro family who employed him, and there he was welcomed into a small white sectarian college, where he ran a little student laundry of his own. A classmate's father helped him enroll and secure a job as janitor at Iowa State College, and there his warmly interested instructors, including two future Secretaries of Agriculture, afforded major stimulation. Though barred from the school's dining hall, he was elected class poet. Confirmed in his conciliatory attitudes, he never became an active opponent of the color line during fifty years at Tuskegee, despite repeated insults from whites, both in Tuskegee, where he was expelled from public parks when he wandered in to look at the flowers, and in New York, where he was barred from a hotel when he was in the city to make a network broadcast.

Just came from upper-class colored folk of Charleston. Light brown himself, he went to a fine New England academy, working during the summers at ocean resorts, and then to Dartmouth, where again he worked his way, and lived in the dormitories without prejudice, graduating with Phi Beta Kappa honors. From Dartmouth he went directly to Howard, where he remained all his life except for a leave to earn the Ph.D. degree at the University of Chicago. Imes, C. H. Turner and T. W. Turner took Ph.D.'s at Michigan, Chicago and Cornell, respectively; Lewis and Hinton, as we have seen, took doctorates at Chicago and Harvard.

Lewis had been born in downstate Illinois, where his parents, Berea College graduates, were public-school teachers. The elder Lewis had been born in slavery, but, as the son of a white man, enjoyed a comfortable slave childhood. By the time Julian was ready for college, Negroes were excluded from Berea by state law, and his parents sent him to the University of Illinois. After a segregated but frictionless boyhood, Julian was unprepared for the coolness that he and the twelve other Negro Illinois students encountered in Champaign-Urbana. Anticipating increased enrollment of Chicago Negroes, the university officials were also growing nervous and, when Lewis was elected captain of his ROTC company, Dean Clark transferred him to a hastily contrived ceremonial office in the corps to prevent possible trouble. Sometimes the science club, of which he was a member, failed to inform him of meetings because they were to be social affairs, but no other overt campus discriminations came to his attention during his four years at Illinois. At the University of Chicago, however, he was freely elected to social and honorary groups, and after his formal education, his professional progress was accelerated by a Guggenheim Fellowship.

Frequently honored by Negroes as a scientist was Matthew Henson. Born to light-skinned parents, he was reared in Washington, and went through the seventh grade. After several years as a cabin boy in the China trade, he found a job as stock boy in a Washington haberdashery, where a chance meeting with Commodore Robert E. Peary led to his employment as Peary's orderly and companion. Negro America thrilled at the news that Henson stood at the North Pole with Peary in the spectacular dash of 1909. Pressure upon Congress later brought him a messenger's job in the New York Customs house and, in 1945, a belated medal for "outstanding service to the Government of the United States in the field of science."

It was almost impossible for Negroes to gain a foothold in the legal profession in the years when this generation was maturing, for colored clients preferred to take their chances in court with white men as their advocates. In the South, where seven eighths of the country's colored folk were still concentrated at the turn of the century, only Howard University's Law School afforded respectable training, and in the North the social and economic obstacles to securing a law degree were still formidable. As late as the 1930's, moreover, it was still possible for a brilliant young Negro law graduate to find no opening waiting for him. Indeed, by 1936 there was still only one Negro attorney for every ten thousand Negroes in the country while there was one white lawyer for every seven hundred whites. In Mississippi there was one Negro lawyer for every 168,286 Negroes, and one white lawyer for 804 whites.

It is hardly surprising, then, that we find only five lawyers prominently noticed in the historical record. Four were in Washington, all of them men of relatively light complexion: Perry Howard and James A. Cobb, in the capital's leading Negro law firm, which often argued civil-rights cases before the Supreme Court; Charles H. Houston, vice dean of the Howard Law School, and legal counsel for the NAACP; and William H. Hart, also of the Howard staff, former United States District Attorney, and architect of a notable victory against Jim Crow in the Maryland courts. The fifth was Scipio A. Jones, public officeholder and lodge official of Little Rock, noteworthy especially for his defense before the Supreme Court of the United States of the victims of disturbances at Elaine, Arkansas, precipitated by sharecropper peonage there. He won fame also for legal battles against the convict lease system and against efforts at legal disfranchisement of Arkansas Negroes.

We have already noted Perry Howard's atypical background. Cobb's was no less unusual. Born in 1876, he was the son of a white Louisiana lawyer and landowner. His ex-slave mother became a servant at her former owners' boardinghouse, and sent James to a plantation school where he was the only Negro. She was a woman of great integrity, keenly ambitious for her son. She sent him through the secondary course at Straight University, New Orleans, where all his instructors were whites, one of whom, a woman, made extraordinary efforts to help him toward a professional career. From Straight he went to Fisk and then to Howard Law School, earning his fees as a Pullman porter and in other summer employment. As a young man he worked so earnestly for Roosevelt's renomination in 1904 that the Colonel rewarded him with the municipal judgeship of the District, and until he died in 1958, two warmly inscribed photographs of Roosevelt ornamented Cobb's office walls.

Hart, after his pre-Civil War Alabama childhood, became the secretary of Senator Evarts of New York, and Jones was invited to read law in a white attorney's office after he had impressed the partners by his audacious, if unsuccessful, effort to enter the state law school in Arkansas. After admission to the bar, he made a foothold in the profession as court-appointed counsel for indigent defendants. Houston's rise was rapid, for he was the son of a prominent lawyer, public official and Howard Law professor, and one of the group of bright young Washington Negroes who went to Amherst. There he made Phi Beta Kappa honors, before going to Harvard Law School, where he was an editor of the *Law Review,* took two law degrees, and was awarded a travelling fellowship for study abroad—a record substantially duplicated by his cousin and future law partner. William H. Hastie, today the highest-ranking Negro on the federal bench. Once admitted to the bar, Houston immediately found a place on his father's law firm and built a reputation as a Negro-rights lawyer. It was Houston who was the real author of the NAACP strategy which was elaborated with meticulous care until it produced the 1954 school decision.

In business and industry, it was only in the separate economy that a few Negroes attained leadership. Not only were they excluded by caste barriers and by want of experience from desirable positions in the general economy; even in the heart of the ghetto—whether in Detroit or the rural South, in Harlem or Atlanta—the bulk of the Negro market was in the hands of whites, for it was they who had the capital resources, the managerial experience and the opportunities for training, and—fully as important—the confidence of the colored shopper.

Negro enterprise subsisted on crumbs in little corners of the economy that white entrepreneurs spurned as either economically unpromising or socially demeaning. Whites willing to sell automobiles to Negroes would not think of cutting Negroes' hair or embalming their dead, so the Ford agency would be a white firm, and the richest Negro in the community a "mortician" or the proprietor of a chain of barbershops. Shrewder, more venturesome men, who but for their race would turn their energies to constructive and legitimate speculations, might find an equivalent in shady enterprise, the only "big operation" open to them.

Negroes were hopelessly divided over an economic strategy for the race. The pinched masses bought where credit and bargains could be had; others spent "double-duty dollars" with Negroes only, to promote colored business and employment. Still others denounced this "self-segregation" and pressed for economic integration through "color-blind competition" and by patronizing those whites who employed Negroes.

With only three exceptions, the "famous" Negroes in business in this era were identified with colored banking and insurance, or with a racial product. In the latter group were "Madame" C. J. Walker, Anthony Overton, Roscoe Conkling Bruce and Robert R. Taylor. Bruce, the fair-skinned son of Senator Bruce, was a Phi Beta Kappa Harvard graduate, who, before becoming manager of the Dunbar Apartments in New York, had tried several Negro business ventures and had been assistant superintendent of schools in Washington. Though a leader in promoting employment opportunities for the race, he supported a plan for segregated schools in New York.

Taylor, the manager of a Chicago housing project, had similar advantages. One grandfather was a Scotsman and the other a Creole member of the Louisiana legislature. Both parents were college graduates, often associated with white professional folk, and Robert was reared, insulated against racial strain, on the Tuskegee campus, where his father, a graduate of Massachusetts Institute of Technology, was resident architect and an intimate of Booker Washington. Taylor was introduced to The Problem at Howard's preparatory school, a fortunate preparation, as it proved, for as a student at the University of Illinois he was kept, by both town and campus, in painful subjection to Jim Crow. There was no bitterness, however, for the Taylors' racial attitudes had been molded by Yankee missionary teachers. The family in fact looked after an aged couple who had been Mrs. Taylor's college instructors, enabling them to retire to their old home in Connecticut.

Overton, markedly Caucasian like Taylor and Bruce, was born in bondage but became, after law training in Kansas, a municipal judge in Topeka and a merchant in the Oklahoma territory before becoming a Chicago banker, insurance executive, newspaper publisher and manufacturer of toiletries for Negroes. Far humbler were the antecedents of Mrs. Walker, to this day the most famous name in Negro industry. Born in Louisiana to ex-slave, dark-skinned paupers; orphaned at six, married at fourteen, widowed at twenty; the washerwoman concocted in 1905 a hair "conditioner" for Negroes, mixed the preparation in her washtubs, and peddled it from door to door. She soon added to her line a device for applying the "straightener," and a cream for "improving" skin color. She advertised in the Negro press, took to the road to preach the cosmetic gospel, and before long had a large factory in Indianapolis and a school for training colored agents and beauty culturists. She died in 1919 at fifty-one, a millionaire.

Three who had roles beyond the ghetto were famous among Negroes because they furnished the race with reassurance of its capacities. Granville Woods, an inventor, acquired practical education in a machine shop, where he was a chore boy, and then added to it by night-school instruction in engineering. Early successes enabled him to give his full time to invention, chiefly in the field of air brakes and electrical equipment. Most of his 150 patents were sold to firms such as General Electric, Westinghouse Air Brake and American Telephone and Telegraph, a market with every incentive for encouraging builders—whatever their color—of better mousetraps.

Archie A. Alexander, from the 1920's until his death in 1958 the most famous colored construction engineer, had doggedly worked his way through the State University of Iowa's Engineering School, needled by the dean's efforts to dissuade him. A decade later, by then a partner of a white classmate, he constructed a conduit for the university's heating plant, and eventually was selected as the outstanding graduate of the class of 1912. Hiring workers from both races (he once removed racial signs over the toilet facilities and substituted "skilled" and "unskilled"), he built power plants, airports, sewage plants, bridges and a three-million-dollar freeway at Washington, and took time to serve as an officer of the Des Moines NAACP branch.

By the late 1920's, Paul Williams had become—and he remains—the race's most prominent architect. Eventually his specialty was office buildings, but he also planned luxury housing for more than a score of leading Hollywood film folk. In 1937 he wrote a remarkable article in which he recounted the obstacles he had faced, and professed himself still committed to the Tuskegee philosophy of forty years earlier.

A fair-skinned Negro, he met no racial tensions in childhood in his mixed Los Angeles community until he began seeking after-school jobs. Then his rejection pushed him through successive stages of shock, inarticulate protest, resentment, and finally, "reconciliation to the status of my race." Disdaining the warning of his instructors, he decided while in high school that he would be an architect. The white man, he argued, had a reasonable basis for his prejudice and an understandable inclination for lumping all Negroes together but was fair-minded enough to give the individual Negro a chance to prove himself not just another Negro, but "Paul Williams, an *individual* Negro."

After taking a degree at the University of California, he began a canvass of all the architects in Los Angeles until he found an employer. When he opened his own office, callers would, upon suspecting his race, edge toward the door, but Williams would maneuver them back into a chair, airily declare that he had no time for small contracts, but would offer some advice. As a growing number overcame their hesitation, he concentrated upon giving the client an undoubted bargain, and perfecting a number of tricks. While others required a week to submit preliminary sketches, Williams delivered within twenty-four hours. What clients did not know was that he dropped everything for the emergency and worked twenty, even twenty-four, hours without rest. Or, again, he mastered a facility for drawing upside down so that the client sitting across the table could discuss a living room as it took shape, in the belief that he and Williams were designing the room together.

While his income rose as he designed some of the finest homes in California, he continued in the belief that his hope for success in the white man's world lay in respecting the patterns of separation. He lived in a modest house in the shabby end of town; he never attended social functions where white women were present; he acknowledged that Negroes were as yet deficient in skills and achievements and must concentrate upon the task of narrowing the gap by tireless industry.*

Negro America, living on the ragged edge of poverty and cut off from the entrepreneurial function, was in these years unable to support a well-developed banking system. From 1888 to 1934 no less than 134 banks (typically established as repositories for fraternal funds) were organized, but most were short-lived, so that the number in being at any one time was always small. In 1905 there were only seven, in 1936 a mere dozen.

Negro insurance businesses grew out of the nickel-and-dime burial plans maintained by churches and lodges. The reluctance of big white companies to

* It should be remembered that this was 1937. Williams in 1959 is a resolute and independent man. In the years here described, and even later, even so manful a fighter as Robeson was taking what would later be considered "Uncle Tom" motion picture roles; and Shirley Graham, today a forthright militant and the wife of W. E. B. Du Bois, wrote stage productions such as *Little Black Sambo.*

enter the field gave Negro enterprise its opportunity, but as colored income levels and life expectancies rose, the white companies conquered their fears, moved in on the fields that Negro business pioneers had tilled and were soon writing most of the insurance carried by the race. The harassed Negro firms formed a National Negro Insurance Association (there were twenty-eight members by 1936) and appealed to race loyalty. The white companies countered by simply hiring colored agents and by stressing their firms' superior security, and the colored companies carried on with a mere fraction of the race's insurance business.

The banking and insurance leaders most prominently noticed in the annals for these years were Jesse Binga, Truman K. Gibson, A. F. Herndon, Frank Gillespie, John Merrick, Anthony Overton, Harry Pace, Heman Perry, R. W. Rutherford, C. C. Spaulding, Maggie Lena Walker, Joseph E. Walker and R. R. Wright, Sr. Binga was born in Detroit to free Northern folk, but all of the others were born in the South, four of them in bondage and the rest the children or grandchildren of slaves. They were a remarkably light-skinned group; some had white fathers or grandfathers and several testified that it was a hard-working mother who kept a fatherless clan together.

They had advantages that favored them above the newly freed blacks. Binga's mother owned rental properties; Wright's parents were "upper-class" slaves; Herndon, though born a slave, found his white connections—he was at least seven-eighths white—an immense social advantage in establishing his businesses in Atlanta. Merrick, another casually begotten son of a white father, found his ancestry an incalculable advantage in finding employment, and Overton was another who found a markedly Caucasian appearance extremely convenient.

Maggie Lena Walker was the child of pampered mulatto slaves whose post-War position as headwaiters at Richmond hotels, combined with Maggie's instruction from a war-impoverished Southern lady, eased her advance. Similarly, Rutherford owed much to the continued interest taken in the colored Rutherfords by the owners who had permitted the boy's grandfather to earn his family's freedom. Spaulding, for thirty years before his death in 1952 the race's favorite tycoon, was the grandson of slaves, and one of fourteen children in a hard-working, pious, rural North Carolina family, living on their own land. Perry had an introduction to business in his father's tiny grocery store, but Joseph E. Walker had no discoverable advantages as a fatherless boy in the Mississippi Bayou.

The group ranged from barely literate to university-trained men. Merrick probably never attended school at all, and Herndon and Rutherford for perhaps one year. Perry managed to get through seven grades and Spaulding, after a few semesters, returned to the fields until he was twenty, and then resumed his education when he had begun his business career—sitting awkwardly in a schoolroom with children less than half his age. Gillespie progressed to the third year in high school, Maggie Walker attended a high school in Richmond, and Binga, after three years of high school in Detroit, read law for two years with a Negro attorney.

Wright graduated with the first class at Atlanta University, where Pace and Gibson enrolled many years later. Gibson, during his years at Atlanta, encountered Harvard men, including Du Bois, who kindled his ambition to follow their example. He found employment as a waiter at the Harvard Faculty Club, and became one of a dozen colored students at the University. He studied under President Lowell himself, was a guest in his home, and when he finished the business course, he was graduated with honors.

Overton was a product of Washburn College and the University of Kansas Law School, while J. E. Walker, after completing the course at an industrial college, earned a medical degree at Meharry, and began as a physician. Gibson was the only member of the group whose higher education was oriented specifically to a business career; all the rest were pioneers, improvising their skills as they went along.

It may be assumed that the motives of these men paralleled those of white leaders in business and industry, but there were joined with the more conventional values certain racial desiderata as well. Major Wright's Philadelphia bank, his leadership in the Negro Bankers' Association and his later venture into Haitian coffee-importing were clearly directed toward race-improvement. When Merrick and A. M. Moore projected the North Carolina Mutual and then remained for years in the background without salary while leaving the management of the enterprise to Spaulding, they were genuinely interested in providing the Negro people both with business opportunity and a service they greatly needed.

In Binga's aggressive financial empire-building in Chicago there was more than race pride—indeed a defiance that offended whites from big Loop bankers to race-hating thugs who bombed his house. The proud, self-assertive, belligerent Binga, the only Northern-born Negro in the group, was the furthest removed, socially and geographically, from slavery. While Binga encountered enormous hostilities, Spaulding, a pious, pacific Negro, steeped in the American Gospel of Work, could in the Southern heartland adapt himself to a society that forbade him to take a meal in buildings he himself owned, while it honored him as a "good Negro" and relied on him to speak the word that would steady the Negro population of Durham in unquiet times—as on the occasion when disturbances flamed after the Louis-Schmeling fight that toppled the race's beloved champion. Negroes were not surprised when Spaulding was invited to confer at the White House; nor were they surprised that Binga never was.

The paths to prominence illustrate once more a variety of selective mechanisms. Major Wright, for thirty years a Georgia college president in the first post-Civil War generation, when education was the freedmen's most insistent need, found, upon his mandatory retirement, a second social frontier in the urban North in thirty years of pioneering as one of the country's leading bankers in the next generation, when his folk, now literate, struggled for economic emancipation.

The case of Herndon exemplified nothing so much as the old story of the American farm boy's will to success. Leaving the farm for Atlanta at twenty-one, he learned the barber's trade as a porter in a white man's shop, and gradually accumulated a string of barbershops catering to whites. With his growing capital, he struck off into side ventures: real estate, a loan company, a cemetery, a bank, a theater, a drugstore and a project that grew into the Atlanta Standard Life Insurance Company. All the while, his strongly Caucasian appearance, intimate association with white Atlanta businessmen, and his reputation as a good citizen insulated him from aggressions. Once when white barbers tried to ruin him by invoking an old racial zoning ordinance, other influential whites had the ruling amended to exempt his shops.

In college, Joseph E. Walker chose medicine simply because physicians enjoyed the highest status to which a bright Mississippi colored boy could aspire. Fresh from Meharry, he went to Indianola, Mississippi, to begin practice and found the town in a ferment over a Negro postmistress—appointed by Theodore Roosevelt—from whom whites refused to accept their mail. The young doctor was so great a curiosity that not a few colored rustics concluded that Mr. Roosevelt had sent him, too. The husband of the postmistress was a prosperous Negro landowner, one Cox, just then making an effort to found a bank, and he immediately made the bewildered young physician president. Neglecting his practice, Walker preached the gospel of thrift at schools and churches, and before he knew it, the wobbly Mississippi Life Insurance Company made him its president also. When it came under new control, the company was sold to a white firm, but Walker then formed a company of his own, and after a period of desperate struggle, his Universal Life Company was solidly established.

For Merrick, insurance was a side line. Beginning as a bricklayer, he became the owner of a cluster of barbershops in Raleigh before joining A. M. Moore in acquiring a tottering little religious-fraternal insurance program. In its early days, Spaulding was its salesman, bookkeeper, advertising department and janitor. A solemn, meticulously groomed young man, he affected a high collar to awe the customers, for they were slow to find a Negro businessman credible. When the first death claim was filed—for forty dollars—the company seemed ruined until the directors dug into their own pockets for the emergency. Spaulding rushed to present the check to the startled widow, and for months thereafter found the signed receipt his most persuasive argument. He shrewdly engaged Negro schoolteachers as agents, and his impeccable conduct won for him the friendship and advice of white actuaries, insurance agencies and solid North Carolina citizens. Success came after years of missionary work on foot and by buggy over rutted roads, and by door-to-door canvassing. His card became a familiar sight in the colored press; and Negro stores, offices, churches, lodge halls and homes were showered with advertising novelties—pencils, matches, fans, calendars, thermometers, paperweights, clothes brushes and cuspidors—carrying the gospel of North Carolina Mutual.

Binga, besides looking after his mother's properties, was cashier in his father's barbershop until he established one of his own in a tent on the Seattle water front. Next he became a Pullman porter, a land speculator in Idaho and a Chicago real-estate man, controlling more than a thousand apartments and residences, a foundation upon which he operated one of the largest Negro banks in the country, until its failure in the Depression. He was a curious mixture of the tight-fisted tycoon and the race crusader, pushing outward the walls of the ghetto, and quietly putting colored boys through college. The collapse of his business empire brought him a prison term, but he was eventually released on the plea of Clarence Darrow, who argued that he had been driven to dubious practices by cruel discrimination.

Maggie Walker's rise in banking was linked to her position as head of a vast benevolent-fraternal organization of Negro women, while Rutherford advanced by way of white industry. He left the farm, a grown man, to cut cordwood until a white woman brought him to the attention of her son, a district manager for the Singer Sewing Machine Company. The latter gave him the job of porter for the company, but he rose until he became a repairman and at last a sales representative. It was then that he went to Washington and there laid the foundation for the National Benefit Life Insurance Company, making his collections on a bicycle.

Two others entered business through white firms. Gillespie, after leaving law school, sold insurance for a Chicago company until he learned the business, and then organized the Liberty Life Insurance Company. Perry, after a brief success as a cotton sampler for a Houston firm, also acquired valuable experience with white agencies, both as solicitor and in the home offices. He cultivated the acquaintance of white actuaries, who shared their specialized knowledge with him, then went to Atlanta and, to the amazement of skeptics, managed by enormous exertions to assemble the one hundred thousand dollars in capital that the law required for the launching of an insurance company. He brought into the organization the college-trained Harry Pace for his managerial talent, while Perry himself continued to look after his laundries and dry-cleaning establishments.

Pace, like Gibson, was criticized for preferring nickel-and-dime insurance enterprise over the learned professions after his college training. Both came into insurance on the invitation of uneducated pioneers wishing to "professionalize" their firms. Pace, fresh out of Atlanta University, had a varied experience before his connection with a Memphis bank brought his business talents to the attention of Perry. After parting with Perry, he joined W. C.

Handy in music publishing and in the Black Swan Recording Company. Later insurance connections won him a foremost reputation in Negro business, and, at the peak of his career, he directed the merger of three companies to form the supreme Liberty Life Insurance Company of Chicago, to be headed by Gibson, already noted for bringing college men into the business and raising its technical standards.

Gibson made his start under Herndon when the latter was building up a small sickness- and accident-insurance business he had lately acquired, and for which he was delighted to secure the young Harvard man. When a speech Gibson delivered before the Negro Business League brought him an offer from a firm in Cincinnati, he was reluctant to leave Herndon and Atlanta, but he finally made the move for the sake of wider opportunities for his children. Soon thereafter he established the Supreme Life and Casualty Company while his friend, Gillespie, was building the Liberty Life Company in Chicago. It was the merger of these companies and another that produced the Supreme Liberty Life Insurance Company.

The armed forces remained virtually closed as an avenue to distinction. A tiny scattering of colored cadets were admitted to the service academies in the seventy years after 1865, but none graduated at Annapolis and only three at West Point. Of these, the first was court-martialed, the second died in early manhood, and the third was Charles Young. A man of strong character and great personal force, Young was a great favorite of Negroes, and the only famous colored soldier until General Davis, in the next generation, unless one includes Private Henry Johnson, an Albany redcap, venerated by Negroes as the first American soldier to win the *Croix de guerre* in World War I.

Born in a Kentucky log cabin, the son of an ex-slave private in the Union Army, Young was named to West Point in 1884, and graduated well up in his class. He eventually served with distinction—usually with colored cavalry units—in Cuba, Mexico, Haiti and Liberia. There was occasional friction; when white troops refused to salute him he stripped off his coat and commanded them to salute the buttons. While the war moved far younger officers quickly to the ranks of colonel and brigadier general, and the command of the Negro officers' training camp at Des Moines was given to a white man, Young was called up for medical examination and retired for "ill health." The apparent subterfuge renewed demands for his advancement to a brigadier's rank and a combat command, and Young made a dramatic horseback ride from Chillicothe, Ohio, to Washington to demonstrate his fitness, but the War Department recalled him only for obscure duty in Illinois and then in Liberia, where he died.

While Negro fraternal potentates came and went, J. Finley Wilson and William C. Hueston stood out in the record. Wilson, as Grand Exalted Ruler of the Elks, was one of the best-known Negroes in America, an effusive little man who dominated his empire, and exercised a tremendous influence in Republican patronage and platform drafting. He was born into a huge family in Tennessee, the grandchild of self-emancipated slaves. At thirteen, in Denver, he joined Coxey's army in the famous march of 1894, only to be snatched out of ranks at Council Bluffs by an aunt who had been apprised of his coming. He drifted from job to job, in Chicago, Arizona, Alaska and Kansas City, with a keen eye for cultivating useful friendships, and then began to rise.

Hueston came to be best known as the Elks' Commissioner of Education, supervising its far-flung program of scholarships for Negro youth. His father was the son of a white horse fancier of Lexington, Kentucky, who reared the boy in his own home on his thousand-acre horse farm. William's mother, whose family name he bore, was also the child of one of the ante-bellum households where the master of the house raised simultaneously two lines of children, in this case under one roof.

Willie's mother was an eager reader, extremely ambitious for the boy's education. He went to an American Missionary Association school, and then, with a $150 oratory prize and $200 supplied by local whites, he went to the University of Chicago for two years, living at the home of President William Rainey Harper, as houseboy. From there he went to the University of Kansas —again living in the president's house—where he was not only captain of the baseball and debating teams, but also the salaried head guide, showing visitors about the campus.

He took a five-year combined arts and law course and was soon conducting a brisk bi-racial practice in Kansas City. In 1920 he moved to Gary, Indiana, at the urging of the leading Senate Republican, James Watson, who with Senator Beveridge made him a major Republican figure among Negroes. After serving as an elected city judge in Gary, he became, again through Watson, Assistant Solicitor of the Post Office, in Washington, and a ranking Negro Republican party official until the advent of the New Deal. Thereafter he devoted himself increasingly to the Elks, whose Department of Education he had organized in 1925.

The years 1900–1936 added to our list an impressive array of athletes. In slavery days, giant Negroes were frequently set upon each other like gamecocks, while frenzied onlookers urged them on and wagered upon the outcome. Big slaveowners, in fact, groomed particular Negroes for local bouts, much as they bred and trained horses to challenge the trotters of neighboring racing enthusiasts. One variant was the "battle royal" in which several Negro gladiators—commonly drawn from various plantations—were thrown together into the cockpit to maul each other until a solitary, dazed champion remained on his feet.

Historians of American sport celebrate the pugilistic exploits of Bill

Richmond and Tom Molyneux, who rose out of the slave-boxing background; and of George Godfrey, Charlie Hadley and Peter Jackson who in the post-Civil War decades fought their way to the very edge of supremacy only to be denied an encounter with John L. Sullivan, whose decision to "draw the color line" met with the country's approval. At the turn of the century, George Dixon, Joe Gans and Joe Walcott were dominating the lighter-weight divisions, but it was Jack Johnson, king of the heavyweights, who became, in 1908, the first nationally prominent colored champion.

A jet-black stevedore from Galveston, he served an apprenticeship as a sparring mate for professional Negro boxers, participated in several "battle royal" bouts, travelled from town to town as a tramp fighter, and took to the road with an amusement company as a travelling strong man, taking on all comers who could be persuaded to try to win a five-dollar prize for knocking him down in four rounds. In Southern states, where "mixed boxing" was outlawed, his white opponents were advertised as boxing teachers and the bouts as "demonstrations." Even this precaution did not protect one of the exhibits from a raid by a Texas sheriff and his five rangers; both Johnson and his adversary were jailed for a month.

Soon Johnson began meeting the foremost Negro pugilists, and his prowess moved sports reporters and spectators alike to join him in his demand for a chance at the heavyweight crown. He literally pursued the touring champion, Tommy Burns, for four years, heckling him all the while with his widely reported challenges, so that the reluctant Burns was at last shamed into compliance. The battle was staged in Australia, and Johnson returned to the United States as champion of the world. The Negro masses were beside themselves with pleasure—these were the years of lynching at its worst—and it may be assumed that this racial triumph afforded a greater lift to the black millions than did the formal launching of the NAACP five months later. On the other side of the color line, the disaster kindled new racial rancors and initiated an anxious search for a "white hope." The quest, incidentally, added that expression to the American language, but it has since lost nearly all its racial connotation. When Jim Jeffries was finally prevailed upon to come out of retirement for the honor of his race, the nation's leading journalists converged upon Reno to cover the combat. Johnson's victory touched off a chain of minor riots and disturbances across the country, and whites took what comfort they could find from Brand Whitlock's sneer that Johnson could also lick Tolstoi or Theodore Roosevelt, for that matter, and it proved nothing.

Johnson's subsequent life as a bon vivant and flashy spender diminished his stature, and his marriage to a succession of white women made him extremely unpopular among whites (and eventually among Negroes), and precipitated the enactment of laws against intermarriage in several Northern and Western states. His refusal to fight Sam Langford was widely interpreted as an intramural drawing of the color line, and his apparent preference for white associates, plus the widespread belief that he threw away his championship in a "fixed" fight, cost him much of his remaining reputation in colored America. In his later years and after his death in 1946, highly responsible white and colored commentators insisted that a hostile press had created Johnson's unfortunate reputation, and that he was in fact an intelligent, sensitive and level-headed man, whose smiling exterior concealed the hurts of countless slights and insults.

Sam Langford, Joe Jeanette and Sam McVey are still fondly remembered by old-timers, and sport writers still argue over what might have been the outcome of a match between Jack Dempsey and Harry Wills, whose assiduous efforts to secure a championship bout with Dempsey were uniformly rebuffed. In the 1920's, the childlike religiosity of Tiger Flowers, of Atlanta, who won the middleweight championship under the management of a white Atlantan, and the exemplary conduct of "Kid" Chocolate, who won the featherweight crown, went far to win back the friends of Negro boxing whom Johnson and other Negro champions had alienated by high living and a weakness for white women. In 1935 John Henry Lewis, a twenty-one-year-old light-skinned boxer, who had been trained from boyhood by his ex-pugilist father, won the light-heavyweight title, just as America was beginning to hear of the greatest champion of them all—Joe Louis, a quiet, unassuming boy from Detroit, who, in the first year of the next generation we are to chronicle, began the longest and most impeccable reign in the history of the heavyweight-boxing throne.

Other sectors of the sport world were as yet closed to Negro leadership. There was an occasional colored favorite from college football in the sports pages of the newspapers: William H. Lewis at Harvard (1892, 1893), Fritz Pollard of Brown (1916), Paul Robeson of Rutgers (1917, 1918)—all of them Walter Camp All-American selections—achieved an eminence that was not again attained until 1938 when Jerome "Brud" Holland made his spectacular record at Cornell. In baseball one name was well known beyond the ghetto: Leroy "Satchel" Paige.

Paige's career had run its course before the barriers went down in major-league baseball, but even though he was confined (until 1946 when he was engaged by the Cleveland Indians as a relief pitcher) to the limited arena of the Negro circuits, he remains a legend in the annals of American sport. Many of the most celebrated pitchers in the history of baseball have called him the greatest hurler the game has produced. In 1952, when he was still probably the most valuable relief pitcher in the American league, he was about fifty years old. The secret of his age has been the jest of baseball enthusiasts for decades. He came up from Alabama, where he had perfected his throwing style during four years in a reform school before he was seventeen. After advancing through sand-lot, semi-professional and Negro League baseball, he was booked for many years as a solo star, on barnstorming tours, and pitching for any teams who would meet his price, "nine strike-outs in three innings guaranteed." At one time he was travelling thirty thousand miles and earning $35,000 a year, adding steadily all the while to his staggering record of no-hit games and of games won. In 1939 in a single month he pitched on twenty-nine consecutive days and lost but one game. In the thirty years of his prime, he is said to have won 2,000 games of 2,500 played, but his prodigies were barred, by the color line, from the official record books. His first significant place in organized baseball, outside the ghetto leagues, came in the 1930's when he was on the pitching staff of a semi-professional club in Bismarck, North Dakota. His belated adoption by the major leagues came in time to permit him to participate in his first World Series game in 1948. A convivial, amiable fellow who had his share of trouble with what he called "the polices," his notorious unpunctuality and his vast and artless humors and unconcerns endeared him to thousands, though some regretted his lack of public solicitude over his race's infelicities.

One other area—track—saw a few Negro notables at the end of this generation. It was the 1932 Olympic games that brought Eddie Tolan and Ralph Metcalfe to world notice, but four years later even they were surpassed by Jesse Owens, who broke three world's records and who is now invariably listed with the greatest athletes in the history of American sport. The seventh of eleven children born to Alabama sharecroppers, who were so poor that they sometimes subsisted on potato peelings, he moved with his family to Cleveland in childhood. From the sixth grade through high school he worked as a shineboy in a shoe-repair shop, but his years at school were singularly free from racial friction. His track coaches in junior high school and at high school industriously trained and exercised him on the sidewalks of Cleveland, and his school fellows liked him well enough to elect him president of the student council. He was cordially welcomed by the track team at Ohio State University, where he worked his way through college as a freight-elevator operator in a warehouse, a gasoline-station handyman and a page in the Ohio House of Representatives.

The triumphs of Owens and of Metcalfe (who was on the United States Olympic Team for the second time) were doubly relished by white and Negro Americans—including many without the faintest interest in sports—because the games in 1936 were held in Berlin. The racial disaster was witnessed by the Fuehrer himself. Though Hitler found it convenient to leave the stadium abruptly before the ceremonies were concluded, the Nazi sports writers showed greater resilience: the American team, it appeared, had not won the games after all; confessing its inadequacies, it had been forced to rely upon its "black auxiliary force."

The first three and a half decades of the twentieth century had been fateful years for the Negro vanguard and for the race's rank and file. And yet, so sharply was progress toward the Promised Land accelerated in the years that were to follow that it has become a commonplace to say that the advance of the twenty years from the middle 'thirties dwarfed everything that came before. The thesis has been endlessly reiterated in the Negro press—and indeed by the NAACP—and evokes nowadays no serious contradiction from the informed.

The strictures of America's critics who belabor her race record in terms of 1935 have been rendered preposterous by the facts of the 1950's, just as the old clichés about the robber barons and Wall Street domination of the country have been made forever ridiculous by the Big Change that Frederick Lewis Allen has described. But it is instructive to remember that they once were solidly grounded in fact—as recently as twenty years ago. Let it be remembered that for all the achievements by the vanguard, for all the social and economic changes that were recasting the Negro community in the years 1900–1936, the relationships between the races *en masse* had shown little objective change—perhaps because such change could come only after other transformations had laid the groundwork for them.

Race relations in 1934, wrote one of the most respected and influential editors of the Negro press in 1953, were not notably different from those in 1900. The Negro's status as a second-class citizen—as a hewer of wood and a drawer of water—was still embodied in law and usage. Colored America was still tightly trapped in urban and rural slums with no prospect for breaching the wall and finding better housing, no appeal from the restrictive covenant. The Negro wage earner's income in the early 1930's still stood at a mere third of that of white workers. The Jim Crow train, bus and trolley was still the inflexible rule for most Negroes, and even in New York, hotel and restaurant facilities were fundamentally segregated. In the churches and the Christian Associations no crack in the color line could yet be discerned, and in hospitals and medical services the lines were just as tightly drawn.

The entry of the first Negro into major-league baseball was still a dozen years in the future, and suggestions for desegregation in the armed forces seemed unrealistic to the most incorrigible visionary. Voting and jury service in the South were brazenly thwarted by legal connivance, if not by legal requirement, and a Negro announcing himself for public office in the South and most of the rest of the country would have been considered mad. Not a Negro was enrolled in a graduate or professional school in the South—where the race was still largely concentrated—and the prospect of opening up the elementary and secondary schools to all comers without regard to race could hardly have seemed more remote.

It is against such a backdrop that the great transformation, taking its rise in the middle 1930's and now at flood stage, should be viewed.

Part Three

1936–1959: Behold the Promised Land

The Negro vanguard of the years since 1936 made their careers in an America where the pace of change was hugely accelerated. Income levels of the race rose at a rate almost twice that for whites, so that by 1958 instead of a mere third (as in 1936), the urban colored wage earner was paid two thirds as much as his white counterpart, and the diminishing farm population climbed increasingly into the small-landowner class. And while the quality of instruction still fell far short of national norms, educational standards were rising, and purely quantitative measures of Negro literacy and elementary school enrollments were approaching virtual parity with the figures for America at large. Negroes in the country's colleges and universities indeed nearly equalled the number of white students in Britain. Health standards inched steadily upward until the race's lag in life expectancy was narrowed to six years, and though occasional acts of violence still marred the record, the day when organized mobs descended upon the Negro quarter to kill, burn and plunder was fading into an evil memory. Genuine lynchings dwindled from an annual toll of more than a hundred in the early 1900's to two, one, or even none in individual years in the 1940's and 1950's.

The 1947 Race Relations Institute at Fisk University, summarizing the gains of the preceding decade, pointed to the Negro's entry into the great labor organizations, the collapse of the last major "legal" obstacles to voting, the growth of fair-employment legislation in several states, the steady progress toward equalization of educational opportunity in graduate and professional schools, the outlawing of segregation in interstate travel, the growing absorption of colored workers into industry and public employment (including Negro policemen in the South). The 1958 session of the Institute added to the list the astonishing achievement of integration in the armed forces, the levelling of barriers in professional sports, the multiplication of appointed federal and elected state, county and local officials; the outlawing of segregation and discrimination in public places in the national capital, the judicial invalidation of racial restrictive covenants, the Civil Rights legislation of 1957; and, above all, the Supreme Court decision of 1954, decreeing the end of segregation in the common schools and other public facilities.

Most of America's vast geographic expanse—as so much of the outside world seemed unable or unwilling to understand—had, of course, since the Emancipation of 1863, never maintained *de jure* segregation, and now, at the opening of 1959, a fourth of all the bi-racial school districts in the South had begun desegregation, while more than half of the former all-white public institutions of higher learning were admitting some Negroes, as were nearly half of the church-related and more than a fourth of the other former all-white private colleges.

No less extraordinary was the changing attitudes of whites, as they conquered old hostilities. The mass communications media quietly shelved old stereotypes. Churches and schools educated countless whites in the civilities —and in the very *vocabulary*—of racial tolerance, and the sober *Scientific American* reported at the close of 1956 that one of the most careful opinion surveys ever conducted had revealed that while, in 1942, half of Northern and four fifths of Southern whites believed Negroes to be less intelligent than whites, by 1956 the figures had shrunk to a seventh and two fifths, respectively. To be sure, the quickened tempo of change, so rich with promise, still left untouched the lives of millions in the South's rural slums and the Northern ghettos. Millions of colored Americans still encountered the rejections, the antipathies and spiritual brutalities that their fathers had known. Yet, so tremendous had been the gains of recent years that Thurgood Marshall, the insistent legal voice of the NAACP, declared in the turbulent summer of 1958, "I can see absolutely nothing to be pessimistic about"; and the head of the Urban League exulted that "Negroes are now in the full stream of the current . . . learning to swim . . . moving toward our goal of absolute equality of opportunity and achievement."

It is easier to multiply examples than to account for the race's accelerated drift toward the mainstream. The momentum of America's spiritual and ideological history, the unfolding logic of her tradition, continued, it may be presumed, to shape our ends, no less in the modern era when history is made swiftly than in the past when it moved with statelier tread. It is clear, too, that the reforming mood of the country in the years of the New Deal supplied materials for social transformation, and then World War II and its aftermath threw into the chemistry of change another potent catalyst. The national emergency increased the Negro's economic and political bargaining power, and the protracted post-war boom sustained for another decade a highly favorable man-job ratio. America's identification with the cause of democracy focused her own, her friends', and—for other reasons—her very enemies' concerns upon the plight of her chief minority, and considerations of both conscience and policy came powerfully to the race's rescue.

Greater economic and social security, rising living standards, growing political power, sharply augmented educational attainments and a perceptibly rising respectability in America at large—all of these operated upon each other reciprocally as cause and effect. They fostered a new self-confidence and militancy in a growing colored middle class, doubly confirmed now in their traditional allegiance to American values and tenets, and responding in intensely American ways to un-American provocations. The maturing of such a class was in itself a major agent of change both because—like the lengthening list of distinguished Negroes who compelled both white and Negro Americans to reconsider their estimate of the Negro potential—it helped to break down the white man's stereotypes, and because it supplied leaders for the struggle. When, during World War II the United States named more than a dozen of its newly constructed Liberty Ships for celebrated Negroes, thoughtful citizens recalled how preposterous would have been such a suggestion in the earlier war only a little over twenty years in the past.

As the paralyzing influence of Social Darwinism gave place in the American creed to an ameliorative social philosophy, religious, humanitarian and civic agencies threw themselves into the cause of racial democracy with appeals to the national conscience. By the middle 1950's, every major church denomination in the country had condemned racial segregation in principle, and nearly a hundred tax-supported city commissions and 345 semi-official agencies were working to advance racial harmony. The proliferation of a huge literature by scholars and polemicists, white and Negro, brought to a growing audience scientific data on race overwhelmingly on the Negro's side, and virtually unchallenged by a literature of rebuttal.

Related to these innovations were the northward migrations, urbanization and social and economic diversification. By 1958 two fifths of the country's Negro population was outside the South and nearly 95 per cent of these were urban folk, two thirds of them in Greater New York, Chicago, Detroit and Philadelphia alone. The three fifths of the nation's Negroes who lived in the South, meanwhile, were now divided almost equally between rural and urban areas.

The steady drift into industry as laborers, semi-skilled workers and skilled draftsmen, and into clerical and professional roles produced wide, and typically American, diversities in wealth, education, sophistication and "respectability." Still, while the growing middle class conformed to American middle-class living standards and values, its evolution was arrested just short of acceptance into the "real" American bourgeoisie. The group was trapped in the ghetto, largely rejected by the white middle class, often estranged from the Negro masses, but held together in their own social groups in a common alienation. Some found contact with the larger world through unions, professional, religious and political groups, and the confraternities of artists, scholars, writers, entertainers, students and athletic organizations. But unyielding *de facto* residential segregation held such breaches in the color line to a minimum, and many adjusted themselves to their catastrophic rejection either by flight into unreality and the world of make-believe that Franklin Frazier has described in *Black Bourgeoisie,* or, as

Kardiner and Ovesey have argued, capitulated to frustration or were broken by the tensions that accompanied the "mark of oppression."

But even after the worst has been said, it must be added that Negroes had moved into more fields of endeavor than ever before. Genuine leaders in these fields, leaders by national standards, were still extremely few. Indeed, a preoccupation with "leaders" distorts the picture. In a simpler era, the Negro vanguard had been effectually confined to its "celebrities" standing apart from the undifferentiated mass. But now the cutting edge that the race presents to the color line is not so much the relatively small company of "big names" as the growing, unsung contingent of advance troops, the trained and industrious strivers, the optimists, the gallant, tough-minded, intrepid outriders who brave the discouragements, the heart-wounds, the counsels of despair. It is these who are moving, on merit, into the periphery of American business and industry, the professions, the arts, government and the sciences —not as protégès and prodigies, cheered by humble blacks and patronizing whites who still apply the double standard, but as advance agents of honest assimilation, forming a reservoir out of which genuine leaders can be recruited in the future, when the training, experience and seasoning, until now not available, have been accumulated.

Because this study is concerned, however, with those who have been most prominently noticed in the printed historical record, our focus continues to rest upon the colored celebrity. One index of such distinction is the listing of Negroes in *Who's Who in America,* admittedly a precarious measure. For purposes of our inquiry, the volumes for 1935–1936, 1944–1945, 1950–1951 and 1954–1955 were analyzed. The first of them lists 92 Negroes (one for every 341 non-Negroes), and the last 190 (one for every 252 non-Negroes). The entire company is contained in a very small number of categories, nearly three fourths of them in the Negro colleges and churches, most of them listed *ex officio.* The rest, nearly all of them operating in the Northern Negro milieu only and not widely known beyond it, were a sprinkling of writers, public officials, musicians, editors, social workers, lawyers and other professional people. Over 85 per cent of all the colored Americans in *Who's Who* in these twenty years were born in the South, at a time when over 90 per cent of the nation's Negroes were still massed there. Still, as the two decades progressed, a few were winning notice for attainments in which racial considerations were decreasingly determinative, and it is notable that the proportion of the whole list who were college-trained was approximately the same as the proportion of college-educated persons among the white listees.

All these folk matured before 1920—many of them before 1900—and their early development was not, therefore, eased by the later ameliorations we have been describing. They were still persons who grew up in the rural and smalltown South, where whites and Negroes alike placed an extremely low estimate upon the Negro's capacity and his "place." In the 1954–1955 volume, seventy-one of the Negro listees (including nearly all who were not in the categories of religious and educational leaders, as well as a few who were) were persons living in the North, only four of them west of Chicago. Twenty were Chicago residents, only two of whom had been born there; and thirty-five were New Yorkers, not one of them native to the city. Almost none had behind him a tradition of Northern urban living.

Our roster of members of the vanguard for 1936–1958 whom we have selected for study includes some of the *Who's Who* listees plus a larger number of others well known but not so listed. It is a sampling only, for lists of accomplished colored Americans now grow hopelessly unwieldy by reason of sheer length and diversity, and it becomes increasingly fruitless to lump them together for purposes of generalization as they exhibit ever wider variations in social origins, in their adaptation to the environments supplied by geography, community, family, vocation and class, in their individual adjustments to The Problem, and in their particular position on the issue of the racial goals, strategy and tactics best suited to the times.

The growing complexities of Negro American society, the multiplying differentiations and stratifications, the intricate interrelations with America at large: all of these rendered absurd any effort to define what "the Negro" thinks, hopes, feels, or what he can or cannot do. There is among Negroes every conceivable attitude on every conceivable issue. There are, to be sure, rough concurrences and tides of opinion, but the quest for a precise definition of either the full freedom, to which perhaps nearly all Negroes yearn, or of the means for its realization, discovers among Negro "leaders" no stable consensus.

Characterization of the contemporary generation of Negro notables is handicapped by the want of perspective and a sifted historical record. We can only confine ourselves to those who seem now, in the recent and current press, to be most widely noticed. These deficiencies are somewhat counterpoised, however, by the availability of many of this generation's vanguard for direct interview, by a lengthening list of book-length biographies, and by the growing attention to Negro achievers in the white periodical press—for the successful Negro has suddenly become good copy.

Noteworthy, too, is the gap between opportunity and preparation that recent changes have exposed. Doors are opening for which there are few qualified Negroes, only because the openings came sooner than the race could realistically have been expected to prepare for them. It is no less clear that many on our roster achieved their rank precisely because they fixed their eyes in youth upon goals which their contemporaries—and, as some candidly confess, which they themselves—thought unattainable. Squarely in the American tradition, they were simply trying a little harder for the impossible, and with a little more help from accident and fortuitous advantage, than were their fellows.

That the more orderly processes of change were disturbed by white resistance to the epochal court decree of May, 1954, few would dispute. But even fewer, perhaps, would venture to assess the decision's net effect. If it stiffened the contrariness of white extremists, it correspondingly energized Negro and white liberal resolution; in the North and the border states—and even in more Southern communities than many realized—it released new public and private concessions and liberalizations at countless points. If it frightened and forced thousands of Negroes off the rolls of the NAACP, it produced in the same years triumphant militancy in Montgomery, as well as the most aggressive program of the NAACP, backed by the largest cash receipts, in its history. It also fathered in New York (which now contained as many Negroes as South Carolina) comprehensive legislation to combat every major form of racial discrimination.

Eminent Negroes between the years 1936 to 1958 were typically born between 1880 and 1915, a mere generation or two from slavery, a social heritage no less remote from the context in which they achieved their distinction than Chicago is from Sumer and Akkad. Some, indeed, there were, listed in *Who's Who in America* as late as 1942, who had in fact been slaves. Many who in 1958 were still fully active were the children of parents one or both of whom were ex-slaves, and most of the Negroes whose eminence belongs to the two decades after 1936 grew to maturity in the rural South, in the receding shadows of the slavery past. They rarely alluded to their lowly origins; indeed, one senses that they preferred to forget them. While whites boasted of log-cabin births and penniless ancestors, Negroes regarded their humble origins with mingled sorrow and shame.

The race's own scholars emphasize the tenacity of reflexes that such a heritage bequeathed. Like the mouse in the maze, which learns that the easy path leads to an electric shock and the circuitous one to a pellet of food, the post-Civil War generations were profoundly conditioned by experience. People whose parents and grandparents had been chattels, people whose own maturing came in a time of slow transition before World War I, were still harassed by old anxieties and uncertainties. Even where half or more of the whites in a community were relaxing former severities, a young Negro soon learned that the safest course was to expect the worst, to flee for refuge at the first hint that he might be hurt again. This was hardly an environment in which even a bright and aspiring young Negro could strike out boldly on untried paths.

Many who grew up in the South found Negro society as yet primitively uncomplicated; others in Northern urban areas before 1915 likewise lived in a comparatively undiversified milieu. The colored population in Northern cities was then still deployed in little clusters, some in superior neighborhoods, where they were servants of the well-to-do, while others, domiciled in white neighborhoods, earned their livelihood as laborers, domestics, Pullman porters, dining-car waiters and postal workers. With the huge northward migrations after 1914, however, the "Old Families" found themselves engulfed in tidal waves of "new people," and very soon nearly all, regardless of background or achievement, were crowded into tight Negro pockets.

In this new environment, class lines hardened by 1930 into a rough hierarchy of lower, middle and upper classes. The lower classes, thickly populated with recent migrants from the rural South, showed the high incidence of family disorganization, illiteracy and law-breaking that are the portion of the swarming poor everywhere in the cities of the world. Doing menial work, and often on public charity, they were held together in a stability of a sort by their churches and lodges.

The middle class, often described as being of lighter average complexion, though the exceptions were so numerous as to attenuate the generalization, numbered many whose residence in the city was of longer standing, who showed pride in their group and an attachment to stable families, conventional moralities and bourgeois virtues. They often pulled away from their darker kinsmen. They aspired to skilled jobs, and if they failed to rise above the rank of domestics and service workers, labored to exhaustion to raise the educational and vocational levels of their children. In the upper stratum, again a shade lighter than those in the stratum below, were folk whose family connections, general culture, occupation, income, education or special achievement set them apart from their fellows. The disinclination of whites to take upper-class Negroes seriously often led the latter to an exaggerated preoccupation with "Society," to a multiplication of functionaries and an insistence upon deference from their underlings for their rank and "entitlements," and to habits of conspicuous consumption, which often required the earnings of a second, after-hours employment or of a working wife.

After the 1930's, the importance of skin color seemed to decline as a status symbol, as more rational criteria became operative and as—with the steady lightening of the average complexion of Negro America—the scarcity value of lighter skin diminished. Paul Laurence Dunbar and Robert S. Abbott were, like so many other very dark members of the vanguard of earlier years, spurned for this shortcoming by girls whom they courted, despite their extraordinary promise; but by 1940 such penalties were less common. The Negro masses exhibited a growing hostility to this intramural color prejudice, especially as more and more dark Negroes, through education, native talent, industry and marriage pushed their way into the upper class.

In the Negro colleges, in the 1920's and 1930's, dark-skinned students were brazenly excluded from fraternities (and, even more, sororities), but twenty years later students and young colored intellectuals in general showed a mounting disposition to reject whiteness as a standard of excellence, and even to stress darker skin as evidence of superior moral inheritance. That color consciousness had by no means disappeared, however, is attested by the immense sales of skin and hair preparation among less sophisticated colored folk. While magazines like *Ebony* still relied to no small degree for revenue upon advertisements of such products, they chided their readers for straining toward whiteness; and while they showed a predilection for light-skinned, Caucasoid subjects as cover girls and "cheesecake," they offered editorials, citing numerous living examples, to prove that the dark Negro's achievements are in no way less memorable than those of mulattoes.

Dark or light, it was the colored elite who found segregation most intolerable, precisely because they had so fully assimilated the white man's culture that further postponement of first-class citizenship could no longer, they felt, be defended. While fearful whites saw in the processes of integration the ultimate flooding of Negroes into their neighborhoods, their churches, their most intimate clubs and their very families, Negro gentlefolk insisted that the same pride that moved them to demand the end of organized segregation would prevent them from entering doors where they encountered strong hostility. Far from being motivated by a hidden desire to be white —so ran the argument—Negroes lamented the segregator's implication of their inherent inferiority far more than they resented the objective exclusions *per se*.

They grieved also over the white man's habit of holding the Negro responsible for the *results* of segregation, and of his citing those very results as justification for perpetuating the patterns that produced them. Under the galling confinements of a life of poverty in the swarming ghetto, smarting from the repeated slamming of doors in their faces, the lowest stratum of the second-class citizenry accounted for an appalling incidence of crime, illegitimacy, venereal disease, family disorganization, coarse conduct and the grossest improvidence. The educated, cultivated Negro was made answerable for these deficiencies by those whites to whom all Negroes look alike; the colored respectables insisted that it was unjust to blame the better class for them, and that even the classes who committed them could scarcely be held accountable for the consequences of the life to which discrimination condemned them. As some expressed it—Nannie Burroughs among them—take the Negro out of the alley and you take the alley out of the Negro.

Although the ownership of homes—and of automobiles and television sets—was vastly more common among American Negroes than among the generality of European people, housing was still the one commodity that the upper-class Negro could not purchase in an unrestricted market. His choice was limited to the Negro section whose most reputable fringes were perpetually falling before the encroaching slum. "Transition" neighborhoods, little outlying oases, or "exclusive" neighborhoods (like Harlem's Sugar Hill where an incredibly large fraction of the cream of Negro society lived at 409 and 555 Edgecombe) afforded temporary sanctuary, but always the egregious shortage of housing for a steeply rising Negro population accustomed to paying fantastic rents and to doubling up and taking in lodgers —at immense peril to family stability and healthy human relations—eventually doomed the best of colored neighborhoods. A measure of relief was afforded also by public housing projects where discrimination was legally forbidden, but the tide of population beat insistently upon the outer edges of the enclave, forcing back the walls, occasionally spilling over in irregular patterns, and evoking frantic resistance from property owners and the real-estate boards.

Even so, a few upper-class Negroes who were determined to flee the squalor and to find fresh air, green grass and better companions and schools for their children, challenged the line in spite of such outbursts of violence as those in the Chicago area at Cicero and Trumbull Park. Marian Anderson at length found a suitable country place in Connecticut, but Judge Delany was repulsed in his effort to find in a white New York neighborhood the kind of fine housing he could well pay for. John Hope Franklin, moving up from Howard to become chairman of the department of History at Brooklyn College, met repeated humiliations with quiet fortitude before finding satisfactory accommodations in a "mixed" area in Brooklyn. The scientist, Percy Julian, upon purchasing a fine home in Oak Park in 1951, encountered threats to his person, harassment of his children and serious attempts to bomb and burn him out. But he stood his ground (hiring private watchmen for two years to guard the place) and finally won acceptance as a respected citizen of that upper-class Chicago suburb. Jackie Robinson, on the other hand, was able to purchase a fine home in Stamford, Connecticut, and Harry Belafonte, after adamant refusals, found a suitable apartment in a good white neighborhood in New York.

Life in the vast Northern ghettos, with all its frustrations, was still preferred above life in the South, however. Nearly all of the country's most famous Negroes, if we except those associated with the separate Negro churches and schools, were massed there, and there was a steady streaming of colored population to these centers, with no discernible reverse flow. The bulk of Harlem's Negroes, for example, were still depressed by labor standards markedly lower than the national average, but no organized citizens' councils thwarted their progress, and no responsible agency, no respected public servant called for the perpetuation of discriminatory practice. The city and the state had rejected segregation in principle, and if a Negro had a complaint, the law and the courts were on his side. A comprehensive and still-growing network of laws and commissions was cutting away discrimination in employment, in schools and other public facilities, and even in housing. Residential segregation operated to neutralize these guarantees, as in the case of elementary and junior high schools, whose pupil assignment is strictly zoned, but the high schools and municipal colleges were blanketed by no such prescription, and the lower schools have begun desegregation.

New York's governing structure was, moreover, now studded with colored public officials. Besides a growing army of lesser functionaries, there has been a member of Congress; a borough president; the state's rent commissioner; the New York City Commissioner of Water, Gas and Electricity; a city councilman; a school-board member; a deputy police commissioner; numerous high-ranking judges, and the assistant to the mayor. Indeed, the growing power of the Negro vote and the liberalization of white public attitudes produced impressive machinery for coping with public discrimination. It was the subtler, private pressures that preserved the Northern ghettos: the hostility of white communities and individuals; the money-lending agencies; the racial restrictive real-state covenant (in effect illegal since the Supreme Court's decision in *Shelley* v. *Kraemer,* 1948); the machinations of real-estate operators; the neglect of the Negro market by private builders and lenders; the fear that improved housing will only attract still more Negroes to the neighborhood.

Housing aside, other economic indices showed notable gains everywhere in the North. Widening opportunities absorbed into the general economy thousands of skilled and semi-skilled workers, and hundreds of white-collar employees in the banks, insurance companies, the communications and transportation industries, and particularly in the profession of engineering. Physicians were, however, still excluded from white hospitals, and there were as yet no Negroes in any major symphony orchestra in the land.

Especially after 1936, the race was steadily losing its old belief in its own inherent inferiority. Upper-class Negroes repudiated it categorically, persuaded that by natural endowment they could in the absence of barriers (as indeed many in the presence of barriers had already done) equal the white man's achievements in every particular. The colored masses had not yet moved so far in their attitudes, and they constantly disappointed their leaders by their sluggish response to appeals that they register as voters, join the NAACP, use the educational facilities available to them, and cultivate industry, temperance, frugality and higher standards of conduct.

The successful Negro was often embarrassed by the vulgarities of the masses, and this estrangement within the ghetto bred strain and a persistent suspicion among lower-class folk that the Big Negro was trying to "go white." The colored aristocracy of talent and attainment and wealth, in their cultural isolation, sought community of interest within their small circle in such organizations as the Boule, and in exclusive clubs like the Frogs of Pittsburg, the Snakes of Chicago, the Mu-so-lit in Washington, the Cosmos in New York, the Nacirema (a significant anagram!) in Detroit. They express themselves poignantly—though rarely in print—on the difficulties (so long as they are exposed to pain and humiliation at the hands of any cracker who chooses to torment them) of maintaining a sense of achievement and self-respect. How, they plead, can a man stand erect as a hero to his community, his family, or even to himself, if in his supremest moments his larger environment still sharply reminds him that his Negroness is the overarching fact of his life, and that millions of his countrymen still believe that every Negro is, when all is said, the inferior of every white man in the world? Such painful misgivings can drive the most gifted men to elaborate devices to reassure themselves and each other that their claim to status is real.

Although the harsher outlines of discrimination in travel had been smoothed by judicial decrees, survivals of Jim Crow on trains and buses in the late 1950's still exposed the Negro elite, no less than their humbler kinsmen, to emotional shock and reminders of inferiority. The immense importance that the race attaches to automobile ownership and its preference for air travel, are in part explained by the desire to escape humiliation. Annual "vacation guides" in Negro periodicals and the yearly *Travelguide* volumes afford tourists some assistance in finding the relatively scarce accommodations where they may expect to be welcome. Another safety valve is the practice of vacationing in Europe or in the Caribbean Islands, but less prosperous folk content themselves with the small number of all-Negro resorts or with unsegregated national and state parks, which, in the absence of ready accommodations, they frequently reach after day-and-night driving, subsisting on basket lunches to avoid humiliation in public restaurants.

The most distinguished Negroes still found that discrimination was in fact highly indiscriminate. In the 1940's the grave, polished William S. Braithwaite, residing in Atlanta as guest professor of the university there, was still hailed as "boy" by the clothing-store clerk; L. K. Williams, head of one of the largest religious bodies in America and a power in Republican politics, could be refused Pullman space on the plea that it was sold out, when whites had no difficulty buying berths; C. C. Spaulding could be roughed up by a petty clerk in Raleigh, when he ordered a soft drink at a little stand adjoining a building owned by his thriving insurance firm; Roland Hayes could be assaulted by police in Georgia, and Rayford Logan could encounter infuriating obstacles in buying steamer accommodations in New York.

Sometimes Jim Crow is more amusing than angering. Langston Hughes could not have his shoes shined at a shop whose window advertised his forthcoming public lecture. Once when he tried to buy a Sunday *New York Times* in the white waiting room of a Southern railway station, a policeman forbade him to depart by the door through which he had entered and instructed him to leave by way of the platform and walk down the tracks to the grade crossing that would put him back on the city street leading to the colored waiting room.

A bitter reminder of his curious status confronted the Negro when the time came to explain discrimination to his children. The *Negro Digest* in the 1950's ran a touching series by famous Negro Americans entitled, "How I Told My Children about Race." Parents uneasily put off the evil day, but late or soon the occasion arose when the child demanded an answer, and the parents' carefully prepared speech, intended for some more convenient day, had suddenly to be tailored to the emergency. Pulitzer Prize poet Gwendolyn Brooks, strolling with her little son near the University of Chicago, was startled by an automobile load of young toughs shouting obscenities and hurling a shower of rocks; Arna Bontemps, on the morning after a Fisk-Xavier football game which his five-year-old son had found so exciting, was asked why the Nashville papers published pictures of the Vanderbilt games but ignored the Fisk contest. Others were called upon to account for jeers or to explain why there were no photographs of colored brides in the daily papers or why colored folk always moved to the back of the bus.

Some highly talented, ambitious Negroes were broken by the disabilities laid upon them, and others were driven to a sullen despair or belligerency that effectually thwarted their rise to distinction. A few well-known achievers tried to flee their constraints by leaving the country, a resort available only to a few: a tiny corps of writers, artists, musicians and entertainers. Henry O. Tanner, smarting from racial rebuffs and reluctant to expend upon racial conflict energies that his creative function could ill share with another preoccupation, was followed in succeeding decades by other artists who made extended, though rarely permanent, stays in Paris. Richmond Barthé went to the West Indies and E. Simms Campbell, the illustrator and cartoonist, took up residence in Europe. Ollie Harrington, the *Pittsburgh Courier's* gifted cartoonist-satirist, in the 1950's was mailing in his weekly cartoons from his home in France.

Among the contemporary writers, Richard Wright became a permanent Paris resident; Frank Yerby and Wallace Thurman established homes in France; Ralph Ellison, James Baldwin and the late Claude McKay sojourned extensively abroad; Frank Marshall Davis settled in Hawaii. Of the musicians, Anne Wiggins Brown, Dean Dixon, Kenneth Spencer and Sidney Bechet took up legal residence in Europe, and Paul Robeson lived for several years in London. Several, like Tanner, Wright, Davis and Dixon, married white women; Miss Brown became the wife of a Scandinavian of distinguished family.

Expatriation was, in fact, extremely rare. Recent years have seen, however, a few examples of retirements of aging Negro notables abroad, though not in Europe. Shelton Hale Bishop, after his retirement as a religious leader in Harlem, moved to Hawaii; the noted physician, U. G. Dailey, established his home in Haiti; Herman E. Moore, former United States District Judge for the Virgin Islands, made the islands his permanent home after stepping down from the bench.

The same general class which furnished the few examples of "voluntary exiles" also supplied most of the rare instances of inter-racial marriages: writers, musicians and entertainers. There were, though, as we have noted, earlier examples like Lemuel Haynes before the Civil War, and in the later nineteenth century such members of the vanguard as Frederick Douglass, William S. Scarborough, Archibald Grimké, and, somewhat later, Daniel Hale Williams. Jack Johnson was one of several prize fighters who "married white." Among contemporary notable Negroes who have taken white marriage partners (most of them after an earlier marriage to a colored spouse) are popular entertainers Harry Belafonte, Lena Horne, Pearl Bailey, Katherine Dunham and Pearl Primus; concert artists Mattiwilda Dobbs and Adele Addison; composer William Grant Still; journalists George Schuyler and Horace Cayton; playwright Louis Peterson; the late NAACP secretary, Walter White; and the prominent Chicago physician, N. O. Calloway.

The traumas attendant upon cultural isolation and the efforts at adjustment to catastrophic rejection by white society moved Franklin Frazier to sketch a somber picture of the black bourgeoisie—which significantly evoked angry dissents from scores of colored reviewers. But more optimistic Negroes pointed out that the gains of the whole race, and notably of the upper stratum, in moving toward white acceptance, had in the past twenty years been more extensive than the most sanguine prophet in the 1930's would have predicted for the next fifty years. Intellectuals were cheered to note especially that at least some members of the vanguard now stood on a wavering color line, making frequent contact with whites who were according them some tentative acceptance, especially in the arts, the sciences, religion and in the scholarly disciplines.

Poised on precarious social frontiers, and keenly aware of the fateful role they were playing as symbols of the race, a majority of the colored elite took their responsibilities with utmost gravity. They redoubled their efforts to demonstrate the race's potentialities, and meticulously avoided every gaucherie that might lend credence to old stereotypes, even to giving up favorite foods and innocent amusements. William H. Jernagin, for example, long past eighty, once had occasion, after a long soaking bath at his hotel, to transfer to another floor where delegates to a religious conference were housed. When shown to his new room, he was asked if he would require a bath at once. He answered with a vigorous affirmative, lest he give support to a hoary fable about the race's inherent distaste for bathing.

The members of the vanguard for 1936–1959 grew up, as we have noted, in a vastly simpler and more homogeneous Negro society than the one in which they were to make their mark. But urban centers in the South as well as a few Northern cities already had a substantial class of postal clerks, mail carriers, petty railway officials and others whose economic base often lay outside the local community: comparatively secure folk, given to religious orthodoxy and puritanical conduct and cleanliness; folk with a little leisure for relaxation and study; as yet unbruised by the vulgarities of the ghettos that would later swallow up their sons; folk determined to see their children educated and established in reputability.

From such antecedents, many of the contemporary generation's notables sprang. Others were the sons of teachers and preachers. Some had mothers who had been teachers or fathers whose diligence had earned for their families a little farm of their own or a dependable income from semi-skilled and skilled labor. In these sturdy segments of the Negro population the matriarchate was now superseded by a family structure steadied and consolidated by the father as a dependable breadwinner, rejoicing in his family's fidelity to the middle-class virtues, dedicated to his church and his lodge, proud of the home that he owned. By no means all of the vanguard came from such comparatively favorable origins, but a large fraction of them did. Yet, even these shared the handicaps that were the common lot of Negro children: there was still the burden of extremely modest material means; the universal expectation that the Negro keep his "place"; the notion that education would spoil him. Public provision for the education of Negroes beyond the elementary grades was still unknown in the South in which most of them were born.

Many contemporary Negro leaders inform the writer that the increasing complexity of the Negro status system in recent years has reduced the importance of family connection as a qualification for status and achievement, but few deny that it was in earlier days a major determinant. That it was a decisive factor in the rise of many who in 1936–1959 stood at the head of the race is more than hinted by the extraordinary links between this and the previous generation's celebrities. After compiling the roster of Negro notables of the past half century, we can, confining ourselves entirely to those names identified in this study, trace out an intricate web of family relationships that argues a high degree of intermarriage and consanguinity. One notable feature of the pattern is the emergence of a number of families, who, now in their third generation since the Civil War, have produced an extraordinary number of outstanding leaders in a variety of fields since the founders of the clans came to prominence in the mid-nineteenth century—people like the Bonds of Tennessee, the Huberts and the Nabrits of Georgia, the Tanners of Pennsylvania, the Clements and the Delanys and Joneses of North Carolina, the Churches of Memphis.

A page or two of examples will serve to illustrate the point. With the aid of the index the reader may identify all of those named, for each was, in his own right, a member of the vanguard. Father and son combinations included R. R. Wright, Sr. and Jr.; Richard H. and Henry Allen Boyd; James M. and William Monroe Trotter; James S. and James A. Russell; the elder and the younger Adam Clayton Powell; James M. and Horace M. Bond; the P. B. Youngs; John E. and Carl Murphy; C. C. Diggs, Sr. and Jr.; the elder and the younger William J. Trent; Benjamin Tucker Tanner and Henry O. Tanner; Isaac and James Lane; the first and second Matthew

Wesley Clair; J. W. E. Bowen, Sr. and Jr.; Truman K. Gibson and his son of the same name; Jesse and Doyle Mitchell; C. C. Spaulding the elder and younger; A. F. and Norris Herndon; William J. and Leigh Whipper; Joshua H. and Gilbert H. Jones; Archibald Carey, Sr. and Jr.; the two Luther H. Fosters; R. R. Church, the first and second; the elder and younger William A. Fountain; Blanche K. and Roscoe C. Bruce; George C. and Rufus E. Clement; B. O. Davis, Sr. and Jr.; Benjamin J. Davis the elder and younger; E. M. and Benjamin G. Brawley; James E. and A. Maceo Walker; Henry B. and Hubert Delany; Elijah and Miles Mark Fisher; Will Marion Cook and Mercer Cook. Angelina Grimké was the daughter of Archibald Grimké.

Other blood relatives were Robert S. Abbott and John Sengstacke; C. C. Spaulding and Asa T. Spaulding; John Mercer Langston and Langston Hughes; Frank S. and Lena Horne; P. B. S. Pinchback and Jean Toomer; composer William L. Dawson and the Congressman of the same name; Hiram R. Revels and Horace Cayton. Brothers were James Weldon Johnson and J. Rosamond Johnson; Archibald and Francis J. Grimké; Horace and J. Max Bond; James M. and Samuel M. Nabrit; Archibald and Willard Motley; Paul and Benjamin C. Robeson. Brother-sister combinations included Rufus Clement and Abbie Clement Jackson, and R. R. Church, Jr. and Mary Church Terrell. Robert C. Weaver is a nephew of Harry Burleigh; the wife of John W. Davis was a granddaughter of Jefferson Long; Clarence Cameron White's first wife was a cousin of Meta Warrick Fuller, and William H. Hastie is a cousin of Charles H. Houston.

Examples of eminent Negroes married (or formerly married) to each other are afforded by David and Susie Williams Jones; Adam Powell and Hazel Scott; William Warfield and Leontyne Price; Joe Louis and Rose Morgan; George E. and Elizabeth Ross Haynes; Midian O. and Maudelle Bousfield; Raymond P. and Sadie Tanner Alexander (Mrs. Bousfield and Mrs. Alexander are also members of the Benjamin T. Tanner clan); Georgia Douglass and Henry Lincoln Johnson; Claude Barnett and Etta Moten; Abbie Mitchell and Will Marion Cook; Robert H. and Mary Church Terrell.

Other examples of marital ties between noted families may be instanced. Countee Cullen married a daughter of W. E. B. Du Bois; children of David D. and Susie Williams Jones are married to children of Louis T. Wright and Mordecai Johnson; William H. Dean was the son-in-law of Channing Tobias, and the younger Archibald Carey's sister married Shelton Hale Bishop. Julian Lewis is the son-in-law of Anthony Overton, and Bindley Cyrus, after his first marriage to an adopted daughter of Booker T. Washington, married the daughter of U. G. Dailey. Sidney Poitier and Archie Moore married a pair of sisters. Judge Delany's first wife was a daughter of Emmett J. Scott, and his brother's wife is a sister-in-law of Franklin Frazier. Lester Walton's wife is the daughter of Fred R. Moore, and the sister of Rufus Clement and Abbie

Clement Jackson is the wife of J. Max Bond and the sister-in-law of Horace M. Bond; Frederick D. Patterson married the daughter of R. R. Moton before succeeding him as president of Tuskegee.

The recent and contemporary record suggests at least thirty-three* religious leaders to be added to our roster for the new era, besides more than a score of men prominent in the previous generation who were still outstanding personages in the 1940's and 1950's. Although the church continued, in the mid-twentieth century, to be the most influential institution in Negro America, it attracted fewer of the race's ablest young men as the opportunities and achievements of colored Americans in a growing number of secular fields multiplied. Martin Luther King, as a student at Morehouse, had at first grave doubts about the "intellectual respectability" of the ministerial calling in the new age, but eventually, under the urging of President Mays, elected the church rather than medicine or law. His subsequent emergence, before he was thirty, as one of the best-known Negro leaders in the land, combined with the mounting participation of other pastors in social action, have for the present renewed interest in the ministry.

While the day-to-day mission of the church was conducted by an army of relatively obscure pastors, the men of widest reputation were the leading Methodist bishops, presidents of Baptist conventions, denominational secretaries and administrators and pastors of huge parishes who, besides directing the church's religious and social programs, participated in a wide variety of community and reform activities, including political action and various pressure tactics. The big names, in short, were organizers and executives, rather than theologians, mystics, or saints.

If the general membership of the church was prepared to acknowledge the integrity of the bulk of its leadership, it continued to be distresssed by startling charges of political jockeying and downright malfeasance hurled at each other by leading ecclesiastical statesmen. The conferences and conventions of the major denominations were still rocked by disclosures of official misconduct, factional in-fighting and suspensions of bishops and college heads

* Many of the religious leaders whom we have previously listed for the period 1900–1936 were still prominent in the more recent period. New names to be added for the years following 1936 follow:

Connie Cornelius Adams	Bravid W. Harris	D. Ward Nichols
Cameron C. Alleyne	John A. Haywood	Adam C. Powell, Jr.
William H. Borders	William Lloyd Imes	Benjamin C. Robeson
John W. E. Bowen, Jr.	Abbie Clement Jackson	James H. Robinson
Robert N. Brooks	Joseph H. Jackson	Shelby Rooks
Nannie H. Burroughs	David V. Jemison	James A. Russell
Archibald J. Carey, Jr.	Martin Luther King, Jr.	Marshall L. Shepard
Matthew W. Clair, Jr.	Harold M. Kingsley	Howard Thurman
Miles Mark Fisher	Edgar A. Love	C. Ewbanks Tucker
Sherman L. Greene	Benjamin E. Mays	Dougal O. B. Walker
Robert Harrington	Solomon L. Michaux	Frank T. Wilson

on charges of the gravest sort. Disputes were carried to the courts and injunctions sought to strip denominational leaders of jurisdiction or to restrain newly elected functionaries from assuming office. In 1946 the AME Bishops' Council was convoked to try nine bishops on charges ranging from "drunkenness" to "accepting money under false pretenses" and "immorality and maladministration through conspiracy." An astonishing contest between two elder bishops, each claiming the right to preside, precipitated a tumult that city police were powerless to quell. A few months later the *Pittsburgh Courier* described "the biggest court fight in the history of the Negro people," a contest in which rival factions employed thirty-three lawyers for legal action that reached into the federal courts. The wounds were far from healed in 1959. For more than a decade the moves and countermoves, the suspensions and reinstatements, continued to be chronicled in detail in the race's press, a protracted wrangle that involved some of the biggest names in the AME fold.

Other denominations were by no means exempt from such distresses. The 1952 AMEZ conference was a turbulent one, and in 1958 a power struggle threatened the peace of the body as rivals bandied accusations of autocracy, "political strategy," and "bogus publicity." Similar competitions menaced the tranquillity of the National Baptist Convention. Disputes there centered annually about the succession to the presidency, an office of immense prestige and a lucrative one as well, for it carried a salary beyond the incumbent's regular pastoral emoluments, free transportation passes and opportunities for delivering well-remunerated addresses. Baptist leaders have worked hard to achieve the office and have been singularly reluctant to relinquish it.

In the 1941 meeting of the National Baptist Convention, a contest over delegate apportionment precipitated a near riot; the platform was mobbed by shouting disputants, and order was finally restored when squads of city police marched into the hall and the convention officers changed the order of business temporarily to prayer and hymn-singing. Another floor fight was touched off when a group of "independents" sought to commit the convention to secret ballots.

When David V. Jemison retired as president in 1953, Joseph H. Jackson, of the strategic Olivet Church in Chicago, defeated five rivals after twelve hours of balloting. An active candidate for years, he had appealed, the press reported, to his congregation for a vote of confidence shortly before the 1953 meeting. Weeks before, a faction in the parish had formally denounced him, but now his supporters gave him a rousing endorsement and presented him with funds for "traveling and campaign expenses." In 1957, when he was elected for a fifth term despite a new four-year tenure rule, there were cries of fraud; galleries were packed, said his detractors, demonstrations were rigged and microphones "killed." Attorneys of the disaffected group promptly challenged his title to the office, but a few days before the 1958 meeting a United States District Court ruled the tenure-limiting amendment illegal, and the last major obstacle to a sixth term fell away. He was triumphantly re-elected at what proved to be a remarkably harmonious session.

A recent issue of *Ebony* magazine gives a candid description of the 1956 quadrennial conference in Miami, where five AME bishops were elected from an initial slate of 102 candidates. When the storm cleared, only one of the successful aspirants (from Capetown, South Africa) was an independent. The other four were Southerners, "members of a slate called 'The Combination'," reportedly financed by a forty-thousand-dollar campaign fund.

The conference, said *Ebony,* was preceded by the usual pre-convention campaign. Candidates came to the meeting with blocks of instructed delegates pledged to them. Some—perhaps four fifths—were only sending up trial balloons, with an eye to a later convention, four, eight, even twelve years distant. The 1676 voting delegates were besieged by placard-carrying spectators, women wearing lettered shawls and sashes, claques wearing campaign hats, and by receptions and "goodwill dinners," one of which cost one of them nearly five hundred dollars. Scattered about the headquarters were free sandwich counters graced with electioneering posters, "information tables" and huddled groups analagous to the floor caucuses of political conventions. Many partisans wore sashes emblazoned with the slogan "Play Ball with Ball, Florida's Strong Man." Ball, one of the four-man combination slate, did indeed win. He had, *Ebony* reported, started with a block of 800 votes, the fruit of four years of hard campaigning, and was now swept into office. The convention ended with the traditional solemn consecration service.

This side of ecclesiastical politics cannot, in honesty, be left out of our account, but undue emphasis upon it gives a false picture. Not only are these irregularities candidly exposed and condemned by the Negro church's adherents, but they are sharply rebuked by most of those whom we have listed in our roster, as well as by thousands of dedicated clergymen who continue to be the most important corps of counsellors, teachers and intercessors for a fundamentally devout people, deeply loyal to America's historic Christian heritage.

It is the Protestant communions that still hold the Negro's allegiance. Ten thousand colored members are added annually to the Roman Catholic Church and there were by 1958 more than a half million Negro American Catholics, but this was far below the proportion of the Catholic population of America at large. Less than a hundred colored priests ministered to these folk, and there has not been, since Bishop Healy, another Negro bishop with jurisdiction in the United States.

The social origins of the thirty-three religious leaders whom we now add to our roster show significant uniformities. All but four were born in the South, and two of the exceptions in the British West Indies. Fully half were the children of clergymen (eight of them sons of church leaders whose prominence placed them in our roster for 1900–1936), and thus early exposed to literate, cultivated, intellectually stimulating home environments. Several had the further boon of living near Negro colleges. At least ten were children of ex-slaves, and most of the rest were only one or more generations removed from unfree forebears. The group exhibited the whole spectrum of Negro pigmentation, from dark-skinned men like Robeson, Robinson and Mays, to extremely fair men like Carey, Imes and Rooks (to name six of the most respected and beloved members of the group).

While several felt drawn to the ministry in childhood by a "call"—in some cases reinforced by parental expectation, or by a sudden conversion—others confessed that exclusion from other vocations drew them to the ministry as the most accessible alternative. As late as 1930, the great majority of active Negro clergymen still had no seminary training at all, and had, in fact, not progressed beyond the elementary grades. In this respect also our list is far from typical, for they were, with only one exception (a radio evangelist), college-trained. Twenty-eight had their basic college education in the Negro colleges (many of which were still staffed by white administrators and professors), and four had Northern college courses. And while a few had little or no formal theological instruction, most of them had bachelor's and some of them master's degrees in theology, and two had earned the Ph.D. Approximately a third of the theological degrees were taken at Negro seminaries, the other two thirds at major Northern institutions: Union, Drew, Garrett, Chicago, Boston, Northwestern, Colgate, Crozer, Yale, Oberlin and Columbia.

Some had far graver obstacles to overcome than did thousands who never rose out of obscurity. Howard Thurman, Dean of the Chapel of Boston University, sprang from the humblest family antecedents, in Florida, and was reared by his ex-slave grandmother. He was able to go to high school in a distant city only because a cousin took him in and gave him one meal a day. After working his way through Morehouse College by long hours of outside labor, and winning virtually every student prize, he managed to enter Colgate Rochester Divinity School.

Benjamin Mays, president of Morehouse and a Baptist leader of world reputation, was born to penniless South Carolina ex-slave sharecropper parents, only one of whom could trace out the easier words in the Bible. They were prevailed upon by a clergyman to send their bright child to a sectarian elementary school, and then the boy was released from farm work for three or four months of the year to attend high school at a state "college" a hundred miles from home. When he finished there, he suffered the distress of "praying against" his father for a chance to go to a Northern white college. Stimulated by a high-school teacher who rebuked laggards with the scornful comment that "the white boys at the state university can work these problems without half trying," young Mays was determined to prove, in direct competition with whites, that the God he worshipped had endowed the races equally.

Catalogs from leading New England colleges persuaded him that his fragmentary schooling failed to furnish the credentials for college entrance, but after a year at Virginia Union he entered Bates College in Maine. He finished the full course with distinction, and then summer employment as a Pullman porter, self-help campus jobs, and scholarships enabled him to go to the University of Chicago Divinity School (where he was elected president of a student discussion group). A few years later he returned to take a Ph.D. degree.

Similar hardships were mastered by James H. Robinson, today pastor of a huge community church and a commanding figure in civic, welfare, political and NAACP affairs in New York. A very dark child of the poorest sort of folk, he was rebuked by his own family for his boyish taste for reading, an exercise for which, they insisted, Negroes lacked all capacity. He was taken out of school at a very early age and put to work, but secretly attended a junior high school across town at the same time. A cash scholarship from the Presbyterian Board of Missions enabled him to set out for Lincoln University, but he lost the money to a pickpocket before he got there. Arrived on the campus, he addressed a letter to every pastor in the Cleveland presbytery, begging for funds for "a poor Negro student studying for the ministry." A generous response saw him through his first year.

Later, self-help jobs, scholarships and periodical cash gifts from an elderly white lady carried him along. His benefactress, he learned later, was a devout Presbyterian, a public-school teacher who helped many Negro students, in expiation, she said, for the sin of her town, Tonawanda, New York, in driving out its Negroes some years before. At Union Theological Seminary, again driven by poverty, he worked as much as forty or fifty hours a week at outside employments to remain in school. When his health broke, he was sent to a hospital for observation, and there an examining specialist took him to a lecture hall and commented on his case before an audience of interns and and physicians.

"This boy," (Robinson was thirty at the time) "is a Negro," he said. "You can see there's nothing wrong with him. His pain's imaginary."

The diagnostician went on to point out that his patient was only a few generations removed from savagery and was now making the foolish error of attempting to compete with men of an advanced race. To Robinson's indignant retort that many Negroes had distinguished themselves, the doctor coolly replied that men like Walter White, John Hope and Mordecai Johnson were men of mixed blood who only "achieved in proportion to that white superiority which they have absorbed." By now thoroughly infuriated, the badgered student shouted, "What about Harriet Tubman, Howard Thurman, George Washington Carver . . . Sojourner Truth? They are black as I am!"

Ben Robeson had his share of youthful hardships, but by contrast with Robinson was fortunate. No high school in his New Jersey community would take the colored boy, but the rugged character of his college-trained father—who had been assisted to freedom by Harriet Tubman—and the moral and intellectual influence of his mother—the descendant of several generations of Pennsylvanians, with Quaker blood in her veins—was a unique heritage. His parents sent Ben to North Carolina for high school and college at Biddle University whose campus proved a haven insulated from white hostilities.

William Lloyd Imes, a Presbyterian leader and famous Negro-rights champion, was also fortunate in his ancestry. His freeborn father had migrated to the South in the late Reconstruction, to labor on the new religious frontier as teacher and preacher. No high school was available to William, but he was surrounded by books, periodicals and cultivated house guests, and the elder Imes undertook to prepare the boy for college himself, with help from his ex-slave, but educated, wife. Just as the elder Imes had been trained by old-line Yankee-Calvinist-Abolitionists at Oberlin, William caught the same moral fervors at Fisk, a spiritual offshoot of Oberlin. And just as his father had named William for William Lloyd Garrison, he in turn named his son (destined to die in battle in World War II) Wendell Phillips. At Union Theological Seminary, Imes's lot was free from friction, and he later served on the seminary's board of trustees.

Upon his retirement at Harlem's St. James Church, he was succeeded by Shelby Rooks, another, who, though his gentle spirit was frequently bruised on the color line, applied himself to improve the advantages he had inherited. He derived from extremely fair-skinned North Carolina ex-slave stock, linked by blood with several white families of the area, who had purchased their freedom well before the Emancipation. His parents, skilled tradespeople of scanty means, encouraged the boy to realize his educational ambitions. The proximity of the Negro state teachers' college at Fayetteville enabled him to begin his college career, and he went next to Lincoln University, finishing in debt despite scholarship aid and earnest efforts to earn his way. He next became a redcap in a Philadelphia depot until a chance conversation with an elderly Quaker Pullman passenger led to an offer of financial help for further studies. The money took Rooks to Union Theological Seminary and, with further funds he earned at menial tasks, he completed the program.

Archibald J. Carey, Jr., is today a leading AME pastor in Chicago, member of a prosperous downtown Chicago law firm, chairman of President Eisenhower's Committee on Government Employment Policy, a former Chicago alderman (after eight years on the City Council, he lost his seat to Ralph Metcalfe, Negro hero of the 1932 and 1936 Olympics), Republican nominee for Congress, and alternate delegate to the United Nations General Assembly. As the son of a prominent Chicago AME bishop and political leader, he had a privileged boyhood. He won the thousand-dollar prize in an annual Chicago *Daily News* oratorical contest for the city's high-school population, and secured all of his college, theological and law degrees in his home city. Ten European nationalities are blended with the Careys' African blood; family relationships link them with Napoleon and Jefferson. Archibald Jr.'s mother was the near-white daughter of a prominent Reconstruction legislator. On his father's side he is the fourth in an unbroken line of Methodist pastors. Just as Bishop Carey had helped William Hale Thompson become mayor, Thompson helped Carey to his bishopric and to significant posts in city government.

His father's prominence put the boy on easy terms with religious, civic and public dignitaries. He was even introduced to Theodore Roosevelt, William Jennings Bryan and Woodrow Wilson. He frequently accompanied his father on professional rounds and, because they were constantly mistaken for whites, frequently heard severe disparagement of Negroes. On one such occasion, when their electric car stalled after toiling up the long hill near Blue Island, repairmen discussed a proposed assault upon the Chicago Negro neighborhood, planned for July 4, 1919. The tip gave Bishop Carey time to warn his friend, Mayor Thompson, and when the now historic flare-up occurred—on July twenty-seventh, as it turned out—the police were forewarned, and confined the riot to a smaller compass than it might otherwise have attained.

Carey's fair skin has sometimes brought him into difficulties. Years ago he was hustled out of Jim Crow cars, accused of misuse of railway passes stamped "colored," and he sometimes found his complexion a political liability among ghetto voters. Once, when he picked up a hitchhiking sailor near the Great Lakes Station, he asked the youth for his opinion of the colored trainees at the post. The unsuspecting serviceman rattled off the usual charges of Negro uncleanliness, laziness and stupidity.

J. W. E. Bowen, of Atlanta, another son of a famous father, was sent to the finest schools in New England: Phillips Exeter, Wesleyan and Harvard. His father was one of the best-known leaders of the Negro wing of the Northern Methodist Episcopal Church besides being one of the first two Negroes to earn the Ph.D. degree and one of the first who sincerely believed and asserted that the Negro is inherently the white man's equal. Miles Mark Fisher, of Durham, North Carolina, was also fortunate in being the son of one of the leading Baptists in his day. After attending his father's alma mater, Morehouse, the younger Fisher was welcomed at Northern Baptist Seminary, Chicago, as its only colored student. His sound preparation at Morehouse enabled him to help his white classmates with Greek and Hebrew assignments in exchange for carfare and lunch money. It is instructive to note how close he still is to the slavery past. Not yet past sixty in 1958, with doctoral training at the University of Chicago, listed in an *Ebony* article as one of the ten outstanding Negro clergymen, he was born of ex-slave parents, one of whom he himself taught to read in her maturer years.

Abbie Clement Jackson and Matthew Wesley Clair, as children of celebrated bishops had impressive advantages, as did Martin Luther King. After splendid training at Morehouse in Atlanta, where his father is still a foremost religious leader, King was in comfortable circumstances when his father sent him first to Crozer Seminary in Philadelphia and then to Boston University for the doctorate. His excellent record at Morehouse had brought him several offers of scholarships, but the elder King insisted that these be reserved for more impecunious young men.

Adam Clayton Powell, Jr., better known as a Congressman, inherited his pastorate of Abyssinian Baptist Church in Harlem as well as some of his political prominence from his father. The senior Powell was well able to send young Adam to Colgate, and though the young man worked in summers as a redcap, he was not dependent upon such earnings. Indeed, a New York *Post* interview once represented Powell as disclosing that his mother, the daughter of a wealthy white man, had been supplied, over the years, with huge sums of money by her father, much of which she turned over to her exuberant son in his college days.

The catalog of extra-church affairs in which the leading clergymen were deeply involved still marked them as some of the most influential men in colored America, deeply affecting its politics, its economic, social and cultural life, and its relationships with white America. Nearly all were affiliated with the NAACP, several as life members, and some—Mays, Imes and Robinson among them—as major officers.

After 1950 they were perhaps superseded by the race's educational leaders as the chief reservoir for advisers and members of public and reform agencies, but from the point of view of the breadth and depth of their reach into the lives of their people, the clergy continued to be more important than the college presidents and scholars, who had a far smaller constituency. One of them, Rev. Martin Luther King, leader in the Deep South of the surprisingly effective campaign against Jim Crow by passive resistance and "meeting the enemy with Christian love," was in 1958 the most famous race leader in the land—a circumstance acknowledged by President Eisenhower when, in the summer of 1958, he invited King, Philip Randolph, Roy Wilkins and Lester Granger to confer with him on the condition and prospects of the race.

Steeply increased enrollments in the Negro colleges, coupled with the shift from white to Negro administrators and instructors—thanks to a growing supply of well-trained Negro professors and stiffening demand, at least at some schools, from students that their institutions be administered by their own people—gave the Negro educator a wider opportunity. The multiplication of college presidents, deans and professors in fact proceeded at such a pace that it was no longer realistic to regard the bulk of them as members of the race's vanguard. The 1954–1955 *Who's Who in America,* for example, lists nearly a hundred colored educators, many of whom are not well known by either Negroes or whites. The traditionally modest remuneration for professors, of whatever race, and the expanding opportunities for bright and ambitious young colored men in medicine, law, engineering, chemistry and other learned callings reduced the attractive power of teaching. The dubious future of Negro colleges, now that the country was officially committed to desegregation, also gave pause to young Negroes fearful of competition with whites for places in institutions still dominated by the latter.

The most conspicuous educators were still principally administrators rather than scholars, and for the same reason that an earlier chapter suggested. Meanwhile, fateful changes seemed already in progress. By the 1950's some of the race's ablest scholars were being drawn from Negro college faculties to white institutions, and colored students gave evidence of a similar drift to white schools. White students, moreover, began to appear at state-supported Negro colleges. In the wake of the 1954 Supreme Court desegregation decision, West Virginia State College and Lincoln University, for example, had nearly three hundred and two hundred white students, respectively, by 1957. Standards at the Negro colleges were creeping upward, and the old animus against "academic" training had so far receded that Tuskegee itself initiated a comprehensive liberal-arts program.

The old isolation of Negro educators was slowly disappearing as contacts with colleagues on white campuses and at annual meetings of professional groups multiplied. The latter showed a growing disposition to select their annual convention sites with a view to the availability of accommodations for their colored members. Negro scholars began to be elected to high office and to read papers before these scholarly associations, and to participate in such agencies as the National Education Association, the American Association of University Professors, the American Council of Learned Societies, the Social Science Research Council, the Fulbright Board of Foreign Scholarships, the American Council on Education and the Ford Foundation's Committee on Fellowships.

Many of the leading college administrators had theological training or were ordained ministers with a history of pastoral experience, but the theological influence was now apparently declining. The sectarian schools naturally drew upon the clergy for presidents and deans, and many of the public institutions also have long been led by churchmen, but more recently chosen college heads perhaps illustrate a break with this tradition. Some see in the tendency a reflection of changed objectives of Negro colleges, an emphasis on making money rather than an education for "making men." Many of the better-known educational statesmen came from the homes of preachers, teachers and physicians, and several from communities where a Negro college was immediately at hand.

Colored college presidents continue, as in the past, to draw fire as tyrants before their faculties, and pliant trimmers before their trustees, the foundations, legislators and other influences. Like their white analogues, some were chosen for outstanding qualities of scholarship and administrative skill and others were not. Many climbed the ladder of preferment by joining the faculty of their own alma mater, then rising through department headships and deanships to the presidency after years of playing a game of safe politics, adroitly ingratiating themselves with factions both on and off the campus, avoiding controversy and demonstrating the kind of moral and intellectual neutralism that a conformist age identifies with "stability."

In the state schools unworthy men have sometimes inherited the throne by the grace of white politicians dispensing partisan plums. Less reprehensible choices were commonly wished upon both public and private institutions by pressures from trustees, foundations, state officials, church bodies and private philanthropists. It is common knowledge that a crucial king-making role has also been played by respected racial diplomats who had the ear of these agencies: men like the white Will W. Alexander of Atlanta, director of the Commission on Interracial Cooperation, and Negroes like Charles S. Johnson, Frederick Patterson and Channing Tobias; men whose associations with white philanthropists of the YMCA, the Phelps Stokes Fund, the Interracial Commissions, the General Education Board, the United Negro College Fund, religious bodies and an intricate web of similar agencies, invested them with extraordinary influence in the distribution of academic patronage.

Educators showed wide disparities in their attitudes toward The Problem. Nearly all were heads of Southern schools. Some, as Saunders Redding has written, were lickspittle opportunists, taking orders from whites with grinning acquiescence, swaggering before their faculties, and deliberately training their wards for second-class citizenship on the theory that the Negro is capable of nothing better. But some of the most eminent were in their several ways articulate militants: Benjamin Mays of Morehouse, a member of the National Board of Directors, and a cochairman of the Life Membership Committee of the NAACP, conductor of a hard-hitting weekly column in the Negro press, a forthright spokesman for equality; and Aaron Brown, who months before the 1954 desegregation decision so boldly defied white supremacy forces by joining NAACP efforts to increase Negro voting that he was dropped by the Georgia Board of Regents as president of the state college at Albany. Similarly, J. R. Otis of Alcorn (Mississippi) was eased out of office by politicians unable to appreciate his failure to discipline students who had publicly censured a pro-segregation instructor. Private schools enjoyed greater immunities, but some heads of public institutions have shown a surprising independence, as in the case of John W. Davis of West Virginia, Martin Jenkins of Morgan State (Baltimore), and Charles H. Wesley of Central State (Ohio). Several are national officers of the NAACP, and in 1956, Rufus Clement, Mordecai Johnson, Charles S. Johnson and Professor A. L. Harris of Chicago were among the seven Negroes on the National Committee of the American Civil Liberties Union.

The group as a body is still caught in the cross fire of divided counsels and conflicting demands, and in recent years pressures from students make the lot of the straddler an unhappy one. The irony that the Negro educator who fights for integration is fighting for the right to lose his position is a further source of strain. Meanwhile, expanding opportunities for Negro teachers at Northern colleges threatens the quality of the Negro college faculties in the South.

The first major integration of publicly supported colleges, the merger of Miner (Negro) and Wilson (white) teachers' colleges in the District of Columbia, proceeded smoothly and without displacement of Negro staff.* Duplicate division headships and one presidency had to be eliminated, but the chairmanships of the newly combined departments were awarded, without regard to color, to the officer for whom the best case could be made on the basis of professional experience. The rearrangement resulted in the appointment of four division heads from each race. The presidency was retained by the former head of Wilson, but President Matthews Whitehead of Miner, his junior in point of service, was made dean of a newly introduced graduate program. Some construed the creation of the new division as a ruse for denying Whitehead a more genuinely second-in-command post, like that of Dean of Undergraduate Instruction in the newly merged single institution.

The supply of Negro Ph.D.'s continued to be small. Before 1920 there had been about twenty in the nation; by 1936 only a hundred more had been added, followed by an annual increment of a dozen or so. Scholarship and fellowship opportunities for colored graduate students became significantly more numerous, though there was still a residuum of opposition. Investigators for the Carnegie-Myrdal study learned, for example, that a few years earlier a candidate for a graduate fellowship at Harvard—whose record would, if he had been white, have guaranteed the appointment automatically—was the subject of discussion by the granting committee. One member objected that the award might, because of the limited employment opportunity for highly educated Negroes, make the grantee "bitter like Du Bois," but the fellowship was granted.

Family connections were still important when these men were on the rise. Several were sons of college presidents; some virtually inherited positions

* An earlier amalgamation was the absorption by the University of Louisville of the Louisville Municipal College, a union that could hardly be described as a merger. In this case there was much displacement of Negro faculty.

their fathers had held before them. Felton G. Clark succeeded his father as president of Southern University; Frederick Patterson followed his father-in-law as president of Tuskegee, and Robert P. Daniel was born on the campus where he was to preside, and where his father had been secretary.

Of 117 educators found by the writer in four volumes of *Who's Who in America* for the decades 1936–1955, most were college presidents, some deans, and a small scattering of department heads, librarians and professors with some reputation as scholars. All of the schools with which they were associated were in the South, except that three or four were at the only Negro colleges in the North: Lincoln University and a state teachers' college in Pennsylvania; and Wilberforce University and Central State College in Ohio. Two thirds had had their basic college training in Negro colleges (but fifteen had gone back for a second bachelor's degree from Northern white colleges), and the rest at strong institutions like Chicago, Amherst, Brown and Northwestern.

Of the twenty-one Negro educators listed in the 1936–1937 *Who's Who,* sixteen had graduate degrees, including five Ph.D.'s, but of the 91 schoolmen in the 1954–1955 volume, 56 held doctorates, more than half of them from Chicago, Harvard, Columbia, Cornell and Northwestern. Of nearly 75 master's degrees in the later list, only nine were from Negro schools, and the rest from first-rank Northern universities. Those appearing in the 1954–1955 volume listed fifty major scholarships and fellowships, led by Rosenwald, General Education Board and Guggenheim grants; university scholarships; and awards from the Rockefeller Foundation and the Social Science Research Council. Of the educator-listees from all four volumes, about 95 per cent were born in the South, and of the tiny number who were native Northerners, all were either on Northern faculties or in the Negro colleges of the Southern periphery: Washington, West Virginia, Baltimore and St. Louis.

Their publications, very modest in quantity (for they were principally administrators rather than creative scholars), showed, as did the titles of their master's and doctoral dissertations, an almost exclusive preoccupation with Negro themes. Some, like the important papers on Negro learning capacity, by Jenkins, afforded significant correctives to pseudo-scientific efforts to prove the race's inherent inferiority.

The group as a whole was drafted for an astonishing array of public, quasi-public and civic services, but it was still difficult to avoid the inference that the Negro educator was drawn into these activities as a token member for the Negro minority rather than simply as the tenth American—except perhaps in the realm of pure scholarship, or, as in the case of professors Bunche and Frazier of Howard, when they were called into service by the United Nations.

We have selected as our nominees for the contemporary vanguard the best known (whatever their title to the honor) of the educators listed in *Who's*

Who, and two younger men not yet so noticed.* They must serve to represent a company now grown too large to incorporate in full. Reserving for a separate listing those known primarily as scholars rather than as school officials (two, however—Johnson of Fisk and Wesley of Central State—are listed in both categories), we have enumerated thirty-five who were college or university presidents, and five deans. Others are four librarians (Delaney, Rollins, Jones and Reason); an "educational administrator" (J. Max Bond); directors of philanthropic funds (Trent and Patterson); and one (Caliver), who is chief of the Division of Adult Education in the United States Office of Education.

Several sprang from families widely known in Negro America. The Clement and Bond dynasties, each of which produced two members for our general roster for 1936–1959, contributed besides, like the Huberts a decade or two earlier, a surprising number of persons distinguished in many fields. The Daniels of Virginia descended from whites mixed with free-Negro property holders of the sober, industrious, "Black Puritan" class. Their respect for learning, industry and upright conduct inspired second- and third-generation Daniels, in whom college training and successful careers became a habit. President Daniel was one of six children, all of whom their half-white father sent to college. Their home environment on the Virginia State College campus was extremely favorable. The family was formally organized, with a chairman, a secretary, a treasurer and other officials, and at the death of the elder Daniel, when Robert was fourteen, the organization efficiently co-ordinated family efforts to put each through college, to co-operate in home-buying, and other joint undertakings.

Frederick Patterson's father was a Texas teacher, editor and politician when he moved to Washington, D.C. on the strength of a promise of a political office. Offered a mere messenger's job, he undertook a law-school course at

* Carried over from the 1900–1936 list were the following, still prominent in the years following 1936: Mary McLeod Bethune, Ferdinand Bluford, Charlotte Hawkins Brown, John W. Davis, John M. Gandy, Dwight O. W. Holmes, Joseph W. Holley, Mordecai Johnson, Gilbert H. Jones, Lawrence C. Jones, David D. Jones, James F. Lane, James E. Shephard, William J. Trent, Sr., Eugene E. Clark, and the scholars Alain Locke and Carter G. Woodson. Names to be added now —comprising about half of those listed during the period in *Who's Who in America* plus two younger men whom I have added—are:

Rufus B. Atwood	Luther H. Foster	St. Clair Price
John A. Bacoats	Charles G. Gomillion	Samuel D. Proctor
William A. Bell	George W. Gore	Joseph H. Reason
Horace M. Bond	Charles L. Hill	Charlemae Rollins
J. Max Bond	Jerome H. Holland	Sherman D. Scruggs
James P. Brawley	Martin D. Jenkins	James W. Seabrook
Aaron Brown	Charles S. Johnson	Frank M. Snowden
Ambrose Caliver	Ralph W. E. Jones	Charles M. Thompson
Felton G. Clark	Virginia L. Jones	Harper C. Trenholm
Rufus E. Clement	Raphael O'H Lanier	William J. Trent, Jr.
James A. Colston	Hardy Liston	Cornelius V. Troup
Robert P. Daniel	Benjamin E. Mays	William J. L. Wallace
Walter S. Davis	Alonzo G. Moron	Charles H. Wesley
Sadie P. Delaney	William Stuart Nelson	Harold D. West
Albert W. Dent	Frederick D. Patterson	Matthews Whitehead
Alfonso Elder	Willa B. Player	Stephen J. Wright

middle age, but died when Frederick was very young and already motherless. Charlamae Rollins, the Chicago public librarian, noted for efforts to induce publishers of children's books to eliminate materials that injure the sensibilities of colored children and instill prejudice in the minds of young whites, was the daughter of parents descended from white male ancestors who kept up a close relationship with their mulatto offspring. When, after Emancipation, the latter were excluded by Klansmen from their lawful inheritance, they made their way to the Oklahoma Territory and became hard-working landowners. Several were children of teachers, clergymen and physicians, but some had no family advantages. Joseph Reason's father, for example, born a slave, never knew who his parents were. After the Emancipation he was simply turned over to a freedman's family and had no educational opportunities at all. A Lousiana sawmill worker, he served as treasurer for his church and his lodge, and young Joseph looked after his papers and read and wrote for him.

Several (even in the Deep South, as in Louisiana or in Negro college towns) were in childhood quite unconscious of racial exclusions and imputations of inferiority. President Jenkins's father was a skilled carpenter, the son of a slave, and moved to Terre Haute, Indiana, where he became an active politician and holder of a modest federal job and prospered in his trade. But even in such sheltered communities the Negro child soon met sporadic jeers from white children, and was puzzled by separate schools and other forms of discrimination, and by the monopoly of whites in positions of wealth and authority.

Horace Bond remembers the family's brusque ejection one summer's day in 1912 from Wyandotte Park in Louisville, when they had entered without knowledge of new segregation ordinances. He remembers, too, his dismay when his father—a dignified Berea graduate and Fisk faculty member whose equalitarian-humanitarian creed had led him to name his son Horace Mann—was arrested in 1917 as the first Negro to move into a neighborhood not yet declared open to the race. And he recalls white children's incessant chant of "Nigger, nigger, nigger!"

Ambrose Caliver lost his father in early childhood and went to work in coal mines at the age of eleven, while his mother went out to domestic service. He was aware of no racial feeling until he went to live in Knoxville with his grandmother. There, while a secondary school student, he suffered a grave shock when he saw in a store window the notorious volume, then just recently jublished, Charles Carroll's *The Negro a Beast* (1910), its shocking title emphasized with lurid illustrations.

Jenkins had, in Terre Haute, no consciousness of racial handicap in his all-Negro elementary school, but he was deeply disturbed in the mixed secondary school when the teacher, after seating the white children alphabetically, instructed the small number of colored children to find places in the rear.

Later Martin joined other children in protesting their exclusion from the swimming classes, and swimming was dropped from the school's program. The colored children were barred from the high-school dances—which they never dreamed of attending anyway—but Martin was elected captain of the track team. Commencement was held at the city opera house, and custom required the colored graduates to sit in the balcony while their white classmates occupied the stage. All but one of the twelve colored graduates in Martin's class protested the discrimination by staying away from the exercises.

Dean Thompson's father was so well regarded in his community that the sheriff himself smiled when the elder Thompson thrashed a white salesman who had been rude to Mrs. Thompson. But to this day the dean remembers with what emotion he heard the town banker confide to his father, "Thompson, it's a shame you're a nigger."

Dean Snowden's parents had come up from Virginia to Boston to improve their children's chances. The elder Snowden was a civil servant, who during the First World War attained the rank of colonel, and his wife was a Hampton graduate. The future dean had his secondary training at the famous Boston Latin School, and grew up in a neighborhood where Negroes were very few and racial tensions wholly lacking. It was in employment that Boston Negroes felt their burden, and the senior Snowden pressed his son to enter a profession in which the handicap was minimized. The boy went directly from the Latin School to Harvard, assisted by scholarships and summer employment at a summer camp in Maine.

Others in the group recall that it had been parents or perhaps a teacher or a preacher who had pressed them to choose teaching or preaching as a vocation. Especially in the rural areas, when a Negro child showed any precocity he was promptly earmarked for one of these callings. The experience of Benjamin Mays was typical. The youngest of eight children, his ability to rattle off the alphabet and to count to a hundred made him a local celebrity. His declamations in Sunday-school exercises delighted his elders, and when a visiting preacher added the authority of his word to the general acclaim, there was little for Ben to do but to live up to the expectations that others had of him.

The struggle for higher education was, as always, a major force in winnowing out the future comers, and in most cases it was a hard fight. Snowden's experience was relatively favorable, as was that of Jenkins. Of the twelve Negro boys in Jenkin's high-school class, eleven finished college, most of them at the unsegregated state teacher's college in their own Terre Haute. He had earlier had two years at Howard, helped by a lucrative job as elevator boy in the national Capitol, secured for him by his politician father. His undergraduate career was undistinguished, but when he went to Northwestern, the skeptical attitude of white professors and classmates so stimulated him to exert himself that the record he had made when he took his Ph.D. in 1935 is still a legend there among older professors.

In the industrious, systematic Daniel family, Robert and his brothers were faithful exemplars of the ambitious American boy of that era. He had a paper route in Richmond, which he built up to such dimensions that he employed others to work under him, and as an undergraduate he was janitor at the Richmond YMCA. The orphaned Frederick Patterson, with the help of a sister and his own dogged industry, entered Iowa State college where he worked so hard as dishwasher, clothes presser, hotel waiter and delivery boy that he had no time to notice exclusions from athletic and social affairs in which he had no interest anyway. Later a General Education Board grant enabled him to earn the Ph.D at Cornell.

Once through a Northern graduate school, young colored scholars before World War II had to seek places in the Southern colleges, but because nearly all had been reared there, they were prepared for Southern life. It was the Northern men who felt the shock. Snowden went to Spelman, excited by the chance to associate with men like Du Bois, Braithwaite and Reid, at that time lecturing at Atlanta University. But the young Harvard-trained aristocrat was soon being called "nigger." When his car was struck by a Negro ruffian, he found police vastly uninterested, since both parties were colored. Once when he and his wife were shopping for a suit at a men's clothing store, the clerk smilingly boasted that he knew "another boy at Atlanta U; boy named Braithwaite." To Snowden's unfamiliar ears the clumsy bonhomie stung like a whiplash. He cancelled the order on the spot, and was loudly cursed as a "black son of a bitch" for his sensitivity. On another occasion at Concord, North Carolina, a filling-station attendant miscalcuated by twenty-eight cents the charge for fuel. When Snowden mentioned the slip, the outraged mechanic roared at him and threatened to kill him on the spot with a crowbar, but then relented far enough to vent his rage by pouring twenty-eight cents' worth of gasoline over Snowden's car, and profanely ordering him off.

A few leading Negro scholars may be considered here separately. Like white learned specialists, they are not widely known to the masses, but they are familiar to the American academic community. Easily the foremost historians in recent years have been John Hope Franklin and Rayford Logan, but Lorenzo Greene, Charles H. Wesley, Luther P. Jackson, Lawrence D. Reddick, A. A. Taylor and Benjamin Quarles have also written works respected by specialists. Merze Tate is a recognized authority on international relations, and in sociology and social psychology Franklin Frazier, Charles S. Johnson, Allison Davis, St. Clair Drake, Horace Cayton and Ira Reid are preeminent. Perhaps less well known are younger sociologists like Hylan Lewis and Mozelle Hill; the anthropologist Lawrence Foster; and the psychologist Herman Canady. In economics much the most famous is A. L. Harris.

Languages and literature have a few recognized Negro experts; the best-known include Lorenzo Turner, Mercer Cook, John Matheus, Arthur P. Davis, Ulysses Lee and the previously noted Sterling Brown.

Of the twenty-five, twenty-one were natives of the South—three fourths from the border South. Nearly all were Ph.D.'s, typically from Harvard, Chicago, or Columbia, and two fifths had their undergraduate training at Northern white schools. Two of the four who did not hold doctorates had extended graduate study beyond the master's degree at the University of Chicago; one studied abroad, and the fourth had field research experience equivalent to doctoral training. Nearly all in the group concentrated upon race-related themes, but compared with earlier professional students, they showed a notably greater objectivity. Indeed, their excellence in this regard, while it won the respect of academic America, exposed them to criticism from Negroes who expect their scholars to shoulder their pens and ride off to the racial wars.

These scholars have been participants in learned societies, contributors to leading professional journals and recipients of the same academic honors that came to whites. Their works have been issued by leading presses and accorded the reviews that their importance required. Ralph Bunche (after he had left teaching) was elected president of the American Political Science Association and in 1959 was elected a member of Harvard University's Board of Overseers; Charles S. Johnson headed the Southern Sociological Society, and Frazier, the Eastern Sociological Society. The latter even became president of the august American Sociological Society. Matheus headed the West Virginia State Foreign Language Association and Canady the West Virginia Psychological Association. If the pressure to confine themselves to Negro themes has been relaxed, the preference persists because materials for such study—comparatively unexploited by whites—are most readily available. Logan, Franklin and Harris have, besides works on Negro subjects, produced volumes wholly outside that field, and Merze Tate has confined her published works wholly to non-racial themes.

Fellowships and grants-in-aid were in recent years so generously heaped upon these students that several insist that no Negro scholar can longer plead his race as an excuse for failure to acquire superior graduate training and to produce significant publications in his field. They were successfull in competing for awards from the American Council of Learned Societies, the Social Science Research Council, the General Education Board, the Fulbright Board of Foreign Scholarships, the Carnegie, Rockefeller and Ford Funds, the Guggenheim Foundation and from the universities they attended. There were, besides, aids specifically intended for Negroes, supplied by the Rosenwald Fund, Negro lodges and scholarships at particular colleges, endowed by Negroes for allocation to Negroes only.

Charles S. Johnson declined an appointment to the Harvard faculty in the 1940's, but younger men were slowly drawn into the white academic community. Abram Harris and Allison Davis became professors at the University of Chicago, and Drake and Turner at Roosevelt University. Ralph Bunche was once elected to a Harvard professorship, but never entered upon the office; Reid is a department chairman at Haverford; and Franklin heads the department of History at Brooklyn College. Atlanta University's sociology department recently lost its chairman, Mozelle Hill, to Teachers College, Columbia University, and some in this group, as well as those still at Negro colleges, have served leading universities as guest professors.

Early in their careers the men we have named faced resistances which have now largely disappeared. Libraries and other research repositories, now freely accessible to them, were formerly closed or available on painfully restricted terms. Hostilities at professional meetings have now all but vanished. Only a few years ago it was sometimes necessary for Negro scholars who read papers at such sessions to use the freight elevators in the hotels where the meetings were held.

Family backgrounds of the group were often highly atypical. Merze Tate, for example, sprang from long-free Negroes who had migrated to Michigan before the Civil War to become landowners. Cayton was the grandson of United States Senator Revels, and his father, the son of a runaway slave whose wife was the white daughter of a slaveholding family, had established himself as a newspaper editor and ward politician in Seattle. Mercer Cook was the son of two famous people—Will Marion Cook and Abbie Mitchell—and Charles S. Johnson's father was a prominent Baptist clergyman in Virginia, born on a plantation where his mother was a favorite slave, whose master himself tutored her child in Latin, Hebrew, Greek, and English and American literature. The elder Johnson, in his turn, provided his son with a home rich in books and intellectual stimulation.

Lorenzo Turner's father had been born free in North Carolina twenty years before the Emancipation, and his mother was the child, by her white owner, of a woman of mixed blood. Legally denied education until he was a grown man in 1865, the elder Turner went to school to Yankee missionary folk, walking nearly twenty miles daily. Soon he himself founded what was to become the North Carolina State Teacher's College at Elizabeth City. Tightening Jim Crow practices after 1900 drove him up to Washington to improve his children's prospects.

Rayford Logan's colored maternal grandfather was the son of a white woman. The historian's father, the son of a white man (reputedly a general) by a Negro-Indian woman, was a butler and hotel bellman with far less schooling than his wife. It was the latter who always insisted that their child should go to college. Logan remembers that his parents were partisans of Du Bois in his contentions against the Tuskegee philosophy, and outspokenly hostile to the newly established Jim Crow usages. He now considers his youth a fortunate one, both because of the character of his parents, and because of the availability of the famous Dunbar High School. His unlimited access to the Library of Congress was another boon that provided intellectual stimulation, self-respect and a love of learning.

Franklin Frazier's father, a bank messenger in Baltimore, never had a day at school in his life, and his paternal grandfather was a self-emancipated slave who bought his family's freedom. The boy's mother was also an ex-slave. He heard in the family's table talk strong condemnation of Jim Crow and vigorous insistence that he secure a college education. So effective was his conditioning that, as a boy walking to school, he habitually spat upon the Johns Hopkins University buildings because he knew he could not aspire to enroll there.

Two generations removed from slavery, John Hope Franklin grew up in Oklahoma. Both parents were persons of strong intellectual interests and excellent education. He was still very young when the family moved to tightly segregated Tulsa, where the elder Franklin established a law practice. They felt relatively free from racial strain because the community was endeavoring to keep the separate facilities genuinely equal. Their father was too strong a believer in the free mind to force his views upon the Franklin children and he never permitted himself to discourage their aspirations, not even John's boyish resolve to become the first Negro President of the United States.

It was one of the extraordinary upper-bourgeois families that produced Arthur Davis. His grandfather, William Roscoe Davis, was the son of a white sea captain by a slave woman of mixed blood. His owners taught him to read and made him their plantation overseer. He was associated at the end of the War with Yankee missionaries, eventually as a lecturer for the American Missionary Association to solicit funds in the North for the education of Southern freedmen. He subsequently assisted General Armstrong in the founding of Hampton Institute. He had four sons and two daughters, all born in slavery. By 1950, their descendants numbered among them two Ph.D.'s, an M.D., a D.D., an LL.B., five M.A.'s, fourteen A.B.'s and three Phi Beta Kappas. The degrees were earned at Harvard, Columbia, Chicago, Dartmouth, Oberlin, Fordham, Hunter, Pratt, Howard, Virginia Union, Fisk and Hampton, and their holders were linked by marriage with other prominent persons, including Charles Anderson, the New York Collector; P. B. Young, Jr., the publisher; and A. L. Harris.

Harris's slave-born ancestors cannot be clearly traced, but his forebears included self-purchased people of mixed blood, and a Scots grandfather who purchased a woman of color whom he called wife. Harris grew up in Richmond, where his father, the only Negro butcher employed by a large market, and his mother, a graduate of a normal school conducted by Yankee missionaries, had a fairly comfortable home, well supplied with books, and where a good high school with white teachers was available to the boy. Ira Reid's father was a West Indian clergyman, educated in London, who came to America in manhood. Reid's mother's people descended from white planters by slave women, and had betaken themselves to West Virginia to escape the loose family arrangements of the slave kingdom.

With few exceptions the group attended segregated elementary and secondary schools which, in retrospect, they learned to recognize as inferior to those of whites. Taylor, Davis, Logan and Cook, as Washington residents, had very good schools, however, and then went, with ample scholarship aid, to Michigan, Williams, Williams and Amherst, respectively. In each case there were only one or two other Negroes at these institutions, but the colored youths formed warm, lasting friendships with white classmates. Others were well received at Washington State, the University of Kansas, Columbia, Western Reserve and Western Michigan College, with only occasional reminders of racial handicap. Of those who studied at Negro colleges, several admit that they would have entered Northeastern schools if they had had the means.

Ira Reid, however, had high praise for the Hope-Archer-Brawley triumvirate at Morehouse, and Franklin feels that the Fisk of his student days offered excellent training, its bi-racial faculty taking greater pains with their five hundred students than was common at Northern schools. He planned a career in law, but fell under the influence of his history professor, Theodore S. Currier, a white New Englander, whom he still regards as "just about the best teacher I know." Franklin's Fisk education prepared him fully for Harvard graduate study. Currier arranged a loan for him and Franklin at first earned part of his support by clerical work, but later he won grants from the university and the Rosenwald Fund. His researches were subsequently supported by a Guggenheim Fellowship, a Brown University Fellowship and grants from the Social Science Research Council. He was invited to lecture as a visiting professor at Wisconsin, Cornell, Cambridge and California universities and at the Salzburg Seminar.

All of the group worked at self-help employment. The commonest sort was summer work as Pullman porters, dining-car waiters, bellhops and porters at summer resorts. Employers recruited such workers at Negro colleges, prompted by the preference of white travellers and vacationers for smiling, white-jacketed colored boys. Lorenzo Turner worked an eight-hour shift at a Cambridge dining room while carrying a full master's program at Harvard and subsisting on four hours of sleep per night. For two years, while accumulating savings to pursue the doctorate, he taught at Howard until noon, worked and slept in the afternoon and early evening, then worked through the night as a federal employee in Washington. Later, however, his researches in African dialects and cultural survivals were supported by the Rosenwald Fund, the American Council of Learned Societies and the Fulbright Program.

The scholars acknowledge a debt to Du Bois and Randolph, whose *Crisis* and *Messenger* stimulated their interests and indignations, and some were prompted to a career in scholarship as a form of ideological warfare. Others, devoted to pure scholarship, as the cool objectivity of their works argues, separated their roles as creative intellectuals from those as participants in the race's struggles.

Until recently travel exposed these scholars to affronts which they tried to minimize by purchasing automobiles even before they could afford them. Dining-car and Pullman facilities and unsegregated waiting rooms were not generally available until lately, and even now many still take the precaution of telephoning for reservations or sending whites to pick up tickets, lest they be put off on the pretext that the space had been sold. Even automobile travel was until a few years ago vulnerable to brazen insult. Once when Charles S. Johnson, returning to Fisk with some colleagues, was following the car in which Frazier was driving another group, Frazier stopped to buy fuel. After paying his bill he noticed that Johnson was no longer behind him so he asked the attendant where "the gentleman in the Hudson" had gone.

"That nigger in the Hudson went across the street," he shouted; and, thrusting his head into the car window, he added, "Nigger, do you know where you are? You ain't up there in Tennessee . . . and I am going to show you how we hang niggers like you in Alabama." Then as the fellow threw a glance at the loafers about the station, Frazier slipped into gear and shot out of the station, preferring for the present, he later laughed, "not to become a martyr to social research."

Another kind of discrimination, now no longer possible, but which several on this roster had to cope with in youth, occurred in military service during World War I. Rayford Logan, for example, fresh out of Williams, with Phi Beta Kappa honors, was commissioned a lieutenant and sent overseas on a rigorously segregated troopship. The insults he suffered throughout a term of service that included heavy action in the Argonne Forest so wounded him that he remained in Europe for five years before he concluded, under the prodding of a beloved Williams classmate, that his problem was not solved by flight. He returned home, earned a Ph.D. at Harvard, and made a brilliant career. In World War II he labored to democratize the armed forces, as chairman of the Committee for the Participation of Negroes in the National Defense Program, as co-drafter of the anti-discrimination section of the Selective Service Act, as a spokesman for Negro groups who pressed President Roosevelt to liberalize the commissioning and assignment of Negro officers, and as a participant with Randolph, White, Granger and Crosswaith, in the March on Washington Movement.

Several of the scholars were called upon for their specialized knowledge by various groups. Franklin and Logan were consulted by NAACP lawyers in the Supreme Courth segregation cases; Johnson, Frazier and Logan were drafted for service in federal and United Nations agencies; Logan, Reid and Canady lectured for the American Friends Service Committee; and Franklin, Logan and Cook have represented their country abroad as cultural spokesmen.

While the names we have singled out as foremost in the category of "race leaders" for the last two decades continue, as in the case of the preceding generation, to be drawn chiefly from the organizations specifically created to plead the race's cause, we must hazard some plain speaking on the problem of identifying and defining Negro "leaders."

Before 1865, the typical "leader" was the man who struck some telling blow for the destruction of the slave system. Before that stupendous object all other considerations were dwarfed. Negro heroes, whether slaves or freemen, were men whose exploits hastened that consummation: abolitionist agitators, saboteurs of slavery, or men whose attainments of mind or character helped to heap up the evidence that the Negro, too, was fashioned for the life of the free American.

After the Emancipation, the condition, the aspirations and the capacities of the race *en masse* were still sufficiently uniform to enable spokesmen, like the more militant Douglass at first and the less aggressive Washington later, to speak for the race and to articulate its hopes and expectations. Such leadership was, moreover, closely dependent upon the collaboration and approval of whites. This first post-slavery generation placed initially a heavy confidence in politics, under federal protection, and then upon white philanthropy to underwrite its schools and colleges and its projects for social salvation.

Then, in the first three and a half decades of the twentieth century, while colored society was undergoing steady stratification and differentiation, the old near-unanimity as to goals and methods gave place to a new and characteristically American pluralism. While the business of "race work" gravitated to full-time professionals, other "leading Negroes" became instead more simply the race's foremost church, educational, or business leaders; or artists, writers, scientific or technical experts. There was still ample opportunity, however, for such persons who headed particular segments of Negro life to exert a generalized pressure upon the color line, supplementing the more highly organized exertions of professional improvers in the NAACP, the Urban League, the chauvinistic Negro nationalism of the Garvey Movement (led, curiously, by an alien, who is, therefore, not within the scope of this book), and lesser agencies.

As the "talented tenth" increasingly deputed to the professional reformers the task of pressing the Negro's case for first-class citizenship, they themselves could shift their emphasis to the raising of standards within the colored group in order to disarm those opponents who thundered against social amalgamation with a people whose levels of health, literacy, personal conduct, sexual morality, industry, prudence, religion and taste were still, in the wake of the lately abandoned slave condition, far below national norms.

In the recent period, now to be surveyed, these trends were quickened. "Race work" became more than ever the task of professionals. The attack upon violations of constitutional and statutory guarantees of civil rights and equal protection of the laws had fallen so largely to the NAACP as to make the association virtually a public agency. Its epic court battles, from the 1938 *Gaines* case forward, were so uniformly successful that each new litigation was almost tantamount to the announcement of new concessions. And if the NAACP was the race's war department, the Urban League was its state department. Not directly involved in combat, it brought the arts of negotiation and parley to the effort to find opportunities hitherto closed to the race by private proscription. Other agencies, like the widely assorted National Negro Council, the March on Washington, the Montgomery Improvement Association and the Southern Leadership Conference concentrated their effort upon similar objects.

President Eisenhower's conference in 1958 with the executive secretaries of the NAACP and the Urban League, the head of the Pullman Porters' Union and the leader of the Montgomery Improvement Association doubtless put him in communication with a huge segment of the race, but the day when a single spokesman could parley with the government with real authority has now long passed. Leadership in Negro society is, in fact, widely diffused, and profoundly conditioned by the larger social environment that imposes its sanctions and expectations upon a beleaguered minority. Scholars have yet to trace the influences which produce leadership in the race and which set the limits and the circumstances in which it may operate. Little is as yet known, for example, about the relative importance, in the natural history of race leaders, of such factors as childhood conditioning, educational opportunities, the role of caution and of calculated dissimulation, the deferential pose, and the qualities that Negroes on the one hand and whites on the other value in Negro leaders.

Some direction is exerted upon Negro life by its higher educators—usually cautious, conciliatory "realists" like the widely differing Patterson, Hancock, Charles S. Johnson, Clement, Horace Bond, Shepard, and occasionally a more outspoken voice like Mays. Johnson, for example, was highly regarded by whites and recognized by them as one of the race's foremost diplomats, whose hands were on the purse strings of numerous foundations and whose voice was heard in the counsels of national and international agencies directly or indirectly connected with race relations; and Patterson has been a favorite emissary peculiarly acceptable to whites. Another kind of influence has been exerted by writers like Hughes and Wright, and artists like the Robeson of old, and Marian Anderson—again, people whose authority was augmented by their reputation in white America. Leftists, like Ben Davis, Jr., James W. Ford, and democratic Socialists like Randolph and Crosswaith had a specialized following, as did such widely disparate politicians as the younger Powell, Dawson, Ben Davis, Sr., A. T. Walden and a fraternal leader like the Elks' Robert H. Johnson.

There are, of course, also "leading Negroes" who have little or no following: specialists of various sorts, creative personalities, absorbed (like, A. L. Harris at the University of Chicago for instance,) in enterprise of which the race as a whole is quite unconscious. Others are *ex officio* leaders, the temporary custodians of the power with which their office invests them. And even the real race leaders—by the technical definition—have an extremely limited reach, often confined to upper-class Negroes who, in turn, are so variegated as to philosophy that the force of the leadership that penetrates to them is fragmentized. Tests have shown that colored college students cannot recognize the names of the great majority of "big Negroes" who are usually listed as the foremost members of the race. Perhaps the most pervasive influence upon the Negro masses continues to be the church, but even here it is quite absurd to impute to any individual or group of individuals any kind of centralized control over this influence.

Local leadership of a sort is wielded by an upper class who set the standards by which lowlier Negroes fix their course: doctors, lawyers, educators, clergymen, civil servants, editors, labor leaders and businessmen. Negroes seem agreed that the ascendancy of such folk is in varying degrees accounted for by factors like family connection, wealth, education and contacts with whites and with other prominent Negroes. Data concerning the bearing of skin color as a factor in hindering or helping the career of the aspiring Negro leader are so contradictory that it has become quite impossible to pronounce upon the point, though there is, paradoxically, a notable disposition to acknowledge that the proportion of light-skinned leaders is perhaps abnormally high, and that successful Negroes seem disinclined to select spouses who are darker than themselves. The older advantages of light complexion in the competition for place are vanishing as a growing proportion of the members of both races cast off—under the urging of accumulating scientific data—old doubts about the inherent equality of endowments of all races.

It is sometimes remarked that Negro leaders in general—just as in the case of bishops and college presidents—are often misfits because the scarcity of leadership opportunities leads to a ruthless competition which awards the prizes to unworthy men. And it is often said that there is no longer any effective general leadership of the race because the leaders show no more inclination to "get together" than do the mass of colored Americans. Others deplore the tendency of highly placed Negroes to pursue a timid course, fearful of white displeasure for themselves or the agencies or movements they direct, though it is often pointed out in extenuation that a leader must often fight the very people whose support he needs if he is to function effectively.

They are often accused also of withdrawing from the very masses for whom they presume to speak, affecting superiorities and pretentions that invite the verdict that the Big Negro, in the status-starved ghetto, cannot stand success or power. The colored American who wields any considerable power is in fact in a painful quandary: the greater his influence, the more shrill the aspersions hurled at him from both left and right.

The extremely limited reach of genuinely competent Negro leaders compared with that of some popular idols has long been the despair of the race's intellectuals. White politicians, for example, have in recent decades made extensive use of the most famous Negro heroes of the entertainment and sport world as political-campaign speakers—no matter how inarticulate—even though they forgot, as they mumbled their inanities, to mention the name of the presidential candidate they were hired to urge upon gaping colored voters. The barely literate—but internationally beloved—tap dancer, Bill Robinson, could command a respectful attention for an "address" on the United Nations where a Du Bois or a Lester Granger could not. Such recruitment of colored celebrities as manipulators of influence is not always so ridiculous. A national favorite like Jackie Robinson, upon retiring from baseball, became an immensely valuable figure in the NAACP, and Lena Horne, again, a national, as well as a racial, favorite, has been an effective mouthpiece for the advancement of the race.

Race leaders, both acknowledged and self-anointed, run the whole gamut of racial ideology. They include bold fighters, brilliant, high-minded, fearless, incorruptible, self-assertive men: editors like Roscoe Dunjee and Carl Murphy; lawyers like Raymond P. and Sadie T. M. Alexander, Earl Dickerson, Hubert Delany; clergymen like Imes, Walls and Jernagin; scientists like Louis Wright and Montague Cobb; public servants like Robert Weaver and Hastie. Others with a reputation for intrepidity are in fact mere opportunists or rabble-rousers. Another category are the cautious moderates—men who not infrequently extort for the race the half-loaf which may exceed by exactly half a loaf the gains captured by the more uncompromising members of the militant camp. Still others are undercover agents and emissaries of foundations, political parties and other interest groups; and some are symbolic leaders who inherit the apparatus of leadership along with the offices they succeed to. Yet another—and widely various—kind of authority emanates from the big names which the white world honors: Roland Hayes, Marian Anderson, the pre-World War II Robeson, Louis Armstrong, C. C. Spaulding, Ralph Bunche. To name yet another species, there are the retired old warhorses, recalled from pasture to be displayed by whites on ceremonial occasions, such as national nominating conventions or presidential inaugurations.

An instructive sample list of Negro leaders was compiled and defended by Roi Ottley in the country's most widely circulated Negro magazine in 1948, the mid-point of the period we are now discussing. The article "The Big Ten who Rule Negro America," designated three educators: Mordecai Johnson, Charles S. Johnson and Frederick Patterson, the presidents of Howard, Fisk and Tuskegee; William E. B. Du Bois, whom Ottley calls the "Elder Statesman;" A. Philip Randolph, "the Mystic Radical" and head of the Pullman Porters; Willard S. Townsend, head of the redcaps, and behind-the-scenes labor statesman who brought the Negro into the CIO; Paul Robeson, "The Othello of the Struggle," by that time leaning far to the left and risking heavy personal and financial penalties to take his defiant stand; Mary McLeod Bethune, "The First Lady of the Struggle," an important political symbol in the Roosevelt and Truman administrations, and a forceful leader of women's organizations; Walter White, then executive secretary of the NAACP and the race's most powerful lobbyist; and Channing Tobias, at that time head of the Phelps Stokes Fund (and now chairman of the NAACP board), included in the list by Ottley because of his lifelong and influential position as a YMCA leader, a leading churchman, a firm, if moderating, force in a vast complex of civic, social and political agencies, a frequent caller at the White House, and one of the two Negro members of President Truman's Civil Rights Committee.

It will be noted that several of the ten whom we listed in the pre-1936 category of race leaders were still of major importance a decade or two later. Several of Ottley's ten were in fact still conspicuous in 1958: Mordecai Johnson, Robeson, Du Bois, Randolph, Patterson and Tobias; and the other four had only recently passed on. Others, besides these, also carry over from our pre-1936 list into the 1940's and 1950's: Mary Church Terrell, William Pickens, George E. Haynes, Elmer A. Carter, Frank Crosswaith, Max Yergan and Daisy Lampkin.

Some of those from the pre-1936 roster who continued to be among the most prominent leaders in the succeeding generation made significant shifts to the left or right while others kept squarely on course. Mrs. Terrell was until her death at ninety an immensely respected symbol in the fight against separate facilities, and Haynes is still elder statesman of the inter-racial co-operation strategy. Carter became a member and eventually chairman of the New York State Commission against Discrimination, and Crosswaith an organizer for the International Ladies Garment Workers Union and a member of the New York City Housing Authority. Randolph's stoutly liberal and anti-Communist position remained substantially unchanged.

Du Bois, replaced as the dominating influence in the NAACP by younger, less passionate men, went briefly to Atlanta University to found and edit

Phylon, and moved steadily leftward, functioning chiefly as a lecturer, social scientist, essayist, and even something of a poet. At ninety, he was completing a trilogy of novels as another blast against the color line. Like Robeson, he was at one point denied a passport because of his Marxist views, but, once again permitted to travel in 1958, he made an extensive European tour and was lionized, particularly—though not exclusively—in leftist circles. Though his defection to the far left was widely deplored by the race, he was still, for his past achievements, venerated as the greatest living fighter for the advancement of Negro America. Upon the appearance of the sixtieth anniversary volume of *Who's Who in America,* he was still listed in that index of distinction as he had been in every number since it first appeared in 1898.

Pickens, meanwhile, shifted to a more moderate position than he formerly occupied. He joined the United States Treasury Department in 1941 and soon thereafter was dropped from the NAACP leadership because of his partisan political activities. Yergan shifted to the far left in the later 1930's, but eventually married a prosperous white physician, repudiated his Marxist confrères, and, like many a white, repentant Fellow Traveler, swerved sharply to the right, acquiring a reputation as an ultra-conservative, accused of expressing approval of Prime Minister Malan of South Africa, and applauding the nomination of James F. Byrnes as a member of the American delegation to the United Nations.

The NAACP's directorate is surprisingly little known to the Negro millions, though most are doubtless more familiar with its objects than was the supplicant who wrote asking that the association for the advancement of colored people advance *him* twenty dollars. The membership has never been large. In 1957 it stood at about three hundred thousand (nearly half of it in the South), a decline of nearly fifty thousand from the previous year in the face of growing hostility in the South. By 1958 approximately nine tenths of the members were Negroes, but nine of ten colored families had no NAACP member at all.

The year 1958 marked the mid-point of the association's ten-year "Fight for Freedom" to achieve by the centennial of the Emancipation "complete elimination of all vestiges of second-class citizenship." It was meanwhile, for the first time compelled to fight for its right to exist in the South, where the group was usually bracketed—even by editors, educators and other intellectuals with a reputation for liberalism—as an "extremist" group of misguided fanatics at best, and at worst as desperate subversives. Yet, in other sections, the association had the support and good wishes of civic and religious agencies, humanitarians (including many a stodgy conservative), and counted among its members the most respected white artists, writers, United States Senators, governors, jurists, lawyers, theologians and educators.

Strained by the new necessity to defend itself at the very time of its maximum effort, it operated in the late 1950's on an annual budget of a million dollars. It continued its long-term strategy of pressing, in the courts, for no more than a bona fide beginning of compliance with existing constitutional and statutory guarantees, in the confidence that it was on the right side of a moral issue, and on the side of history and the American creed.

The years following 1936 witnessed a succession of NAACP victories in the courts that steadily chipped away the barriers to first-class citizenship, notably in the franchise, in interstate travel and in public educational opportunity—a development that clearly prefigured the Supreme Court decision of 1954. This, in turn, reduced the proponents of segregation to obstructive subterfuges, which the association countered by new suits as rapidly as they appeared. Progress that had brought the race perhaps halfway, in ninety years, to the enjoyment of the Constitution's guarantees was, in the view of NAACP leaders, considerably short of "moderate," and a growing number of their countrymen wondered if the NAACP in asking for compliance with the law by 1963, after a century's delay, was not better described as "moderate" than were its opponents.

In 1955, the late Walter White was succeeded as executive secretary by Roy Wilkins, who had been on the association's staff since 1931. An even-tempered, hard-working man, he is a dark-skinned, college-bred Negro, two generations removed from the slavery past. His parents left Mississippi when they married in 1900 and settled in St. Louis, where the college-educated elder Wilkins obtained employment in a brick kiln. Roy's mother died when he was only three, and the three Wilkins children were sent to live with relatives in St. Paul, Minnesota. Here, unsegregated schools and a respectable home in an unsegregated community insulated the future NAACP official from racial hurts.

The only separate institution Wilkins remembers from his childhood was the AME Church. In high school he was editor of the school's magazine, and at the University of Minnesota, where he majored in sociology and took a few courses in journalism, he became issue editor of the university daily, a newspaper with a circulation of ten thousand. A lynching in Duluth prompted him to enter the university's oratorical contest with a strong anti-lynching speech which won him first prize. After graduation he found a place on the Kansas City *Call,* one of the race's largest weeklies, and quickly rose to the managing editorship.

Kansas City's large Negro population contrasted sharply with the smaller, comfortably situated Negro group in St. Paul. His confrontation with Jim Crow facilities, and personal indignities to which he was now for the first time subjected, shocked Wilkins into the role of a crusader almost at once, the more so because the stream of race news that came across his desk forced his attention constantly upon the plight of his race. In 1930, his vigorous campaign against an anti-Negro United States Senator from Kansas led to his appointment to the NAACP staff.

If Wilkins is now the strategist for the NAACP, others are also prominently associated with its program. Thurgood Marshall, its gladiator-in-chief, will be considered later in these pages when we identify the race's most prominent lawyers. Others in the group's headquarter's staff—like Henry L. Moon, director of publicity; James E. Ivy, editor of *Crisis;* Clarence B. Mitchell, director of the association's Washington Bureau; John Morsell, assistant to the executive secretary, and Gloster B. Current—are also far removed from the rough-hewn, slaveborn warriors who were in the forefront of the race's struggles scarcely half a century earlier. They are all college men, almost without exception with postgraduate training at foremost universities. They were recruited for the NAACP staff after responsible experience as journalists, labor-organization officials, social workers, race-relations advisers, YMCA secretaries, college teachers and government officers. Not only are such highly-trained, cultivated men brought into the association from federal, state and municipal posts; the movement is sometimes reversed. Madison Jones, for example, once assistant to the executive secretary of the NAACP, recently became, at fifteen thousand dollars a year, consultant in race relations for the New York City Housing Authority. And passing mention at least should be made of a new kind of NAACP hero: Daisy Bates, the strong-willed president of the Arkansas Conference of NAACP branches and heroine of the Little Rock episode, who, as *Ebony* reported, "deployed her meager forces with consummate skill and artistry," though she herself insists that the Negro children who bore the stress of the first integrated school year at Central High School were the real heroes of that epic struggle which resounded throughout the world.

Allusion has already been made to Martin Luther King, Jr., as one of the most famous Negro clergymen of the middle 1950's, and before passing on to other race leaders we should at least remark here that the young Alabama preacher was suddenly catapulated into an ascendancy no less—and for a time perhaps even more—authoritative than that of professional leaders of the NAACP and the Urban League. Not only because of his identification with the most successful peaceable boycott ever conducted against the American color line, but also because of his immense influence over Negroes of the South where, because it is still pre-eminently the home of America's Negroes, perhaps the ultimate "solution" must be found. There (again, because of the higher concentration of Negroes) effective resistance to discrimination has always been more difficult and more dangerous than elsewhere. There the new-won freedom of colored passengers to sit where they pleased in a Montgomery bus marked a deeper social transformation than did the most advanced anti-discrimination law in New York City.

Usually considered more conciliatory than the NAACP, the leading figures in the National Urban League are inclined to the good-will-interracial-co-operation strategy which many of the more resolute Negroes deplore.

Yet, the ideological distance between the groups is not so great but what there is much overlapping in membership, leadership and financial support. Originally established to help the Negro newcomer to the city make the transition to urban life, it has been dedicated to "gathering facts about racial conditions and using them to improve working and living conditions of Negroes and to promote better understanding between whites and Negroes," co-operating with health and welfare agencies, and addressing itself to the improvement of housing, vocational guidance and employment opportunities.

The direction of the League fell in 1941 to Lester B. Granger, a polished, affable man—frequently drawn into civic, welfare and public service. During World War II he was Special Adviser to the Secretary of the Navy. He has been criticized as an "ultra moderate," but he is an indisputable patrician, and his high rank in the Negro vanguard is beyond challenge.

His father, Richard Randolph Granger, the son of a peace officer of Barbados, made his way to the United States as a cabin boy and found lodging with Philadelphia Quakers, who helped him enter Bucknell University. He married a very fair, upper-class Negro schoolteacher of Richmond (the granddaughter of a white Virginia planter), one of a group of beautiful, refined and well-educated sisters. Resolved upon a career in medicine, he took his training at the University of Vermont, entered practice in Arkansas and Oklahoma, and then moved to Newport News, Virginia, where the couple settled to raise six sons.

When Virginia established its Jim Crow laws in 1904, the proudly independent physician moved again, this time to New Jersey, though it meant leaving his practice and facing a new State Board examination. Here the boys —thus far taught by their mother, who declined to enroll them in inferior Jim Crow schools—entered unsegregated schools and enjoyed a childhood virtually free from racial affronts. The oldest entered Dartmouth on an athletic scholarship and he drew all but one of his brothers after him. The other took a dentistry course at the University of Pennsylvania.

When Lester entered Dartmouth, there were three Granger brothers enrolled simultaneously. The other two had established a clothes-pressing business which now became "Granger, Granger and Granger." They occupied their own little shop ("We work while you sleep," it advertised), and their earnings, eked out by summer work as redcaps in New York's Grand Central Station, saw them through college. The Dartmouth years were a rich experience, but not without heartaches. In high school Lester had been a campus notable, but at college he was excluded from several activities, and smarted under the rule that no Negro might have a white roommate. Athletics were open, but the glee club barred him because its concert season included a tour of women's colleges.

White boys avoided sitting with the Grangers in chapel and dining hall, but the brothers sedulously avoided self-segregation. The unwritten rule of all the colored students was to avoid being seen with more than one fellow Negro at a time. After college, Lester served in World War I as a lieutenant, taught for a year at St. Augustine College, and secured some graduate training in social work in New York before entering the employ of the Urban League.

Two men whose position in the country's economic structure invested them with extensive influence in the race were A. Philip Randolph—the race's foremost labor leader well before 1936 and already noted in these pages—and Willard S. Townsend. Both sat on the Executive Board of the mighty AFL-CIO as the highest-ranking Negro officers in the hierarchy of American labor. Randolph, still in 1959 one of the three or four most commanding figures in Negro America and perhaps its most majestic patriarch, came into the newly merged AFL-CIO directorate by virtue of his presidency of the Pullman Porters (an AFL union). Townsend, as head of the United Transport Service Employees (CIO) was before the merger a CIO vice president, and now joined the governing council of the combined organization.

While Randolph and Townsend towered over other Negro labor officials, there were also by the middle 1950's at least sixty significant positions held by Negro labor chiefs, representing the million-and-a-half colored workers lately added to America's unions. These officers included vice presidents, housing consultants, and directors of fair employment practices, civil-rights and political-action divisions of several of the most powerful trade and industrial unions in the land. Their emergence testified to the remarkable upsurge in the Negro labor movement since the 1930's. The AFL and other groups had long barred Negro members, but the number of major unions now excluding Negroes by formal rules has dwindled to a mere five: the four independent railway brotherhoods, and an association of postal transport workers.

It is noteworthy that Townsend and Randolph were both intellectuals —scholarly men who spoke and wrote impeccable English, and were deeply informed in economics, history, political science and public affairs. They were welcome and at ease among the country's civic, educational and public leadership, far removed from the popular image of the bluff and uncouth labor boss.

Townsend was, unlike Randolph, a man of light-brown complexion. His people had lived in the North for several generations and in his lineage were a Pennsylvania Dutch grandfather, a granduncle who had helped found Oberlin College, and several upper-class people of color who had been educated there. Young Willard grew up and went to school in a wholly unsegregated neighborhood in Cincinnati, where he worked at the usual schoolboy after-hours jobs that ambitious urban boys of his generation pursued. He was the child of separated parents and lived with his grandfather, a funeral director with a taste for reading, and a good home library. After two years of high school he worked as a redcap at Cincinnati's Union Station, and became by turns a dining-car waiter and a steel worker.

In World War I, he pounded a typewriter in an all-Negro stateside unit. When he mustered out, he was still virtually unscathed by racial affronts, still unmoved by any crusading impulse. After his military service he worked with the Canadian Pacific Railroad, completed his education at the Royal College of Science in Toronto and then returned to dining-car work in Chicago before joining the ranks of the redcaps, in those days unorganized and deriving their earnings from tips alone. New Deal legislation gave the redcaps their opportunity, and Townsend, intimately acquainted with the plight of the Negroes who comprised the bottom rank of the country's railway workers, now found an outlet for the new militancy which recent years had instilled in him as he played the role of the servile worker (in sharp contrast to his sheltered youth), ordered about as "George" or "Sam" by patronizing passengers.

He and his associates in building the redcap union saw clearly that labor organization had an additional dimension for Negroes, as part of the larger thrust toward first-class citizenship. And, once strong leaders like Randolph and Townsend moved, along with lesser Negro union leaders, into the councils of the American labor movement, the campaign against the color bar, supported by multiplying union committees on minority affairs, discrimination and inter-racial participation, moved rapidly forward. Townsend was drawn into a long list of advisory committees, boards and commissions, by both government and private welfare, reform and humanitarian agencies, and his untimely passing in 1958 was widely mourned across the country.

The press since 1936 has moved on much the same lines that had been laid down earlier. It continued to be a fighting instrument, but less dominated by individual crusading editors, for, as in the general American press, personal journalism had given place to big-business newspaper publishing, conducted by staffs grown conspicuously more "professionalized." The founders of the twentieth-century newspapers had passed on or retreated to less active roles, and the reins were often turned over to sons or nephews, who came to their tasks with a background of college education and experience which the pioneers had not enjoyed. Abbott's *Defender,* for example, passed to his nephew, John Sengstacke, and to Louis E. Martin (who also published the *Michigan Chronicle*), the son of the Sengstacke's physician. Carl Murphy gradually relinquished his direction of the *Afro-American* papers to younger members of the Murphy dynasty, and P. B. Young's *Journal and Guide* was entrusted to his sons, P. B. and Thomas W. Young, while Robert Vann was succeeded as the *Pittsburgh Courier's* publisher by his wife.

Several of the pioneer editors and publishers of the previous generation continued active into the 1950's, and newcomers to the list included, besides those just named, such figures as Clilan B. Powell of the New York *Amsterdam News* (a physician-businessman, he bought the paper in 1936); William O. Walker, of the Cleveland *Call and Post;* E. W. Rhodes, of the Philadelphia *Tribune;* C. A. Scott of the Atlanta *Daily World;* Frank L. Stanley, of the Louisville *Defender,* and W. Beverly Carter, of the *Pittsburgh Courier.*

In the previous generation, William Stanley Braithwaite, T. Thomas Fortune, Lester Walton and Eugene Brown were contributing to important white papers, but only later were colored members brought into major dailies as regular staff people. In 1948 there were some fifteen and by 1955 the number exceeded thirty, serving Northern metropolitan papers from Oregon to New Jersey—ordinarily young men, some of them Nieman Fellows, who covered "Negro news" as part of their larger assignments. Publishers otherwise willing to engage Negroes demurred because colored reporters were refused entry where a white could move freely to get his story.

The best known of the journalists on white newspapers were Theodore R. (Ted) Poston, of the New York *Post;* Roi Ottley, of the Chicago *Tribune;* and Carl T. Rowan, of the Minneapolis *Tribune.* All three wrote also for the general periodical press, and Ottley and Rowan were authors of popular books on Negro American life. Poston, a Kentuckian, established himself in the Northeast upon graduating from Tennessee's state college for Negroes, serving on the staffs of the *Amsterdam News* and the *Pittsburgh Courier* before joining the New York *Post* in 1937.

Ottley was born in New York City to immigrants from the British West Indies who had never been members of a declassed minority. As a boy in Harlem, he felt himself rejected by the tribe, and during his student years at the University of Michigan was affably tolerated as an eccentric Negro who had yet to learn his station. Although his books, *New World A'Coming* (1943) and *Black Odyssey* (1948), sold well, a position as a radio commentator was closed to him because, he believes, of the white man's reluctance to take the Negro intellectual laborer (as compared with Negro entertainers) seriously. The barrier, he concedes, is not one erected by the communications industry, but by the wider public whose preferences cannot without grave financial penalty be offended.

Carl Rowan came from a rural community at the foot of the Cumberland hills in Tennessee. The usual drab boyhood and youth of the black boy in a Southern small town was profoundly transformed when, during his year at Tennessee State College for Negroes, he was admitted by examination to naval training for World War II. While he was at home awaiting assignment, his unique position as an apprentice seaman for a navy where the Negro was extremely rare, raised his expectations and ambitions. His subsequent reception as an equal, at a Kansas college where he was the only

Negro in a company of 334 naval trainees, fortified his resolve to rise above the anonymity of the ghetto. Some years later, as an Oberlin graduate and a reporter for the Minneapolis *Tribune,* he returned South to gather material for his book, *South of Freedom,* to explain "how it feels to be a Negro in the South."

In his adopted state he is invited to address college convocations and civic organizations, but when the city editor dispatches him to cover a story, Rowan is never certain whether he will find hotel accommodations, whether his scrambled eggs will be mixed with shells, whether it is indeed true that town *X* will permit no Negro to tarry overnight.

Negro journals, too, have some brilliant reporters and editors (one thinks of Dan Burley, columnist, barrel-house pianist and expert on "Harlem jive"). No longer the firebrands of old, they are neither overzealous nor heartsick but, commonly hardheaded, disciplined, race-conscious businessmen. Less widely known than Poston, Ottley, or Rowan, they are mainly Southern-born, college-educated men—frequently with professional training at Northern universities—associated with the race's larger weeklies. (There were in 1958 as yet only two Negro dailies: the Atlanta *World* and an edition of the Chicago *Defender*.) The papers now carried notably more general advertising by white firms, suddenly grown aware of the eighteen-billion-dollar Negro market.

The colored press's National Newspaper Publishers Association maintains a bustling Washington bureau, a White House correspondent, and accredited members of the Congressional Press Gallery and the National Press Club. In 1958 it sponsored a "summit conference" on the race's economic and social prospects, bringing together editors and publishers with some two hundred more or less famous Negroes. The assembly was addressed by President Eisenhower, whose exhortation that they cultivate "patience and forbearance" disappointed, if it did not exasperate, his hearers.

Resolutions drafted by the conference illustrated the press's enduring goals. The race was admonished to combat the juvenile delinquency, intemperance, coarse behavior, illegitimacy and family instability that slavery and the ghetto had fostered. The delegates called for increased registration of colored voters and the avoidance of blind adherence to any party. They urged Negroes to support their own business enterprises while pressing for integration in the general economy, and demanded firmer federal and state action on civil rights, and the withholding of federal funds from housing and hospital facilities which discriminate against Negroes.

In the 1950's, the press took what comfort it could from the reflection that its failure to grow derived from the race's appreciating fortunes. The plain fact was that the Negroes' sense of grievance, their hurts and their humiliations, had so far diminished that they felt less need for their own tribunes. The white press was showing a greater respect for the race—though its reporting of positive achievements and of Negro personal, "society" and church news was still so nearly totally ignored that the colored press still filled a real reporting need, heedless of occasional sneers that it was unduly preoccupied with social gossip and exaggerated estimates of Negro attainments. Editors sometimes pointed out that the end of prejudice and proscription for which they contested would bring with it the end of the Negro press, for it would then have no further reason for being.

Recent years saw rising standards of taste in the papers' columns, but it was, if slender revenues were to be eked out, still necessary to pander to untutored popular appetites and to accept dubious advertising. During World War II its "Double V" slogan ("Victory abroad and at home") at a time when the race's bargaining leverage was strong ("Buy another bond, but keep them squirming!") evoked from some sanctimonious whites the charge that the Negro papers were disloyal, "irresponsible, inaccurate and inflammable," but the censorious mood soon passed.

While colored popular magazines multiplied, the *Crisis* entered its fifth decade in 1950 as an NAACP house organ, and *Opportunity* ceased publication in 1949. *Phylon,* the scholarly journal launched at Atlanta University by Du Bois in 1940, continued its distinguished career under Mozelle Hill and Hylan Lewis, while the *Journal of Negro Education,* edited by Charles H. Thompson at Howard earned its reputation as one of the finest publications of its kind. The *Journal of Negro History* remains the major repository for Negro studies by scholars throughout the world. Long brilliantly edited by Harvard-trained Carter Woodson, its Harvard tradition was continued in his successors, Rayford Logan and William M. Brewer.

It was the popular magazines however, which saw the most spectacular development. Here the undisputed leader was John H. Johnson of Chicago, who in 1951 (like Rowan in 1953) was designated by the United States Junior Chamber of Commerce as one of America's "Ten Outstanding Young Men." His *Ebony* magazine is patterned closely upon *Life,* even to its literary style. Founded in 1947 when Johnson was twenty-seven, it has a circulation of nearly half a million. Nine tenths of its large editorial staff are college graduates. The general tone of the magazine has, from the beginning, been exuberant, optimistic and "positive," depicting the "bright side of Negro life."

"On the whole," said the publication at the end of its first decade, "the Negro has had a good life in America during that period. . . . The chief criteria we use in determining the suitability of any story is [sic] success and achievement in any field." *Ebony's* function is to stimulate the Negro's self-respect and pride in his race, to "promote interracial understanding by emphasizing the positive and minimizing the negative aspect of race relations" and to "give hope and inspiration to our young people," and prove "that their dreams too can come true."

Once firmly rooted, *Ebony* sent out three offshoots: *Tan,* a "romance and confessions" magazine; *Jet,* a pocket-size illustrated weekly; and *Hue,* a "miniature *Ebony.*" Together the publications reached by 1957 a circulation of nearly a million and a half. An earlier Johnson venture was the *Negro Digest,* modelled upon the *Reader's Digest.* Established in 1943, it was dropped in 1951, when experience proved that the general press did not provide an adequate selection of pieces suitable for condensation in a Negro digest. The enormous circulation of Johnson publications attracted white advertisers —who often used colored models to illustrate their spreads—but *Ebony* and other popular Negro magazines still carry advertising of "skin brighteners" and "hair conditioners," promising a skin "several shades lighter," and hair "longer, softer, and straighter." The Johnson magazines avoid dogmatism on racial questions, but despite their conservatism, they award editorial applause to what they have called the "shouting militance" of Philip Randolph and Congressman Powell, as well as to the "gradualism" of C. C. Spaulding and Frederick D. Patterson.

Johnson himself is a fascinating variation on the American success theme. A very dark descendant of slaves whose family records cannot be traced, he was long denied full acceptance by "high-class" Negroes because of his utter lack of social advantages. His parents had separated when he was very young, and he was reared in bleakest poverty by his mother, a woman of scant schooling but ample "mother-wit." When Johnson was nine, his mother married a levee worker whose employment compelled the family to move about, living not infrequently in tent colonies where the boy's mother worked as a cook for construction gangs.

When Johnson reached high-school age, he and his mother moved into an apartment in the Chicago black belt, a part of which they rented to roomers to supplement her earnings as a domestic. At the Negro Du Sable High School, embarrassed by his rural-South origins—which his thick speech and outlandish clothing loudly proclaimed—Johnson worked doggedly at his studies, steeped himself in success books, and became editor of the school paper, manager of the year book and president of the student council. A sober lad, fiercely determined to make his mark, he haunted the local branch of the Chicago Public Library, devouring books about leading Negroes. While the most successful symbols in the squalid Chicago ghetto seemed to be policy kings, racketeers, and reckless adventurers, the colored heroes he met in the public library's volumes proved the most important single inspiration of his youth, he later told this writer.

He even saw in his humble origins a possible advantage: Southern migrants without "connections," he concluded, were challenged by their handicap, while boys native to the slum had been vulgarized and unmanned by it. A chance meeting with insurance executive Harry Pace, while the latter was visiting the school Johnson attended, led to employment in the afternoons as

Pace's assistant in reviving a house organ for the Supreme Liberty Life Insurance Company; in the mornings, Johnson attended the University of Chicago.

Five years of close association with Pace gave him a sound grounding in business and journalism, and when Pace lent him as a "political secretary" to Earl B. Dickerson, a brilliant Negro member of the Chicago City Council and a major officer in Supreme Liberty Life, the youth acquired yet another sound counsellor. In office space allotted him by Dickerson, young Johnson launched his *Negro Digest,* with five hundred dollars in capital borrowed on his mother's furniture. It was conceived as a purely personal business venture, with no backers or investors, no façade of big names on an "editorial board." It was to rise or fall on its own consumer appeal. He excluded advertisements because the *Reader's Digest* carried none, for he operated on the principle that whites knew this business best. In its first six months the little periodical grew so rapidly that he was compelled to resign his place with Supreme Liberty Life to give his whole time to it. A remarkable career had begun, and as in the case of many another self-made man in the long catalog of real-life Alger-Heroes, America had won another impassioned booster. The writer has heard from few Negroes as emphatically as he has heard from Johnson the judgment that the United States is incomparably the world's best home for Negroes.

Continuing urbanization both swelled the number of Negro voters and facilitated the pooling of their strength. In some centers colored voters were now so numerous as to give them what was essentially a balance of power, and white politicians of the two competing major parties were under new necessities to court their favor by admitting them to a larger share in office holding; by combating old injustices; by broadening public employment; by routing out differential treatment by police and the courts; by expanding public facilities and services; by restraining private discrimination in employment, housing and public accommodations. So strong, indeed, were these new compulsions, that public authorities were perpetually apprehensive that the race or its friends might raise the cry of racial bias even where none was intended. The dropping of white employees from an overstaffed bureau or the curtailment of some service for whites might be defended on grounds of economy. But, in the case of Negroes, such retrenchments often were politically impossible because they were branded as discriminatory.

The Negro's enlarged political leverage in these decades was reinforced by other influences: the country's liberal mood; the war; the weight of world opinion in a context of international ideological conflict, and the race's own improved economic status. In the earlier generation, a few patronage plums were distributed to placate a few colored hacks and a scattering of respected clergymen and college presidents. Heading the list were the ministerships to Haiti and Liberia and two ceremonial functions: the Register of the Treasury and the Recorder of Deeds for the District of Columbia. The number of such federal consolation prizes had sharply declined after the return of the Democrats in 1913 and the losses were not recovered until still another Democratic administration moved into power twenty years later. The Treasury post was in fact not restored until 1953—at a salary of $10,500—and by that time the place had become so unexciting that the appointee, Louis B. Toomer, a Georgia banker and professional Republican politician, soon resigned rather than suffer the restraints upon his Georgia politicking that his tenure of the office imposed on him by way of the Hatch Act. Another recent incumbent as Recorder of Deeds has been Marshall Shephard, a high official in the National Baptist convention.

When the New Deal brought its trainloads of bright young men into government service, a few colored members came with them, recruited, like many of the whites, with scant regard for party affiliation or political obligation, and in most cases drawn fresh from college faculties: men like Robert C. Weaver, James C. Evans, William H. Hastie, Frank S. Horne, Ambrose Caliver, Rayford Logan, Ira Reid, William J. Trent, Jr., Campbell C. Johnson and Ralph Bunche. With them as a sort of mother superior was Mrs. Bethune who, with Weaver, unofficially presided over the "Black Cabinet." With the Presidential blessing they were enlisted by Harold Ickes, Clark Foreman, Aubrey Williams and Will W. Alexander, and then by other department and agency heads as the practice spread. Soon editors such as Robert Vann and "race leaders" like Eugene K. Jones and William Pickens were in the circle, working (often as "Adviser on Negro Affairs," or "Consultant for Minority Affairs") in the Interior, Justice, Treasury and War departments, the National Youth Administration, the Social Security System, the Farm Credit Administration, the Federal Emergency Relief Administration, the Federal Works Agency, the Housing Authority, the Office of Education. Transferred from one agency to another, as the experience gleaned in one became pertinent to the other, they were particularly entrusted with the introduction of Negroes into the rank and file of government service, and with keeping a sharp eye on the interests of the race in the administration of the agencies' functions. Some drifted out of government after a few years. Several, however, found entirely different posts in federal, state and city units, or, long after their original function had been discharged, gradually assumed permanent agency posts at the policy-making level, and in capacities unrelated to race.

By 1940, more than a hundred Negroes had been brought into federal agencies, and though there were still only a single member of Congress and a dozen state legislators, it was noteworthy that the new development reached into the South. As early as 1935, Charles W. Anderson, an able young attorney from Louisville, began the first of several notable terms in the Kentucky legislature. In the Northern states, there were also in 1940 a few elected and appointed city officials, such as judges, civil service commissioners, assistant prosecutors, city attorneys and members of library boards, health departments and school boards.

Negro voting was all the while on the increase, most conspicuously in sections where it had been only lately repressed. In 1940, registered Negro voters in the South barely exceeded 200,000, but ten years later they numbered 1,200,000. In the biggest Northern cities there were no obstacles to the Negro franchise. Colored voters there could now elect some of their own people, and compel appointment of many more, and they showed a growing political sophistication in pressing for positive, progressive measures instead of merely voting against discriminations. They were strengthened, too, by multiplying ties with unions and other white liberals and party leaders, to say nothing of the maturing leadership from the race's own best brains, the organized race-advance agencies and religious and fraternal bodies.

On a single election day in 1946 some thirty-six officials were elected, including two members of Congress, thirty state legislators (among them three representatives in Missouri, and senators in Ohio, Michigan and Indiana), and two county commissioners. By 1956 there were forty state lawmakers, several women among them, drawn from Southern border states like Kentucky, West Virginia, Tennessee, Maryland and Missouri, as well as from New York, Illinois, Michigan and Pennsylvania. Well before that year there were elected members of city councils and school boards in such Southern cities as Greensboro, Winston-Salem, Durham, Gastonia, Chapel Hill, Atlanta, Richmond, Knoxville and San Antonio. In the first three years of the Eisenhower administration, some three hundred colored appointees with salaries of $6000 or more were in service in Washington. By the middle 1950's, Negroes held offices in all the branches—executive, legislative and judicial—at all three levels—federal, state and local—and only a few of the most conspicuous attracted attention.

In 1940 less than ten Negroes were in the foreign service. Lester Walton as minister to Liberia (1935–1946) headed the list, and the remaining seven included consuls, vice consuls and a doorman. By the middle 1950's Negroes were no longer unusual in the corps. The Liberian ministership was held in 1946–1948 by Raphael O'Hara Lanier, an early New Deal NYA official. The post was raised during the tenure of attorney Edward R. Dudley (1948–1953) to an ambassadorship. Others in the service were consuls and vice-consuls. Frank Snowden, a classical scholar, was, before becoming dean of the college at Howard, American cultural attaché in Rome; and Giles Hubert was chief of Educational Mission in Afghanistan, and has also served in India.

Ralph Bunche's career with the United Nations will be noted below. Another promising future in the service of the UN was cut short by the untimely death, by his own hand, of the brilliant William H. Dean, economist for the trusteeship council. A succession of Negroes have served as alternate delegates to the General Assembly: attorney Edith Sampson; attorney and clergyman Archibald J. Carey, Jr.; Channing Tobias; attorney Robert L. Brokenburr; and singer Marian Anderson. Charles H. Mahoney, a Detroit lawyer and insurance executive, became in 1954 the first Negro to serve as a full delegate to the UN Assembly.

In the legislative branch there were in 1958 four Negroes in the United States House of Representatives, and the federal bench had also by then been occupied by several colored jurists. But when Robert N. C. Nix of Pennsylvania became in 1958 the fourth Congressman the event excited less attention in the Negro press than do the exploits of the race's athletes in major league baseball. Municipal judgeships in the District of Columbia (another federal appointment) have been held by Negroes for more than half a century. Recent incumbents have included E. B. Smith and Armond Scott, but it was not until the appointment of William H. Hastie in 1937 as United States District Judge for the Virgin Islands that a man of color presided over one of the regular federal courts. When he resigned in 1939, he was succeeded by Herman Emmons Moore, and in 1958 by Walter A. Gordon.

In the states, the most numerous high officials were the legislators, but a few administrative offices were also in the late 1950's held by persons of color. Robert C. Weaver, one of the nation's foremost housing experts, occupied a New York cabinet-rank position as State Rent Administrator, and Joseph Bibb of Illinois sat in the cabinet of that state as Director of Public Safety. In New York, Elmer A. Carter became a member and then chairman of the State Commission against Discrimination, created to administer the state's fair employment practices statute. In Pennsylvania, Andrew M. Bradley became a member of the Governor's cabinet when he assumed, in 1955, office as budget secretary, and then—at a $20,000 salary—secretary of Property and Supplies for the commonwealth. In 1958 Harold J. Ashby, a Newark attorney, was appointed chairman of the State Parole Board of New Jersey.

The 1940's and 1950's saw the election of Negro members of city councils and school boards, not only in New York, Chicago, New Haven, Philadelphia, Milwaukee, Boston, Buffalo, Canton, Cincinnati, Toledo, Cleveland and a score or more of other Northern cities—but in a few Southern cities as well, including Atlanta, Houston, Greensboro, Louisville, Nashville, Winston-Salem, Durham, Gastonia and Richmond. Cincinnati and Gary elected colored vice mayors. Trenton, New Jersey, made Frank H. Wimberley president of its school board. The highest municipal executive post thus far to be held by a colored American is that of President of the Borough of Manhattan, to which Hulan Jack was elected in 1953.

Most startling of all to those unfamiliar with the pace of social change in America was the multiplication of Negroes who sat in judgment and passed sentence upon white men—and women. The past two decades have seen some fifty Negroes ascend the bench, concentrated in New York and Chicago, but scattered as far west as Minneapolis, Denver and Los Angeles. In Detroit, Wade McCree was one of the youngest and highest-paid Negro judges with a salary of $26,000 before he was forty. In Chicago, Henry Ferguson and Fred Slater were municipal judges and Wendell Green a circuit judge in the 1950's. In New York, Charles A. Toney and James S. Watson began, in 1931, long terms as municipal judges, and in the same year Myles Paige entered upon a long and distinguished career as a jurist. By 1950 the city had eight Negro judges: Thomas Dickens of the Municipal Court, Francis E. Rivers of the County Court, Harold A. Stevens of the General Sessions, Myles Paige of Special Sessions, Jane Bolin, Hubert Delany and Herman Stout of Domestic Relations, and Henry Reddick of the magistrate's court. By 1956, C. DeWittt Baker and Louis Flagg went to Brooklyn Municipal Court, while Edward R. Dudley succeeded Delany in Domestic Relations. In December, 1957, Stevens was elevated to the state supreme court, at a salary of $37,000, well in excess of the salary of nearly every state governor in the country, and greater than that of the Chief Justice of the United States.

The social origins of these public servants show the usual variations. The examples of three of the Congressmen are instructive. Representative Diggs of Michigan was the heir of his father, who had come to Detroit from Mississippi, developed the largest Negro funeral business in America, achieved prominence as a civic and fraternal leader and politician, and won election to the state Senate. His son, Charles, Jr., earmarked to succed him in his funeral and insurance enterprises, was educated at the University of Michigan and at Fisk.

The boy grew up in comfortable circumstances, and at the university found that a colored lawmaker's son could enter doors closed to other Negro students. When he was twenty-nine, Diggs, a quiet, hard-working sort, had already followed his father in the state Senate and was established in the Diggs business interests. The family's social position in a district suddenly so heavily Negro that the race could demand its seat in Congress made the youthful state senator—still only thirty-three and an able campaign orator—an obvious choice for the place.

William L. Dawson's rise was a different matter. The grandson of slaves, and the child of a sober Alabama barber and a hard-working mother, young Dawson struggled through Fisk, graduated with honors and struck out for Chicago's fast-growing Bronzeville. He attended law classes at night, volunteered for war service and opened a desultory law practice, giving his chief energies to politics. He began as a menial in the precinct, inching his way forward in ward politics. As a Republican stalwart of the old Thompson machine of the 1920's, he won five terms (1933–1943) in the city council, and then moved, on the New Deal tide, into Mayor Kelly's Democratic organization, with the perquisites of dispenser-in-chief of patronage, favors and fixes in the swarming ghetto. If critics accused him of manipulation of police captaincies and protecting gamblers, racketeers and vice kings, his defenders countered that it was never a question of personal pelf but always one of political organization.

He went to Congress in 1943, and in 1958 his hold on the place was stronger than ever, thanks to his tight control of five wards and his offices as precinct captain, ward committeeman, vice chairman of the Cook County Democratic Organization and vice chairman of the Democratic National Committee. He sometimes disappointed educated Negroes by his conservatism on racial matters, but his pragmatic realism, his seniority, and his invincibility at home, where all comers had direct access to him without previous appointment, and where thousands are dazzled by his sheer strength, his war record and his dogged spirit in spite of physical handicap (he lost a leg in a railway accident), make him one of the few Negroes who are genuinely in the country's power structure. In Congress he has climbed the seniority ladder to become chairman of the House Committee on Government Operations, and his quiet work and shrewd political strategy have won the respect of congressional leaders.

Different again is the case of Adam Clayton Powell. A tall, dazzlingly handsome man, he combines the influences of superior family and social heritage with a lusty taste for politics. The son of a famous father, whose preeminence as a Harlem church and political leader he inherited, he has modified the inheritance by his own mercurial qualities. When his parishioners objected to his plan to marry an actress, he threatened to resign, and had his way. He later married another night-club entertainer, and further offended the timid in his flock by his predilection for swank foreign sports cars.

His penchant for high life had ended his student days at City College with expulsion and persuaded his father to send him to Colgate, a men's school. There he is said to have passed as a white student until his father visited the campus and was introduced as a Negro. Once out of college and established in his church and in a publishing venture, he assumed the role of a fighting radical, vociferously identifying himself with the "marching blacks," and professing a burning ambition to avenge the injuries suffered by his branded slave grandfather. With leading Harlem pastors, he helped promote Negro job opportunities in Harlem's white business firms in the early 1930's, and in 1941 was elected as the first Negro city council member when Channing Tobias and Max Yergan withdrew from the contest to prevent a division in the Negro vote.

The help of his congregation, his personal popularity and his impassioned oratory brought him the congressional nominations of Democrats, Republicans and the American Labor Party and easy election to the House of Representatives in 1944. Thereafter his stentorian arguments for civil rights and other legislation favorable to Negroes more than offset his reputation for absenteeism in Congress. In 1958, when he was facing indictment for tax irregularities and was repudiated by the regular Democratic organization, he was triumphantly renominated (in the Republican and Democratic primaries) and elected for an eighth term, heavily defeating Negro city councilman Earl Brown, a staff member of *Life* magazine, and the author of municipal anti-bias legislation.

Leaders in the NAACP, though deploring Powell's "extreme racialism," have supported him because he has "fought courageously and vigorously for civil rights throughout the years," and other highly respected voices of Negro America in the 1958 crisis in his career rallied to his defense. Democratic regulars were enraged by his defection to the Eisenhower camp in the 1956 campaign, but some eminent supporters argued that efforts to purge him from the party and to hound him with tax litigation were inspired by Southern reactionaries determined to banish him from national politics. Powell's free-wheeling success would have been impossible in Dawson's Chicago, a tightly knit "precinct town," where organization, regularity and rewards at the local level determined political contests. There, personal popularity and prestige would count for little. New York's less cohesive Negroes, political newcomers relatively undisciplined by party, were more easily moved by "glamor," slogans and ideological appeals.

The Congressmen were elected officials, but most of the colored public officers were appointed—chosen, perhaps, in obedience to the demands of political strategy that an increasingly enfranchised minority exerted upon a two-party system, but chosen with surprising regard to their competence, training and experience. The appointments tended to come in clusters, at times of crisis, when some concession to Negroes might inspirit, conciliate, or pacify. In the previous generation, purely ceremonial figures and party hacks were elevated with the calculated design of anticipating, holding down and disarming potential Negro political leverage, but many saw in the newer appointments an emergent disposition to *yield* to the pressures, rather than to smother them—a willingness to experiment in enlightened co-operation with the inevitable.

A review of the influences that operated in the careers of some of the best known of them will illustrate some of the factors in the evolution. In recent years four of the most notable federal officeholders have been J. Ernest Wilkins, E. Frederic Morrow, Campbell C. Johnson and James C. Evans—all four, incidentally, sons of preachers.

Johnson's emergence in 1940 as assistant to the director of Selective Service has been explained as the result of an acute political pressure which only dramatic measures could relieve. A few days before the 1940 elections, Mr. Roosevelt delivered a major campaign speech at Madison Square Garden. As the President's party prepared to entrain for Washington at Penn Station, his press secretary, Stephen Early, finding his way barred by a cordon of police, angrily jostled the nearest officer to the ground. The policeman was a Negro. The anti-Roosevelt press gleefully exaggerated the injury and, as an added propaganda fillip, falsely described Early as the grandson of a Confederate General. The train had hardly left the station when screaming headlines were already on the streets.

Frantic White House aides promptly telephoned Robert Weaver at midnight to "get the boys together and turn out a really rousing speech which the President can give in Baltimore" to salvage what was left of the Negro vote. ("The boys" were, Hastie among them, in fact assembled at the poker table in Weaver's basement.) A mere speech, Weaver shrewdly hinted, would not suffice. Invited to suggest what the crisis required, he and his associates transmitted their recommendation to the White House, and Roosevelt approved the program on the spot. Forty-eight hours later the country had its first Negro general in Benjamin O. Davis; an assistant to the Selective Service Director in Campbell Johnson; a civilian aide to the Secretary of War in William Hastie.

This may well be the explanation of Johnson's advancement, but the appointee was not whistled up from obscurity. A refined, soft-spoken man, the son of a slaveborn Baptist minister who had been the personal servant of Gen. Phil Sheridan, young Johnson grew up in upper-class Negro Washington, took bachelor's and law degrees at Howard, and had, before 1940, a long career as a Howard instructor, an army reserve officer, executive secretary of the Washington YMCA, and an official of countless Washington civic, welfare and public agencies—characteristically as the only Negro, sitting as his race's representative.

James C. Evans descended from white and colored ancestry, including some Negroes who were free well before the Civil War. He was the child of sober, respectable folk eager to see their sons enter the professions. After taking an A.B. degree at a Negro college he entered Massachusetts Institute of Technology and, with assistance from his parents and some scholarship aid, made his way with remarkably little social strain to B.S. and M.S. degrees in electrical engineering. Employment opportunities, however, were virtually closed to him and he joined the faculty of West Virginia State College. An inventor, and the winner of a Harmon Award in Science, he was early invited into the public service in various New Deal agencies, originally assigned to personnel problems and the absorption of colored employees into the federal service. By 1943, he was a full-time official as Civilian Aide to the Secretary of War, and continues now in the Defense Department where he is concerned with manpower problems and the

"People to People Program" as a fully "integrated" official in the Pentagon.

Morrow's is another story. In the summer of 1952, the Republican party needed a personable Negro for the presidential candidate's campaign train. Morrow accepted the post, but soon realized that he was travelling as a mere exhibit to win Negro votes in the platform crowds. When he expressed his dissatisfaction, Sherman Adams quickly presented him to Mr. Eisenhower, who promptly made him a bona fide consultant to scrutinize all passages of particular interest to Negroes in the candidate's speeches and press releases. After Mr. Eisenhower's election, the President gave him the position of Administrative Officer for Special Projects, with impressive quarters in the White House Office, where many callers having business with the President are referred to Morrow. Occasionally one of them impatiently tries to push his way past the Negro, insisting that he be taken "directly to Mr. Morrow."

Whatever the original motive for his appointment, Morrow was not a pliant flunky, picked at random, who could be counted upon to hold his peace. He was at the time a member of the Columbia Broadcasting System's Press Information Department—a position he achieved with assistance from the New York State Commission Against Discrimination. During the war he had earned the reputation of a troublemaker by his outspoken criticism, while in the service, of discrimination in the army, and before his enlistment had been on the staff of the NAACP.

His father, the son of a white man, had been taught along with his master's sons, and his mother had been brought north to Williamstown, Massachusetts, as a domestic by a white family. While other Negro boys grew up under the tutelage of parents who were cowed by their handicap, his parents encouraged him to aim high and to ignore the advice of his teachers that he forego hopes of college. His stimulating, happy years at Bowdoin began with a dash of luck. The college was admitting one Negro a year, and when he reached the campus the quota had already been filled. Morrow had, however, been admitted by mail, without knowledge of his race. The thunderstruck college officials, once he stood before them, accepted a *fait accompli.*

Wilkins, Assistant Secretary of Labor from 1953 to 1958, was another example of an appointment in which considerations of merit at least temporarily superseded political calculations. The son of a mulatto minister of unknown male parentage, he was evidently at first attracted to the President's advisers by his prominence as a Chicago attorney with a bi-racial practice in the Loop, and by his high office in the predominantly white Methodist Episcopal Church. He is also known as the father of several precocious sons, one of whom, J. Ernest Wilkins, Jr., a Phi Beta Kappa, took a Ph.D. in mathematics at the University of Chicago at nineteen. Wilkins had served briefly as vice chairman of the federal Committee on Governmental Contracts, a body which also included the Secretary of Labor, and it was this association that led to Wilkins's selection for the Labor position.

Of the numerous judges, some of the most widely noticed have been William H. Hastie, Irvin Mollison, Herman E. Moore, Harold A. Stevens, Francis E. Rivers and Hubert Delany. Each was born in a section remote from the scene of his later distinction, four of them in the South. Not one is a dark Negro; each had a mother who had been a schoolteacher and a father who was in the professional class. These parents considered their sons' education the first claim upon the family budget after the barest necessities had been guaranteed.

Stevens's father owned a thousand-acre plantation in South Carolina, but died when Harold was three. The mortgaged estate was lost and the widow returned to schoolteaching and soon married a preacher. Her father had been a clergyman also, a graduate of the University of South Carolina in Reconstruction days, who had a career in business and Republican politics. Rivers's father, the last Negro member of the post-Civil War Tennessee legislature, was the unacknowledged son of a white pastor. The senior Rivers became for forty years a pastor in Washington, and it was there that Francis Rivers passed most of his youth in superior schools and a refined home. His father was a scholarly man and his mother, a former college teacher, a woman of great intelligence.

Rivers's parents impressed upon their children the notion that race was a fiction. Utterly incapable of craven deference, the senior Rivers all his life avoided association with whites. No less stubborn in his refusal to acknowledge the relevance of race, the younger Rivers, on the other hand, met the problem by conducting himself as if race were in fact a fiction. He found so many of his companions among whites that his campaigns for office elicited the criticism that he was too remote from colored folk, in blood and in sympathies, to speak for them. He early fixed his goal upon some non-racial role in the mainstream, aiming originally at a seat in Congress.

Judge Mollison is the fair-skinned son of an Oberlin-educated lawyer who had held public office in Mississippi before establishing a practice in Chicago. The judge's mother had been reared by a white family and had attended Fisk. Delany's father, though born a slave, was a Protestant Episcopal Church leader in the denomination's college in Raleigh, North Carolina, where both he and his slaveborn wife had been educated. One of Judge Delany's grandfathers was white; one grandmother was extremely fair, and a great-grandmother was a native African who married a freeborn shipbuilder. Hastie was reared in Washington. His mother was a college-trained schoolteacher, and his father, a native of Ohio, came to Washington as a clerk and, though trained as a pharmacist at Howard, remained in the federal service until his death.

Stevens's interest in law was awakened when, as a college student, he witnessed a multiple lynching. Delany's parents hoped to see their son enter the ministry, but he was offended by his father's status as a second-class "suffragan bishop" because of his race. Mollison had the example of his father to thank for an early inclination to the law, and Rivers and Hastie were pushed toward high aspirations by their families. All but Stevens went to leading Northern undergraduate colleges, and for their professional legal training Hastie chose Harvard; Mollison, Chicago; Rivers, Columbia and Harvard; Delany, New York University; and Stevens, the Jesuit Boston College Law School.

Stevens's years at Boston College were happy ones; but Rivers, the only Negro in the Yale class of 1915, was never wholly comfortable there. He was barred from athletics but worked off his discontents in long hours of self-support employment and by earning Phi Beta Kappa honors. Three decades later, at a class reunion, a speaker remarked that Rivers was in 1915 perhaps considered the least likely among his classmates to succeed, but that he was now, with Dean Acheson, one of the most celebrated members of his class. Mollison sensed no hostility in his classes at Chicago, but winced when Southern classmates freely used the word "nigger" without rebuke from professors. Once he was hired by mail by the famous constitutional historian, McLaughlin, as a grader, only to be discharged when the professor returned to the campus and discovered that his assistant was a Negro. Hastie was one of the Dunbar High boys in Washington who won scholarships to New England schools. He made a brilliant record at Amherst (including junior-year election to Phi Beta Kappa), and upon graduation he was comfortably assimilated at the Harvard Law School, where his classmates elected him to the board of the *Law Review*.

Hubert Delany began as a boy to work in summers, going as far afield from North Carolina as the Connecticut tobacco farms, to earn the means to attend a Northern college. City College afforded him excellent instruction, but he was forced to carry an enormous work load (he had, at the same time, four sisters in college) to remain in school. His white classmates were able to earn more on Saturdays than he could accumulate in a week. After hours he carried bags at Penn station, studying as he found opportunity in the subway, in the locker room, and at lunchtime. He took first prize (after one of the judges held out for an hour against giving the award to a Negro) in an oratory contest at CCNY. A city judge, himself a former winner of the prize, was attracted by the youth's feat, and helped promote Delany's appointment as an assistant United States Attorney. Young Rivers also benefited from the hospitality of white lawyers who took him into their firm, and Hastie acknowledges a debt to former Harvard associates, who pushed him forward at crucial stages in his career. Rivers, shortly before becoming a judge, was denied admission to the American Bar Association, but his chagrin was softened by the indignant withdrawal from the association by the distinguished Arthur Garfield Hays.

Stevens and Rivers owed their success to support from powerful district leaders in New York's party machinery. Stevens, after his arrival in the city as a fledgling lawyer, plunged into precinct politics as a party work horse and his labors were rewarded by Tammany's Harlem leaders with a seat in the General Assembly, to represent a predominantly white district. Years of experience as counselor for the Pullman Porters' Union, his forthright efforts during the war in behalf of Negro railway workers, and his record as a Catholic lay worker also recommended him as a strong contender for Irish as well as Negro votes.

Rivers, on the Republican side, also threw himself into the "legwork" that marks party regulars and brings them their rewards. He was elected to the Assembly in 1929, and in 1930 barely missed election as a city judge. In 1932, 1936 and 1940 he was assistant director of the Republican campaigns in the Eastern states, in charge of work with Negro voters. Then, in 1943, after five years as assistant district attorney, appointed by District Attorney Thomas E. Dewey, he was named (by Governor Dewey) to fill a vacancy as justice of the City Court. This put him in a strong position to win the regular ten-year term by election.

His nomination by the Republican and American Labor parties rallied an extraordinary army of campaigners. The Negro community was organized in various groups: lawyers, women, clergymen, lodges and general voters. More help, financial and organizational, came from whites, both separately and in close association with the Negro campaigners. Party workers functioned with unwonted energy and even many Democrats helped with a benevolent neutrality, rather than support Rivers' Democratic opponent, a professional officeholder of conventional qualities. The treasurer of Rivers's campaign, a white Yale classmate, raised a goodly sum from the Yalemen of '15, and a Columbia Law School alumni group entered the hustings in their classmate's behalf. New York newspapers, from the *Times* to the *Worker,* endorsed him, and when the victory was won, it appeared that three fourths of his vote had come from whites. Race was involved in the contest only in the sense that Rivers's backers, determined to elect him on his merits, felt that unusual exertions would be needed to offset the handicap, but the question of color *per se* was little heard except from political opponents in his own race who argued that he was too light-skinned and too aloof from colored folk to represent them. His triumph moved many to agree with *The New York Times* that the electorate had demonstrated that "what the public welfare demands is careers open to talent and character, regardless of racial origin. Mr. Rivers can confidently take his seat on that basis."

Hubert Delany was not conspicuously active in politics before his first appointment to municipal office. Mayor La Guardia, interested in proving that Negroes could be competent public servants, and concerned also about shortages in the revenue department's accounts, made Delany Tax Commissioner, responsible for handling the city's enormous revenues. Delany had by that time, as an assistant federal attorney, acquired a reputation for courage and unswerving incorruptibility and had made, at the age of twenty-eight, a remarkable showing as a Republican candidate for Congress. In 1942, La Guardia appointed him to the Court of Domestic Relations, an office he held until 1956, when Mayor Wagner, despite pressures in Delany's behalf from civic and lawyers' groups, replaced him with a Negro Democrat, in response to both partisan and religious opposition to the judge's allegedly ultra-liberal affiliations, and some unpopular decisions from the bench.

The four Negro federal judges appointed during these years had had experience in partisan politics and as spokesmen for Negro advance. Herman E. Moore, Judge of the District Court for the Virgin Islands, had been a Chicago lawyer, a working Democrat and an assistant commissioner of the Illinois Commerce Commission, as well as an official of Chicago's Urban League and NAACP chapter. Mollison worked with Chicago's Republican organization in the twenties, but switched to the Democrats in 1936 and put himself in their debt for his organizing efforts in De Priest's Republican satrapy. Mayor Kelly gave him respectable, if unremunerative, posts on the library and school boards. He practiced law meanwhile and dropped suggestions that a federal judgeship would be acceptable. The professionals smiled, but he insisted that President Truman would recognize the value of appointing a few judges from the colored bar, and his appointment to the United States Customs Court came early in Truman's administration.

Like Mollison, Hastie had his color to thank for his elevation to the federal bench, and like Mollison, he was fully qualified for the place. The first, and now the highest-ranking, of colored federal judges, his successive promotions in the government service usually coincided with political crises for which the advancement of a prominent Negro promised relief. He entered government as an Assistant Solicitor in the Department of the Interior in the early days of the New Deal. With strong support from the NAACP, influential Harvard Law School friends among alumni and professors and prominent Negroes, he was urged upon Mr. Roosevelt. Confirmation of his appointment was blocked for months in the Senate Judiciary Committee by Senator Eastland, and when his name was finally sent to the Senate floor, opponents of confirmation thundered against his highly active NAACP and "leftist" affiliations.

After two years as a judge in the Virgin Islands, he resigned to return to Howard Law School as its Dean, but soon the Roosevelt administration's apprehensions (quickened by the Stephen Early incident) about the colored electorate brought him into the War Department as Civilian Aide. Two years later he resigned in protest (expressed in some spirited published articles) against the department's inertia with respect to segregation in the armed forces. Hastie was now more than ever a hero to Negroes, and two years later he was appointed by Truman as Governor of the Virgin Islands, once again the beneficiary of the race's wartime pressures upon the government, and of the President's comparative liberalism. In 1948 Hastie campaigned energetically for Truman—while the President's very cabinet members hung back, convinced that his cause was lost. Soon after his re-election, Truman, pressed to appoint several Negro judges, disappointed the race's expectations by naming only one, but the disappointment was tempered by the fact that the place went to Hastie, and that it was a seat on the exalted Court of Appeals.

Robert C. Weaver was in 1958 an outstanding example of a cabinet-rank officer in a state administration. One of the contingent of bright young university men brought into the New Deal agencies in 1933, he was moved from one assignment to another, usually as assistant to some agency head, with responsibility for minority problems. The author of two important volumes and numerous journal articles on Negro housing and labor, he returned to academic work after a decade in Washington. When Governor Harriman made him State Rent Administrator, he had not been active in politics and electioneering, but was well known as vice-president of the National Board of Directors of the NAACP, as a member of the Fulbright Scholarship Selection Committee, chairman of the National Committee against Discrimination in Housing, a member of the board of directors of the Health and Welfare Council for New York City and as the director of the Whitney Foundation's "opportunity fellowship" program.

Here is an example of the highly trained expert, comparatively aloof from party politics, who is drafted by a liberal administrator, in part as a concession to the Negro electorate, in part for his own qualifications, and then retained for his proven worth. Men like Hastie, Bunche and Weaver received more recognition than whites would for similar achievements but were also able to accomplish particular objects where whites, perhaps, could not have succeeded. Fifteen years after these trail blazers began their careers in government, the able young Negro with some spectacular achievement in his record could move forward more rapidly in public life than could many whites, and still answer the need for "Negro representation"—to the dismay of the older colored political hacks and spoilsmen.

Weaver's was the old story of social advantages improved by his own industry and character. His grandfather, Robert T. Freeman, was a graduate of the first dental class (1869) at Harvard. His parents, in the respected civil-servant class, descended from whites and slaves who had been self-redeemed artisans before the Civil War. They lived in Washington where, as the tidal wave of newer colored migrants swirled over the small Negro elite, the Weavers struggled harder than ever to preserve their genteel middle-class standards, giving a high priority to superior education for their sons, and residing where few Negroes had yet settled. The boys had to attend segregated schools, but their parents taught them to strive for high achievement, accepting humiliation from no one. Though rigorously drilled in the polite forms, the boys were forbidden to use terms like the servile "yessir."

Young Robert won the Harvard scholarship that fell to Dunbar High boys, and at Harvard was greatly stimulated by the presence of Negro graduate students like Bunche, Hastie and Percy Julian. He was welcomed into a graduate dormitory during his junior year and was a member of the Harvard debating team. Graduating cum laude, he indignantly rejected the opinion of the eminent Professor Taussig that Negroes had no aptitude for graduate work in economics, and he took the Ph.D. in that field with a doctoral examination which, according to Professor William Z. Ripley, "showed exceptional ability."

Arthur C. Ford, President of the New York City Board of Water Supply, is an outstanding example of Negroes holding high municipal office. His career shows the usual pattern of the favored youth, sound education and the happy situation of being ready at the right place at the right time when opportunity came. His father was a coachman for Justice Joseph P. Bradley of the United States Supreme Court. When United States Senator Thomas C. Powers of Montana purchased the Bradley estate, the coachman was included in the transaction, and the Fords moved to Helena, where the small Negro population had excellent unsegregated schools and lived in the best parts of town near the leading families whom they served. The public library was open to young Ford and he participated fully in his high school's athletic teams. He became the first Negro graduate of Montana State College, earning his way as chauffeur for Senator Powers's family. His engineering degree had small market value in Montana, however, and when his efforts to enter the Army Air Corps in World War I were repulsed, he secured, by examination, a place in the Ordnance Bureau in Washington.

In 1924 he was employed by the New York City Board of Transportation and thereafter rose steadily, always by civil-service examination, in the city's public work agencies. Then, in 1950, a Democratic district leader, a total stranger to Ford, needed a candidate for the job of Consulting Engineer for the Borough of Manhattan, a man who was at once a professional engineer and—as a reward to colored Democratic voters—a Negro. Ford was not even a Manhattan resident nor an active partisan, but he was pressed for an instant decision, and on the next day was inducted into office by Borough President Robert F. Wagner, Jr. When Wagner became mayor he made Ford Commissioner of Water Supply and then President of the Board of Water Supply, a lifetime, twenty-thousand-dollar-a-year job.

Frank S. Horne, chairman of the New York City Commission on Intergroup Relations, is another trained specialist, aloof from the rough and tumble of politics. Like his famous niece, Lena Horne, he is of light complexion and derives from irregular ancestry, which on his mother's side probably descended from John C. Calhoun. His mother had a college education, and his father's intellectual capacities equipped him for more than his modest employment in the Fire Inspection Service. The Horne household was well supplied with books, good conversation and refined Negro guests. Young Frank was reared in Brooklyn in a lower middle-class neighborhood of Irish, Germans, Jews, Italians and a few Negroes. The public library was as important to him as were his mixed schools, and the free City College enabled him to continue his education while earning a small wage delivering telegrams. He studied optometry in Chicago, but was advised by his doctor to move into the South. His mother, a civic leader of some prominence, was a friend of Mrs. Bethune, so he set out to visit the latter. He stopped, however, at Fort Valley College in Georgia and remained there for ten years in close association with president Henry A. Hunt, serving on his faculty, writing publicity for the college, and adding to his reputation as a writer of verse. Hunt and Mrs. Bethune were instrumental in placing him in federal-housing agencies and he remained there until 1953, when he joined the Commission on Intergroup Relations.

Strikingly different is the case of Hulan Jack, Borough President of Manhattan, who governs a constituency that includes Park Avenue and Wall Street as well as Harlem—a population four fifths of whose voters are whites. When in 1953 the Republican and Liberal parties both nominated prominent Negroes (Elmer A. Carter and Rev. James H. Robinson) for the place, Tammany Hall gave the Democratic nomination to Jack. He had worked his way through evening high school and had gone to work for a paper-box company in which he eventually won a vice-presidency, but his real interest lay in politics. He joined a Democratic club when still very young, and then hard work as a Tammany man, at precinct and ward levels, in a notoriously tough and corrupt district, eventually won him a seat in the general assembly. By the early 1950's, when Negro voters were greatly increased by the inflow from Puerto Rico, the Tammany organization picked Jack, in no small measure because, as a hard-working, loyal organization man, a Catholic and a native West Indian, he was a "natural," though other prominent Negro politicians, including Congressman Powell, were interested in the place.

Some notice has already been taken of the Liberian ministership. In 1948 the place went to Edward R. Dudley, who heroically accepted the appointment on the eve of the 1948 election, after the nomination was cleared with party regulars and the patronage dispensers of what seemed to most observers to be a doomed administration. Here was another example of a traditional plum awarded to a thoroughly competent appointee. A faithful doorbell ringer in local Democratic politics when he was a law school student in Brooklyn, he was rewarded with minor party patronage crumbs, and then joined the NAACP legal staff. In 1945 his service to the party, and his acceptability to Negroes, whom the party was anxious to woo, brought him a political appointment as legal aide to Governor Hastie of the Virgin Islands.

After his retirement as Ambassador to Liberia (where most of his subordinates were whites), he rejoined the NAACP staff until he was designated to the New York Court of Domestic Relations.

Dudley's forebears were North Carolina slaves. His family on both sides had a record of Reconstruction officeholding, and his paternal ancestors were presumably owned by Governor Edward R. Dudley of North Carolina. His aunts and uncles numbered several teachers, an Assistant United States District Attorney, a dean of Shaw University Law School, a founder of Fort Valley College, and the first Negro legislator of New York State. Dudley grew up in Roanoke, Virginia, in an upper-class Negro home—his father was a dentist—at a time when race relations were still remarkably easy there. The family was one of the first in Roanoke to own an automobile. A few hundred miles farther South, a Negro family before World War I who, like the Dudleys, owned a car and kept its home painted and its hedges clipped, ran the risk of white aggressions. One of Dudley's uncles had been hustled out of North Carolina on just such grounds, and established himself in the real-estate business in New York.

The Liberian ambassadorship continues to be a political appointment. President Eisenhower's first choice was Jesse D. Locker, an attorney and active Republican who had served several terms in the Cincinnati city council. Locker was succeeded by Richard Lee Jones, an Alabama-born businessman. He came to Chicago in 1922 from Louisville, served as business manager of the *Defender,* and then became general manager of a large ghetto department store. He was noticed also because he attained the rank of reserve brigadier general in the Illinois National Guard. His ambassadorial appointment was in no small part ascribable to the accident that he was on the scene as director of the "Point Four" program in Liberia when Ambassador Locker died suddenly; but he was also an acceptable candidate by virtue of his prominence in the country's second largest Negro community as a business, civic, YMCA and Boy Scout leader.

Perhaps the most honored Negro in America in the 1950's is Ralph Bunche, the highest-ranking American in the United Nations Secretariat. The Noble Peace Prize, more than forty honorary degrees, and uncounted awards, medals and citations spangle his history. Another of the bright young Negroes drafted for government service with the backing of former Harvard associates, liberals and the NAACP, he began with the Office of Strategic Services as a social science analyst for colonial areas. By 1946 he was director of the UN's Trusteeship Department and in 1948 was sent to the Middle East, where it fell to him to contrive an Israeli-Arab truce. The settlement brought its author instant fame and the office of Undersecretary of the United Nations.

He had in the meantime declined appointment as American Assistant Secretary of State because of his reluctance to rear his children in the then still-segregated Washington. (He himself was excluded from first-class restaurants and sometimes purchased movie tickets by ordering them in French.) When he returned from his diplomatic successes in Palestine, a leading Washington hotel refused the Middle East Institute the use of a banquet room for a session where Bunche was to speak. In New York it was otherwise, however; there he was offered the presidency of City College.

His Harvard training, his post-doctoral field studies abroad under Rosenwald and Social Science Research Council grants, and his work with the Carnegie Myrdal study in 1939 afforded solid preparation as a specialist in problems dealing with racial minorities. During his year with Myrdal, he and the Swedish scholar carried their investigations into the Deep South, separating at night while Bunche hunted up accommodations in the Negro quarters. Sometimes, Bunche recalls, they were threatened and "found it necessary to make a run for it in my V-8.'"

His early years were shadowed by poverty and Jim Crow. In his lineage the blood of whites and blacks were freely mixed. His ex-slave grandfather migrated to Detroit and reared three daughters, one of whom married Fred Bunche, a barber who kept his shop in a decayed two-story structure where his family lived in the congested ghetto. The boy sold newspapers and shined shoes; when he was twelve, his father and mother were dead and he was living with relatives in a crowded household in Los Angeles. When he graduated near the top of his high-school class, his misty-eyed principal, thinking to pay him the ultimate compliment, assured him, "We are sorry to see you go, Ralph. We never thought of you as a Negro."

An athletic scholarship at the University of California and a job as a janitor in the women's gymnasium enabled him to put himself through college, while sharing with his grandmother and aunts the burden of supporting the family. Severe illnesses postponed his graduation for a year, but he made a distinguished record as a scholar and athlete and won a tuition scholarship to Harvard Graduate School. Negro women rallied to raise, from colored businessmen and church and social groups, a thousand-dollar fund to enable him to meet other expenses. After earning an A.M. degree, he went to Washington to teach at Howard and to pursue his studies at the Library of Congress, but before long he returned to Harvard for the doctorate, assisted by scholarships. He was soon known as a vigorous defender of the race, identified with the NAACP program. His liberal affiliations have drawn the fire of a few reactionaries, but America has covered him with honors.

Even more significant as an augury of the race's rising prospects than Bunche's dazzling record was the steady increase of Negroes in career positions in the foreign service. In the two decades following the establishment of the career service in 1924, only one Negro of the thirty-odd in the State Department was in this professional, non-political service: Clifton R. Wharton, born in Baltimore and educated at Boston University Law School. He entered the service in 1924, took his career examination, and was sent to Liberia with the lowest rank, vice-consul and third secretary. The department was not wholly to blame for this isolation, for it learned that some European countries which were most censorious of America's racial usages, were unwilling to accept a colored American envoy. Wharton served at "Negro posts" until 1957 and then was quietly appointed United States Minister to Rumania. So accustomed was America by that time to seeing colored citizens in high office, that the dispatching of this first Negro American diplomat to head a European legation excited almost no notice at all, even in the Negro press.*

When Rupert Lloyd became the second Negro in the career service, few expected that he or Wharton would ever break out of the "Negro beat." Indeed, when the State Department created another Negro post at Madagascar, a third Negro career man had to be recruited to man it, because the department still forbade the setting of Negro officers over white stenographers. By 1949 none of the three had yet served at a white post. By 1955, however, the three had grown to six (Wharton, Lloyd, William George, William Boswell, Charles M. Hanson and Clinton E. Knox) and all were at non-Negro stations in Europe, Asia and in Washington. As early as 1950 the only remaining all-Negro station was Liberia, and soon it too became a fully integrated embassy, and the most serious limitation upon the recruitment of Negro career diplomats was simply the dearth of qualified applicants.

Lloyd's rise was roughly typical for the group. His father, the natural son of a white Army officer, was a physician in Manassas, Virginia. His mother's people had grown up as field hands in slavery. The elder Lloyd provided his children with superior material and cultural advantages, but his wife, far less disposed to accept racial discrimination, sent young Rupert to high school in Pennsylvania. After a year he transferred to Dunbar High in Washington. Once again, it was the familiar story of a promising lad groomed for a New England college. He won the scholarship to Williams, and the only racial affront he remembers from his college days was the refusal of the town barber to cut his hair for less than ten dollars. Lloyd was one of three Negroes in his class. All three worked their way to eke out their scholarships; all three achieved junior-year election to Phi Beta Kappa; all three took highest honors in their major fields. One was class valedictorian, one received a graduate scholarship to Yale, and another won a scholarship to Brown.

Lloyd took a master's degree in Philology at Harvard, but the war interrupted his study (on a scholarship from the Institute of International Education) for the doctorate at the University of Paris. He entered the foreign service in 1941, serving until 1949 in Liberia, and then went to Paris as Consul

* Since this was written, John Howard Morrow, chairman of the Department of Modern Languages at North Carolina College, was appointed ambassador to the new state of Guinea—again, without excitement in the Negro press.

and First Secretary. There followed tours of duty at Budapest and Karachi and a return to Washington in 1957 for a period with the department.

Powerful Negro figures in the Republican party structure, supplied by Southern pocket boroughs, have been reduced until in 1958 only the durable Perry Howard remained as the senior member of the Republican National Committee. A remnant of Robert Church's old influence in party counsels survives in his daughter, Roberta Church, the holder of a master's degree from Northwestern University, and a political appointee with the title of Minority Groups Consultant for the Department of Labor. Somewhat the same function is supplied by Val Washington, Director of the Minorities Division for the Republican National Committee. A university graduate, he had had a career in business and journalism in Chicago and several years as a member of the Illinois Commerce Commission, and became an adviser to the party's national chairman as early as 1946.

In Wisconsin, Mrs. Vel Phillips, a young Negro housewife, lawyer and member of the Milwaukee City Council, became that state's member of the Democratic National Committee in 1958. She began her professional career as her husband's law partner and after two years in the city council was elected to the national committee by the state's Democratic convention, with vigorous backing from white CIO, liberal-labor, "egghead" groups and by Negro intellectuals. Old party regulars complained that the party was denying well-earned rewards to its old war horses and elevating Mrs. Phillips simply because she was a Negro.

Another innovation was the emergence in the Deep South of a Negro Democratic "boss," Austen T. Walden, a blunt foe of discrimination and Jim Crow. He has been head of the NAACP in Atlanta, a member of the association's national legal committee, chairman of the Atlanta Urban League and of the YMCA, legal counsel for the National Baptist Convention and the Knights of Pythias, and president of a powerful Negro voters' organization. A quiet, self-effacing man, his industry, shrewdness and strategic offices have made him the dean of Georgia's Negro leaders. He was trained at Atlanta University and the law school of the University of Michigan. His law practice, which included numerous civil-rights cases and some successful prosecutions of whites, made him a target of the Klan, but the report that he had been an infantry captain in World War I frightened off potential attackers.

After the Supreme Court had struck down the white primary in 1944, colored citizens were still apathetic, so Walden, through churches, fraternities and business organizations, spurred the establishment of Democratic clubs. In two years colored registrants increased from 20,000 to 100,000. New forces had, in fact, been astir in Atlanta since the early 1930's when Walden and his following, seconded by a teachers' association, began a drive for Negro registration. In 1934, railway mail clerk John Wesley Dobbs, a Republican and leader of Negro Masons, joined the organizing efforts and in that year the

Atlanta Civic and Political League brought Atlanta's Negroes together in an effective action group which, with energetic assistance from the Atlanta *World* and the NAACP, pressed for still more extensive Negro registration. Finally, in 1949, the Democrats under Walden and the Republicans under Dobbs, joined hands to form the Atlanta Negro Voters League.

It was political action of this sort that helped to elect Rufus E. Clement, President of Atlanta University, to the city school board in 1955, as the first Negro holder of elective office in Georgia since the Reconstruction. He defeated a white encumbent who had held the position for twenty-six years, winning by a wide margin, despite a spirited effort of the Democratic Executive Committee to stop him. In the closing hours of the contest the mild Clement—frequently rebuked for his conservatism by the Negro press—was openly accused of being a Communist, but the vituperation heaped upon him by white supremacy extremists so outraged the sensibilities of white voters that he was swept into office, and with him Miles G. Amos and Walden as members of the party's executive committee. In 1957 Clement was re-elected, again by a bi-racial vote, in an election in which whites and Negroes alike rallied once more to Mayor William B. Hartsfield, whose reputation for racial fairness helped rather than hindered his campaign for a sixth term. This second election of Clement was widely cited in the press as evidence that, despite the excitements stirred up by the Brown decision in 1954, anti-Negro rancors in the Deep South had, at least in some quarters, relaxed.

The extraordinary resistance of Negroes to the Communist appeal has been variously explained on the grounds that "it's tough enough to be black without being red too," and that the Negro sees more promise in the gradual realization of the American creed than in its repudiation in favor of another. In any case, the Negro's emphatic rejection of importunate bids for his allegiance has held to a minimum the number of Negro Marxist leaders. Two prominent colored communists, however, have been James W. Ford and Benjamin J. Davis, Jr.

Ford, the Communist candidate for Vice-President in 1932, 1936 and 1940, was born in Alabama and reared in a climate of poverty and implacable Jim Crowism. At thirteen he was a water boy for a railroad gang, and soon thereafter became a steel worker. His work-worn mother sent him to Fisk, but he left to serve in World War I. His experience in the segregated army left him bitter. After the armistice he worked in the Chicago post office until discharged as an "irresponsible agitator." Then, after some experience as a left-wing labor organizer he entered the Communist Party.

Ben Davis had a sharply different history. The son of Benjamin Jefferson Davis, the prominent Atlanta Republican leader of the previous generation, Ben, Jr. was reared in a family whose affluence (they were among the first to own a car in Atlanta), fine home and prestige shielded him from many of the cruelties of prejudice. White politicians fawned upon his father, but some upper-class Negroes snubbed him because of his iron-handed tactics as a political and fraternal potentate.

Young Ben went to the nation's finest schools. At Amherst he was a classmate of Mercer Cook, William H. Hastie and W. Montague Cobb, and together they made up a remarkable quartet, all four of them Southern boys of color destined to become distinguished. Davis was comparatively happy at Amherst, though he was occasionally disturbed by the sting of being called "nigger" and by his exposure, especially when playing varsity football against Princeton, to savage mauling by athletic opponents determined to bait their colored adversary.

Like Hastie, he took his law degree at Harvard, and then returned to Atlanta to look after his ailing father's affairs. One of his most vivid memories was the burning of crosses by the Klan on his family's front lawn, a shock which hastened his mother's death. He seemed, however, to be making a normal adjustment to Negro life in Georgia after eight years in Massachusetts, when the Herndon case changed his life. Angelo Herndon, an eighteen-year-old Negro, was snatched into court, under an archaic statute, as an insurrectionist, when, in the dismal autumn of 1932, he led a crowd of unemployed to the capitol steps in Atlanta to harangue them and ply them with Marxist leaflets. Davis, a minor celebrity as a Harvard-trained lawyer, was importuned to enter the case, and agreed to conduct the defense without fee.

Herndon was threatened with violence in the very courtroom; and Davis, deliberately badgered and abused, was called "nigger" and "darky lawyer" by the prosecutor with no objection from the judge. The latter added to Davis's exasperation by turning his back on him and reading a newspaper while Davis was presenting his case. Herndon was sentenced to twenty years in a road gang, and the affair hurled Davis straight into the Communist camp. He moved to New York City, joined the staff of the *Daily Worker,* and in 1943 won election to the City Council—the only avowed Communist to hold elective office in the United States.

His election victories (he was re-elected by an impressive majority) were in no sense a measure of Negro Communist strength, for his support came also from many conservative Negroes as a tribute to his integrity, his engaging personality and his effective appeals to audiences of both races. He drew votes from all over Manhattan under the proportional representation plan then still in operation. As councilman he won the applause of Negroes for winning significant concessions for his race, but in October, 1949, he was convicted as one of the eleven Communist leaders charged with advocating the overthrow of the Government of the United States. By a rare double coincidence, he was imprisoned in the federal penitentiary in his native Atlanta, and was sentenced in the same week that saw the elevation of his old Amherst and Harvard companion, Hastie, to the highest judicial office ever held by a Negro American.

Still productive in the new generation were writers who had risen to prominence before 1936. Langston Hughes was adding steadily to his volumes of poetry, autobiography, plays, popular Negro history, fiction and the irrepressible "Simple" sketches. Braithwaite, Sterling Brown, Bontemps, Thurman, Hurston and Horne were still publishing in the 1940's, but new names now rivalled theirs: Richard Wright, Ralph Ellison, James Baldwin, Frank Yerby, Ann Petry, Willard Motley, Chester Himes, John Killens, Waters E. Turpin, William Attaway, Saunders Redding and Era Bell Thompson in prose works; Gwendolyn Brooks, Margaret Walker, Frank Marshall Davis, Owen Dodson, Melvin Tolson, Robert Hayden, M. Earl Holman in poetry; and Louis Peterson in drama.*

Again, they defy categorization from any point of view—their social origins, their education, their styles, their preoccupations, their daily employments, their several attitudes toward the problem of living and writing in a white man's world. Some were still close to the slavery past. With others it was a fading tradition that one read about in books. Peterson, for example, was born and reared in New England, of a long-established line of Northern free folk; but Redding's boyhood home was much under the influence of grandmother Redding, who had escaped slavery as a young woman and kept the recollections of bondage vividly alive.

Gwendolyn Brooks's freeborn ancestors had long since fled the South for Kansas, but she was reared in the Chicago black belt and attended bi-racial public high school and junior college, relatively unbruised by racial hostilities but too shy (she was a plain, dark child) to avail herself of the wide-open opportunities for inter-racial friendships. Her parents were well educated and kept their children supplied with books of their own and from the public library. Wright, by contrast, was born to people who were slaves until the Emancipation in Mississippi, where his dissolute father and toil-worn mother lived in circumstances little better than those of their fettered forebears. Attaway was also born in Mississippi, but his father, a physician, took his family North. Half of the whole group were born in the South, and most of these a mere generation or two removed from bondage. Even so, more than half came out of households with cultural advantages far above those of the generality of Negroes. Many had parents in the professional class, descended from white planters and favored house servants.

At one extreme we have the record of Wright's brutal childhood, in his autobiographical *Black Boy* and the Federal Writers' Project's *American Stuff*. Reared in poverty, violence, squalor and depravity; an arsonist at four, a drunkard at six, he was turned over, a "foul-mouthed brat," to an orphanage

* To these may well be added Shirley Graham, who made her mark as a composer of folk operas, and, more recently, has produced a long list of popular biographies of Negro symbols: Jean Baptiste Du Sable, Benjamin Banneker, Phillis Wheatley, Frederick Douglass, Booker T. Washington, Paul Robeson, and George W. Carver among them.

by his mother when his worthless father abandoned the family. He attended a wretched school, but despite his brutalizing life, he early developed a hunger for reading that he gratified by handing to the attendant at the public library notes to which he forged a prominent white citizen's name and which read "Please let this nigger boy have some books." Repeated wounds forced him at last to "calculate his chances for life in the South," and it was, he wrote, his reading that created the sense of terror that finally drove him to flight, first to Chicago, and then to Harlem and the temporary fellowship of the Communist Party.

Saunders Redding, reared in the upper South, by Howard-educated parents, has, like Wright, written a poignant account of his youth. It could hardly have been more remote from Wright's, but there were in it the same inexorable rejections. Grandmother Redding, black, proud, embittered by memories of slavery, continually shrilled her hatred of whites, while the boy's middle-class parents sought a neutral ground. The elder Redding, an ex-schoolteacher, became a minor functionary in the postal service. His light-skinned wife, another former teacher, raged when a second Negro family moved into their tidy neighborhood. When Saunders's father pointed out that they were "our own people" she would retort, "Yours, but not mine!" The boy's bewilderments were compounded by his colored maternal grandmother's insistence that "a black skin was . . . a blemish, a taint of flesh and bone and blood." The emotional corrosions engendered by color conflict were sharpened in his classrooms. Teachers and children in the lighter-skinned majority taunted the darker children, and when young Redding, a light-brown child, was adjudged the winner in an oratorical contest over a black boy who had clearly won, he was so sickened by the injustice that he kept away from school for a week. The pressures of the color line shaped in his youthful mind an image of the white man which required years to erase. Grandmother Redding's stories of her slave days; the Negro papers which his father took; the editorials of Du Bois; the fiction in *Crisis* and *Opportunity;* tales of peonage, bastardy and lynching; all compounded into a picture of the "typical Southern white," as a "soulless creature of the devil, drooling blood and venom, ignorant . . . but also cunning beyond belief; filthy, lecherous, murderous; cowardly, superstitious, . . . barefoot, in . . . dirt-encrusted blue denim breeches within which he concealed a bottle of red whisky and a horse pistol."

Peterson, growing up in white neighborhoods in Hartford, was so far removed from racial bruises that his father, a bank messenger, sent the boy to Morehouse College, partly because the sojourn in Atlanta would acquaint the lad with "his own people." Ann Petry's childhood in a small Connecticut town was also free from racial self-consciousness, except for occasional disasters. The first shock came when the Sunday-school class of seven-year-olds in which she was the only colored child was picnicking on a beach, and onlookers took up the chant of "Nigger, Nigger, Nigger!" The frantic teacher prevailed upon the scoffers to withdraw, but, minutes later, a huge, red-faced guard startled the party anew with the shout, "Niggers ain't allowed on this beach!"

Baldwin, growing up in Brooklyn, was also comparatively safe, but minor insults accumulated at last into unendurable pain. While working in a defense plant in New Jersey, he was often refused service in the cheap lunchrooms where the workers took their meals. On one such occasion he flew into a rage and hurled a pitcher at a waitress's head. He was promptly borne down and beaten by whites, but kicked his way to freedom and ran.

The group was, as a whole, a highly schooled lot. At least sixteen of the twenty-one attended college (Wright, Motley and Baldwin were among the exceptions) and of these more than two thirds studied at Northern white colleges. Nine or ten took postgraduate study at Northern universities, some of them to the Ph.D. degree. Several concentrated in literary studies with a view to teaching, but others had, at least for the present, other vocational goals. Ellison majored in music at Tuskegee; and Petry, at the University of Connecticut, took a degree in pharmacy.

The Federal Writers' Project of the WPA provided several in the group (Wright, Ellison, Motley, Thompson, Walker and Hayden among them) with a fortunate opportunity to cultivate their talent without the handicap of a hostile market. Many had also the benefit of subsidies and prizes to enable them to mature their gifts. A dozen, for example, held Rosenwald Fellowships, and a half dozen Guggenheim Fellowships were shared by them. Important also was the hospitality of the columns of *Crisis* and *Opportunity* (and later of *Phylon*), always alert to emergent Negro talent. After publishing early stories and poems in these Negro journals, they began appearing in periodicals like *Story, Poetry, Atlantic,* the *Yale Review, Esquire, Harper's, Coronet, Partisan Review* and *The New Yorker*.

Several have remarked upon the ambitions that animated them. Some aspired to vindicating the race in the white man's eyes; others, once begun as writers, felt that Negroes would be judged by their work and were thereafter much under the pressure of this awareness. Some expressed a debt to other colored writers whose earlier examples had inspired them and smoothed their way by preparing white publishers, critics and readers for a more hospitable reception of Negro literary artists. Wright was moved by a compulsion to cry out against the cruelties of the Southern and Northern ghetto life, while Ellison, though sharing similar indignations, was in fact more inspired by the achievements of Wright than by his own resentments. He was so stirred by his first reading of Wright's early poetry that he sought out the gifted Mississippian for advice and even joined him in a short-lived magazine-publishing venture. Attaway was electrified by the example of Langston Hughes whose work was called to his attention by his white high-school teacher. He had always been taught that the successful Negro was the Negro in the learned professions, but this first acquaintance with Negro verse which was included in high-school anthologies so fired his imagination that only a writing career could interest him thereafter.

Ann Petry began in pharmacy but her marriage took her to journalism and social work in Harlem, and she was stimulated to set down the ghetto life she was witnessing. Era Bell Thompson, at a small denominational college in North Dakota as the only Negro student (she lived in the president's home), was so remote from Negro life that she had not heard of Marian Anderson or Paul Laurence Dunbar until she was halfway through college. In high school and college she wrote verse and humorous bits for the school papers, but doubted that she could find a satisfactory place in journalism, and when, upon her graduation, she went to Chicago, she found only modest clerical employment.

A few of the twenty-one eventually became real professionals, as Hughes had done. Wright, after the success of *Native Son* and *Black Boy,* derived a substantial income from his writing, and Yerby, since 1946, has earned a princely income from his annual best-sellers. Others were sustained by scholarships, fellowships and other subsidies, and some made their living as journalists. Peterson had a desk job with the Treasury Department, and Attaway, after earlier dependence upon menial jobs, earned (as did Peterson) substantial fees by writing and consulting for the film and television industries. Gwendolyn Brooks has long insisted that she is a housewife and mother first, and a writer only in her spare hours. Her fellow poet, Frank Horne, left Fort Valley College to enter government service, first as a federal-housing official and then as a New York City race-relations expert. College teaching, at Negro schools in the South, gave employment to more of the writers than did any other vocation—among them Turpin, Dodson, Tolson, Walker, Holman and Redding.

Others struggled with poverty and hardship. Himes is said to have begun publishing while in prison; before leaving America he had worked as a farm hand, coffee packer, cannery hand and shipworker. Ellison was a counterman at the Negro YMCA in Harlem, a photographer, a receptionist for a psychiatrist, and trumpeter in a jazz band. Motley lived in a Chicago slum, gathering raw data for his novels about lower-class whites, while making a precarious living as a short-order cook, Christmas-card salesman, shipping clerk and vagabond, sustained for a while by the WPA. While working on his novel, *Knock on Any Door,* he lived in a shabby building that had once housed a stable. His room contained no stove to fend off the harsh Chicago cold so he burned paper in a tin can to warm his hands as he labored over his manuscript.

The avenues to public recognition were various. Some slowly came to notice by publishing pieces in the "little magazines." Gwendolyn Brooks, after earlier ventures for her high-school paper and the Chicago *Defender,* was invited to participate in the annual Mid-Western Writers' Conference, and there came to the attention of publishers' agents who invited her to submit samples of her work. Ann Petry's first appearance in the *Crisis* emboldened her to try a novel. She sent the first half-dozen chapters to Houghton Mifflin for criticism and the firm responded by offering her a $2,400 Literary Fellowship to enable her to complete the work for them.

Motley spent eight years on his first novel, trying vainly all the while to place stories in magazines. He sent the completed manuscript off in a tomato crate to a succession of publishers, who rejected it as too raw; but with support from Newberry and Rosenwald fellowships, he revised it and reduced its enormous bulk by half. When Macmillan published it, he became a celebrity overnight. Miss Walker was launched when she won the Yale University competition for younger poets, and Wright found his first considerable audience after he won, for his *Uncle Tom's Children,* the five-hundred-dollar prize offered by *Story* magazine in a competition for Federal Writers' Project workers.

Yerby's first recognition came when his story, "Health Card," appeared in *Harper's* in 1944. A bitter story of the Negro's rejection, it promised a fruitful literary career. Yerby was at the time a young defense-plant worker, a former English teacher in a small Negro college. He had earned a master's degree, but his funds ran out and he was obliged to forego the Ph.D. degree which would doubtless have consigned him for life to genteel poverty on a Negro campus. He had already essayed a "protest novel," but it proved a dismal failure—perhaps, he thought, because he had encountered little friction and felt little of the anger that animated a Wright or an Ellison. He decided to write simply to entertain a mass audience, with no pretensions at literary excellence.

In 1944 came his first best-seller, *Foxes of Harrow*. Spurned by reviewers as "drugstore fiction," it was precisely the compound of romance, sex and swashbuckling historical pageantry that the millions buy. Thereafter he has annually turned out his best-selling thrillers—all of them book-club selections, and many of them filmed by motion-picture makers. In ten years he published a round dozen, with an average sale of more than a million per title. His publisher has sedulously avoided mention of the author's race, and Yerby himself has discouraged publicity. He is, from a commercial standpoint, not only the most successful Negro writer who ever put pen to paper, but is in fact one of the most successful writers of whatever race. Hundreds of thousands of his readers have no knowledge of his color and are quite unaware that he has long since gone to live abroad.

If Yerby won the greatest material rewards, others garnered other kinds of approbation. Their works were published by leading houses and cordially reviewed in the country's press. Wright's *Native Son* and *Black Boy* were both Book-of-the-Month selections, and have invited comparison with the best of

Dreiser and Farrell. A Pulitzer Prize went to Gwendolyn Brooks, and a National Book Award to Ellison (when Hemingway was a competitor). Redding, a stylist of extraordinary gifts, was awarded one of the annual Mayflower Prizes for the best volume by a resident of North Carolina. Ann Petry and James Baldwin appeared in the best short-story anthologies, and others, like Tolson and Hayden, have been honored by less widely known literary prizes.

Both to escape the constraints that have burdened travel in their homeland and to see what life without a color line was like, Negro writers, like the most successful Negroes in every calling, have tried somewhat earlier and harder than have whites in similar economic circumstances to manage a sojourn abroad. But it has been only the writers—plus a sprinkling of artists and entertainers—who have manifested any disposition to remain in Europe, once they have savored life on the Continent. This singularity is often ascribed to the independent status of such people as compared with colored businessmen, physicians, educators, lawyers (or numbers tycoons), who would find no clientele in Europe. At least four of the leading novelists (Wright, Himes, Yerby and Motley) are expatriates. Others, like William Gardner Smith, William Demby, Ben Johnson and Richard Gibson, may be added to this list. Still others have tarried abroad until their funds ran out or a need to renew home ties overtook them. Attaway, Hughes, Baldwin, Ellison and the journalist Ottley have made extended stays abroad, but always rejoiced to return to the American motherland. Ottley's *No Green Pastures* reports in detail his disillusionment with the European "haven" and strongly hints that some of the expatriates are lonelier than ever in Paris or Rome, but too proud to admit that flight had been a mistake.

The most famous exile is Wright. Praised by critics for his undeniable insights into human motivations, he remained a tortured soul, chafing under the frictions of color prejudice and also from rejections by Negroes, who deplored his leftist loyalties and his depiction of coarse and blasted Negro lives. After his *affaire du coeur* with communism, now repudiated, he fled to Paris. Remote from the Negro life he portrays, he now writes like a man who has been abroad too long, and as if nothing had changed since the days upon which his bitter memories dwell.

Yerby, though far from bitter, finds life on the Riviera far more conducive than life in New York to producing his romances. Others have expressed a preference for Paris or Rome (Motley and Davis, however, chose Mexico and Hawaii), quite apart from racial considerations, because of the presumed greater hospitality to intellectuals than the great American metropolitan centers afford. Still others have pointed out that a year abroad tempts younger Negroes to stay at least a while longer. "The bright young white boys," Richard Gibson has said, "after . . . their Fulbright scholarship, are able to return with reasonably light hearts to the dens of Madison Avenue or to the provincial Ph.D. factories," but for the young Negro, it still requires a kind of audacity to plunge back into the surviving uncertainties.

The Negro writer was still fighting his way out of the stereotype that boxed him in. He had always found greatest acceptance where his artistic expression was "flattering and obsequiously entertaining to the majority ego," as Margaret Just Butcher has explained in her book, *The Negro in American Culture*. His recognition was, in fact, longer delayed than that of other colored artists, because the white man's image of the unspoiled child of nature—easy enough to identify with the "born" singer, dancer, or painter—is too much at variance with the popular myth, for literary genius presumes a degree of intellectuality which whites have been reluctant to concede to Negroes. These preconceptions conspired to keep the race's literary production at a low plane—either pliantly imitative, provincial and immature, or distorted by defiant racialism, chauvinism and strident protest.

The writer was, of course, not alone in this predicament. Just as the idea of a truly competent Negro literary craftsman, dealing with universal themes, was somehow inconceivable to whites (and therefore his reality was denied even by the white man who was looking at one), so also the Negro businessman, for example, was too much for many white minds to grasp. That the Negro is inherently incapable of responsible economic enterprise is for many whites so much an article of faith that the exception is not recognized as an exception at all, but only as a man—perhaps a Spaniard or a "South American" —who must be mistaken about his race.

No less an obstacle to the maturing of a distinguished literature was the patronizing double standard of criticism, which took the form both of indiscriminate praise and of the myth of a "Negro literature," as a thing apart, corrupted if it presumes, as Charles Glicksburg has said, to express anything but "the soul of the black folk; their exuberance, their earthy sensuousness, their childlike mind and innocent eye, their African sense of rhythm."

Critics often argued that the cultural isolation forced upon the Negro disqualified him as a commentator on anything but the Negro community, and even within that contracted sphere, the choice of themes must still conform to the preconceptions of the race which dominates the literary market. A "literature of manners," for instance, has long been frustrated by stereotypes. Jessie Fauset and Nella Larsen's pioneer efforts won little approval from publishers and the public because, as Braithwaite has said, whites were not ready to "appreciate the delicate evocations of such human situations among Negroes, a race which was considered without emotional refinements and the dignity of personal ideals." Negroes themselves, moreover, demanded of their imaginative writers "a lustiness of challenge and the biting bravado of censure."

By 1950 critics of Negro books were abandoning these stubborn presumptions, but surviving obstinacies among publishers, forced upon them by the public, continued to favor the writer who conformed. Even the best of the new realists were rebuked for craven conformism, as Braithwaite argues, for "low life characterization, tragic abandonment to violent impulse, and an exultant trespassing of moral codes which victimized women of both races." It was a striking back, he suggests, a subtle propaganda against the mistreatment that the Negro has so long endured. But for all its passionate protest, its intense feeling, it was still painfully narrow in scope, still a kind of subservience to pressures from whites which bound rather than liberated the Negro writer. Some Negro intellectuals argued that the case-study portrayals of Himes's, Wright's, and Ellison's warped Negro males were only new stereotypes, demanded by a changing literary market, and that they only reinforced existing prejudice and discrimination.

Perhaps so. But the current, however slow and fitful, bore steadily in one direction: toward the coming of age of the Negro's writing; toward emancipation from the compulsion to produce "Negroid" poems and stories; toward a genuinely American literature that would find its themes in universal concerns. In the 1950's the whole of life was increasingly recognized as the Negro writer's proper study. When he treated Negro life (and he did so most of the time, for it was still what he knew best) it was often from a universal perspective, unconfined by Jim Crow aesthetics, depicting (to quote Mrs. Butcher again) "Negro life and expression . . . with a third dimension of universalized common-denominator humanity." In growing measure he used racial characters and situations as symbols and dealt with universals through the experience of people who happened to be colored. Others, after earlier success with Negro protest novels, shifted their interest as social changes relaxed the fetters that bound them.

Involved in the changing literary currents was the gradual conjunction of Negro life with the American mainstream. The fading color line relieved the artist of the imperative to defend or explain the Negro, and diminished his own sense of separateness and inferiority, drawing him to general subjects. The same social changes, as they brought the races into closer communion, enabled whites to delineate Negro life more accurately, so that the Negro writer found in his white counterpart a competitor, whether he wrote of the general American or the Negro environment. The progress of integration created real dilemma for the colored writer. Until lately, when systematic discrimination was approved by the country, a literature of exposure dominated the interests of the most independent among the race's authors. But by 1955, although integration had scarcely proceeded beyond token dimensions, the old protestantism became anachronistic, for the nation was now officially on the Negro's side. The spiritual climate of integration had come to stay, and further advocacy would be anticlimax.

This change, writes Arthur P. Davis, caught writers unprepared. In the 1940's the best of them were still churning out protest fiction and poetry. Maturer writers found the transformation too great a wrench and either fell silent or continued to intone the old litanies. Younger writers fared better, but several never again repeated their old success. Some illustration of the shift is indicated by the contrast between Himes's mordant *If He Hollers* (1943) and his *Third Generation* (1953), the latter a study of color conflict not between the races but within a Negro family. The second novel of the indignant Wright, appearing a decade after *Native Son,* also exhibits the change. Perhaps only the very newest writers were at home in the changed social landscape, though the poets, Hughes, Tolson, Hayden and Brooks successfully weathered the dislocations.

Colored critics like Davis, Brown and Braithwaite now confidently looked forward to the successful exploitation of the richer materials of Negro life in America at large to be set down by artists under fewer constraints, free, without self-consciousness, to explore the humorous, the tragic, the pathetic, in the life of their own people, in universal human terms, and judged by a single standard of criticism. Negro writers are still largely excluded from editorial posts and are rarely asked to review any but books and manuscripts by and about Negroes. But their revolt against stereotype, encouraged by the literate white community's growing willingness to agree with them, is in full career, and with it marches an insistence that there is no "Negro art," no "Negro writing," no unique cultural pattern, but only a Negro life stamped with the same cultural pluralism that marks the life of whites.

In "serious music" the three most famous Negro names—Anderson, Robeson and Hayes—of the previous generation still dominated the next. The aging Hayes was in the 1950's still making European tours, but in America was increasingly confined to Negro houses after his seventieth birthday. Miss Anderson's concerts became less frequent as the years burdened her voice, but her fame was never greater than in 1958. Her tour of the Orient under State Department auspices (a protracted ovation) and her telecast *Lady from Philadelphia,* elicited unstinted praise from her countrymen and an appointment by the President as alternate delegate to the United Nations General Assembly.

Vastly different was Robeson's later history. Repeated injuries to himself and a brooding despair over the race's plight (sharpened, it may be, by an impressionable, crusading temperament) drove him at last to the far left in the racial struggle, and—more damaging to his personal fortunes—into vigorously avowed admiration for "scientific socialism" and for the Soviet Union which had long and assiduously courted his favor.

He had, however, long been an outspoken enemy of Jim Crow. Upon his return to America in 1939, he carried his war against racial bias to the very concert stage in firmly worded but good-humored little speeches at scattered points in his concerts. Some of his listeners were moved by his candor and courage, but others found the propensity annoying. He continued to be enormously lionized in the early 1940's, and his annual income from concerts kept him among the highest-paid singers in America. In the middle 1940's he was still appearing as soloist with foremost symphony orchestras and on leading network programs. In 1944 he campaigned for the Roosevelt-Truman ticket, and in the same year was appointed, with Sumner Welles, to the editorial board of Phi Beta Kappa's quarterly *American Scholar*.

In 1947 his popularity began to slip, and the Negro press began to deplore his extremism. His identification with the Wallace campaign in 1948 and his association with Marxist groups persuaded even liberal, anti-Jim Crow white Northerners to join in checking him with congressional investigations, boycotts and the "silent treatment" in the press. Finally, his public outcry, often misquoted in the press, that it was "inconceivable" to him that Negro Americans would ever join their American oppressors in a war against Russia evoked angry repudiation by former admirers. Before another year had passed his concert career came to an abrupt halt, and his income dwindled to a mere two thousand dollars, provided by an occasional recital at Negro churches or for left-wing audiences.

Robeson's rejection by hurt and uncomprehending whites and Negroes so swiftly bolted the door that a man of his pride could not negotiate for reinstatement. Many insisted that his fabulous success, prestige and financial returns should have tempered his indignations, but even conservative whites sometimes countered that Robeson's very achievements made racial insults the more unendurable to him. His long habit of success, the adulation that had been his portion since college days, had unsuited him for steeling himself against racial affronts; and—so ran the argument—when the provocations became too great, he had no defense to which he might retreat. Negroes sprang readily to his defense when whites rebuked him, reiterating that when an artist who has been wildly applauded in every major country of the world can, fresh from an ovation at Carnegie Hall, be relegated to the freight elevator at a hotel, or refused a glass of water to wash down his aspirin in a Times Square drugstone, the instinct to rebel is stronger than in a humble domestic. He had, after all, everything to lose by his defiance; and lose it he did.

European music lovers—particularly leftists and critics of American racial practices—continued to clamor for him but the State Department cancelled his passport, cutting off escape from his lonely exile in Harlem, where he lived quietly with his wife and in close association with his clergyman brother. It was only in 1957 that he began to be heard again in modest church concerts. Bigger church engagements followed and then, now sixty years old, he resolved to resume his career. A Carnegie Hall concert in 1958, his first important New York performance in a decade, persuaded critics that he was still a man of magnificent vocal endowments, still proud and unrepentant, still disposed to use the concert stage for a rostrum.

A television network arranged a program for him and then dropped it before the date came around. Municipal auditoriums were still closed to him, but his prospects changed sharply for the better when the State Department removed the long-standing ban on travel. He promptly went abroad for what proved to be a triumphal concert and television tour of England, the Continent and the Soviet Union. On both sides of the Atlantic old friends began to hail his return to the musical world. Meanwhile, his earnest, plain-spoken book *Here I Stand* (1958), went far to persuade many Americans to reconsider their judgment of the man. Former admirers in both races who had abandoned him were softening their estimates, but still hoping that he too would see that the time had come to erase the memory of ancient injuries—that the Rutgers which had expected him to keep his "place" could now elect a colored student as president of the senior class; that the era which had produced his grievances had lost its hold on the future, giving place to a more liberal generation which was providing a vastly changed environment and opportunity for his own younger successors.

The concert stage was, after 1936, shared by a growing number of younger singers, three of them (Dorothy Maynor, Anne Wiggins Brown and Todd Duncan) before 1945, and at least a dozen who came to real prominence in the next decade: Adele Addison, Carol Brice, Gloria Davy, Mattiwilda Dobbs, Ellabelle Davis, Robert McFerrin, Leontyne Price, Kenneth Spencer, William Warfield, Camilla Williams and Lawrence Winters.

Duncan was reared in Indianapolis where his parents were in better circumstances than most Negroes. He had his first lessons from his music-teacher mother, but not until his student days at Butler University did he become seriously interested in a musical career. He studied voice and theory at an Indianapolis conservatory, and after taking a master's degree at Columbia went to Howard as a voice teacher. An appearance in a Negro production of *Cavalleria Rusticana* in New York in 1935 brought him to the notice of George Gershwin, who promptly engaged him for the male lead in his *Porgy and Bess*. For the next nine years it was his chief role. Between times he was cast in the standard vehicles which provide the few parts available to colored singer-actors, and also made some moderately successful concert tours in Europe and Latin America as well as some American concert, motion-picture and radio appearances, but he emerged a decade too early to achieve roles in first-rank opera.

A more spectacular success came to Dorothy Maynor, who flowered in her first professional season, 1939–1940 as one of the nation's leading sopranos. The daughter of a Norfolk, Virginia, pastor, she went to Hampton Institute for her secondary and college training, and there came under the tutelage of Nathanael Dett. She sang in his choir in the soprano section and as a soloist, accompanying the group in cross-country tours and on a European trip. Dett, impressed by her extraordinary voice, made every effort to induce her to transfer to a musical course, and when she remained unmoved, peremptorily directed the college registrar to change her status from that of a home economics major to that of music student.

In the summer after her graduation she sang for a minister's conference on the Hampton campus, and there her performance so startled the president of the Westminster Choir School of Princeton, New Jersey, that he offered her a scholarship. With funds from a benefactress—Harriet Curtis, a Hampton dean and Boston blue blood—she spent three years at Westminster and then several more under private teachers in New York, again as the protégée of her New England patron.

In 1939 she went to the Berkshire Music Festival and through the efforts of Mrs. Gorham Brooks of Brookline, Massachusetts, was invited to sing for the celebrated Koussevitsky at a private picnic he had arranged for members of his orchestra and a corps of critics. The maestro's extravagant praise led to generous press notices and a Town Hall debut before a full house. Her instant fame brought agents, in quest of another Anderson, hastening to her side. Once under professional management, she had access to hundreds of stages in the United States and Canada. In the South, however, only her own home town included her in its regular series, of which only whites could be subscribers.

In her second season she was already among the ten most highly paid concert artists in America. She had been a guest soloist on radio and with the country's foremost orchestras, and had twice been the soloist at Presidential inaugural ceremonies, but continues to be an extremely shy person of gentle, childlike manner, and devout religious loyalties—a plump little woman standing less than five feet tall, unnoticed in a crowd even in her own neighborhood. Her prodigious travels across the United States and the world, and her constant association for twenty years with sophisticated folk have left her unchanged. When she travels under professional management, she can usually secure first-class hotel accommodations, but even in the middle 1950's it was still sometimes necessary for her agents to hunt up overnight lodging for her in private homes. When she travels with her husband, Shelby Rooks, she still betrays all the reactions of a Negro who has never known anything but Negro life, ready like millions of sensitive colored Americans to run for cover at the first hint of hostility. For all her world fame, she is barred from fashionable resorts. When her husband was scheduled to attend a ministerial conference at a fine hostelry in the Pocono Mountains in 1957, she was happy to be invited to accompany him because she would not otherwise have the chance to see what life in such places was like.

Three of the most famous contemporary singers (William Warfield, Camilla Williams and Carol Brice) were interviewed for this study, and biographical data concerning five others are available. Of these eight, six were reared in the South and nearly all were born into the colored upper class. Miss Dobbs is the daughter of J. Wesley Dobbs, the Atlanta fraternal and political leader. Miss Williams's father, as a domestic for a prosperous white physician, enjoyed, because of his connection with reputable whites, a kind of preferred position that brought more advantages to his family than membership in the colored elite might have afforded.

Not one resembles the artless, untutored prodigy of legend. All were trained at leading conservatories or by outstanding teachers in the Northeast, and nearly all had had a college education before beginning advanced professional studies. Nearly every one acknowledged a heavy debt to white patrons or sponsors who helped them with funds and crucial introductions, and all came under the management of leading agents and toured under the auspices of leading concert bureaus. Though most of them had extended European tours, the European imprimatur was no longer an important credential for American acceptance. In fact, several now declared that finding a European audience was easier because a sophisticated Negro from America was still an exotic spectacle to Europeans long after he was a commonplace in the United States. A few of the rising young Negro artists who went to Europe remained there: Kenneth Spencer, Anne Wiggins Brown and Mattiwilda Dobbs—the latter two because they had married Scandinavians.

Nearly all were guest soloists on radio and television networks and with major symphony orchestras, notably the Philadelphia, the Boston and the New York Philharmonic. After Marian Anderson's admission to Metropolitan Opera, three younger colored singers followed: Robert McFerrin in 1955; Miss Dobbs in 1956, and Gloria Davy in 1957. Warfield and Miss Price won leading operatic roles in "highbrow" television productions, and several toured Europe and Asia under State Department sponsorship.

Williams, Davy and Dobbs all won Marian Anderson scholarships to finance their advanced professional training, and nearly every one of the eight was helped by foundation or conservatory fellowships or personal gifts from patrons. All affirmed that opportunities for genuinely talented singers are now wide open. Typically they built their initial reputations in local church concerts, and then in well-worn Negro vehicles or in standard operas, operettas, or recitals produced by the City Center of New York, the Young Women's Hebrew Association, or the International Ladies Garment Workers Union. Once seasoned by such experience, they would, precisely like white artists, hazard a debut at Town Hall, usually by "papering the house," to place themselves before the critics. A debut costs upwards of a thousand dollars and ticket sales were small.

The leading colored concert artists feel that the day of the single standard of criticism has just recently dawned. In the first era, before World War II, Hayes, Anderson and Robeson were demonstrating the race's right to a respectful hearing. In the second, and briefer, period, extending to the early 1950's, whites applauded Negro musicians simply because they were Negroes, with little regard to their competence. In the newer era the really deserving colored virtuosi were being recognized as American musicians. The South, however, still posed the old dilemma: should the Negro refuse to sing to all-white audiences, or should he demonstrate to them that the Negro deserved full acceptance as creative artists? Should he sing to a house where his kinsmen were impounded in a separate section? In the 1940's Robeson refused to submit to discriminations, but his bookings were so full that he did not feel the loss of the Southern audience. The less contentious Anderson and Hayes, however, continued to sing for Jim Crow houses, and lesser figures had still so little bargaining power that the futile protest might only prevent their recognition at all.

In the 1940's Negro singers, especially those still on the make, freely accepted all-Negro audiences in the South, usually under college, church, fraternal or Christian Association sponsorship. But as early as 1940, Marian Anderson—because she was a world figure, long past the need to struggle for a hearing—felt the pressure to take her stand. In that year, when the New Orleans municipal auditorium reserved a "peanut gallery" for Negroes at a major concert, she was urged by progressives in both races to cancel. She went through with the program, but in 1941 omitted New Orleans from her itinerary. In 1944 the race rejoiced when an Anderson concert in the Louisville city auditorium permitted colored patrons to occupy a special section on the main floor; and eight years later it was still big news when a similar concession was made in Miami. By that time, however, liberals had raised their sights. In 1951 Miss Anderson was booked for a recital in a huge Richmond auditorium, and a large block of very desirable seats was reserved for Negroes. She was importuned to cancel, and when she declined was formally boycotted by the local NAACP chapter with the result that she sang to a half-empty house—and a totally empty Negro section. In 1953 she was still barred from a leading Baltimore concert hall on any terms. Finally in 1957, during the Little Rock excitement (when Louis Armstrong, soon warmly seconded by Lena Horne and Eartha Kitt publicly rebuked the President for his vacillation), Miss Anderson, then on her famous good-will tour of the Far East, announced that she would accept no more engagements for segregated audiences.

The race's leading musicians are still far from agreed upon the solution. Warfield, now the most successful colored baritone, takes a fairly typical stand. He prefers to leave the South out of his tours, except for unsegregated audiences in regular concert series at liberal colleges and universities, but he is disinclined to censure those who play or sing to segregated houses, for he can see conceivable gains for the race when hugely popular entertainers like Armstrong, Basie and Ellington evoke standing ovations from the most adamant white supremacists in the Deep South.

Three of the most eminent of the new generation of singers may be taken as examples to illustrate the web of circumstances that went into the making of the artists' careers: Carol Brice, Camilla Williams, and William Warfield.

Carol Brice was the fourth child of a pastor (he served in World War I as a chaplain overseas in her infancy) and a schoolteacher. Both parents were college trained and had more than ordinary musical gifts. Carol was reared on the campus of Palmer Institute in Sedalia, North Carolina, a haven untouched by the ghetto psychology, where her father became head of the English department and her mother's "foster sister," Charlotte Hawkins Brown, was president. At a very early age she toured with the school's glee club as a prodigy.

At Palmer, the future contralto received excellent voice training from a Talladega graduate who influenced her to enroll in the music curriculum at his alma mater when she finished the academy course at Palmer. Her expenses were paid in part by a New England lady who had been helping Mrs. Brown for many years. She kept the examples of Hayes, Robeson and Anderson steadily before her, in spite of Aunt Charlotte's admonition that whites would recognize only one Negro contralto and that Miss Anderson had a lifetime claim upon the place. At the urging of a Negro public-school teacher, she went to New York on funds supplied by her New England benefactress, to compete for a conservatory scholarship, and was awarded a year's tuition (subsequently renewed for four more years) at Julliard, where, with the exception of Dean Dixon, she was the only Negro.

During her last year at Julliard, she married and entered a competition for which the prize was a Town Hall debut. She won the audition a scant month before her first child was born. During her earlier years at Julliard she had secured, through Harry Burleigh, a salaried place in the choir at the fashionable St. George's Episcopal Church, and later a place as a soloist at a white Congregational church in East Orange. Her husband, it chanced, had business connections with a resident of Westport who happened to be a neighbor of the conductor, Fritz Reiner. By prearrangement, Miss Brice and her husband were invited as weekend guests at the businessman's home. Reiner was invited to a party to join the group in hearing Miss Brice sing, and she so impressed the conductor that he invited her to be guest soloist with his Pittsburgh Symphony orchestra. Another guest at the party took immediate steps to place her under the best professional management. Additional guest appearances with the Pittsburgh Symphony and with Koussevitsky's Boston Symphony added to her reputation and soon a distinguished career was well under way. Performances on radio network programs and recordings for the Columbia Masterworks series added to her audience. Her Southern tours were under Negro auspices for Negro audiences, supplied by schools, churches and fraternities, but as her bookings on the regular concert circuit took more and more of her time, she soon, somewhat regretfully, found herself singing almost wholly for whites.

Camilla Williams evidently inherited some talent from her grandfather, a tobacco worker adept at sight-singing. The Williams home had a piano, and all the children were provided with music lessons. Their parents, ill-educated themselves, sent all of their children to college. Camilla began singing in church before she was six, but the public schools for the colored children of Danville, Virginia, offered no musical instruction. The deficit was partly supplied by church, Sunday school, and private lessons. Excluded, because of her color, from concerts in her community, she had seen only one opera when she became the first Negro to sing with a major opera company.

Her father's employers and other prominent white Danville families helped the Williams children in college. A white music teacher at a neighboring college coached her for the title role in *Madame Butterfly* for a Philadelphia performance by the West Virginia State College chorus. After Camilla graduated at Virginia State, a friend of her father's employer prompted a New England acquaintance to arrange a concert for her in Connecticut to which the operatic soprano Geraldine Farrar was invited. The stratagem succeeded. Miss Farrar became Camilla's sponsor and eventually steered her into just the opportunities she needed. A European teacher who had heard her in Philadelphia invited her to become her pupil, and—overriding kinsmen and acquaintances who warned her against so dubious an undertaking—the singer accepted the challenge. With her parents' blessing and a "Camilla Williams Fund" raised by Danville teachers, friends and neighbors, and her college's alumni, she went to Philadelphia, began her training, and won the first two annual Marian Anderson scholarships. Then in 1946, with help from Miss Farrar, came an offer of the lead in a *Madame Butterfly* production of the City Center of New York. She was the only Negro in the cast, and the fee for her make-up man consumed her entire honorarium, but the event soon led to other operatic roles at the Center, and concert tours under Columbia Artists management, interspersed with recitals at Southern colored colleges. From 1955 to 1957 she made five tours in Europe, but her own native Danville did not give her any sort of formal public recognition until 1959.

Warfield also exemplifies a conjunction of fortunate circumstances in an improving social climate. A huge, dark man, he was born in Arkansas, but reared in Rochester, New York, where his father, a common laborer, hoped to secure night-school training as a pastor, and was soon cast in the double role of minister and garbage hauler. (Robeson's father had also been obliged to eke out his pastoral income by working as a coachman and ash collector.) Young William thus grew up in a modest parsonage where industry and a taste for scholarship elevated the family's interests and aspirations. The Warfields lived in a polyglot, emigrant neighborhood, and the boy was scarcely aware of The Problem. At his white high school he was vice-president of the student government, and a favorite of the music teachers. When he was about sixteen, he found himself wondering why all of the choice jobs were monopolized by whites, but it was not a serious preoccupation, and he enjoyed his school days and the music which had been cultivated in him from his earliest years by his father's church organist. He sang in the high-school choir, and one of his white teachers was so enthusiastic about his promise that she gave the boy voice lessons at her home and without fee.

His teacher also prepared him for a competition sponsored by a national music teachers' association, and protected him from exploitation when invitations to sing for local white groups began to inundate him. His high-school principal, president of the Lions Club, boasted of his colored student at every opportunity. The school, the teachers, the Rotarians, the Lions and the Kiwanians were vociferously proud of him, not as a Negro prodigy, but simply as a local boy who was sure to be heard from. In the music association's contest he won his way, as the only Negro, to the finals, and then emerged as national champion. The prize was a full-tuition scholarship to the conservatory of his choice and he elected to go to Eastman School in his home city.

After taking his bachelor's degree, he spent three comfortable years in military service with the army recreation program at Camp Ritchie, where nearly all the personnel were whites, training himself meanwhile as a jazz pianist as a possible source of supplementary employment for the future. After the war he returned to Eastman for a master's degree, but before he finished the course, joined a road show at $250 a week for a year, and then drifted into night-club work, playing the piano and singing everything from boogiewoogie and ballads to operatic airs. One night in Toronto, a fascinated patron drew him aside and asked why he was not working at something better. Warfield replied that he was considering a Town Hall debut when he could find the funds. The man, a Toronto stock broker named Walter Carr, returned a few days later to say that he wanted to sponsor the debut both because he was interested in Warfield as an artist and because he himself had once been helped at a crucial time.

The concert was booked in March, 1950. A few weeks later Warfield's patron was dead and the young baritone was in Australia on a concert tour launched by his Town Hall success. In his Camp Ritchie days, one of his associates had been Larry Goodkind, formerly with the motion-picture industry. The two met again at a party, quite by chance, after Warfield's return to New York, and Goodkind, emboldened by his acquaintance with the entertainment world, persuaded Warfield to permit him to try his hand as a concert agent. From that time forward, Goodkind was Warfield's manager and steered him into a concert career of the first magnitude. On one of his trips to Europe, Warfield met Leontyne Price, then starring in a revival of *Porgy and Bess,* and the pair eventually married.

Warfield and Miss Price are frequently booked as guest soloists with the foremost symphony orchestras and with superior television shows, and both have made extensive foreign tours under State Department auspices. Miss Price was born in Mississippi, where her father was a carpenter and her mother a midwife. The white Chisholm family, who employed her aunt, took an interest in the gifted child, and after her graduation at Central State College (Ohio), enabled her to go to Julliard for voice training. Her splendid record there brought invitations to the Tanglewood festival, and then in 1952 the role of Bess in the *Porgy* revival. Additional television operatic roles were followed by her "adoption" by Columbia Artists and Goodkind, and a concert career much like her husband's.

Such recognition as the country has accorded to Negro concert artists has been confined to vocalists. Two symphonic composers who won minor notice after 1950 were Howard Swanson and Ulysses Kay. Swanson was the only American composer represented at the 1951 Edinburgh Festival, where his *Short Symphony* was performed. Kay, the son of a Tucson, Arizona, barber, is a graduate of the University of Arizona, and the Eastman School of Music, with advanced study at Tanglewood, Yale, and (under the GI Bill) Columbia. The winner of two Rosenwald fellowships and two fellowships of the American Academy in Rome, he is best known for his "Of New Horizons" and some film and television scores.

The most famous composers, however, were Still and Dawson, whom we encountered in the previous generation. Both continued to be productive in the 1940's and 1950's. Still, though perhaps more at home with whites than with Negroes, has repeatedly refused to produce music in the "Uncle Tom" tradition when his radio and motion-picture employers called for music that conformed to the stereotype of "Negro music." Dawson was associated with choral music in recent years, but was occasionally invited to be guest conductor at musical conventions, and, like Still, sometimes heard his works performed by America's most distinguished orchestras.

The first Negro American to win international acclaim as a symphonic conductor is Dean Dixon. Born in Harlem to highly educated West Indian parents, he was trained at Julliard Institute and Columbia University (assisted by three years of fellowships at Julliard and two Rosenwald grants) and struggled to develop an orchestra of his own in New York. In 1941 David Sarnoff, head of RCA and a member of Governor Lehman's committee to combat racial bias, invited the twenty-six-year-old Dixon to fill in as summer conductor of the NBC Symphony. Other guest-conductor appearances with famous orchestras followed this success, but it was apparent that the country was not ready for a Negro maestro and he went to Europe. After a few years with symphony groups on the continent, he was selected both as permanent conductor of the Gothenburg Symphony Orchestra and as director of classical music for Radio Köln in West Germany. With his Swedish wife he made his home in Sweden.

The 1940's and 1950's produced no violinist to challenge the supremacy of

Clarence White. White, whose earlier career we have reviewed, was still a fruitful composer in the 1940's and 1950's, still heard by Negro audiences, and was briefly a headline figure when, in 1955, he won the first "restful music" prize competition sponsored by a capitalist of Greensboro and New Orleans. When White's composition, a delicate elegy, was adjudged the winner and a wire invited him to come to New Orleans to receive the prize at a public ceremony, he was in a quandary. As it turned out, however, his color proved no obstacle and the presentation program was held in excellent spirit.

The best-known Negro pianist, Philippa Duke Schuyler, daughter of the journalist, George S. Schuyler, was in fact no real exception to the rule that a colored instrumentalist is trapped behind the color line. Her American reputation belonged largely to her career as a child prodigy. She had been presented in radio and concert-hall recitals before she was ten; her compositions were performed by the New York Philharmonic when she was twelve; she was guest soloist with that orchestra at fourteen, and had by that time repeatedly won the annual Young Composers' award. But once she reached maturity, her solid artistry no longer interested the nation. Her heavy concert schedule was thereafter increasingly restricted to European, Caribbean, South American and African tours, and, in America, to Town Hall recitals and the Negro concert circuit.

Dawson and Still, though performed by venturesome conductors like Stokowski and Barbirolli, and despite their demonstrated capacity for abstract and universal materials, are still largely identified in the public mind with African and Negro American themes. The same constraints conspire to keep all colored instrumentalists in obscurity while vocal artists move forward. One hears occasionally of a Negro violinist or woodwind player with a symphony orchestra—Jack Bradley of the Denver Symphony comes to mind—but they are only the exceptions that prove the rule.

Several factors explain the rarity of Negro concert artists other than singers. First, there are far more very good white musicians than the market can absorb, and the particular advantages that single out the few, particularly through sound (and lucky) "public relations," are unavailable to most musicians and to virtually all Negroes. Second, the enormous cost in money, time and effort, with little prospect of success, cuts off the potential Negro musician, either choking off a musical career entirely or diverting it to jazz and popular music where the prospect is more inviting. Third, there is no Negro musical literature for instrumentalists like the spirituals and ballads which enable the vocalist to win his first hearing. Once established, the latter may move away from this esthetic ghetto, but it is indispensable to him in winning his initial reputation, and this resort is not available to the violinist, pianist, or oboist.

Indeed, even the most famous singers must still keep close to the Negro idiom to retain the good will of concert-goers and reviewers. It is a rare review that does not ring the changes on the old cliché: "Excellent as were the opening numbers of *X*'s program, it was when he turned to the beloved old spirituals and sorrow songs of his people that he was genuinely . . . (etc. etc.)." Negro musicians also point to the want of a cultivated Negro audience, and to the conservatism of the wealthy whites to whom opera companies and symphony orchestras must look for largesse. Still another deterrent is the pride and esthetic integrity of colored musicians who decline to play *as* Negroes *for* Negroes and who seek acceptance not as Negro prodigies but only as good musicians.

Not only was the Negro's pre-eminence in jazz and related popular musical forms more marked than ever after 1936; the idiom itself had grown impressively in popular acceptance. On the precise definition of "real jazz" the connoisseurs, performers and the listeners who knew what they liked disagreed as stoutly as ever, but the genre had now fully arrived. Its votaries multiplied in every social class; collectors of recordings talked learnedly of the new "discography"; high-brow columns of jazz criticism and history ran regularly in the *Saturday Review* and *The New Yorker;* and the country saw an astonishing proliferation of annual jazz "cavalcades," "festivals" and "institutes," as well as formal concerts by Negro jazzmen—even as guests of symphony orchestras—at Carnegie or Town Hall.

The Government itself, quick to sense the opportunity both to gratify a vast jazz-hungry overseas audience and to exhibit the triumph of Negro-Americans, dispatched colored trumpeters, drummers, piano thumpers and blues shouters to world capitals and lonely frontiers. In 1957 the State Department coolly defended, before a Congressional Committee, the expenditure of $140,000 to send Dizzy Gillespie on a "good will" tour through the East and Latin America, and a few months later Americans grinned over a *New Yorker* cartoon depicting a conference of ranking diplomats solemnly debating the alternative of sending John Foster Dulles or Louis Armstrong on a delicate mission abroad. Only recently the durable "Ambassador Satchmo," in Africa, had stepped before one of the largest throngs of humans ever assembled anywhere for any purpose, tucked his trumpet under his arm, and grinned, "Dig this folks, this trumpet ain't no cannon." He was only one of many Negro jazz artists who could evoke a tumult of applause where diplomats and the Vice-President of the United States drew catcalls and brickbats.

Their audience now hugely enlarged by long-playing records and high-fidelity sound reproduction, some Negro performers commanded enormous incomes. A few earned more than a quarter of a million dollars a year, but others drew only modest financial returns, blocked by surviving—if diminishing—discriminations, or by inept management, by high living, or perhaps by an artistic integrity that rendered them indifferent to commercial considerations. The latter, however, was more rarely an obstacle to economic success than formerly, for the inspired virtuoso had by now a sufficient following to guarantee him substantial material rewards. It is noteworthy also that historians of jazz freely acknowledged that it was Negro rather than white jazzmen who were the principal innovators. The development of Modern Jazz, for example, is usually ascribed to such colored outriders as Charlie Parker, Dizzy Gillespie, Thelonious Monk, Bud Powell and Kenny Clarke. They point out too that a major factor in the fantastic jazz boom after 1936 in America was the steady waning of racial prejudice.

As in the previous generation, Negro names dominated the roster of jazzdom's titans and, once again, our selections, far from definitive, reflect not subjective judgments but only the priorities which the printed record seems to assign. The sifting of names from a literature now grown too vast to be completely canvassed has yielded some sixty-nine names.* We exclude some who have only recently achieved prominence, and include a few whose popularity as singers of popular and folk music entitles them to special notice even though the jazz enthusiast may object to their inclusion. A few are better known as popular entertainers in media other than music, and two —Mahalia Jackson (an authentic heir of the blues in the Bessie Smith tradition) and Clara Ward—are identified with Gospel hymns only. Most of the rest are genuine jazz artists: vocalists, band leaders, composers, or masters of the jazz piano, trumpet, saxophone, drums, trombone, clarinet, guitar, bass viol, violin, or vibraphone.

* Many of those listed in the roster for the previous decades were, of course, still in full career after 1936, and could with equal logic have been incorporated in this newer list instead of the older. Similarly, many names appearing here might well have been placed in the pre-1936 roll of jazz musicians. We have, however, elected not to duplicate. Those now added are:

Albert Ammons
Lil Armstrong
Pearl Bailey
Harry Belafonte
Barney Bigard
Jimmy Blanton
Earl Bostic
Bill Broonzy
Cab Calloway
Harry Carney
Benny Carter
Sid Catlett
Charlie Christian
Kenny Clarke
Buck Clayton
Cozy Cole
Nat King Cole
Miles Davis
Sammy Davis, Jr.
Dorothy Donegan
Roy Eldridge
Billy Eckstine
Ella Fitzgerald
Erroll Garner
Dizzy Gillespie
Earl Grant
Lionel Hampton
Eddie Heywood
Johnny Hodges
Billie Holiday
Lena Horne
Mahalia Jackson
Illinois Jacquet
Jay Jay Johnson
Jo Jones
Jonah Jones
Louis Jordan
John Kirby
Andy Kirk
Meade Lux Lewis
Carmen McRae
Johnny Mathis
Thelonious Monk
Ray Nance
Sy Oliver
Oran Page
Charlie Parker
Oscar Peterson
Oscar Pettiford
Bud Powell
Max Roach
Jimmie Rushing
Hazel Scott
Charlie Shavers
Stuff Smith
Willie Strayhorn
Maxine Sullivan
Billy Taylor
Joe Turner
Sarah Vaughan
Dinah Washington
Ben Webster
Josh White
Cootie Williams
Mary Lou Williams
Lester Young
Trummy Young
Clara Ward
Teddy Wilson

Fully half of the newer group of Negro jazz musicians were natives of large Northern urban centers, notably New York, Chicago and Pittsburgh. Southern-born members of the group came from the upper South and urban environments rather than from the Delta or the rural and small-town Deep South. Nearly all were now the products of common schools, many had attended high school, and not a few had some college training. While a substantial proportion were the children of the colored bourgeoisie, with a history of modest economic security and social respectability, several of those who came from larger metropolitan areas of the North and upper South were buffeted and scarred by an underprivileged childhood.

Several who came from cities of the deeper South had a background of pinching poverty and unstable families. Mahalia Jackson was an orphan at six on the tough New Orleans water front. She was washing and ironing for whites before she was ten, and at sixteen was working in a Chicago factory for little more than a dollar a day. Farther north, Billie Holiday came out of a brutalizing background which goes far toward explaining her subsequent disastrous struggle with the narcotics habit for many years while she was one of the greatest blues singers in the history of the art. "Mom and Pop were just a couple of kids when they got married," she begins in her candid autobiography, *Lady Sings the Blues*. "He was eighteen, she was sixteen, and I was three." At six she was running errands for an East Baltimore madame; she was raped at ten, jailed for prostitution at fifteen, and harassed by color prejudice during bitter childhood years in a slum, eked out by petty thieving and the pittances she could earn by scouring the stone front stoops of the city. Harry Belafonte, earning about $750,000 a year by 1958, could recall a childhood in the late 1920's, and early 1930's in a succession of Harlem tenements. He was so constantly embroiled with youthful gangs during the bleak Depression years that his alarmed mother moved back with her two children to her native West Indies for several years before returning with the boys to New York, this time to live in a white neighborhood where, Belafonte recalls, "the fights were more frequent and vicious than ever."

Such examples were in no sense typical of our group of sixty-nine, for they were recruited from every level of Negro society. No less various than their social origins were the artistic conditioning, the formal training and professional beginnings that launched them upon their careers. Most of them grew up in family environments with more than average opportunities for musical growth. Josh White, Charlie Christian, Louis Jordan and Stuff Smith had systematic musical training from their fathers, and Benny Carter from his mother and sister. Buck Clayton's father, who played several instruments and led a church orchestra, taught his child what he knew of the piano, and Nat Cole's brother directed a sextet which included Nat. Lester Young's first music teacher was his father, a Tuskegee-trained violinist, choir leader and carnival musician.

Gillespie's father, a bricklayer, directed a band and kept a houseful of instruments, while Hazel Scott's mother led an all-girl orchestra and prepared Hazel for piano recitals before the child was six. Kenny Clarke, Bud Powell and Jimmy Rushing grew up in households where at least three others—parents, brothers and sisters—were musicians. Sammy Davis, Jr., was in a road show with his father when he was four, Dorothy Donegan's mother was a guitarist, Illinois Jacquet's father a bassist with a railroad band and Billie Holiday's father was briefly a guitarist with Fletcher Henderson. Sy Oliver had his trumpet lessons from his parents, both of whom were music teachers. Erroll Garner's father and several of his sisters and brothers were musicians, and Erroll himself began picking out tunes on the piano at three. Pettiford's father, a veterinarian, organized a family band made up of his wife (a music teacher) and their eleven children.

Mahalia Jackson, Sarah Vaughan, Dinah Washington, Josh White and Cab Calloway were among the many who sang in church choirs as children. Nat Cole played the organ in his father's church in Chicago, and Thelonious Monk was a church organist at twelve. Several benefited from musical instruction in public elementary and high schools, and some were instructed by professional music teachers. Billie Holiday was permitted by the East Baltimore call girls for whom she ran errands to listen to their records of Bessie Smith and Louis Armstrong, and Roy Eldridge also became a close student of Armstrong records, while Mahalia Jackson found models in recordings of Caruso, Tibbett, Bessie Smith and Grace Moore.

While many made their way without professional training, the drift was in the other direction. They were increasingly, as Leonard Feather writes, "products of a new tradition of musical literacy and restless ambition," bent upon technical expertness, fame and fortune, to the alarm of devotees of the abandoned spontaneities of old. Many of the Negro vocalists (Ella Fitzgerald, Sarah Vaughan, Billie Holiday, Billy Eckstine, Harry Belafonte, to name a few), like white popular singing idols, were to all intents untrained.

The same surprising musical "illiteracy" still marks some of the most gifted instrumentalists. Garner, perhaps the greatest living jazz pianist—he has made more records than any other and appears as a concert artist under the management of the nation's leading impresario, Sol Hurok—still reads no music. Lil Armstrong, on the other hand, prepared at Fisk for a concert career; Teddy Wilson was a music-theory major at Talladega; Earl Bostic studied harmony and theory at Xavier; Miles Davis and Hazel Scott were trained at Juilliard; Milt Jackson studied music at Michigan State; and Dorothy Donegan had solid classical training at the Chicago Conservatory under Rudolph Ganz. Some, indeed, turned to jazz only because the way to a concert career seemed barred.

Dorothy Donegan, her conservatory training and a sparkling concert debut behind her, had to be content with a beginning in a shabby Chicago gin mill, and then moved by way of "souped up" classics into jazz. Many with less impressive training made similar beginnings in grubby black-and-tan clubs, speakeasies, basement bistros and local movie houses in urban black belts and, eventually—often as emergency stand-ins—in swank Negro clubs like the de Lisa in Chicago or the Café Society in Harlem. In time they joined name bands or became conductors of their own groups. Some, until rescued by alert scouts like Norman Granz or John Hammond, or enterprising managers like Joe Glaser, found their efforts to develop a real jazz style impeded in night clubs where drink-dulled patrons called either for pallid popular songs and show tunes or pornographic ballads.

Amateur contests, an invention of the 1930's which gave aspiring entertainers an opportunity to compete before well-filled neighborhood theaters for a chance at a limited engagement that might prove a steppingstone to bigger things, provided fortunate beginnings for Sarah Vaughan, Eckstine, Fitzgerald, Monk and Oscar Peterson, among others. Once under way, burgeoning careers were accelerated by record-cutting dates with more prominent groups or "sidemen." The recording sessions were not always profitable for the Negro entertainer, however. Billie Holiday's discs sold in tremendous volume, but sometimes, through mismanagement or sheer exploitation, brought her incredibly small returns. In more recent years favorite performers like Fitzgerald (twenty-two million records sold in 1936–1954), Belafonte, Armstrong, Jackson and Johnny Mathis, sold their platters by the millions and earned fabulous royalties.

Progress toward the assimilation of colored entertainers by American show business at large was steady but slow. Negro bands and individual performers were still largely excluded from radio and television—not so much by the entertainment business itself as by nervous advertisers fearful of offending the Southern market. Appearances as guest stars on radio were not unusual, however, in the 1940's and beyond, and more recently big-name Negro jazz musicians have been commonplace on network television shows like those of Steve Allen, Ed Sullivan, Jack Paar, Arthur Godfrey, Dave Garroway, Edward R. Murrow, Dinah Shore, Garry Moore and Perry Como. Anti-discriminationists sometimes declare that such *guest* performances are readily accepted only because they do not seriously imperil the pre-eminence of whites.

In the middle 1940's Nat Cole was the only Negro with a major, commercially sponsored radio network program. Ten years later (1956–1957) he became the first—and at this writing still the only—Negro entertainer with his own television show. For sixty-four weeks the network "sustained" the show but waited in vain for a sponsor to pick it up. Conscious that he was the Negro test case of television, Cole gave the program his best efforts. He plowed part of his salary back into the series, rejected a half-million dollars in dates in order to be on the scene, brought in the nation's most distinguished white guest stars (who often worked for token fees to help make the program go). He had a huge audience and critics praised the program, but no commercial sponsor dared to assume the cost of the series, and it was dropped. Friends of the race who were disposed to blame the advertising profession were sobered when they learned that the network was inundated with indignant letters from the South and that Cole's own home city of Birmingham, Alabama (where he had been physically assaulted in 1956 on a stage upon which he was performing for an unsegregated audience), banned the program at the local television outlet.

In other sectors of show business less sensitive to advertising pressures, assimilation was more rapid. "Mixing" in big-name bands and combos had begun in the 1930's when Billie Holiday was singing with Artie Shaw's band, and Benny Goodman employed a succession of Negro artists including Teddy Wilson, Lionel Hampton, Fletcher Henderson, Charlie Christian and Cootie Williams. The trend was accelerated in the 1940's. Though white sidemen were occasionally engaged by Negro orchestras, most of the mixing went the other way, perhaps because underpaid Negro bands could not compete with white bands in buying the best talent. Such mixing still encounters sporadic resistance in the South in the later 1950's, but Negro "singles" such as Lena Horne, Pearl Bailey, Belafonte, Eartha Kitt, Sammy Davis, Jr., Erroll Garner, and scores of others were making extended engagements all over America at plush night clubs, supper clubs and hotels, like the Chez Paree, the College Inn and the Palmer House in Chicago, the Waldorf-Astoria and the Statler in New York, and even the Eden Roc and the Americana Hotel in Miami.

The white jazz historian, Leonard Feather, one of the severest critics of racial discrimination in jazz and popular music, and one least likely to overstate the case for an optimistic evaluation, concluded in 1957 that remaining discriminatory practices were sharply on the wane, but reminded his readers that outrages still occasionally marred the vastly improved record. Casting a retrospective eye over the 1940's and early 1950's, he cited examples ranging from physical assaults like that upon Nat Cole in 1956 and the attempted bombing of a hall where Armstrong was performing, to refusal to rent halls for mixed combos or to grant membership in unions without segregation. He pointed to examples (which sound absurdly incredible in 1959) of whites in blackface, playing the parts of Negro jazzmen in Hollywood pictures. He recalled trumped-up arrests of traveling jazz masters on flimsy charges of gambling or possession of narcotics; discrimination in performers' fees and royalties; hostility of a few scattered diehards (one was enough to spoil an evening) in audiences where whites performed with Negroes. The colored giants of jazz, he pointed out, were still being denied television sponsorship while insipid white orchestras and vocalists who offered only pallid caricatures of jazz, won lucrative contracts.

Some who were engaged as featured performers by the finest white bands —and fervently envied by less favored artists—had occasion to repent of their success. Billie Holiday, travelling with Artie Shaw's group, drew frenzied applause so long as she was on stage, but once off, encountered monstrous insults and brutalities—from obscene sneers to refusal of meal service or consignment to rear entrances and freight elevators. On one occasion, Roy Eldridge, in a piteous interview in *Down Beat,* spoke for many a sensitive colored jazz master who has travelled with a white group. First while appearing with Gene Krupa's band, and then with Artie Shaw's—for both of whom he had only the highest praise—he was, he said, repeatedly refused room space, even when it had been reserved in advance, while his comrades checked into their hotel. "Then . . . I lug that baggage back into the street and start looking around again."

Sometimes they were denied entrance to the very halls where their names blazed on the marquee. In one such crisis, "I got to brooding," Eldridge mourned. "The tension got so bad I flipped. I could feel it right up to my neck while I was playing *Rocking Chair;* I started trembling, ran off the stand, and threw up. They carried me to the doctor's. I had a hundred and five fever; my nerves were shot." At other times he gave way to convulsive weeping while the sympathetic Shaw soothed him and forced his tormentors to apologize. When he had had enough, Eldridge swore "I'll never in my life work with a white band again." In 1956, when he had been a distinguished professional for thirty years, he auditioned for a studio job with a late night television show, only to be bludgeoned by Jim Crow. This time it took the form of a Negro-baiting director, who stung him first with a warning that he had better not perform while drunk, and then asked him how well he could read.

The day of full and final acceptance of Negro jazz artists had not yet arrived, but over-preoccupation with these scattered incidents seriously distorts the picture. Even Feather, after his indignant recital of the colored jazzmen's grievances, concluded in his *Book of Jazz* (1957) that race was steadily becoming irrelevant in a segment of American culture whose votaries were perhaps less given to racial bias than almost any other group of similar size united by a similar interest. Most of the few remaining big bands were, to be sure, still all-white or all-Negro, but the combos, far more important to the development of jazz as a whole, were fast losing their last tinges of color consciousness.

Individuals in the group showed wide differences in their accommodations to the pressures to which their profession exposed them. The frenetic pace of their lives, the corroding round of one-night stands and more protracted post-midnight revels, coupled with the jarring reminders of color prejudice, took their toll in a few cases in the form of addiction to liquor, marijuana, and—though not so frequently as popular legend had it—in sexual aberrations and heroin. The incongruities were enough to shake any man's equipoise. A man might be one of the most famous Americans in the world, lionized in

Stockholm, Paris, Amsterdam, Rio, New York, Chicago and San Francisco; he might be the admiration, to the point of fatuity, of sophisticates, advanced poets and beatniks who made a cult of aping his every eccentricity (from his bizarre language and personal conduct to his wine-colored sports jacket, green beret, dark glasses and goatee); and yet in some corners of America he would be forbidden to sit at a lunch counter in the very halls where jukeboxes blared out his recordings.

Aberrant behavior in the newer generation was in fact less marked than it had been in the first generation of jazzdom's history. A few still burned themselves out with debaucheries or prodigal expenditures of energy and creative elan. Ammons, Catlett, Kirby, Holiday, Page and Prez Young collapsed and died in their forties. Charlie Parker—one of the greatest of them all—was a slave of the needle at fifteen, a psychiatric ward patient for several months at twenty-six, an attempted suicide at thirty-three, and dead at thirty-four. Bud Powell suffered the first of a series of mental breakdowns at twenty-one and in the next decade spent much of his time in mental hospitals. Charlie Christian was dead at twenty-two, blasted by pneumonia, tuberculosis, stupendous dissipations and a fanatical devotion to his art; and the fragile Jimmy Blanton, one of the greatest of the bassists, was dead of tuberculosis at twenty-one. The Negro press regularly reported also the repeated encounters of some of the more exuberant and dissolute with the police and the courts, but such news items were far from representative of the great majority of the musicians of the 1940's and 1950's.

Resistance to the still painful, if waning, discriminations varied greatly from one performer to another. Some shrugged them off philosophically while others occasionally struck out angrily at insult and deprivation. Hazel Scott, for example, in 1947 cancelled an appearance at the University of Texas and forced the management to refund the admissions paid by a segregated audience of seven thousand when she was refused a room at a co-operative dormitory on the campus. Duke Ellington, on the other hand, in 1951 cancelled a scheduled program for a segregated house in Richmond only when the NAACP boycotted the concert mere days after the Duke had generously played a fourteen-thousand-dollar benefit engagement for the Association. When he protested the boycott, the NAACP replied that the effort was part of a campaign to press Virginia to repeal its Jim Crow laws.

In the middle 1950's a growing number of big-name jazzmen were announcing an intention to appear before no more segregated houses, but others continued to make an exception of the Southern states, where two thirds of the nation's Negroes would otherwise be deprived of a chance to hear them—to say nothing of the loss to the region's white audience. Negro attitudes on this point continued to vacillate. The *Pittsburgh Courier,* for example, in 1950 thought it unfair when liberals pressed entertainers to forego the Southern market while millions of Negroes in the South were still drawing a livelihood from the segregated economy. But in March, 1957, the same paper shouted "Negro bands and entertainers, stay out of Dixie!" and deplored the continued performances there by some of the most famous musicians such as Ellington, Armstrong, Basie and Cole. Such "sacrifice of principle," it now argued, was excusable twenty years earlier, but had no more place in the America of 1957.

Many leading artists who continued to bend to the fiats of Jim Crow, in both North and South, were by no means pliant weathercocks. Some of the vocalists—Josh White, Belafonte, Holiday, for instance—included songs of militant protest in their programs. Miss Holiday's *Strange Fruit*—a haunting, impassioned outcry against lynching—was a startling case in point. Others spoke out bluntly. In the fall of 1957, during the school segregation crisis in Little Rock, "Satchmo" Armstrong publicly rebuked President Eisenhower's conduct as "two-faced" and irresolute. The nation gasped; but, though both whites and Negroes disagreed over the propriety of the outburst, Armstrong elicited spirited applause for his candor and thousands were cheered by its symbolism. The *Courier,* quoting *Down Beat,* spoke for much of the American press, and for the Government itself, when it exclaimed:

> [Armstrong] showed the world that an American Negro can stand up and talk back to the President of the United States, and nobody, absolutely nobody, raises a hand against him. He does not go to jail. His property is not confiscated. He is just as free to travel and to work as he was before. . . . Louis's statement dramatizes one aspect of how superior [the American-Negro's situation] is to [that of], say, the ordinary citizen of Russia. Let some of them issue a statement criticizing Khrushchev and let's see what happens.

The penetration of Negroes into motion pictures, theater, radio, television, the dance, and supper and night-club entertainment was still not very deep in 1959; yet it was here that the race made some of its most notable gains after 1936. Attainments that excited surprise twenty years ago have now no news value at all. As recently as 1949, even in the upper South, the scenes in which Lena Horne appeared in innocuous bit parts were cut out of films and her name was deleted from the newspaper and billboard advertising of motion-picture houses. In 1958, by contrast, class-A Hollywood pictures in which racial themes were boldly, even passionately, presented by Negro actors playing leading roles opposite whites were not only exhibited uncut everywhere, but held over for weeks in deep South cities, by popular demand.

The eighteen-billion-dollar Negro market also commanded respect that insulated the race from offensive stereotypes and provided new reasons for making concessions to Negro preferences. Besides, a widening circle of whites were enlisted in the campaign against bias, and these too had to be taken into account. All but vanished from radio, television, motion pictures, cartoons, comic strips and magazine fiction were the old racial jests, the chicken-and-watermelon fables, the darkey-dialect humor, the head-scratching buffoon and the "burly" Negro brute. In the television business, hundreds of aging films revived for exhibition often proved unusable because their disparagements of minorities had rendered the ten-year-old pictures as obsolete and offensive to American sensibilities as the bear-baitings, gander-pullings and gouging matches of an earlier era. So far, indeed, had these solicitudes for the feelings of Negroes been pressed that some well-intentioned zealots insisted on purging familiar American folk songs and banning *Huckleberry Finn* from the libraries because of an occasional "the darkies are gay" or a "Nigger Jim."

Negro actors and show people rejected roles in which their race was even faintly patronized. Sam Goldwyn, projecting a highly budgeted remake of *Porgy and Bess* in 1957–1958, met blunt refusals from colored actors to whom he offered parts until he had taken very considerable pains to reassure them that this version would reflect the race's increased self-respect. Still, when radio and television networks, the advertising business, the theater and motion pictures had to choose between clearly apposite pressures from the general economy and the Negro market, there could be little doubt of the outcome. "You can't blame them," said one colored actor to this writer. "It's like asking a banker to be a good fellow and lend his money to people who need it most and are least likely to pay it back."

Two other considerations countered the drift across old barriers. Movies, plays and other entertainment forms find their themes in romantic love and marriage—an area in which "integration" is still, in the minds of Negroes no less than in the minds of whites, dominated by taboos. (Not a few whites were alarmed by the predilection of some entertainers for interracial marriages. They pointed to the cases of Hilda Simms, Harry Belafonte, Dorothy Dandridge, Lena Horne, Pearl Bailey, William Walker and Katherine Dunham, and they worried about the rumored romantic interest of Sammy Davis, Jr., in a white actress and reports of Eartha Kitt's friendship for Orson Welles.) There was also the problem of the "integrity" of a play, a movie, and even a comic skit. There are, after all, many roles and statuses in which a Negro actor is not yet believable because such positions are still denied him in real life or because they have so recently become available to Negroes—there are Negro Congressmen, but the stock stage figure of a Congressman must still for years to come be white—that the lag has not yet been overcome. A colored actor in such places is still a distraction, for he cannot be genuinely plausible so long as viewers are conscious of race or any other considerations not germane to the action. The most advanced egalitarian would still be saying to himself, "Why, that is a colored actor; how decent of them. I must write them a letter."

As early as the 1930's, motion pictures brought in Negro jazz personalities, hoofers and comics as incidental entertainment, and in the 40's such people were sometimes featured members of otherwise white casts. The late 1930's and the 1940's saw also the increase of staple "natural" vehicles for Negroes, productions which were sometimes remade in successive versions: *Show Boat, Carmen Jones, The Green Pastures, Porgy and Bess, Cabin in the Sky;* but these were supplemented by more serious dramatic films which presented Negroes with dignity and compassion deep in the context of their problem, as in *Dust Be Their Destiny, Intruder in the Dust* and *The Sound and the Fury.* Meanwhile, the old stereotypes of the bustling mammy, shiftless males, pickaninnies, servile oafs and uniformed maids were slowly being shelved. Still bolder pictures with racial themes appeared as the years passed, notably in the wake of World War II and the Supreme Court's desegregation decisions: *Home of the Brave; The Quiet One; Cry, the Beloved Country; Lost Boundaries; Kings Go Forth; Island in the Sun; The Defiant Ones* and *Anna Lucasta,* in which some of the prickliest, most pathetic, tragic and explosive implications of the color line were sensitively delineated.

These developments were paralleled on the stage, especially in off-Broadway and New York City Center productions. Langston Hughes's *Mulatto,* Richard Wright's *Native Son,* as well as plays by white authors such as *Anna Lucasta, Strange Fruit, Deep Are the Roots* and *Member of the Wedding* were some of the contributions to this growth. In the 1950's a few Negro authors had plays produced on Broadway. In 1954, Louis Peterson (whom we have listed earlier as a writer) saw his *Take a Giant Step* run for several weeks and go to Hollywood for movie adaptation. Charles Seebree and Greer Johnson's *Mrs. Patterson* had a short run in 1954, and Langston Hughes's *Simply Heavenly* had a year's run (1957). Ranking Negro stage actors also found opportunities in other white plays, but with no adequate Negro theater as a "feeder" and with a scarcity of suitable vehicles, they still suffered grave want of roles and of opportunity to acquire professional training and experience.

The most considerable dramatic success was *A Raisin in the Sun,* written and directed by Negroes and performed by an all-Negro cast headed by Sidney Poitier. Described by *The New York Times* as "a homely play about the day-to-day anxieties of a Negro family on the South Side of Chicago," it was by turns comic and harrowing. Neither a morality or a message play, it confined itself to a practical narrative of the life of a family. It argued no causes, treated both Negro frustrations and white aggressions with remarkable objectivity, and provided some of its principle comic lines in lampooning the belligerent racism of the college-girl daughter of the household.

The play promptly settled into what at this writing promises to be a very long run. It won the New York Drama Critics' Award for 1958 and was bought by Columbia Pictures for a movie version at a price reported in the press as three hundred thousand dollars. The play's creator, Lorraine Hansberry, only twenty-seven when she wrote it, is a University of Wisconsin graduate who gained her practical knowledge of dramatics from university and community theaters. She was born to an upper-class Negro family in Chicago, where her father was a wealthy businessman and a former United States Marshal. A sturdy race-advance man, who had carried restrictive covenant litigation to the Supreme Court, he eventually despaired of the Negro's future in America and was preparing at the time of his death in 1945 to move to Mexico. Miss Hansberry now insists that his pessimism was a tragic mistake. The product of a newer age and newer opportunities, she told a *New Yorker* interviewer that she herself feels singularly free, and confident of the Negro's future in America.

We single out here some thirty-five of the leading Negro stage and motion-picture actors, omitting those who (like Louise Beavers, Hattie McDaniel, Leigh Whipper, Bill Robinson, Ethel Waters and Etta Moten), though mentioned in an earlier chapter, were still prominent in the 1940's or 1950's. We include some whom we have noted in the present or previous chapters as musicians or other entertainers, but who appeared prominently also in motion pictures after 1936. A conscientious effort is made to compile a list of the most conspicuous, with the addition of a representative sampling of those who are somewhat less famous.*

Only a few in the group played what could be called "starring roles." Some had literally hundreds of briefer "character" parts in either motion pictures or television, some of them in fact very exacting, and several were cast as Indians, Egyptians, Arabs, Chinese, Filipinos, Mexicans, and even as whites, far more often than as American Negroes. The face of the light-skinned, delicate-featured Miss Dandridge was sometimes darkened to make her more plausible as a Negro or as a South Sea Island girl.

Lena Horne, one of the most successful as a supper-club, radio, motion-picture and television performer, and more recently as the star of *Jamaica,* a hugely successful Broadway musical, was the child of a broken home, and travelled as a very young child with her mother on the latter's modest stage tours. Before she was twenty-one, she had become a prominent night-club singer with Noble Sissle's orchestra and at the Cotton Club. She never completed high school, but is a woman of marked refinement and, still, at the peak of her career in 1959, has a long-standing reputation as an outspoken defender of her race. She was first drawn into vigorous social action by Paul Robeson,

* Eddie Anderson
Louis Armstrong
Ruth Attaway
Pearl Bailey
Count Basie
Harry Belafonte
Diahann Carroll
Nat King Cole
Maidie Comfort
Dorothy Dandridge
Sammy Davis, Jr.
Ruby Dee
Todd Duncan
Duke Ellington
Juanita Hall
Juano Hernandez
Lena Horne
Earl Hyman
Rex Ingram
Sarah Jane Johnson
Eartha Kitt
Canada Lee
Claudia McNeil
William Marshall
Juanita Moore
Clarence Muse
Maidie Norman
Frederick O'Neal
Dorothy Phillips
Sidney Poitier
John Silvera
Hilda Simms
William Walker
Fredi Washington
Frank Wilson

and has long been a courageous figure in the NAACP and in action groups of the anti-communist, liberal left.

William Marshall and Henry Scott had professional instruction in dramatics, the former at an actors' studio in New York and the latter at Columbia University. Hernandez, a native of San Juan, never attended a school of any sort. He began as a street singer in Brazil and became an extraordinarily versatile actor. Another educational background is exemplified by the cast of the new multi-million-dollar Goldwyn version of *Porgy and Bess*. Of the forty-six Negro players in the group, no less than four have master's degrees, four others have bachelor's degrees, two hold law degrees, and at least eight more have had some study at colleges, universities, or professional schools, almost without exception in the North.

Clarence Muse, perhaps the best-known Negro motion-picture actor in the early 1940's, when first-rate roles for Negroes in class-A pictures were not yet available, was trained as a lawyer at a Northern university, and then worked with Negro theater groups for which he wrote, produced and acted. Then followed a period with the Lafayette Theater group in New York and with a dramatic school for Negroes in Chicago before he began winning motion-picture parts. Canada Lee ran away from home at fourteen and never finished high school, because his parents forbade him to plan for a concert violinist's career. He became by turns a jockey, a prize fighter, and a jazz-band leader before drifting into the Federal Theater Project of the WPA, where Orson Welles took him in hand, worked with him in *Macbeth,* and finally steered him into his most important role as Bigger Thomas in *Native Son.*

The most successful of Negro straight dramatic actors is Sidney Poitier, celebrated alike for his stage role in *A Raisin in the Sun* and his motion picture parts in (to name a few of his films) *No Way Out; Cry, the Beloved Country; Blackboard Jungle; Edge of the City; Something of Value; Band of Angels; Mark of the Hawk; The Defiant Ones,* and the new *Porgy and Bess.* He was scheduled to appear in 1959 in still another film, cast this time as a master sergeant in an outfit made up largely of white troops. He is now in every respect a first-rank Hollywood star, the first Negro to be fully recognized in that grade. In 1959 he was nominated for a Motion Picture Academy best-actor award. Neither singer, dancer, mimic, nor comic, he owes his success solely to his acting genius, and though he denies being a crusader, he declares that "as the cats say in my area, I'm out there wailing for us all."

Poitier was born in the West Indies, entered school at the age of eleven, and at fifteen when his total formal education had come to less than two years, he was sent by his family to Miami, Florida. Repulsed everywhere by the color line while making a precarious living in the South, he entered the army as an under-age volunteer, and after the war answered an advertisement of the American Negro Theater of New York calling for actors. His painful mumbling at his audition was so unintelligible that he was urged to drop his ambitions for the theater. Challenged by the disaster, he bought a cheap radio set, carefully studied the speech of announcers and radio actors for several months and then returned to the ANT, this time persuading them to give him acting lessons in exchange for his work as a janitor and handyman. The connection led quickly to very minor roles on and off Broadway, and then to important motion-picture assignments.

In radio, colored concert artists and show-business personalities have been presented as guest performers since the 1930's, but these, of course, have been radio stars only incidentally. There have been occasional foils like the gravel-voiced "Rochester" (Eddie Anderson) on the Jack Benny program, and Eddie Green on *Duffy's Tavern,* and others associated with such presentations as the *Beulah* series have reached wide audiences. A growing number of Negroes are entering radio and television as technicians and writers (Richard Gibson, the young novelist, was recently hired as a regular staff member of the CBS Radio news desk), and a few radio stations are Negro-owned, but their staffs and entertainers have only local reputations.

There is in 1959 only one national "Negro program," a variety show, carried by transcription by some sixty stations on Sunday mornings, with Sid McCoy as master of ceremonies. Sponsored by the Pet Milk Company, the series is aired by fifty-two stations in the South and one in each of eight Northern cities with large colored populations. When colored performers participated in network programs in recent years, an unwritten code hedged them about, but most of these constraints were relaxed after 1950. In the early 1940's for example, when the biggest Negro name in radio was that of Rochester (who embarrassed educated and race-proud Negroes while he was earning his $150,000 a year), the tacit rules decreed that colored performers on radio could not be introduced or referred to as "Mr.," or "Mrs.," or "Miss" (Bing Crosby boldly defied the tradition in 1942 by presenting the celebrated baritone as *Mr.* Robeson); that the race should be represented in dramatic productions only by servants, comics, or ignorant underlings; and that all mention of Negro contributions to the war effort should be omitted from sponsored programs.

In television, we have noted, Negroes have been even more tightly confined than in radio to guest appearances. Perhaps the one segment of show business most hospitable to Negro performers by 1958 was the night-club, supper-club, and hotel circuit; but because the audiences for such shows were necessarily limited, the general public is little aware of the Negro's share in this branch of show business. Popular Negro jazz figures and comedians have in recent years been performing regularly in the nation's finest night spots and hotels, including some in the South. Lena Horne, Pearl Bailey, Erroll Garner, Sammy Davis, Jr., Eartha Kitt and Ella Fitzgerald, for example, have had extended engagements at the leading clubs and hotels of New York, Chicago, Miami, Los Angeles and San Francisco.

The barriers that confined Negro dancers to tap-dancing and buck-and-wing routines began to fall away in the early 1940's when Katherine Dunham emerged as one of the nation's foremost creative dancers and choreographers, and in the 1950's her pre-eminence was shared by Pearl Primus, a concert dancer of the first magnitude, and Janet Collins, premiere danseuse of the Metropolitan Opera. Others—Avon Long, Donald McKayle, and Geoffry and Carmen Holder come to mind—were also achieving national prominence, but Dunham, Primus and Collins were still, in 1959, the best known, Dunham and Primus in primitive and modern dance and choreography, and Collins as a ballerina.

Miss Dunham who, with her famous troupe, has been associated both with Hollywood and the concert stage, began dancing as a child in Joliet, Illinois, and came early under the tutelage of a former member of the Moscow Art Theater. She worked her way through the University of Chicago by running a dancing school in an old unheated barn. Public recitals brought her to the attention of the Rosenwald, Rockefeller and Guggenheim foundations, all of which eventually supported her studies in dance and anthropology in the West Indies, before she became known as "the Marian Anderson of the dance."

Pearl Primus is a native of Trinidad, her dominant African ancestry blended with the blood of Scottish, Jewish, Spanish and Indian forebears, while Miss Collins was born in New Orleans of mixed Negro, French-Creole and Indian ancestry. The Primus family migrated to New York, where the head of the household found work as a janitor, and Miss Collins's father, a proud, self-assertive tailor, preferred to take his family to Los Angeles rather than expose his two daughters to the hazards that beset handsome, light-skinned young girls of color in Louisiana.

The earliest effort of each of the three to enter a dancing career met with the objection from directors that they would either have to build special numbers around her or make her up to pass as a white girl, and all three were warned that it would be necessary to excel their white rivals if they were to succeed. Pearl Primus entered college with a view to a career in medicine, but fell under the spell of a dance teacher and eventually moved into dancing by way of the WPA (to which Miss Collins also owed much of her opportunity). Both were also greatly assisted by the Young Men's Hebrew Association in New York, which arranged appearances for them and placed them prominently before critics and the public.

In the fine arts several (like Motley, Woodruff and Barthé) who became prominent before 1936 were still productive in the late 1950's, but new recruits for the vanguard had emerged, notably the painters Charles Alston, Romare Bearden, Jacob Lawrence, Norman Lewis, Charles White, Charles Seebree,

Elzdier Cortor, Merton Simpson, Walter Simon, Ellis Wilson and Horace Pippin; sculptors Selma Burke, Sargent Johnson, Marion Perkins, John Rhodes and William Edmondson, and the cartoonist-illustrators E. Simms Campbell and Ollie Harrington. Indeed, the sheer number of younger artists —exhibiting a notable vigor, wide stylistic variety and a growing preference for non-racial themes—is perhaps even more newsworthy than are the achievements of those whom we are citing as examples. The group has in recent years found ready opportunities for one-man shows, for gallery affiliations, and for entering competitions, and has been especially cautious about the perils of uncritical praise and of conformity to stereotypes.

The depression-born Federal Artists Project afforded several of them an opportunity to perfect their youthful gifts, but, like artists everywhere, most were unable to earn a living by art alone. Two or three, like Alston and Lawrence, have earned their principal income from painting, but even they have devoted some time to teaching, Alston at the Art Students' League and Lawrence at Pratt Institute. Others have relied on full-time teaching and other employments. Bearden is a social worker in New York; Selma Burke was an art teacher during her most productive years; Edmondson was a general handyman and tombstone cutter, and Perkins, in his prime, was still a freight handler. The self-taught Pippin was a Pullman porter, while Simon was one of the several who were art teachers at Negro colleges.

Some have picked up commissions as illustrators, portraitists, muralists, or advertising artists, but the group as a whole showed a remarkable disinclination to commercialize their talent. Their work ran the whole gamut of abstractionism, expressionism, caricature, schematic muralism, naive primitivism, realism and social protest, and if it has shown a preoccupation with "Negro life," the predilection is to be set down to propinquity and to the pressure of galleries, dealers and the picture-buying public rather than to an "instinctive" expression.

In recent years, the single standard was at last becoming a fact in critical circles. So insistent were the new Negro artists that their art is not racial, but American, and that they be judged by performance only, that they have been reluctant to exhibit as "Negro painters." Alston goes so far as to condemn the Harmon awards for distinguished Negro achievements as "racial chauvinism." When the International Business Machine Company planned an extensive prize competition for Negro paintings to be sent on tour, the leading colored artists in the country declined the opportunity. Most of the group, while shying away from competitions for Negroes, have little objection to exhibiting in all-Negro shows where, without implying differential evaluations, they may demonstrate (like, say, an exhibit of Ohio or women painters) what a particular group is doing, and thus combat rather than confirm stereotypes. At the same time, an Alston, who refuses to compete or exhibit either as a "token

Negro" or with an all-Negro group, draws his materials from Negro life because it is the life he knows best.

Pippin and Edmondson were self-taught "primitives." In the middle 1940's Pippin had perhaps more canvases in museums than any other Negro painter, and his pictures commanded high prices. Edmondson was an especially appealing figure to patronizing romantics. He had, he said, been suddenly called to preach and carve religious sculpture at God's command. His work, a collection of simple, rude religious figures and symbols, carved by a semi-literate happy craftsman inspired by a religious ecstasy, was discovered by a New York photographer and soon exhibted at the Museum of Modern Art. He worked at his art in a Nashville ghetto, his front yard littered with tombstones for the Negro trade. A few months after his death in 1951, his work was exhibited in Paris alongside that of Barnard, Saint-Gaudens and Epstein.

Pippin and Edmondson were not typical of the group. Several were college graduates, and nearly all were trained in excellent art schools, often with the help of Guggenheim or Rosenwald fellowships, and in some cases after an excellent start under competent instructors in the Federal Artists Project. Several encountered stout resistance from their parents when, in childhood, they talked of becoming artists; but some of the younger members of the company found in the example of Simms Campbell and others who had become successful commercial artists, an argument that reassured their anxious elders that a Negro could make a living in the arts. They show the usual tendency to derive from middle-class folk—teachers, preachers and other white-collar parents. Alston, a very fair man, was the son of a light-skinned North Carolina minister. His mother, the daughter of a white man, was, like her husband, a graduate of the Negro Episcopal college in Raleigh. When the Alstons moved to Harlem, young Charles had some happy years in his predominantly white high school. He was elected to an exclusive club, whose meetings he was unable to attend because they were held at the Young Men's Christian Association where the color bar excluded him, even though he was almost the only baptized Christian (the others being Jews) in the group. His years at Columbia were pleasant though marred by occasional slights. His freshman English instructor invited small groups of the class to teas at his home, but omitted Alston from the invitation list. When he was invited to join a fraternity, he went—so unfamiliar to him was the etiquette of segregation—to the rush party only to be repulsed when the fraternity discovered that he had Negro blood. He later spent a year in the South to learn about Negro rural life and to feel what it was to be a Southern Negro. He stored up sensations that were as vivid two decades later as when they first occurred—above all the visceral spasm that every Negro sooner or later feels when he is called "boy" or when he braces himself for the waitress's reaction: a request for his order or a request to leave the hall.

Bearden, even fairer than Alston, was the son of recent migrants from North Carolina to New York, both of whom were well-educated civic leaders in the Negro community and municipal public servants. The elder Bearden, notaby darker than his son, was on one occasion during a visit to the South picked up by police on suspicion and jailed for a night. He never returned to the section except to attend dedicatory services at Bennett College nearly two decades later.

Selma Burke's North Carolina childhood was brightened by her whittling and clay modelling, but her ambition to become a sculptor was thwarted by her parents, and she studied nursing instead. Her father, a minister, died in Selma's youth, and she entered the home of a white superintendent of schools as a housemaid in exchange for a home, private tutoring and the use of public-library books which he secured for her. After a brief beginning in nursing in Winston-Salem, she resolved to try an artist's career and set out for New York. Supporting herself as a model at Sarah Lawrence College, she entered Columbia University on a scholarship, and, with help from the Rosenwald Fund spent a year in Europe in study and travel before returning to the United States and the Harlem WPA.

Campbell was the group's foremost commercial success. Overruling his parents' objections to his ambitions, he left his St. Louis home to live with an aunt in Chicago in order to attend high school and the Art Institute. Upon completing his course, he could find no better employment than that of dining-car waiter. Between meals he made pencil sketches of waiters and passengers until a sampling of his work persuaded a white St. Louis commercial artist to hire him. He longed to establish himself in the North, however, so he left his lucrative advertising job for an inferior one in New York. He took further training at the Academy of Design, and soon, with helpful advice from a former Chicago schoolmate, now a successful cartoonist, he was contributing to *Esquire, Life, Judge, College Humor,* the *Pittsburgh Courier,* and the Hearst King Features Syndicate. His best-known work were his *Esquire* cartoons of rosy harem girls, whose mildly salacious *mots,* delivered in wide-eyed innocence, delighted thousands of readers who never guessed that the artist was a Negro. For a time he lived in a fine Westchester County home, but he eventually moved to Europe. Ollie Harrington, another famous Negro cartoonist, was also an expatriate who sent his weekly contribution to the *Pittsburgh Courier* by mail.

Alston made a successful start in advertising and magazine-cover illustration, but soon found that the high income it brought him was no adequate compensation for the constraints upon his freedom as an artist, so he turned to "serious" painting. Bearden began as a cartoonist with some coaching from Campbell, but was drawn into painting by his advanced training and the encouragement of a white "angel," Caresse Crosby, a patroness who assisted aspiring young American artists. She helped Bearden to his first one-man show in her New York gallery and, under her urging, he went to Paris for two years of study. Cortor had strong encouragement from a white schoolteacher and from a woman editor of the Chicago *Bee,* an art enthusiast who gave the youth the art supplies he could not afford to buy. Even so, his family's opposition was so strong that they broke with him over the issue until newspaper notices of his talent softened them. After gaining a foothold as a painter, he worked at advertising art to supplement his income from his more ambitious painting.

Several in the company produced pictures with a strong protest motif, but they kept their polemics subordinated to artistic considerations. Lawrence, a dark-skinned, sensitive young painter, who passed through a serious illness, created some powerful canvases and a series of panels for *Fortune* magazine, in which the drearier side of ghetto life and the theme of anti-Negro violence were vigorously presented. Harrington's cartoons, for all their good humor, have often been social documents, mordantly critical of Negro-baiting whites and of Negro gaucheries alike.

If family opposition bedevilled some aspiring young Negro artists, others had loyal family support from the earliest awakening of their esthetic interests. Simon, reared in a white, predominantly Jewish, section of Brooklyn, had been instructed by his parents to "walk as if you own the street." They gave him a set of paints when he was only eight, and three years later helped set him up as a youthful entrepreneur, supplying him with printed cards reading, "Walter A. Simon, Jr., Portrait Painter. $2.00 and up." The Brooklyn papers brought the child prodigy to the notice of his neighbors. While still in high school he studied art at Pratt Institute, but later when his interest flagged, he was dismissed from New York University and drifted into menial employment in Washington until he was taken in hand by Alain Locke and some young painters. After a brief military service, he resumed study in New York under Woodruff and became an art teacher, first at Negro colleges and then at New Jersey State Teachers' College.

Lawrence, though he had the advantage of a Northern rearing, suffered the handicap of a broken home, and as a boy was left with foster parents until his mother, a domestic, took him to New York to live with her. By a fortunate coincidence, the neighborhood settlement house where he spent many of his childhood hours had Charles Alston on its staff, in charge of arts and crafts instruction, and Alston was to be a source of encouragement to him from that time forward.

The success of men like Alston, Bearden and Lawrence owed much to their membership in good commercial galleries. In the 1930's Negroes could not yet aspire to such affiliations, but the 1940's saw some exceptions in favor of the leading Negro artists. Then in the 1950's almost any competent Negro artist could look forward to a good gallery connection; once the precedents were established, Negro artists could rely on the artistic community's freedom from prejudice and condescension to level the remaining barriers.

In the sciences, as elsewhere, the most ponderable triumphs were being made not so much by a few big names as by hundreds of lesser ones, moving without fanfare into places formerly closed to the race. Critical shortages and softening attitudes carried highly trained Negroes into university teaching and research staffs, public and private laboratories, and research divisions of industrial corporations, not excluding textile, tobacco and chemical industries in the South. When the doors opened, qualified Negroes were in short supply, and the rewards went as usual to the optimistic striver who was ready because he had begun his preparation in advance of opportunity. Important also were the greater hospitality to colored students in universities and professional schools, and the rising economic standards and multiplying scholarships that enabled colored youth to improve the wider opportunities.

In medicine, similar ameliorative influences were at work, but barriers against hospital affiliation for Negro surgeons and against training as specialists persisted. Genuinely inter-racial hospitals are still rare. Only one of Chicago's four-score hospitals had Negroes on their staffs of affiliated doctors in 1956, and in New York a third of the Negro doctors had no affiliation and the bulk of those who had them were confined to three institutions in the ghetto. When the American Medical Association in 1949 pressed its component county and state societies to reconsider their discriminatory membership policies, some saw in it an attempt to wean colored physicians from a preference for "socialized" medicine. In any case, AMA membership came to be common in the North, and in several Southern states the AMA's county and state affiliates opened the doors. In all but two states in the South, at least some county societies let down the bars.

The race was still seriously undersupplied with physicians in 1959. There were still only two Negro medical schools, accounting for two thirds of the country's annual increase of colored doctors, and the shocking undersupply of medical schools in the nation at large operated disastrously to reduce the accessibility of places in medical classes to Negroes. Meanwhile, even though the white man's predilection for lumping all Negroes together deprived them of one of the principal spurs to achievement, colored doctors and scientists felt keenly their responsibility for winning respect for their race in an America that accorded an exalted status to its doctors and scientists.

In the new generation there was no successor to Carver as the nation's favorite Negro scientific wizard, but the new corps of specialists, even if they did not conform to the stereotype of the docile, childlike genius, reproduced familiar American patterns and exemplified the spirit of the age. Held over from the previous generation—some of them still prominent in the late 1950's

—were Drs. Dailey, Murray and Wright, and pathologists Lewis and Hinton. The new leaders included a baker's dozen more or less prominently noticed in the historical record if not in the popular press, and many more could be cited.*

Eight, mainly men of light complexion, were in the medical profession: Harold D. West, president of Meharry Medical School, and John A. Lawlah, Joseph L. Johnson and Robert Jason, successively deans of Howard Medical School; W. Montague Cobb, an anatomist and physical anthropologist on the Howard Medical staff; Charles R. Drew, head of the department of surgery at Howard, and Theodore K. Lawless and Nathaniel O. Calloway, practicing physicians.

By residence, institutional connection, and in their daily rounds, they were trapped in the Negro enclave, but they were active in a network of predominantly white professional associations. They read papers before scientific congresses and meetings and published articles in the profession's scientific journals. Lawlah, who had been the director of Provident Hospital in Chicago before heading the Howard Medical faculty, (and who later left his deanship to direct his private radiological practice) was a highly productive scholar whose papers appeared in foremost technical journals. Cobb wrote articles especially for the (Negro) *Journal of the National Medical Association,* which he edited, but the larger scientific community also saw his contributions in other learned periodicals. He was also a major figure in the NAACP as well as in professional associations. He has been a vice-president of the American Association for the Advancement of Science and in 1957 was elected president of the American Association of Physical Anthropologists.

Calloway, a specialist in internal medicine with an extensive practice in Chicago, and a member of the faculty of the University of Illinois College of Medicine, is the author of scores of professional papers and a Fellow of the American College of Physicians. His researches are chiefly non-racial, but he has drawn attention to the physical toll of discrimination by demonstrating the high incidence of hypertension in Negro mortality tables, a phenomenon he attributes to social stresses and particularly to what he calls the "compulsive servility" required of colored workers.

Drew, whose career was cut short by his early death, made a major contribution to the strengthening of Howard Medical School. He had his bed equipped with a buzzer so that he could be awakened to observe every important emergency that came to the school's hospital. His fame, however, derived from his innovations in blood preservation, surgical shock procedure, fluid balance in surgery and in banked blood. He organized a blood-collecting service for the British government in the early days of World War II, while

* While I list here those whose names I found most frequently noticed in the literature, I learn from conversations and correspondence that there are many others whose achievements are as notable as those I mention. David Blackwell, a specialist in mathematical statistics at the University of California; S. O. Johnson, a psychiatrist with the army and the Veterans Hospital at Tuskegee, Alabama; and J. Ernest Wilkins, Jr., a mathematician now in industry, are examples.

the American Red Cross was still, at the insistence of alarmed racists, segregating the blood of Negroes. Drew's admirers are fond of pointing out that while the treatment of American war casualties with front-line transfusions owed much to Drew, he himself, had he needed blood in an emergency, would have been supplied from Jim Crow stocks. The Red Cross has since eliminated the distinction, in no small degree as a result of Drew's dramatic identification with this revolutionary technique.

Lawless is the director of his own dermatological clinic in the heart of the Chicago black belt. His reputation has brought him an enormous bi-racial clientele. On any day his waiting room may be crowded with the humblest blacks, middle-class whites, a wealthy banker flown in from Atlanta, a dowager from Detroit, an oilman from Texas. He exacts the same modest fees from all comers and exasperates the profession by his preference for "volume practice" rather than confining his skill to cases which less able men cannot control. A sad-faced, tense bachelor, with a taste for music and the arts, he is equally famous as a philanthropist who has bestowed princely benefactions upon Negro colleges and hospitals.

Robert P. Barnes and Lloyd Ferguson of the Howard University Chemistry Department, both dark men, confound those who associate Negro distinction with light complexion. Barnes (appointed by President Truman to the board of the National Science Foundation) and the students he trained were in recent years publishing more papers in the *Journal of the American Chemical Society* than were all the other chemistry professors in Negro colleges combined. Ferguson, his young colleague, produced a chemistry textbook used in scores of colleges and universities in addition to papers for scholarly journals. A member of many professional associations, a Guggenheim Fellow, a reader for scientific publishing houses, and a research grantee of the National Science Foundation, the Office of Naval Research and the United States Quartermaster's Corps, he is a full member of the American scientific community, who happens to be on the staff of a Negro college. Like his colleague, Herman Branson, chairman of the Howard Physics Department and another productive scholar, Ferguson insists that the openings for qualified Negro scientists so far exceed the number qualified to fill them that the strongest scientific departments in colleges and universities compete with government and industry for Negro specialists.

The most widely noticed living Negro scientist in 1959 is Percy Julian. Originally an academic chemist at Howard and DePauw Universities, he became director of research for a corporation in Chicago and then established his own Julian Laboratories, best known for its soya products, hormones and pharmaceuticals. Lloyd Hall, another famous industrial chemist, like Julian holds numerous patents and is the author of scores of monographs. Hall, a specialist in food products, is technical director of the otherwise all-white Griffith Laboratories in Chicago.

The thirteen medical and natural scientists had their professional training in the best white Northern universities and professional schools, assisted by scholarships, or as teaching fellows instructing white students. Several were aided by subsidies from the Rosenwald Fund, the General Education Board, the National Science Foundation, the National Research Council and the Guggenheim Foundation. They acknowledged that professional training for gifted Negroes, once they had gained a foothold in college, had become so freely available that the sense of exclusion had by the late 1930's been greatly reduced.

Cobb, Barnes and Drew are three more examples of bright young Negroes who had the advantage of growing up in Washington and attending Dunbar High. All three won scholarships to Amherst and made outstanding records there. Cobb descended from free folk established in New England before the Civil War. One grandfather was a government messenger, a tax-assessor for the District of Columbia and a bibliophile. Cobb's father, a printer by trade, was fair enough to be mistaken for white, and never discussed his ancestry with his son. Young Cobb's mother was a graduate of a "normal school" in Washington and together the elder Cobbs provided their children with a devout, genteel home environment and a profound respect for education. The senior Cobb was a sturdy "race man," who, when he saw his child overburdened by an employer, snatched the boy out of his exploiter's employ. He sometimes took the child to white theaters to show him how much more whites were given for their money than Negroes received.

At Dunbar High, Cobb's teachers held before him the example of other Dunbar alumni who had distinguished themselves at Amherst and Williams. He was moved toward a medical career by a boyhood job in a pharmacy during the 1917 influenza epidemic, and after his four years at Amherst chose Howard Medical School because of the availability of jobs in his home city. Once established as a leader in his field, he seized the opportunity, under the protection of his scientific reputation, to become a spokesman for Negro rights in medicine. A typical stroke for the cause was his pamphlet "Old Clothes to Sam," whose trenchant arraignment of Jim Crow medicine did little to endear him to the American Medical Association, already offended by his championship of national health-insurance legislation. In the professional associations in which he was a respected participant, he skillfully pressed for resolutions to confine the annual conventions to cities where colored members would not be exposed to insult.

Drew, besides making a memorable scholarship record at Amherst, was captain of the track team and a football halfback of more than local fame. When he took his medical training at McGill in Canada, he again attracted wide notice as an athlete, and when he was invited to join the Howard Staff, he was selected for special training under a General Education Board Fellowship at Columbia Medical School.

Barnes, who preceded Cobb and Drew at Amherst, was, like them, a product of the Washington Negro middle class. His parents, the children of illiterate slaves, had moved from Maryland to Washington to improve the children's prospects, and all four of their sons went to college and into professions. Robert went through Amherst and Harvard Graduate School on fellowships. The Barnes boys thought segregation inevitable and felt less troubled by it than by intra-racial discrimination imposed by lighter-skinned Negro classmates and instructors. It was the distinguished records made by men like Charles Houston and Rayford Logan at Amherst and Williams that provided other Washington boys like Barnes, Cobb, Drew, Weaver, Hastie, Rupert Lloyd and Sterling Brown with the incentive to extend the tradition of brilliant scholarship by colored students at Amherst, Williams and Harvard.

Ferguson's parents were both employed, and entrusted their only child to his grandparents in Los Angeles, where he grew up in mixed neighborhoods, attended unsegregated schools, and made his way through college by working as a redcap in the mornings and evenings, subsisting on the barest minimum of sleep. He pushed himself through to the Ph.D. at the University of California, having never spent a day in a colored school until he became a member of the Howard faculty.

Jason ascribes his rise to the fact that his parents were well-educated Negro missionaries in Puerto Rico in an environment untouched by racial disabilities. He came to the United States for his college training at Lincoln University (Pennsylvania), where the kindly white faculty occasionally shocked him by the racial etiquette they observed, but where he was helped by philanthropic white families. Lawlah's parents, hard-working, uneducated Alabama folk born to ex-slaves, maintained a neat and respected home. His mother was an enthusiast for higher education, but his father was not persuaded of the market value of a college education for Negroes. Most of his youthful companions, Lawlah remembers, looked forward to menial jobs, but the four Lawlah boys, spurred by their mother, went to college. Dr. Lawlah took his undergraduate work under the stimulating influence of Hope, Archer and Brawley at Morehouse and his professional training, subsidized by the Rosenwald Fund, at Rush Medical College.

Lawless's parents were the children of ex-slaves but were substantially educated. His father was a Congregational minister and his mother a schoolteacher. Himself meticulously trained in medicine at Kansas, Northwestern and Columbia universities and at several European medical centers, he became a member of the Northwestern medical faculty. After several years there he realized that promotion was being postponed by one stratagem after another, so he resigned, and in a few years was better known than were the men who had denied him advancement.

Hall, a barber's son, descended from freeborn Northern ancestors. He himself never attended a segregated school or lived in a ghetto. He worked his way through college, and after initial disappointments was hired by telephone by the Western Electric Company, only to be repulsed when he reported for duty. Shaken by the rejection, but still hoping that a mistake had been made, he telephoned the personnel office again, and met the shouted reply, "We don't take niggers!" Shortly thereafter he was employed by mail by a firm in Buffalo. Again he was rejected when he presented himself. This time his abashed employer made partial amends by granting him six months' salary. In a matter of days he found a still better place and began a long career in industrial chemistry. Today most of his social and professional relationships are with whites, and he makes his home in the Chicago Hyde Park-Kenwood area, an upper-class neighborhood housing both white and colored professional people and Old Families whose attachment to the dignified neighborhood was not disturbed by the absorption of a few upper-class colored households.

Percy Julian's entry into an all-white upper-class community in 1950 was greeted with less tolerance. An urbane, light-skinned, strong-willed man, he became embroiled with the university administration when he was on the Howard faculty. When he bought a fine home in the Chicago suburb, Oak Park, the resistance he met moved friends to beg him to back down rather than risk so valuable a reputation in a hopeless cause, but he stood his ground in the face of bombings and incendiary attempts, coolly pointing out that he only sought housing commensurate with his position and that he wanted good schools for his children. The house was under guard for more than a year, but in time Julian and his wife (a social worker with a Ph.D.) became prominent citizens in their church and community, and their child was elected president of the student body at the public school. Julian himself was named Man of the Year in Greater Chicago by one of the city's big daily papers.

Julian's father, as a railway clerk in Montgomery, Alabama, was a member of the Negro elite. At DePauw University, young Julian slept in the attic of a white fraternity house where he worked as a waiter. When he graduated, with Phi Beta Kappa honors, as valedictorian of his class, his mother was so delighted that she moved the family to Greencastle to enable the other five Julian children to attend college, and in time they took fourteen college and university degrees. The head of the house, meanwhile, remained at his job in the Deep South and sent the bulk of his wages to his family to enable his brood to realize their ambition. After finishing at DePauw, Julian went to Harvard on a scholarship and then to Vienna, with the help of a wealthy college classmate and a General Education Board grant, to complete his professional training there. It is not without interest that Julian, one of the country's leading scientists, a trustee of Roosevelt University, trained at the University of Vienna, and perennially listed in *Who's Who in America,* is the grandson of a slave who suffered mutilation of his right hand as a punishment for learning to read.

The recent advance of the race was at once cause and effect of the rise of its lawyers. Besides several from the preceding generation still prominent in the next, two dozen new attorneys may be listed in the vanguard for the 1940's and 1950's. The most renowned is, by common consent, Thurgood Marshall, but other leaders were George N. Leighton, James M. Nabrit, Earl B. Dickerson, Raymond Pace Alexander, Sadie T. M. Alexander, William R. Ming, William H. Hastie, Scovel Richardson, J. Ernest Wilkins, Truman K. Gibson, Jr., Edith Sampson, Archibald J. Carey, Jr. and Hubert Delany. Others well up in the front ranks were Pauli Murray, Euclid Taylor, William H. Huff, William T. Andrews, Bindley Cyrus, Wendell Green, Loren Miller, Z. Alexander Looby, Charles W. Anderson, Leon A. Ransom and George E. C. Hayes.

Still others were perhaps more successful or more celebrated as practicing attorneys, but our concern is with those most widely publicized. Negro lawyers continued to increase and their share of the Negro clientele was enlarged, though in the South their practice was still sharply limited and would have been smaller still but for cases thrown their way by the NAACP, a "meal ticket" which some of them shamelessly exploited. In the larger Northern cities Negro law business, especially in criminal practice, tended to go increasingly to colored attorneys, a small minority of them taking the bulk of the clientele.

The lawyers we have named were famous not as leaders in the American bar, but for their part in the racial struggle or for roles incidental to their legal practice. Marshall is an obvious example. Nabrit is a Howard law professor specializing in civil rights, and noted for participation in crucial constitutional cases relating to the franchise, equal educational facilities, and racial restrictive covenants. Ming, now in lucrative bi-racial practice (in 1958 he won a thirty-two-million-dollar case for the Commonwealth Edison Company, according to *Ebony*) became noted as an attorney for state and federal agencies, as a full professor of law at the University of Chicago, and as an NAACP legal strategist in white primary- and public-school cases. Dickerson served as a Chicago alderman and a member of President Roosevelt's Fair Employment Practices Committee, as a major officer of the NAACP and Urban League, as a crusader against restrictive covenants, and became president of the North's largest Negro insurance company. He missed his ambition to go to Congress by his independent course in Chicago politics where the principal requisite for preferment was a degree of loyalty to the Kelly machine that the forceful, cultivated and proud Dickerson was never minded to pay.

Edith Sampson was alternate delegate to the UN. Raymond P. Alexander's prominence derives from his membership in the Philadelphia City Council and from his championing of civil liberties—notably his fight to gain admission for Negroes to Girard College. His wife won distinction as a pioneer woman attorney and as a member of President Truman's Civil Rights Commission. Wilkins was conspicuous as Assistant Secretary of Labor and as the only Negro on the Civil Rights Commission that was called into being by the legislation of 1957. Scovel Richardson was chairman of the Federal Parole Board and Judge of the United States Customs Court. Hastie's fame rests largely on his law-school deanship and the high federal posts he has held.

Gibson is notable chiefly for his appointment as Hastie's successor in the War Department, and for his leading position as a promoter in professional boxing. Carey, though associated with a prosperous downtown law firm in Chicago, is better known as a church leader and holder of important public appointive and elective positions. Other famous lawyers, like Miller, Looby and Hayes, owe their prominence primarily to their identification with civil rights cases, typically as spokesmen for the NAACP, while Cyrus, a member of a bustling Chicago law firm, earned a reputation in politics and in efforts to promote intra-racial harmony between West Indian and native American Negroes. Pauli Murray is best known as the author of a sprightly family history and of the scholarly *States' Laws on Race and Color,* while Ransom and perhaps others are better known as law professors than as attorneys. Andrews owes his repute to his seat in the New York legislature, and Anderson to his long tenure as the first Negro in the Kentucky legislature since the Reconstruction. Huff's reputation rests upon his battles against debt peonage and upon his teaching, while Green, a hard-working organization Democrat in Chicago was a civil-service commissioner before becoming a municipal judge.

Two of the group, born in the West Indies, had the problem of adapting themselves to American mores. Cyrus, for example, after a period of employment on the Panama Canal, came in his youth to America, armed with credentials from the great Goethals, and totally ignorant of American ways. He worked first as a messenger, and when he was handed a tip by a wealthy manufacturer, he drew back, protesting that he did not accept "gratuities." The startled industrialist undertook at once to lecture him on the structure of the American economy.

Only six of the group had their undergraduate training in Negro colleges and the rest attended Northern state universities or leading private colleges. Only five, including two of the most eminent (Marshall and Richardson) attended a Negro law school, all of them at Howard. Very few attributed their choice of law primarily to a desire to fight the race's battles; more of them reported that they were drawn to it by expectations of financial success—either in general practice or in Negro business enterprise, which drew heavily upon lawyers for leadership. Still others were fascinated by the supposed opportunities for dramatic self-expression that courtroom practice promised. They were drawn mainly from the upper stratum of Negro society, often unconscious of racial tensions in their youth. Several, however, began to feel the sting of prejudice and proscription in college, and nearly all were compelled by economic stringencies to earn their way through law school.

Dickerson recalls some influences that impelled him to leave Mississippi to carve out a career in Chicago. The sight of his widowed mother, an intelligent, hearty, industrious woman, reduced to a backbreaking life bending over a washboard made a deep impression, in no way softened by the inclination of white children to taunt him with the old chant of "Nigger, Nigger!" and to upset the laundry in the city streets as he delivered the bundles to their owners. Once a kinsman was shot and seriously wounded, before his very eyes, for having brushed by a white in the town square without the proper degree of deference. The trains rumbling through from Chicago also turned his mind to thoughts of fleeing North, an intention he carried out when he was fourteen. He found a job with an educated Negro family who steered him into a fine preparatory school in Evanston, where he earned his way at menial employments. Next he entered the University of Illinois, and once again it was a Negro who came to his aid—an employee of the college of agriculture who hunted up jobs for Chicago colored boys who came to Urbana. He decided to become a lawyer, for he had long been outraged by the absence of recourse for the Negro who met brutality. Transferring from the state university to the less hostile University of Chicago, he found another spur to success when the college librarian drew him aside to urge him to disprove an old campus legend that no Negro could get through the law school. He became the first Negro to take a law degree at the Chicago school.

The Philadelphia boyhood of Raymond Pace Alexander was virtually free from overt discriminations. His stimulus came from a large family's pressing economic need. By the time he was seven he was working at the city market and on newspaper routes and, when he was thirteen, began an eight-year period as handyman at the city opera house, supplemented, after he became eighteen, with work as a redcap, waiter, and Pullman-car cook to put himself through college. The fortunate opera-house-connection had come when its proprietor was impressed by the tireless labors of the colored newsboy and deliveryman whose incredibly skinny frame stood up so manfully under the exactions laid upon it. Valedictorian of his largely white high-school class, Raymond attended the University of Pennsylvania on scholarships, and then supported himself through Harvard law school as a redcap in summer and as assistant in the Harvard economics department during the school year.

His impressive record at Harvard led the law school to recommend him to a leading Philadelphia law firm. Responding with high hopes to the firm's request that he come for an interview, he was crushed when the lawyers, thunderstruck to find that he was a Negro, explained that they could not engage a colored assistant. He wept bitterly as he went down the elevator and walked the street for hours, unable to confront his father with his humiliation. Soon thereafter he married Sadie Tanner Mossell (the holder of a doctorate in economics and a law degree from the University of Pennsylvania, and the first Negro woman to win admission to the Pennsylvania bar), and the two established a notable partnership. Mrs. Alexander became a prominent civil libertarian as did Alexander himself. The firm accepted a large number of civil-rights cases without fee. Alexander also attracted notice as an organizer of Democratic election campaigns in Philadelphia and by his appointment in 1958 as a municipal judge.

Gibson, the son of a prominent Negro family, was at his predominantly white high school an oratory champion and member of the football squad and the honor society. His Columbus (Ohio) mixed neighborhood had a tradition of easy race relations. He worked at the usual occupations that engaged ambitious boys of both races and when he was ready for college enrolled at the University of Chicago at the urging of a Rosenwald Fund representative. During five years at the university he was an assistant to Harold Gosnell, then at work on his study of the Negro in Chicago politics.

Ming, born into the Negro bourgeoisie in Chicago (his father was in the civil service), was a classmate of Gibson at Chicago. At Englewood High School and Crane Junior College, both municipal institutions with a small proportion of colored students, he encountered no serious racial friction, and he kept in spending money by working at an A&P store managed by whites. During his years at the university he won several athletic numerals and was elected to the *Law Review*. With Gibson and Benjamin O. Davis, Jr., he helped break up a Negro club as an unnecessary form of self-segregation. He was admitted to the Order of the Coif but was not eligible to membership in any social fraternity except the campus's one all-Negro Greek-letter society. He began his legal career in the office of Earl Dickerson, and his subsequent political appointments as well as Dickerson's backing made him one of the best known of the country's young Negro lawyers.

Nabrit, in addition to his favorable family background, had the further advantage of following his father to Morehouse college, in those years one of the most remarkable recruiting grounds of Negro leaders in the country. Then, at Northwestern University Law School he found a hospitable reception, followed by an easy transition into the profession by the opportunity to work in the offices of the future federal judges, Mollison and Moore, and of the future "little cabinet" member, Wilkins. When he returned to his native Georgia to establish a practice of his own, he found himself so inadequately prepared for the peculiar role of advocate for the disfranchised and disinherited Georgia Negro that he retreated to the Howard Law School and developed the notable course in civil rights that was to make a strong imprint on a whole generation of Howard-trained attorneys.

Wilkins lost his father when he was very young, and because his impoverished mother could contribute little to his education, he left his Farmington,

Missouri, home, where there was no Negro high school, to attend a school in Jefferson City, supporting himself all the while. He then entered the University of Illinois (chosen for reasons of economy), where the anti-Negro atmosphere drove him to work with such intense application that he earned election to Phi Beta Kappa even while maintaining a heavy schedule of self-help work. At the University of Chicago Law School he was far more comfortable.

Edith Sampson, whose spokesmanship abroad for the American Negro has been criticized (but more often praised, because of the Negro's propensity for defending America when charges of extreme racialism come from foreign quarters), was relatively unscarred by childhood racial incidents. Her middle-class family was in pinched circumstances and at fourteen she was scaling and boning fish in a local market. Her chance came when the Associated Charities of Pittsburgh, desiring a Negro social worker, sent her to New York for training. At Columbia University she was urged, because of her good work in a law course, to enter the legal profession. In her childhood she had been much influenced by a truant officer's advice that her best hope lay in preparing herself for the time when the doors of opportunity should open. After taking the first law degree awarded a woman by Loyola University, she became a Chicago municipal officeholder and private attorney, and a women's club leader. As a member of the Town Hall tours she developed her reputation as an able exponent of the I-like-America line which later made her an attractive appointee as alternate delegate to the UN.

Thurgood Marshall's Baltimore youth was also relatively untroubled by racial strain. After working his way through Lincoln University as bellhop, dining-car waiter and pinochle player, he entered Howard Law School. He threw himself into his course with an energy that is still a legend at the school. After five years of ghetto practice, he found that his Negro-rights cases brought him wide respect and deep personal satisfaction but little financial return, so in 1938 he joined the NAACP's staff and before long was its chief legal voice, exerting an influence as a mover and shaker of American society that few of his white contemporaires in the profession could match.

The architect of an impressive series of crucial Supreme Court victories, he attained his greatest renown in *Brown* v. *Board of Education* (1954), whose implications made a nation gasp. It was only with the emergence of the generation of young lawyers like Marshall, Edward R. Dudley, Ming, Nabrit, Hayes, Alexander, Dickerson, Looby, Miller and others, that the race could at last, with its own corps of advocates, enter the lists in dead earnest against legal proscription. Success came faster than they expected. Hoping at first merely to erode the foundations of legal discrimination by pressing for *de facto* equality in the separate facilities accorded to Negroes in the South, they soon saw the very principle of separate-but-equal repudiated. So far had the Court moved by 1954 in the direction of a literal reading of the

Fourteenth Amendment's equal-protection clause, that the Brown decision should have surprised no one. Beginning with the Gaines case in 1938, and moving on through the Sipuel, Sweatt, McLauren and Henderson cases a decade later, the Court had entered upon a process that could end only with the conclusions reached in the Brown action.

In business and industry, as in science and medicine, the chief gain was in the closer approach of the whole race to the mainstream rather than in achievements of the celebrities whom the record thrusts forward. Real income increased threefold from 1936 to 1957 and compounded into an eighteen-billion-dollar "Negro market." In 1959 most adult Negroes could remember a hard-scrabble childhood on Southern farms, but now a mere sixth were in the rural South. Half of the country's colored population was in the non-farm South; two fifths were in the urban North and West. Five sixths of all Negroes were in cities, where the war boom and its sequel sucked them into sectors of the economy from which they had formerly been excluded. The cutting off of European immigrants also operated to enlarge the colored American's opportunity in an expanding economy.

A closer view admonishes us to temper our estimates, however, for per capita income still lagged fully a third behind the national figure and three eighths of the nation's colored families still subsisted on less than two thousand dollars a year. They still held the least desirable jobs, and when employment levels sagged were the first to be discharged. The relaxation of old racial barriers in the unions was a major accelerating factor, but the employment of Negroes in Southern industry, where unions were weakest, was still lagging. In the North the race's economic advantages were diminished by crowded ghetto conditions. In New York City, where, with the possible exception of Washington, the race's status was perhaps higher than anywhere else in the land, the colored population was so tightly crammed into Harlem that the same population density for the entire nation would be achieved by packing all of the 170 million Americans into greater New York City alone.

The professions were still undersupplied. Teachers and preachers were plentiful enough, but in 1955 the annual increase of graduate engineers was about 150, and the yearly crops of lawyers and doctors stood at about 200 each. And while Negroes everywhere encounter closed doors in the general economy, they do not command the Negro market. They may operate half of the ghetto's firms, but they are the marginal firms, accounting for a mere tenth of Negro spending. Even the grocery business in Harlem is not theirs. Indeed it is largely in personal service that Negro enterprise must find its opportunity, where the white investor is not interested: in the funeral business, beauty shops, barbershops and the like. There was still, in 1956, no first-class hotel owned by Negroes. The famous Theresa in Harlem was not in fact a Negro business. So precarious were the sources of Negro venture capital that the most impressive Negro-owned hotel in America was owned by a colored numbers tycoon who had made his fortune in the policy racket because exclusions and proscriptions closed legitimate enterprises as an outlet for his business talents.

Popular accounts of Negro business greatly exaggerate its importance. They do give employment to some Negroes and opportunity for roles closed to them in the general economy, but they do not add much to the economic improvement of the race. In the large Southern cities, the presence of a few colored businesses does little to relieve surplus-labor conditions in the Negro community. The condition of colored labor in Baltimore, where there is far less Negro enterprise than in Atlanta, is markedly better because the race is being more extensively assimilated in the general economy there than in Atlanta. The economic fortunes of the race are more dependent upon the winning of a secure place in the American economy than upon the elaboration of a separate Negro economy. It must still in all candor be set down that in 1959 Negroes are nowhere genuinely in the economic "power structure," and that they are still almost totally excluded from a share in significant economic decision-making. The continued enforced economic subservience to whites constitutes perhaps the race's most catastrophic exclusion, by which all other barriers are reinforced. This iron constraint is only now for the first time being seriously challenged, now that the colored Americans have achieved political strength and a spending power equal to that of the entire Canadian dominion.

While the levelling of barriers is multiplying the number of colored participants in formerly all-white employments, one hears of no colored directors of corporations, factories, railroads, or utilities. Still, the Negro press faithfully records the precursors of an expanding future: the first stewardesses, pilots and junior executives in aviation; the first cameramen, stage managers and editors in television; the first engineers, chemists, mathematicians in industrial laboratories; buyers for large department stores; accountants and statisticians for industrial plants; photographers for the nation's largest picture weekly; skilled, semi-skilled and unskilled workers for the nation's industries.

The best-known Negroes in business and industry are still men in Negro firms, serving a Negro clientele. Paul Williams in architecture and Archie Alexander in engineering continued to be the principal exceptions. Other, younger men, associated with engineering, architecture and construction, were climbing to responsible positions in the general economy, but were not widely known. Here and there was an occasional all-Negro radio station or a white-owned station employing a Negro staff and beaming its broadcasts to the colored market.

The most successful colored enterprisers in the separate economy were usually of local importance only: real-estate and property management men like Robert Y. Browne in Chicago, Augustine A. Austen in New York and Everett Watson in Detroit; heads of funeral establishments like Robert A. Cole in Chicago and the elder C. C. Diggs in Detroit (both of whom spread their interests to insurance also); "beauticians" like Rose Meta Morgan of New York, and a tycoon like A. G. Gaston of Montgomery, who expanded from insurance into a wide range of ghetto enterprises. The record identifies an inventor or two, like the self-taught Frederick M. Jones, an ex-racing-car driver who became a refrigerator engineer and the holder of sixty patents.

Colored businessmen often question the logic of Negro industrial undertakings and argue that the better strategy is to increase the number of colored technicians who can move into the periphery of American industry and then penetrate more deeply. Colored manufacturing for a national Negro market is rare and confined to "race products," notably hair and skin conditioners, embalming supplies for colored undertakers, and Negro dolls and Christmas cards. Perhaps the largest Negro firm is the S. B. Fuller Company of Chicago, manufacturers and distributors of toiletries, cosmetics, kitchen supplies and patent medicines, sold by door-to-door canvassers, Negro and white, to both races. Another important augury of expanding economic horizons is the Practical Electronics Manufacturing Company, of Chicago, headed by Louis G. Alexander, a firm which has in 1959 government contracts totalling nearly two million dollars for its electronics products.

Here and there one finds a large-scale local contractor building Negro housing. Perhaps the best-known engineer in 1959 is Lewis K. Downing, training young men at the country's only full-scale colored engineering school at Howard, outside the engineers' workaday world. The demand for his graduates exceeds the supply. Recruiters from leading manufacturing, construction, electrical and civil engineering firms visit the Howard campus annually to sign up the young colored engineers, who begin in comfortable berths at salaries above those of many of their college instructors.

Downing's paternal grandfather went to Sunday school to Stonewall Jackson, and his maternal grandfather was an AMEZ bishop. His light-skinned father, a pastor, was born in bondage in the closing days of slavery, but worked his way through Lincoln University before marrying an Oberlin student. All five of their children became college-bred professional folk. Downing took engineering degrees at Howard and Massachusetts Institute of Technology, working during the summers with the Maryland Highway Department. His work fellows accepted him, but the problem of finding lodging proved so difficult that he used a motorcycle to commute between his jobs and his Washington home. He gained practical engineering experience in minor jobs with some of the finest construction firms in the country, earned still another degree, in highway transport and traffic control, at the University of Michigan, and then became Howard's first Negro engineering dean. He eventually became, after earlier snubs, a member of the American Society of

Engineers and recently had the satisfaction of securing a charter for a Howard University student chapter.

The Johnson Publishing Company and some of the race newspapers are among the largest Negro businesses, but the leading interest continues to be insurance, followed by banking and the savings and loan business. There were still only thirteen banks in 1958, and the number of savings and loan associations was somewhat larger. In 1958 there were sixty-five insurance companies, all but ten of them in the South. Together they employed about 8,000 Negroes and claimed a total of $250 millions of insurance in force—a figure that loses its impressiveness when one notes that the Metropolitan Life Insurance Company alone writes more Negro insurance than do all the Negro companies combined. Similarly, in cities served by colored banks, the bulk of the Negro trade is in the hands of whites.

Negro insurance and banking provide capital for colored enterprise and stimulate the interest of white banks and insurance companies in the Negro market. A minor revolution in housing has been wrought by these Negro businessmen, for they demonstrated that the colored American gives a high priority to home ownership, particularly in the South where Negro housing is less dominated by white-owned tenements in egregiously overcrowded ghettos. Once colored lenders proved that colored borrowers could be sound risks, the availability of white capital to Negroes was greatly enlarged.

A dozen names in Negro banking and insurance came prominently to the writer's attention: William J. Kennedy, Earl Dickerson, Maceo C. Martin, Jesse and Doyle Mitchell, Asa T. Spaulding, John H. Wheeler, Norris B. Herndon, George Beavers, J. Lorimer Milton and A. Maceo Walker. These and lesser-known businessmen are typically the sons or nephews of the pioneers who established the businesses these younger men now head. They had, usually, a background of college training and experience that had not been available to their elders. They entered Negro business when it was a going concern, and the skepticisms of whites and colored had been quieted.

Five of those we have mentioned may serve as examples of Negro business leaders: Kennedy, Martin, Mitchell, Spaulding and Wheeler. Mitchell, a fair-skinned man, never discussed his ancestry with his son and successor, Doyle Mitchell. His immediate slave forebears elected to remain near the old home place in Texas, but young Jesse, after working his way through Prairie View College, went to Washington, where he worked as a government clerk, attended Howard Law School in the evening, and married a daughter of ex-slaves. His education completed, he made a modest beginning in real estate and, with his savings, became a silent partner in a commercial bank, which failed in the banking crisis of 1933. In the following year he organized what was to become the largest Negro bank in America—a primacy it has since surrendered to the Citizens Trust Company of Atlanta. The firm became the chief reliance of colored borrowers in the District of Columbia, specializing in small loans. Upon his death in 1955, Mitchell was succeeded by his son, B. Doyle Mitchell, who had begun working in the bank as a boy, and had taken a degree in commerce and mathematics at Howard, and had further study at the Wharton School of Finance.

Maceo C. Martin, president of a Danville, Virginia, bank, and of the (Negro) National Bankers' Association, is another second generation businessman. As the son of a pioneer banker and himself the father of a cashier in the largest bank in America, he symbolizes the progress of Negro business. Both of his parents, the children of literate house slaves, were schoolteachers and sturdy exemplars of the colored elite in their Virginia community, conspicuous in church affairs, and warm exponents of education and tireless effort. Young Martin heard the same values preached at Virginia Union University. The elder Martin and a local minister had established the Danville bank in 1917, less for financial gain than for race advance. Maceo Jr. entered the employ of the bank when it opened and by the time he was twenty-two was running it.

The head of the largest Negro business in America in 1958 was William J. Kennedy, president of the North Carolina Mutual Insurance Company. His father, a self-taught schoolteacher and the son of slaves of uncertain ancestry, had been identified with a small fraternal burial benefit program, and an uncle, a letter carrier, was a part-time insurance agent. Kennedy's paternal grandfather had been a skilled artisan in slavery and upon his emancipation built bridges for neighboring communities. He prospered and bought a square mile of land at Andersonville, Georgia, a plot including the site and the surviving stockade of the infamous Civil War prison.

The Kennedys were intermittently employed by the national military cemetery at Andersonville, and young William had his first business experience accumulating army buttons and belt buckles and carving walking sticks from the timbers of the prison stockade for sale to visiting Union veterans. He had only a secondary-school education before securing a place with the young North Carolina Mutual. He spent a year during World War I in a tightly Jim-Crowed camp in the South, an experience which threw him into association with colored bumpkins from Mississippi, who had never seen a railroad car before they had been drafted. Their tales of the colored boy's plight in the Deep South led Kennedy to regard himself as the very button on Fortune's cap. After the war he returned to North Carolina Mutual, adding to his knowledge of the business by extensive reading and by correspondence courses. As a life member of the NAACP and a leader in boys' club and religious work in Durham, he has lent his weight to the struggle for Negro advance. His high reputation was attested when he was appointed by the governor of North Carolina to serve on the state's nine-man Board of Higher Education which oversees the state's colleges, universities and teacher training institutions.

John H. Wheeler, president of the Farmers and Mechanics Bank of Durham, is another figure respected on both sides of the color line. His father, the son of a white man, left a Negro-college presidency to join North Carolina Mutual. His mother, like her husband, was educated at Wilberforce and both were members of the devout, thrifty colored ultra-respectables. They encouraged their son to work his way through Morehouse, a stimulating training ground for ambitious young Negroes, where the more industrious hired other students to work for them. (The Scott brothers, for example, ran a thriving business of selling umbrellas and hosiery, with fellow students as their agents, and eventually bought from Heman Perry an old printing works and established what eventually became the Atlanta *Daily World*.)

After Morehouse, Wheeler went to North Carolina Mutual and then to the bank affiliated with it. The bank was admitted to the state's Bankers' Association, then dropped because of nervousness over dinner meetings, and later reinstated. Leaders in both the insurance company and the bank have in recent years supported the NAACP program and have contributed funds to push school-integration cases. They have done so without losing the respect of Durham's white leadership. Wheeler, in fact, like many Southern Negroes, believes that Southerners are more liberal than they admit to each other, but continue to reiterate old clichés under the apprehension that it is expected of them.

The Spaulding family continued to be represented in North Carolina Mutual by C. C. Spaulding, Jr., an attorney, and by his cousin, Asa T. Spaulding, who became president upon Kennedy's retirement in 1959. As a member of the Spaulding clan, he was from boyhood earmarked for the insurance business, and as a student at New York University he earned a degree in mathematics with magna cum laude honors. His professor of business mathematics was so impressed by his performance that he went to Durham to persuade the North Carolina Mutual board to permit him to coach the young man with a view to making him the country's first Negro actuary. The elder Spaulding thereupon talked with the state's insurance commissioner to inquire if a Negro actuary would be recognized. The assurances were given and young Spaulding went for two years to the University of Michigan and attained his goal. On the occasion of the inauguration of President Tubman of Liberia, Spaulding was sent by the Department of State as an American representative, and in 1956 he was a delegate to the ninth general conference of UNESCO in India.

The integration of the races in the armed forces—not by protracted legislative steps, not by slow judicial clarification of old constitutional and statutory provision, but by swift, massive action of the federal executive, initiated and vigorously prosecuted by the Democratic President Truman and concluded by the Republican President Eisenhower—wrought one of the most profound changes in American racial patterns since the Emancipation.

As late as 1949, colored servicemen were still tightly segregated in 220 all-Negro units. Within five years these outfits had been reduced to a mere fifteen; in 1958 there were none, and for all administrative and practical purposes the Army was completely integrated. The Air Force made the change-over in mere months; and if the Navy resisted somewhat stubbornly, there too, by 1958, colored servicemen were at their posts, on every class of vessel in the fleet. The roads to officer commissions were thrown open to the race and in 1958 the Defense Department could furnish this writer a list (by no means complete) of some fifty Negro colonels and lieutenant colonels assigned to virtually the entire range of staff and field commands. The social revolution in the armed forces was at this writing still so recent that there had not yet been time for the emergence of candidates for the Negro vanguard.

Another innovation was the appointment of Negro cadets by white Congressmen, now that the latter were increasingly awarding these prizes on the basis of competitive examinations without restrictions as to race. West Point had graduated three Negroes in its 125 years prior to 1936, and the first colored midshipman was graduated at Annapolis in 1949. But in 1950 the Military Academy contained eight Negroes simultaneously, and the Naval Academy was no longer a closed preserve.

Considerations of world opinion and of maximum utilization of the nation's manpower forced serious attention to the demands of white liberals, Negroes and coldly practical military policy-makers that the segregation of the military be re-examined; but significant change was postponed until after the War. Even so, an anti-discrimination clause, drafted by a Committee on Participation of Negroes in the War, was incorporated in the Selective Service Act of 1940, and a few weeks later, in circumstances that we have already described, William Hastie was made civilian aide to the Secretary of War; Col. Campbell C. Johnson was appointed special aide to draft director Lewis B. Hershey, and Col. Benjamin O. Davis was promoted to the rank of brigadier general.

Two years later, Hastie resigned in indignation and published an attack upon the government for its failure to proceed against segregation in the Army. Far from being proscribed for his hard-hitting strictures, Hastie was soon recalled to government service by President Truman to be governor of the Virgin Islands. Further attention was drawn to the problem when Truman K. Gibson, Jr., Hastie's youthful successor as civilian aide, investigated charges of grave failures and misconduct by Negro troops in combat. Gibson, instead of denying the charges, confirmed them and coolly accounted for them as the products of Jim Crow and the troops' encirclement by circumstances egregiously destructive of morale.

Hastie, Gibson, Colonel Johnson and James C. Evans were conspicuously identified with the military in essentially civilian capacities, but the years after 1936 also produced in Brigadier General Davis and his son, of the same name and rank, two heroes of the vanguard well before the Army's big switch from Jim Crow. They were the first, and remain the only, Negroes to achieve the rank of general in the regular army. Davis senior, in 1959 living in Washington in dignified retirement, is still every inch the Old Soldier, an authentic link with the Old Army of spit-and-polish, leather and horseflesh. He looks back upon the longest troop service in the history of our army: fifty years of garrison duty as a cavalryman at home, and in the Philippines, interspersed with stateside service as military instructor at Tuskegee and Wilberforce; combat duty in the Spanish-American War, the Philippine Insurrection, the Mexican Border Incident, and World War I; and finally as commanding general of the all-Negro Fourth Cavalry in 1941–1944, special adviser to the commander of the European Theater in 1944–1945 and assistant to the Inspector General, 1945–1947.

A grave, erect, soft-spoken, and abstemious man, magnificently preserved at eighty-two, he is the son of a copper-colored freeborn Virginian who had settled in Washington after the Civil War as the household retainer of General John A. Logan, then a Congressman. His mother was the child of a white slaveowner and a light-brown house cook. The future general was virtually untouched by segregation in his childhood in the Washington of the 1880's, and attended a "mixed" county school. Early in his army career, however, he met his first direct rebuff when his promotion from the ranks was overruled. The discrimination moved General Logan's wife to lay the youth's case before President McKinley, with a plea that he be admitted to West Point. Nothing came of it, and Davis re-enlisted in the Negro 9th Cavalry, determined to earn a commission. He was assigned to duty as post schoolteacher, and his superior officer engaged him as a tutor for his small daughter to give him the opportunity to use his library and prepare for the examination which afforded an avenue to a commission. In less than two years he became a lieutenant.

The general insists that he rarely met with affronts, partly because "I never embarrassed my white or colored friends and I never went where I was not wanted." He kept away from social functions at the Officers' Club. He never called upon brother officers in quarters except when regulations required, and then was careful to say that he was making the call under orders. When white troops failed to salute him, he bore the snub with soldierly fortitude, and only in flagrant cases demanded that the delinquent salute at least his tunic. "I always tried," he told this writer, "to be sufficiently competent to compensate my officer for the trouble of having me on his hands." Thirty-two years of service brought him a full colonelcy in 1930, to all appearances the ceiling of his career because the normal pressures from politicians and brass hats for further promotion were not available to him. But when, in 1940, while commanding the Negro 369th Infantry in the New York National Guard, he was advanced to the rank of general, he was, he says, "the most surprised man in the country."

His son had nearly finished college at the University of Chicago when Congressman De Priest offered him an appointment to West Point. His rigorously disciplined father made no effort to influence the boy's decision, but when young Ben entered the Academy, Colonel Davis was overjoyed. In the years when the colonel taught military science at Tuskegee he amused himself by drilling a "kid company" of his own and other Tuskegee faculty children. Even at home Ben, Jr., and his sisters were held to a military schedule: breakfast at six thirty, all properly dressed and in good formation; bed check at seven.

Cadet Davis's first year at West Point was a harrowing and lonely ordeal, but thereafter he became one of the most respected men in the corps. When he was graduated in 1936 near the top of his class, he was assigned to duty at Tuskegee in his father's old position. In 1942 he was ordered to the newly created Negro-pilot training center at Tuskegee, and a year later was commanding the all Negro 99th Fighter Squadron, operating in the Mediterranean area. In 1944 he was a full colonel and his highly decorated unit was expanded to form the 332nd Fighter Group. He returned to the United States in 1945, his tunic spangled with the insignia of the Legion of Merit, the Silver Star, the Distinguished Flying Cross, four Air Medals and ribbons of the American Defense and European Theaters. A decade later, long since promoted to the rank of brigadier general in a completely integrated Air Force, he served as commander of Task Force Thirteen in Formosa and became Chief of Staff of the Twelfth U.S. Air Force, based in Germany.

The resounding collapse of racial barriers in sports dates from the middle 1940's, when professional baseball instituted changes which within a decade all but abolished the color bar in the national game, and rolled on into other realms of sport to sweep away barriers which most Americans had thought to be impregnable. The same national and international forces to which we have ascribed the Negro's status revolution in the years since the middle 1930's, go far toward explaining also the race's startling advance in athletic competitions. And then, in 1959, one of the last barriers to the Negro's full participation in sports was levelled when the United States Supreme Court ruled that state laws barring racially mixed sports contests are unconstitutional. The ruling specifically struck down statutes that prohibited mixed boxing, but also extended to athletic contests generally.

These influences were significantly reinforced by other impulses internal to the Negro community itself. For many, sports seemed to offer the shortest and most exciting road to riches and applause in an economy where words of praise for the Negro were still few and where millions of humble colored folk had to be content with the leavings. But there were other considerations. Some of the new sport heroes have declared that it was a combination of the liberalized social climate plus the example of older Negro sport idols that provided their incentives. Others confide that it is because the race's emancipation has proceeded further in sports than in other segments of American life where Negroes can earn both status and a living, that a disproportionate number of young men make a desperate attempt at finding fulfillment in athletics, sometimes with the added object of working off—in the stimulating contentions of sport, often before cheering multitudes—the frustrations and rejections that still plague them in other corners of their lives. To some, the prospect of close personal combat with the white man, of giving him a thorough drubbing, and then shaking his hand in a generous gesture of conciliation, affords a heady ecstasy.

Still others have emphasized that bitter experience with disabilities and discouragements toughens the fiber of those whose spirit survives these cruel siftings, strengthening both their resolve and their capacity to excel rivals who have not passed through the same rigorous school. Some, it is clear, were pushed forward also by whites interested in promoting racial equality or simply in raising the standards of performance in a particular sport.

There has been considerable diversity among the Negro athletes in the matter of "race effort." Some, like Roy Campanella, have kept themselves resolutely apart from the racial struggle, accepted their opportunities as they found them, and sought their satisfactions on the playing fields. At the other extreme have been a very few, who, after they achieved success, have, like Jackie Robinson, come to regard themselves primarily as crusaders for racial justice. In the center have been those who, without entering the polemics of the struggle, have, like Althea Gibson, been concerned about The Problem, but have hoped that their individual achievements would speak for themselves as an advertisement for the race.

Robinson has made no secret of his contempt for the most celebrated Negro baseball stars who adopt racial attitudes of conciliation or surrender. Some of the conservatives have expressed public disapproval of Robinson's aggressiveness, and some moderates have seen a need for a plural adjustment. "The difference between me and Jackie Robinson," says Miss Gibson in her autobiography, *I Always Wanted To Be Somebody* (1959), "is that he thrives on his role as a Negro battling for equality, whereas I shy away from it. . . . [but] if he hadn't paved the way, I probably never would have got my chance."

America had long before 1936 become accustomed to colored boxing champions, but the year 1937 marks the beginning of a new era of Negro ascendancy in pugilism, for it launched Joe Louis on the longest reign (twelve years) as the world's heavyweight king in the history of the sport.

The same year brought the featherweight crown to Henry Armstrong, who —under the rule that permits a boxer to compete in divisions above his own weight—promptly went on to hold the featherweight, the lightweight and the welterweight championships simultaneously, and then, in 1940, to fight the middleweight champion to a draw in a bout for that division's title.

Another master boxer emerged when "Sugar Ray" Robinson won first the welterweight championship in 1946, and then the middleweight crown in 1951, the latter of which he regained for the fifth time in 1959.* So uniformly successful were colored boxers after 1936 that six of them, five of whom were United States citizens, held the world's championships in the six highest weight divisions in 1958, and 60 per cent of all professional boxers in the United States were Negroes. In that same year, Truman K. Gibson, Jr., the Negro lawyer, had become president of the International Boxing Club, designated at the time by some sports writers as "the biggest man in boxing." Confronted by such a record, no one could longer complain that racial discrimination bedevilled the prize ring.

When sports columnists fell to accounting for the "Negro monopoly" in boxing in the 1950's, they brushed aside the arrogant observation of the few who sneered that the phenomenon was only one further proof of the race's essential animality. Most of them agreed that economic pressures—supplemented by the earlier successes of Louis, Armstrong and Robinson—were the prime factors in drawing into the prize ring young men who suffered discriminations in most of the more conventional employments. Still others point to the symbolic importance which fighting carries for disadvantaged minorities, and they bolster their case by citing the boxing successes of Jewish fighters like Max Baer, Barney Ross, Benny Leonard, Abe Attell, Louis Kaplan, and the former Irish-American champions such as John L. Sullivan, Billy Smith, Kid McCoy and Terry McGovern.

Joe Louis's readiness to risk his crown far oftener than the rules required; his modesty; his scrupulous sportsmanship; his quiet personal conduct; his patriotic war service as an enlisted man and in armed-service benefit performances; his devastating defeat of the Nazi Schmeling in one of the swiftest and most catastrophic knockouts in the prize ring's history; and his "deadpan" expression, maintained even in his supremest moments of victory (his handlers reminded him that the jubilant smile of Jack Johnson as he stood over

* Negro champions in the years after 1936, together with their divisions and the years in which they first won the titles, follow: *Heavyweights:* Joe Louis (1937), Ezzard Charles (1949), Jersey Joe Walcott (1951) and Floyd Patterson (1956); *Light heavyweights:* Archie Moore (1952); *Middleweights:* Ray Robinson (1951), Randy Turpin (1951); *Welterweights:* Henry Armstrong (1938), Ray Robinson (1946), Johnny Bratton (1951), Kid Gavilan (1951), Johnny Saxton (1954), Virgil Akins (1958); *Lightweights:* Henry Armstrong (1938), Beau Jack (1942), Bob Montgomery (1943), Ike Williams (1945), Jimmy Carter (1951), Wallace Bud Smith (1955), Joe Brown (1956); *Featherweights:* Henry Armstrong (1937), Chalky Wright (1941), Sandy Saddler (1948), Percy Bassett (1953), Hogan Kid Bassey (1957); *Bantamweights:* George Pace (1941), Harold Dade (1947); *Flyweights:* none.

his defeated white opponents had antagonized thousands of Americans), made him a national hero until his retirement.

Louis was born Joe Louis Barrow in a household of Alabama sharecroppers. Joe was three when his father abandoned the family, leaving his penniless wife and seven children to make their way to Detroit's black belt where they became relief clients and Joe found employment in the Ford Motor plant. The boy's rise in prize fighting owed much to the opportunity afforded to all aspiring boxers by the newspaper-sponsored Golden Gloves Tournament, and to his systematic grooming by three men, all Negroes: John Roxborough, a Detroit lawyer and real-estate operator and civic worker; Julian Black, a Chicago business associate of Roxborough, who managed hopeful Negro boxers; and Jack Blackburn, a trainer and former prize fighter.

Armstrong was the eleventh of fifteen children in an impoverished Mississippi sharecropper family which later moved to St. Louis. There he had the advantage of attending high school, "working out" at a colored YMCA, and finding opportunities to fight other colored boxers in a segregated Negro boxing association until he became its regional featherweight champion. Rejected by managers who declined to take on a colored fighter, he rode freight trains to California and there entered professional boxing.

Robinson (born Walker Smith) grew up in the Detroit ghetto, where his divorced mother toiled to keep the family off the relief rolls. Disciplined by hard work from the age of seven—shining shoes, washing windows and hawking newspapers—Ray resisted the pull of street loafers and poolroom toughs, and spent his time at a gymnasium where he watched Joe Louis train. Inspired by the Brown Bomber's success, he entered the Golden Gloves Tournament, and won first its featherweight championship in 1939 and then its lightweight crown in 1940. After wartime military service, he returned to the ring as a professional, and in 1946 found himself welterweight champion of the world. He later made barnstorming trips to Europe, sometimes as a night-club entertainer, and vigorously defended America against the charge that it still denies Negroes the opportunity to rise.

Impressive as was the performance of Negroes in boxing, professional baseball made still bigger news. Before 1947 not a single Negro was on the roster of any major-league club, but in May, 1959, the race filled fifty-seven positions in fifteen of the sixteen league teams: approximately 15 per cent of the total roster of the National and American Leagues. Again, when a seventh of the nation's big-league ball players were drawn from a race that comprised a tenth of the country's population, it was a sour critic, indeed, who could still complain of the color bar in professional baseball.

But the major leagues were not the whole story. The minor circuits showed the same heavy influx of colored players, and—even more astonishing to students of race relations—professional and semi-professional teams in scores of Southern cities let down the bars. Deep in the old Confederacy, a brilliant pitching performance, a home run, or a spectacular catch by a Negro player was as loudly cheered by white spectators as if it had been the work of a white.

No less surprising than the rapid assimilation of Negroes into organized baseball was the quality of their performance. Two years after Jackie Robinson became the first Negro big-leaguer, he won the Most Valuable Player Award in the National League, and two years later the same honor went to his colored teammate, Roy Campanella, who, until his widely regretted disablement in an automobile accident in 1958, was frequently called the greatest catcher in baseball. Other Negroes have won the Most Valuable Player Award (Willie Mays in 1954, Don Newcombe in 1956, Hank Aaron in 1957 and Ernie Banks in 1958); have led their respective teams and leagues in batting averages, home runs and runs batted in; and at this writing it is a Negro, Willie Mays, who is generally regarded as the leading performer in organized baseball. His salary, incidentally, was eighty thousand dollars in 1959, more than any ballplayer had ever been paid before that year. The salary of Banks, perhaps the best shortstop and recently the home-run king of both leagues, was fifty thousand dollars in 1959, and several other Negro players were among the highest-paid professional athletes in the world. In recent years, Larry Doby, Minnie Minoso and Wes Covington have been pre-eminent outfielders; Hank Aaron has been one of the game's leading batters, and Don Newcombe and Sam Jones have been among its outstanding pitchers—while at mid-season in 1959, Frank Robinson and Orlando Cepeda were ranked among the finest first basemen. In the 1958 annual All-Star game (in which the foremost players of both leagues are pitted against each other) there were six Negroes on the two opposing teams: Mays, Aaron, Banks, John Roseboro, and George Crowe for the National League, and Elston Howard for the American.

The revolution began in 1945 when Branch Rickey, President of the Brooklyn Dodgers, determined both to break the color line in the sport and to strengthen his team, assigned Jackie Robinson (discovered by Rickey's scouts in an East-West Negro championship game in Chicago) to the Montreal Royals, a Brooklyn "farm," and then moved him directly to the Dodgers' lineup in 1947. Robinson's own teammates were so startled by the innovation that in his first season he trained, not with his fellow Dodgers, but with his former Montreal club. Rickey was sharply criticized for breaching the baseball color line, and the quick-tempered Robinson himself was at first the constant butt of opposing players and spectators. Negro sports writers complained that before the season was two months old he had been hit seven times by pitched balls, whereas in the entire 1946 season no player had been struck more than six times.

But Robinson's brilliant playing, and his unflinching race pride, won him quick acceptance and promptly opened the way for others of his race. (When he retired from baseball in 1956, he became vice-president of a New York restaurant chain, and a vigorous spokesman for the NAACP). The rapidly growing number of Negro players continued, in diminishing degree, to face hostile opponents and spectators and to be humiliated sometimes by hotels, restaurants and railroads, but the day when a team found itself padlocked out of Southern parks where it had planned to hold spring training, and was forced to find suitable training climate outside the country, in Cuba, Venezuela, Panama and the Dominican Republic, as did the Dodgers in 1947 and 1948, was by the middle 1950's a curious memory.

In 1958 and 1959, Negroes were playing in every position: pitchers, catchers, outfielders and infielders. They were no longer being recruited primarily from Negro leagues, but, like other players, were "spotted" by scouts and brought into the major leagues, either directly or through minor-league affiliates. They were native big-city boys, Southern small-town boys, farm boys from every section of the country, and not a few were Puerto Ricans, Mexicans and Cubans. Like white players, they derived from widely various backgrounds. Some came up through high-school or college teams, sometimes on athletic scholarships; some had all their preprofessional experience on obscure sand-lot teams. Sports writers seemed agreed that the fifty-odd Negro players in major-league baseball in 1959 were, man for man, abler than any random sampling of fifty-odd of their white teammates, probably because a colored boy still had to be extraordinarily good to impress a scout.

Those we have mentioned so far are among the most celebrated, but others were perhaps equally so. For our purposes, we can only list those who had a better press than the rest, for the number of colored players who had had a place in big-league baseball since 1947 was, by 1959, fast approaching a hundred.*

Colored football players were far less in the public eye than were baseball heroes, but much the same kind of steady assimilation was going forward for the former as for the latter. In college football, both Negro and "white" colleges and universities gave colored athletes a wider opportunity. When Levi Jackson became Yale's first colored captain in the late 1940's, the national

* Hank Aaron	Wes Covington	Clifford Johnson	Dick Ricketts
Felipe Alou	George Crowe	Sam Jones	Frank Robinson
George Altman	Bennie Daniels	Willie Kirkland	Humberto Robinson
Ossie Alvarez	Larry Doby	Brooks Lawrence	Jackie Robinson
Ruben Amaro	Solly Drake	Hector Lopez	Andre Rodgers
Gene Baker	Joe Durham	Felix Mantilla	John Roseboro
Dan Bankhead	Chicao Fernandez	Lee Maye	Willie Tasby
Ernie Banks	Curt Flood	Willie Mays	Joe Taylor
Earl Battey	Bob Gibson	Roman Mejias	Tony Taylor
Julio Becquer	Junior Gilliam	Minnie Minoso	Valmy Thomas
Joe Black	Ruben Gomez	Charlie Neal	Hank Thompson
Bob Boyd	Jim Grant	Don Newcombe	Bob Thurman
Bill Bruton	Lenny Green	Jim Pendleton	Harry Simpson
Joe Caffie	Pumpsie Green	Juan Pizarro	Al Smith
Roy Campanella	Elston Howard	Vada Pinson	P. C. Stevens
Orlando Cepeda	Monte Irvin	Vic Power	Leon Wagner
Roberto Clemente	Lou Jackson	Larrie Raines	Bill White

press took note of the event, but in succeeding years, Negro football heroes were becoming commonplace. In 1957–1958, Jim Pace, All-American star of the University of Michigan and the Big Ten's "most valuable player", shared headlines with Sidney Williams, of the University of Wisconsin, the Big Ten's first Negro in the crucial position of quarterback, and Prentiss Gautt, of the University of Oklahoma (which ten years earlier had no colored students at all), the first Negro to participate in a major university athletic team south of the Mason-Dixon line. In professional football also, Negroes began to appear on the squads of the major leagues, the most conspicuous of the gridiron stars being William Willis, who joined the Cleveland Browns in 1946, after a career in college football at Ohio State, and became the first Negro listed in the All-Time All-Star team of professionals in the National Football League's *Football Encyclopedia.* Another example was Emlen Tunnell, who in 1958 completed his tenth season with the New York Giants, the most durable halfback in professional football. Like Willis, he is considered one of the "all-time all-star" football professionals, and he is one of the two players in the history of the sport who had, by 1958, been named to every "Pro Bowl" game.

Golf was more resistant to Negro entry, but changing attitudes were heralded when Charles Sifford of Philadelphia became the first Negro to win a major golf tournament (the Long Beach Open) in 1957. Basketball, both college and professional, opened up in the 1950's, so much so that the 1958 selection of the ten All-American stars from major-college teams and small-college teams included no less than eight Negroes. In professional basketball, meanwhile, the barriers came down, and the race produced in Reece ("Goose") Tatum and Wilt ("The Stilt") Chamberlain, two of the nation's leading athletes. Chamberlain in 1959 signed a one-year contract for more than thirty thousand dollars with the Philadelphia Warriors and became the highest paid basketball player in the history of the National Basketball Association.

In track and field sports, Mal Whitfield established Olympic 800-meter records in 1948 and 1952, while Harrison Dillard was the Olympic sprint champion in the same two international competitions. In 1958, Rafer Johnson, a student at the University of California, where he was president of the student body, won world-wide attention by establishing a new world's record in the decathlon at Moscow before a vast and incredulous Russian audience.

In tennis, no other Negro has had a record like that of Althea Gibson, by 1957 the foremost woman tennis player of the world. The hard climb had been not a little eased by important helps. She was born in a tiny South Carolina hamlet and reared in Harlem, in whose congested streets she participated in far rougher sports than her favorite paddle tennis. When she was fifteen, Harlem's Cosmopolitan Club (whose tennis professional, Fred Johnson, had trained her) sent her to the colored American Tennis Association (ATA) championship matches at Lincoln University, Pennsylvania. She lost the match, but returned in 1944 and 1945 to win the association's girls' singles crown, and then, moving out of the juvenile class, reached the finals in the women's competition when she was eighteen.

Her professional promise interested two tennis-playing doctors of North Carolina and Virginia, who undertook to groom her for major championship play on the other side of the color line. When her first United States Lawn Tennis Association (USLTA) invitation to Forest Hills came in 1950, it was in no small part because of the indignant insistence of the famous champion, Alice Marble, who pressed the USLTA hard to put down the color bar and open its competition to Miss Gibson.

As late as 1955, when she had been a champion of the ATA for a decade, but had been defeated at Forest Hills, she lost hope of winning the ranking "White" championships and prepared to enter the Women's Army Corps, but the State Department, just in time to save her career, offered her, with the joint sponsorship of the USLTA, an eight-month world tour. On her travels in 1956 she picked up a string of European and Asian tennis crowns, and then in 1957 she made a clean sweep of the Wimbledon, England, international matches in June; the National Clay Courts competition at Chicago in July; and the Nationals at Forest Hills in September. Upon her return from Wimbledon, she was welcomed by the traditional Broadway ticker-tape parade, led by the Mayor of New York and witnessed by a crowd of a hundred thousand. In 1958 she repeated her Wimbledon success, taking both the international singles and doubles championships, and narrowly missing the mixed-doubles crown.

This roll call of the Negro Vanguard must, of course, be terminated at a point far short of a full roster of the colored movers and shakers of American social history. Then let it end here with this symbol: an angular, solemn colored girl, who rose from a sharecropper's cabin in South Carolina, by way of the streets of Harlem, to be crowned queen of the genteel courts of Wimbledon and Forest Hills, the applause of her countrymen ringing in her ears, and messages of congratulation from the President of the United States and the Governor of New York in her hands.

This work was undertaken as straightforward history and, as I believe, without fear or favor. But no one can live long with this theme without yielding to an impulse to reaffirm his faith in America. While these last pages were being written in the spring of 1959, the world was shocked and saddened—but not more shocked and saddened than America was—by the outbreak once more, perhaps for the last time, of a lynching on the old, now nearly forgotten, model, this time in Poplarville, Mississippi. But the very revulsion, the anguished cry that it elicited from the country as it recoiled before this specter from the past, was itself the best proof that America wants nothing more than to put these evil memories behind her.

The pity is that the Poplarville story reverberates throughout the world; and this egregious incongruity, this unbelievable anachronism, will for some time now be the message from America to many who might better ponder the story of the Negro Vanguard. They have conquered the last domestic frontier of the United States, these colored Americans. These exemplars of our pioneers are incorporating at last into the larger commonwealth what was formerly an outlying colony.

By their courage and their faith, their strength and their skills, they have opened doors where the millions may follow. For every Negro now knows in his heart, if he considers the record of this vanguard (despite all the surviving hostilities and social rigidities in some corners of America, and still countenanced in some degree by most Americans in every quarter of the country), that the law and the momentum of the American tradition are on his side. He knows that any colored child born in the 1950's, if nature has equipped him for it, may realistically hope for a place of pre-eminence in any art, in any science, in any profession, in any industry, without the fear that mere color will thwart his dreams. And for the more modestly endowed who march in legions behind the vanguard, and who make up the bulk of every race, there will be room for the Negro, too, in every employment in the land.

And let it be remembered that the Negro did not make his way alone. The white man also had to fight off his primal fears, his parochial prides, through uneasy years of doubt and discipline, before he came to see that here, too—to borrow the image of Donne—no man is an island, entire of itself; the Negro community is a piece of the continent, a part of the main; and any Negro's lessening diminishes America, for the Negro, too, is now, at last, truly involved in America.

Essay on Authorities

For the current generation of Negro leaders, much the most important source for both information and interpretation was the personal interviews I had with more than 130 of the most celebrated Negro Americans, in a wide range of fields. A few of the interviews were very brief, but in most cases they ran to ninety minutes or two hours, and some were considerably longer. My choice of interviewees was somewhat limited by geographical considerations; most of them were concentrated in New York, Chicago and Washington, with an additional scattering from the South. Several whom I hoped to see could not be reached because they were abroad or ill. A very few persons of whom I requested an audience declined to grant it, but the majority were extraordinarily kind and cooperative. In many cases information was given in confidence, some of it not to be made public at all but offered to aid me in forming conclusions and impressions, and some of it to be used with adequate safeguards for the anonymity of the deponent.

In no case was my evaluation of a particular interviewee based exclusively on my conversation with him, and it is not to be supposed that my informants are responsible for the character I give them in my book. In some cases I found it difficult to induce them to enlarge upon the grounds upon which their distinction rests; but if anything surprised me more than the candor of these persons and their eagerness to promote the objects of my study, it was the singular lack of bitterness; the resilient faith in the essential health of American society and the ultimate triumph of full justice and opportunity for all Americans. None of them spoke in anger—conceivably, it was the angry ones whom I failed to reach—but many of them, as they ran their recollections over their own past and that of their forebears, talked with manifest emotion, some of them giving way to sobs and then begging me to forgive them for their "foolishness" when they recovered themselves. To all of them I am, of course, deeply grateful. The notes in the latter portion of this bibliographical essay will identify, at appropriate points, the persons with whom I talked.

I. Basic Bibliography

The quantity of literature on Negro life and history in America is enormous and growing rapidly. Notice will be taken here only of materials directly exploited by this study. In this first section will be presented the general sources which proved useful in the enterprise as a whole. A second section combining notes with bibliography will follow the organization of the volume and comment on the materials from which my narrative was, at least in some measure, derived.

The starting point was *Dictionary of American Biography,* Allen Johnson and Dumas Malone, eds., (20 vols., plus supplements, New York, 1928–), a monumental work of scholarship, prepared under the supervision of the American Council of Learned Societies. It contains biographical sketches of notable Americans from early colonial times to 1936, not including individuals still living at the latter date. Nearly sixteen thousand persons appear in the work, only one hundred of whom are Negroes. There is no guide to Negro biographies in the index, and it was necessary to scan all the biographical sketches in the *DAB* to find those that treat persons of color. Eighty-nine of them are identified in my article, "The Distinguished Negro in America, 1770–1936," *American Historical Review,* LX (Apr., 1955), pp. 527–547. Since that paper was published another *DAB* volume (Supplement Two) has appeared, listing eminent Americans who died between Dec. 31, 1936, and Dec. 31, 1940, including the following Negroes: Robert S. Abbott, Marcus Garvey, John Hope, James Weldon Johnson, John R. Lynch, Kelly Miller, Robert R. Moton, Joseph ("King") Oliver Gertrude ("Ma") Rainey, Bessie Smith and Henry O. Tanner.

For the period after 1936, a careful search was made of four volumes of *Who's Who in America* (Chicago; volumes for the years 1936–1937, 1944–1945, 1950–1951 and 1954–1955). Because of the high critical standards of the *DAB,* all persons there listed who are known to be Negroes are included in my roster of distinguished Negro Americans. In the case of the *Who's Who* volumes, I was more selective, checking the claims of prospective candidates against testimony supplied by other sources in the list of authorities here under discussion.

The number of Negroes in the *Who's Who* volumes rose from 82 (out of a total of 31,434 listees) in 1936–1937, to 192 (out of a total of 48,650) in 1954–1955, but because the task of singling them out from so large a volume of names is enormously tedious (they are, of course, not identified as Negroes in the biographical sketches), some—but, it is believed, very few—may have been missed. Some characterization of those who achieved *Who's Who* notice—and a note on the limitations of such listing as an index of "distinction," is available in my essays, "The Negro in *Who's Who in America,* 1936–1955," *Journal of Negro History,* XLII (October, 1957), pp. 261–282; and "Negro Religious and Educational Leaders in *Who's Who in America,* 1936–1955," *Journal of Negro Education,* XXVI (Spring, 1957), pp. 182–192. Also useful, both for determining which persons to include in the present study, and for the biographical data they afford, were successive volumes of *Who's Who in Colored America* (Yonkers, 1927, 1928, 1930, 1933, 1941, 1950).

The standard general histories of the Negro in America—all of them written by Negro scholars—were examined both for background and to discover which persons in the Negroes' past receive most prominent notice from their own historians. These include John Hope Franklin, *From Slavery to Freedom* (New York, 1947); Carter G. Woodson, *The Negro in Our History* (Washington, 1945, eighth edition); Benjamin G. Brawley, *A Social History of the American Negro* (New York, 1921); George Washington Williams, *History of the Negro Race in America* (2 vols., New York, 1882). Franklin's is a balanced treatment, written in the tradition of modern critical scholarship; the others are in varying degrees "race-advance conscious." A recent, thoughtful survey of special aspects of the story, based on materials left by Alain Leroy Locke, is Margaret Just Butcher, *The Negro in American Culture* (New York, 1956), and an excellent brief history published as a paperback is Rayford Logan, *The Negro in the United States* (Princeton, 1957). Also of interest for the frank intention which the title implies, is Merle Eppse, *The Negro, Too, in American History* (Chicago, 1939).

A readable popular, if somewhat uncritical, running history of the Negro in America is Roi Ottley, *Black Odyssey* (New York, 1948), and a valuable recent addition to the *Mainstream of America* series is Saunders Redding, *The Lonesome Road; the Story of the Negro's Part in America* (New York, 1958). Redding's earlier work, *They Came in Chains* (New York, 1950), spreads a wider net and is charmingly written. Three older works, uncritical and clearly animated by the purpose of celebrating the race's potential and its achievements, and of generating race pride, but useful on several particulars, are Clement Richardson, ed., *National Cyclopedia of the Colored Race* (Montgomery, 1919); William J. Simmons, *Men of Mark; Eminent, Progressive, and Rising* (Cleveland, 1887); and William Wells Brown, *The Black Man: his Antecedents, his Genius, and his Achievements* (New York, 1863).

Some major (and controversial) works of scholarship shedding further light on Negro life in America in general but also on the problem of selecting the most eminent are E. Franklin Frazier, *The Negro in the United States* (New York, 1949); *idem., The Negro Family in the United States* (New York, 1939); and *idem., The Black Bourgeoisie* (Glencoe, 1957). A balanced survey is Maurice R. Davie, *Negroes in American Society* (New York, 1949). Extremely valuable to this study from other points of view were William E. B. Du Bois, *Black Folk Then and Now: an Essay in the History and Sociology of the Negro Race* (New York, 1939). Pertinent both for general background and as a guide to the choice of names for inclusion in my roster of distinguished Negroes was that treasury of information assembled under the sponsorship of the Carnegie Corporation of New York, by Gunnar Myrdal and his associates, *The American Dilemma* (2 vols., New York, 1944). Vernon Loggins, *The Negro Author; his Development in America* (New York, 1931), by a white scholar, had a much wider relevance to this study than the title suggests. Immensely useful also was William E. B. Du Bois and Guy B. Johnson, eds., *Encyclopedia of the Negro* (preparatory volume, New York, 1946), a catalogue of all the topics, including persons, that were to have been the subjects of sketches in that projected work.

There is a profusion of books offering collections of biographical sketches of celebrated Negroes, all of them, in varying measure, written with a view to emphasizing the race's contribution and achievement, to stir a spirit of race pride and emulation in the Negro community, and to argue the case for a greater appreciation of Negro accomplishment on the part of white Americans. They vary greatly in sophistication, reliability, literary merit and the types of readers to whom they are addressed. Some of the titles in this category include Arna Bontemps, *Story of the Negro* (New York, 1948); Langston Hughes, *Famous American Negroes* (New York, 1954); Ben Albert Richardson, *Great American Negroes* (second edition, revised by William A. Fahey, New York, 1956); Benjamin G. Brawley, *The Negro Genius* (New York, 1947) *idem., Negro Builders and Heroes* (Chapel Hill, 1937); *idem., Early Negro American Writers* (Chapel Hill, 1935); Elisabeth Ross Haynes, *Unsung Heroes* (New York, 1921); Phillip Lotz, ed., *Rising Above Color* (New York, 1943); Mary White Ovington, *Portraits in Color* (New York, 1927); Edward Embree, *13 Against the Odds* (New York, 1944); E. P. Derricotte, G. C. Turner and J. H. Roy, *Word Pictures of the Great* (Washington, 1941). Others in this numerous category that I perused are Ralph W. Bullock, *In Spite of Handicaps* (New York, 1927); John Edward Bruce, *Short Biographical Sketches of Eminent Negro Men and Women . . .* (Yonkers, 1910); George F. Bragg, *Men of Maryland* (Baltimore, 1914); Hallie Quinn Brown, *Homespun Heroines and Other Women of Distinction* (Xenia, 1926); Arthur Huff Fauset, *For Freedom* (Philadelphia, 1927). The authors of most of the foregoing were Negroes, and their works were of interest for this study, even when the sketches themselves were poor, because the selection of persons included bore upon our problem. A special type of work is represented by some of the titles of Joel A. Rogers, an indefatigable amateur historian and columnist for the Negro press, who enjoys a considerable reputation among Negroes as an authority on their past. Some of his titles, all of which make startling claims for the Negro celebrities with whom they deal, are *Sex and Race* (New York, 1940); *From Superman to Man* (fifth edition, New York, 1941); *World's Greatest Men and Women of African Descent* (New York, 1935); *World's Great Men of Color* (New York, 1946–1947), and *100 Amazing Facts about Negroes* (New York, 1934). Special attention is given in these works to the putative Negro blood in the descent of famous world and American figures.

Two recent volumes of high quality particularly important for this study for the choice of Negro heroes they select, are Langston Hughes and Milton Metzner, *Pictorial History of the Negro* (New York, 1956), and Lucille Arcola Chambers, *America's Tenth Man* (New York, 1957). Both present a pictorial review of the Negro's contribution to American life, and both stress individual Negro personalities. The latter volume has introductions and digests by a dozen contemporary Negro leaders in various fields of effort. Less satisfactory is an older work, Thomas O. Fuller, *Pictorial History of the American Negro* (Memphis, 1933), and less ambitious, but offering more biographical details concerning the many well-known Negroes it selects, is the folio-size picture pamphlet, Fletcher Martin, *Our Great Americans* (Chicago, 1954).

Additional data to guide the scholar in gauging Negro opinion as to the identity of foremost Negro Americans of recent decades are afforded by the volumes in the *Negro Handbook* series (Florence Murray ed.; 1942, 1944, 1947, 1949); and the successive issues of Monroe N. Work and Jessie P. Guzman, eds., *Negro Year Book; an Annual Encyclopedia of the Negro* (Tuskegee, 1912–). These works also are clearly conceived as "inspirational" books rather than as purely informational compendia. The Association for the Study of Negro Life and History (ASNLH), founded by Carter G. Woodson in 1915, accounts for a copious flow of published material, frankly designed to stimulate race pride among Negroes, to spur their youth, and to lay before the white world the Negro's credentials for the white man's full acceptance and respect. Their productions range from the scholarly *Journal of Negro History,* the country's chief repository for professional papers dealing with the history of the race; the monthly *Negro History Bulletin,* aimed at the popular—and especially the youthful—audience; and great quantites of promotional materials, including pictures for framing, dramatic skits and biographical data, supplied by the association to help celebrate Negro History Week in schools and communities throughout the country. The emphasis in all these materials is on Negro achievement and particularly on leading personalities. The files of the *Journal of Negro History* and of the *Negro History Bulletin* were searched for the purposes of this study. Also associated with the ASNLH is a book-publishing firm which formerly accounted for a considerable quantity of books on the Negro, again, centering upon achievement and upon outstanding Negro personages in the American past.

Another scholarly journal whose files were studied with profit was the *Journal of Negro Education* (Washington, 1932–). A number of leading Negro periodicals of a more popular character were also combed both for clues to aid in the selection of our roster of distinguished Negroes and for information about these individuals. Of great importance was the file of *Crisis,* the organ of the National Association for the Advancement of Colored People, founded by William E. B. Du Bois in 1910 and edited by him until 1936. During its first quarter century it was an immensely important magazine, brilliantly edited and containing an amazing variety of offerings. As other Negro periodicals developed, some of the older functions of the *Crisis* were supplanted, and it was modified to suit the more particular needs of the NAACP as a house organ. The files yielded a tremendous quantity of evidence that bore upon this study. Another significant publication in the same general category was *Opportunity,* published by the National Urban League from 1923 to 1949, and edited first by Charles S. Johnson and then by Elmer A. Carter. The *Messenger* (New York, 1917–1928) edited during its brief but important life by A. Philip Randolph and Chandler Owen, of the philosophical Negro left, also proved useful, as did the conservative *Southern Workman* (Hampton, 1872–1939), an organ of Hampton Institute.

Two more recent journals, *The Negro Digest* (Chicago, 1942–1951), and *Ebony* (Chicago, 1945–), also yielded a very considerable fund of information about outstanding Negro personalities and about Negro opinion as to who the Negro hero is. The first, frankly patterned upon the *Reader's Digest,* and the second, a Negro counterpart of *Life* magazine, were both founded by John H. Johnson. *Ebony* enjoys an enormous circulation but, like the now suspended *Negro Digest,* is a disappointment to some intellectuals because, though it has the ear of more Negroes than any other publication of the race, it follows a conservative and conciliatory line and, it is alleged, too often panders to unsophisticated tastes, wasting the opportunity to serve as a major force for the enlightenment and social progress of the Negro. Whatever the merits of the criticism, the enterprise is a robust commercial success and is evidently pretty much what its readers want it to be.

From the long list of Negro newspapers available to the student, the one chosen for analysis was the *Pittsburgh Courier* (1910–). Other leading journals include the Baltimore *Afro-American* (1892–), the Chicago *Defender* (1905–), the Norfolk *Journal and Guide* (1901–) and the New York *Age* (1880–). Only two "white" newspapers give considerable attention to Negro personalities in recent decades: the now-defunct *PM* (New York, 1940–1948), and the Communist *Daily Worker* (New York, 1922–), from the columns of both of which important data were gathered for this study by way of the clipping files at the Schomburg Collection of the New York Public Library. Occasional biographical sketches in the monthly *Current Biography* (New York, 1940) proved useful, as did feature articles and "profiles" on leading Negro Americans in such periodicals as *The New Yorker, Collier's, Life, Time, Newsweek, The Saturday Evening Post, Look,* the *Saturday Review* and the *American Magazine.*

Help in the selection of a roll call of distinguished Negroes is afforded by the list of winners of the Harmon and Spingarn awards, both established for the triple purpose of providing Negro talent with rewards not adequately supplied by the larger American community; to furnish incentive for potential Negro talent; and to call the attention of both colored and white Americans to the Negro's capacity and attainments. Other miscellaneous aids to the identification of the Negro's heroes are the lists of low-cost, black-and-white portraits of eminent Negroes sold by commercial publishers, and wall calendars, characteristically featuring a Negro hero-of-the-month and noting for every day of the year significant anniversaries of Negro American history (particularly the birthdays of notables). Not overlooked were the dozen Negro Americans for whom Liberty Ships were named during World War II.

There are a number of special studies which give major attention to leaders in particular fields; these will be noted at appropriate places in the second section of this essay on authorities. Of particular interest, of course, is the long list of autobiographies and biographies now available. Full-length life histories of more than a hundred of the Negro notables identified in this study were examined, comprising perhaps nearly all of the extant biographies of famous and near-famous Negro Americans, thanks to the facilities of such libraries as the Harvard University Library, the Howard University Library, the New York

Public Library, and the libraries of Bennett College, the Woman's College of the University of North Carolina, the University of North Carolina at Chapel Hill, North Carolina College and Duke University. The Schomburg Collection alone came very close to possessing all of them.

These biographies exhibit extreme unevenness as to factual reliability, soundness of interpretation and literary merit. The great majority of them must be used with caution and balanced against other available evidence, considering the "inspirational" objects they were written to serve. This is no less true of the later works in this category than of the earlier slave narratives that make up a fraction of the list. The latter were frequently ghostwritten or "edited" by Abolitionists, and their circulation was vigorously pushed by crusaders as an important phase of the antislavery struggle.

Another type of testimony turned up in the course of the perusal of all of the foregoing were lists of famous Negroes compiled by various persons and for a variety of purposes. *Ebony* magazine, for example, has its Negro Hall of Fame, and papers like the *Defender* and the *Pittsburgh Courier* frequently play the game of drawing up rosters of celebrated Negro Americans, either from the whole range of their history in America or in particular fields of endeavor or for particular eras. The popular-magazine press runs feature stories on the greatest Negro preachers or the most famous Negroes in art, or government, or music, and the like. These periodicals, time and again, in articles putting forward the race's claim to first-class citizenship, rely chiefly on the achievements of the race's most eminent sons and daughters, and such writing almost invariably invokes its sanctions by calling the roll of the Negro greats. Even blotters and posters, distributed for use in homes and offices and commercial establishments, serve these ends. A good example of the latter is a large wall map of the United States, published recently by the Friendship Press of New York, on which events and personages conspicuous in the history of Negro life are illustrated, and along the borders of which are entered the names of more than a hundred leading Negroes of the past and present.

The Associated Publishers of Washington, D.C., long identified with the Association for the Study of Negro Life and History and its revered founder, Carter G. Woodson, mailed out a brochure in 1958 offering for sale pictures of more than 150 celebrated Negroes. The brochure urges Negro Americans to learn "the history of the Negro race told with the pictures of its great men and women," and suggests that they "frame them and decorate your home with them. Hang them on the walls of your schoolroom." For my purpose the list was useful in drawing up the roster of the Negro Vanguard. I do not know what importance to ascribe to the fact that the largest lithographs—nearly life size—include only seven Negro Americans: Mary McLeod Bethune, Benjamin O. Davis, Sr., Frederick Douglass, Paul Laurence Dunbar, George Washington Carver, Booker T. Washington, and Phillis Wheatley. Pictures of the next largest size (11 x 14 inches) add nine more to the foregoing: Marian Anderson, Ralph Bunche, W. E. B. Du Bois, Roland Hayes, James Weldon Johnson, Kelly Miller, Henry O. Tanner, Carter G. Woodson and Charles Young.

I have also seen at the Schomburg Collection a list of seventy-one names, drafted in 1940 by L. D. Reddick and others for purposes of Negro History Week, and still another of forty-two names of Negroes inscribed on the panels of the American Commission at the 1939 World's Fair. A particular interest attaches also to a profusely illustrated pamphlet called *The Negro in America,* and clearly marked "Distributed by the United States Information Service," and widely distributed abroad with the frank intention of putting America's best foot forward. It bears a heavy emphasis upon achievements of colored celebrities, specifically mentioning some thirty Negroes, from both past and present, who are here introduced with evident pride.

Finally, the Schomburg collection supplied two other rich sources of information: a vertical file of newspaper and magazine clippings and other miscellaneous papers, with a separate folder for each personality, the folders being alphabetically arranged (I have examined a similar file at the Johnson Publishing Company in Chicago); and a vast body of materials in typescript and conveniently bound, assembled by the associates of Gunnar Myrdal and the Carnegie Corporation of New York in preparing the celebrated study, *The American Dilemma* (cited), and its allied volumes. Of particular value for the present study were the following memoranda: Sterling Brown, "The Negro in American Culture," particularly the section dealing with sports; Ralph Bunche, "Conceptions and Ideologies of the Negro Problem," "The Programs, Ideologies, Tactics, and Achievements of Negro Betterment and Inter-racial Organizations," "The Political Status of the Negro," and "A Brief and Tentative Analysis of Negro Leadership"; E. Franklin Frazier, "Stories of Experiences with Whites"; Guion G. Johnson, "A History of Racial Ideologies in the United States with Reference to the Negro"; and Edward A. Shils, "The Bases of Social Stratification in Negro Society."

A remarkable collection of photographs of celebrated Negro Americans, assembled by Carl Van Vechten, a close student of Negro culture, is in the Yale University Library.

II. Notes on Authorities

It is, of course, impossible to cite here all of the printed sources for the nearly one thousand persons with whom this book is concerned. Only selected bibliographical aids and some basic documentation are offered. Abridged citations are used for the second and subsequent references to particular titles, and full citations of works are not repeated if they were listed in the Basic Bibliography, above. The *Pittsburgh Courier* will be cited as *Courier;* and a few titles, after their first mention in these notes, will be indicated by initials thus:

CB *Current Biography* (*Yearbook*)
DAB *Dictionary of American Biography*
JNH *Journal of Negro History*
ND *Negro Digest*
NHB *Negro History Bulletin*

Part One: 1770–1900 (Pages 17–97)

Prologue. Pages 3–16.

The general argument of this section was influenced by a study of the works cited in the Basic Bibliography, and by years of perusal of the Negro periodical and newspaper press, as well as by conversations with Negroes, both famous and obscure. Although I am inclined to the view that circumstances pushed the Negro American's African past into the background, the question of African cultural survivals is one upon which I must decline to dogmatize. There is, I am aware, impressive evidence to refute my tentative conclusions on the point. Those interested in examining the case for the persistence of the African heritage may well begin with the works of two scholars who had the advantage of studying African culture on the scene, notably Melville J. Herskovits, *The Myth of the Negro Past* (New York, 1941), and Lorenzo D. Turner, *Africanisms in the Gullah Dialect* (Chicago, 1949).

The perplexities of defining a "Negro"

may be traced in Pauli Murray, ed., *States' Laws on Race and Color* (Cincinnati, 1950). For information about the Negro family in slavery times I have relied on Kenneth M. Stampp, *The Peculiar Institution* (New York, 1956); Arthur W. Calhoun, *A Social History of the American Family from Colonial Times to the Present* (3 vols., New York, 1945); Otto Klineberg, *Characteristics of the American Negro* (New York, 1944); E. Franklin Frazier, *The Negro Family in the United States* (Chicago, 1939) and *The Negro in the United States* (New York, 1949). See also my paper, "Social Origins of Distinguished Negroes, 1770–1865," in *Journal of Negro History,* XL (July, 1955), pp. 211–249. Some discussion of miscegenation in slavery times and beyond is available in E. B. Reuter, *Race Mixture; Studies in Intermarriage and Miscegenation* (New York, 1931), and *The Mulatto in the United States* (Boston, 1918). Testimony by social scientists on the general character of Negro life in America and on the effect upon the Negro personality of discrimination and segregation may be assembled from the books and learned journal articles of the "lengthening list of scholars" to whom I refer on page 15. They would include, among scores of others, Ralph Bunche, Horace Cayton, Allison Davis, John Dollard, St. Clair Drake, William E. B. Du Bois, E. Franklin Frazier, Buell G. Gallagher, Burleigh B. and Mary R. Gardner, Melville J. Herskovits, Charles S. Johnson, Guy B. Johnson, Abram Kardiner, Otto Klineberg, Hylan Lewis, Howard Odum, Lionel Ovesey, Robert E. Park, Arthur F. Raper, Ira A. Reid, Richard Sterner, Rupert Vance and Lloyd Warner. Besides the many books that touch upon these themes, the psychology and sociology of discrimination and segregation is now increasingly discussed in such professional journals as the following: *The American Journal of Sociology* (1895–); *American Sociological Review* (1936–); *Journal of Social Psychology* (1930–); *Journal of Abnormal and Social Psychology* (1906–); *Journal of Personality* (1932–).

The statement of Pauli Murray on page three is from her *Proud Shoes* (New York, 1956), p. 270. Langston Hughes's words on page five are from his "The Need for Heroes," *Crisis,* XLVIII (June, 1941), p. 206. Saunders Redding's observation on page seven concerning the average Negro's attitude toward his more prosperous fellow Negro, is from his article "What the Negro Believes," in Norfolk *Journal and Guide,* Nov. 27, 1943 (condensed in ND, II, Jan., 1944, pp. 3–4). Robert Purvis's retort to Douglass, quoted on page nine, is from the *Liberator,* Sept. 16, 1853, and is quoted in Loggins, *Negro Author,* p. 67. Walter White's remark about "passing" is from his autobiography, *A Man Called White,* p. 4. Sources for the quotations on page eighteen about irregular family relationships under slavery are from William Wells Brown, *Narrative,* p. 13, pp. 88–89, and *idem., Black Man,* p. 86; Henry Bibb, *Narrative,* p. 38; and Frederick Douglass, *Narrative* (1845 edition), pp. 2–3.

(*Pages* 17–24) Background for the period, 1770–1800.

The most convenient accounts of life in slavery are the two titles by the conservative, pro-Southern Ullrich B. Phillips, *American Negro Slavery* (New York, 1918), and *Life and Labor in the Old South* (Boston, 1929); Kenneth M. Stampp, *The Peculiar Institution,* which in the judgment of many historians is the best account in print; and the illuminating observations of a perceptive traveller in the 1850's, Frederick Law Olmsted, whose *Cotton Kingdom* has been reissued under the editorship of Arthur M. Schlesinger, Sr. (New York, 1953). For my remarks on the ante-bellum free Negro class I made use of Edward Raymond Taylor, *The Negro in Pennsylvania; Slavery—Servitude—Freedom, 1639–1861* (Philadelphia, 1899); James W. Wright, *The Free Negro in Maryland,* 1634–1860 (New York, 1921); John Russell, *The Free Negro in Virginia, 1619–1865* (Baltimore, 1921);

Luther P. Jackson, *Free Negro Labor and Property Holding in Virginia, 1830–1860* (New York, 1942); and John Hope Franklin, *The Free Negro in North Carolina, 1790–1860* (Chapel Hill, 1943). The best account I have seen of self-purchase of slaves is in Herbert Aptheker, *To be Free; Studies in American Negro History* (New York, 1948), pp. 31–40. The quotation from Douglass, on page 18, is from his *Life and Times* (1881 ed.), pp. 48–49.

(*Pages* 24–29) Leading Negro Personalities, 1770–1800.

There are sketches of Attucks, Wheatley and Hammon in the *Dictionary of American Biography.* On Derham, see Kelly Miller, "The Historic Background of the Negro Physician," *Journal of Negro History,* I (Apr., 1916), pp. 99–109. Accounts of Banneker are in Benjamin Brawley, *Early Negro American Writers* (Chapel Hill, 1935); Henry Baker, "Benjamin Banneker, the Negro Mathematician and Astronomer," *JNH,* III (Apr. 1918), pp. 99–118; William B. Settle, "The Real Benjamin Banneker," in *Negro History Bulletin,* XVI (Jan.–Apr., 1953, pp. 90–91, 105–108, 129–135, 153–158; and Shirley Graham, *Your Most Humble Servant* (New York, 1949). Prince Hall is treated in Harry E. Davis, "Documents Relating to Negro Masonry in America," *JNH,* XXI (Oct., 1936), pp. 411–432; and in Loggins, *Negro Author,* pp. 84–85. Hammon, Wheatley and Vassa are discussed in Loggins, *Negro Author,* pp. 9–29, 40–47; and Brawley, *Early Negro Writers,* pp. 21–74. See also Shirley Graham, *The Story of Phillis Wheatley* (New York, 1949), and Edward D. Seeber, "Phillis Wheatley," *JNH,* XXIX (July, 1939), pp. 259–262. Gustavus Vassa's autobiography is entitled *The Interesting Narrative of the Life of Oloudah, Equiano, or Gustavus Vassa* (2 vols., London, 1789).

(*Pages* 29–42) Leading Negro Personalities, 1801–1831.

Background for this era was drawn from the sources given above for the 1770–1880 background. Some, especially Chicagoans, press the claims of Jean Baptiste du Sable for recognition as a leading Negro of this early period. A free Negro of Haiti, he came to America, built a cabin on the present site of Chicago in 1779, and prospered as a fur trader. See Mercer Cook, "Chicago's Haitian Ancestor," *Americas,* IV (Feb., 1952), pp. 24–27, 41–42; and Shirley Graham, *Jean Baptiste Pointe du Sable: Founder of Chicago* (New York, 1953). All older accounts of the career of Richard Allen are superseded by Charles H. Wesley's scholarly *Richard Allen, Apostle of Freedom* (Washington, 1935). This work also sheds light on the careers of other religious leaders who are on our roster. Two other works which discuss several of these men are Carter G. Woodson *The History of the Negro Church* (Washington, 1921), and Loggins, *Negro Author.* See also John W. Davis, "George Liele and Andrew Bryan, Pioneer Negro Baptist Preachers," *JNH,* III (Apr., 1918), pp. 119–127; Miles Mark Fisher, "Lott Cary, the Colonizing Missionary," *JNH,* VII (Oct., 1922), pp. 380–418; W. Sherman Savage, "The Influence of John Chavis and Lunsford Lane on the History of North Carolina," *JNH,* XXV (Jan., 1940), pp. 14–24; G. F. Bragg, *Men of Maryland,* pp. 37–40; Wright, *Free Negro in Maryland* 217n.; Henry Noble Sherwood, "Paul Cuffe," *JNH,* VIII (Apr., 1923), pp. 153–229; Ray Allen Billington, "James Forten, Forgotten Abolitionist," *NHB,* XIII (Nov., 1949), pp. 31–36, 45. On Haynes see Timothy Mather Cooley, *Sketches of the Life and Character of the Rev. Lemuel Haynes . . .* New York, 1837); and W. G. Morse, "Lemuel Haynes," *JNH,* IV (Jan., 1919), pp. 22–32. For Nat Turner, consult Rayford W. Logan, "Nat Turner: Fiend or Martyr?", *Opportunity,* IX (Nov., 1931), pp. 337–339. And see Henry Highland Garnet, *Walker's Appeal, With a Brief Sketch of His Life . . .* (New York, 1848), and John M. Lofton, Jr., "Denmark Vesey's Call to Arms," *JNH,* XXXIII (Oct., 1948), pp. 395–417.

(*Pages* 42–58). Antislavery leaders, 1831–1865.

Again, the chief reliance for the background has been the works cited in the Basic Bibliography, above, and in the special studies listed for descriptions of the two previous eras. The abolitionist movement in the larger context of the antebellum reform effort is satisfactorily discussed in Alice Felt Tyler, *Freedom's Ferment; Phases of American Social History to 1860* (Minneapolis, 1944). An excellent introduction to the abolitionist movement itself is Gilbert H. Barnes, *The Antislavery Impulse, 1830–1844* (New York, 1933); but see also Herbert Aptheker, "Militant Abolitionism," *JNH,* XXVI (Oct., 1941), pp. 438–484. Some account of the Convention Movement may be found in John W. Cromwell, *The Early Negro Convention Movement, The American Negro Academy, Occasional Paper No. 9* (Washington, 1904); Bella Gross, "The First National Negro Convention," *JNH,* XXXI (Oct., 1946), pp. 435–443; Howard H. Bell, "National Negro Conventions of the Middle 1940's; Moral Suasion vs. Political Action," *JNH,* XLII (Oct., 1957), pp. 247–260. For special accounts of Negroes in the antislavery movement see Charles H. Wesley, "The Negro in the Organization of Abolition," *Phylon* II (third Quarter, 1941), pp. 223–235, and, by the same author, "The Negroes of New York in the Emancipation Movement," *JNH,* XXIV (Jan., 1939), pp. 65–103; Herbert Aptheker, *The Negro in the Abolitionist Movement* (New York, 1941); Carter G. Woodson, *The Mind of the Negro as Reflected in Letters during the Crisis, 1800–1860* (Washington, 1926). There is extended discussion of Negro participation in slave rescue operations in Wilbur H. Siebert, *The Underground Railroad from Slavery to Freedom* (New York, 1898); William Still, *The Underground Railroad* (Philadelphia, 1872); Henrietta Buckmaster, *Let My People Go* (New York, 1941); and William Breyfogle, *Make Free; the Story of the Underground Railroad* (New York, 1958).

Autobiographical works—notably the "slave narratives," some of which were ghostwritten—were themselves an important element in the antislavery struggle, for they were written as abolitionist propaganda. Autobiographical sketches ascribed to persons in the vanguard we have identified are Henry Box Brown, *Narrative of the Life of Henry Box Brown; Written by Himself* (Manchester, England, 1851); William Wells Brown, *Narrative of William W. Brown, a Fugitive Slave. Written by Himself* (Boston, 1847); Henry and Ellen Craft, *Running A Thousand Miles for Freedom* (London, 1860); Frederick Douglass, *Narrative of the Life of Frederick Douglass, an American Slave. Written by Himself* (Boston, 1845); *idem., My Bondage and My Freedom. . . .* (New York, 1855); *idem., Life and Times of Frederick Douglass . . .* (Hartford, 1887); Josiah Henson, *The Life of Josiah Henson, Formerly a Slave . . as Narrated by Himself* (Boston, 1849); Lunsford Lane, *The Narrative of Lunsford Lane, Formerly of Raleigh, N.C. . . .* (Boston, 1842); Jermain W. Loguen, *The Rev. J. W. Loguen as a Slave and as a Freeman. A Narrative of Real Life* (Syracuse, 1859); James W. C. Pennington, *The Fugitive Blacksmith; or Events in the History of James W. C. Pennington . . .* (London, 1850); Sojourner Truth, *Narrative of Sojourner Truth: Northern Slavery* (Boston, 1855); Samuel Ringgold Ward, *Autobiography of a Fugitive Negro: His Anti-Slavery Labours in the United States, Canada & England* (London, 1855). Other volumes in this category, although their authors do not appear in our roster, are illuminating; they are listed in Frazier, *Negro Family in the U.S.*, 662–667, and in Loggins, *Negro Author,* 408–457, *passim.* I have drawn directly from a few of them: Henry Bibb, *Narrative of the Life and Adventures of Henry Bibb, an American Slave, Written by Himself* (New York, 1849); Linda Brent (*pseud.*), *Incidents in the Life of a Slave Girl, Written by Herself*

(Boston, 1861); Austin Steward, *Twenty-two Years a Slave, and Forty Years a Freeman . . .* (Rochester, second edition, 1859); Francis Frederick, *Autobiography of Francis Frederick, of Virginia* (Baltimore, 1869); Moses Roper, *A Narrative of the Adventures and Escape of Moses Roper, from American Slavery* (Philadelphia, 1838). Biographical sketches of the following appear in *DAB:* Bell, W. W. Brown, Burns, Delany, Douglass, Garnet, Henson, Loguen, Nell, Pennington, Ray, Remond, Roberts, Roye, Russwurm, Saunders, Scott, J. McC. Smith, Still, Tubman and Ward. There are several book-length biographies, other than the narratives cited above. See F. T. Ray, *Sketch of the Life of Charles B. Ray* (New York, 1887); Frank A. Rollin, *Life and Public Service of Martin R. Delany . . .* (Boston, 1868). The numerous lives of Frederick Douglass include: Shirley Graham, *There Was Once a Slave . . . The Heroic Story of Frederick Douglass* (New York, 1947); Benjamin Quarles, *Frederick Douglass* (Washington, 1948); Booker T. Washington, *Frederick Douglass* (Philadelphia, 1907); Charles Waddell Chesnutt, *Frederick Douglass* (Boston, 1899); and Philip S. Foner, *The Life and Writings of Frederick Douglass* (3 vols., New York, 1954). The standard Biography of Sojourner Truth is Arthur Huff Fauset, *Sojourner Truth, God's Faithful Pilgrim* (Chapel Hill, 1938). The other leading Negro woman abolitionist is portrayed in Sarah E. Bradford, *Harriet, the Moses of Her People* (New York, 1886); Earl Conrad, *Harriet Tubman* (Washington, 1943); and Ann Petry, *Harriet Tubman, Conductor of the Underground Railroad* (New York, 1955). On Josiah Henson see Brion Gysin, *To Master—a Long Goodnight; The Story of Uncle Tom* (New York, 1946), and Jessie L. Beattie, *Black Moses; the Real Uncle Tom* (Toronto, 1957). A contemporary view of Lane is offered by William George Hawkins, *Lunsford Lane, or, Another Helper from North Carolina* (Boston, 1863). There is a section on Lane in John Spencer Bassett, *Anti-Slavery Leaders in North Carolina* (Baltimore, 1931), pp. 60–74; and a chapter on Crummell in William E. B. Du Bois, *Souls of Black Folk* (Chicago, 1903), pp. 215–217. Sojourner Truth is pictured in Saunders Redding, *Lonesome Road,* pp. 65–82, *passim.* Brief articles, some of them unsigned, on most of the colored antislavery champions whom we have selected are scattered through the files of *NHB.* Somewhat more dependable are papers appearing in the *JNH:* Monroe N. Work, "The Life of Charles B. Ray," IV (Oct., 1919), 361–371; Savage, "Influence of John Chavis and Lunsford Lane" (cited); W. B. Hartgrove, "The Story of Josiah Henson, III (Jan., 1918), pp. 1–21; William M. Brewer, "Henry Highland Garnet," XIII (Jan., 1928), pp. 36–52; *idem.,* "John B. Russwurm," XIII (Oct., 1928), pp. 413–422; Irving Dilliard, "Dred Scott Eulogized by James Milton Turner," XXVI (Jan., 1941), pp. 1–11; Dorothy B. Porter, "David M. Ruggles, an Apostle of Human Rights," XXVIII (Jan., 1943), pp. 23–50. Most of the thirty Negro rights champions whom we have listed for this generation are treated in Loggins, *Negro Author,* and in the several works of Brawley which we have mentioned, as well as in Simmons, *Men of Mark.*

(*Pages* 58–61) Other Leaders, 1831–1865.

For Victor Séjour, consult *DAB,* XVI: p. 565; A. E. Perkins, "Victor Séjour and his Time," *NHB,* V (Apr., 1942), pp. 163–166; T. A. Daley, "Victor Séjour," *Phylon* IV (first quarter, 1943), pp. 5–16. Thierry is sketched in *DAB,* XVIII: p. 417. An enlightening article on Rillieux is George P. Meade, "A Negro Scientist of Slavery Days," in *Scientific Monthly,* LXII (Apr., 1946), pp. 317–326. It is reprinted, with extensive notes by Sidney Kaplan, in *NHB,* (Apr., 1957), pp. 159–164. The beginnings of the Negro on the American stage are traced in Edith J. R. Isaacs, *The Negro in the American Theater* (New York, 1947). On Ira Aldridge, see *DAB,* I:160; Brawley, *Negro Genius,* pp. 91–93; Charles S. Johnson, "Ira Aldridge," *Opportunity,* III (March, 1925), pp. 88–90; Henrietta Buckmaster, "A Forgotten Othello: Ira Aldridge," *Crisis,* LI (March, 1944); and Herbert Marshall and Mildred Stock, *Ira Aldridge, the Negro Tragedian* (New York, 1959). Beckwourth appears in *DAB,* II:122, and is the subject of T. D. Bonner, *Life and Adventures of James P. Beckwourth, Mountaineer, Scout and Pioneer and Chief of the Crow Nation of Indians* (n.p.? 1856); and of W. Sherman Savage, "James Beckwourth—Negro Fur Trader," *NHB,* XVII (March, 1954), pp. 123–124. Elizabeth Taylor Greenfield is noticed in Brawley, *Negro Genius,* pp. 96–99; and summaries of the careers of Horton, Vashon, and Mrs. Harper are in Brawley, *Early American Negro Writers,* pp. 110–122, 261–278, 290–298, and in Loggins, *Negro Author*, pp. 107–117, 235–239, 245–248, 324–325, 342–344.

(*Pages* 61–63). The post-Civil War generation, 1865–1900.

Once again, the Basic Bibliography supplied the factual substructure. Specialized works which shed further light on the period are Henderson H. Donald, *The Negro Freedman* (New York, 1952), Rayford W. Logan, *The Negro in American Life and Thought; the Nadir, 1877–1901* (New York, 1954); George B. Tindall, *South Carolina Negroes, 1877–1900* (Columbia, S.C., 1952); C. Vann Woodward, *Origins of the New South, 1877–1913* (Baton Rouge, 1951), and *idem., The Strange Career of Jim Crow* (New York, 1955). For the Reconstruction years, the reader should balance the old accounts in the Rhodes-Dunning-Fleming-Schouler tradition by looking into Howard K. Beale, "On the Rewriting of Reconstruction History," *American Historical Review,* XLV (July, 1940), pp. 807–827. A. A. Taylor, "Historians of Reconstruction," *JNH,* XXIII (Jan., 1938), pp. 16–34; T. Harry Williams, "An Analysis of Some Reconstruction Attitudes," *Journal of Southern History,* XII (Nov., 1946), pp. 469–486; William E. B. Du Bois, *Black Reconstruction* (New York, 1935), and, by the same author, "Reconstruction and its Benefits," *Amer. Hist. Rev.,* XV (July, 1910), pp. 781–799. The Southern Senator quoted on p. 63 was James K. Vardaman, and the statement is printed in Paul Lewison, *Race, Class and Party* (New York, 1932), pp. 84–85.

(*Pages* 63–74). The Negro in Politics, 1865–1900.

Besides the kinds of sources indicated in the preceding paragraphs, I made extensive use of unpublished materials in the Carnegie-Myrdal study in the Schomburg Collection, New York, notably the typescript of Ralph J. Bunche, "The Political Status of the Negro"; *National Cyclopedia of the Colored Race,* Clement Richardson, ed., (Montgomery, 1919); *DAB* (which lists Bruce, Cain, Lynch, Pinchback, Langston, Rainey, Revels, Smalls, Smyth, J. M. Turner and Wright); Eighty-first Congress, Second Session, *Directory of the American Congress, 1774–1949* (*House Document no. 607,* Washington, 1950); Simmons, *Men of Mark;* Francis B. Simkins and R. H. Woody, *South Carolina during Reconstruction* (Chapel Hill, 1932); files of *NHB, Crisis, Opportunity, Negro Digest, Ebony* and *Phylon*. There is much useful information in William F. Nowlin, *The Negro in American National Politics* (*1868–1930*) (Boston, 1931). The standard account of the colored Congressmen, Samuel Denny Smith, *The Negro in Congress, 1870–1901* (Chapel Hill, 1940), though written under the spell of the older Southern scholarship, was immensely useful. Some articles of special interest in the *JNH,* are Alrutheus A. Taylor, "Negro Congressmen a Generation After," VII (Apr., 1922), pp. 127–171; E. David Houston, "A Negro Senator," VII (July, 1922), pp. 243–256; R. H. Woody, "Jonathan J. Wright, Associate Justice of the Supreme Court of South Carolina, 1870–1877," XVIII (Apr., 1933), pp. 114–131; Irving Dilliard, "James Milton Turner: a

Little Known Benefactor of His People," XIX (Oct., 1934), pp. 372–411; Roy Garvin, "Benjamin, or 'Pap', Singleton and his Followers," XXXIII (Jan., 1937), pp. 50–92; John G. Van Deusen, "The Exodus of 1879," XXI (Apr., 1936), pp. 111–129. See also A. E. Perkins, "Oscar J. Dunn," in *Phylon,* IV (second quarter, 1943), pp. 105–121; Marcus B. Christian, "The Theory of the Poisoning of Oscar J. Dunn," *Phylon,* VI (third quarter, 1945), pp. 255–266; and Walter L. Fleming, " 'Pap' Singleton, the Moses of the Colored Exodus," *American Journal of Sociology,* XV (July, 1909), pp. 61–82. The biographies of politicians of the period are Maud Cuney Hare, *Norris Wright Cuney; a Tribune of the Black People* (New York, 1913); John Mercer Langston, *From the Virginia Plantation to the National Capitol; or the First and Only Negro Representative in Congress from the Old Dominion* (Hartford, 1894); Dorothy Sterling, *Captain of the Planter; the Story of Robert Smalls* (New York, 1958); Geraldine E. Wheeler, "Hiram Rhoades Revels; Negro Educator and Statesman," (unpublished dissertation at the University of California, Berkeley, 1949); and William H. Heard, *From Slavery to the Bishopric of the A.M.E. Church* (Philadelphia, 1924).

(*Pages* 74–88). Religious and educational leaders, 1865–1900.

For information about the post-Civil War development of the Negro church and school and their leaders, I am indebted to the files of *Crisis, Opportunity, NHB,* newspaper files, and the volumes of Loggins, Simmons, and Clement Richardson, all previously cited. I have drawn also from the early volumes of *Who's Who in America* (Chicago, 1899–), and from John William Gibson and W. H. Crogman, *Progress of a Race or, the Remarkable Advancement of the Colored American* (Naperville, Ill., 1920). Special accounts of Negro church leaders were found in abundance in Woodson, *History of the Negro Church;* William Wells Brown, *Black Man;* and *Progress and Promise, 1863–1910,* William Newton Hartshorn, ed., (Boston, 1910). Of the twenty-five religious leaders we have listed, the following have sketches in the *DAB:* Boyd, Brown, Gaines, Holly, Holsey, Hood, Love, C. H. Payne, D. A. Payne, Perry, Sanders, Tanner, Taylor, Turner, Wayman. Biographies and autobiographies are Albert S. Foley, *Bishop Healy: Beloved Outcaste* (New York, 1954); Isaac Lane, *Autobiography of Bishop Lane, LL.D., with a Short History of the C.M.E. Church . . .* (Nashville, 1916); Horace C. Savage, *The Life and Times of Bishop Isaac Lane . . .* (Nashville, 1958); Silas Xavier Floyd, *Life of Charles T. Walker, DD., the Black Spurgeon* (Nashville, 1902); M. M. Ponton, *Life and Times of Henry M. Turner* (Atlanta, 1917); William Jacob Walls, *Joseph Charles Price; Educator and Race Leader* (Boston, 1943); Josephus Roosevelt Coan, *Daniel Alexander Payne, Christian Educator* (Philadelphia, 1935); Daniel A. Payne, *Recollections of Seventy Years* (Nashville, 1898); E. A. Randolph, *The Life of Rev. John Jasper,* (Richmond, 1884); Levi J. Coppin, *Unwritten History* (Philadelphia, 1919); L. H. Holsey, *Autobiography, Sermons, Addresses and Essays* (Atlanta, 1898); Alexander Wayman, *My Recollections of A.M.E. Ministers, or Forty Years Experience in the African Methodist Episcopal Church* (Philadelphia, 1881). For the educational leaders, I have drawn from the standard accounts of Negro education, such as Horace M. Bond, *Education of the Negro in the American Social Order* (New York, 1934); and Dwight O. W. Holmes, *The Evolution of the Negro College* (New York, 1934). The volumes of the *Journal of Negro Education* supply information on every phase of the development. Biographies of Booker T. Washington include his own *Up From Slavery* (New York, 1902); Basil Joseph Mathews, *Booker T. Washington, Educator and Interracial Interpreter* (Cambridge, 1948); Shirley Graham, *Booker T. Washington, Educator of Hand, Head, and Heart* (New

York, 1955); Benjamin Franklin Riley, *The Life and Times of Booker T. Washington* (New York, 1916); Emmett J. Scott, *Booker T. Washington, Builder of Civilization* (New York, 1916); Samuel R. Spencer, *Booker T. Washington and the Negro's Place in American Life* (Boston, 1955); Anson Phelps Stokes, *A Brief Biography of Booker Washington* (Hampton, Va., 1936). I have also been influenced in my evaluation of Washington by my reading of Du Bois, *Souls of Black Folk,* chap. III, and August Meier, "Toward a Reinterpretation of Booker T. Washington," *Journal of Southern History,* XXIII (May, 1957), pp. 220–227. On Crogman, see *Crisis,* VIII (May, 1914), pp. 14–15, XXVII (Nov., 1923), p. 8, and XXXIX (Feb., 1932), p. 51; and *Twentieth Century Negro Literature,* D. E. Culp, ed., (Atlanta, 1902), p. 6–7. There is some account of Cook in *Crisis* XXXIX (Feb., 1932), p. 50, and of William Jefferson White in Ridgely Torrence, *The Story of John Hope* (New York, 1948), pp. 54–55, and Simmons *Men of Mark,* pp. 704–705.

(*Pages* 88–97). Other leaders, 1865–1900.

Greener, Grimké and Williams are in *DAB,* but see also Angelina Grimké, "A Biographical Sketch of Archibald H. Grimké," in *Opportunity,* III (Feb., 1925), pp. 44–47; Mary Anthony, "An Abolitionist and His Nephews, *ND,* IX (December, 1950), 22ff; John Hope Franklin, "George Washington Williams, Historian," *JNH,* XXXI (Jan., 1946), pp. 60–90; and a sketch of Greener in *NHB,* VI (Dec., 1942), p. 58. Johnston, Duncanson, Bannister and Edmonia Lewis are considered in the surveys of Negro American art provided by Alain Locke, *The Negro in Art* (Washington, 1940) and James A. Porter, *Modern Negro Art* (New York, 1943). See also Brawley, *Negro Genius; Crisis,* XL (March, 1933), p. 248; *Opportunity,* (July, 1923), p. 211; Isaiah A. Woodward, "Joshua Johnston: Baltimore's First Slave Artist of Distinction," *NHB,* XXI (Apr., 1958), p. 166; James A. Porter "Robert S. Duncanson Midwestern Romantic Realist" *Art in America* XXXIX (Oct., 1951), pp. 97–154; and (on Miss Lewis), *NHB,* I (Nov., 1937), pp. 6–7. The musicians mentioned in our list are treated in Brawley's *Negro Genius,* and in Maud Cuney Hare, *Negro Musicians and their Music* (Washington, 1936). On Bland, see John Jay Daly, *A Song in his Heart* (Philadelphia, 1951), and on Blind Tom Bethune see Kurt Juhn, "Black Beethoven," condensed from April, 1945 *Pageant,* in *ND,* III (June, 1945), pp. 33–38. Consult also Arna Bontemps, *Chariot in the Sky, the Story of the Jubilee* Singers (Philadephia, 1951). For information about the pioneers in business and invention, see the *DAB* accounts of Wormley, Lafon, McCoy and Matzeliger; Henry E. Baker, "Negro in the Field of Invention" (cited); Sidney Kaplan, "Jan Earnst Matzeliger and the Making of the Shoe," *JNH,* XL (Jan., 1958), pp. 8–33. See also *NHB,* IV (May, 1941), p. 189, and V (May, 1942), p. 187, and VII (Oct., 1943), p. 6, 20; *Crisis,* VI (Aug., 1913), p. 172; Hughes and Meltzer, *Pictorial History of the Negro,* pp. 52–53; Edward T. Clayton, "Four Chicago Pioneers," *ND,* VIII (Sept., 1950), 91ff; and Dan A. Rudd and Theo Bond, *From Slavery to Wealth. The Life of Scott Bond . . .* (Madison, Ark., 1917). Numerous references to A. A. Whitman, Dunbar and Chesnutt may be found in the indexes of Loggins, *Negro Author;* Brawley, *Negro Genius;* and Sterling A. Brown, Arthur P. Davis and Ulysses Lee, *The Negro Caravan* (New York, 1941). The standard biography of Dunbar is Benjamin G. Brawley, *Paul Laurence Dunbar: Poet of his People* (Chapel Hill, 1936); The quotation from Brawley on p. 95 is from page 77 of this last mentioned work, and a good recent life of Chestnut is Helen M. Chesnutt, *Charles Waddell Chesnutt: Pioneer of the Color Line* Chapel Hill, 1952). I have also benefited from a sketch of Dunbar in typescript, in the Schomburg Collection, written by Harry M. Lydenberg. For details concerning T. Thomas Fortune, see the typescript of G. James Fleming, "The Negro Press," in the Schomburg Collection, and also an account in the *Pittsburgh Courier*, November 13, 1926.

Part Two: 1900–1936 (Pages 99–202)

For contemporary commentary on general conditions and the progress of social change, I was increasingly dependent upon Negro periodicals, both scholarly and popular, and the race's newspapers—especially the *Crisis* and the *Courier*, both of whose files I combed from the year 1910 forward. "White" periodicals and newspapers were still virtually ignoring the Negro community and the Negro's contribution to American life during these years. Besides a large note file which I built up from the *Crisis* and *Courier* and other general Negro journals, the clipping files of the Schomburg Collection were very productive. I gained much also from the article "Negro Problem" by Abram L. Harris and Sterling D. Spero, in E. R. A. Seligman and Alvin Johnson, eds., *Encyclopedia of the Social Sciences* (15 vols., New York, 1933), XI, pp. 335–356; and from the Carnegie-Myrdal typescript materials now held by the Schomburg Collection. The autobiographies and biographies for the new period, more competently written, on the average, than were their predecessors, proved a prime source, as did my interviews with several of that generation's leaders who were still living in the 1950's, and who took a lively interest in the objects of my study without pushing their own claims for inclusion in the roll call of the Negro Vanguard. The *Ebony* article referred to on page 103 is Edward T. Clayton, "Famous Negro Sons of White Fathers," in vol. V (October, 1950), pp. 96–100; and the quotation from Woodson on page 104 is from the *Courier*, Feb. 3, 1940.

(*Pages* 105–120). Religious leaders.

My interviewees from this list were John H. Johnson, William Y. Bell, Shelton Hale Bishop, Robert E. Jones, Willis Jefferson King, William Jacob Walls and William H. Jernagin; and there are sketches of the following in the *DAB:* Clinton, Proctor, Russell, Walters. Autobiographies for the group include Heard, *From Slavery to Bishopric* (cited); Charles Henry Phillips, *From the Farm to the Bishopric* . . . (Nashville, 1932); Adam Clayton Powell, Sr., *Against the Tide* . . . (New York, 1938); Henry Hugh Proctor, *Between Black and White; Autobiographical Sketches* (Boston, 1925); Reverdy C. Ransom, *The Pilgrimage of Harriet Ransom's Son* (Nashville, 1949); Alexander Walters, *My Life and Work* (New York, 1917). See also Miles Mark Fisher, *The Master's Slave, Elijah John Fisher* . . . (Philadelphia, 1922). There is a "profile" of Walters, by Rufus E. Clement, in *Phylon,* VII (first quarter, 1946), pp. 15–18. The *Crisis* and the *Courier* devoted a great deal of space to the Negro church in this generation. Also useful were the following sources, previously cited: *Opportunity, Phylon, National Cyclopedia of the Colored Race, Who's Who in America, Who's Who in Colored America, Ebony, ND,* Simmons, *Men of Mark;* Woodson, *History of the Negro Church;* Myrdal, *American Dilemma,* chap. 40; Davie, *Negroes in American Society,* chap. 7; and Frazier, *Negroes in the U.S.,* chap. 14. Useful also were Benjamin E. Mays and Joseph W. Nicholson, *The Negro's Church* (New York, 1925) and U.S. Bureau of the Census, *Religious Bodies,* 1936, Vol II Parts 1 and 2. *Statistics, History, Doctrine, Organization, and Work* (Washington, 1941). For documentation of some of the internal struggles, stormy politics and scandals at denominational conventions and conferences, see *Courier*, Apr. 14, 1923; Apr. 28, May 19, June 2, 1928; Aug. 22, Nov. 20, 1931; May 14, 1932; May 16, 1936. And consult *Crisis,* X (July, 1915), pp. 129, 132; XII (July, 1916), pp. 117–118;

XIII (Nov., 1916), p. 19; XXXIX (July, 1932), pp. 220–221, 234, 236.

(*Pages* 120–135). Educators and scholars.

The same periodicals, newspaper files and reference volumes which were cited in the preceding paragraphs devoted much attention to Negro education, especially to institutions of higher learning and their leaders. Of particular value were the chapters (and accompanying bibliographies) in Davie, *Negroes in American Society,* chap. 6; Myrdal, *American Dilemma,* chap. 41; and Frazier, *Negroes in the U.S.,* chaps. 17 and 18. The volumes of the *Journal of Negro Education* were indispensable, as were the titles listed in the bibliography (above) for the educators of the previous generation. Of special interest are three pieces from *Crisis:* Arthur P. Davis, "The Negro Professor," XLIII (April, 1936), pp. 103–104; Charles H. Thompson, "75 Years of Negro Education," XLV (July, 1938), pp. 202–205, 240; and William E. B. Du Bois, "Colleges," XXXIX (Sept., 1932), p. 298. Of the persons listed on page 120. Aggrey, Ellis, Hope, Miller, Moton, Wilkinson, Young and Scarborough are in *DAB,* and others will appear in forthcoming supplementary volumes of that work. I interviewed Charlotte Hawkins Brown, John W. Davis, William E. B. Du Bois and Mordecai Johnson, and searched through the following biographies: Warmoth T. Gibbs, *President Matthew W. Dogan of Wiley College; a Biography* (n.p., n.d.) Edwin W. Smith, *Aggrey of Africa . . .* (New York, 1930); William E. B. Du Bois, *Dusk of Dawn: an Essay Toward an Autobiography of a Race Concept* (New York, 1940); Joesph Winthrop Holley, *You Can't Build a Chimney from the Top; the South Through the Life of a Negro Educator* (New York, 1948); Ridgely Torrence, *The Story of John Hope* (New York, 1948); Leslie Harper Purcell, *Miracle in Mississippi: Lawrence C. Jones of Piney Woods* (New York, 1956); Lawrence C. Jones, *Piney Woods and its Story* (New York, 1922); Robert Russa Moton, *Finding a Way Out: an Autobiography* (New York, 1921); and Elizabeth Ross Haynes, *The Black Boy of Atlanta* (Boston, 1952), a life of Richard Robert Wright, Sr. The following *Phylon* profiles were read with profit: "Carter G. Woodson," by Rayford W. Logan, in VI (4th quarter, 1945), pp. 315–321; "John Hope," by W. W. Alexander, in VIII (first quarter, 1947), pp. 4–13; "Kelly Miller," by Dwight O. W. Holmes, in VI (second quarter, 1945), 121–125; and "Benjamin G. Brawley—Teacher and Scholar," by John W. Parker, in X (first quarter, 1949), pp. 15–23. An obituary sketch by Du Bois, "Moton of Hampton and Tuskegee," in *Phylon,* I (fourth quarter, 1940), pp. 344–351, suggests that Moton, like his predecessor, Washington, was in his last years moving away from his earlier "softness" toward segregation. See another obituary notice in *JNH,* XXV (July, 1940), pp. 404–406. Other biographical articles of interest are Leonard S. Kenworthy, "James K. Aggrey, Reconciler of Races," *Jour. of Neg. Ed.,* XV (Spring, 1946), pp. 181–190; Charles H. Wesley, "Carter G. Woodson—As a Scholar," *JNH,* XXXVI (Jan., 1951); pp. 12–24; and Jessie P. Guzman, "Monroe Nathan Work and his Contributions," *JNH,* XXXIV (Oct., 1949), pp. 428–461.

(*Pages* 135–142). "Race leaders," 1900–1936.

Discussion of race leaders (in the sense of "race improvement" and "Negro rights" effort) is voluminous and often spirited in the works listed in the Basic Bibliography, and especially in the race's periodical and newspaper press. Particularly valuable were the typescript memoranda of the Carnegie-Myrdal study, in the Schomburg Collection: Ralph J. Bunche, "Conceptions and Ideologies of the Negro Problem," "The Programs, Ideologies, Tactics, and Achievements of Negro Betterment and Interracial Organizations," "A Brief and Tentative Analysis of Negro Leadership"; and Guion G. and Guy B. Johnson, "A History of Racial Ideologies in the United States with

Reference to the Negro." The student who wishes to find his way through the tremendous bulk of writing on this general theme may well begin by searching the files of *Crisis,* 1910 ff., and by studying the following chapters (and their bibliographies): Myrdal, *American Dilemma,* Chap. 35; Davie, *Negroes in American Society,* chap. 20; and Frazier, *Negroes in the U.S.,* chaps. 20, 21. For some additional side lights, see Roi Ottley, *New World A-Coming* (New York, 1943), pp. 236–253; Benjamin E. Mays, "What's Wrong with Negro Leaders," *ND,* VI (Jan., 1951), 45 ff; and an editorial "In Defense of Negro Leadership," *Ebony,* IV (August, 1949), pp. 62–63. See also a series by Kelly Miller in the *Courier,* Jan. 8–Feb. 26, 1938.

For details of the lives and careers of the sixteen individual leaders I have identified, I found much material in *Crisis, Opportunity, ND, Ebony, Southern Workman, Messenger,* the *Courier,* and in the clipping files at the Schomburg Collection and the Johnson Publishing Company. Fully as important were published biographies and my own interviews. I had long talks with William E. B. Du Bois, A. Philip Randolph, Channing Tobias, George E. Haynes and Elmer A. Carter; and I canvassed the following biographies: Catherine O. Peare, *Mary McLeod Bethune* (New York, 1951); William E. B. Du Bois, *Dusk of Dawn;* William Pickens, *Bursting Bonds* (Boston, 1929), Mary Church Terrell, *A Colored Woman in a White World* (Washington, 1940); Walter White, *A Man Called White* (New York, 1948). There is a section on Ida Wells in John E. Bruce, *Short Biographical Sketches. . . .* (cited); and see also *Daily Worker,* July 1, 1951. On Mrs. Bethune, see also *ND,* IX (December, 1950), 27 ff; *Crisis,* XLII (July, 1935), p. 202; and *CB* for 1942, pp. 79–81. For estimates of Randolph, see Allen Morrison, "A. Philip Randolph; Dean of Negro Leaders," *Ebony,* XIII (Nov., 1958), pp. 103–114; Brailsford R. Brazeal, *The Brotherhood of Sleeping Car Porters* (New York, 1946), Redding, *Lonesome Road,* pp. 249–265, and *passim.;* and a profile by Oswald Garrison Villard, in *Phylon,* VIII (third quarter, 1947), pp. 225–229. Of the thirteen leaders, eight may be found in the volumes of *CB* for the years indicated: Du Bois and Randolph, 1940; Bethune, Terrell and White, 1942; Tobias, 1945; Haynes, 1946; Yergan, 1948.

(*Pages* 142–146). Journalists.

The principal source for my observations on the press was a direct examination of the files of leading Negro periodicals and newspapers, but I made use also of the discussion and bibliographical leads in Davie, *Negroes in American Society,* chap. 8; Myrdal, *American Dilemma,* chap. 42; and Frazier, *Negro in the U.S.,* chap. 19. Also important was John H. Burma, "An Analysis of the Present Negro Press," *Social Forces,* XXVI (Dec. 1947), pp. 172–180; P. L. Prattis, "The Role of the Negro Press in Race Relations," *Phylon,* VII (third quarter, 1946), pp. 273–283; *idem.,* "Race Relations and the Negro Press," *Phylon,* XIV (fourth quarter, 1953), pp. 373–383; and G. James Fleming, "The Negro Press," typescript in the Schomburg Collection. Of the thirteen leading personalities whom I list on page 143, only one, Abbott, is in the *DAB,* and the following talked with me at length about their own careers and about Negro journalism: Claude A. Barnett, George S. Schuyler and Lester Walton. There is one full-length biography: Roi Ottley, *The Lonely Warrior; the Life and Times of Robert S. Abbott* (Chicago, 1955). On Monroe Trotter, see the profile by William Harrison, in *Phylon,* VII (third quarter, 1946), pp. 237–245; *New York Times,* April 7, 1934; and Charles W. Puttkammer and Ruth Worthy, "William Monroe Trotter, 1872–1934," *JNH,* XLIII (Oct., 1958), pp. 298–316. George Forbes, mentioned on page 145, an important figure who deserves to be better remembered, is considered in *Crisis,* XXXIV (July, 1927), pp. 151–152; and for Dunjee, consult *Crisis,* LXIII (Jan., 1956), pp. 23–26. Robert Vann is sketched in Norfolk

Journal and Guide, April 21, 1934, and *Opportunity,* XVIII (November, 1950), p. 343.

(*Pages* 146–150). Politicians.

For light on Negro politics and politicians, I drew chiefly from the columns of *Crisis* and the *Courier,* and the clipping files at the Schomburg Collection; but I also made use of the Bunche typescript, "Political Status of the Negro"; and Harold F. Gosnell, *Negro Politicians; the Rise of Negro Politics in Chicago* (Chicago, 1935); and Myrdal, *American Dilemma,* chaps. 20–23. I found no biographies for the period, but I interviewed Perry Howard and the widow of Henry Lincoln Johnson.

(*Pages* 151–156). Writers.

For Negro writers and writing, I depended on *Crisis, Phylon* and *Opportunity* (especially the contributions of Alain Locke to the latter two); Brawley, *Negro Genius;* Brown, Davis and Lee, *Negro Caravan;* Alain Locke, *The New Negro* (New York, 1925); and Margaret Just Butcher, *The Negro in American Culture* (New York, 1956). Biographies and my conversations and correspondence with leading colored literary figures of this and the next generation were also informative. I benefited greatly from an exchange of letters with William S. B. Braithwaite. Those in the list on page 151 whom I interviewed are Braithwaite, Brown, Du Bois, Hughes, Mrs. Johnson and Schuyler; and I had some correspondence with Arna Bontemps. Corrothers and J. W. Johnson are in *DAB.* Biographies I used were James D. Corrothers, *In Spite of the Handicap . . .* (New York, 1916); Du Bois, *Dusk of Dawn;* Langston Hughes, *The Big Sea* (New York, 1938), and *I Wonder as I Wander* (New York, 1956); Zora Neale Hurston, *Dust Tracks on a Road* (Philadelphia, 1942); James Weldon Johnson, *Along This Way* (New York, 1938); Claude McKay, *A Long Way From Home* (New York, 1937); and Walter White, *Man Called White.* See also a series of autobiographical essays by Braithwaite, "A House Under Arcturus," appearing in *Phylon,* II (second, third and fourth quarters, 1941), and III (first quarter, 1942).

(*Pages* 156–181). Musicians and entertainers.

For basic information about "serious music," and its Negro performers, I have used Brawley, *Negro Genius;* Hare, *Negro Musicians and Their Music;* and the periodical and newspaper press. I have had interviews with Abbie Mitchell, composer William L. Dawson, and Clarence Cameron White, and talked with Rev. Benjamin C. Robeson about his famous brother. I have also had a fruitful exchange of letters with William Grant Still. There are a few biographies for the group: MacKinley Helm, *"Angel Mo" and her Son: Roland Hayes* (Boston, 1942); Marian Anderson, *My Lord, What a Morning* (New York, 1956); Kosti Vehanen, *Marian Anderson: a Portrait* (New York, 1941); Paul Robeson, *Here I stand* (New York, 1958); Eslanda Goode Robeson, *Paul Robeson, Negro* (New York, 1930); and Shirley Graham, *Paul Robeson, Citizen of the World,* (New York, 1946). There is a tribute to Robeson called "Colossal Bronze," in Alexander Woollcott, *While Rome Burns* (New York, 1934), 121–131. See also Redding, *Lonesome Road,* pp. 275–286, for a recent sketch of Robeson. The literature of jazz and popular music and their Negro makers is vastly more copious. Not only did I draw a mass of notes from the Negro press and general magazines; the quantity of competent book-length histories and critical studies of jazz and the growing number of biographies made interviewing unnecessary. (I did, however, spend a profitable evening of conversation with Noble Sissle, whose long career in jazz brought him into close company of scores of the historic figures in the development of the form.) For a sampling of books on jazz and jazzmen see: Dave Bexter, Jr., *Jazz Cavalcade* (New York, 1946); Rudi Blesh, *Shining Trum-*

pets: A History of Jazz (second edition, New York, 1958); Rudi Blesh and Harriet Janis, *They All Played Ragtime* (New York, 1957); Leonard Feather *The Book of Jazz* (New York, 1957); Leonard Feather, *Encyclopedia of Jazz* (New York, 1955); Sidney Finkelstein, *A People's Music* (New York, 1948); Elliot Paul, *That Crazy American Music* (New York, 1957); Winthrop Sargent, *Jazz: Hot and Hybrid* (New York, 1946); Marshall Stearns, *The Story of Jazz* (New York, 1956); Ralph de Toledano, *Frontiers of Jazz* (n.p., 1947); Barry Ulanov, *A Handbook of Jazz* (New York, 1957); Barry Ulanov, *A History of Jazz in America* (New York, 1952); Louis Armstrong, *Swing that Music* (New York, 1936); Louis Armstrong, *Satchmo; My Life in New Orleans* (New York, 1954); Jeanette Eaton, *Trumpeter's Tale: the Story of Young Louis Armstrong* (New York, 1955); Robert Goffin, *Horn of Plenty: the Story of Louis Armstrong* (New York, 1947); Barry Ulanov, *Duke Ellington* (New York, 1946); W. C. Handy, *Father of the Blues* (New York, 1941); Alan Lomax, *Mister Jelly Roll* [*Morton*] (New York, 1950); Ethel Waters (with Charles Samuels), *His Eye is on the Sparrow* (New York, 1951). Collections of shorter biographical sketches are in Nat Hentoff and Nat Shapiro, *Hear Me Talkin' To Ya—the Story of Jazz by the Men who Made It* (New York, 1955); Hentoff and Shapiro, *The Jazz Makers* (New York, 1957); and Studs Terkel, *Greats of Jazz* (New York, 1957).

In addition to giving major attention to music, the contemporary Negro press devoted much space during this generation to the other entertainers who are discussed in pages 175–181. Enlightening also are Tom Fletcher, *100 Years of the Negro in Show Business* (New York, 1954) and, at a more sophisticated level, Margaret Just Butcher, *Negro in American Culture*. And see also James Weldon Johnson, *Black Manhattan* (New York, 1930), and Alain Locke, *New Negro*. Abbie Mitchell shared with me her recollections of a long career as a dramatic artist, and Mercer Cook gave me an oral account of his father, Will Marion Cook. Bert Williams, Richard Harrison and Charles Gilpin are in the *DAB*, and besides the biography of Ethel Waters, just cited, there is one more biographical volume for this group: *Bert Williams, Son of Laughter*, Mabel Rowland, ed., (New York, 1947).

(*Pages* 181–197). Artists, scientists, lawyers, and businessmen.

Background material about the fine arts and biographical data about the artists were drawn especially from *Crisis, Opportunity, NHB*, and *Messenger*, and from the volumes of Locke, Butcher, Porter and Brawley, which we have cited. In addition, I have also been instructed by Alain Locke's "The Negro's Contribution to American Art and Literature," *Annals of the American Academy of Political and Social Science*, CXL (Nov., 1928), pp. 234–247. There are no published biographies of any of the sixteen artists I have named, but William Eduoard Scott and Hale Woodruff talked at length with me about their own development and about the rise of their predecessors and contemporaries. The *New York Herald Tribune* for May 26, 1937, has an informative obituary sketch of Tanner, and there is an account of him in *DAB*. (Vol. XXII; Supplement Two). For the field of science and medicine, much the most useful accounts for my purpose were Lewis K. Downing, "Contributions of Negro Scientists," *Crisis*, XLVI (June, 1939), pp. 167–169, 187; Herman Branson, "The Negro in Scientific Research," in *NHB*, XV (Apr., 1952), pp. 131–137; and *The Negro in Science*, Julian H. Taylor, ed., (Baltimore, 1955). For the special case of medicine, the most convenient source on distinguished achievement by Negroes is the volumes of the *National Medical Association Journal* (Tuskegee, etc., 1909–). W. Montague Cobb, "Progress and Portents for the Negro in Medicine," in *Crisis*, LV (Apr., 1948), pp. 107–122, and his "Medical Care and the Plight of the Negro," in *Crisis*, LIV (July, 1947), pp.

201–211, are penetrating. The *Crisis* and the general Negro press for the period proudly set forth the achievements of Negro scientists which the white press ignored. Another source for these scientists were my interviews with Peter Marshall Murray, Julian Lewis, and with Margaret Just Butcher, who talked with me about her father, Ernest E. Just. There is a popular life of Williams: Helen Buckler, *Doctor Dan; Pioneer American Surgeon* (Boston, 1954); but see also Redding, *Lonesome Road,* pp. 128–148, 154–178. There are several biographies of Carver: Arna Bontemps, *The Story of George Washington Carver* (New York, 1954); Shirley Graham and George D. Lipscomb, *Dr. George Washington Carver* (New York, 1944); Rackham Holt, *George Washington Carver; an American Biography* (New York, 1943). Reservations about Carver's stature are expressed by Herman Branson in Taylor, *Negro in Science,* 7. On Just, see also Branson in *ibid.*, pp. 6–7, and the profile by S. Milton Nabrit in *Phylon,* VII (second quarter, 1946), pp. 121–125; and on Louis Wright, see *Crisis,* XLVII (Jan., 1940), pp. 14–15, 27. There are two biographies of Matthew Henson: Bradley Robinson, *Dark Companion* (New York, 1947); and Matthew Henson, *A Negro Explorer at the North Pole* (New York, 1912).

For the Negro in the legal profession, see Carter G. Woodson, *The Negro Professional Man and the Community* (Washington, 1924); Raymond Pace Alexander, "The Negro Lawyer," *Opportunity,* IX (Sept., 1931), pp. 268–271; and W. E. B. Du Bois, "Wide Opportunities for Negro Lawyers," *Crisis,* XLI (Dec., 1934), p. 371. On Charles Houston, see *CB* (1948); *Crisis,* XLII (July, 1935), p. 208. Of the lawyers I have listed I interviewed two who were still living in 1957: Perry Howard and James A. Cobb. For light on the evolution of Negro business in this generation, see the volumes of the *Crisis, Opportunity,* and *Messenger,* and the newspaper press. Consult also Robert H. Kinzer and Edward Sagarin, *The Negro in American Business* (New York, 1950); Abram L. Harris, *The Negro as Capitalist; a Study of Banking and Business among Negroes* (Philadelphia, 1936); Davie, *Negroes in American Society,* chap. 5; Myrdal, *American Dilemma,* chap. 14; Frazier, *Negroes in the U.S.,* chap. XVI. I learned much from conversations with Truman K. Gibson, Sr., Robert R. Taylor, W. J. Kennedy, and Asa T. Spaulding, prominent business leaders. "Madame" Walker is in the *DAB,* and the following biographies are available: T. J. Johnson, *From the Driftwood of Bayou Pierre* (Louisville, 1949), a life of Joseph E. Walker; R. McCants Andrews, *John Merrick; a Biographical Sketch* (Durham, 1920); Wendell P. Dabney, *Maggie L. Walker . . . the Woman and her Work* (Cincinnati, 1927); Elizabeth Ross Haynes, *Black Boy of Atlanta* (cited). C. C. Spaulding was widely noticed in the Negro press in his time. See his "What America Means to Me," in *ND,* VII (April, 1949), p. 15. On Alexander, see *Ebony,* IV (September, 1949), p. 58; and consult *Opportunity,* III (July, 1925), p. 222, and *Courier,* March 7, 1925, for accounts of Gillespie. Rutherford is sketched in the *Messenger* VI (May, 1924), pp. 147–150; Harry Pace in the *Amsterdam News* (Dec. 15, 1929); and Heman Perry in the *Courier,* January 5, 1929. On Binga, see Inez V. Cantey, "Jesse Binga; the Story of a Life," *Crisis,* XXXIV (December, 1927), 329, 350. For Paul R. Williams, see his article, "I am a Negro," in *American Magazine,* CXXIV (July, 1937), pp. 59, 161–163; but compare with Du Bois, "A Good Architect," *Crisis,* XLIV (Sept., 1937), p. 273, *Courier,* Dec. 4, 1943, and *Ebony* I (Feb., 1946), pp. 25–29. Granville Woods is noticed in Baker, "Negro in the Field of Invention" (cited).

(*Pages* 197–202). The armed forces, fraternal orders, and sports.

For the Negro and the armed forces, 1900–1936, I have relied upon my conversations and correspondence with James C. Evans of the Department of Defense, and Brigader General B. O. Davis (Retired).

There is an autobiography of Henry Flipper, *The Colored Cadet at West Point* (New York, 1878). See also obituary notice about Flipper in *JNH,* XXV (July, 1940), pp. 403–404; and Wesley A. Brown, "Eleven Men of West Point," *NHB,* XIX (Apr., 1956), pp. 147–157. Information about Col. Young I drew from *Crisis* XI (March 1916), pp. 240–242; *ND,* IX (Nov., 1950), 29ff; *Opportunity,* I (July, 1923), pp. 218–219; Johnson, *Along This Way,* p. 345; and from a letter of Col. H. O. Atwood (Retired) to James C. Evans, 28 July, 1958. For data on Negro fraternal orders I made use of *Ebony* V (Nov., 1949), pp. 19–23; Edward T. Clayton, "183 Years of Negro Masonry," *Ebony,* XIII (Sept., 1958), pp. 26–34; and an interview with William C. Hueston. For general background as well as specific information about sport heroes I used Sterling A. Brown, "The Negro in American Culture; Section I, Sports," typescript, 1940, in Carnegie-Myrdal tmaterials, Schomburg Collection. Additional data were supplied by Edwin Bancroft Henderson, *The Negro in Sports* (revised edition, Washington, 1949); and the Negro periodical and newspaper press, especially *Crisis, Courier, ND* and *Ebony.* It was these sources also, and a correspondence with the editors of *Sports Illustrated,* that determined my choices of the leading colored athletes for the period. On Jack Johnson see his own *In the Ring and Out* (Chicago, 1927); Denzil Batchelor *Jack Johnson and His Times* (London, 1956); and John Lardner, *White Hopes and Other Tigers* (New York, 1951). Nathaniel S. Fleischer, *Black Dynamite; the Story of the Negro in the Prize Ring from 1782–1938* (4 vols. New York, 1938–1939), is basic. There is some notice of Leroy Paige and other Negro baseball heroes in Harry Grayson, *They Played the Game; the Story of Baseball Greats* (New York, 1944); Robert M. Smith, *Baseball; a Historical Narrative of the Game. . . .* (New York, 1947); and A. Young, *Great Negro Baseball Stars, and How they Made the Major Leagues* (New York, 1953).

Part Three: 1936–1959 (Pages 203–341)

Because there is as yet no sifted historical record for the contemporary generation, heavy reliance was placed upon interviews. The other major resort was the Negro press, for the general American magazines and newspapers still had relatively little to offer. Biographical data drawn from the press, though voluminous, were for the most part extracted from hundreds of brief accounts and news items, and it is, therefore, not possible to cite them in detail. For background, the basic bibliography and other works given as authorities for the introductions to previous generations continued, but in decreasing degree, to be useful. Myrdal, *American Dilemma* (for which the research was conducted in 1938–1940), and even Frazier's *Negro in the United States* (1949) and Davie, *Negroes in American Society* (1949) were, by 1959, no longer abreast of the race's progress, for the last decade had brought Negro Americans forward so rapidly that a ten-year-old work is in many respects outdated. The race's press, especially after World War II, was optimistic, and much given to remarking upon the accelerated advance of colored Americans. See the annual surveys of Negro gains for 1953 and 1958, for example, in *Ebony,* IX (Jan., 1954), pp. 17–24, and XIV (January, 1959), pp. 86–90; and also a ten-year review, for 1945–1955 in XI (November, 1955), pp. 134–138. An earlier decade, 1937–1947, is summarized in the *Courier*'s report on the 1947 Fisk University Race Relations Institute, in the issue for July 28, 1947.

Commentary on the race's improving prospects came also from writers least likely to overstate it. The grand old man of the Negro left, William E. B. Du Bois, wrote, well before the desegregation decision of 1954, an optimistic and clairvoyant piece, "The Negro Since 1900: a Progress Report," in *The New York Times Magazine,* Nov. 21, 1948, pp. 24, 54–59; and, more recently, Walter White, then the NAACP's chief spokesman, published an even more optimistic book-length evaluation, *How Far the Promised Land?* (New York, 1955). Another example of a "progress report," by a liberal white scholar, is Guion G. Johnson, "The Changing Status of the Negro," *Journal of the American Association of University Women,* LI (May, 1958), pp. 217–220. I have drawn also upon *Courier's* account of the 1958 Race Relations Institute, in its issue for July 26, 1958; and such newspaper summaries as those in *The New York Times,* April 23, 1951, and *Christian Science Monitor,* June 12, 13, 1956. Further description and analysis—not all of it optimistic, and much of it controversial—is in Albert P. Blaustein and Clarence Clyde Ferguson, Jr., *Desegregation and the Law* (New Brunswick, 1957); E. Franklin Frazier, *Black Bourgeoisie* (Glencoe, 1957); Robert C. Weaver, *Negro Labor* (New York, 1946), and *The Negro Ghetto* (New York, 1948); *What the Negro Wants,* Rayford Logan, ed., (Chapel Hill, 1944); Thurgood Marshall, "What the Negro Wants Now," *Ebony,* XIII (March, 1958), pp. 66–72; Wilma Dykeman and James Stokely, *Neither Black Nor White* (New York, 1957); Harry S. Ashmore, *The Negro and the Schools* (Chapel Hill, 1954); Eli Ginzburg and others, *The Negro Potential* (New York, 1956); Wilson Record, "The Role of the Negro Intellectual," *Crisis,* LX (June-July, 1953), pp. 329–335; Charles H. Wesley, "Do Negroes Believe in Themselves?" NHB, XXI (Oct., 1957), pp. 2, 9–15; Charles I. Glicksburg, "Psychoanalysis and the Negro Problem," *Phylon,* XVII (first quarter, 1956), pp. 41–51; Abram Kardiner and Lionel Ovesey, *The Mark of Oppression* (New York, 1951). See also an issue of *The Nation,* CLXXXIII (July 7, 1956), devoted largely to the plight of the Negro in the middle 1950's. I have also drawn upon the inconclusive discussion of Negro class structure in Frazier, *Negroes in the United States, passim;* and Edward A. Shils, "The Bases of Social Stratification in Negro Society," (typescript in Carnegie-Myrdal materials, Schomburg Collection). The opinion survey cited on page 204 is reported in H. H. Hyman and P. B. Sheatley, "Attitudes on Desegregation," *Scientific American,* CXCV (Dec., 1956), pp. 35–39.

The annual *Current Biography* cumulated volumes (cited hereafter as CB) published since 1940, by 1959 contained biographical sketches (with useful bibliographies) of more than a hundred of the country's best-known Negroes. And for the period after 1936 an increasing number of colored Americans have been appearing in *Who's Who in America.* See my paper, "The Negro in *Who's Who in America,* 1936–1955," JNH, XLII (Oct., 1957), pp. 261–282.

(*Pages* 218–225). Religious leaders.

Mention of such men as "Father Divine," "Prophet" Jones, "Daddy" Grace, and other leaders of exotic cults has been omitted because they are almost never mentioned in lists of distinguished Negroes compiled by persons of color. Elijah Muhammed, a Chicago leader of Muslim Negroes has in 1959 a considerable following, but I have encountered little mention of him in the literature I surveyed except in the *Courier,* for which he writes. Sources previously noted in sections dealing with the Negro church were again drawn upon for this period. See also my paper, "Negro Religious and Educational Leaders in *Who's Who* in America, 1936–1955," *Journal of Negro Education,* XXVI (Spring, 1957), pp. 182–192. Those in the list on page 218 whom I interviewed at length were J. W. E. Bowen, Archibald Carey, Miles Mark Fisher, William Lloyd Imes, Benjamin Robeson, Shelby Rooks and Frank T. Wilson. Biographical sketches of the following are in *CB,* for the indicated years: Powell (1942), King

(1957) and Howard Thurman (1955). There is autobiographical material in Adam Clayton Powell, *Marching Blacks* (New York, 1945). Two other biographical volumes are L. D. Reddick *Martin Luther King, Jr., Crusader Without Violence* (New York, 1959); and James H. Robinson, *Road Without Turning.* (New York, 1950). There is a "cover story" on Martin Luther King in *Time,* LXIX (Feb. 18, 1957), pp. 17–20; but see also his own *Stride Toward Freedom* (New York, 1958), and consult Jean Burden, "Howard Thurman," in *Atlantic Monthly,* CXCIV (Oct., 1954), pp. 39–44. For the sordid side of ecclesiastical politics see, for example, "How AME's Elect Bishops," in *Ebony,* XI (August, 1956), pp. 17–23; and assorted news stories in *Courier,* Sept. 21 and Oct. 5, 1946; Feb. 1, Mar. 15, Sept. 20, 1947; May 14, 1948; Mar. 24, and Aug. 10, 1951; Mar. 9, May 17, 1952.

(*Pages* 225–239). Educational leaders.

General sources cited on page 358, above, were still useful for the present period. See also Ginzburg, *Negro Potential,* chap. III, and my paper "Negro Religious and Educational Leaders in *Who's Who. . . .*" just cited. A sharp attack upon Negro colleges and college presidents by a prominent colored writer is in Saunders Redding, *No Day of Triumph* (New York, 1942), pp. 119–139; but see also "The End of Uncle Tom Teachers," in *Ebony,* XII (June, 1957), pp. 68–72. For the progress of integration in institutions of higher learning see the files of *Southern School News* (Nashville, 1954–) and Guion G. Johnson, "Quiet Revolution in White Colleges," *Journal of Amer. Assoc. of University Women,* LII (March, 1959), pp. 133–136. Even before the 1954 Supreme Court decision, Negroes were faculty members of seventy-two "white" colleges and universities. Walter White, *How Far the Promised Land?,* 9. Educational leaders for the period, who are in *CB* (with dates) are Robert P. Daniel (1952), R. E. Clement (1946), Benjamin E. Mays (1945), Frederick D. Patterson (1947), Charles S. Johnson (1946), Mordecai Johnson (1941) and Charles H. Wesley (1944). I had some fruitful correspondence with Dr. Wesley and Dr. Bond, and interviews with the following educators and scholars on my list: R. E. Clement, M. Johnson, J. A. Colston, R. P. Daniel, John Hope Franklin, Martin D. Jenkins, Benjamin Mays, William S. Nelson, Patterson, Charles W. Thompson, Frank M. Snowden, Ambrose Caliver, Matthews Whitehead, Mercer Cook, Franklin Frazier, Rayford Logan, A. L. Harris, Lorenzo Turner, Merze Tate, and S. A. Brown, and the librarians, Charlemae Rollins and Joseph Reason. Those whom I have cited separately as scholars, who are in *CB,* are Horace Cayton (1946), St. Clair Drake (1946), Frazier (1940), Alain Locke (1944), Carter Woodson (1944) and Du Bois (1940).

(*Pages* 239–249). "Race Leaders."

To sources listed on pages 358 may now be added Wilson Record, "Extremist Movements Among American Negroes, *Phylon,* XVII (first quarter, 1956), pp. 17–23; Roi Ottley, "The Big Ten who Rule Negro America," *ND,* VI (Sept., 1948), 4–9; Calvin Kytle, "The Story of the NAACP," *Coronet,* XL (Aug., 1956), pp. 140–146; "The World's Biggest Law Firm," *Ebony,* VIII (Sept., 1953), pp. 17–21; "New Look at Negro Labor," *Ebony,* XI (Sept., 1956), pp. 25–28; "300,000 Members Note 50th Birthday of National NAACP," *Courier,* Feb. 7, 1959. Besides talking with Du Bois, Tobias, Randolph and Haynes about the present generation, I also interviewed three more recent additions to the roll of race leaders: Roy Wilkins, Lester Granger, and the late Willard Townsend. The only full-scale biography is that of King, by Reddick (cited), but brief life histories of Granger, King, Thurgood Marshall, Wilkins and Townsend are in *CB* for 1946, 1957, 1954, 1950 and 1948, respectively. See also "Daisy Bates, First Lady of Little Rock," *Ebony,* XIII (Sept., 1958), pp. 17–24, and the references to King cited above.

(*Pages* 249–254). Journalists.

Besides authorities cited in previous sections on journalism, I used "Summit Conference of Negro Leaders," in *Ebony,* XII (July, 1958), pp. 125–130; "The *Ebony* Story," *Ebony* XI (Nov., 1955), pp. 121–173. There are no biographies except Rowan's *South of Freedom* (New York, 1952); but editors, publishers and staff writers whom I interviewed were Louis Martin, Roi Ottley, Carl Rowan, Dan Burley, John H. Johnson, George S. Schuyler, Era Bell Thompson, Charles H. Thompson, William M. Brewer and Rayford Logan; and there are *CB* sketches of John Sengstacke, Ottley and Rowan in the volumes for 1949, 1943 and 1958, in that order. For an article on "Negroes on White Newspapers," see *Ebony* XI (Nov., 1955), pp. 77–82.

(*Pages* 254–275). Government and Politics.

See, again, sources cited on page 360, above. The only biographical volumes are Powell, *Marching Blacks,* and J. Alvin Kuglemann, *Ralph J. Bunche, Fighter for Peace* (New York, 1952). There is a discussion of the expanding role of the Negro in politics in White, *How Far the Promised Land?,* pp. 65–86. In my list of officeholders and practising politicians, several are in *CB:* Hastie (1944), Bunche (1948), Diggs (1957), Dawson (1945), Powell (1942), J. E. Wilkins (1954), Wharton (1958) and Clement (1946). The following granted me generous time for interviews: J. C. Evans, Frank Horne, Ambrose Caliver, C. C. Johnson, Edward R. Dudley, Elmer A. Carter, Francis Rivers, Hubert Delany, C. C. Diggs, William L. Dawson, J. Ernest Wilkins, E. Frederic Morrow, Irvin Mollison, Arthur Ford, Hulan Jack, Rupert Lloyd, R. E. Clement, and Perry Howard. On the four current Congressmen, see John Madigan, "The Durable Mr. Dawson of Cook County, Illinois." *Reporter,* XV (Aug. 9, 1956), pp. 38–41; Robert Gruenberg, "Dawson of Illinois," *Nation,* CLXXXIII (Sept. 8, 1956), pp. 196–198; also, on Dawson, *Ebony,* X (Jan., 1955), pp. 17–24; "Mr. Diggs Goes to Congress," *Ebony* X (April, 1955), pp. 104–109; "Capital Welcomes Fourth Negro Congressman," *Ebony,* XIII (Sept., 1958), pp. 98–102; (on Powell) *Courier* Oct. 11, 18 and 25, 1958; a series of five articles by Irwin Ross, "Adam Clayton Powell, a Post Portrait," in *New York Post,* March 26–30, 1956; Albert N. D. Brooks, "Profile of a Fighter (Powell)" *NHB,* XX (May, 1957), pp. 170, 191. For the Negro's resistance to communism, see an important study by Dr. Wilson Record, *The Negro and the Communist Party* (Chapel Hill, 1951). Concerning Benjamin J. Davis, Jr., the following are enlightening: his own "Why I am a Communist," in *Phylon,* VIII (second quarter, 1947), 105–116; Walter White, "Portrait of a Communist," *ND,* IX (Feb., 1951), pp. 84–85; and C. A. Bacote, "The Negro in Atlanta Politics," *Phylon,* XVI (fourth quarter, 1955), pp. 333–350. Other articles of interest are "Negro Judges," *Ebony,* XI (Feb., 1956), pp. 61–65; Alvin Rosenfeld, "Red Cap to Jurist," (Delany), *ND.,* III (July, 1945), pp. 79–81; B. Smith, "First Negro Governor," *Saturday Evening Post,* CCXX (Apr. 12, 1948), 15–17.

(*Pages* 276–284). Writers.

Besides drawing again upon the sources listed on page 360 above, I made much use of Butcher, *Negro in American Culture,* and my correspondence and talks with W. S. B. Braithwaite and Langston Hughes, but none of these is responsible for my conclusions. I have also leaned upon Arthur P. Davis, "Integration and Race Literature," *Phylon,* XVII (second quarter, 1956), pp. 141–146, and the annual evaluations of Negro writing in *Phylon* in the 1950's. Charles I. Glicksburg, "The Alienation of Negro Literature," *Phylon* XI (first quarter, 1950), pp. 49–58, and Allan Angoff, *American Writing Today* (New York, 1957), pp. 96–110, also influenced my judgments. Hugh M. Gloster, *Negro Voices in American Fiction* (Chapel Hill, 1948), was informative. The autobiographical volumes for the period are James Baldwin, *Notes of a Native Son* (Boston, 1955); Redding, *No Day of Triumph* (cited); Era Bell Thompson, *American Daughter* (Chicago, 1946); and Richard Wright, *Black Boy* (New York, 1948). I interviewed William Attaway, Era Bell Thompson, Gwendolyn Brooks, and Louis Peterson and found accounts of the following in *CB:* Wright (1940), Frank Yerby (1946), Ann Petry (1946), Attaway (1941), Brooks (1950) and Shirley Graham (1946). Other biographical articles of interest are "Mystery Man of Letters; Frank Yerby . . ." *Ebony* X (Dec., 1955), pp. 31–38; and another on Yerby in *Crisis,* LV (Jan., 1948), pp. 12–13. See also William Gardner Smith, "Black Boy in France," *Ebony* VIII (July 1953), pp. 32–42. There is a piece on Ann Petry in *Ebony* I (Apr., 1946), pp. 35–39; and there are items on Motley in St. Louis *Post Dispatch,* July 2, 1947; *Ebony* II (Sept., 1947), pp. 47–50; and "The Return of Willard Motley," *Ebony* XIV (Dec., 1958), pp. 84–90. See also a brief article on Ellison in *Crisis,* LX (March, 1953), pp. 154–158.

(*Pages* 284–303). Musicians and entertainers.

There are no full-length biographies of the newer concert musicians I have listed, but Mattiwilda Dobbs (1955), Todd Duncan (1942), Dorothy Maynor (1951) and Camilla Williams (1952) may be found in *CB.* I interviewed Carol Brice, Miss Williams, and William Warfield (who gave me also an account of his wife, Leontyne Price), as well as Shelby Rooks, who is Dorothy Maynor's husband. Printed sources were much like those mentioned on p. 360, above. For side lights on the later, and controversial, Robeson, see *Courier,* Sept. 3, 10, 17, 1949, on the "Peekskill Riot;" an editorial, "The Strange Case of Paul Robeson," *Courier,* May 1, 1947; William E. B. Du Bois and Walter White, "Paul Robeson, Right or Wrong" *ND,* VIII (March, 1950), 8–18; Earl Schenck Miers, "Paul Robeson, Made by America," *Nation,* CLXX (May 27, 1950), pp. 523–525; Walter White, "The Strange Case of Paul Robeson," *Ebony,* VI (Feb., 1951), pp. 78–84; Robert Alan, "Paul Robeson—the Lost Shepherd," *Crisis,* LVIII (Nov., 1951), pp. 569–573; Carl Rowan, "Has Paul Robeson Betrayed the Negro," *Ebony,* XII (Oct., 1957), 31–42; and Irving Kolodin, "Paul Robeson in Carnegie Hall," *Saturday Review,* XLI (May 24, 1958), p. 35. The foregoing, much of it severely critical, should be balanced by a reading of Robeson's own *Here I Stand* (cited). In late 1958 and 1959 even conservative Negro journals were proudly reporting Robeson's new triumphs in Europe on the concert stage and in the theater. See also, on Dean Dixon, the article "World's Foremost Negro Conductor," *Ebony,* XIII (Dec., 1957), pp. 48–56.

For jazz and popular music, the same general sources that served for the previous generation are pertinent. To them may be added biographies of later arrivals: Lena Horne, *In Person, Lena Horne* (New York, 1950); Billie Holiday (with William Dufty), *Lady Sings the Blues* (New York, 1956); and William Broonzy, *Big Bill Blues* (London, 1955). Interesting also is Gilbert Millstein, "Jazz Makes it up the River," *The New York Times Magazine,* (Aug. 24, 1958), pp. 14, 50–56. My allusion to the persistence of discrimination and segregation in jazz are founded on Leonard Feather, *Book of Jazz,* chap. 5. The quotations of Eldridge are from pp. 47–48, and from Shapiro and Hentoff, *The Jazz Makers* (cited), pp. 303–305. See also Nat Hentoff, "Race Prejudice in Jazz: it Works Both Ways," *Harper's,* CCXVIII (June, 1959), pp. 72–77; and Langston Hughes, "Culture via the Back Door," *ND,* IV (July, 1946), pp. 47–48. Of the newer generation of jazz artists and popular musicians, the following are in *CB:* Mahalia Jackson (1957). Dizzy Gillespie (1957), Ella Fitzgerald (1956), Nat King Cole (1956), Harry Belafonte (1956), Cab Calloway (1945), Hazel Scott (1943), Sammy Davis, Jr. (1956), Lena Horne (1944), Josh White (1944), Pearl Bailey (1955), Billy Eckstine (1952) and Sarah

Vaughan (1952). For actors, dancers and night-club entertainers, see again the sources listed on page 361, above, and consult White, *How Far the Promised Land,* pp. 203–211. There is an autobiography by Eartha Kitt, *Thursday's Child* (New York, 1956), and (besides those just mentioned) *CB* lists Geoffrey Holder (1957), Canada Lee (1944), Eartha Kitt (1955), Sidney Poitier (1959), Frederick O'Neal (1946), Pearl Primus (1944), Katherine Dunham (1941) and Hilda Simms (1944). I have interviewed Janet Collins, Pearl Primus and Louis Peterson. Additional data were taken from "Belafonte Becomes 'Big Business'," *Ebony* XIII (June, 1958), pp. 17–24; and the cover story on Belafonte in *Time,* CXXIII (March 2, 1959), pp. 40–42. Also enlightening are Nat King Cole, "Why I Quit my TV Show," *Ebony,* XIII (Feb., 1958), pp. 29–32; Thomas M. Pryor, "A 'Defiant One' Becomes a Star," *The New York Times Magazine,* Jan. 25, 1959, p. 21; Lerone Bennett Jr., "Hollywood's First Negro Movie Star," *Ebony* XIV (May, 1959), pp. 100–108. On Miss Hansberry, see "Negro Playwrights," *Ebony,* XIV (Apr., 1959), pp. 95–100; and "Playwright," *The New Yorker,* XXXV (May 9, 1959), pp. 33–35. See also "Do Negroes Have a Future in Hollywood," *Ebony,* XI (Dec., 1955) pp. 24–30; and, in addition, the annual reviews of "The Negro on Broadway," in *Phylon* in the 1940's and 1950's.

(*Pages* 309–319). Artists and Scientists.

I have relied again upon the titles listed on 361, above, and especially upon Butcher, *Negro in American Culture,* and Porter, *Modern Negro Art,* and upon several interviewees: Hale Woodruff, Charles Alston, Romare Bearden, Jacob Lawrence and Elzdier Cortor. There are no book-length biographies and *CB* sketches only Simms Campbell and Horace Pippin. But see L. D. Reddick, "Walter Simon; the Socialization of an American Negro Artist," *Phylon,* XV (fourth quarter, 1954), pp. 373–392; "Most Exciting and Tragic Job was her FDR Plaque," a sketch of Selma Burke, in *Ebony* V (Mar., 1947), pp. 34–35; and a profile of Campbell in *Ebony* II (Aug., 1947), pp. 9–15. See also an illuminating article, "Leading Young Artists," in *Ebony,* XIII (Apr., 1958), pp. 33–38. For the men of science, see again the citations for the corresponding section in Part Two, above. *CB* lists only Charles Drew and Percy Julian, but I had extensive interviews with W. Montague Cobb, T. K. Lawless, John Lawlah, Robert Jason, Lloyd Ferguson, Robert Barnes and Lloyd Hall. A revealing description of the position of the Negro physician is in Thomas Roy Peyton, *Quest for Dignity; an Autobiography of a Negro Doctor* (Los Angeles, 1950). Other items of interest are "Charles R. Drew, 1940–1950," an obituary article in *National Medical Association Journal,* XLII (Oct., 1951), pp. 501–506, 555. There is a profile of Julian in *ND,* IX (Mar., 1951), pp. 1, 52, and some account of his housing difficulties in Carl T. Rowan, "Why Negroes Move to White Neighborhoods," *Ebony* XIII (Aug., 1958), pp. 17–24. Lawless is depicted in "Doctor with a Big Heart," *Ebony,* XIII (Jan., 1958), pp. 51–56.

(*Pages* 320–330). Lawyers and businessmen.

Besides sources previously cited for leaders in the legal profession—particularly the files of *Crisis, Ebony* and *Courier*—I have again put my chief reliance upon personal interviews. Those with whom I talked were Earl B. Dickerson, W. Robert Ming, James M. Nabrit, Edith Sampson, J. Ernest Wilkins, Truman K. Gibson, Jr., Archibald J. Carey, Jr., Hubert T. Delany and Bindley Cyrus. There are no biographical volumes and *CB* includes only Thurgood Marshall (1954), Mrs. Sampson (1950), Judge Hastie (1944) and J. E. Wilkins (1954). But see also the article in *Ebony,* II (Apr., 1947), pp. 15–18; the "cover story" on Marshall in *Time* (Sept. 19, 1955); and (on Raymond Pace Alexander), G. James Fleming, "Philadelphia Lawyer," *Crisis,* XLVI (Nov., 1939), pp. 329–331, 347–348. For a note on Ming, see *Ebony,* X (Dec., 1954), p. 23; and on Looby, see *Courier,* May 19, 1951. There are items on Dickerson in *ND,* VI (Jan.,

1948), p. 2, and *Courier,* Oct. 27, 1951; and a brief account of the Alexanders in *Ebony* IX (Jan., 1954), p. 73.

For the businessmen I used much the same sources that are listed on page 362. Newer material was drawn from Ginzburg, *Negro Potential,* chaps. 1 and 2; and from Hughes, "The Negro's New Economic Life," *Fortune,* LIV (Sept., 1956), pp. 126–131. See also a reply to the latter, by Phyllis Wallace in *Fortune,* LIV (Oct., 1956), p. 32. There is a very strong statement of the unimportance of Negro business in Frazier, *Black Bourgeoisie,* chaps. 2 and 7. On the retreat of Jimcrowism from organized labor see Walter White, *How Far the Promised Land?*, pp. 187–193; and "New Look at Negro Labor," *Ebony* XI (Sept., 1956), pp. 25–28. For some details on S.B. Fuller, consult *Fortune,* LVI (Sept., 1957), p. 76, and the article, "Genius of Direct Selling," in *Ebony* XIII (Nov., 1957), pp. 119–124. Conversations with Lester Granger, Elmer A. Carter and Truman K. Gibson, Sr., supplied me with additional data about contemporary developments in Negro enterprise. There are no biographies of the businessmen and enterprisers whom I discuss in this chapter, and none has been noticed by *CB,* but I had enlightening interviews with Lewis K. Downing, William J. Kennedy, Earl B. Dickerson, Asa T. Spaulding, John H. Wheeler, Maceo C. Martin and Doyle Mitchell.

(*Pages* 330–333). Armed forces.

For developments in the armed services I have turned to Lee Nichols, *Breakthrough on the Color Front* (New York, 1954); Ginzburg, *Negro Potential,* chap. IV; Office of the Assistant Secretary of Defense, "Integration in the Armed Services," (Pamphlet, Washington, 1955); and "Integration in the Armed Forces," *Ebony* XIII (July, 1958), pp. 17–24, as well as to conversations and correspondence with James C. Evans of the Department of Defense. In addition, I made use of White, *How Far the Promised Land,* chap. III, and had a long conversation with Brig. Gen. B. O. Davis, Sr.

(*Pages* 333–340). Sports.

Besides works mentioned in the bibliography for the section on sports in Part Two, above, many newer biographical materials were examined. Biographies of boxing champions included Joe Louis, *My Life Story* (New York, 1947), and Margery Miller, *Joe Louis, American* (new edition New York, 1951); Gene Schoor, *Sugar Ray Robinson* (New York, 1951); Henry Armstrong, *Gloves, Glory, and God; an Autobiography* (New York, 1956). On Louis, see also Redding, *Lonesome Road,* pp. 286–301. Louis (1940), Ezzard Charles (1949), Robinson (1951), Joe Walcott (1949) and Randy Turpin (1951) may be found in *CB.* Baseball heroes mentioned in that compilation are Aaron (1958), Mays (1955), Campanella (1953), Banks (1959), Jackie Robinson (1947). Book-length biographies available are Ken Smith, *The Willie Mays Story* (New York, 1954); Willie Mays (with Charles Einstein), *Born to Play Ball* (New York, 1955), Dick Young, *Roy Campanella* (New York, 1952); Bill Roeder, *Jackie Robinson* (New York, 1950); Jackie Robinson (with Wendell Smith), *My Own Story* (New York, 1948); and Arthur W. Mann, *The Jackie Robinson Story* (New York, 1951). Althea Gibson is in the 1957 *CB,* and is the author of an autobiography, *I Always Wanted to be Somebody* (New York, 1958). Materials were also drawn from assorted pieces: "Negroes Make Clean Sweep of Boxing," *Ebony,* XIII (Oct., 1958), pp. 90–94; A. S. Young, "A Visit with Boxing's Elder Statesman" (Archie Moore), *Ebony* XIII (Jan., 1958), pp. 63–72; "The Negro Comes of Age in Baseball," *Ebony,* XIV (June, 1959), p. 41–46; Tom Meany," Jackie's One of the Gang Now," *ND,* VIII (Nov., 1949), pp. 11–17; "The Toughest Man in Football," (Tunnell), *Ebony,* XIII (Nov., 1957), pp. 99–104. See also *Time's* "cover story" on Althea Gibson in LXX (August 26, 1957), pp. 44–48; and "Negroes in Pro Basketball," *Ebony* XIV (Feb., 1959), pp. 55–58.

Index